Britain's Gulag

Britain's Gulag

The Brutal End of Empire in Kenya

CAROLINE ELKINS

THE BODLEY HEAD
LONDON

Published by The Bodley Head 2014

11

Copyright © Caroline Elkins 2014

Caroline Elkins has asserted her right under the Copyright, Designs
and Patents Act 1988 to be identified as the author of this work

First published in the United States in 2005 by Henry Holt and Company, LLC

First published in Great Britain in 2005 by Jonathan Cape

Published in 2005 by Pimlico

The Bodley Head
20 Vauxhall Bridge Road,
London SW1V 2SA

www.bodleyhead.co.uk
www.vintage-books.co.uk

Addresses for companies within The Random House Group Limited can be found at:
www.randomhouse.co.uk/offices.htm

The Random House Group Limited Reg. No. 954009

A CIP catalogue record for this book
is available from the British Library

Maps by James Sinclair

ISBN 9781847922946

Penguin Random House is committed to a sustainable future for
our business, our readers and our planet. This book is made from
Forest Stewardship Council® certified paper.

Printed and bound in Great Britain by Clays Ltd, Elcograf S.p.A.

To Brent

CONTENTS

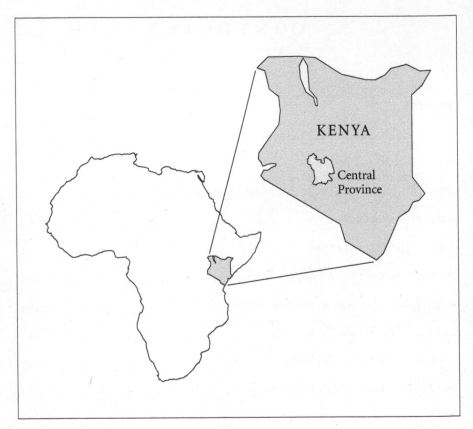

Kenya

PREFACE

LOOKING BACK TO THE START OF MY RESEARCH IN THE SUMMER OF 1995, I had no idea that nearly ten years later I would write a book about wide-scale destruction in colonial Kenya and Britain's vigorous attempts to cover it up. I was a Harvard graduate student during those early days and had become fascinated with the history of the Mau Mau uprising, a movement launched by Kenya's largest ethnic group, the Kikuyu, who had been pushed off part of their land in the process of colonization. From the start of the war in October 1952, tales of Mau Mau savagery spread wildly among the white settlers in the colony and at home in Britain. Mau Mau was portrayed as a barbaric, anti-European, and anti-Christian sect that had reverted to tactics of primitive terror to interrupt the British civilizing mission in Kenya.

Mau Mau seized the world's attention in the early 1950s, not just in Britain and the Commonwealth countries but also in the United States, Western Europe, and the Soviet bloc. *Life* and other magazines presented photographic spreads with chilling pictorial evidence of Mau Mau's savagery that contrasted dramatically with images of the local British settlers. While the Mau Mau insurgents claimed they were fighting for *ithaka na wiyathi*, or land and freedom, few people in the Western world took seriously the demands of these so-called savages. The Mau Mau were said to be criminals or gangsters bent on terrorizing the local European population, and certainly not freedom fighters.

The British mounted two parallel responses to the rebellion. The first was in the remote mountain forests of Kenya, where security forces engaged in a drawn-out offensive against some twenty thousand Mau Mau guerrilla insurgents. In difficult forest terrain it took over two years and twenty thousand members of Britain's military forces, supported by the Royal Air Force, to gain control over the Mau Mau insurgents, who were armed largely with homemade weapons and who had no military or financial support from outside Kenya.

The second and lengthier campaign was directed against a much larger civilian enemy. The British and their African loyalist supporters targeted some 1.5 million Kikuyu who were believed to have taken the Mau Mau oath and had pledged themselves to fight for land and freedom. The battlefield for this war was not the forests but a vast system of detention camps, where colonial officials reportedly held some eighty thousand Kikuyu insurgents.

I couldn't help but find these camps a compelling subject for my dissertation, particularly since no one had written a book about them. So in 1995 I embarked with great interest on the research I would need to do to capture the details of this story. I began with a preliminary sift through the official archives in London, where files stuffed with dusty, yellowed memos and reports told a seductive story about Britain's civilizing mission during the last years of colonial rule in Kenya. According to the documents, the detention camps were not meant to punish the rebellious Kikuyu but rather to civilize them. Behind the barbed wire, colonial officials were reportedly giving the detainees civics courses and home-craft classes; they were teaching the insurgents how to be good citizens and thus become capable of running Kenya sometime in the future. The colonial government did report some one-offs, or incidents, as it called them, of brutality against the detainees but insisted they were isolated occurrences. At this early stage in my research, I had little doubt about the story slowly unfolding from Britain's official archive. When I presented my dissertation proposal to my department in the winter of 1997, I was intending to write a history of the success of Britain's civilizing mission in the detention camps of Kenya.

I soon returned to Britain and then went on to Kenya for an exhaustive look into the official colonial records. It wasn't long before I began questioning my earlier view of the camps and the British colonial government. I found that countless documents pertaining to the detention camps either were missing from Britain's Public Record Office and the Kenya National Archives or were still classified as confidential some fifty years after the Mau Mau war. The British were meticulous record keepers in Kenya and elsewhere in their empire, making the absence of documentation on the camps all the more curious. I came to learn that the colonial government had intentionally destroyed many of these missing files in massive bonfires on the eve of its 1963 retreat from Kenya.

To give a sense of the destructive scale, three different departments within the colonial government kept individual files for each of the reported eighty thousand detainees in the camps. This means there should have been at least 240,000 individual detainee files in the official archives. I spent days and days searching for them in the catalogs of Britain's coldly efficient Public Record Office and in the dusty but orderly file shelves of the

Kenya National Archives, but in the end I unearthed only a few hundred in Nairobi and came up empty-handed in London.

After years of combing through what remains in the official archives, I discovered that there was a pattern to Britain's cleansing of the records. Any ministry or department that dealt with the unsavory side of detention was pretty well emptied of its files, whereas those that ostensibly addressed detainee reform, or Britain's civilizing mission, were left fairly intact. This was hardly accidental and explains why my first cursory reading of the official files in London generated a picture of a relatively benign system of detention in colonial Kenya.

Even the most assiduous purges, however, often fail to clean up all the incriminating evidence. I spent years going through file upon file of official documents looking for anything that pertained to the detention camps. Some days I found nothing of use; other times I discovered nuggets of information that I added to a growing pile of evidence. It was a tedious and sometimes frustrating process as I struggled simply to identify all of the different camps—there is no single remaining document that lists them all—and to reconstruct the chain of colonial authority responsible for their day-to-day operations. Many times I would grow weary of finding little of any use, then hit on a document that provided just another small piece to the puzzle. Mercifully, there were also the handful of days when I would come across entire files filled with rich evidence, files like the ones bursting with letters written by detainees during their time in the camps and addressed to high-ranking colonial officials. In them, the detainees provided vivid accounts of what their lives were like behind the wire, accounts that challenged any notion that the British detention camps were civilizing.

Other revelations in the archives came not from any single document or file but rather from the cumulative effects of sustained research. Over time, I developed a certain sense that told me when something just didn't seem right. For instance, given the sheer number of detainees referenced in the files, the official number of eighty thousand detained began to seem more and more suspicious to me. Upon closer scrutiny it was clear that the British had provided misleading detention numbers, giving "daily average" figures, or net rather than gross figures. In other words, the official number did not take into account all those detainees who had already entered and exited the camps. By going back through the documents and piecing together the intake and release rates, I determined that the number of Africans detained was at least two times and more likely four times the official figure, or somewhere between 160,000 and 320,000.

Something else nagged at me about these numbers. Except for a few thousand women, the vast majority of the detention camp population was composed of men, despite several files discussing the steadfast commitment of Kikuyu women to Mau Mau and their role in sustaining the movement. I soon realized that the British did detain the women and children, though not in the official camps but rather in some eight hundred enclosed villages that were scattered throughout the Kikuyu countryside. These villages were surrounded by spiked trenches, barbed wire, and watchtowers, and were heavily patrolled by armed guards. They were detention camps in all but name. Once I added all of the Kikuyu detained in these villages to the adjusted camp population, I discovered that the British had actually detained some 1.5 million people, or nearly the entire Kikuyu population.

These revelations alone were not enough to reconstruct the full story of detention in British colonial Kenya. I had to build upon the fragmented remains in the official archives with written and visual materials from private collections, as well as from missionary and newspaper archives. I also had to track down as many people as I could find who had directly experienced the detention camp system. While I was working in Kenya in 1998, I bought an old Subaru station wagon and together with my research assistant, Terry Wairimu, set off into the heart of Kikuyuland in Central Province in search of survivors willing to speak with us about their experiences in the camps and barbed-wire villages.

Meeting these elderly Kikuyu men and women was initially a challenge. Many of my introductions to them were made by their children or nieces or nephews whom I had met in Nairobi and who, at my request, agreed to take me upcountry to meet their mother or father or aunt or uncle who had lived through the camps and villages. At first the former detainees and villagers were uncertain of me and my motivations. Some thought I was a Catholic sister and wanted me to bless their livestock. Others thought I was British and refused to speak to me until I convinced them that I was an American. This was my first introduction to the intense bitterness engendered by British colonial rule in Kikuyuland, a bitterness that still seethes today.

Together with Terry, I would live in the rural countryside among the survivors in modest mud-and-wattle homes for days or weeks. We would eat meals of *ugali* and *sukuma wiki,* help with the *shambas* (farms), play with grandchildren, and talk around the kitchen fire late into the night over milky, sweet tea. I quickly found that my hosts were as interested in me as I was in them, and on several occasions had to explain why I was there in the Kikuyu countryside living with them rather than at home with my husband producing children.

In time, many of the elderly Kikuyu felt comfortable sharing their pasts with us, and I soon found that my initial difficulty in meeting and earning the trust of the survivors gave way to a new problem. After almost every interview the former detainees and villagers would ask if I would like to meet other survivors, for example, their next-door neighbor or a sibling or cousin who lived up the road or on the next ridge. Once I had been accepted within a local Kikuyu community, I was overwhelmed by the number of men and women who were willing to share with me the often painful details of their detention experiences. In total, we collected in 1998 and 1999, as well as in subsequent years, nearly six hundred hours of interviews with some three hundred ex-detainees and villagers. We also worked very hard to find Kikuyu loyalists who were willing to share their stories with us, though these interviews were significantly more difficult to conduct. In many areas former loyalists, or Kikuyu who had supported the British occupiers during the Mau Mau war, refused to acknowledge their previous status, and many who did were very reluctant to speak. Eventually a handful candidly told us about their participation on the side of the British during Mau Mau, but often on condition of anonymity.

There were also scores of colonial officials, missionaries, and European settlers who were willing to speak with me, though many would offer their vivid accounts only if I agreed not to reveal their names. To meet with them, I would often take my old Subaru out to one of Nairobi's posh suburbs or to the Muthaiga Club, Kenya's most exclusive country club and a vestige of its colonial past, where we would discuss the camps over afternoon tea or a gin and tonic served to us by African houseboys or waiters. Other times I met with former British settlers on their glorious estates near Lake Naivasha in the Rift Valley. There they told me about their roles in suppressing Mau Mau and casually admitted appallingly brutal behavior.

Almost a decade after I first started my research, my view on the detention camps, as well as on broader British colonial policy in Kenya, has changed dramatically. An integrated reading of all the sources—written, oral, and visual—yields an astonishing portrait of destruction. I've come to believe that during the Mau Mau war British forces wielded their authority with a savagery that betrayed a perverse colonial logic: only by detaining nearly the entire Kikuyu population of 1.5 million people and physically and psychologically atomizing its men, women, and children could colonial authority be restored and the civilizing mission reinstated.

Certainly, the Mau Mau war was a fierce struggle that left blood on the hands of all involved. But in considering the history of this war, we must also consider the issue of scope and scale. On the dreadful balance sheet of atrocities committed during Mau Mau, the murders perpetrated by Mau

Mau adherents were quite small in number when compared to those committed by the forces of British colonial rule. Officially, fewer than one hundred Europeans, including settlers, were killed and some eighteen hundred loyalists died at the hands of Mau Mau. In contrast, the British reported that more than eleven thousand Mau Mau were killed in action, though the empirical and demographic evidence I unearthed calls into serious question the validity of this figure. I now believe there was in late colonial Kenya a murderous campaign to eliminate Kikuyu people, a campaign that left tens of thousands, perhaps hundreds of thousands, dead. Mau Mau has been portrayed as one of the most savage and barbaric uprisings of the twentieth century. But in this book I ask that we reconsider this accepted orthodoxy and examine the crimes perpetrated by colonial forces against Mau Mau, and the considerable measures that the British colonial government undertook to conceal them.

BRITAIN'S
GULAG

CHAPTER ONE

PAX BRITANNICA

Pax Britannica

The expansion of Europe during the last century has been the story of crime and violence against backward peoples under the cloak of protective civilisation.
—CAPTAIN RICHARD MEINERTZHAGEN[1]

LIKE SO MANY OTHER AREAS OF THE BRITISH EMPIRE, EAST AFRICA was opened to colonial domination with the building of railroads, the symbol of imperial achievement. By the early twentieth century thousands of miles of tracks crisscrossed Africa and Asia, opening the territories to the forces of Pax Britannica. Beginning in August 1896, the British government financed and directed the laying of 582 miles of track stretching from the coastal port of Mombasa all the way to Lake Victoria and beyond. The line cut through the lush and exotic landscape of the Indian Ocean coast, then through the arid, lion-infested plains of Tsavo, and finally upcountry toward the Eden of the interior highlands. Completed in December 1901, it was called the Uganda Railway for it linked the inland territory of Uganda to the outside world. For its time the Uganda Railway stood as a remarkable feat of modern engineering.

But building the railway took an enormous toll in capital and man-power. Britain spent over £6.5 million on the project and imported over thirty thousand "coolies" from India, nearly a third of whom were killed or maimed by the punishing work, disease, and frequent lion attacks. Lord Salisbury's Tory government reasoned that the railway would help to civi-lize East Africa by facilitating the spread of Christianity and the destruc-tion of the slave trade. It would also make it easier to counter any possible foreign invasion into Uganda, with its precious Nile headwaters. In one of the more foolish and paranoid scenarios ever imagined, the British feared one of their rivals, particularly Germany, would seize Uganda and dam up the headwaters of the Nile, thereby desiccating Egypt. Such an ecological disaster would, in turn, force the British to withdraw their forces from the area around the Suez; without control of the prized canal, so the logic went, Britain would also lose control of India. Such a scenario would have re-quired the invading foreign government to mobilize and import the mas-sive equipment and manpower necessary to dam not just the White Nile but also all of the Nile's other tributaries. Somehow the railway would pro-vide the British with quick, military access to the interior so as to frustrate any such invasion. The British public could not understand this convo-luted logic. As cost overruns and horrific stories of man-eating lions ap-peared in the British press, the Uganda Railway came to take on a new name: the "Lunatic Express."[2]

The building of the railroad would seem a relatively minor feat com-pared to the looming challenge of repaying the debt to the British taxpay-ers incurred by its construction. In 1902 Sir Charles Eliot—the first commissioner of the British East Africa Protectorate, as Kenya was called until the 1920s—surveyed the territory and its people for economic poten-tial and found the Africans lacking in nearly every respect.[3] In Eliot's eyes not only were they black and uncivilized, but there were just too few of them to form a nucleus of cash-crop producers and future paying cus-tomers for the railroad.

Eliot's negative assessment was further skewed by the actions of his own government and military. The number of Africans living in close proxim-ity to the railway would decline significantly between the time the British arrived on the scene in the 1880s and the completion of its lunatic line. The Kikuyu were hard-hit, as they traditionally occupied the highlands of the interior that had been traversed by the rail line. Thousands of Africans died at the hands of the British who came to pacify the local population in preparation for effective occupation, as formal colonial rule in Africa was called at the end of the nineteenth century. The British military launched punitive expeditions that established an enduring pattern of virulent racism and white violence, and their social acceptability within the colony. Francis Hall, an officer in the Imperial British East Africa Company, initiated a series of raids against the Kikuyu and remained so incensed by their continued resistance that he wrote to his father, a British colonel, "There is only one way of improving the Wakikuyu [and] that is wipe them out; I should be only too delighted to do so, but we have to depend on them for food supplies."[4] A few years later, Captain Richard Meinertzhagen, a Harrow-educated British army officer, took pride in his elimination of the Kikuyu who refused to capitulate to British rule; he launched several attacks that included wiping out an entire village of men, women, and elderly (the children were spared) using bayonets, rifles, machine guns, and fire.[5] Part of the Kikuyu population of some five hundred thousand migrated farther into the interior and away from the British advance. They were fleeing not just the armed invasion but diseases like smallpox that came with the foreign imperialists. Tragically, a series of natural disasters, including a locust plague, a prolonged drought, and an epidemic of rinderpest (a cattle disease), hit the region in the same years as British imperial pacification and took a heavy toll on the Kikuyu. By the time Eliot arrived on the scene to undertake his economic assessments, the losses of life and livestock, together with the migration, made parts of Kikuyuland appear to be more vacant than they truly were.[6]

It became urgent in London to find a reliable group of people to develop the colony's production, make use of the railway for export, and pay back the unprecedented sum of public capital that seemed to have been so unwisely invested. Various options were considered. The most serious was to create in East Africa a Zionist state for persecuted European Jews. Ultimately, the British colonial government decided to launch a campaign to attract settlers of British stock to the colony, people who could capitalize on the territory's agricultural potential and provide cash crops for the world market.[7] Settlers were urged to come to East Africa, where there was plenty of cheap land, abundant labor, and large potential profits. Advertisements, like the following, were published in British newspapers enticing would-be settlers to pick up their stakes and move to the colony.

Settle in Kenya, Britain's youngest and most attractive colony. Low prices at present for fertile areas. No richer soil in the British Empire. Kenya Colony makes a practical appeal to the intending settler with some capital. Its valuable crops give high yields, due to the high fertility of the soil, adequate rainfall and abundant sunshine. Secure the advantage of native labor to supplement your own effort.[8]

Eventually, thousands of settlers responded to the call, migrating to Kenya in search of their fortunes. They came determined to forge "White Man's Country."[9]

In many ways, the story of the pacification and effective occupation of Kenya was no different from what happened all over Britain's empire at the close of the nineteenth century. Across Africa and Asia entire populations were dispossessed of their land through suspect but useful alliances with illegitimate rulers, deceitful treaties, and the barrels of guns. Resistance campaigns like those in East Africa were played out to their grim end all over the world. But bravery was no match for the British and their Maxim gun, and imperial warfare more resembled big-game hunting than it did combat.

The drive to amass African colonies at the end of the nineteenth century represented a change in Britain's overseas strategy, reflecting a shift in geopolitical tactics that had its roots in the onset of Britain's economic decline. For decades, the British were able to dominate their European competitors, keeping open the doors of international commerce through what has been called the "imperialism of free trade."[10] The British had not needed formal colonies in many parts of Africa, Asia, and Latin America because their global economic dominance rendered those regions informal but de facto British territories; other European powers simply could not compete economically with Britain in the free market. Certainly the British did maintain formal colonial possessions, such as India and Hong Kong, but much of the world remained under Britain's less costly and economically advantageous informal control merely through the forces of the international marketplace. As the economic depression of the late nineteenth century hit Britain at the same time that other Western powers—particularly Germany and the United States—were successfully industrializing, a serious threat to British economic dominance was on the horizon. Together with changes in local domestic economies, and new alliances in European geopolitics, this shift in industrialization fed an appetite for new colonies in Africa, and to a lesser extent the Middle East and Asia.

The Scramble for Africa, Europe's move to partition the continent, is one of the most written-about processes in imperial history.[11] Until the Scramble the colonial map of Africa—with the notable exception of the strategic seaports on the West and East African coasts and colonies in South Africa and Egypt—was blank. But in a few short decades, the European powers—including Britain, France, Germany, Portugal, Italy, and the infamous King Leopold II of Belgium—carved up the continent and divided the spoils. This began at the Congress of Berlin in 1884–85, when European imperial bargaining was the first step in the establishment of nonsensical territories that divided unified ethnic groups and trading networks, while forcing together other groups of Africans who would have preferred to remain separate. These territories—some forty colonies and protectorates in all—would later provide the basis for the modern nation-states of Africa.

Queen Victoria sat on Britain's throne during much of the African partition, and by the end of the nineteenth century she reigned over the most expansive empire in her country's history. Along with her new African territories were those her imperialist negotiators picked up in the Scramble in East Asia, including Malaya, parts of Borneo and New Guinea, and numerous islands in the Pacific such as Fiji and the Solomons. These were added to an already impressive list of formal colonies, including the prize of India and various islands in the Caribbean, as well as numerous territories claiming dominion status such as Australia, New Zealand, and Canada. The British Empire encompassed nearly 13 million square miles or roughly 25 percent of the world's total landmass. Queen Victoria presided over some 445 million subjects around the globe. Not included in these figures were territories that retained their informal colonial status with Britain, places like Argentina and Brazil. Based upon the amount of British capital invested in these countries and their trading dependence on Britain, these territories were British colonies in all but name.[12]

Though disparate, Britain's far-flung empire was united by a single imperial ethos, the "civilizing mission." For the British, imperialism was not solely about exploitation; in fact, if one believed the official rhetoric of the time, exploitation was hardly a factor at all in motivating Britain's global conquests. With their superior race, Christian values, and economic know-how, the British instead had a duty, a moral obligation, to redeem the "backward heathens" of the world. In Africa the British were going to bring light to the Dark Continent by transforming the so-called natives into progressive citizens, ready to take their place in the modern world. According to their own line of reasoning, the British were not actually stealing African land or exploiting local labor but were instead self-appointed trustees for the hapless "natives," who had not yet reached a point on the evolutionary scale to develop or make responsible decisions on their own. With proper British guidance, and tough paternalistic love, Africans could be made into progressive men and women, though it would take many decades or more

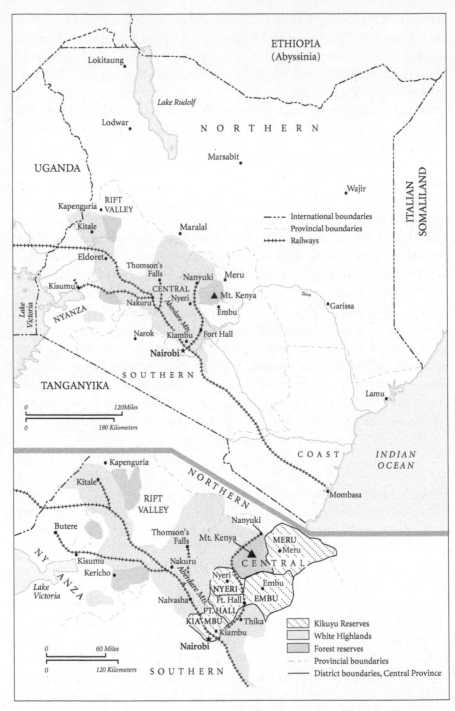

Kenya with Kikuyu Reserves and the White Highlands Inset

likely centuries for such a radical transformation to take place. At first such attitudes were called "Victorian aspirations," although British sanctimony about so-called native peoples remained relatively unchanged throughout much of the twentieth century.[13] This was cultural imperialism par excellence. This was the "White Man's Burden."

Administering the empire was a much bigger challenge than legitimating it rhetorically, though here too a single credo prevailed. In London and throughout the empire the various levels of British colonial government were always to "trust the man on the spot." This made great sense considering the enormity of Britain's imperial holdings; any form of micromanagement from London would have been financially and administratively impossible, particularly under Britain's tight budget for colonial administration. The empire was never to be a burden on British taxpayers, and every colony was expected to be self-financing. This policy would place an enormous burden on both local indigenous populations and colonists to generate enough income to pay for Britain's colonial infrastructure, like railways, roads, telegraph systems, and administrative personnel.[14] It also meant there would be little funding for the schools, clinics, and other social and community institutions that presumably would form the backbone of Britain's civilizing mission. Colonial fiscal policy also translated into enormous responsibilities and challenges for the men on the spot, who were expected to rule over hundreds of thousands of colonial subjects with very little guidance and even smaller budgets. While there was a strong consensus for the British imperial mission, there were never any hard-and-fast rules about how this mission should be carried out on the ground. Again, this may be partly explained by the fiscal limitations of British colonial governance. But there was another important reason why these men on the ground would be given so much latitude: they were the only colonial officials with the experience and local knowledge necessary for on-the-spot decision making.

Thus the most defining characteristic of British colonial governance in Africa, and throughout most of its empire, was the looseness of its decentralized control. The empire was managed largely through a prefectural style of administration that incorporated peculiarities rooted in the unique features of each colony.[15] In practice administrative responsibility for the empire was vested primarily in three institutions, which together made up the British colonial government. For most of British Africa, the apex of imperial governance was the Colonial Office in London.[16] It was headed by the secretary of state for the colonies, also known as the colonial secretary, who reported to the prime minister and who held the status of cabinet minister. Given the scope of the empire, the Colonial Office had a tiny staff. In 1929 there were thirty-five administrative class officials, and ten years later fewer than fifty. This made it absolutely impractical for the Colonial Office to oversee anything in the various colonies but the broadest areas of policy. Even then, blanket official orders issued by London were rare. Intervention from the Colonial Office would be most significant at the beginning and end of empire, or in the structuring and dismantling of a colonial government on the ground. In the intervening years several major programs aimed at fostering development in Kenya and elsewhere in Africa were broadly conceived by the Colonial Office in London, though they were almost entirely implemented by local colonial officials.

Throughout Britain's empire there was an elite cadre of officers who functioned as the Colonial Office's agents on the ground. It was these men who engaged daily in the trench warfare of British colonial rule. They were responsible for the day-to-day imposition of colonial authority and for adapting the broadly conceived notions of British imperialism to their local and particular circumstances. For most Africans they were the white face of British colonial rule. In Kenya these colonial officials were members of the Administration, as it was called. The Kenya Administration was at the bottom of the colonial governing hierarchy and was made up of provincial and district commissioners, as well as their subordinates, dispersed throughout the colony.[17]

These men on the spot were not just any men. They were handpicked by the Colonial Office in targeted recruitment campaigns that openly sought future colonial rulers with backgrounds common to the dominant ruling class in Britain. This was believed to be absolutely critical to the functioning of the empire. While diffuse and decentralized, colonial rule would be strengthened, it was thought, by recruiting men who would conform instinctively to British imperial principles: establishing and maintaining control over local populations, promoting fiscal self-sufficiency, and civilizing the Africans and other indigenous groups with paternalistic authority. They would not need direct day-to-day supervision because they shared with their superiors in London a common ideology of aristocratic social superiority and thus were ipso facto equipped to rule. Recruits were often the younger sons of aristocratic families, or if not they shared a similar privileged pedigree rooted in the principles of noblesse oblige. They attended public school and then generally went on to either Oxford or Cambridge, where they were steeped in the ideals of honor, duty, and discretion. When they were shipped to their remote posts, such as in Kenya, often what they found was little more than a single hut that functioned as an office, local courthouse, and bunk. They were startlingly young, some barely twenty years of age, and had received very little formal training for what awaited them; some former administrators from Kenya recalled their arrival in the "bush" as analogous to being "thrown in at the deep end,"[18] where they sank or swam. This rite of passage only tightened their solidarity and purpose as a group. Kenya's Administration was by all accounts a brotherhood with its own unwritten code of conduct, the most important detail of which was steadfast loyalty to one another and to the Crown.[19]

Between the Administration in the field and the Colonial Office in London was the colonial governor and the colony's central government. From London's perspective, the governor was the most important man on the spot. In Kenya's case he was in charge of devising and implementing policies in his colony; he was responsible for his various members or ministers who administered departments like Native Affairs, Health and Housing, and Finance. The governor also had to cope with the colony's Legislative Council, or LegCo, and the many vested European interests that held seats in this lawmaking body. And he had to make certain that the young colonial officers in the field were doing their jobs. The governor's role was not to be envied. He and his central government stood foursquare in the vortex of colonial pressures, simultaneously balancing and resolving the often conflicting demands of the Administration in the field and the Colonial Office back in London.

The governor was ultimately an agent of the British Colonial Office who had immense discretion in running Kenya. The poor communications linking London to its empire meant that the Colonial Office had little choice but to devolve a significant share of decision making to the local man in charge. Even when communications improved significantly, the colonial secretary still continued to operate by proxy through his governors, rather than trying to control these faraway imperial agents' day-to-day decision making. The effectiveness of the link between Kenya and the Colonial Office depended almost entirely on the personal relationship between the colonial secretary and the governor, their shared ethos of imperial domination, and their ability to reach consensus through bargaining and negotiation. It was understood that the Colonial Office in London would not directly intervene in Kenya or elsewhere in the empire, except to defuse embarrassing situations that might threaten the reputation and legitimacy of Britain's civilizing mission. Even when such problems would crop up, local colonial agents would still be given great latitude in remedying the situation.

What made Kenya unique in British Africa, along with Southern Rhodesia (today Zimbabwe) and South Africa, was the settlement of white colonists who were expected to form the economic backbone of the colony. Kenya's settlers were a mixed bag, roughly falling into two socioeconomic groups: small-scale farmers and aristocratic big men. Less affluent white immigrants largely from South Africa were among the first to arrive. They brought hardened social attitudes and racist views of so-called native rights that had been honed in Britain's colonies south of the Zambezi River. Hardly ideal contributors to Kenya's burgeoning economy, they were often undercapitalized. Each was settled on about a thousand acres or less of cheap land. Together they quickly became a drain on the colony's limited resources, demanding infrastructure like schools, roads, and hospitals, though offering little in return. In contrast, the settlers arriving from Britain were some of the most aristocratic immigrants ever to populate the British Empire. Though noble by birth, many of these settlers suffered from a weakening economic position in Britain with family inheritances increasingly divided up by new generations and where younger sons—as many of these men were—were often excluded from the privileges of primogeniture. By 1905 nearly three thousand settlers had landed by ship in Mombasa, prepared to re-create the seignorial lifestyle in the highlands of Kenya that had been increasingly difficult to maintain at home. At the coast Africans loaded these lords and ladies onto railcars, along with their countless bags, crates of fine china, hand-cranked gramophones, bathtubs, and other necessities, for the overnight trip to their new homes upcountry. When the train stopped in Nairobi, the colony's capital and hub of social and economic activity, the settlers still had to bounce through miles of roadless territory—often called "miles and miles of bloody Africa," or simply "MMBA"—on oxcarts before reaching their final destinations.[20]

They acquired estates of enormous size. Lord Delamere, the popular settler leader in the early days of the colony, owned the largest, receiving title to some one hundred thousand acres in 1903 and acquiring another sixty thousand acres a few years later. Other landholdings, though smaller, were nonetheless impressive in size. They were all located in the fertile and temperate highlands of central Kenya, an area which was to become the heartland of White Man's Country. These wealthy families did not come to Kenya to work, but rather to take advantage of the British government's offer of land, labor, and capital, an offer which the settlers interpreted rather generously. Kenya's new aristocrats shared Lord Delamere's ambition to create a plantocracy modeled on the American South. Like the colonial officers, they were united by their cultural and social values. Many of them were old Etonians, or from similar public-school backgrounds, and accustomed to a life not of working but of overseeing the work of those around them. And they expected all levels of the British colonial government to support them in this vision.[21]

Kenya's big men quickly established a leisurely lifestyle aspired to by all Europeans in the colony. On their estates or farms or in European neighborhoods in Nairobi, every white settler in the colony was a lord to some extent, particularly in relationship to the African population. They all had domestic servants, though the wealthier families would have dozens. Some servants would have but a single responsibility, like tending a favorite rose garden or, as in the case of Karen Blixen, carrying the lady's favorite shawl and shotgun.[22] They enjoyed game hunting and sport facilities, with the Nairobi racetrack and polo grounds being one of the most popular European social spots in town. Beyond such gentrified leisure, these privileged men and women lived an absolutely hedonistic lifestyle, filled with sex, drugs, drink, and dance, followed by more of the same. In Nairobi, where some settlers lived a full-time urban, professional life, they congregated in the Muthaiga Club, also known as the Moulin Rouge of Africa. They drank champagne and pink gin for breakfast, played cards, danced through the night, and generally woke up with someone else's spouse in the morning. At the Norfolk Hotel, better known as the House of Lords, settlers rode their horses into the Lord Delamere Bar, drank heavily, and enjoyed Japanese prostitutes from the local brothel. Outside of Nairobi part of the highlands became the notorious Happy Valley, where weekend houseguests were often required to exchange partners, cocaine and morphine were distributed at the door, and men and women compared their sexual notes when the debauchery was over. The colony's settlers were notorious worldwide for their sexual high jinks, and the running joke in Britain became, "Are you married or do you live in Kenya?"[23]

The large landholding settlers were also a political force to be reckoned with, even in the early days of the colony. Settlers influenced colonial decision making using their political ties back in London—many fathers, brothers, and uncles sat in the House of Lords—as well as because of the economic promise they represented to the colony. From the start settlers made strident demands on the British colonial government and were quite successful in gaining concessions that placed their own interests above those of the African population. They insisted upon and were granted low-interest loans, reduced freight charges, and government subsidies for their crops; they pushed for and won an extension of their land leases in the highlands—from 99 to 999 years. Most important, they gained access to the central institutions of the colonial government in Nairobi when their representatives—like Delamere and later other notables like Ferdinand

Cavendish-Bentinck and Michael Blundell—became members of the Kenya Legislative Council. Here they had a direct role in the formulation of the colony's laws and regulations. Once the British colonial government decided to base Kenya's economy on the production of export commodities from the settler estates, it agreed in principle to ensuring that there would be ample land and labor to sustain settler production—land and labor which of course would come from the Africans.

Settler self-interest was predicated on a sense of entitlement that resulted not only from the shared aristocratic pedigree of many British immigrants but also from a perception of profound racial superiority that infused every rung of the colony's white socioeconomic ladder.[24] By virtue of their skin color, whites of all classes were the master race and therefore deserving of privilege. To the settlers there was nothing noble about the African "savage." Many believed the African to be biologically inferior, with smaller brain sizes, a limited capacity to feel pain or emotion, and even different nutritional needs, requiring only a bowl of maize meal, or *posho*, to maintain their health. African men had to be controlled; they were unpredictable and sexually aggressive, threatening both white women and the maintenance of their idealized chastity as well as the racial purity of the colony's European community.[25] Virulent racist ideology grew more intense over time as the so-called native was moved along the racist spectrum from stupid, inferior, lazy, and childlike to savage, barbaric, atavistic, and animal-like. This shift in characterization would correspond closely to the Africans' increasing unwillingness to be exploited by the colonial economy, and with their desire to reclaim land they considered to be rightfully their own.

Though all indigenous groups were affected by British colonial rule in Kenya, none experienced a transformation as intense as the Kikuyu. This was the ethnic group most affected by the colonial government's policies of land alienation, or expropriation, and European settlement.[26] The Kikuyu were agriculturalists who lost over sixty thousand acres to the settlers, mostly in southern Kiambu, a highly fertile region just outside of Nairobi that would become some of the most productive European farmland in the colony. After the British military assault and natural disasters of the late nineteenth century, many Kikuyu migrated back to their ancestral territory in the highlands, only to find Europeans living on their land. To make matters worse, the Kikuyu had for centuries relied upon territorial expansion into surrounding frontiers to alleviate population pressures or to defuse internal civil struggles. In particular, young men would typically set

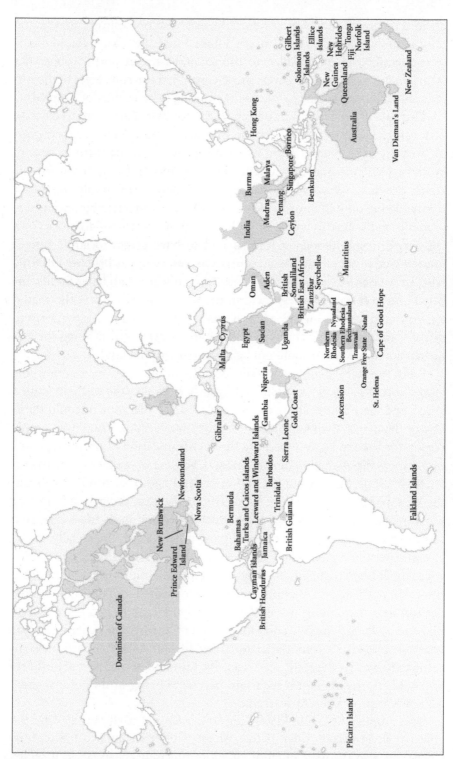

The British Empire in the Early Twentieth Century

off into the forests to colonize new land, establish homesteads, marry, and raise a family. But with the coming of colonial rule, the Kikuyu found themselves hemmed in on all sides: to the south, east, and north were settler farms, to the west were the government-controlled forest reserves of the Aberdares, and to the southeast was the expanding urban center of Nairobi.

This loss of land was devastating to the Kikuyu. They were to have an increasingly difficult time sustaining themselves, particularly as their population began to recover from its earlier losses with the introduction of Western medicine and subsequent declining mortality. By the 1930s the land's productivity began to deteriorate as there were simply too many Kikuyu living on it. But for the Kikuyu there was also a terrible social consequence to the British landgrab. To be a man or a woman—to move from childhood to adulthood—a Kikuyu had to have access to land. A man needed land to accumulate the resources necessary to pay bridewealth for a wife, or wives, who would in turn bear him children. Land and family entitled him to certain privileges within the Kikuyu patriarchy; without land a man would remain socially a boy. A woman needed land to grow crops to nurture and sustain her family; without it in the eyes of the Kikuyu she was not an adult. A Kikuyu could not be a Kikuyu without land.

From the start there was a bitter emotional intensity surrounding the land issue. The Kikuyu complained angrily over the loss of their "stolen land," and there was nothing the British colonial government could do to assure them that their remaining territory was secure. There was ample reason for Kikuyu anxiety, because the very foundation of the settler community was the alienation of African land. Settlers were determined to create their White Man's Country, and once land had been confiscated from the local population they were singularly focused on protecting it against any possible threat of its loss. After much lobbying, the settlers extracted several guarantees from the colonial government about the racially exclusive and permanent nature of white settlement in the highlands, now calling it the White Highlands. Seeking to expand their numbers and increase the value of their land, they also successfully pushed for continued immigration into the colony. After World War I the empire became a logical place to resettle demobilized British soldiers. Lieutenant generals, major generals, brigadiers, colonels, majors, captains, and their subordinates all came to Kenya. By the early 1920s over five hundred of these former officers and soldiers, together with their families, were living in the colony, some on newly expropriated African land.[27]

The promise of White Man's Country was only partly fulfilled by the colonial government's offer of free, or relatively free, land to the settlers. There was also the issue of labor, or more precisely cheap labor. It seems not to have mattered whether settlers were relatively well-capitalized aristocrats, poor whites from South Africa, or former British soldiers; among all classes agricultural productivity was pathetically low, at least until the economic boom brought on by World War II. Curiously, settlement policy in Kenya seemed to be focused more on numbers of immigrants than on potential economic production.[28] Many British immigrants had little or no farming experience before arriving in the colony, and many of those coming from South Africa left because they could not make ends meet there, despite the incredible economic favoritism given to the white population over the African majority. In Kenya there was considerable tension between inadequate settler production on the one hand and, on the other, the settlers' desire to make the colony into a white man's enclave. It was not the inherent strength of their agricultural productivity that entitled the settlers to racial privilege and political power, but rather a highly interventionist colonial government that did everything it could to promote the settlers' economic success and, by extension, the financial viability of the colony.

It grew increasingly clear that the local African population was going to be sacrificed on behalf of settler agricultural subsidies and productivity. Labor was the one factor in the economic equation that the settlers and the colonial government could jointly manipulate, and they did so ruthlessly. Rather than offering wage incentives, the European employers relied upon coercion by the colonial government to recruit African labor, which was, more often than not, drawn from the Kikuyu population then living on the edges of the White Highlands. The government's guarantee of cheap and bountiful Kikuyu labor was based on a complex set of laws aimed at controlling nearly every aspect of Kikuyu life. Over time, four regulations, together, pushed the Kikuyu off their remaining land and into the exploitive wage economy.

First, the colonial government established African reserves, which were defined rural areas, eventually with official boundaries, much like the homelands in South Africa or the Native American reserves in the United States, where each African ethnic group in the colony was expected to live separately. The Kikuyu had their own reserves in the Central Province districts of Kiambu, Fort Hall, and Nyeri, the Maasai resided mostly in the colony's Southern Province, the Luo lived in Nyanza Province, and so forth. This practice of divide and rule was also a cornerstone of the colonial government's labor policy. With insufficient land in their reserves many Africans had little choice but to migrate to the European farms in search of work, and survival.[29]

But confining the Africans was not enough to force them all into the wage economy. As an additional tactic of control, the British colonial government taxed them. The second colonial regulation called for a hut tax and poll tax, together amounting to nearly twenty-five shillings, the equivalent of almost two months of African wages at the going local rate. In response, thousands of Kikuyu began to migrate in search of work. It was at this point that colonial officials decided to introduce the third regulation, this one to control the movement of the African workers and to keep track of their employment histories. By 1920 all African men leaving their reserves were required by law to carry a pass, or *kipande*, that recorded a person's name, fingerprint, ethnic group, past employment history, and current employer's signature. The Kikuyu put the pass in a small metal container, the size of a cigarette box, and wore it around their necks. They often called it a *mbugi*, or goat's bell, because, as one old man recalled to me, "I was no longer a shepherd, but one of the flock, going to work on the white man's farm with my *mbugi* around my neck."[30] The *kipande* became one of the most detested symbols of British colonial power, though the Africans had little recourse but to carry their identity cards at all times; failure to produce it on demand brought a hefty fine, imprisonment, or both.

From the start the Africans, who were deeply resourceful and in fact often much more accomplished agricultural producers than the settlers, did everything they could to negotiate their way through the new colonial economy, and to avoid being captured in the coercive and exploitative labor contracts on the settler estates. In Central Province Kikuyu who had enough land adapted to the new colonial economy by increasing their own maize production and selling their surpluses in the expanding internal market. Some Kikuyu were so efficient that they were able continually to undercut the price of settler-grown maize. In the early days, most Europeans in the colony understood that African peasant production was expanding. Quick to appreciate the significance of this threat, and to do everything in their power to stymie it, the settlers again put pressure on the colonial government to intervene. Though colonial officials harbored doubts about settler productivity, the commitment to agricultural production by European settlers had been made, and with it the entrenchment of a vocal, and formidable, white minority. There was no turning back. As its fourth strategy for forcing Africans into the wage economy, the colonial government sought to limit African agricultural production for the marketplace. Africans were forbidden to grow the most profitable cash crops such as tea, coffee, and sisal though they were able to produce and sell maize freely until marketing boards were established after the Second World War that required Africans to sell their grain at a set price. These marketing boards would throw up roadblocks against African agriculture, further forcing the indigenous population to turn to wage labor for income.[31]

These four measures were clearly designed to subordinate African peasant agriculture to that of the settlers, but this subordination did not happen overnight, nor did it always take the form preferred by the colonial
government and the settler population. There was another, more feudal labor relationship that took hold in the White Highlands precisely because
the settlers could not capitalize effectively on their embarrassment of land.
Africans relentlessly and often subtly sought to negotiate their way
through and outwit the very system that afforded the settlers more land
than they possibly could farm. A form of sharecropping called *squatting*
evolved on cash-strapped European farms throughout the colony and
would quickly provide the Kikuyu with access to alternative arable land
outside of their reserves. Shortly after the settlers' arrival, thousands of
Kikuyu left for the White Highlands with their families and livestock and
settled on European farms, where, in return for laboring for the European
owner for about a third of the year, they could cultivate a plot of land, graze
their cattle and goats, and raise their children. These Kikuyu were not wage
laborers who migrated back and forth between the reserves and the White
Highlands; instead they left the reserves for good and set off to forge new
lives and communities on the European farms. Squatters relieved the population pressures in the Kikuyu reserves, at least temporarily, and they also
kept alive the myth that the frontier of migration was not entirely closed
off, but rather took on a new form with settler colonialism. There was a
common fear among the settlers that Kikuyu squatters, particularly those
living alongside the poorest settlers, would start to demand tenant rights.
Still, there was no way of ending the squatting phenomenon, because without these so-called Kaffir farmers the settler economy would likely have
collapsed prior to the Second World War.[32]

The squatters and the settlers remained, however, in an unequal economic and political relationship, with Europeans relying on the support of
the British colonial government to protect their interests against those of
the tenant farmers. Like the settlers, the squatters believed themselves to be
pioneers with long-term potential claims, but in reality their years as residents on European-owned land were numbered, and those that remained
would increasingly become more punitive and less profitable. The squatters enjoyed a golden age of relative freedom and thriving productivity until the end of World War I. But in 1918 the British colonial government
introduced the first of several Resident Native Labourers Ordinances. Together, these ordinances would drastically reduce squatter wealth by limit-
ing the amount of cattle they could own and the size of their tenant farms
on European land, while increasing the number of days Africans were required to work for their settler landlords. As the settlers gradually became

more efficient agricultural producers, the squatters simultaneously became more and more an economic anachronism. Moreover, the growth of independent squatter communities, where the Africans collectively organized self-help organizations and elders' councils, were perceived as a threat to political stability in the White Highlands. The settlers doggedly pushed for further legislation that would control the squatters, to the point of forcing all of them into the role of virtual wage laborers. For their part, the Kikuyu living on European farms fought back by illegally cultivating crops and grazing their cattle, organizing go-slows, sabotaging settler machinery and livestock, and striking outright. While such strikes were handily put down, squatters occasionally managed to wrest small concessions from their European farmer landlords.[33]

The squatters, though, lacked one critical option. They could not return to their reserves, having given up their land claims when they migrated to the White Highlands. Indeed, many became squatters in the first place because either they did not have access to land in the reserves, or that to which they did have claim was insufficient in acreage or quality, or both, to support their families. When the most draconian piece of resident native legislation was introduced in 1937, transferring virtually all responsibility for the squatters to the settler-controlled district councils, squatters simply had no choice but to search for new and perhaps more radical ways to fight off this encroachment on their way of life.

Until World War II, there were at most eighty men in the Kenya Administration, and they had day-to-day responsibility for the approximately 5 million Africans living in the colony. In practice this meant that administrators in the field needed African subordinates willing to exercise delegated power, and they found them in colonial-appointed chiefs. Throughout Britain's African empire colonial rulers sought out collaborators who would be willing to assume an authoritative role within the colonial government, beneath the provincial and district administrators to be sure, but decidedly above the rest of a colony's African subjects. This was the basis of indirect rule, a way of administering the empire on the cheap by co-opting local African leaders, using them to enforce discipline and control over local populations, and in return providing them with generous material rewards. Such a system was predicated upon the European stereotype of traditional African political systems, which always placed the chief at the top of the hierarchy; the chief, in turn, had the fundamental role of maintaining "tribal order."[34]

But the Kikuyu did not have chiefs. Prior to colonialism, they were a stateless society, governed by councils of elders and lineage heads. In

Kikuyu districts these new chiefs were a phenomenon of colonial rule. They were created by the colonial government and thus wholly illegitimate in the eyes of ordinary Kikuyu people. By accepting British authority, the chiefs were granted a monopoly of power in the African districts and given a great deal of autonomy to exercise it. Their primary jobs were labor recruitment, or labor encouragement, as the colonial government called it, and tax collection—two colonial demands that the ordinary Kikuyu attempted to avoid, or at least negotiate. But the chiefs had sufficient incentives to enforce these measures with impunity. If they did not perform, they would be dismissed and replaced, and sacking would mean the loss of their bogus chiefly title and all of the political power and socioeconomic privilege that went along with it. So the chiefs ruled with an iron fist, earning a reputation for both corruption and oppression. They traveled with their own semiofficial entourages of "tribal retainers," many of whom did the dirty work of collecting taxes and procuring labor. This labor was not only for the agricultural support of the settlers but also for the colonial government. In the early days of Kenya the colonial government was the largest—and rumored to be the worst—single employer of African labor, which it put to work building the colony's infrastructure of roads, secondary railways, and the like.

The introduction of chiefs brought with it a bitter internal conflict within the Kikuyu community, a conflict that only intensified over time. This is not to say that there was no internal differentiation among the Kikuyu prior to colonial rule. The Kikuyu certainly did not live in a precolonial socialist utopia without class divisions. The competitive environment that spawned the chiefs was a direct result of the intense internal competition for resources and wealth that peaked at the time of colonization. The chiefs merely capitalized on the opportunities that came with the power they derived from colonial rule. Catapulted into the new colonial hierarchy by their self-interest, they proceeded to do away with local Kikuyu competition by forcing the entrepreneurial masses out of the peasant economy and into the colonial wage market. To add insult to injury, the chiefs were rewarded for their loyalty to the colony and the Crown with larger and more fertile parcels of land in the reserves, superior seed, licenses to conduct internal trade, and access to local cheap labor, all ingredients for success in the peasant agricultural sector. Throughout its rule the colonial government would accelerate and manipulate socioeconomic differentiation in Kikuyu society. While the Kikuyu could easily be described as the most exploited group of Africans in Kenya, at the same time a tiny minority of them would become among the greatest beneficiaries of colonial rule.

. . .

The hypocrisies of British colonialism did not escape the Kikuyu. By the early 1920s a small group of progressive and educated young men formed a political organization called the Kikuyu Central Association, or KCA, to challenge the colonial establishment. Politically savvy and knowledgeable about the intricacies of the British colonial government, these men pursued their complaints through the limited channels of petition and constitutional redress. They took their demands on matters of land and forced labor from the local field level of the Kenya Administration to the colony's central government in Nairobi and ultimately to the final arbiter, the Colonial Office in London. Working through formal channels for several years, the KCA would leap into the spotlight when it waged a cultural battle against the British colonial government over the issue of female circumcision.

Leading the KCA as its general secretary in the late 1920s was a young Kikuyu by the name of Johnstone Kenyatta. Like the KCA's other members, Kenyatta was relatively conservative and upwardly mobile, and was seeking to capitalize on the opportunities made available by the new colonial system, though denied to him because he was not an appointed chief. Importantly, Kenyatta and his fellow KCA members were products of a missionary education. The missionaries had a leading role in Britain's civilizing mission in Kenya, as they did throughout most of the empire. Missionaries were determined to convert the Africans not just to Christianity but to an entire Western way of life. They competed with one another for African souls, with each denomination carving out its own spheres of influence throughout Britain's colonies. In the Kikuyu reserves the Presbyterians, the Anglicans, the Methodists, and the Catholics dominated the Christian scene, establishing mission stations—which included churches, schools, and medical clinics—condemning the heathenism of Kikuyu religious and cultural practices, and preaching the values of Christianity, commerce, and civilization. For the colonial government, missionaries offered civilization on the cheap. To the degree that any education or welfare services were provided to the local African population, they were delivered largely by missionaries. Of course, the Africans would have to pay school fees and health-care costs; in fact, to earn the right to buy these services the Kikuyu, like all other colonial subjects, had to renounce their own religion and convert to Christianity.[35]

When Protestant mission societies launched an attack on the Kikuyu custom of female circumcision, the KCA responded vigorously by defending their cultural practice. The issue exploded in the 1920s after several missionaries banned the practice for their converts. In response to missionary pressure, colonial officials in Nairobi altered their typical hands-off approach toward African customs and urged the Local Native Councils in the Kikuyu districts to restrict and regulate female circumcision. By 1929, thousands of Kikuyu were protesting and leaving the established churches to form their own independent churches and schools, which would permit the practice to continue. This single cultural issue mobilized the Kikuyu peasants for the first time and, in so doing, provided the KCA with a mass political base.[36]

The repeated, reasoned demands that were issued by Kikuyu politicians on the subject of circumcision brought home the realities of Britain's civilizing mission in Kenya. The colonial government responded to the KCA with unequivocal hostility, labeling it a dangerous and subversive organization that was unrepresentative of the Kikuyu majority. This reaction was a reflection of both British imperial self-interest and a twisted sense of colonial paternalism, particularly on the part of the Administration in the Kikuyu reserves. Despite the fact that these men on the spot, the young members of Britain's ruling elite who considered themselves to be the protectors of "their natives," were watching Kikuyu country rapidly deteriorate around them, many continued to believe they had come to Africa to oversee a slow, organic change from savagery to civilization. They were trustees who acted in the best interests of the African, who after all had to be protected from himself. Though this paternalistic notion permeated all ranks of the colonial government, it was particularly strong in the African reserves, where the members of the Administration re-created their own public-school drama, taking the role of the tough but loving headmaster and casting the Africans in that of the young and artless innocents.

Kikuyu political leaders had no role in this script. They were a rival leadership, outside of the colonial hierarchy, and, according to colonial officials, betrayed the dangers inherent in educating Africans too quickly. Their demands for responsibilities for which they were assumed to be ill-equipped rendered them, in the eyes of the colonial government, detribalized or semi-educated agitators. In the wake of the female-circumcision controversy, KCA members were no longer simply agitators but also atavistic, anti-Western, and anti-Christian agitators. It became the duty of the British colonial government to protect the hapless Africans from these troublemakers.

In hindsight it is difficult to assess how much British colonial officials actually believed their own delusional rhetoric. They could not fail to see the destructive impact of British colonialism on the Kikuyu population, though colonial logic always seemed able to find fault with presumed

African inefficiencies, or customs, or inherent racial inferiority rather than the injustices of colonial rule. Such myopia freed colonial officials from responsibility for the collapsing Kikuyu society. At the outbreak of the Second World War the British colonial government outlawed the KCA, on the pretext that Kikuyu political leaders were secretly contacting fascists in the nearby Italian colony of Ethiopia, in preparation for an armed invasion. As Kenya readied itself for war, colonial officials believed that with the elimination of the self-interested Kikuyu politicians and with even more paternalistic British guidance, the Kikuyu could aspire to someday achieving the lofty standards of British civilization.

The Second World War brought vast changes to Kenya, changes that exposed the inequities of British colonial rule, galvanized Kikuyu discontent, and channeled it into a mass peasant movement that would be called Mau Mau. The war converted the settlers into a powerful economic force in Kenya. The economic boom resulting from wartime demand at long last transformed their agricultural production into a profitable venture, and profits would continue for the next twenty years. The colonial government continued to intervene to satisfy the settlers' wartime labor needs, conscripting Africans onto European farms. Meanwhile, the Administration in the African districts, and particularly the Kikuyu reserves, followed the directives of their superiors in Nairobi and London and pushed the local African farmer population to produce as much as possible for the war effort, a complete about-face from the explicit discouragement of peasant production in previous decades. Under increasing pressure, the Kikuyu were left with little choice but to abandon such traditional farming practices as crop rotation and resting land with fallow periods, and instead intensely cultivate every available parcel in their reserves.

The settlers were poised to take advantage of a notable change in Kenya's relationship with the British government. A tighter economic bond between the colony and London persisted after the war as Britain looked to its empire to help the nation through its reconstruction. A series of Colonial Development and Welfare Acts were passed that provided unprecedented sums of capital to the colonies. Misleadingly named, these infusions of cash were not intended to strengthen colonial trusteeship of the Africans, but rather had the clear objective of lifting Britain's economy out of its postwar crisis. These capital investments were targeted largely at the settler economy in Kenya, in response to its recent expansion of scale and profitability. By ramping up settler agricultural production, the British government planned to purchase European-produced products like coffee, tea, and pyrethrum through local government-controlled marketing boards, then resell the same products on the world market at higher prices. Since many of these goods were going to the United States, the British government would in exchange receive dollars that were critical to paying off its wartime debt to the Americans. For their part, the settlers benefited from unprecedented government support and financial intervention calculated to ensure the expansion and increased profitability of their estates.[37]

In spite of their hard work, after 1945 the Kikuyu way of life suffered a serious decline, particularly in relationship to the settlers. After decades of intensive farming, the reserves were on the brink of an agricultural crisis, and the Kikuyu were divided between the rich but tiny chiefly minority and the majority, who had endured not just exploitation but loss of land and status under British rule. Making matters worse, the colonial government was convinced that the so-called traditional and primitive Kikuyu agricultural practices of land-mining, continuous cultivation, and overstocking of cattle and goats were the real reasons for the reduced soil fertility and accelerated erosion. In an effort to mitigate the ill effects of these practices, colonial authorities introduced a series of postwar development projects aimed at averting what appeared to be an incipient ecological disaster.[38]

In practical terms this meant that active steps were taken to prevent the Kikuyu from producing for local markets. Restricted from capitalizing on the expanding colonial economy, the Kikuyu were left to subsistence production in the reserves and forced to work free of charge on a variety of soil conservation programs. This proved to be the most egregious of all colonial programs of coerced labor, with women shouldering the bulk of the strenuous and unpleasant work—such as the creation of hundreds of miles of communal terraces to counteract soil erosion—since most of the men had become more and more dependent upon wage labor. The root of the problem in the reserves was, of course, the simple fact that too many Kikuyu were living on too little land. The only solution was an expansion of the boundaries of the Kikuyu reserves or a change in policy to allow the Africans to own land in the exclusive White Highlands. Neither policy was considered at this time.[39]

The Kikuyu soldiers who returned from war would galvanize the growing popular discontent. As part of the Allied forces, the British government marshaled troops from around its empire. The Kikuyu, like other British subjects, joined the British army and were shipped off to fight in the

Middle East and the India-Burma theaters of war.[40] After the Allied victory, they returned home with a new global awareness of nationalist movements like that in India, as well as a genuine belief that they had fought for the principles of self-determination against the forces of fascism. In Kenya Kikuyu veterans found many of their British counterparts receiving demobilization support from the colonial government in the form of land, low-interest loans, and job creation programs. Ex-servicemen from Britain constituted another wave of immigrants to Kenya, coming to the colony through soldier settlement schemes much like those after the First World War. Kikuyu veterans expected a homecoming different from the status quo, perhaps even one bringing improvements to their daily lives commensurate with their contributions to the war effort. Dismayingly, they found that their fortunes, and those of their fellow Kikuyu, not only had remained unchanged but were steadily worsening.

The basis for a popular Kikuyu movement extended well beyond the boundaries of the reserves. In the White Highlands increased mechanization introduced by European settlers forced thousands of squatters off their farms, and those that remained were forced to work harder and for longer hours. The closing of the squatter frontier created an agitated group of homeless and property-less people in a land they considered to be their own. Some went back to the reserves, though they received a less than warm reception from distant family members who were already struggling. Popular discontent was also taking hold in depressed urban areas, particularly Nairobi, to which many of the dispossessed squatters and impoverished peasants from the reserves migrated in search of work. The African residential areas in the city quickly became overcrowded, unemployment escalated, and inflation skyrocketed. The so-called informal economy—including hawking, beer brewing, and prostitution—offered many urban residents their only hope of survival. It was hardly surprising that the Kikuyu poor, already disaffected by their loss of land and condemned to an alien urban existence, sought to redress their grievances against both the European and African agents of colonialism.

In spite of abundant Kikuyu frustration, there still did not exist the means by which to mobilize. Kikuyu politicians from the KCA, as well as the nascent trade union movement, had been forced underground during the war, only to reemerge in 1944 with the formation of the Kenya African Union, or KAU. Three years later Kenyatta—now calling himself Jomo Kenyatta—returned to Kenya after a sixteen-year stay in Britain, where he studied at the London School of Economics, cosponsored a Pan African Congress with Kwame Nkrumah, and wrote his controversial book, *Facing Mount Kenya*, which was a highly polemical defense of the cultural practices of the Kikuyu, and of their ability to speak for themselves.[41] Kenyatta's return electrified the colony, making it apparent that he was not only the chosen leader of the Kikuyu people but also the popular protagonist for the entire indigenous population in Kenya.

However, it was neither Kenyatta nor KAU who discovered a means for mobilizing the masses, but rather a group of several thousand Kikuyu squatters who had been forced to leave the White Highlands and resettle in an area called Olenguruone. Threatened by the colonial government with yet another eviction, sometime around 1943 the Olenguruone residents radicalized the traditional Kikuyu practice of oathing. Typically, Kikuyu men had taken an oath to forge solidarity during times of war or internal crises; the oath would morally bind men together in the face of great challenges. But at Olenguruone the oath was transformed by the changing political circumstances of British colonialism, and local Kikuyu leaders administered it not only to men but to women and children as well. This oath united the Kikuyu at Olenguruone in a collective effort to fight the injustices of British rule.[42]

Mass oathing spread rapidly as African politicians quickly recognized its potential for organizing, though it was largely limited to the Kikuyu population. Initial grassroots support for oathing largely came from members of the Kikuyu independent schools and churches, which had been formed in the wake of the earlier female-circumcision crisis. By 1950 the scale of the oathing campaign made the movement's detection unavoidable, and the colony's African Affairs Department noted that "secret meetings were being held in which an illegal oath, accompanied by appropriately horrid ritual, was being administered to initiates binding them to treat all Government servants as enemies, to disobey Government orders and eventually to evict all Europeans from the country."[43]

The movement that would be popularized as Mau Mau[44] was quickly seen by colonial officials as a unified force. In reality, however, its leadership, pulled from KAU and other groups, came to be divided over several issues, most notably the methods by which African grievances should be addressed. By 1950 the young militants—many of them drawn from the ranks of the ex-soldier community—began splitting from the moderate political elite of KAU. These radicals assumed control over the oathing campaigns, many of which were now being imposed by force. They introduced several different oaths, each representing a deeper pledge of loyalty to the movement and a deeper commitment to violent action. The militant wing was able successfully to link Kikuyu urban and rural discontent. Preferring violent means, they began to replace earlier constitutional methods of reproach, such as those advocated by Kenyatta and his moderate compatriots, with calls for active, armed resistance. In spite of the August 1950 government ban on Mau Mau, the pace of violence quickened not only in the White Highlands, where the remaining squatters, frustrated at every turn, saw hope in the militants' demands for land and freedom, but also in Nairobi, where the conditions of the urban poor steadily eroded, and in the Kikuyu reserves, where members of the chiefly community were already being murdered by Mau Mau adherents.[45]

Oathing ceremonies, so crucial to the solidarity of ordinary Kikuyu, could number well over one hundred participants. Mau Mau initiates often would enter into a liminal state by passing through an arch of banana leaves and stripping naked, in effect shedding their former status in the community and preparing themselves for their symbolic rebirth as Mau Mau adherents. With some variation, an oath administrator would direct the slaughtering of a goat and then lead the initiates in a ritual. He would sometimes begin by asking them, "[Do you] agree to become a Kikuyu, a full Kikuyu, free from blemish?"[46] The initiates would answer in the affirmative, and they would then bite and ingest a piece of the goat meat. The oath administrator would go on to inquire if the candidate wanted to know the "secret" of the Kikuyu people, and again the initiates would answer in the affirmative and receive instruction in the history of the Kikuyu people and Mau Mau's goals of land and freedom.[47] Various vows were then repeated, followed by the refrain "may this oath kill me." Two of the most common pledges were "If I know of any enemy of our organization and fail to kill him, may this oath kill me," and "If I reveal this oath to any European, may this oath kill me."[48] Following each vow, the initiates would again bite and ingest pieces of meat from the slaughtered goat.

The oath not only created a new status for the Kikuyu as reborn members of Mau Mau but also served as a moral contract. A genuine fear of reprisal infused most of the oath takers, regardless of whether they were willing participants in the ceremony or not. Forced oathing did not make the pledge less binding, and in fact the bind of the oath often prevented them—even under torture or threat of death—from betraying the movement. Just as a Kikuyu one hundred years earlier believed he could not elude the power of an oath, so many Mau Mau adherents believed in the repercussions of breaking their pledge. In an interview one former Mau Mau adherent insisted, "It was a very strong oath, in the Kikuyu belief, just like during the old days when the Kikuyu elders, after having slaughtered a goat, they used to hit the ground with their sticks while uttering the words, 'He who divulges information about the *kiama* [council], may he fall down like this!'"[49] In effect, the Kikuyu believed that if an oath taker violated his or her pledge, then loyalty to Mau Mau would be broken. If someone confessed having taken the oath, that person would suffer the wrath of the Kikuyu creator god, Ngai. His punishment would come in the form of injury—or, more likely, death.

Such beliefs render research into oathing an enormous challenge. To this day, most former Mau Mau adherents believe in the power of the oath and the fatal consequences of divulging its secrets. For example, while traveling in the area of Mathira near the foot of Mount Kenya, I asked Lucy Mugwe, an elderly Kikuyu woman whom I had been interviewing for some time, what had happened to one of her neighbors who was missing. She replied, "Oh, she was walking back up the hill carrying water [which was roughly a fifteen-gallon container strapped around her forehead and swung over her back] when her cow walked in her path and knocked her over. She died not long thereafter." Lucy then leaned over and in a hushed voice reminded me, "But you know it was to be expected . . . that woman confessed the oath years ago."[50] Only after considerable time living in the field did I begin to explore the issue of oathing with former Mau Mau adherents, and even then I only scratched the surface of its history and meaning.

The British colonial government estimated that the first Mau Mau oath, or the oath of unity, was administered to nearly 90 percent of the 1.5 million Kikuyu people.[51] As the movement progressed, the Mau Mau leadership devised seven different oaths, with each successive level representing greater commitment to the movement. Accompanying each new oath was a new ritual that incorporated the drinking of animal and even human blood, and the biting or eating of various animal parts. In one account of the fourth oath, a Kikuyu was bound together with his fellow initiates using a goat intestine, was cut on his arms by the oath administrator, then compelled to lick blood from the fresh wounds of his fellow oath takers. According to the initiate, "After taking the blood, one felt how a woman feels towards her harvest of maize or beans [e.g., protective]. That was how someone who had taken [this] oath felt about his land. He could do anything to protect it, even if it meant death."[52] The seventh and final oath was called the *batuni*, or killing oath. It would become more widespread after Kenya's governor declared a State of Emergency in the colony, and was administered only to those who were prepared to fight in the forests.

Indoctrination into the Mau Mau movement drew upon this adaptation of traditional Kikuyu oathing for the new explosive circumstances of the postwar period. Whereas the colonial government, and certainly the local settlers, viewed oathing as barbaric mumbo jumbo and further evidence of the backwardness and savagery of the Kikuyu, the practice had logic and purpose. It was the rational response of a rural people seeking to understand the enormous socioeconomic and political changes taking place around them while attempting to respond collectively to new and un-just realities.

On the eve of the Mau Mau war, there were hundreds of thousands of Kikuyu who had taken an oath of unity, pledging their lives for Mau Mau and its demand for land and freedom. When the European settlers and the colonial government learned of the movement, land and freedom were clearly understood as demands for the return of disputed land and an end to British colonialism. But for those Kikuyu who pledged themselves to Mau Mau, the meanings of land and freedom were less defined and much more complex than merely tossing off the British yoke and reclaiming the land of their ancestors. In part, the specific meaning of Mau Mau tended to reflect the age, gender, and birthplace of the oath taker. For some of them, land and freedom meant a rejection of the colonial-appointed chiefs and their policies of self-aggrandizement.[53] For many men in the younger generation, it was a demand for a return of the frontier where they could once again earn their adulthood, often with the help of an elder Kikuyu patron.[54] For some Kikuyu women, land and freedom repre-sented an end to the backbreaking terracing projects and other forms of forced communal labor.[55] For others, the slogan represented a future hope of finding farms in the overcrowded reserves that were large enough to feed their children.[56] It was as much the ambiguity as the specificity of Mau Mau's demand for land and freedom that made it so appealing to the Kikuyu masses and such a powerful and difficult movement for the British to suppress.

By 1950 Kenya was on the verge of one of the bloodiest and most protracted wars of decolonization fought in Britain's twentieth-century empire. Mau Mau had enormous grassroots support, and it was clearly directed at both the white and black faces of British colonial rule, notably the settlers and the colonial-appointed chiefs. For their part, the settlers reacted with pre-dictable hysteria and with demands for a draconian response on the part of the colonial government. Though the settlers were by no means a unified ideological force—there certainly existed a spectrum of European opinion in the colony on all issues—they quickly coalesced around the issue of Mau Mau. Whereas for years the proverbial "conservative tail wagged the mod-erate dog"[57] in Kenyan settler politics, with the onset of Mau Mau settler conservatism and overt racism would harden, and local European opinion would collectively move farther and farther to the right.

Alongside the settlers stood the other target of Mau Mau hatred, the colonial-appointed chiefs and their followers who in the upcoming war would be called loyalists. These men became enormously wealthy and powerful at the expense of their fellow Kikuyu. Some even earned the status of senior chief, overseeing vast portions of the Kikuyu reserves, with all the inherent potential for self-aggrandizement. For the Kikuyu masses, senior chiefs like the soon-to-be-famous Waruhiu represented everything that was corrupt about Britain's civilizing mission. The backbone of loyalist support during Mau Mau would come from these men, along with the lesser chiefs and headmen, and their coteries. Importantly, *loyalist* would come to have a very specific meaning for the colonial government and for those who considered themselves loyalists, of which there would ultimately be several thousand. Quite simply, *loyalist* was a term for any Kikuyu who would actively fight on the side of the British government against the Mau Mau movement and who in return would be granted privileges that would far outweigh anything that previously had been granted to the chiefly community during the years leading up to the war.

For Mau Mau followers, those who betrayed their movement had to be eliminated. This included not just the loyalists but also the small minority of devout Kikuyu Christians who were neither Mau Mau nor loyalist, and who suffered persecutions from both opposing factions. The local Christian missionaries would fight endlessly with the colonial government to expand the official definition of *loyalism*, claiming that their Christian flock comprised the most loyal and Western-leaning Kikuyu in the colony. They would have very limited success. Throughout the war these missionaries would play a pivotal role, as many witnessed the atrocities that would unfold in the detention camps and barbed-wire villages. The degree to which they would intervene against—and in some cases abet—colonial violence would be a reflection of their own self-interests and their loyalty to the colonial government.

Overseeing the unfolding Mau Mau drama was Kenya's governor, Sir Philip Mitchell, and the colonial secretary in London, Oliver Lyttelton. Mitchell was a short, pudgy, and by all accounts rather unlikable man who, on paper, appeared to be the governor best suited to take on the job in Kenya in late 1944. He was at the end of a long and distinguished career in Britain's colonial service, which presumably made him the ideal candidate. He was, though, staunchly determined to retire with a spotless record, a goal which took on new meaning when his colony became the new jewel of the British Empire after Britain's loss of India in 1947. When Mau Mau began to emerge as a real force in 1950, Mitchell downplayed its significance and scope to the Colonial Office, as well as the escalating violence and disorder.[58] Anything less would have been an admission of his failure to govern. Right up to his retirement in June 1952, he sent memo after memo to

London inaccurately reporting the peace and progress of his colony. In reality, violence was already reaching serious proportions, with Mau Mau hamstringing settler cattle, burning crops, and murdering Kikuyu loyal to the British. Had he alerted Colonial Secretary Lyttelton, London would surely have intervened, and several senior officials on the spot would have been held accountable and their careers tarnished. Remarkably, Mitchell successfully managed to retire with honor, though his charade would soon be unveiled. During the long summer of 1952, as Kenya awaited its new governor, the situation continued to deteriorate. It was now clear to those on the spot that Mau Mau was preparing to launch an anticolonial and civil rebellion, though few at the time foresaw the level of destruction that lay over the horizon.

CHAPTER TWO

BRITAIN'S ASSAULT ON
MAU MAU

Senior Chief Waruhiu lying dead in his Hudson

IN THE LATE AFTERNOON OF OCTOBER 9, 1952, SENIOR CHIEF WARUHIU stepped into the backseat of his spotless Hudson sedan for what would become a most fateful journey. His driver whisked him and two of his friends away from the controlled order of downtown colonial Nairobi en route to the village of Gachie not far from the White Highlands. The journey along winding, narrow roads would take them past the graceful pink stucco buildings and manicured grounds of the Muthaiga Club. Partway through the journey a gentle rain began to fall as the Hudson climbed the foothills, reflecting the vibrant green of the local coffee plantations and the ever-present banana trees with their tremendous, oval-shaped leaves. As the driver made a sharp turn, three men wearing British colonial police uniforms waved the car to a stop. One of them approached the car, leaned in, and asked for Senior Chief Waruhiu. The senior chief no sooner identified himself than the man drew a pistol and shot him in the mouth and then three more times in the torso. The Mau Mau adherents, masquerading as policemen, shot out the car's tires before making their escape. Despite three eyewitnesses—the driver and the

other passengers were left unharmed—the real assassins were never ap-
prehended.[1]

The murder of Senior Chief Waruhiu came just ten days after Sir Evelyn
Baring arrived in Kenya to assume his new role as governor of the colony.
The settlers had greeted him with hysteria and irrepressible demands to
take action against the Kikuyu who were reportedly ravaging the countryside. In fact, there could be no doubt that in the months leading up to Baring's arrival Mau Mau had struck on numerous occasions, destroying settler
property and murdering several Kikuyu loyalists. The local police also suspected Mau Mau of claiming its first white victim on October 3 when Mrs.
A. M. Wright was stabbed to death by unknown assailants near her home in
Thika, only ten miles from Nairobi. But Baring had received no warning
from either the Colonial Office or his predecessor, Sir Philip Mitchell, about
the escalating violence, despite the fact that both men were fully aware of
the deteriorating situation in Kenya.[2] For his part, Mitchell could not bring
himself to admit the severity of the situation and thus shatter his dream of
retiring with a spotless colonial record. But Colonial Secretary Lyttelton
had received numerous reports in the summer of 1952 from Kenya's acting
governor, Henry Potter, as well as cables from several outraged settlers, that
Mau Mau savagery was increasing at a dangerously fast pace. Lyttelton and
his staff dismissed these accounts, even those coming from his administrative officers in the field, as exaggerated and alarmist. Mau Mau, Lyttelton
felt, could be checked with a few pieces of hard-nosed legislation and some
tougher policing. There was no need to panic.[3]

Baring had yet even to unpack at Government House when he was confronted with the realities of his new post. Awaiting him on his desk was a
memorandum from the colony's chief native commissioner concluding
that Mau Mau had gained control over the three Kikuyu districts, that it
was anti-European and atavistic, and that it was spreading rapidly. Worse,
the colony's security was deteriorating, despite the fact that Potter, the acting governor, had imposed curfews and collective punishments, and had
increased the size of the police force in the months before Baring's arrival.
Jomo Kenyatta, according to the report, was the mastermind behind the
Mau Mau movement, though there was no direct evidence to implicate the
Kikuyu leader as directing either the oathing campaign or the escalating
terror.[4] Other colonial officers with firsthand knowledge of the situation in
the Kikuyu reserves and Nairobi soon briefed Baring, warning him of the
savagery of Mau Mau and of the ominous threat it presented. But the new
governor decided he had to see for himself, and immediately after his
swearing-in he set off on a tour of the Kikuyu areas outside of Nairobi. Of
his stop in Kandara, he later recalled, "I've never seen such faces, they were

scowling, they looked unhappy, they were intensely suspicious. It was an expression I saw a great deal during the early years of Mau Mau."[5] There is no record of Baring ever suggesting during his introductory tour or at any time during the Emergency that the Kikuyu people might have had a genuine social or economic grievance. From the time he arrived in Kenya, he accepted uncritically the notion that Mau Mau was a completely illegitimate movement. On his tour he spoke with no one suspected of Mau Mau sympathies. Instead, he had meetings with Kikuyu chiefs and headmen, all colonial-appointed officials, as well as with teachers from the mission schools. They all painted a desperate picture of a breakdown in law and order, and all emphasized, as Baring remembered, that "if you don't get Kenyatta and those all round him and shut them up somehow or other we are in a terrible, hopeless position."[6]

Evelyn Baring appeared in person and pedigree to be a most capable colonial leader, a man who could navigate Kenya through the Mau Mau storm. He was dashing, strikingly tall and handsome, and particularly majestic when he wore his full gubernatorial regalia, including an oversized white helmet topped with ostrich plumes. Baring's name offered a distinct cachet to the title "His Excellency the Governor of Kenya." Born into Britain's distinguished imperial and financial family, he was the son of the famed Lord Cromer, known as the "Maker of Modern Egypt," whose imperious behavior earned him the other, less honorific nickname of "over-Baring." But Evelyn hardly knew his father. Lord Cromer was already in his early sixties when Evelyn was born, and then spent much of his time in Egypt, leaving his young son behind in Britain. Evelyn was thirteen when his father died in 1917. Since that time, he spent much of his life trying to relive his father's career. After taking First Class Honors at Oxford in modern history, Baring joined the Indian Civil Service, whose decentralized style of colonial rule made a lasting impression on the young administrator. It was in India that Baring honed his understanding of land-based politics and rural administration. He then moved on to Britain's Foreign Office, which dispatched him to the settler colony of Southern Rhodesia and then finally to South Africa, where he took over the coveted post of high commissioner.[7]

Despite his formidable background in imperial governance, the vicissitudes of late colonial Kenya would vex Baring from the moment he arrived in the colony. He was foremost a colonial bureaucrat whose prior success was largely due to his carefully measured, methodical style of governance. In most circumstances this style and these skills were exactly what was needed to run Britain's far-flung empire. But the Emergency in Kenya

His Excellency Sir Evelyn Baring inspecting the troops

would present different challenges. It would demand quick and decisive action by the colony's governor. There would be no time to ruminate while the events of Mau Mau were unfolding at breakneck speed. Lord Cromer would have been well suited for the job but, in several ways, Baring was not his father's son. He lacked "over-Baring's" rough-and-ready mentality; his mind was better suited to his favorite leisure pursuits of wildflower collecting and bird-watching. Finally, he was devoid of the oratory skills that would be needed to ingratiate himself with the local settler population. And though patrician in stature, Baring was hardly robust. He had contracted a severe case of amoebic dysentery in India that had left him with bouts of disabling intestinal pain and severe exhaustion, accompanied by depression, for the remainder of his life.[8] Baring must be characterized, then, as the colonial ideal on paper, a patrician figure who at least superficially seemed to represent everything that was exemplary about British colonial rule—even if he was not the most well-suited man for the job of governing Kenya during the crisis of Mau Mau.

The news of Waruhiu's assassination reached Baring in the middle of his Central Province tour. The governor hurried back to Nairobi and, only a few hours after the senior chief had been murdered, he cabled the Colonial Office seeking permission to declare a State of Emergency. Baring knew

Waruhiu had been one of the strongest supporters of Britain's colonial enterprise in Kenya. The senior chief had embraced Western values, having become a devout Christian, an advocate of British law and order, and one of the most outspoken critics of Mau Mau—earning him the epitaph in the British press of "Africa's Churchill."[9] He also was always careful to look the part of a black Englishman, dressing impeccably in a crisp European suit, pressed oxford shirt, tie, and hat.

Mau Mau adherents loathed Waruhiu and the other senior Kikuyu chiefs who controlled their lives and reaped the benefits of colonial patronage. The senior chief's death was civil justice according to Mau Mau, and so most of Kikuyuland did not mourn, but rather celebrated his murder with dancing and songs, some of which are still remembered today. Simply mentioning the name Waruhiu prompts some former Mau Mau adherents to burst out: "I will never sell out my country, or love money more than my country. Waruhiu sold out his country for money, but he died and left his money."[10] For Baring, the senior chief's death was an outrage that could not be ignored. For the next ten days Governor Baring and Colonial Secretary Lyttelton fired secret memoranda back and forth, working through the details and justifications of the impending State of Emergency.[11] They were convinced it would be over before it started—three months at best. Decapitate the movement and introduce a few more restrictive measures, they reasoned, and Mau Mau would fall apart. The Emergency would in fact be a blessing, avoiding bloodshed by getting rid of the Mau Mau leadership, so bringing peace to Kenya.

Senior Chief Waruhiu's funeral was as much a stage for Kenya's unfolding drama as it was a somber testimonial to a fallen servant of the British Crown. Almost everyone of political importance attended, including both Jomo Kenyatta and the governor, posturing and sizing up the other side. Kenyatta and Baring stood near each other but did not exchange a single word just days before the governor was to sign the arrest order for Mau Mau's alleged mastermind.

With Operation Jock Scott, Kenya's State of Emergency was officially launched. This code-named assault was directed at Kenyatta and 180 other identified leaders of Mau Mau. In the early morning of October 21, 1952, scores of Kenyan policemen, white and black, zealously carried out their arrest orders, rousing suspected Mau Mau protagonists like Paul Ngei, Fred Kubai, and Bildad Kaggia, handcuffing them, and hauling them off to Nairobi police station. Not surprisingly, Kenyatta was given special treatment. With great melodrama, scores of police officers escorted him from his home in the middle of the night and drove him to a waiting plane at the military airfield outside of Nairobi. As the plane took off and passed over the Aberdares, Kenyatta was convinced he was going to be ejected into the forest below, where his body would never be recovered.[12] Instead, he soon found himself in total isolation more than four hundred miles to the north of Nairobi, at a place called Lokitaung—an arid and desolate region where the Turkana pastoralists herded their livestock. There simply could not have been a more remote or inhospitable spot in Kenya.

Operation Jock Scott ushered in the colony's rapid decline. Contrary to official wisdom, Mau Mau did not collapse with the arrest of the politicals, but instead turned more violent as the movement's leadership passed into the hands of younger men, the same men who for months had been pushing Kenyatta and others to adopt a more radical, revolutionary course. Baring and Lyttelton had managed to remove the one person who had been tenuously keeping the young militants in check; in fact, Mau Mau only gained strength when Kenyatta the heroic Kikuyu leader also became, literally overnight, Kenyatta the martyr. Although his political leanings were more moderate than the majority of Mau Mau, Kenyatta became a potent and unifying political symbol. For Mary Nyambura, who lived outside of Nairobi in an area known as Banana Hill, Kenyatta was the man who "would liberate me from the [colonial] district officer who was forcing me to work"; the youthful Hunja Njuki thought Kenyatta was "the leader fighting to give me a rightful share of my land"; and then there was the elderly Magayu Kiama, born before the turn of the century, who believed "[Kenyatta] would destroy the local chief" who had been harassing his wife and helping himself to Magayu's goats.[13] For every Mary, Hunja, and Magayu, there were hundreds of thousands of other Kikuyu men and women who had their own reasons for joining Mau Mau, and who saw them embodied in Kenyatta, the unjustly detained and rightful leader of the Kikuyu people. It is here that Baring and Lyttelton made their other gross miscalculation. Colonial racist orthodoxy refused to allow for independent African thought, let alone sophisticated social and economic grievances. At the start of Mau Mau Kenya's governor, the colonial secretary, nearly all colonial administrators in the colony, and certainly most of the local settlers underestimated the political sophistication of the ordinary Kikuyu. While recognizing the depth of Kikuyu anger, they thought it was the result of Kenyatta's manipulations and the so-called spell of the Mau Mau oath, rather than an outgrowth of legitimate complaints rooted in individual circumstances.

As Governor Baring signed the Emergency order on the evening of October 20, twelve aircraft carrying the first contingent of British ground

British soldiers on patrol in Nairobi

troops landed at Nairobi's Eastleigh airfield. Hundreds of baby-faced soldiers from the Lancashire Fusiliers drove their military vehicles through the streets of the capital to reassure the local Europeans and, in theory, intimidate Mau Mau adherents. At first, this gunboat diplomacy appeared to work as initially there was no major combat. Mau Mau appeared to be a phony war. In reality, this period was the calm before the storm as Mau Mau, caught unprepared by Baring's declaration, went through several months of military buildup both in and outside of the forests of the Mount Kenya and Aberdares mountain ranges, about fifty miles north and west of Nairobi. With the Emergency now in effect, hundreds and eventually thousands of Mau Mau adherents fled to these forests, where a fragmented leadership had begun to establish individual platoons before the Emergency started, and was now responsible for taking young men and women who had never seen combat and turning them into soldiers. Some of these leaders had served in the British army during World War II, had been in combat in Southeast Asia, and were able to draw on their prior military experience to organize their troops in the forests. They adopted British ranks—using titles like field marshal, general, major, and lieutenant—and attempted to instill strict discipline, though they did not always follow their own rules.[14] Outside of the forests, Mau Mau adherents organized an intricate, passive-wing operation that would provide intelligence, weapons, food, and other supplies to the forest fighters. It was the size of this passive-wing organization that reflected the grassroots depth of the movement.

The relative calm in the forests was shattered by a series of gruesome, high-profile murders. In late October on the farming plateau above Naivasha the disemboweled corpse of Eric Bowker, a settler and veteran of both world wars, was found in his home—the brutal nature of his murder a sure sign of a Mau Mau attack, according to the local whites. Less than a month later, an elderly couple living at the edge of the Aberdares forest, near Thomson's Falls, were sitting down for their after-dinner coffee when they were attacked with machetes by Mau Mau guerrillas. The husband, retired naval commander Ian "Jock" Meiklejohn, collapsed while loading his shotgun and died two days later. His wife, a retired doctor, survived despite extensive mutilation of her torso and breasts.[15] Four days later Tom Mbotela's body was found in a muddy pool of water near the Burma Market in Nairobi. An outspoken critic of Mau Mau and an African-appointed member of the City Council, Mbotela was reviled by many Africans and had already escaped one assassination attempt. During the hustle of morning commuting and trade, hundreds of market goers had passed his body until it was discovered by a European passerby. That evening the Burma Market, named in recognition of the Africans who had served on the Burma front during the war, was burned to the ground. According to witnesses, it was the local police who torched the stalls, infuriated by Mbotela's death and the defiant indifference, if not complicity, of the locals.[16]

The European community in Kenya was justifiably terrified by these events. Many living in the White Highlands were on isolated farms without telephones and far from police assistance. They were a tiny white minority, and the fear of "the night of the long knives" that had hung over their colonial idyll for so long was finally upon them. They demanded quick and summary justice against Mau Mau. A "pathological atmosphere"—as Dame Margery Perham, the Colonial Office's own Oxford tutor, called it—had already been present before the Emergency and was now intensifying as settlers started taking the law into their own hands.[17] Governor Baring stood by, although fully aware of ongoing settler justice and the formation of vigilante groups throughout the Rift Valley and around Nairobi. Settlers, with the help of the Administration, were exacting revenge on Mau Mau suspects in unspeakable ways. In the wake of the attacks on Bowker and the Meiklejohns, Baring wrote to the colonial secretary "of Europeans taking drastic action on their own" and went on to forewarn that "this might even lead to something like civil war."[18]

In the midst of this growing settler hysteria, the colonial government, in a risky move, decided to prosecute Kenyatta along with five of his so-called deputies: Bildad Kaggia, Fred Kubai, Paul Ngei, Achieng' Oneko, and Kungu Karumba.[19] On the one hand, an acquittal would have surely created mayhem in the colony, transforming the already uncontrollable settler outrage into virtual anarchy. On the other, a conviction would be interpreted by the Kikuyu as yet another travesty of British colonial justice. There was a viable alternative to trying these men. With the powers of detention that were at his disposal as governor, Baring could easily have kept them safely locked away, as he would later do with many of the others arrested during Jock Scott. But there was a strong sense from the Colonial Office in particular that a trial was necessary, if only to placate some of the anticolonial critics at home who were becoming increasingly vocal in their opposition to the Emergency. Evidence to be introduced in court could offer the legal justification for the Emergency that the government so desperately needed—provided, of course, there was a conviction.[20]

But from the moment Kenyatta was arrested, Baring and his legal advisers knew they had little credible evidence with which to prosecute him. Even after a ton and a half of documents, books, and papers had been confiscated from Kenyatta's home and picked apart by colonial officials, there was virtually nothing.[21] Ultimately, and with the slimmest of evidence, the government decided to charge Kenyatta and the others with "managing an unlawful society"—or, in layman's terms, fomenting a revolution. The evidence in hand provided no basis for a conviction, at least not under British standards of impartial justice. But this was Kenya, and the system of justice accorded to Africans had been a travesty for years. Of course, the stakes were much higher, and those responsible for orchestrating Kenyatta's trial were top-level colonial officials in Kenya, including Baring himself.

Although six men were on trial, the only one who mattered to the government was Kenyatta, whose alleged crimes occurred in Kiambu. Technically, his case should have been tried in a Nairobi courthouse. Fearing demonstrations, as well as an onslaught of unwanted publicity, the government instead sent the trial to Kapenguria, one of Kenya's most remote outposts. Thirty miles north of the settler town of Kitale, near the Ugandan border, Kapenguria had no rail service, hotel, phones, restaurants, or running water. In fact, it did not even have a courthouse. In haste, the government converted an old school building for what would be the trial of the century in Kenya. Kapenguria's isolation and restricted-area status meant that the government could control who came in and out of the town, a power that would be of utmost importance as the trial progressed. The legal technicality of venue, however, was hanging in the balance and required taking Kenyatta to Kapenguria, releasing him from custody, and then rearresting him. Though this maneuver did not change the fact that his alleged crimes had been committed in Kiambu, apparently it was enough to satisfy local legal opinion.

Still, there remained the issue of evidence. Even with the new venue the colonial government had a very weak case—a problem easily solved through a few well-placed bribes. In the first instance, Baring helped to fabricate, or at the very least influence, the so-called witnesses to Kenyatta's crimes by offering them healthy financial incentives. Writing to Lyttelton in November 1952, he said, "Every possible effort has been made to offer them rewards."[22] This approach was also taken with the special magistrate brought in to hear and pass judgment on the case, one Ransley Thacker, QC. Judge Thacker had spent twelve years as a member of Kenya's Supreme Court and was the former attorney general of Fiji. As special magistrate in this case, he would be both judge and jury for the Kapenguria Six, as the defendants came to be called. The aging, potbellied, and bespectacled Thacker apparently had no qualms about selling his verdict long before the trial began. He insisted upon twenty thousand pounds to ensure a conviction, and in what must be described as one of his most self-incriminating moves as governor, Baring complied. The bribe, in fact, did not go through the attorney general's office in Kenya, as others had, but rather was appropriated by Baring himself from a special Emergency fund.[23]

Before their opening argument, Kenyatta's attorneys already knew that Thacker had his mind made up. Indeed, the defense counsel team was a formidable group of advocates—all of whom viewed the trial as simply groundwork for the eventual appeal they would be filing with the Privy Council back in Britain. Leading the team was the robust and gray-haired Dennis Lowell Pritt, QC, one of Britain's most able, and notorious, trial lawyers. Pritt was as well known for his courtroom theatrics as he was for his communist sympathies, which hardly helped Kenyatta, who was already suspected of socialist leanings. Needless to say, the settlers hated Pritt from the moment he stepped off the plane from London—particularly since there were thousands of Africans gathered at the airport to welcome him, counsel for their beloved Kenyatta.

Further inflaming settler hatred was Pritt's utter contempt for the colony's color bar. He surrounded himself with a multiracial defense team that included a Nigerian lawyer named H. O. Davies; Chaman Lall—a member of the Indian Parliament and close friend of Prime Minister Jawaharlal Nehru; and three Kenya residents: Fitz de Souza, Achhroo Kapila, and Jaswant Singh. Throughout the trial this team would daily travel back and forth between Kapenguria and the settler bastion of Kitale, along bad roads that were hardly passable due to the choking dust. In Kitale the mixed-race defense team could neither eat together nor stay in the same hotel, making their legal work extraordinarily difficult. Everyone except Pritt, who stayed in the modest Kitale Hotel, found lodging with local Africans, all of whom were subjected to repeated police raids. Making the situation all the more frustrating was the local district commissioner's decision to limit the defense team's contact with their clients to ten minutes before and after court, invoking Kapenguria's status as a restricted area. Eventually, Pritt successfully contested this mockery, but in no time the atmosphere that enveloped Kapenguria, Kitale, and the thirty-mile stretch between was one of intrigue, fear, and hostility.

When the trial began on December 3, 1952, the scene outside the makeshift courthouse was as comic as it was menacing. Having deprived the defendants of their rights, shackled and imprisoned them, removed them to Kenya's wilderness, and rigged their trial, the government also felt compelled to make a dramatic show of force. Planes circled overhead, and yellow armored cars were positioned threateningly around the makeshift courthouse, which had been ringed with barbed wire and gun-wielding troops, cached behind mountains of sandbags. Inside, press coverage was intense as Deputy Public Prosecutor Anthony Somerhough opened the case for the Crown. "May it please Your Honour," he began. "The charge is that of managing an unlawful society." He went on to spell out the government's case, arguing that

> the Crown cannot bind themselves to any particular place in the Colony where this society was managed. The Society is Mau Mau. It is a Society which has no records. It appears to have no official list of members. It does not carry banners. Some details of its meeting and its rites, the instruments of which are got from the local bush, will be heard later in the proceedings. Arches of banana leaves, the African fruit known as the Apple of Sodom, eyes of sheep, blood and earth—these are all gathered when ceremonies take place.[24]

After his introduction, which went on to accuse the defendants of misguiding the entire Kikuyu population through bestial rituals, and commanding them to drive out or kill Kenya's settler population, Somerhough confidently called his first witness. Rawson Macharia took the stand and testified to the fact that he had been present when Kenyatta had administered the Mau Mau oath to several people in Kiambu. That Macharia conceded that these oath ceremonies took place before the government had even proscribed Mau Mau mattered little to Judge Thacker. When Pritt protested, Thacker nevertheless accepted the testimony on the grounds that if Kenyatta had been administering the oath before the proscription, he must have been engaging in similar illegal oath giving after the ban on Mau Mau. It was Macharia's testimony, the key evidence the judge had for supporting his graft-inspired verdict, that would prove critical in Thacker's ultimate finding. It was hardly a surprise that after his testimony, Macharia took the next flight out for London, where he took up a two-year residence for studies at a local university—all at the expense of the British government.[25]

"I would submit that it is the most childishly weak case made against any man in any important trial in the history of the British Empire," Pritt argued after the prosecution rested its case.[26] Thacker, though, refused to dismiss the charges, gave Pritt a week to pull his defense together, and then went on to spend the recess at the Kitale Club—the area's one exclusive settler club. The judge had set up quarters there for the entire duration of the trial, spending the evenings and weekends socializing with the local settlers—most of whom would make a day of the courtroom proceedings, bringing picnic lunches served to them by white-gloved African houseboys.

It was on the first night of this adjournment—January 24, 1953—that the most sensational European murder at the hands of Mau Mau took place. On a farm not far from where Eric Bowker had been murdered, the Ruck family—Roger, Esme, and their small boy—were hacked to death by their trusted servants, one of whom had tenderly carried home the child, six-year-old Michael, after he fell from his pony, just days prior to the attack. The contradiction between the formerly kind and devoted servants and their now savage behavior electrified the settler community. Making matters worse, newspapers in Kenya and abroad published graphic murder details and postmortem photos, including images of young Michael with bloodied teddy bears and trains strewn on his bedroom floor.

The next day over fifteen hundred settlers marched on Government House in Nairobi, demanding summary justice and the elimination of the Mau Mau movement by any means necessary. Michael Blundell, a leading settler politician and member of the Kenya Legislative Council, intervened and managed to disperse the crowd, though not before the mob sang one last round of "God Save the Queen." Blundell, who would soon become one of the most influential settlers in Baring's government, recalled many years later that the European protesters were "very right wing, a very right wing reactionary, incandescent group." One settler in particular declared, "Michael, you'll never cure this problem, you'll never cure it. You put the troops into the [Kikuyu] villages and you shoot 50,000 of them, men, women and children."[27] This sentiment was becoming all too prevalent within the settler community. The Europeans in Kenya now moved about with guns at the ready. Husbands trained their wives in marksmanship,

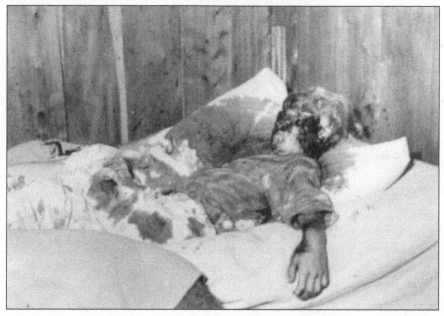

Postmortem photo of Michael Ruck after being hacked to death by Mau Mau insurgents

boarded up their windows, and formed large vigilante groups that claimed to represent the collective will of the settler community. Parents kept children home from school and indoors most hours of the day. No one was thought safe from the Mau Mau threat. Local Europeans chastised the colonial government, and Baring in particular, for being too hesitant in eliminating Mau Mau. Many called for a wholesale extermination of the Kikuyu population.[28]

Baring refused to meet with any of the settler protesters, which only confirmed their opinion that the governor was aloof and ineffective. But a few days after the murder he completely revamped the organization of Kenya's security forces, removing them from the police department and reassigning control to the British military. Baring needed to organize a more effective show of force, and Major General W. R. N. Hinde, better known as "Loony" Hinde, flew in to take charge. At first, Hinde and other members of the security forces scoffed at the Kikuyu and their ragtag militia, but the Mau Mau insurgents quickly exposed Britain's inadequacies in fighting a nonconventional war. Mau Mau became one of the first armed struggles of the twentieth century where superior Western firepower was no match, at least initially, for local knowledge of difficult forest terrain, or for the insurgents' use of hit-and-run tactics. Because it underestimated the strength and shrewdness of Mau Mau, the colonial government withheld from

Hinde the authority and the manpower he needed to seize the initiative and restore local law and order. The security forces were a splintered group partly composed of British military personnel, over whom Hinde had command. But there was also the Kenya Regiment, a volunteer militia of several thousand settlers; the Kenya police force, also with thousands of settlers in its ranks; the Kikuyu loyalists, who would soon begin to fight actively on the side of the colonial government as part of the Home Guard; and the King's African Rifles, a standing force of African men from Kenya, Tanganyika, and Uganda, and their European officers, who were deployed en masse to Kikuyuland at the start of the Emergency. Hinde had little control over these units, which instead remained largely under the authority of either Baring or one of his ministers. He found himself in the unenviable position of having to manage an uncoordinated offensive against Mau Mau. All the while, the settlers were demanding more decisive and draconian action, while the various elements responsible for suppressing Mau Mau—the army, the police, the local militias, and the Administration—generally refused to cooperate, let alone work as a single unit.

When the trial resumed, the Rucks' shadow hung over the Kapenguria courtroom. The settlers demanded retribution, and the virtually uncontrollable lynch mob had its eyes set on Kenyatta, who had become more than ever the universal scapegoat. During the adjournment numerous articles had flooded into the press in Kenya and in Britain—many of which shared an earlier condemnation of Kenyatta in the *Daily Telegraph* as "A Small-Scale African Hitler."[29] By the time Kenyatta took the stand his conviction was a mere formality. In his closing argument Pritt surgically disposed of the prosecution's case and argued powerfully for the legitimacy of African nationalism. If his clients were to have no chance, then at least the QC would publicize their cause. After closing arguments, Judge Thacker continued to make a show of things, adjourning for a month to mull over his findings before delivering his verdict.

While the colony awaited that verdict, two decisive Mau Mau strikes on March 26 shook Kenya, finally dashing any hopes for a brief, nonshooting war. The first raid took place on Naivasha Police Station in the Rift Valley. There, nearly eighty Mau Mau guerrillas executed a well-planned swoop. They broke into the armory, stole a large supply of firearms and ammunition, and released close to two hundred Mau Mau prisoners before making their escape.[30] The British security forces had suffered deep embarrassment, and the Mau Mau were finally recognized by the British military command as a legitimate fighting organization. The second Mau Mau strike took place only a few hours later at Lari, a few miles outside of Nairobi, where a long-standing dispute over land came to a grisly end. After weeks of threats, Mau Mau attacked the homesteads of Chief Luka—a loyalist and beneficiary of a vast land concession from the colonial government— his eight wives, and their followers. The Mau Mau insurgents burned the loyalists in their huts and hacked to death those who tried to escape the fires. They mutilated men and women, old and young alike. In total, ninety-seven Lari residents died, scores of others suffered serious disfigurements, and some two hundred huts were burned and several hundred head of cattle destroyed. With the homesteads still smoldering and the bodies yet to be removed, the colonial government shepherded the press into the area to witness and record the carnage. Official press releases were handed out that described in gruesome detail the carnage resulting from the attack, which the colonial government called the Lari massacre. These releases, though, failed to mention that as many as four hundred Mau Mau were killed by security forces—British and African soldiers, local police officers, and loyalists—during a vengeful reprisal.

By the time Kenyatta's judgment was rendered on April 8, the settlers were in a frenzy and the Emergency appeared out of control. When Thacker handed down his guilty verdict against Kenyatta and the other five defendants, it seemed to provide some measure of psychological relief to the local Europeans. Before passing sentence, the judge gave the alleged Mau Mau mastermind one last opportunity to speak. At the time, it seemed it would be his last opportunity to address the public. Kenyatta spoke of the "discriminations in the government of this country" and denied his involvement in directing Mau Mau. "Our activities have been against the injustices suffered by the African people," Kenyatta implored, "and if in trying to establish the rights of the African people we have turned out to be what you say, Mau Mau, we are very sorry that you have been misled in that direction. What we have done, and what we shall continue to do, is to demand the rights of the African people as human beings that they may enjoy the facilities and privileges in the same way as other people."[31]

It was then Thacker's turn. Looking down upon the defendants—but focusing solely on Kenyatta—he dismissed the evidence presented by ten exonerating witnesses, and delivered his sentence.

> You, Jomo Kenyatta, stand convicted of managing Mau Mau and being a member of that society. You have protested that your object has always been to pursue constitutional methods on the way to self-government for the

African people, and for the return of land which you say belongs to the African people. I do not believe you. It is my belief that soon after your long stay in Europe and when you came back to this Colony you commenced to organize this Mau Mau society, the object of which was to drive out from Kenya all Europeans, and in doing so to kill them if necessary. I am satisfied that the mastermind behind this plan was yours. . . . Your Mau Mau society has slaughtered without mercy defenseless Kikuyu men, women and children in hundreds and in circumstances which are revolting and are better left undescribed. You let loose upon this land a flood of misery and unhappiness affecting the daily lives of all races in it, including your own people. You put the clock back many years. . . . You have much to answer for and for that you will be punished.[32]

He then sentenced Kenyatta and the rest of the Kapenguria Six to the maximum seven years' imprisonment with hard labor, to be followed by a lifetime of restriction. In other words, they were to live in isolation for the rest of their lives. As soon as the trial was over, Thacker hustled out of the courthouse into an awaiting armored car and took the next flight back to London—twenty thousand pounds richer for his five months of work. Kenyatta and the others were destined to spend years in the desolation of Lokitaung, their later appeals dismissed by the higher courts—including the Privy Council in London, which rejected Pritt's petition without offering any reason whatsoever.[33]

Like most wars, Mau Mau was as much about propaganda as it was about reality. From the start of the Emergency the colonial government was masterful in its public depiction of Mau Mau. Directing the colonial propaganda war was Granville Roberts, the Kenya public relations officer based in the Colonial Office in London. Almost daily he oversaw the release of government press office handouts that chronicled the unfolding events. Some of the handouts were mundane reading, others lurid in detailing Mau Mau atrocities. Equally powerful as the photographs distributed by the Colonial Office was the language used to describe Mau Mau. The "horror of Mau Mau" stood in contrast to what the public relations officer called the "peaceful and progressive conditions" of Kenya prior to the Emergency.[34] The "white" and "enlightened" forces of British colonialism were a stark contradistinction to the "dark," "evil," "foul," "secretive," and "degraded" Mau Mau.[35] These descriptions spilled over into the Kenyan and British press, where sensationalist accounts juxtaposed white heroism with African, or Mau Mau, terrorism and savagery.[36] Roberts was not alone. In speeches both Governor Baring and Colonial Secretary Lyttelton

Jomo Kenyatta under guarded escort during the Kapenguria trial

used similar language and would often stop just short of providing graphic details of Mau Mau attacks and oathing ceremonies, further titillating listeners and permitting the public to allow its racist imagination and fear to run wild.

The press releases were not mere spin-doctoring. They also reflected a colonial world that was organized according to a strongly hierarchical scale of humanity. White racial supremacy in Kenya had long manifested itself in various kinds of primitive settler justice, including public floggings, beating deaths, and summary executions.[37] The majority of Africans were at the very bottom of the European settlers' human hierarchy. The nature and demands of Mau Mau led to an even greater pathological fear by whites of the Kikuyu. It was the distinctive quality of Mau Mau oathing rituals, and methods of killing, that transformed the virulent racism that had been the cornerstone of settler racial attitudes for over half a century into something even more lethal. Settlers and colonial officials alike were repelled by the Kikuyu oaths, which used powerful symbols like goats' blood and eyeballs, and ram intestines and scrotums. Mau Mau's method of killing with *pangas*, or machetes, was likewise bloody and helped to further drive local Europeans into a frenzied state of terror.

Settler anxiety did of course have a basis in fact, yet the settlers' dehumanizing view of Mau Mau cannot be completely understood without placing it in its social and historical context. The majority of European settlers who immigrated to Kenya did so with the intention of making Kenya their permanent home; they were establishing farms, schools, and communities not just for themselves but for their children and grandchildren. But after World War II many settlers felt increasingly isolated as the same principles of self-determination that were circulating throughout the world reached Kenya, leaving settlers less certain about the degree of support they might continue to enjoy from their government. Newly repressive colonial policies and practices during Mau Mau would soon create the impression that these fears were somewhat unfounded. But the settlers remained an implacable group, forever suspicious and critical of the "liberals" from London and elsewhere who they believed knew nothing about their country or their "natives."

Mau Mau thus ushered in a critical change in the settlers' already racist hierarchical segregation of humanity. There was a shift in language and belief, from simple white supremacy to one that was overtly eliminationist. In this altered hierarchy the Europeans were clearly positioned at the top, and the Asians and loyalist Africans somewhere in the lower middle. But in the settler imagination, Mau Mau adherents were scarcely part of humanity's continuum; they were indistinguishable in local thought and expression from the animals that roamed the colony. From the early days of the Emergency, this attitude became accepted orthodoxy for much of the Administration. Frank Loyd, who was later knighted for his formidable service in Britain's empire, was stationed in Kenya's Central Province—the heart of Kikuyuland—for the entire Emergency. He thought Mau Mau was "bestial" and "filthy"—an "evil movement" that was "extremely vile and violent."[38] "Mau Mau had to be eliminated at all costs," he later recalled, "something had to be done to remove these people from society."[39] "Mau Mau was a seething mass of bestiality—we had to go to extraordinary lengths to get rid of this thing," remembers Terence Gavaghan, a district officer who was stationed in Central Province before later taking over the detention camps in Mwea.[40] This sentiment would become more and more widespread as the Emergency wore on, in part because the settlers were so effective in promoting their view of the movement and the drastic steps necessary, they believed, to cleanse the colony of the Mau Mau filth. Insofar as the settlers spoke with one voice, and there certainly existed within the settler population varying degrees of the eliminationist mentality with different views on how Mau Mau should be removed, their voice was constantly front-page news in the colony's two leading newspapers: the *Kenya Weekly News*, a highly conservative and pro-government paper, as well as the slightly more moderate *East African Standard*.

Kenya was also a relatively small place for the European population, both settlers and colonial administrators, who lived and socialized there. Weekends were often spent together in places like the Muthaiga Club or Thacker's trial residence, the Kitale Club, where all local whites drank, ate, danced, and enjoyed themselves long into night. Social ties between the Administration and the local European population were also strengthened through bonds of kinship, as many young officers married settler daughters. John Nottingham, who was a young district officer at the start of the Emergency, remembers how influential settler racial extremism was and how many members of the Administration, already colored by a sense of racial and moral superiority over the local African population, easily slipped into its logic. "All we heard was how savage Mau Mau was, shoot to kill. You can't imagine how often I heard, 'The only good Kuke is a dead Kuke.' There was this idea that Mau Mau was savage, just completely atavistic, and somehow had to be gotten rid of, regardless of how it was done. This idea was everywhere."[41] During a brief stop in Nairobi in the spring of 1954, journalist Anthony Sampson likewise observed what he later called the "dehumanization of the enemy" by local settlers and colonial officials. "I heard it everywhere I went," he said. "How many Kukes had to be gotten rid of, how many Kukes did you wink today. [It was] almost like they were talking about big game hunting."[42] The historical record is littered with lengthy descriptions from settlers and colonial officials of Mau Mau "vermin," "animals," and "barbarians," who lived in the "untidy, sprawling heaps . . . hovels, with seething mud and animals in the huts," or in the "bush" with other wildlife. Like other predatory animals, they were "cunning," "vicious," and "bloodthirsty."[43] Thus Mau Mau became for many whites in Kenya, and for many Kikuyu loyalists as well, what the Armenians had been to the Turks, the Hutu to the Tutsi, the Bengalis to the Pakistanis, and the Jews to the Nazis.[44] As with any incipient genocide, the logic was all too easy to follow. Mau Mau adherents did not belong to the human race; they were diseased, filthy animals who could infect the rest of the colony, and whose very presence threatened to destroy Kenya's civilization. They had to be eliminated.

The Colonial Office christened this extremism in Kenya the "Emergency mentality."[45] British colonial officials in London, including the colonial secretary, were well aware of the radical threat to Kikuyu society posed by local whites. Less than two weeks after the start of the Emergency Lyttelton flew to Kenya, where he met with several groups, including the European

Elected Members, as the settler block in Kenya's Legislative Council was called. Michael Blundell, fast becoming a voice of moderation among the extremists, called for "drastic action" against the "80% to 90% of Kikuyu [who had no] mental or moral fibre," and advocated granting all police-men a shoot-to-kill policy. Major Keyser, an archconservative and Blundell's predecessor as leader of the European legislators, reminded Lyttelton that Kenya was "bush country" and implied that only the locals knew how to deal with the natives: "Having lived for thirty-two years in this country, I am quite sure that [shooting down the Mau Mau] is the action that should be taken." But it was the grandstanding of Humphrey Slade that could have left no doubt in Lyttelton's mind about the prevailing sentiment among the "White Mau Mau" in Kenya who were by all accounts gaining control over local opinion.

> Sir, in this matter we are not only speaking for ourselves, we are speaking the views of the people we represent, 40,000 Europeans. It is our view, Sir, rightly or wrongly, that these Mau Mau men are rebels who work by terror-ism. They are fighting a war against this country's Government, the European and the Asians in this country. You can only defeat them by aggressive action against them. You cannot afford to sit back and wait for them to hit you here and there, and only, in return, try to arrest a few of them. They are men who when they have their Mau Mau meetings are actually concentrat-ing for murder and I do submit to you, Sir, and everyone of us feels that the only way of dealing with those men is to treat them as men with whom you are at war. And if you cannot arrest them, as you cannot, the only alterna-tive is to kill them. When you know they are our enemy, it comes to this, that you have to consider the white population here and the real danger that arises from that angle.[46]

How much did senior colonial officials believe in the local characteriza-tion of Mau Mau? On this score, Lyttelton hardly equivocated. In his mem-oirs the colonial secretary wrote, "The Mau Mau oath is the most bestial, filthy and nauseating incantation which perverted minds can ever have brewed. . . . [I have never felt] the forces of evil to be so near and so strong as in Mau Mau. . . . As I wrote memoranda or instruction . . . I would sud-denly see a shadow fall across the page—the horned shadow of the Devil himself."[47] Baring, though more circumspect, certainly felt that Mau Mau was an "atavistic savage sort of affair" that had to be removed at all costs.[48] Both stopped short of advocating, at least at the start of the war, any kind of officially sanctioned violence. Lyttelton had admonished the settler repre-sentatives of the long-term consequences of summary justice: "That is the law of the jungle, and if you fight the law of the jungle with another law of the jungle, you will end by being run out."[49] In the years to come, neither he nor his men on the spot would heed this prescient warning.

Six months after the start of the war things were going from bad to worse in Kenya, and Baring and Lyttelton knew it. Kenyatta's trial, for all of its drama and political grandstanding, did little to release the mounting pressure of the local eliminationist mentality. Secret documents exchanged between their two offices described the security force's "trigger happy" attitude, and allegations of misconduct, which included kill competitions complete with "five shillings a nob" bounties for Mau Mau guerrillas and "scoreboards."[50] The colonial government did its best to keep a lid on the situation as General Brian Robertson, the commander in chief of the British forces in the Middle East, was quick to point out after an inspection of Britain's troops in Kenya. "The most immediate anxiety of the Governor," he reported, "is that some of the settlers will take the law into their own hands, and indeed there have been cases already, fortunately hushed up, of their doing so."[51]

There was little in Granville Roberts's hundreds of press handouts, or in Baring's or Lyttelton's speeches, that mentioned these irregularities, as the colonial government euphemistically called the ongoing atrocities perpetrated against Mau Mau. There was no mention, for instance, of the vengeful aftermath of Lari, when white and black members of the British security forces massacred as many as four hundred suspected Mau Mau adherents. In one case where a British-directed massacre at Kiruara was reported, the murders were apparently justified because "the Police partly opened fire in self-defence."[52] On November 23, 1952, in the marketplace of this small village located in the heart of Fort Hall District, several hundred Kikuyu had gathered to listen to the prophecies of a young man who claimed to have had a vision of the end of colonial rule. According to numerous eyewitnesses, several white police officers arrived on the scene, along with a few dozen black policemen and local loyalists. They ordered the crowd to disperse. When no one moved, the white police officer in charge ordered his men to open fire. "We were all standing there, listening to this young man, and the next thing people were falling down around me," remembers Naftaly Mang'ara. "I just fell to the ground and covered my head. When the shooting was over I rose, only to collapse because the police officers began shooting again."[53] There are various recollections of the precise sequence of events from different Kikuyu men and women who were in the marketplace that day, but they are all in agreement that the police fired several rounds with automatic weapons, nearly one hundred unarmed people were murdered, and many of their bodies buried in a nearby shallow grave.[54] At the time, colonial officials claimed only fifteen Kikuyu were murdered and twenty-seven wounded. Even if these figures are correct, no white or black member of the police force was tried for the crimes committed at Kiruara. This stands in contrast to the Lari massacre, for which over three hundred Mau Mau adherents were tried and scores convicted and hung for their alleged murderous deeds.[55]

In May 1953, General Sir George Erskine, better known as "Bobbie" Erskine, was called in to bring an end to the violence and restore order to Kenya. A short, rather rotund man, Erskine had led troops in World War II and in colonial operations in India and Egypt. A personal friend of Winston Churchill, then the prime minister, Erskine was a no-nonsense commander who, unlike his predecessor, Hinde, was given full operational control over all of the security forces in the colony, including the King's African Rifles, the settlers in the Kenya Regiment and Kenya Police Reserve, and the loyalists. One of his first moves was to reform the security forces, and in June he issued an order to all its members, reminding them that they represented the British government and the forces of civilization, and that they were to stop " 'beating up' the inhabitants of this country just because they are the inhabitants." Further, he ordered the military to "stamp at once on any conduct which he would be ashamed to see used against his own people."[56] Erskine's directive hardly brought the violence to an end; in the months and years ahead there would be countless episodes of similar behavior on the part of the security forces, including the British army. The mere existence of the directive, however, was a strong indication that everyone, including the men at the top, knew that all was not right with Britain's colonial forces of law and order.

As far as Erskine was concerned, Kenya was a political disaster. He made the immediate decision to act as independently as possible, largely because he loathed the local settler population and their virulent racism, with demands for summary justice, and their butting into military policy making. While in Kenya, Erskine could hardly contain his feelings toward them, writing to his wife, "I hate the guts of them all, they are all middle-class sluts. I never want to see another Kenya man or woman and I dislike them all with few exceptions."[57] The feeling was mutual, the settlers equally disliking Erskine's abrupt personality as well as his politics. The general felt that Mau Mau did, in fact, have some basis for legitimacy, declaring, "[The Africans] hate the police and absolutely loathe the settlers. It is not difficult to realize how much the settler is loathed and the settler does not realize it himself. . . . [Mau Mau was rooted in] nothing but rotten administration . . . in my opinion they want a new set of civil servants and some decent police."⁵⁸ Erskine was irritated that he had to participate in the War Council, which was composed of himself, Governor Baring, and Michael Blundell, the settler representative. Established in March 1954, the War Council was responsible for formulating Emergency strategy and, in theory, reaching some kind of consensus on military and civilian operations. The general was outraged that settler interests had a privileged place on the council and took every opportunity to snub Blundell. He also tried to ignore the governor, believing that Baring was in such poor health and lacking in decision-making skills that he was close to incompetent.

Erskine never declared martial law in Kenya, a critically important decision since it meant that he would be responsible only for military operations—in other words, for suppressing the Mau Mau guerrillas. He had no responsibility for dealing with the rest of the civilian population, including settlers, except as it might relate to his military operations. The State of Emergency declared in Kenya was unlike that in Malaya, where General Sir Gerald Templer was directing the British battle against the communist insurgents and had full command of both the military and civilian forces. Had Erskine been granted the same martial-law power, not only would he have had to assume responsibility for the hundreds of thousands of Mau Mau adherents who had taken the oath but remained outside the forests, but he would also have had to contend with the settlers, something he was loath to do and something the settlers wanted to avoid as well. Nevertheless, he carried the ultimate trump card. Erskine had a letter from Churchill authorizing him to declare martial law and assume control of the government at any time. The general kept this handy slip of paper in his glasses case, and whenever he felt the settlers or members of the colonial government were getting out of line, he would stop them in their tracks by snapping the case open and then shutting it.⁵⁹

The Mau Mau guerrilla war has all the ingredients of a stirring military drama, and there are several publications that explore various aspects of the fighting.⁶⁰ Erskine and his successor, General Sir Gerald Lathbury, oversaw the deployment of three British battalions, four battalions of King's African Rifles, the Kenya Regiment, an artillery battery, and an armored car squadron—all with the support of Royal Air Force squadrons of Vampire jets and heavy bombers. Their mission was to defeat a Mau Mau force of some twenty thousand men and women armed largely with homemade weapons. Despite their clearly superior firepower, the British initially could not gain the upper hand in guerrilla combat inside the seemingly impenetrable forests, replete with wild animals and the ubiquitous "African unknown" that seemed to be lurking behind every impenetrable thicket. The British military had to fight for nearly two years before gaining the initiative in late 1954, and then gained the upper hand only after Erskine took his British troops out of the forests and sent them to lock up the perimeter. He replaced them with members of the King's African Rifles, as well as young settlers from the Kenya Regiment who became part of the infamous pseudogangsters. Black-faced, and often Kikuyu- or Kiswahili-speaking, these forces went into the forests with Africans, including captured Mau Mau turned government informants, where they hunted down the last remaining guerrillas platoon by platoon.

Directing the pseudogangster operation was Ian Henderson—a man whose name would become synonymous with brutality, not just in Kenya but elsewhere in Britain's empire as well. Henderson is credited with transferring the torture techniques he perfected as a member of the Kenyan Criminal Investigation Department to the pseudogang military operations that he oversaw in the forests. Guerrillas who were captured alive later recalled stories of unspeakable interrogation methods employed by Henderson and his minions.[61] But in the eyes of the local settler population, the pseudogangsters were Kenya's finest—proving they could pierce the heart of Kenya's forests to hunt down those remaining "savages" who were threatening civilization. Henderson and his crew's most glorious moment came when they captured the famous and elusive Mau Mau guerrilla leader, Field Marshal Dedan Kimathi. The ultimate symbol of Mau Mau resistance, Kimathi was interrogated after his capture and eventually tried and hung. For his role, Henderson won the George Medal and was later dispatched by the British government to Bahrain, where he served for some thirty years as the head of that tiny protectorate's state security.[62]

If Mau Mau was largely a military war, fought between British security forces and the Mau Mau guerrillas, a war that was winding down as soon as late 1954, then why didn't Kenya's governor lift the State of Emergency until January 1960? Given a postwar international climate that was increasingly hostile to colonialism, the extension of the Emergency six years beyond the end of overt military hostilities is even more incredible. If we keep in mind that there was an absence of martial law in Kenya, the answer becomes clearer. Erskine may have won the military war in 1954, but Baring was knee-deep in a vast civilian war, one that was far more complex than anything that had taken place in the forests. According to official government estimates, there were some twenty thousand insurgents in the Mount Kenya and Aberdares ranges. Yet roughly 90 percent of the 1.5 million

Kikuyu had taken the oath for land and freedom. Erskine and his military forces were responsible for defeating about 2 percent of the Mau Mau insurgents. Baring and his men were responsible for breaking the Mau Mau allegiance of well over a million Kikuyu. The assault against the Mau Mau civilian population—orchestrated and executed by Governor Baring with the approval of the Colonial Office—was far more significant in scope and impact than the military's campaign against the guerrillas.

This historical revision compels us to acknowledge that the colonial government in Kenya was willing to go to extraordinary lengths to reestablish and maintain its control of the colony. The maintenance of power and authority drove British colonial decision making not only during Mau Mau but throughout Britain's imperial occupation of Kenya, and in much of Africa and Asia. As with its other colonial territories, the British colonized Kenya first and foremost to exploit its resources, particularly the land and local labor. Like all colonial governments, Kenya's was illegitimate, as it derived its power not from democratic consensus but from a host of repressive laws that forced the local population to obey, using taxation, pass laws, imprisonment, legal floggings, and terror. In its struggle to maintain control over the African majority, the colonial government became ever more dependent on increasingly arbitrary and oppressive laws, which, in turn, reaffirmed its illegitimacy in the eyes of many Africans.[63]

This was most evident at the start of Mau Mau. Between January and April 1953, Governor Baring empowered his government with dozens of extreme and wide-ranging laws, called Emergency Regulations. These included provisions for communal punishment, curfews, the control of individual and mass movements of people, the confiscation of property and land, the imposition of special taxes, the issuance of special documentation and passes, the censorship and banning of publications, the disbanding of all African political organizations, the control and disposition of labor, the suspension of due process, and detention without trial. Emergency legislation extended to the control of African markets, shops, hotels, and all transport—including buses, taxis, and bicycles. During these early months, Baring established enabling powers for the creation of concentrated villages in the African reserves, barbed-wire cordons in African towns and in Nairobi, and concentrated labor lines—or mini-detention camps—on settler farms in the White Highlands.[64]

From the moment Baring declared the State of Emergency, the treatment of Mau Mau suspects, with rare exception, was devoid of any humanity. The convergence of local ideology, or the "Emergency mentality," with the draconian legislation passed by Baring meant that these laws worked to reestablish colonial domination and satisfy to some degree the vehement demands of local settlers for the tightest possible control of the Kikuyu. A critically important factor in understanding the effect of the Emergency Regulations is to know who actually had the day-to-day job of enforcing these harsh laws. Who were Baring's foot soldiers? They were in many cases the same men who had been calling for summary justice to purge the colony of the so-called Mau Mau vermin. Baring delegated his Emergency powers not only to his Administration in the field, most of whom were unsympathetic to the oath takers, but also to hundreds of settlers, many of whom would be drafted into the colonial government as temporary district officers, and to Kikuyu loyalists, who were poised to be incorporated into the British colonial government as members of the Home Guard.

Selecting who was best suited to implement Emergency Regulations on a day-to-day basis was partly dictated to the governor by the budgetary and administrative hand that was dealt him. He was hardly unaware of the extremist attitudes gaining ascendancy with the settler population, and with members of his own Administration, particularly after the well-publicized Mau Mau attacks on local whites and at Lari. But throughout the Emergency, Baring constantly struggled with financial and manpower shortages. He and his finance minister, Ernest Vasey, despaired that Mau Mau was not communist. Had it been, the British government would have given them a blank check to suppress the movement, as it had done with General Templer and the communist uprising in British colonial Malaya.[65] Baring instead found himself having to finance the entire civilian war on a shoe-string budget. His lack of personnel only worsened as the war dragged on, and he was forced to delegate huge responsibilities to many young district officers, local settlers, and loyalists, and with them unprecedented powers to act. To the governor, at least, there appeared to be no alternative.

Forced removals marked the colonial government's first major assault against the civilian population of Mau Mau suspects, setting an alarming standard for acceptability. In the midst of Kenyatta's trial in late 1952, Governor Baring decided to deport all suspicious Kikuyu living outside of the reserves, particularly those who were living as squatters on European farms, back to Kikuyu districts in Central Province.[66] Ndiritu Kibira still remembers vividly the night the forced removals began on the Kiringiti Estate. The farm was in Molo, in the heart of the Rift Valley Province, and its owner decided it was time to get rid of the "rats," as he called them, that lived on his land.[67] Ndiritu had been a gardener on the farm ever since he was a young boy; in fact, his family had lived on the Kiringiti Estate for several decades before the start of the Emergency. It was, as far as they were concerned, their home. Ndiritu remembers, "The door to our hut was smashed in by some *Wazungu* and Africans whom I didn't know. My parents and sisters hurried around picking up our belongings, but there just wasn't enough time. We had no warning. They were loaded into the back of a lorry and carried off into the night. Later I heard they were sent back to the [Kikuyu] reserves. I was spared, only to be arrested later."[68] Ndiritu's family was part of the first wave of Kikuyu deportations that began in December 1952 and rolled through other settled areas of Kenya, eventually on to Nairobi and Mombasa, and finally to the neighboring British colonies of Tanganyika and Uganda, where thousands of Kikuyu had migrated in search of land and employment after their displacement during the early years of British rule.[69] The removals were massive and indiscriminate, with the deportations often carried out shortly after Mau Mau strikes against Europeans or loyalists, a clear reaction to the outcry from European settlers.

Local colonial administrators in the Rift Valley executed the Emergency Regulations with particular zeal. By the beginning of 1953 they had packed thousands of Kikuyu into railcars and lorries for shipment back to the already overcrowded reserves. The volume of humanity was staggering, and members of Kenya's Legislative Council commented again and again that the "trickle [of repatriates] became a stream."[70] As of May of that year, over one hundred thousand Kikuyu had been deported from their homes and returned to the Kikuyu reserves, a place many of them hardly knew, having been squatters all their lives. Scarce consideration was given to the conditions awaiting them. One young colonial servant had just arrived in Kenya to take his post as a district officer in Nyeri. He remembers vividly the forced removals, having had to cope with their effects in the Kikuyu reserves.

These Kikuyu were packed into lorries, and they were carrying pots and pans mostly. There were small children being carried and pulled along, even women trying to nurse their infants. They had no money. There was this broad assumption by those in charge of this whole operation that these people would be welcomed with open arms by the Kikuyu in the reserves, that they would feed them and let them live on the land. But these people just exacerbated the land issue; they weren't wanted. I was totally overwhelmed. I couldn't deal with this problem at all. They usually arrived late in the day, sometimes hundreds of them. They had no food, and I wasn't given any rations to give them. They just slept wherever they could outside at this place called the Showground. The whole thing, it affected me in a way I had never been before. Of course, this was just the start of what I call the horrors.[71]

Kikuyu women and children being held at Thomson's Falls Transit Camp
after their forced removal, December 1952

In a halfhearted attempt to control the flow of deportees, the colonial
government established transit camps in the European areas intended to accommodate thousands of Kikuyu awaiting their final deportation to the reserves. The largest camps were located in Nakuru, Gilgil, and Thomson's
Falls, and they quickly became notorious for their squalid and overcrowded
conditions. Thousands in the transit camps suffered from malnutrition,
starvation, and disease—hardly surprising given that the transit camps had
inadequate sanitation or clean water and insufficient rations, if any at all.
Most Kikuyu had no means of purchasing food, having been deported
without compensation for their livestock or outstanding wages. They depended heavily on assistance from voluntary organizations, particularly the
Red Cross, for food and medical assistance. Thousands of the repatriates
languished in the transit camps for months or more, in part because there
was simply nowhere to put them in the Kikuyu reserves.[72] Clearly, despite
the denials of the colonial government, the socioeconomic basis for Kikuyu
anger that manifested itself in the Mau Mau demand for *ithaka na wiyathi*,
or land and freedom, was, in fact, a reality. There simply was not enough
land, and that which was set aside for the Kikuyu in the reserves was col-

lapsing ecologically from overuse. Governor Baring, his ministers, and officers in the field knew the reserves could not accommodate another single Kikuyu, time and again calling the land "oversaturated."[73] At the height of the deportations, Desmond O'Hagan—then the provincial commissioner for Central Province—demanded a temporary end to the returns. "This is a very serious problem," he wrote, "for to each of the Kikuyu Districts some 20,000 to 30,000 people have been returned. . . . It is certain that the Native Lands cannot absorb all those who have returned."[74]

Nevertheless, the deportations continued. In Kenya's Legislative Council, the majority advocated even more severe punishment for the Kikuyu. Major Keyser captured this retributive sentiment when he declared, "The Kikuyu tribe is going to suffer very greatly by the congestion that is going to take place in the reserves, by the lack of food that is going to take place in the reserves, by the amount of strife that is going to take place in the reserves, and all I can say . . . is that they brought it on themselves and unless they are going to suffer very considerably, they will not see the advantage of putting down this rebellion and of supporting the Government."[75] Shirley Cooke—who represented settlers living in Coast Province, far from the Mau Mau conflict of central Kenya—was the lone voice of European reason. Addressing the deportations, Cooke was blunt: "I have no hesitation in calling Government's policy a complete negation of good government," and further warned, "The reputation will live for years about these Transit Camps, and they will probably get the reputation of the concentration camps after the Boer war, memories of which live even to-day."[76] He demanded an investigation into the extraordinary power being exercised by the colonial administrators and settlers who were carrying out the forced removals. Not only was his motion resoundingly quashed, but the Member for African Affairs, Eric Davies, publicly scolded Cooke. "I do not believe what may be described as a witch hunt—an inquiry—should take place now," Davies insisted, "this indeed is not time for such things." A similar refrain from various British colonial officials resisting other calls for independent inquiries—first into the transit camps and later into the detention camps and barbed-wire villages—would be heard throughout the course of the Emergency.[77]

Appeasement and retreat were always available to Baring and Colonial Secretary Lyttelton, but in the early years of Mau Mau these options were unthinkable to them. They were committed to regaining control of Kenya and to reaffirming white minority rule over the colony. Certainly, there was some overarching plan to grant Africans their independence someday, but

Women and children being screened at a transit camp

the timing for Britain's future decolonization of Kenya was vague, at best, particularly in the face of Mau Mau.[78] In late 1952, even the most liberal officials in the Colonial Office anticipated that an imperial retreat would be at least a generation away, and even then would take the form of some kind of multiracial democracy in which the white settlers would maintain a strong foothold in Kenya's political institutions. Additionally, there was a single-mindedness shared by most colonial officials in Nairobi and London, and local European settlers, that the future African leaders of Kenya had to be hand-cultivated moderates who would help safeguard British interests and protect the settlers after colonial retreat. As regards the Kikuyu, the moderate politicians would come from the ranks of the loyalists. These loyalists—some of whom, like Waruhiu, had been prominent senior chiefs during the years leading up to Mau Mau—were known locally as the "rock on which to rebuild a common future," or the backbone of enlightened Kikuyu leadership.[79] During the remaining years of formal colonial rule, and beyond, they would move in lockstep with the British to ensure their common collective interests.

Neither Governor Baring nor Colonial Secretary Lyttelton, nor his successor, Alan Lennox-Boyd, set out to annihilate the Kikuyu population. There is nothing in the historical record to indicate that Kenya suffered from its own version of Adolf Hitler. But maintaining colonial rule while simultaneously preventing a massacre of Kikuyu oath takers was nearly impossible in light of the realities and constraints of late colonial Kenya. Rather, the British colonial government would not lose sight of its ultimate objective of reestablishing colonial domination in Kenya—even if it meant perverting judicial processes, creating one of the most restrictive police states in the history of the empire, and deploying unspeakable terror and violence. In 1953 the end of the Emergency seemed nowhere in sight, despite the now steel-fisted grip of colonial control. In retrospect, the next logical step in restoring and protecting British domination was to round up the entire population of Mau Mau suspects, detain them, and force them, somehow, to submit to colonial authority.

CHAPTER THREE

SCREENING

Hooded loyalist screeners

Undu umwe itakariganirwo ori ni screening. *Ngeretha acio matiaiganagira, mendaga o ndimahe uhoro ona itari naguo. Makiihura, makiihurira, kuu borithi station kuu* detention *ona villagi.* Screening *yahanaga ta kwa ngoma.*

(One thing I will never forget is screening. Those British were never satisfied; they just wanted more information from me but I didn't have any. They just beat me and beat me in the police station, in detention, and in the village. Screening was hell.)
—GACHECHE GATHAMBO, *February 22, 1999, Mathira, Nyeri District*

SCREENING IS THE ONE WORD IN KIKUYULAND TODAY THAT IS SYN-onymous with British colonial rule during Mau Mau. In recounting their days in the detention camps and barbed-wire villages, Kikuyu men and women never translate *screening* into their own language. Instead, they pause in their Kikuyu or Kiswahili and enunciate the English word *screening* in a slow, deliberate, colonial British accent. This is because there is no word in Kikuyu or Kiswahili that captures the same meaning.

In British colonial Kenya, *screening* was the preferred term for interrogation. *To screen* meant to get information from a Mau Mau suspect and, as the Emergency wore on, to persuade him or her to confess Mau Mau affiliations. When interrogations of Mau Mau suspects by colonial officials turned bloody, *screening* took on a more sinister connotation. For former Mau Mau adherents and even for those Kikuyu who never took the oath, screening was indiscriminate, and no one escaped it. It was an experience they would prefer to forget, although their memories often prove uncooperative. The practice began not long after the start of the Emergency when British security forces, European settlers, and the Kenya police force together spearheaded a campaign to interrogate anyone suspected of Mau Mau involvement. No Kikuyu—man, woman, or child—was safe from the screening teams. Every Kikuyu was a suspect.

When the mass deportations of Kikuyu to the reserves was started in early 1953, the colonial government began setting up screening centers throughout the Rift Valley and Central provinces. Local settlers and colonial officers funneled thousands of repatriates through these centers, where they were interrogated for hours and sometimes even days. Baring and General Erskine had ordered their men to screen all Mau Mau suspects in search of intelligence, especially information about future Mau Mau operations, guerrilla support in the reserves and on the settler farms, and names of other Mau Mau, particularly passive-wing organizers and oath administrators. Suspects branded as dangerous were shipped off to a detention camp, while others were slated for final deportation to the reserves, often via a transit camp.

In the field the teams of interrogators, known as screening teams, were ruthless in their pursuit of information. Even in government-approved screening centers like Subukia and Bahati, where presumably there was closer scrutiny of interrogation tactics, the third degree (as the local settlers called it) was the method of choice for extracting information and confessions from Mau Mau suspects. D. H. Rawcliffe, himself a settler, wrote in 1954 that the third degree was so widespread that "every European in the security forces knew about these beatings, talked about them, and very often had ordered them or participated in them."[1] Even the Christian missionaries were aware of the brutality, calling the government's screening center at Thomson's Falls a "cruelty camp."[2] Such abuses could hardly have been surprising, considering those who were typically in charge. The screening centers were often staffed by local European settlers whom Baring had appointed as temporary district officers in charge of screening.

Christopher Todd, the first settler appointed as a screening officer, had a major role in devising the screening system on the settler estates and elsewhere in the colony. Todd was a longtime resident of Naivasha and a leader among the local settlers there. Fresh from his service in the First World War, Todd arrived in Kenya in 1920 to take up a government land grant in the Rift Valley, or Happy Valley, as the local settlers called it. His view of the natives, as he referred to the Africans, was not unlike that of his fellow European colonists. Stereotypical in his British paternalism, Todd displayed a common colonial attitude of the time.

> There was no depth of thought [with the native]. As for culture, compared with European and Asian standards, there was none. These men were pagan barbarians but none the less likeable for that. . . . They were naturally lazy and had continually to be kept up to the mark. Perhaps their greatest curse was, and is, the way in which their whole lives are governed by superstition—that, coupled with their colossal vanity, makes them such an easy prey for the unscrupulous agitator.[3]

During the Second World War Todd fought again for the Allied forces, this time narrowly escaping death. Returning to Kenya in 1950 after two years of convalescence in Wales, he remained paralyzed for the remainder of his life. His physical condition did not prevent him from joining the Kenya Police Reserve at the outbreak of Mau Mau. Along with his close friends in the Kenya Legislative Council, settlers like Cavendish-Bentinck, Todd was resoundingly critical of what he described as Baring's too soft Emergency policies. Together with his neighbors, he formed the Vigilance Committee for Naivasha. As he later recalled in his memoirs:

> A number of farmers in the district became so exasperated by the lack of action taken by Government to suppress the menace that they formed a Vigilance Committee, to take the law into their own hands for the purpose of protecting the lives of their families should the occasion arise. The Police soon got word of this "subversive society." After discussion with the members, they persuaded them to join the KPR where they would have legal protection.[4]

Baring did not seek to disband the Vigilance Committee, but rather wanted to be certain it was incorporated into his government and protected by the same laws that would also shield his police force from outside scrutiny and possibly later prosecution for Emergency abuses. By appointing settlers like Todd as temporary officers, he bestowed on them the protection of the Crown in return for their manpower and local knowledge.

By his own account, Todd and his fellow screening officers felt they needed shielding by the colonial government to do their interrogation work effectively. He candidly remembers, "I did not believe in obtaining information under threat of violence, although there are cases where such methods are necessary, such as in a case of emergency."[5] Typically, screening would begin with a long question-and-answer session, but Mau Mau suspects generally sat silently or were "sullen and arrogant," as one settler described them.[6] Occasionally, the interrogators would give up, frustrated and exhausted, and either release the suspect for final deportation to the reserves or hold him for another round of screening. The more likely scenario, though, was similar to the experiences of Njama Ireri, Ndiritu Kibira, and Kirigumi Kagunda—three detainees who years later described what had happened to them. Bound to a chair in the screening center at Subukia, Njama Ireri was tortured by a white settler and several Kikuyu loyalists. Although he recognized the Africans as some of the workers with whom he had labored on the Subukia Estate, Njama did not know the *Mzungu*, or European, who extinguished cigarettes on his back during the interrogation. Today he still bears the scars of the cigarette burns and walks with a limp from the beatings given him by his loyalist interrogators.[7] Njama's experience in the screening center was hardly unique. At the Kiringiti Estate in Molo, Ndiritu Kibira was working as a gardener when he was rounded up with nearly one hundred other Kikuyu workers and shipped by lorry to the Bahati screening center in Nakuru. There, according to Ndiritu,

> we were taken to a camp in a farm [Bahati] owned by a settler whom we had nicknamed Nyangweso. That was where we were screened. We would be asked whether we had taken the oath, and those who denied having taken it were beaten badly until they were forced to confess or at least gave them some information. Many died from the beatings. . . . The black *askaris* [guards] were the ones who were doing most of the beating, but the white settlers and policemen were there as well, directing it and also beating us.

Kirigumi, a Kikuyu squatter who was forcibly removed from the Rift Valley, recalled his screening experience.

> We would be sent to the camp where we would be interrogated. To be interrogated meant to be beaten. It wasn't just to be asked questions. It was to be beaten—holding yourself like this. You would be hit there. . . . You would be beaten here [on the stomach and back] very hard. You would also place your legs thus, and be hit on this ankle and the other which would go this way and was hit again to go back. Then you would be asked to stand up and someone else would take your place.[8]

Scores of former Mau Mau adherents whom I interviewed offered similar recollections. Teams made up of settlers, British district officers, members of the Kenya police force, African loyalists, and even soldiers from the British military forces demanded confessions and intelligence, and used torture to get them. If the screening team was dissatisfied with a suspect's answers, it was accepted that torture was a legitimate next resort. According to a number of the former detainees I interviewed, electric shock was widely used, as well as cigarettes and fire. Bottles (often broken), gun barrels, knives, snakes, vermin, and hot eggs were thrust up men's rectums and women's vaginas. The screening teams whipped, shot, burned, and mutilated Mau Mau suspects, ostensibly to gather intelligence for military operations, and as court evidence.

Identifying who exactly perpetrated screening crimes is difficult largely because the Kikuyu oath takers knew their interrogators often only by nicknames. Though they rarely knew a European's name, they could generally identify a screener's colonial affiliation based on his uniform: a German-style SS cap meant he was part of the Kenya Police; the Kenya Regiment uniform was also distinctive, as was that of the members of the Administration, many of whom the locals knew well before Mau Mau. The Kikuyu nicknamed nearly every colonial agent who had an impact on their lives, whether bad or good, a practice that had been ongoing throughout Britain's occupation of the colony. For the Kikuyu victims of screening, nicknames not only identified someone but were also a form of empowerment. How better to insult a much-hated young settler than to call him Muru wa Itina, or the Son of the Buttocks? Not surprisingly, his father was simply Itina, or the Ass. But when the Emergency started, less humorous and more sinister names appeared, like Kiboroboro, or the Killer. There was also More More, the Whip, the Man with No Shirt, and the One with the Crooked Nose. This list goes on and on and would become more impressive when Mau Mau suspects began filling the detention camps, where even fewer Kikuyu knew the Christian names of the British camp commandants or the African warders.

Self-described screening experts like Christopher Todd claimed to know merely by the look of a suspect whether or not he or she was Mau Mau. When a suspect refused to talk, the screeners used this extraordinary intuition to justify their use of the third degree. Todd would later boast of his screening prowess: "When I became more practiced, I could get a very good idea as to how many oaths a man had taken just by looking at him.

There was something about the ideas and whole demeanour, an aura of evil which emanated from the man or woman which showed the state of utter degradation to which a once normal human being had been reduced by the foul oathing ceremonies."[9] Most British settlers and colonial administrators agreed there was a sense of evil that manifested itself in devil-like eyes and sinister and sullen expressions—they called it the Mau Mau look. Margery Perham, on visiting some of the Mau Mau detainees, noted "the dark look upon their faces, which seemed to add an extra darkness to the colour of their skin, and their look of settled hatred as they sat motionless on the ground."[10]

Bahati and Subukia, where Todd was stationed, were not the only screening centers using abusive tactics. There existed dozens of technically illegal, or unregistered, screening centers throughout the Rift Valley and Central provinces. In fact, of the scores of interrogation facilities in both the settled areas and the reserves, only fifteen were ever officially sanctioned by the colonial government. Governor Baring knew that illegal screening centers were operating and tacitly approved of them, partly because he had neither the manpower nor the funds to establish additional government-sponsored interrogation units.[11] Some of these centers were actually mobile, like the one operated by the local settler R. E. Fellowes. Together with a team of other settlers and Kikuyu loyalists, Fellowes would travel from farm to farm in the White Highlands and conduct massive, on-the-spot screening.[12] Most of the screening operations took place in permanent sites, generally in the offices of the Administration or in outposts on settler farms. In the Rift Valley, for example, one settler who operated his own screening camp was known as Dr. Bunny by the locals. It was his experimental prowess when it came to interrogating Mau Mau suspects that earned the doctor his notorious nickname: the Joseph Mengele of Kenya. One settler remembers her brother, a member of the Kenya Regiment and a pseudogangster, boasting of Dr. Bunny's exploits, which included burning the skin off live Mau Mau suspects and forcing them to eat their own testicles.[13] Another former settler and member of the local Moral Rearmament Movement also recalled Dr. Bunny's handiwork. He, too, remembered skin searing along with castration and other methods of screening he would "prefer not to speak of."[14]

Margaret Nyaruai, a young woman at the time of Mau Mau, was taken to the screening hut on the estate of her settler employer near Kabaru not long after the start of the Emergency. There she was beaten by a white man whom the Kikuyu had nicknamed Karoki, or He Who Comes at Dawn, and by the young settler turned British colonial officer nicknamed YY. While being screened, Margaret was asked:

Questions like the number of oaths I had taken, where my husband went, where two of my stepbrothers had gone (they had gone into the forest). I was badly whipped, while naked. They didn't care that I had just given birth. In fact, I think my baby was lucky it was not killed like the rest. . . . Apart from the beatings, women used to have banana leaves and flowers inserted into their vaginas and rectums, as well as have their breasts squeezed with a pair of pliers; after which, a woman would say everything because of the pain . . . even the men had their testicles squeezed with pliers to make them confess! After such things were done to me, I told them everything. I survived after the torture, but I still have a lot of pain in my body even today from it.[15]

Margaret's confession did not earn her release. Instead, Karoki forced her to labor without pay on his estate throughout most of the Emergency. From time to time the screening teams, hungry for any information, continued to interrogate her, often thrusting hot eggs into her vagina to force her to talk.[16]

Ratcheting up the violence in the screening centers were the Kikuyu loyalists who worked side by side with the British colonial officers to interrogate Mau Mau suspects. Many loyalists were known by the local settlers, members of the Administration, and the Mau Mau adherents for their ruthlessness. Nonetheless, the British colonial government was utterly dependent upon them for their knowledge of Mau Mau activities; interrogations would have been impossible without them. On one level, they became the henchmen for the European officers in charge of screening operations. With few exceptions, the loyalists beat and murdered Mau Mau suspects on command; other times they tortured the oath takers without any prompting or supervision. But some loyalists had been conscripted into colonial service and for this reason were less reliable deputies. There were also those who dangerously played both sides, loyalist during the day and Mau Mau by night, either in an attempt to save their own skins or opportunistically to hedge their bets before knowing who would be the eventual victor. And then there were the true double agents, as Mau Mau called them, oath takers who had infiltrated the colonial government by joining the Home Guard. The ruse did not always work; in some cases when Home Guards refused to follow orders, they suffered detention and torture just as the Mau Mau suspects they had helped detain. In Kiamariga, for example, Kamau Githiriji remembered that he and five other men had been arrested and brought behind the district commissioner's office. There the "white man in charge," as Kamau remembered him, "ordered [the loyalists] to shoot us, but [they] refused to comply. For that, they were relieved of their duties." The same white man then loaded the loyalists on the back of the lorry with Kamau and the other Mau Mau suspects and sent them all to Nyeri Prison, where they were held for several weeks before being transferred to Athi River Detention Camp.[17]

Loyalist behavior was motivated by much more than simply desiring to follow the orders of their white superiors. Many of them hated the Mau Mau and everything they represented; the oath takers had launched a direct attack on the loyalists' privilege, and greed, and targeted most of their aggression on those individuals who had collaborated with the British and allegedly profited at the expense of their Kikuyu neighbors. Loyalists were determined to eliminate Mau Mau, or as one former Home Guard from Kiambu district stated bluntly, "I wanted to kill them all; they wanted to ruin everything."[18]

By empowering the loyalists to participate as equals in the screening operations, the British colonial government was fueling a smoldering civil war in Kikuyuland and providing loyalists with the opportunity to settle old scores. They could identify adversaries as belonging to Mau Mau, torture them during interrogation, and confiscate their property. In some cases the loyalist interrogators stood barefaced in front of Mau Mau suspects, identified them as oath takers, and beat them senseless, sometimes killing them.[19] In other cases, loyalists' identities were protected, and they became the notorious hooded informants of Nairobi and the White Highlands. Their heads covered with a *gakunia*, or sack, the loyalists would peer out at the accused Mau Mau through two small eyeholes. Colonial officers directed countless screening parades in which lines of Mau Mau suspects filed past the hooded loyalists. His identity protected, the loyalist could send a man or woman off to a screening center or a detention camp with a nod of the head. One former Mau Mau suspect recalled such a screening parade that took place outside Nairobi during the early years of the Emergency.

We went through a kind of identification parade, whereby one was ordered to pass in front of a parked vehicle inside which there was a person in a hooded, flowing robe. The informer's face was completely covered, except for the eyeholes. When a suspect passed in front of the vehicle the informer would say "yes" and the suspect would be sent aside, or "no" and the suspect would be allowed to go past. . . . In my case, the informer said "no" and I was allowed to go past, but for only a few steps because seconds later I heard someone call, "Hey, you man with a long coat; arrest that man in the long coat." I then felt someone grab me by the collar of my coat and I was put into the enclosure where those arrested were being held.[20]

Colonial authorities were keenly aware of the civil dimension of Mau Mau and knowingly exploited it in the reserves. Many of the chiefs had begun organizing their own private police forces for protection of themselves and their families, and these private armies merged with some several hundred Tribal Policemen, an organization formed in the late 1920s and composed mostly of the sons and close relatives of the chiefs and headmen. By 1953 the colonial government had recognized these groups as so-called islands of resistance to Mau Mau and therefore ready recruits in the war against it. Baring gave Major General Hinde authorization to convert these private militias into the officially sanctioned Home Guard, or Kikuyu Guard, but first the chiefs and the local British district officer had to vet each potential recruit. Refusal to serve actively in the anti–Mau Mau campaign rendered a Kikuyu, a priori, a Mau Mau. To become a colonial-appointed Home Guard meant you were, in theory, willing to fight and kill your oath-taking neighbor. Local senior chiefs—like Njiiri and Ignatio in Fort Hall, Muhoya in Nyeri, and Makimei of Kiambu—would vouch for their mercenaries and then force each one to *kuhungwo mahuri,* have their "lungs cleaned." In other words, they had to proclaim openly that they had never taken a Mau Mau oath.

Still, in the early days of the Emergency, Mau Mau retained the upper hand in the reserves, often savagely attacking many of the loyalist leaders. In late October of 1952 Mau Mau murdered Chief Nderi. The district commissioner struck back, levying a collective fine of nearly ten thousand head of livestock on all suspected Mau Mau adherents in the area; he later redistributed the livestock to the local loyalists. Undeterred, Mau Mau also targeted loyalist informants for elimination. In Fort Hall a district officer reported:

> There was one murder of an old man at Ruathia; he was chopped in two halves because he had given evidence against Mau Mau in Court at Fort Hall. Further down the road the whole family of a Chief's retainer had been murdered because the retainer had given evidence, and down in the river below Gituge we found the corpse of an African Court Process Server who had likewise been strangled for informing against Mau Mau.[21]

Other attacks were against loyalist witnesses slated to testify against Mau Mau in local courts. Several such potential witnesses were hacked to death, burned inside their huts, or they simply disappeared.[22] Then came the infamous Lari Massacre of March 1953, during which ninety-seven loyalists, most of whom were members of Chief Luka's family, were slaughtered. Within a month, the colonial government armed some 20 percent of the

Home Guard with shotguns and provided them with uniforms and rations. Major General Hinde recruited Colonel Philip Morcombe and appointed him commander of the Home Guard. Eventually, nearly the entire corps of Kikuyu Home Guard, numbering some fifteen thousand in early 1953, would be armed with precision weapons or spears and outfitted with uniforms and easily recognizable silver armbands. Hinde also insisted that the Home Guard should come under the day-to-day command of European officers, or district officers, Kikuyu Guard. Many of these officers were recruited directly from the ranks of the British settlers; others were career colonial servants. Thus those in day-to-day charge of the Home Guard were not trained military personnel but local settlers out of the Kenya Regiment or career colonial officers, most of whom were quite junior.

One such junior officer was J. A. Rutherford, who in 1954 took it upon himself to compile a history of the Kikuyu Guard and the Europeans responsible for its activities. Utterly disdainful of the oath takers, Rutherford and his fellow district officers were dedicated to maintaining the morale of the Home Guard, despite the fact that they knew the loyalists were routinely "pay[ing] off many old scores against Mau Mau."[23] The colonial government knew that loyalist *fitina*, or intrigue, was rampant in the reserves. Most colonial officers believed the loyalists were as justified as the British colonizers in brutalizing the Mau Mau. Rather than trying to stop loyalist predation, they worried more about keeping their Kikuyu supporters firmly on the side of the colonial government. Rutherford was hardly circumspect in pointing out how he and his fellow colonial officers supported the loyalists.

> The District Officers in the field were quick to sense this feeling [of low morale] and made it clear that the Government would have to take definite action to maintain the loyalty and aggressive spirit of the Guard. Action was soon taken. The Guard was told that its members would, when conditions improved, receive preference in every possible way and be considered before the masses who, by their oathing and obedience to Mau Mau ways would have to work their passage back to recognition. Words were not enough. The Guard was given material assistance in a number of ways. . . . The Guard was never paid because it was felt that would make them mercenaries whereas they were in fact engaged in eradicating a disease which afflicted the majority of their tribe. They were assisted in a number of ways; they were let off the Special Tax the tribe had to pay as its contribution to the costs of the Emergency. They were helped with the school fees of their children; they were given free issues of clothes from time to time. Where the battle did not allow any form of trade to be carried on, such as the export of wattle bark or charcoal, they only were given permits.[24]

In return for their active help in suppressing Mau Mau, the colonial government guaranteeed the loyalists the best of everything—the biggest and most fertile plots of land, trading licenses, tax exemptions—not to mention carte blanche to settle old scores with their Mau Mau neighbors, even if that meant torturing and murdering them. Mau Mau were getting what they deserved, as O. H. Knight, a district officer in charge of the Kikuyu Guard in Kitale, made perfectly clear: "I have just been reading the unmentionable foulnesses of the Mau Mau oaths, and I can only say, in the words the Jews used against St. Paul, 'Away with such fellows from the earth, for it is not fit that they should live.' "[25]

By the spring of 1953 the Kikuyu loyalists were working side by side with British forces to cleanse the Kikuyu countryside of the Mau Mau scourge. The Home Guard had become an officially recognized armed unit, fighting on behalf of the colonial government, which needed these loyalists to defeat Mau Mau in the reserves. Together with members of the Kenya Police Reserve, the Kenya Regiment, the King's African Rifles, British military forces, and officers from the Administration, the Home Guard joined in launching the screening campaign that so terrorized the suspected Mau Mau population in the Kikuyu reserves and the White Highlands. Ostensibly, the British forces were in Central Province to hunt down the armed guerrillas operating in and near the forests. But in practice little distinction was made between the Mau Mau forest fighters and the civilian population. They were all Mau Mau savages, and treated as such. In southern Kiambu the Kenya Regiment launched a murderous campaign from its post in Thigio, near the Rift Valley escarpment. Farther north, in what was then called Fort Hall (today Murang'a District), there were numerous massacres like the one at Kiruara in November 1952. In 1953 a series of yet more assaults was launched against the civilian population at the hands of the British-led forces. Thousands of young men, both white and black, cut their battle teeth in the Kikuyu reserves—men like Idi Amin, whose King's African Rifles company had been dispatched from nearby Uganda to fight in the war. Then in 1954 came the massacre after the Mau Mau attack at Kandara, in the heart of Fort Hall District. Once the battle was over, the "British security forces just went crazy," recalled one woman who survived. "They had stripped the local people naked and started beating them. Some were led off and shot; others were executed right there. Later, the whites ordered them buried beneath the road and tarmaced it over again. But for a long time you could see the dried blood that had oozed to the surface and out of the sides."[26]

Similar episodes unfolded in Nyeri District. In March 1954 the King's African Rifles massacred a reported twenty-two civilians—an event that apparently led to a court-martial, though the relevant files still remain sealed in Britain's Public Record Office.[27] In many locations, the wives and mothers of the Mau Mau guerrillas were often targeted by the British security forces. When Molly Wairimu was awakened in the early morning hours to the sound of rifle butts breaking open her door, she knew she had been singled out. "There were many young British soldiers and some African soldiers as well," she later recalled. She then went on, describing the events that followed.

They informed me that they had just killed my husband at a place called Muumbuchi, and then they started beating me. They were using their gun butts to hit me. One would hit me, and the blow would throw me to the other, who would hit me and throw me to the next. Nobody cared about where they were hitting me. I was beaten until I was confused and I didn't care anymore if they killed me. My two-year-old son, who had been woken up by the noise and my screams, ran to me, passing between the legs of the soldiers. As I was being thrown by the blows, from one soldier to the next, my son was trying to hide himself between my legs. They were then shouting at me, telling me that they were giving me the independence that my husband had gone to get for me. They did not seem to care that there was a small child, scared to death and screaming his head off. As I was being thrown from one soldier to the next, my son fell down and was trampled by the frenzied soldiers. . . . I was beaten so much that my body had grown numb, until I could no longer feel the pain. They then took me outside, and the last thing I saw was my son's [dead] body lying on the floor of my house.[28]

The collective devotion that these troops displayed in terrorizing the locals is striking. Many of the members of these forces had been officially instructed to hate. Throughout Central Province, men and women recalled drills that impressed a dehumanized image of Mau Mau into the minds of the British forces and encouraged them to take violent action. "They would parade up and down the main road here in their rows with their backpacks on," recalled a man from southern Kiambu. "The white man in charge would shout, 'Who are the bloody savages?' and the other white soldiers and their black *askaris* would respond, 'Mau Mau.' He would then say, 'What are your orders?' and they would reply, 'Kill them.' "[29]

But this state-sanctioned terror hardly eliminated Mau Mau from the reserves. The local populations had established, and through all the terror continued to operate, an intricate supply line to the Mau Mau guerrillas in the surrounding Mount Kenya and Aberdares forests. Food, ammunition, intelligence, medical supplies, and clothing were all collected and disbursed to the forest fighters. Prearranged sites, or *postas,* as many former Mau Mau adherents called them, were the distribution method of choice, though there were other far riskier handoffs. In some instances, women would wrap bullets around the thighs of their infants, tie the young children onto their backs with a cloth, and make a delivery to the forest edge. Older children, too, were used as conduits. Many were scouts, collecting information and passing it to the forest fighters through a relay system. As one man who was ten at the start of the war recalled, "We would run around chasing our hoops, looking like we were playing. But in fact we were listening all of the time and knew how to convey information to the fighters in the forest. Sometimes we were given guns and ammunition to take to them because the British officers didn't usually suspect that children like ourselves would be carrying these things."[30] On other occasions, the guerrillas might come in the middle of the night demanding supplies. The owner of the targeted homestead had no choice but to comply, despite the fact that such an encounter put everyone in jeopardy.

Oathing also continued. Despite tightened surveillance, Mau Mau adherents in the reserves organized nighttime oathing ceremonies, often indoctrinating the recently arrived repatriates whom the colonial government had forcibly removed from the White Highlands, and elsewhere, at the start of the war. Even if those coming to the reserves had already joined the movement, their new neighbors took no chances. A homestead would be chosen for the oathing, and young children would be left outside to scout the perimeter for Home Guards or British patrols. Inside, with the requisite banana leaves and sacrificial goat, the oath administrator would begin. Though there were variations in the ritual process, it was invariably punctuated by political instructions, the meaning of which were clear—at least according to those who took the oath. Muringo Njooro was among those who were indoctrinated during these upheavals, and, according to her recollection, the oath administrator led them through the ceremony where they ingested the meat and blood of the slaughtered goat. After the ceremony, she said,

[we were] told that we were fighting for our land, the land of the Kikuyu, which had been taken by the white people who had taken it for themselves. They could do whatever they wished with the land. A white man could come and declare land for miles as his, without having to ask for anybody's permission or buying it from us. If you as a Kikuyu happened to graze on that land the white man declared as his, you could be beaten or killed. That was where the anger started. . . . We could see that we were being op-

pressed, because when something belonging to you had been taken by someone else and then you are treated like slaves on the land that once was yours, you're bound to feel angry about it, aren't you?[31]

The step-up in oathing reflected the hardening ideological battle lines of the war. There continued to be a sizable minority of Kikuyu Christians who refused to take the oath. "It was not because we disagreed with the principles of Mau Mau," one such devout Christian later recalled. "It's just that we had taken the blood of Christ, so taking the blood of the goat would have been blasphemous."[32] Mau Mau adherents often dealt swiftly with these Christians, though not without cause—at least according to the oath takers. "We generally left the Christians alone," recalled one forest fighter. "But if they informed on us, we would kill them and sometimes cut out their tongues. We had no choice. If they had just kept quiet, we would not have bothered them. But you know, it was impossible for them to be neutral. The British would not allow it."[33]

Then there were those oath takers who became, in the language of the time, *migaru*, or turncoats. The fear of the colonial government or the temptation of material gain, or both, compelled some of these Mau Mau adherents to defect and join the ranks of the Home Guard. As the war progressed, scores of poor Kikuyu fought actively against their former Mau Mau comrades as loyalists enforcing British law and order. There were men like Frederick Kinyanjui who, with no land of his own, decided to give up and join Chief Mathea's Home Guard unit in Kiambu. "It was because of the beating I received, and the pain of seeing my wife being beaten until she miscarried what would have been our firstborn baby," he said. "I decided to confess in order to save my life, to have a chance of getting other children. I would have died without leaving any children."[34]

But few gave in during the early years of the war. To break Mau Mau support in the reserves, the colonial government continually turned up the heat. First came forced communal labor. When this was not enough, Baring ordered collective punishments and the further confiscation of property and land. According to Emergency Regulations, the governor could issue Native Land Rights Confiscation Orders, whereby "each of the persons named in the Schedule . . . participated or aided in armed or violent resistance against the forces of law and order" and therefore had his land confiscated. Additionally, colonial officers in the Kikuyu districts could seize livestock and other items, like bicycles, from suspected Mau Mau sympathizers. By early 1954 tens of thousands of cattle, goats, and sheep were taken and, according to many former Mau Mau adherents, never returned.[35] In the North Tetu Division of Nyeri District, for example, Wachehu

Magayu later recalled: "The British officer would come with the Home Guards and take our animals, calling us the bloody Mau Mau. They said that our cows were getting their *wiyathi* [independence], and that we would get ours if we weren't careful. But there was nothing that was going to get me to give up. The British took our land, and we wanted our freedom back, and I had taken the oath and was prepared to die for it."[36]

Magayu Kiama never expected to survive screening. Facedown in a pool of his own blood, Magayu raised his head, only to be kicked in the face again and finally knocked unconscious by one of the Home Guards in Aguthi Location, in Nyeri District. When he came to, he was naked and slumped over in a ditch of cold, insect-infested water.[37] Here he was left to await more screening in a *ndaki*, or pit, inside one of the Home Guard posts that had sprung up all over the Kikuyu reserves. Initially, these posts were an easy target for Mau Mau attacks, because they were poorly designed and sited by the chiefs. After 1953 Baring's government overhauled the posts, and they became the physical symbols of loyalist power in the reserves. Magayu likened the one in his location to a fortress. The post was surrounded by a huge trench filled with wooden spikes, the high walls were laced with barbed wire, and a watchtower soared above the rest of the structure (a trademark for all of the posts throughout the Kikuyu reserves). Magayu also recalled several buildings within the post: a large courtyard, the same place where he had first been beaten, and a long row of individual cells where the *ndaki* was located. He remained in his cell for nearly ten days and was screened daily by the Home Guards and a European officer before finally being sent to detention.

Magayu, like thousands of other Mau Mau suspects, was picked up and brought to the post for screening, with the specific objective of extracting a confession and intelligence. There was, however, a callousness in the behavior of the white and black interrogators that exceeded the mere objectives of war. Few escaped the Home Guard posts, whatever the age or gender. Undoubtedly, the screening task was massive, and to some degree the loyalists and the handful of overseeing colonial officers had to have been overwhelmed by the sheer numbers they were required to screen. Yet the use of sadistic screening techniques reported by numerous survivors and other eyewitnesses suggests that the loyalist Home Guards and their white superiors took perverse pleasure in their various physical assaults on Mau Mau suspects. Word quickly spread among the locals about what awaited them in the Home Guard posts, and many struggled fiercely to stay out. Living in Mathira at the start of the Emergency, Ndiritu Goro remem-

Home Guard post and watchtower in Kianjogu village, Nyeri District

bers the scene in late 1953 at the gate of the post in his location: "I held on to a fence post with both my hands, and refused to go. The Home Guards pried my fingers from the post and overpowered me. We were headed to where Ngotho's dead body was; they had just shot him dead. When we neared the place, Allan, the headman, loaded his gun, ready to shoot me."[38] Unlike Ngotho, Ndiritu lived. Another headman named Kiana intervened, though his reasons were not entirely sympathetic. He wanted additional information and realized Ndiritu was more valuable alive than dead.

The loyalists' violent anger was not solely reserved for screening sessions in the Home Guard posts but was also expressed all over the markets and homesteads of Kikuyuland. There were instances where all pretense of intelligence gathering was dropped and retribution took on a naked and brutal face. When Mau Mau forces murdered one of Senior Chief Njiiri's sons in Fort Hall in early 1953, the consequences for the local Mau Mau population were devastating. For most members of the Administration, the senior chief epitomized colonial loyalty; he was their darling who ruled over the most substantial island of Mau Mau resistance in Fort Hall's biggest location, Location 2. J. A. Rutherford praised him endlessly, and Frank Loyd, Fort Hall's district commissioner at the time, later recalled, "Senior Chief Njiiri was a bedrock for colonial values. We needed more people like him; he was a true example and leader of loyalist forces."[39]

Among the local population, however, the senior chief was known largely for two things: his wives—he had over sixty of them—and his cruelty. When his son was killed by General Kago, one of the legendary Mau Mau guerrillas fighting in the Aberdares, he unleashed his rage. Kago and his forest gang had made their attack not far from the village of Mununga, near the forest edge. Within a few days the senior chief and the district officer in charge of the local Home Guard entered Mununga with several hundred Home Guards from Njiiri's stronghold of Kinyona. They were not, however, seeking to screen the locals for knowledge about Kago or the assassination. Instead they told the men, all of whom had already been forced for several months to dig a trench between their village and the forest, to put down their tools and make their way to the market. Before many of them could reach the market square, they saw smoke coming from the surrounding huts. The Home Guards were burning everything in sight: homes, crops, bicycles. Then the gunshots began. Everyone scattered, but the Home Guards had formed a cordon around the village, and no one could escape. One eyewitness, Njuguna Robinson Mwangi, who was a teenager at the time, recalled the massacre (as he termed it).

> When the first round of shooting was over, the European Home Guard leader called each Home Guard one by one and asked him how many bullets he had used. He then replaced the used bullets with new ones. He then instructed [the Home Guards] to start beating without using their guns, so they started using their *pangas* [machetes] and clubs. My father was beaten mercilessly and could not walk. . . . So many people were killed. The Home

Guard did not want to pass over the dead, so they tried to walk around them, but they couldn't, there were just too many. They then called all of the survivors to the market square, where they were being paraded one by one in front of the shops. When a person reached a certain point, he was just shot dead. I was in that very line. I saw a small passageway between the shops and took a chance. I ran and they shot at me, but they missed. I hid in the forest, and when I came out there was nothing left, just ash and smoke where our village used to be.[40]

Other survivors of Mununga recall similar stories of Njiiri's revenge. Along with Njuguna, Karuma Karumi and Paul Kimanja vividly remember the day, and the corpses that remained.[41] The Home Guard dumped several hundred of them in the communal latrine, where "no one could dare to bury them."[42] In fact, some of the bodies remain there today, under a row of small shops. The rest of the dead were left exposed, to be consumed by hyenas and other local wildlife. Many survivors believed the massacre was meant as an example for other Mau Mau supporters in the district. News of it spread, and even some fifty years later Kikuyu men and women from throughout the region remembered what happened at Mununga and insisted that other forms of British colonial revenge were widespread. "Mununga was not an isolated incident," recalled Muthoni Waciuma. "There was Kiruara, the massacre after the battle of Kandara, and many other such attacks by the colonialists and the Home Guards happening all over the Kikuyu reserves."[43]

In the early years of the Emergency two men working for the British government in Fort Hall were renowned for enforcing colonial control. The first was Sam Githu, better known as Sam Speaker because of his rapid speech. Later it was said that his nickname took on another meaning: Speaker could make anyone talk. Also called the "horror of horrors," the "face of the devil," and more commonly "pure evil," he was a loyalist from Chomo in Fort Hall who had risen through the ranks of the local colonial government. At the start of the Emergency, Speaker was an assistant district officer who appeared to occupy a multitude of roles other than his official one of clerical staff. Working alongside him was a young British settler nicknamed YY by the local Kikuyu. Around twenty years of age at the start of the Emergency, YY and his reign of terror were legendary from Fort Hall all the way through to northern Nyeri District, a distance stretching some fifty miles. Like the sons of many settlers, YY joined the Kenya Police Reserve when the war began and from the start advocated harsh justice for any civilians suspected of Mau Mau sympathies. He was a

Napoleonic figure who more than made up for his diminutive stature with his imperial bravado. Dressed in a police uniform complete with a black leather sash and hat pulled down closely over his eyes, YY walked carrying a riding whip, which he snapped in time with his pace.

In 1953 Speaker and YY moved throughout Fort Hall, helping direct massive screening parades and individual interrogation sessions. In some instances they personally disposed of suspects, often making an example of them for the rest of the Kikuyu population. On one occasion in early 1953 they brought two suspects to the Kandara police station. Prior to the Emergency, the building had been the dispensary and home of the local clinician and his family; when Mau Mau started, the police took over the dispensary space but allowed the man and his family to remain in their attached living quarters. From their window, the two daughters had a perfect view from which to witness what went on at the police station when YY arrived with two Mau Mau suspects. Muthoni Waciuma, the younger of the two sisters, recalled:

> We were standing right next to our fireplace, resting our chins on the bricks and looking directly at the police station; it was just a few feet away. We then saw Kamiraru [YY] pull up with two men. They took the first man and hooked him up to the engine of the Land Rover while it was still running and his body just shook all over. But they weren't finished with him. . . . Kamiraru and some other Kikuyu Home Guard took him over to the generator that was in the back of the police station's garage. They then hooked him up to this generator and electrocuted him. After that, Kamiraru and Speaker turned to the other man, who was still standing there. They tied him to the back of the Land Rover and made him run behind them as they drove off. He was running, and of course he falls. They drove him until he died in pieces. That was being done to really show people that if they didn't confess and give up Mau Mau that that would be their fate. I have never seen anything so cruel. And we were scared stiff, so we did everything we could not to have something like that done to ourselves. You just kept quiet. It was really a traumatic time. . . . There was so much suffering. People will not believe that we have survived such things. A lot of atrocities like this one were done.[44]

This example typifies the priority given by white and black alike to inflicting punishment and suffering upon the population of Mau Mau suspects, and the extent to which the brutality was intentionally committed in plain view. While some screening was conducted behind closed doors, it was also a public spectacle, empowering the perpetrators and terrorizing the civilian population.

Local police preparing to screen Mau Mau suspects, November 1952

. . .

Baring generally refused to do anything to rein in the Home Guards' sadistic tactics, arguing along with his officers in the field that wrist slapping or prosecutions would undermine loyalists' morale. However, in one rare instance six Home Guards were tried in late 1954 for brutally forcing confessions and for summarily executing a Mau Mau suspect in the Ruthagati Home Guard post in Nyeri District. Presiding over the case, Judge A. L. Cram convicted headman Eliud Muriu and the five other Home Guards of murder. In explaining his verdict, Cram deplored the system that permitted the Home Guards to arrest anyone at will, torture the individual until extracting a confession, and then either try the victim solely on the basis of the forced confession or use the same confession as a pretext for sending the suspect to a detention camp. The men on trial were guilty of not just murder; they were committing atrocities on what Cram believed to be a daily basis. He focused particularly on the Home Guard post at Ruthagati, which he said resembled the "stronghold of a robber baron," and elaborated that

it was a barbed wire enclosure surrounded by a staked moat and provided with a drawbridge—a primitive keep, in fact. The sort of place from which prisoners could not readily escape, and it was presided over by [Headman Muriu] and a team of men who had one function in life and that was to extort statements or confessions by fear and if necessary by violence from every hapless person sent or brought there, innocent or guilty. . . . The reign of terror is well advanced [in this area].[45]

Predictably, Cram absolved the district commissioner from any wrongdoing, remarking that "the DC states he made it amply clear that his instructions were that no violence of any sort was to be used in extracting confessions."[46] But just days before Cram handed down his verdict, G. Hill, the district officer in charge of Eliud Muriu and the rest of the Home Guard at Ruthagati, wrote a memorandum denouncing the prosecution of the six loyalists, arguing, "The conclusion is that the K.G. [Kikuyu Guard] may consider it better to join the Mau Mau and reactivate the fighting war than stay in a post and be liable to serious charge."[47] Far more damning, though, was his argument that the colony's attorney general, John Whyatt, had "no personal knowledge or experience of the physical side of the war"—implying that physical violence was justified given the nature of Mau Mau.[48] Hill well knew what was going on in the Home Guard posts, and it would have been likely that he informed his superior officer, the district commissioner. Throughout the Emergency, variations on Hill's argument, that only those in the field truly understood the mitigating circumstances of colonial violence, would be used time and again to justify brutality and avoid prosecution.

Screening abuses were also being perpetrated in nearby Tanganyika, where a British judge adamantly supported the view that colonial violence was justified during Mau Mau. In October 1953, Governor Baring dispatched Brian Hayward and twenty-one African loyalists to the Northern Province of Tanganyika, to which thousands of Kikuyu had earlier migrated after the British colonial incursion. Tanganyika's governor Edward Twining greatly feared that Mau Mau would spread to his colony. Hayward and his men came to screen local Kikuyu and repatriate any of the so-called bad hats back to Kenya, where they would be detained. All of nineteen years old, Hayward was the son of a British settler in Kenya who had been steeped in local white beliefs about Mau Mau. Baring picked Hayward for his firsthand experience in screening. He was already a temporary district officer in charge of screening in the Kikuyu reserves and had been sent on a brief tour of the screening centers in the Rift Valley (like Subukia and Bahati) before leaving. In less than a week, Governor Twining reported to the Colonial Office that "rumours were heard that the screening teams were being very rough with the Kikuyu, and a European farmer—Colonel Minnery—confirmed these rumours." Unlike Baring, who refused to follow up on such allegations, Twining ordered an immediate, official investigation that revealed

> violence, in the form of whipping on the soles of the feet, burning with lighted cigarettes and tying leather thongs round the neck and dragging the victims along the ground, had been used on the interrogated. Between 170 and 200 were interrogated, of whom at least 32 were badly injured, and others received some injury. Hayward himself took an active part in the chastisement of the Africans and is said to have threatened to shoot one man after pointing his revolver at him.[49]

Hayward and ten African members of the screening team pleaded guilty on all twenty counts of assault occasioning "actual bodily harm." Most revealing, though, were the judge's summary remarks. In passing sentence, he told the courtroom, "It is easy to work oneself up into a state of pious horror over these offenses, but they must be considered against their background. All the accused were engaged in seeking out inhuman monsters and savages of the lowest order."[50] He fined Hayward one hundred pounds, which was paid by a local group of settlers, and sentenced him to three months' hard labor, which Hayward performed by doing clerical work in a hotel. The loyalist screeners were fined one hundred shillings and sentenced to a day of imprisonment.[51]

By and large, any limits placed on screening techniques were introduced independently by a handful of white colonial officers or, occasionally, a Kikuyu Home Guard. Early in 1953, Magayu Kiama was accused by the local Kamatimu, or Home Guards, of harboring Mau Mau fighters in his home. He recalled "two white men and several African soldiers" burning down his house. Magayu continued: "My wife was shot. A lady visitor was shot, and several suspected Mau Mau fighters were shot. Their bodies were burned in the inferno. I do not know who came to take my children away, or my wife. I was in shock, and I spent the night outside my burned-out homestead. In the morning, the police came for me, and I was taken to the chief's camp, where I stayed several days." Like other suspects held there, Magayu was slated for summary execution. A white officer intervened just in time. He reprimanded the chief, according to Magayu, saying, "I had not been at fault, because it just happened that Mau Mau came to my house to demand sheep for slaughter. . . . That was what I had told [the chief]. I could have been killed, were it not for [this white officer]. . . . [But still] I had been badly beaten and could hardly walk. The Home Guard in charge lied to the white officer that I was sick, to hide the fact that I had been beaten."[52]

In Pascasio Macharia's case, he was picked up by the Kenya Police and Home Guard in Nyeri and shipped to his home location in Fort Hall District, where he befriended a Kamba guard who then saved his life. At the Kahuro camp, he remembers,

> I was removed from the truck. The order was given by the headman from my place, who said that I was to be beaten because I was the worst person. The *askaris* set on me and beat me until I fell unconscious, and they left me for dead. When they locked up the others, I was left outside, but some guards were there, just in case I regained consciousness. I came to . . . and looked around, and I noticed someone smoking. I asked him for a cigarette. It was a Kamba *askari*. I then asked him for a drink of water, and he gave me one. . . . Just before dawn, the guards who had been guarding me wanted to put me into a pit that was close by. They dragged me toward it, but fortunately, the same Kamba who had given me the cigarette appeared and told them to leave me alone.[53]

But Pascasio's troubles were not over. He was then sent to the office of the Criminal Investigation Department, or CID, where local Home Guards and a white officer interrogated him some more. "Things were bad there; they were exterminating a lot of people," Pascasio said. Luckily, his uncle was a friend of the headman, who agreed, for two crates of beer, to spare Pascasio's life. Instead of a single bullet to the head, the local execution style of choice, according to Pascasio, he was transferred to a detention camp.[54]

Had Baring wanted to control the abuses, he would have had a difficult time imposing his authority on the diverse multitude who had a hand in screening. Interrogators included the European settlers, the district commissioners and their officers in the White Highlands and reserves, the Home Guard, a separate phalanx of security forces under Erskine's command, as well as the Special Branch and the Criminal Investigation Department, who were effectively the colony's gestapo, according to one member of the force.[55] The local colonial press, generally sympathetic to the forces fighting Mau Mau, particularly in the early days of the Emergency, published an article titled "Law and the People," in which it raised the matter: "That any member of the public held in custody as a suspect can be handed over to a body which has no standing or statutory duty in the investigation of crime, for the purpose of extracting confessions or evidence that the police have failed to obtain by normal method of examination, is something which should cause very real concern."[56]

The Kenya Police, of which the Kenya Police Reserve and the Special

Branch were parts, were a special category. Many whites in the police force were a lowbrow corps of recruits who, in keeping with their racist up-bringing, routinely roughed up the local Africans. With the Emergency, the ranks of the police swelled more than twofold, with white officers like YY coming either from within the settler population, or from a pool of British recruits with few career alternatives other than a post in remote Kenya, or from Rhodesia and South Africa, where similar law-and-order policies were applied to the so-called native populations. Side by side with the whites were African recruits, most of whom came from remote parts of Kenya and who were untrained in policing policies. These new white and black policemen were wholly unprepared for the Emergency situation in Kenya. Even Baring remarked that "the members of the Kenya Police Reserve were tough, that the Police Force was rotten."[57]

Many Europeans in the police force felt entitled to any means at their disposal to fight the war against Mau Mau. Interrogating men and women as they pleased, they created among the Kikuyu a terror of capricious violence. In his autobiographical account of the Emergency, William Baldwin candidly recalls the callousness of the Kenya Police. Himself a member of the Kenya Police Reserve, Baldwin was a nomadic young American seeking adventure in Africa. He seems to have found it in Kenya, where he proudly worked to rid the colony of the Mau Mau baboons, as he called them, freely admitting to murdering Mau Mau suspects in cold blood during eight different interrogations. Some he slowly killed with a knife while forcing other suspects to watch.[58] Former Mau Mau suspects living as far south as Thigio in Kiambu District and as far north as the northern edge of Nyeri District, a hundred miles away, confirmed scenarios similar to the young American's account, leaving little doubt that his behavior was typical. John Nottingham, the young British district officer who was outspoken both during and after the Emergency about his colleagues' behavior, underscores this point. In a 1987 interview for Grenada television's *End of Empire* documentary, Nottingham emphasized:

I think there was nothing that the local Europeans in these various organizations didn't do. . . . I've seen old men kicked into my office in Nyeri by settler sons who are very surprised that I should feel this was the wrong thing to do. The only crime the gentleman had committed was to take an oath. I've seen KPR [Kenya Police Reserve] in charge of, for example, Kiriaini police station in Murang'a District, just put eight people against a wall and had them shot. . . . There were really no limits that they wouldn't go to.[59]

Police brutality during screening and throughout everyday life was hardly a secret in Kenya or in Britain. In March 1953 Tony Cross, a temporary British officer posted at Gekondi Police Station in Nyeri, sent a letter to his former colleagues at Streatham Police Station in South London bragging about what he termed the "Gestapo stuff" that was going on in the ranks of the police force and Home Guard. Soon picked up by the press in London, the letter made the headlines in the *South London Press* and the *Daily Worker*.

> We have formed 3 home guards on this manor, each about 50 strong—and they get out and bring in the information—some are pretty good—then we go out and raid, and knock a few off—don't ask me why—just because the home guard say they are bad men—of course some are wanted—anyways after persuasion they usually confess something. It's not uncommon for people to die in the cells—these home guards are unmerciful bast—s. Since I've been here I inspect all prisoners brought in—and if they are a bit dubious I refuse to have 'em—get called to a dead body the next day—and proceed normally. The rule here is if you are on patrol and you find some men hiding in the bush—you call upon them to stop and if they don't—they are shot—or rather shot at—these boys I've got are such rotten shots they can't hit anything—so I grab the first bloke's rifle and have a go—anyway I've been giving them some intensive training and they are getting better now.[60]

Like Cross, other police officers offered accounts of brutality. In one case, Peter Bostock wrote that it was "quite common to shoot prisoners 'while [they were] trying to escape'" and that one officer had told him proudly that he "got nine of the swines [*sic*] in that way." After recalling various acts of terror, Bostock then went on to report, "I can truthfully say that only one act of cruelty towards a Kikuyu ever revolted me during my service in the Police. With two other Europeans I was questioning an old man. His answers were unsatisfactory. One of the white men set his dog at the old fellow. The animal got him to the ground, ripped open his throat, and started mauling his chest and arms. In spite of his screams, my companions [i.e., fellow police officers] just grinned. It was five minutes before the dog was called off. I can still hear that old man's screams."[61]

Then there were the South African imports Heine and Van Zyl, two Special Branch officers who were known as particularly sadistic torturers, no small distinction given the situation in Kenya.[62] In fact, some British settlers nicknamed the Special Branch "Kenya's SS" because of its notoriety for torturing Mau Mau suspects behind closed doors. Nottingham highlights this police unit in his description of the screening camps.

When you come to what happened in the various camps, the screening camps, whether they were the local areas, the police stations or whether they were the bigger camps and so forth again there were very few limits that people seemed to observe. The Mau Mau Investigation Center at Embakasi outside Nairobi was nothing less than a torture area which used everything. And it was run by the Special Branch and I would say people were killed there without any news of this being allowed to escape or anything happening at all.[63]

There is little in the colonial record documenting what happened at the famous Mau Mau Investigation Center, the brainchild of the Special Branch. If there were records, they have been destroyed or are still to be declassified. "This [Mau Mau Investigation Center] is where we liked to send the worst gang members when we captured them sent to the forests," recalled one settler who had joined the ranks of the Kenya Regiment sent to the Aberdares. "We knew the slow method of torture [at the Mau Mau Investigation Center] was worse than anything we could do. Special Branch there had a way of slowly electrocuting a Kuke—they'd rough up one for days. Once I went personally to drop off one gang member who needed special treatment. I stayed for a few hours to help the boys out, softening him up. Things got a little out of hand. By the time I cut his balls off he had no ears, and his eyeball, the right one, I think, was hanging out of its socket. Too bad, he died before we got much out of him."[64]

Rhoderick Macleod, a British settler, member of the Kenya Police Reserve, and brother of Iain Macleod, the future colonial secretary, summed up the attitude of many members of Kenya's police force and the Administration in the reserves when he commented: "[The Emergency] was a state of anarchy, in which the book did not work. It was as simple as that."[65] Worse, everyone seemed to know about colonial violence and to condone it, at least tacitly if not explicitly. Fitz de Souza, a respected attorney in Nairobi and defender of Jomo Kenyatta, remembers that a consensus of British political leaders in the colony endorsed a shoot-to-kill policy: "[The idea of shooting people on the spot] was quite, quite, quite widely spread. I was surprised to find that many reasonable educated people, some of them in fact later became members of Parliament and to a very responsible position in independent Kenya, supported this idea of arresting a hundred people from nowhere, just shooting thirty, and sending the seventy to tell the tale of who was the boss."[66]

Screening was not only a way to terrorize the Mau Mau population. Though hardly a streamlined system even by the end of the Emergency, screening made it possible for the colonial government to amass huge files of information about Mau Mau activities. Torture, or fear of it, compelled oath takers to give details about their oathing ceremonies, including names or revealing the locations of the caches of arms or food supplies for Mau Mau fighting the forest war. Some of this intelligence was accurate and some pure fiction, fabricated on the spot by Mau Mau suspects trying to save themselves. The colonial government nevertheless used the information to convict some thirty thousand Kikuyu men and women of Mau Mau crimes and sentence them to prison, many for life. "Far from being concerned about possible disregard of human rights," Cyril Dunn, a correspondent for the *Observer,* would later comment, "Europeans here [in Kenya] are apt to argue that British notions of justice are inapplicable. A letter this week in a local newspaper is typical. 'It is stark nonsense,' the writer says, 'to treat these rebels as legitimate belligerents, and to apply to them all the subtleties and intricacies of British law.'"[67]

The vast majority of Mau Mau cases were heard in Emergency assize courts, where due process was suspended, the defense had little if any access to the evidence in the case, and the defendants themselves were often tried en masse and identified for the court not by name but by large numbers hanging around their necks. Along with those convicted and imprisoned, the makeshift court operations in place throughout the Emergency found over one thousand Mau Mau suspects guilty of capital offenses and sent them to the gallows. This is a startling number of executions, given the often slim evidence offered by the prosecution. However, the suspects tried, found guilty, and sentenced to death by the Kenyan system of justice comprised only a very small percentage of those who ultimately would die at the hands of the British colonial government during the Emergency.

The forces unleashed by the screening campaign revealed a darker side of British colonialism than had earlier been seen in Kenya. Virulent racism was certainly endemic to the colony, as was a profound righteousness—a sense that the British were morally superior not only to black Africans but to all other races as well. Kenya's so-called native laws were already notoriously harsh, and would become even more so in the years to come. There were even massacres during the early years of colonization, like the one Richard Meinertzhagen boasts about, in which some one hundred Kikuyu were murdered as the interior was opened up for British settlement.[68] But what happened during the early years of Mau Mau was different. The dedication to torture and killing during screening operations stands apart. The ubiquity of screening from the rural areas to the urban center of Nairobi meant that even those in the colonial government and the local European community of settlers and missionaries who were not directly involved with suppressing Mau Mau had to have been aware of the brutality of the screening process.

The British colonizers continuously defined themselves and their Mau Mau antagonists as polar opposites. How better to save Britain's civilization in Kenya than to eradicate the elements who threatened the colony's very foundation? Like the Jews in Nazi Germany, the Mau Mau had few defenders, except for the small minority of Asian lawyers like Fitz de Souza and Sheikh Amin. Today, when reflecting on the number of Mau Mau suspects killed from the start of screening in late 1952 to the end of detention in 1961, de Souza says: "By the end I would say there were several hundred thousand killed. One hundred easily, though more like two to three hundred thousand. All these people just never came back when it was over. This was a form of ethnic cleansing on the part of the British government, and there is no doubt about that in my mind."[69]

From the start the colonial government fought fiercely to deny any wrongdoing in Kenya, and when caught red-handed, Governor Baring and Colonial Secretary Lyttelton cited mitigating circumstances. At the time, men and women did not talk in terms of guilt or responsibility, because their crimes in the screening centers, police stations, and Home Guard posts were not crimes as far as they were concerned. Mau Mau forced them to fight violence with violence. In effect, they were compelled to do the unthinkable when confronted by the barbaric behavior of the Kikuyu oath takers. Casting themselves as hapless victims, rather than perpetrators of crimes, the British colonial agents sought to evoke sympathy, not condemnation. British reaction was hardly different from that of any other regime trying to face down accusations of wartime crimes. In his reflections on Nazi Germany, the Soviet Union, and Americans in Vietnam, Jan Philipp Reemtsma suggests: "The problem is that societies confronted with their own armies' war crimes often try to get rid of the problem, first by denying the existence of the crimes (it's unjust and insulting to be accused of having committed such crimes), or, if the crimes cannot be denied any longer, by lowering the standards. In both ways people try not to give up the correspondence between reality and self-image in order to be a 'civilized' society, even in war time."[70]

In the case of Mau Mau, the British colonial government was doubly determined, in accordance with colonial rhetoric, to maintain civilization's upper hand over the African savages. Civilization was, after all, the whole point of Britain being in Kenya in the first place. But if British settlers and those who acted on their behalf were as barbaric as Mau Mau, how could

Britain justify its continued presence in and exploitation of the colony? Even the newly arrived temporary officers and young brash settlers, or the Kenyan Cowboys, as the foreign journalists called them, believed to some degree in Britain's paternalistic ethos, or its civilizing mission. In the face of incontrovertible evidence to the contrary—for instance, the castration of a Mau Mau suspect—the British and their loyalist supporters maintained the illusion that their actions were the epitome of civilized behavior. It was as if by insisting loudly enough, and long enough, they could somehow revise the reality of their campaign of terror, dehumanizing torture, and genocide.

At the end of 1953, the Emergency was still in its early stages. Though screening was widespread, there were still but a few thousand detainees in the camps, and the barbed-wire villages had yet to be conceived. But violence against Mau Mau suspects during screening was so extreme, and so widely applied, that there could have been little doubt that it would spill over into the evolving Pipeline of detention camps that was now starting to take shape. The symbiosis between the bloodthirsty views of the British colonizers and the Kikuyu loyalists had already produced the conditions and the drive to destroy, quite literally, the Mau Mau. Although the detention camps in Kenya would never systematically aim to eliminate a whole population as did the Nazi death camps, the conditions were in place by 1953 to transform a fledgling camp system into a far broader locus of torture, hard labor, and killing. Protagonists in this setting were the tens of thousands of Mau Mau suspects who were dehumanized by the British even before they set foot in the camps. While enduring screening, men and women were often reduced to looking and smelling like the animals they were claimed to be. By relentlessly subjecting the minds and bodies of Mau Mau suspects to violence during screening, the British colonizers and their loyalist sympathizers were able to confirm in their own minds that the oath takers were subhuman and themselves paragons of civility.

CHAPTER FOUR

REHABILITATION

IN EARLY FEBRUARY 1953, CANON T. F. C. BEWES OF THE CHURCH MIS-
sionary society held a press conference in London. Addressing a host of
journalists, he accused British security forces of routinely using the third
degree, as he called it, to extract intelligence and to impress upon Mau
Mau adherents the strength of colonial power. He offered the example of
Elijah Gideon Njeru, a former missionary teacher, who had been beaten
by Jack Ruben of the Kenya Regiment and Richard Keates of the Kenya Police Reserve, along with several of their African *askaris,* or guards. Bewes
stated that Njeru was suspected of being Mau Mau and had been "taken
away and beaten, [the beating] continued to make him confess and he
died under beating." He went on to add that "this is not repeat not an isolated case." When members of the press pushed the canon for more details
of the third degree, he said he had extensive evidence of the use of "exces-
sive force by settlers, military forces, [and] police," and that he and the
archbishop of Canterbury would deliver this evidence to Colonial Secretary Oliver Lyttelton.[1]

Canon Bewes's credibility was unimpeachable. He had been a missionary in Kenya for twenty years, from 1929 to 1949, where he lived in Central

Province and worked extensively with the Kikuyu. He had, in his words, "established close relationships with many Kikuyu. I was in and out of their huts in the evenings; sat round their fires; exchanged jokes and riddles with elders; fished and hunted with the lads. . . . Our Kikuyu friends showed great interest in our children. We grew to love them, understand their language, share their thoughts."[2] In 1950 he was living in London, serving as the African secretary for the Church Missionary Society, when he began receiving numerous dispatches from his Anglican missionaries in Kikuyuland describing the "increasing difficulty and tension" there. He decided to return to Kenya to view the deteriorating conditions firsthand, and on January 5, 1953, he left London for the Kikuyu reserves. Bewes returned to England three weeks later, though not before meeting privately with Governor Baring to express his grave concern about what he called the "extreme pressure being used by the Authorities, Police or Home Guard."[3]

Bewes committed his discussion with Baring to a "private and confidential" report that has survived archival purgings. The report, still in the files of the Colonial Office in London, describes the missionaries' concern for their tiny remaining flock of devout Kikuyu Christians, many of whom were growing more afraid of the colonial forces than they were of Mau Mau. When Canon Bewes mentioned this fear to local police, one British officer responded, "Good, that is what we want; when they are more afraid of us we shall get the information we want." To his horror, Bewes realized that terror was being used to intimidate, and eliminate, both Mau Mau adherents and the few remaining Kikuyu Christians. In his private memorandum to Baring, he reiterated:

I reported to you [Governor Baring, during our visit before my return to England] certain statements given by European police themselves. One spoke to me of the methods used by himself to extract information—putting an up-turned bucket on a man's head and then beating it with a metal instrument for up to half an hour when the man usually burst into tears and gave the information if he had any. . . . A second policeman had reported to a missionary concerned that a fellow European policeman had picked up a man, had him laid on the ground with his legs apart, and had him beaten on the private parts in an attempt to extract a confession. . . . Further information along this particular line was that some of the police had been using castrating instruments and that in one instance two men had died under castration, and one had gone to hospital. . . . The same castrating instrument—a metal one had also been reported as being used to clamp on to the fingers of people who were unwilling to give information, and that if the information was not given the tips of the fingers were cut off.

> This information was given to me from such widely separated sources that
> I am sure it was at least based upon fact.[4]

The canon was initially reluctant to go to the media with this damning information, writing to the governor, "I am very anxious that information of this kind should not go into the Press for I am sure that we must do all that we can to prevent inflammation of passions on either side [of the Mau Mau war]."[5] We can only assume that Bewes's press conference resulted from Baring's refusal to take concrete action. The canon went public because no one in the British colonial government would listen to him.

Granville Roberts, chief strategist in the East African Public Relations Department of the Colonial Office, knew how damning Bewes's public accusations were. From the start of the Emergency, the colonial government had made a concerted effort to manage information coming out of Kenya and especially to minimize the impact of any statements about or accounts of torture. In the wake of the canon's press conference Roberts wrote, "It is unnecessary for me to say how very damaging to the Government accusations in these terms are particularly in view of the fact that Bewes told Press he would not give many details but left to go 'straight to the Archbishop with whom he would be completely frank.' This implies that he could have told [a] much worse story if he cared."[6] Roberts was proved absolutely right as Bewes and the archbishop did go on to tell a "much worse story" privately to the colonial secretary, the basic details of which had already been spelled out in his earlier memorandum to Governor Baring.

The colonial government's response of obstruction and obfuscation was becoming predictable. Governor Baring and the Colonial Office first sent secret memoranda back and forth determining how best to handle the ensuing queries from the House of Commons, finally agreeing on a response that would become standard for years to come: "The Governor is investigating the matter."[7] Interestingly, in the same report discussing the public-response language, Baring wrote to the colonial secretary that "there is every reason to believe that this is a case where a Mau Mau man was beaten in order to get information vital in the public interest and died in consequence, although this consequence was not to be expected."[8] The initial internal inquiry conducted by R. A. Wilkinson, a first-class magistrate, urged that the offense be viewed in the light of the panic caused by the recent Ruck murders that had "horrified the whole country." In his recommendation, Wilkinson wrote that the British perpetrators had "quite obviously suffered considerable punishment in the form of worry and remorse." More to the point, British colonial interests had also to be considered. "I do not in any case consider that it is in the public interest," he concluded, "that such action [i.e., prosecutions] should be taken at the present time, when all must unite in the effort to restore this country to a state in which such circumstances as these could not arise."[9]

The public response in Britain to the beating to death of Elijah Gideon Njeru made a trial difficult to avoid. Ruben and Keates—the two Europeans charged with manslaughter in the case—were tried in September 1953. The jury found them not guilty of the manslaughter charge though guilty of the much lesser offense of "assault occasioning actual bodily harm." They were fined fifty pounds and one hundred pounds, respectively. According to the Reuters report at the time, "The jury had recommended mercy 'having regard to the full circumstances of the Emergency and consequent heavy responsibilities placed on a small section of the community.'"[10] Judge Rudd, who presided over the case, endorsed the jury's decision, saying he was sympathetic to its viewpoint, and added, "As far as I am concerned I do not think I would have imposed a very much greater sentence even if the conviction had been of manslaughter."[11]

The verdict caused Canon Bewes to reconsider the public nature of his reproach. The missionaries in Kenya, like elsewhere in Britain's empire, were dependent upon the colonial government's goodwill, and never more so than during the Emergency, when the governor could use his wide-ranging powers to remove missionaries from the colony or greatly circumscribe their activities. The colony's relationship with the churches was, nonetheless, one of mutual dependence as the colonial government relied on the missions to underwrite many of the social costs of Britain's civilizing role. Throughout the Mau Mau war Christian missionaries would carefully balance their outrage over colonial violence with their need to maintain the favor of the government; they wanted above all else to continue God's work in upholding Britain's civilizing mission. In hindsight, it is not surprising that Bewes's press conference was the last of its kind. Moving forward, most missionaries would spend much of the Emergency privately lobbying Governor Baring and the Colonial Office rather than airing their complaints in the public arena. Even then they clearly feared reprisals. When bringing another "incident," as Bewes called it, to the attention of the colonial secretary in October 1953, he wrote, "I would rather the matter were dropped altogether than that anybody should think I had raised it—and this refers to the Governor in particular."[12]

Timorousness of the missionaries aside, the public debates over screening abuses did inflict damage on the British colonial government, coming as they did at a time when Governor Baring was using with increasing regularity his powers to detain Mau Mau suspects without trial. As of July 1953, he had sent over fifteen hundred suspected Mau Mau politicals and militants to the "internee camps," as they were first called. Each of the detainees was incarcerated without trial under Governor's Detention Orders, or GDOs, something that would later distinguish them from the growing camp population of "lesser Mau Maus." The expanding detainee population was a reflection of the Crown's inability to prosecute cases effectively against Mau Mau suspects, so that a GDO functioned as the "next best thing" to a conviction. The colonial government routinely failed to amass enough evidence to convict the vast majority of Mau Mau adherents, often owing to the disappearance or murder of witnesses for the prosecution. As the mechanisms of justice hit a wall, ongoing screening operations still continued to produce thousands of cases against Mau Mau suspects, ranging from consorting with terrorists to possessing ammunition to administering or taking an oath.

The Kenyan courts, financially and administratively strapped like the rest of the colonial government, could not possibly prosecute all these cases. While some of those arrested for directing Mau Mau activities were tried, convicted, and sentenced to prison, Governor Baring used his power of detention without trial for the greater majority of the suspected Mau Mau leaders. At the start of the Emergency Baring and his attorney general divided the leading Mau Mau suspects into two categories: Class I comprised "persons against whom criminal proceedings can be instituted with reasonable success," and Class II was meant for those against whom there was scant evidence for a conviction and who were therefore destined for permanent detention without trial.[13] This meant that men like Bildad Kaggia and Paul Ngei stood trial and were found guilty, along with Kenyatta, for organizing the Mau Mau society, while others such as the Koinange brothers and James Beauttah, who were arguably as involved in the Mau Mau movement, if not more so than those who had been convicted, were detained without trial under a GDO.

During the first year of the Emergency there was only a handful of detention sites for Mau Mau suspects. Some detainees were held in the prisons originally meant to house common criminals that dotted the colony, but the majority were kept in barbed-wire, heavily guarded internee camps. Two of the camps, Athi River and Kajiado, were located just outside of Nairobi and were reputed to hold some of the most politically active and dangerous detainees. The other main camp was on the remote island of Lamu, just off the northern coast of Kenya in the Indian Ocean. Lamu held those Mau Mau politicals considered to be the most militant. The majority of these detainees had been routinely screened at Athi River and then transferred to the island camp, going first in an enclosed railcar and lorry, then, once at the coast, shackled beneath the deck of a boat.[14]

The threat posed by the politicals to colonial society in Kenya was more ideological than military. The men and women at Lamu, Athi River, and Kajiado were the core of the Mau Mau intelligentsia, unlike most Mau Mau adherents who would begin filling the camps a year later. For the most part their arrest proved that the colonial government's intelligence was correct, at least according to the testimony of some of the camps' detainees, among them oath administrators, Mau Mau committee leaders, passive-wing organizers, and Kikuyu culture brokers—men like the famous Gakaara wa Wanjau, who had dedicated his life to writing and publishing Kikuyu cultural and political history in the years prior to Mau Mau.[15]

Detention without trial was a violation of Article 5 of the European Convention on Human Rights and its Five Protocols, to which Great Britain was a party. The Convention had been drafted in the wake of World War II with the intention of averting future catastrophes like those in the Nazi concentration and Japanese POW camps. It took as its starting point the United Nations' 1948 Universal Declaration of Human Rights and was put into force in September 1953. From the start of the Emergency in Kenya, British colonial officials internally debated the applicability of human rights accords like the European Convention on Human Rights and its Five Protocols to their subjects in the empire, despite the extension of the Convention to British territories, including Kenya, in October 1953. They decided ultimately not to challenge the scope of the Convention but rather to invoke a derogation clause. Article 15 of the Convention permitted an abrogation from the accord in times of war or other extreme public emergency that threatened the life of a nation, though such derogations were to be limited "to the extent strictly required by the exigencies of the situation."[16]

The scope of the European Convention extended beyond the question of detention, outlining a list of basic human rights that had to be protected under any circumstance. For example, Article 3 of the Convention states, "No one shall be subjected to torture or to inhuman or degrading treatment or punishment."[17] In addition to the European Convention, there was the aforementioned UN Universal Declaration of Human Rights, as well as the UN Convention Against Torture, which prohibited the use of torture under any circumstance, including states of emergency. The Geneva Conventions were also in effect during Mau Mau, stipulating that during war "at any time and in any place whatsoever" the following were prohibited:

(a) Violence to life and person, in particular murder of all kinds, mutilation, cruel treatment and torture;

(b) Taking of hostages;

(c) Outrages upon personal dignity, in particular, humiliating and degrading treatment.[18]

The colonial government treated Mau Mau detainees as prisoners of war. Governor Baring was clear on this point when he wrote the Colonial Office in July 1953, "[Mau Mau suspects] are a type who in another form of action, would become prisoners of war."[19] The establishment of the War Council in Kenya, for the formulation and execution of British wartime strategy against the Kikuyu, clearly suggests that colonial officials considered their engagement with Mau Mau to be a war. While the colonial government could derogate the European Convention on the issue of detention without trial, it could do so only while a State of Emergency was ongoing, and even then any form of torture or inhumane treatment was strictly prohibited not solely by the European Convention but by other international human rights accords as well.

The detention of Mau Mau suspects without trial seemed perfectly reasonable to many colonial officials. Most thought Africans and Asians not yet civilized, and therefore not entitled to the rights and obligations that went along with the postwar notions of international citizenship. Additionally, Mau Mau suspects were thrown into a category all their own. Their bestiality, filth, and evil rendered them subhuman, and thus without rights. The British argued that Mau Mau threatened not just the life of the colony but that of British civilization as well. Detaining these subhuman creatures amounted not only to saving Africans from themselves but also to preserving Kenya for civilized white people. The world had heard variations of this logic before, most recently when nearly 50 million people had lost their lives in the fight against fascism for the preservation of liberal democracy. Yet only seven years after the end of World War II, Britain found itself in a curious position of constructing its own labyrinth of detention camps in its fight to preserve colonial rule in Kenya.

The colonial government had to justify, at least rhetorically, its use of detention without trial and respond to the allegations of torture being used in a handful of camps already in operation. In Britain, anticolonial critics were beginning to mount an offensive against the Emergency Regulations in Kenya. Leading the attack against the Conservative government's colonial policies were Opposition Labour MPs, particularly Barbara Castle and

Fenner Brockway. With her fiery red hair, Barbara Castle would come to spearhead Opposition outrage over the British government's policies in Kenya, particularly detention without trial. Castle was a self-described fighter who, having been born into a socialist family, would eventually blaze her way "through the political jungle to the Cabinet."[20] From the early years of the Emergency she was relentless in her criticism of the British colonial government, emphasizing that "you were chasing a sense of complacency and cover up by the government in Kenya and at home that made one realise that there was something very wrong."[21]

Castle was certainly not alone, as various Labour MPs joined her condemnations and strident pursuit of the truth. Foremost was Fenner Brockway. In 1950 he had traveled to Kenya, where Jomo Kenyatta, the colony's best-known African intellectual and hence suspected troublemaker, served as his escort throughout Nairobi and the Kikuyu reserves. In the Kikuyu district of Kiambu the Labour MP spent extensive time with former senior chief Koinange and his sons. Koinange was already infamous in colonial circles, having been discharged from government service for his "disloyalty." According to Baring, he was reputed to have become "progressively more extreme in his political views, violently anti European and one of the hierarchy of the Kenya African Union."[22] Not surprisingly, local whites in Kenya were shocked when Brockway declined to avail himself of the comforts of a local European hotel, opting instead to accept the invitation of the ex–senior chief to stay with him and his wives in their traditional *boma* in Kiambu. It was there that the former senior chief explained to Brockway, by way of a Kikuyu parable, why there was so much anger in his reserve. "When someone steals your ox, it is killed and roasted and eaten," Koinange said. "One can forget. When someone steals your land, especially if nearby, one can never forget. It is always there, its trees which were dear friends, its little streams. It is a bitter presence."[23]

Not long after the start of the Emergency, Brockway returned to Kenya with fellow Labour MP Leslie Hale, largely to investigate the arrest and imprisonment of Koinange. The colonial government had charged him and one of his sons with the murder of Senior Chief Waruhiu. Both were acquitted only to be sent to detention, and despite Brockway's vehement protests they remained there throughout much of the Emergency. For the Colonial Office, the former senior chief was a difficult case. He was nearly eighty years old and held under conditions that were by all accounts horrendous. He had been convicted of no crime; nor had any effort been made to address his conditions in detention or the constant threats that were made against his life by European members of the police force.[24] Brockway's visit confirmed for him, as well as for Castle and others in the

Opposition, that only a few whites in Kenya or Britain believed Mau Mau to be anything other than a reversion to atavistic tribalism. The Colonial Office's response to the Koinange case reflected this sentiment.

The colonial government could not, however, silence Labour Opposition quite as easily as it did the Christian missionaries. In fact, the postwar period had ushered in a new era of knowledgeable and persistent debate in Parliament over colonial issues, debate forced by Labour Party members and other politicians and activists on the left. In 1954 Brockway established the Movement for Colonial Freedom and through this interest group consolidated the work of several Labour MPs, as well as organizations like the Congress of People Against Imperialism.[25] Protest against colonial policies throughout Africa, including detention without trial in other British colonies like Nyasaland, became the focus for many in the British government's Opposition. The Labour Party had a history of extraparliamentary organizations that targeted colonialism. The Fabian Colonial Bureau, founded in 1940, was the first of such groups that provided the Labour MPs with the research, networking, and publications necessary to influence the nature of British colonial rule throughout the empire.[26]

By the early 1950s, though, there was a shift in British anticolonial organizations as the Opposition began forming movements to more stridently challenge Churchill's Conservative government. A highly vocal minority was disgusted by the continuation of British colonial rule in Africa and elsewhere, particularly in the wake of the Second World War and the Atlantic Charter. In 1952 the Reverend Guthrie Michael Scott founded the Africa Bureau, bringing together an unprecedented group of diverse individuals interested in advising and supporting Africans who wished to oppose, by constitutional means, British colonial rule.[27] A group of Kenyans living in exile—led by Mbiyu Koinange, a son of the detained former senior chief, and Joseph Murumbi—formed the Kenya Committee to target the Emergency injustices.[28] Together with Brockway's Movement for Colonial Freedom, these organizations represented significant departures from the original Fabian Colonial Bureau. Whereas the bureau sought to influence the direction of colonial development policies, the postwar, anticolonial organizations wanted to expose the injustices of colonialism and bring the anachronistic form of governance to an end. Together they provided blanket coverage of the Mau Mau Emergency, galvanizing public awareness and empowering the Opposition in the House of Commons with the information necessary to challenge the Conservative government's depiction of events in Kenya. As early as 1953, charges that "Africans have been arrested and detained without trial . . . [and] have been, and are being, abused and evicted and gaoled and flogged and hanged, and shot before trial, amid sounds which almost amount to shouts of glee from the dominant race,"[29] were being unleashed, and the British government could not ignore them.

Even before the British colonial government took the extraordinary step of detaining the entire Kikuyu population, Mau Mau was exposing the hypocrisy of British trusteeship. In September 1953 Hugh Fraser, the Conservative MP and parliamentary undersecretary to Oliver Lyttelton in the Colonial Office, was dispatched to Kenya to evaluate the situation and assess what could be done to defuse charges of British misrule. On the one hand, the colonial government was straining to maintain its benevolent image as the advocate and protector of African interests in Kenya, and elsewhere in its empire, while, on the other, it was justifying its need for absolute power under Emergency Regulations. In his final report to the Colonial Office Fraser was unequivocal about what the colonial government needed to do in Kenya, and specifically addressed the growing detention camp problem. "Although there are only . . . about 1,500 detained, the number of detainees may well increase by June next year to some 25,000–40,000," Fraser wrote. He then went on to emphasize, "Should such numbers have to be involved, I have stressed to HE [His Excellency Governor Baring] the importance of the word 'Rehabilitation,' and machinery for this purpose is being set up."[30]

To understand the significance of Fraser's statement, we need to assess what exactly he meant by "Rehabilitation," as well as the "machinery" that was being established "for this purpose." In the spring of 1953 Governor Baring and his ministers had turned their attention to mounting a kind of psychological assault against the Kikuyu. According to extensive memoranda written at the time, there was support within the colonial government for an alternative course in defeating Mau Mau, one that did not rely entirely on violence and repression. The civilizing mission, Britain's raison d'être for colonizing the Kikuyu people, could be introduced to the masses of Mau Mau adherents through a program called rehabilitation. This strategy would offer social and economic change to those Kikuyu who confessed their oaths and then cooperated with colonial authorities in the detention camps, and eventually in the Emergency villages in the Kikuyu reserves. Rehabilitation would be the inducement needed to lure the Kikuyu away from Mau Mau savagery and toward the enlightenment of Western civilization. It would offer Mau Mau adherents opportunities far more alluring than those offered by their own movement. Rehabilitation was to become the colonial government's campaign for the hearts and minds of the Kikuyu.

This would not be the first time that the British government undertook a hearts-and-minds campaign to reorient detainees toward a more Western and civilized way of thinking. During and after the Second World War the British attempted to de-Nazify German prisoners of war in order to cleanse them of their fascist and anti-Semitic beliefs. At the same time the British undertook similar psychological campaigns throughout their empire as part of a larger effort to repress postwar, anticolonial uprisings. During the late 1940s and 1950s nationalists in Malaya, for instance, were demanding their independence, and the British responded by declaring a state of emergency as a way of fighting for their colonial subjects' hearts and minds. These antecedents would have great influence on the shape and direction of the Mau Mau rehabilitation program that was evolving in Kenya in 1953. There is no reference in Britain's declassified colonial files, however, to the Chinese communists' reorientation of their POWs toward an Asian, socialist way of thinking during the Korean War. In fact, the Americans and British both denounced Chinese ideological reorientation efforts as brainwashing, a psychological and physical trauma. But whether derisively labeled brainwashing or euphemistically termed hearts and minds, the psychological campaigns undertaken in each situation were strikingly similar: they were experiments in disciplinary power aimed at forcing individuals to reject their own ideas and adopt the purported superior beliefs of their captors.

Of all the British hearts-and-minds precedents, the one undertaken in colonial Malaya ultimately most influenced Kenyan policy. The Federation of Malaya, under the leadership of its governor, General Sir Gerald Templer, had already provided Baring and his ministers with a blueprint for Emergency Regulations. Malaya had been under a state of emergency since 1948, and its British colonial officials had exported to Kenya much of their legal work in drafting all-empowering Emergency legislation. On the issue of rehabilitation Baring also looked to the Asian colony, believing Templer was offering sound civic and social improvements to the communist insurgents and their supporters as a way of luring them back to the capitalist and civilized ways of their British colonizers. Baring telegrammed the general several times, asking to borrow a Malayan civil servant with experience in designing and mounting a hearts-and-minds campaign. Templer refused but did agree to host one of Kenya's colonial officers in Malaya and tutor him in the ways of rehabilitation. By the summer of 1953 Baring needed to dispatch someone to Malaya immediately so he hand-selected Thomas Askwith, who was by all accounts the most logical choice.

. . .

A leader among the small group of liberal-minded settlers and administrators who were disturbed by the racial injustices of British colonialism, Askwith stood alone in his empirical knowledge of African impoverishment and in his perseverance for reform in Kenya. For most Europeans in the colony, Africans were meant to be field hands or houseboys, not social and political equals. But for Askwith and his friends, the inequities of the government's land and labor policies, not to mention its color bar, which segregated Kenya's racial groups and prevented Africans from patronizing most restaurants, hotels, and even taxicabs, somehow had to be redressed. In 1946 Askwith, along with Ernest Vasey, Derek Erskine, and a handful of others, founded the United Kenya Club, a multiracial social club where men and women of all colors could socialize and dine.[31] In light of the extraordinary economic inequalities in Kenya this club may appear to have been a minor achievement, but in the context of the time and place its founding was revolutionary.

Askwith's pedigree did not betray a young man destined to question the racial divides and injustices of Britain's empire in Kenya. Born in 1911, Thomas Garrett Askwith was educated at Haileybury and then went on to read engineering at Peterhouse, Cambridge University. There he became a passionate sculler and oarsman, and eventually distinguished himself as one of the foremost athletes of his time. His image appeared on a Gallagher cigarette card in a series commemorating Britain's sporting heroes, where he was featured with other greats like Fred Perry, Harold Larwood, and Sir Malcolm Campbell. He confirmed his prowess on the river with his crew victories at the University Boat Race, the Grand Challenge Cup, and the prestigious Diamond Challenge Sculls at Henley. He was also a member of the Great Britain Eight in the 1932 Olympic Games in Los Angeles, and later in the 1936 Olympic Games—or "Hitler Games," as Askwith called them—in Berlin. When later recounting this episode, he vividly remembered, "As the German athletes saluted their führer, I felt physically sickened by what it represented. It affected me in a way that I'm not sure I can describe."[32]

After the Berlin Games Askwith set off for Kenya to a future that he called "invigorating, rewarding . . . disturbing, disheartening."[33] A member of the Colonial Service, he initially spent ten years in the Kikuyu reserves as a district officer before taking on the job of municipal native affairs officer for Nairobi, a posting that changed the course of his career. It was there that he witnessed firsthand the lives of the African urban poor and observed conditions scrupulously ignored by most Europeans in the colony. For Askwith, the urban slums epitomized the racial inequities upon which Britain had built its colony in Kenya. Two years later he took on the job of

commissioner of the Community Development Department and also became principal of the Jeanes School, Kenya's adult-education institute for
Africans, from which he promoted his concepts of African betterment and
social change. Askwith's endorsement of self-help principles—the notion
that given the proper knowledge and tools Africans could actualize their
own improvement—underwrote his approach to community development. His belief in the potential for African advancement and his practice
of racial inclusion caused him to be marginalized within official and unofficial circles throughout his career. That he was ostracized for his belief in
racial equality has been confirmed by many of his peers. Petal Erskine
Allen, a longtime British settler from one of Kenya's most distinguished
colonial families, later remarked, "Tom was about a century ahead of his
time, and even then most whites in Kenya will probably think Africans are
of a lesser form of life than they are."[34]

In a heavy summer rainfall that Askwith recalled being "eerily cleansing
and foreshadowing," he boarded a British cargo plane for Singapore. By the
end of his whirlwind fortnight tour he had observed various reform mea-
sures under way in Malaya's detention camps and rehabilitation centers,
Emergency villages, approved schools for young offenders, and prisons.
Templer's staff briefed him on their attempts to secure a lasting peace in
Britain's Asian colony through the reeducation and resettlement of the
communist insurgents and their supporters.[35] Askwith's observations in
Malaya would later provide the outline for similar Emergency policies in
Kenya. According to his rather idealized tour report, issued in August 1953,
the detention camps in Malaya were regarded not as punitive institutions
but as opportunities to alter the attitude of the communist sympathizers
and reinstill confidence in the British colonial government. The administrative structure of Malaya's camps emphasized rehabilitation. Templer
had created a temporary Detention Camps Department under the Ministry of Defence which was completely separate from the Prisons Department. Askwith made careful description of this part of the Malayan system
by noting, "It would not only be wrong in principle for detainees, who are
not convicts, to be placed under the Prisons Department, but also it would
detract from the value of the rehabilitation process itself. The rules and
principles governing rehabilitation are quite different from those concerning convicts, and it was felt that they were incompatible."[36]

The classification of detainees was especially critical to Malaya's apparent
success, according to Askwith. Police Interrogation Units labeled detainees
"black" or "grey," depending upon their level of communist indoctrination.
"Blacks" were hard-core Reds who could not be redeemed and who were
therefore deported. "Greys" had weaker communist sympathies and thus

were ushered through a series of rehabilitation stages, each punctuated with greater opportunities for reeducation and voluntary, paid employment. Askwith also saw immeasurable value in positive interactions between the officers and detainees. For him the quality and training of the staff would be the key to the success of any similar program in Kenya, and he noted in his report that "the value of teaching [in the camps and villages] was . . . secondary to the desire to teach."[37]

In Malaya rehabilitation appeared to stretch beyond the confines of the camps, which symbolized for Askwith a commitment at the highest levels to implementing Britain's civilizing mission throughout the colony, and particularly in those areas most affected by the State of Emergency. Colonial officials in Malaya seemed to be embracing reform. According to Askwith:

> It was generally recognised [in Malaya] that the rehabilitation process could not expect to succeed by itself, unless concrete evidence were given by the Government that it could offer a better future than that promised by the Communists. . . . The Government's over-riding purpose is to remove bitterness among the detainees and general public and to build a better life by meeting the social, economic and political needs of those who form the bulk of the Communist supporters, namely the poor sections of the community. It is almost universally felt that only thus can the ideological war be won.[38]

In effect, rehabilitation was one part of a comprehensive strategy for reconstructing Malayan society, with the work in the camps linked to rural development and social reform measures in the Emergency villages. Those who suffered from communist intimidation in the countryside also needed relief and reform. Moreover, the colonial government had to create future homes and employment opportunities for former detainees in Malaya. The captured hearts and minds of reformed communist insurgents could be lost if they were released into a hostile or impoverished situation.

Governor Baring, delighted by Askwith's findings and his enthusiastic commitment to the principles of rehabilitation, officially appointed him in charge of a Mau Mau psychological and civic reform program in October 1953. Coincidentally, or perhaps not, Askwith's appointment occurred on the heels of Hugh Fraser's visit to Kenya and his written directive on "the importance of the word 'Rehabilitation.' "[39] Thereafter, Askwith's title was expanded to commissioner for community development and rehabilitation, and so too were his responsibilities.[40] He found himself overseeing the hearts-and-minds campaign for some fifteen hundred persons already detained under Emergency Regulations, nine thousand convicts imprisoned for Mau Mau offenses, and, as Baring put it, "the many ex-squatters, and persons returned to the reserves as a result of screening, together with the waverers normally domiciled in the reserves."[41] To finalize rehabilitation policy, Askwith, Baring, and others in the colonial government evaluated precedents both outside of and within Kenya. They assumed the nature of confinement and the rules for the psychological reform of POWs and rebellious civilian populations transcended, to some degree, the peculiarities of individual settings.

In practical terms this meant Askwith did not have to reinvent the wheel but could borrow large portions of his hearts-and-minds program from other campaigns. Among them, the Malayan precedent was still the most important, largely because General Templer had already accomplished the difficult task of streamlining earlier psychological efforts targeted at POWs. Askwith's impressions from his tour of Malaya, and particularly of Templer's emphasis that "the problem . . . was one of rehabilitation and re-settlement or re-employment, not rehabilitation alone," were fundamental to his vision of Emergency reform in Kenya.[42] But to adopt the Malayan policy in toto was going to be problematic. As much as the principles of confinement and the tactics of psychological reform appeared to transcend local particularities, each situation was also unique and had to take into account differences in political circumstances as well as the social and cultural characteristics of the imprisoned or detained population. Mau Mau was not communism, and Africans were not Asians.

For Askwith, the difficulties he faced in Kenya were far more challenging than those that existed in Malaya. First, Templer was able to use the deportation option. More than half of the thirty thousand detainees in Malaya were repatriated by the British colonial government to China, where the communists welcomed back their "victims of imperial persecution" with open arms.[43] Those remaining in the Malayan camps had much "softer" communist sympathies and were easier to convert to the Western or British way of thinking. In Kenya, despite vociferous arguments from Baring advocating deportation to remote islands in the empire, the Colonial Office in London ruled that Mau Mau adherents "belonged to the territory."[44] Unlike many of the Malayan communists, who had allegedly immigrated to the British colony from China, the Kikuyu had been born in Kenya and therefore could not be exiled outside the colony's borders. In other words, Kenya had to deal with its "black" detainees, whereas Malaya for the most part did not.

Askwith also correctly perceived that the reabsorption problem of reformed detainees would be far more difficult in Kenya than it had been in

Malaya.[45] Already over one hundred thousand Kikuyu had been forcibly deported from their homes outside Kikuyuland and were returning to the overcrowded reserves, the same places to which rehabilitated detainees would later be returning upon release from Kenya's camps. Employment opportunities and expanded landholdings would have to keep pace with the release of the detainees. If this were not possible, Askwith predicted, "rehabilitation [would] be a waste of time, money and effort."[46] While job creation for Kenya's African population was challenging enough, the land issue was another story altogether. For the settler population, there was no land issue in Kenya. The colonial government supported this self-serving view and continued to uphold the earlier Carter Land Commission finding that the Kikuyu had ample land for subsistence production, a preposterous assertion.[47]

Finally, there were the oaths. Even for Askwith, whose liberal mind recognized the socioeconomic dimension of Kikuyu unrest, the "oath represented everything evil in Mau Mau."[48] He wrote that Mau Mau adherents had "tortured minds," and insisted that any reeducation program could not begin until their demented psyche had somehow been reached.[49] The European community in Kenya was in complete agreement with Askwith that Mau Mau was a kind of disease or filth that affected the bodies and minds of those who took the oath; it was a type of contagion or "mind-destroying disease."[50] Mass detention provided a form of quarantine where those afflicted with the Mau Mau infection could be diagnosed and treated.[51]

Long before launching rehabilitation, the colonial government enlisted the help of an expert to explain the causes of, and potential remedies for, the so-called disease of Mau Mau. The governor sought the advice not of a historian, an anthropologist, or an expert in political science, but rather that of an ethnopsychiatrist. A member of Baring's government, Charles Mortimer, commissioned the famed Dr. J. C. Carothers, Britain's expert in ethnopsychiatry, to write a report on Mau Mau and its causes. Ethnopsychiatry, or the study of the psychology and behavior of non-Western people, was a colonial science born at the end of the nineteenth century right alongside British colonization in Africa; it faded away around 1960, not coincidentally at the time of independence for most African nations. At its most basic level, ethnopsychiatry employed terms like *normal* and *pathological* to describe groups of people, terms which corresponded rather neatly with racial categories whereby whites were always the definition of normal against which pathological blacks were defined and therefore analyzed by the colonial psychiatrists.

Carothers's investigation in Kenya provided "hard scientific evidence" supporting the settlers' beliefs about themselves and about Africans, and about Mau Mau adherents in particular. In his thirty-five-page report titled "The Psychology of Mau Mau," Carothers argued that Mau Mau was not political but psychopathological, certainly a validation for the colonial government and one quoted time and again by the governor and the colonial secretary. Like so many others, Carothers was appalled by the oath, describing it as similar to those believed to be performed by witches during the European Middle Ages. On the question of whether the oath takers were redeemable, he looked not to the Kikuyu and their history under British colonial rule but rather to the literature on psychopathology. Carothers felt that the worst Mau Mau, as with hard-core criminal psychopaths, could not be saved, though the less indoctrinated, the ones suffering the milder forms of Kikuyu psychopathic behavior, could be reformed using the principles of Christian stewardship.[52] Redemption soon became a subtext that ran through the discussions of a hearts-and-minds campaign in Kenya, with the oath and its confession as the nonnegotiable focal points of rehabilitation policy and practice. For many contemporary commentators, confession was evidence of the Christian principles that underwrote the reform program; but the emphasis on confession can be found nowhere else in Britain's other hearts-and-minds campaigns, although the principles of Christian theology were certainly present. In Kenya, as tempting as it is to attribute rehabilitation's emphasis on confession to the colony's Christian influences, it was actually more strongly rooted in a particular psychology—a perceived psychology—of the Kikuyu people.

It is here that the famed Louis Leakey made a profound contribution to the rehabilitation plan, one that would soon have a great impact on the lives of Mau Mau detainees. Leakey, the well-known archaeologist who had grown up among the Kikuyu, spoke their language, and had even been circumcised with one of their age groups, was uniquely positioned within Kenyan society. During Mau Mau Leakey became the British authority on Kikuyu customs, supplementing the work of Carothers with his own self-professed, unique knowledge of the Kikuyu. In his book *Defeating Mau Mau*, Leakey suggested that traditionally among the Kikuyu the power of an oath could be removed if the initiate confessed having taken it; a traditional cleansing ceremony was then needed to rid his mind and body of the oath's polluting vestiges.[53] Askwith championed Leakey's idea of confession and insisted that a Mau Mau adherent could not partake in any rehabilitation activities until he or she confessed the oath, or, as he put it, "vomit[ed] the poison of Mau Mau."[54]

But Askwith diverged from Carothers and Leakey, and nearly every other European in the colony, on the causes of Kikuyu discontent. For Askwith Mau Mau grievances were legitimate and not the result of some kind of mass psychosis. In his internal reports he punctuated the urgent need for juvenile and adult education, unemployment relief, housing programs, increased wages, social security, and, most important, expanded opportunities to acquire land. Moreover, Askwith emphasized the negative effects of the color bar and the bitterness it engendered among all Africans in Kenya.[55] When W. H. Chinn, the social welfare adviser to the colonial secretary, toured Kenya in 1951, he commented upon the colonial government's obvious lack of commitment to the development and welfare of the colony's African community. He emphasized that a coordinated policy of social development was imperative to the relief of African poverty and to what he called the "training process of citizenship." In a scathing report he explained that "the services which are needed by all communities cannot be provided on an *ad hoc* basis or be dependent on the vagaries of political maneouvres; they must be accepted as government policy and as part of the Development Plan for the Colony."[56] Chinn had hardly minced words: Britain needed to take a hard look at its civilizing mission in Kenya. But Mau Mau was evidence that the colonial government ignored Chinn's recommendations, and in early 1953 Askwith made many of the same points that Chinn had offered two years earlier when he wrote to Baring and the colonial secretary.

> The present Mau Mau disturbances are an indication of how badly Kikuyu society has become disrupted through the impact of European civilisation, and of Government policy practised up to the present. . . . Maladjusted individuals whether they become so through economic, social or ideological causes are very susceptible to such disruptive movements as Mau Mau. It is therefore in my view most important that a plan for Social Welfare should be evolved. Social work in civilised countries became the safeguard of society. Without it hardship would, as it has in the past, lead to brigandage and even revolution.[57]

Looking back at his work during the summer and fall of 1953, Askwith remembered those months as being "the most inspiring and even optimistic time of [his] years in the colonial service."[58] He delivered his final draft for rehabilitation to Baring in October 1953, and it was a complete blueprint for winning the war against Mau Mau using socioeconomic and civic reform rather than destructive violence. The oath takers, behind the barbed wire of detention, would confess their Mau Mau oaths, and in return the colonial government would offer them many of the reforms that it had failed to deliver during the first half century of colonial rule. With Askwith's plan, detention would not be a punitive measure but an opportunity for British colonizers to introduce dramatic changes. Behind the barbed wire the Kikuyu would confess their oaths and then walk in lockstep with the well-trained rehabilitation staff toward redemption and progress. A recipe of paid physical labor, craft training, recreation, and civic and moral reeducation would produce governable men and women.

Askwith termed the system of detention and rehabilitation the *Pipeline*, denoting a Mau Mau adherent's progression from initial detention through ever more benevolent rehabilitation activities to ultimate release. The process would begin at the transit camps, where teams of Europeans and Africans would screen and classify each Mau Mau suspect. Those considered "white" would be repatriated to the African reserves; those labeled "grey" or "black" would be consigned to the reception centers, also known as holding camps. Screening would continue, and those still considered "grey" would be moved along to works camps, where detainees would confess their oaths voluntarily. Kikuyu elders and former Mau Mau adherents would induce a detainee's confession through "reason, cajoling, or ridicule." Once confessed, a "grey" detainee would spend his or her day performing voluntary, paid labor on some of the colony's development projects. Evenings would be spent with the rehabilitation staff in reeducation classes. A marked change in attitude would lead to a detainee's movement down the Pipeline and eventual transfer to an open camp in his or her home district. There, rehabilitation would continue with instruction by local chiefs and headmen, who would decide on a detainee's final release. Those classified as "black," however, were destined for the special detention camps. These camps would hold the hard core and the politicals, most of whom were considered beyond redemption. Even prior to Askwith's appointment Baring had ordered the construction of permanent exile settlements within Kenya for this brand of irreconcilable detainee.[59]

Askwith's rehabilitation policy was ultimately as much about communal reform as it was about changing individuals. The dependents of those in the Pipeline also needed opportunities for social and civic improvement. Askwith called the Kikuyu family the "foundation of African life," though he and most other colonial officials thought that many of the women and children were as steadfastly Mau Mau as the men, if not more so.[60] Hope for a peaceful future hinged on the reconstruction of African motherhood in the British image, with Askwith emphasizing: "It will be necessary to cleanse the women in the same way as the men before they are permitted to rejoin them, as there is evidence that wives have in many cases persuaded their husbands to take the oath and are often very militant. They are also said to be bringing up their children to follow the Mau Mau creed. It is therefore more important to rehabilitate the women than the men if the next generation is to be saved."[61] The colonial government zeroed in on Kikuyu women and children with a plan to pursue a dogmatic program that would break them of their allegiance to Mau Mau and convince them of the benefits and superiority of the British way of life. The plan was for the community development and probation staff to go to the reserves to oversee the rehabilitation of the Kikuyu family. There they would introduce communal confessions, or confessional *barazas*, that would purge the women of their Mau Mau indoctrination and ready them for home-craft, child-care, and agricultural classes.

Despite Baring's public enthusiasm and Askwith's commitment, the Mau Mau war was certainly a peculiar moment for liberal reform. At the very time that Askwith was drafting his rehabilitation program, screening abuses like the ones in Bahati and Subukia were taking place with the public's knowledge in Kenya, and to a lesser degree in Britain as well. Askwith was hardly oblivious to all the violence going on around him but simply could not reconcile the dreadful behavior of his fellow colonial officers, the settlers, and the loyalists with his passionate belief in Britain's civilizing mission. "I knew, I knew, but how can I say it . . ." he recalled in later years. "I just believed in our higher purpose. The oaths were terrible, and we had so much better to offer them. I thought our own bad hats [those perpetrating colonial violence] would come around."[62]

Rehabilitation presumed Britain's inherent moral superiority over the Kikuyu, something Askwith never questioned. When they first thought of introducing a hearts-and-minds campaign, Baring and Lyttelton viewed it as the antithesis of physical violence and summary justice. British colonial violence, however, could and did take many forms, and rehabilitation was no less coercive than some of the brute-force tactics employed in screening operations by Britain's colonial agents. Rehabilitation was an expression of cultural hegemony that assumed Britain's inherent superiority over anything Kikuyu. Nevertheless, on a relative scale rehabilitation was certainly much preferred to, say, the electric-shock torture being used by the Special Branch at the Mau Mau Investigation Center, or castration, or the other forms of physical brutality routinely used during interrogation.

Despite what he knew was going on around him, Askwith's belief in rehabilitation would be unshakable. Out of the ashes of Mau Mau, a reconstructed Kikuyu society would arise and with it the threat of any future uprising stymied. The commissioner had reason to believe that others, including the governor, shared his vision of an impending social counterrevolution.[63] In fact, one month after Askwith submitted his final rehabilitation outline to Baring and Lyttelton the colonial government endorsed it as official policy. The governor made a public spectacle of his government's adoption of a hearts-and-minds campaign, splashing it all over the papers in Kenya, Britain, and elsewhere with the help of Granville Roberts and the public relations offices in Nairobi and London. Even today, if one visits the Public Record Office in London or the Kenya National Archives in Nairobi, there are piles of documents describing Mau Mau rehabilitation, its official launching, and its purported successes. Somehow all of these files managed to survive the purgings.

It appeared that Askwith was poised to become one of the great liberal influences in the late colonial empire. The few historians writing about rehabilitation in Kenya have accepted the colonial government's assertion that it adopted liberal reform in the Pipeline, describing Askwith's revolutionizing role and his program as an example of the civilizing mission, albeit carried out under unusual and strained circumstances.[64] A close read of the historical evidence suggests, however, we need to reexamine the colonial government's agenda and the events that were unfolding in Kenya in the early 1950s. Had there been a broad consensus supporting Askwith's plan, the circumstances of the Emergency would have rendered its implementation difficult, at best. Budgetary constraints, staffing difficulties, the endless repatriation of Kikuyu back to their reserves, screening, and ultimately detention together stretched the British colonial government in Kenya as never before.

From the start rehabilitation hardly elicited widespread support. If prior to Mau Mau the Kikuyu had been at least a generation away from becoming equal citizens prepared to rule Kenya, then once the oath taking began it was not even worth speculating on how long it would take to transform them into governable citizens, let alone future leaders of the colony. Not long after the start of the Emergency Michael Blundell commented on the changing sentiment in Kenya.

In general there is a quiet and steady swing by all shades of European opinion over to the right and quite moderate people have been shocked out of thoughts of eventual partnership by the horrible barbarities which have come to light from the Mau Mau leaders. People are beginning to question whether all Africans however soft spoken and educated are not just the same and whether they are wise to talk about any future relationships with them other than on the basis of strict discipline and rule. I find it hard to counter these arguments as long as our policy is dictated from UK with all its emphasis on political advance regardless of the state of the African people themselves.[65]

For many Europeans who earlier had been considering civic equality in Kenya, Mau Mau erased all doubt, confirming the inherent savagery of Africans and their unreadiness to assume the privileges and benefits of citizenship.

At its most liberal, Kenya's European community advocated a slow, measured pace of reform. The East African Women's League—a conservative voluntary association and mouthpiece for the majority female settler opinion—argued, "The basic fact was not that the African had been held back by racial discrimination, but that he had traveled too far too quickly."[66] The settler women were not alone in believing that an accelerated path toward Western progress had numerous unforeseen and objectionable consequences for the Africans. While Askwith advocated drastic, rapid change, other British colonial officers and settlers saw a type of civilizing retrenchment as the direction to take. European members of the Legislative Council, such as N. F. Harris, pressed for a reevaluation of citizenship in light of Emergency events: "Throughout the British Empire, the Empire which was created by those people who have brought humanity to a great number of places in the world, it is in this Empire that a peculiar uprising of violence is apparent. I wonder whether, in fact, we have not—I say we, I mean the British—have not brought humanity to the people throughout the world, rather quicker than they and we ourselves have learnt the lessons of citizenship."[67] For Harris and others, the Kikuyu were trapped in what was then called a "crisis of transition." Neither primitive nor modern, they were caught in a kind of civilizing limbo. In the language of the day, the Kikuyu were suffering from "detribalization," and most Europeans in Kenya doubted whether rehabilitation was the solution to the problem. Even a relative moderate like Elspeth Huxley equivocated.

> The oath-taker is forced deliberately to flout the very deepest of his tribal tabus, to take actions which plunge him into so bottomless a pit of degradation that there can be no cleansing, no climbing back into the community of decent men. He is damned forever in his own eyes and therefore desperate, hopeless, irreclaimable. What a weapon of psychological warfare! It is impossible not to feel that a mind, or minds, diabolic in their ingenuity still control enemy strategy and that the gentle—perhaps genteel—minds of high officials operate on a level so different that the two cannot mesh. Courses in civics, training in carpentry, can they reclaim these self-condemned people?[68]

A settler sharpening her target skills

This skepticism over reform grew as Mau Mau's alleged savagery seemed to reach unmentionable proportions. Hardly a European in the colony believed Mau Mau to be human beings. They held the oath takers in utter contempt for their apparently obscene, primitive rituals and love of killing. In early 1953, just a few months into the Emergency, Ronald Sherbrooke-Walker went to visit friends in Kenya and candidly remarked upon the local attitude toward Mau Mau.

What do the settlers say? They know the primitive East African mentality and that "black brother" is a thousand years behind the European in outlook, and the "Kuke," who are causing the present trouble, are much inferior to the other Kenya tribes in moral qualities. If Europeans were to abandon the country voluntarily, or be squeezed out politically, without the Pax Britannica it would revert to blood-thirsty barbarism. If they are to remain, the policy of appeasement over the past few years must be halted. Justice must be done more promptly and effectively—and it must be seen to be done. The slow careful process of British justice, so cherished at home, is neither understood nor appreciated by the African mind molded by centuries of rough tribal discipline. This outlook is not changed to order by a dose of the three R's, nor yet by what may often be no more than a veneer of Christianity.[69]

By the end of 1953 the hard-line demand for summary retribution and for control of the Mau Mau population prevailed everywhere, making the adoption of rehabilitation, at least as outlined by Askwith, almost laughable.

This was especially true in the Kikuyu districts where the Administration, the elite cadre of colonial servants that had dedicated itself to uplifting the so-called hapless natives and tutoring them in the ways of British civilization, felt overwhelmed and betrayed by Mau Mau's rising tide. With Mau Mau the Kikuyu had become disobedient and ungrateful. Their movement touched personal nerves, challenging not just British colonial domination but the purported benevolence of the British colonial officers on the spot. The provincial and district commissioners moved quickly to revise their old patterns of control, though some did so with a rage that startled observers. As John Nottingham, a district officer during the Emergency, commented, "There was a dreadful trend in the districts, particularly condoned by the older Administration. You see, rehabilitation or reform, however you wish to call it, had no chance. You must understand that it had no real place in their Mau Mau. They wanted to remind the Africans who was boss, and they did it. They did some terrible, terrible things."[70] Some in the Administration advocated a policy of initial retribution rather than reform in the Kikuyu areas. F. D. Homan, the district commissioner for Meru, was clear on this point.

> Before any palliative measures are introduced Mau Mau must be crushed. We must lead from strength and not attempt to "finesse," for any other approach will be interpreted as weakness. As Winston Churchill said "We can afford to be generous in Victory"— but we must be quite certain first that we have won. . . . It must be clearly stated and obvious to everyone—not only the Kikuyu but also every other tribe—that any interim measures for displaced persons etc are either punitive (in the case of known bad characters) or at any rate framed on a bare maintenance basis.[71]

Others administering the Central and Rift Valley provinces were more restrained in their prescriptions for controlling Mau Mau, but no less determined to restore order using the heavy hand of colonial authority.[72]

It is clear that the colonial government was constructing detention camps in Kenya for punitive rather than rehabilitative purposes. The dominant eliminationist attitude toward Mau Mau overshadowed, even from the outset, any reconstructive hearts-and-minds campaign. Moreover, the liberal plan called for an accelerated civilizing process whose pace exceeded all acceptable limits for the colonial government and for the local settlers. Implementing Askwith's plan and carrying it to its logical conclusion would quite simply have meant African self-government. In 1954 for the British colonizers to agree to a hastening of colonial retreat in Kenya was unthinkable.[73] In fact, the colonial government's main concern was to retain power and reaffirm its position of dominance in the face of Mau Mau, rather than to prepare the colony for some kind of immediate multiracial, liberal democracy.[74] Most ministers within Baring's government envisaged a post-Emergency Kenya where African loyalists would be rewarded and co-opted into the colonial system as instruments of collaboration and control, the purveyors of Mau Mau would be eliminated, and the "rehabilitated" Kikuyu would be granted positions as disciplined subjects, but not citizens.

Governor Baring made several crucial decisions that quickly revealed the true nature of the Pipeline. While he publicly endorsed Askwith's rehabilitation program, the governor refused to approve an administrative structure for the camps that was a critical ingredient in rehabilitation's success. Askwith demanded that the colonial government create an independent department of detention and rehabilitation that would have full oversight over the custody and rehabilitation of the detainees. Baring and his ministers would not consider it. They viewed the detainees as offenders who had endorsed the unthinkable, a violent and savage challenge to the legitimacy of British colonial rule. They instead placed all detainees in the custody of the Prisons Department and its commissioner, John "Taxi" Lewis.[75]

In the years to come, Askwith would be virtually powerless to control or influence the Pipeline he helped to create. He would provide the staff for rehabilitation, but Taxi Lewis would remain fully in charge of the camp commandants, the warders, and the administration of all of the facilities within the Pipeline. On any points of conflict between the two departments, and there would be countless in the years ahead, Lewis and his men would have the final say. A committee of independent observers would eventually recognize the incompatibility between liberal reform and the

Mass roundup of Mau Mau suspects in the Rift Valley, November 1952

mission of the Prisons Department, issuing the strong reminder that "the object of detention is not to punish but to rehabilitate."[76] This suggestion, which came years later at the end of the Emergency, reflected a misunderstanding of the basic purpose of the Pipeline. From the point of view of most British colonizers, Mau Mau adherents were not ready for even the most rudimentary elements of rehabilitation. Indeed, one thought prevailed in Kenya and Britain: how could such savages possibly be remade to be like us, their civilized British colonizers? First they would have to be punished, forced to confess their oaths, and eventually trained to conform; then perhaps in a generation or so they would be ready for the basics of citizenship training on the British model. The actual detention camp structure in Kenya was critical in implementing this version of Britain's civilizing mission.

Apart from the Pipeline, Baring was pursuing several other blatantly punitive and arbitrary official policies. While publicly lauding Askwith's rehabilitation plan, the governor unleashed a policy of forced communal labor. Liberal reform was intended to extend beyond the Pipeline and into the Kikuyu reserves, where the family, the presumed "foundation of

African life," would be uplifted; instead colonial officers on the spot were forcing all Kikuyu men and women to labor, often as a form of collective punishment. Under Emergency law the Kikuyu had to work unpaid ninety days a year on communal projects like bracken clearing, trench digging, and the much-hated land terracing program. If they refused, they could be fined up to five hundred shillings or imprisoned for six months.[77] Work refusal cases rarely made it to court, and Mau Mau suspects instead remember being terrorized by the district officers and the Home Guard, who forced them to work.[78] "Even before the Emergency villages," Marion Wambui Mwai later recalled at her home in Nyeri District, "we went out nearly every day to build the terrace. The loyalists just whipped you and whipped you. Even if you dug faster, they whipped you. They treated us just like animals—and the white officer who oversaw the project would just march about, grinning at our suffering."[79]

The colonial government argued that communal labor was for the benefit of the Kikuyu community, and that the Africans actually enjoyed it. In fact, communal labor was a form of punishment that the Administration in the reserves wielded liberally, and one that several commentators likened to the slave labor policies of the Third Reich. Kenya's communal labor regulation was a violation of the International Labour Organization (ILO) conventions, which stipulated that communal labor could be required only for sixty days per year, and only from able-bodied men between the ages of eighteen and forty-five. British Labour MPs voiced their outrage on the floor of the House of Commons, as well as in partisan tracts. Fenner Brockway's condemnation was particularly powerful.

> When the Nazis carried out collective punishments against the Jewish race during the war, British politicians of all parties, preachers of all denominations, writers of all schools of thought—all voiced their indignant protest. The immorality of punishing innocent people was universally recognised. Now, only a few voices are raised in protest, although the principle is exactly the same.[80]

Criticism also came directly from the ILO, which likened Kenya's forced communal labor to outright enslavement.[81]

The British colonial government's agenda in Kenya had two faces: the one it presented to the world and the sinister one that it tried to conceal from the public. From the very start of the Emergency colonial officials planned to detain permanently thousands of alleged Mau Mau leaders and intellectuals, people of influence whose presence threatened to expose the illegitimacy of colonial rule and potentially incite the anger of the much needed loyalists. Several senior chiefs petitioned Baring and the Colonial Office to ensure the permanent banishment of the Mau Mau leadership, as well as the confiscation of their land and other property. In one case a group of prominent loyalists wrote:

> We feel most deeply that if any of the detained leaders of Mau Mau, or any who receive and serve sentences of imprisonment, or any who are at present at large and who may be arrested in the future, are later allowed to resume life among us once more, they will, inevitably, endeavour to reorganise a similar movement, perhaps under some other name. . . . We therefore most respectfully and sincerely petition Your Excellency to take such steps as may be necessary to insure that no leader of Mau Mau who is sentenced, shall later return to live among us, and further, that no leader of Mau Mau who may have been detained and against whom there is evidence to satisfy Government that he or she is such a leader, shall be later released and allowed to come back to live among us. . . . If such people do eventually return, we are convinced that they would cause further troubles and try to bring about further dissention between the people and Her Majesty's Government.[82]

The loyalists clearly had self-serving motivations consistent with the long-term plans of the British colonial government to retain domination and control through unlimited powers of arrest and detention. Colonial Secretary Lyttelton endorsed a policy of detaining permanently twelve thousand Mau Mau politicals and other irreconcilables who could not be coerced into supporting Britain's continued rule in Kenya. Provided no one "belonging to the colony" was deported, but rather permanently exiled to detention sites within the four corners of Kenya, the Colonial Office approved of "the Kenya Government's policy of building on the 'loyalists' to the exclusion of ex-Mau Mau leaders."[83] This meant that men and women picked up and detained at Athi River, Kajiado, and Lamu camps had no hope of ever being released.

Even with the permanent removal of the Mau Mau leadership Baring was still insecure about his government's ability to rule without the use of arbitrary legislation. At the same moment when he was publicly endorsing liberal reform, the governor was preparing, with the help of the Colonial Office, post-Emergency laws that would legalize the continued use of detention without trial and communal labor. This legislation would also mandate control over African political organization, the circumscription of African movement, and the marketing of African labor. All of these authoritarian and arbitrary laws were eventually enacted in late 1959 and early 1960, further emphasizing the British colonial government's continued unwillingness to commit to reform.[84]

Had they embraced Askwith's program for rehabilitation and his vision of a multiracial future, surely Baring and the colonial secretary would not have envisioned a continued dependence upon arbitrary powers after the lifting of the Emergency. D. F. Malan, the prime minister of the new apartheid government in South Africa, applauded Kenya's use of force and arbitrary rule, and saw it as a model for his own apartheid regime. In his condemnation of the British colonial government Brockway was quick to point out, "Perhaps the severest comment upon the Kenya Government's repressive measures has been the exultant remark of Dr. Malan in South Africa that a British Colony has given him an example of how to treat discontented Africans. The policy of the Kenya Government, supported by Mr. Oliver Lyttelton and the British Government, may destroy Mau Mau only to increase Mau Mauism."[85]

In hindsight, the most surprising turn of events of all would have been Governor Baring's implementation of Askwith's program. The introduction of rehabilitation, as Askwith defined it, would have required a complete shift in the public's perception of Mau Mau, the authoritarian nature of the British colonial government, and its plans for continued imperial domination in Kenya's post-Emergency future. The rehabilitation program enjoyed scant financial support, requiring Askwith to beg other departments and outside donors for contributions. Staffing was minimum, and supplies, from footballs to chalkboards, were hard to come by. There was no indication of the colonial government's dedication to the hearts-and-minds campaign in Kenya. Detainees themselves remember little about colonial-sponsored rehabilitation other than the odd football game, loudspeakers blaring colonial propaganda through the camps, and government pamphlets that provided the latest "news" of the success of colonial forces in the forests and the fairness of Britain's land policies in the reserves.

In keeping with its wish to maintain appearances, the British colonial government highlighted at every turn its endorsement and the purported successes of rehabilitation. When colonial officials would stand accused of torture or misconduct in detention camps or Emergency villages, Governor Baring and the colonial secretary would proudly hold up the success of rehabilitation as mitigation for any "one-off" offenses that may have occurred. Colonial logic had the world believing that the violation of the basic human rights of hundreds of thousands of people could be excused merely because there now existed a bogus and largely nonperforming program of liberal reform. With the notable exception of a handful of humane and reform-minded colonial officers detailed to the Pipeline, re-habilitation was nowhere to be found in the camps or barbed-wire villages of colonial Kenya. Whatever term is given to Askwith's program—rehabil-itation, hearts and minds, liberal reform, the civilizing mission—its imple-mentation was largely a sham. With the camps filling up and public criticism mounting, the British colonial government would not deviate from its misleading rhetoric, deliberately extolling rehabilitation as a legit-imating ideology in order to mask the increasing violence and brutality of detention without trial in Kenya.

CHAPTER FIVE

THE BIRTH OF
BRITAIN'S GULAG

The purging of Mau Mau suspects in Nairobi during Operation Anvil

THE EVENTS OF APRIL 24, 1954, WOULD IRREVOCABLY CHANGE THE detention camp system in Kenya and the lives of tens of thousands of Mau Mau suspects. On this day Britain's military forces, under the command of General Sir George Erskine, launched an ambitious operation to reclaim full colonial control over Nairobi by purging the city of nearly all Kikuyu living within its limits. Quite befittingly, the assault was called Operation Anvil.

In the early morning of Nairobi's "D-day"—as Anvil's launch was called—Erskine began deploying nearly twenty-five thousand security force members whose mission was to cordon off the city for a sector-by-sector purging of every African area.[1] The general took his cue from a similar "clean-up" conducted by the British military before the Second World War in the then Palestinian city of Tel Aviv, where the element of surprise was the key to its success. Likewise in Nairobi, the entire population—African, Asian, and European—was caught off-guard, and what happened next has been described as nothing short of "Gestapolike."[2] Loudspeakers affixed to military vehicles blared directives: pack one bag, leave the rest of your belongings in your home, and exit into the streets peacefully. In some cases, the targets of the sweep had no time to pack. People were picked up on the street or at their places of work, or the security forces knocked their front doors down with swift kicks and rifle butts. All Africans were then taken to temporary barbed-wire enclosures, where employment identity cards were used to determine tribal affiliations. The Kikuyu, as well as the closely related Embu and Meru, were separated from the rest of the city's African population in preparation for on-the-spot, ad hoc screening,[3] while members of other ethnic groups were most likely released and returned to their homes or places of work.

Nelson Macharia was one of the thousands of Africans caught up in the purge. He had been working as a mechanic at an Asian car-repair shop in order to support his wife and children, who were living on a small plot of land in the reserve in Fort Hall. "I was arrested on April 24, 1954, at the garage where I worked," Nelson later recalled. "I had no time to collect any of my things, but I was lucky. When we arrived in the large place surrounded by coiled barbed wire in the middle of Nairobi, there were many people who had obviously been beaten and harassed. They were shaking from fear. When I saw them, I knew we were in trouble, though I had no idea the kind of trouble that lay ahead of us."[4] From there, he and the others were marshaled through a screening parade, where a Kikuyu loyalist— his identity protected by a hood, or *gakunia*—sealed a person's fate within a matter of seconds. As Nelson later explained:

> There were many white police officers about, and I was made to pass in front of the *gakunia* behind the others, in a long file. The person inside the sack, which had holes made in it, would look at you, and if he nodded his head, that meant that he had recognized you [as a Mau Mau], and you would be whisked away by the white officers and put into the screened-in lorry with the rest of the *magaidi* [dangerous people]. But if he shook his head, it meant that he had not recognized you, and you would be set free for repatriation to the reserves. In my case, he nodded his head, and I was taken to Langata Screening Camp, where I was interrogated some more before I was sent to detention.[5]

Langata Screening Camp was the temporary destination for many of the Mau Mau suspects rounded up during Anvil. Like Nelson, Karue Kibicho was also taken there after he was removed from his home on River Road. Karue was typical of thousands of young Kikuyu men who had migrated to the city in the years prior to the Emergency. Born on the farm of *Bwana* Baker in the Rift Valley Province, he never knew life in the Kikuyu reserves, living instead as a squatter on land that neither he nor his father ever had any chance of owning. "I felt like the world was closing in on me," Karue later recollected. "After the [Second World] War things were getting worse for us on *Bwana* Baker's farm, and I knew I had to leave to find better work, so I went to Nairobi. It was the only place for me to go." But on April 24, he too was picked up. According to Karue and others, "the operation was carried out by only white police officers [security force members], whom we had nicknamed 'Johnnies'. . . . They did everything like forcing us into the barbed-wire enclosures, they took our valuables, all the time calling us 'bloody Mau Mau.' "[6] Eventually, he too walked through a screening parade, which, though carried out by a European officer rather than a Kikuyu loyalist shrouded in a *gakunia*, was just as capricious and deterministic as the one experienced by Nelson. Along with the eight other men with whom he had shared a room on River Road, Karue was taken to the bus station.

> The former bus station . . . [was] near where the Hilton Hotel stands today. Coiled barbed wire had been used to surround the place. That was where we were divided according to our tribes. Everyone who was not Kikuyu, Embu, or Meru was taken away, whereas those who were Kikuyu, Embu, and Meru remained. Each of us then passed in front of a white officer, who scrutinized us without asking anything. He would then hand a person a card that was either red or white in color. There was nothing written on the cards; they were just blank. After getting the card, we would go to another white officer, who after noting the card's color would point us to different directions. Those who had white cards would be shown one way, while those holding red cards would be shown another. In my case, I was handed a red card, which I soon realized meant that I was to be detained. We were later loaded onto buses which took us to Langata Camp, where we were put into tented compounds. We knew we had been arrested because of our involvement with Mau Mau, because we were demanding our land and freedom. We did not have to be told.[7]

Dozens of people whom I interviewed had been picked up during Operation Anvil, and each one recalled similar moments of confusion, fear, and verbal and physical abuse. If they moved too slowly, or too quickly, they were beaten with clubs and rifle butts. If they spoke in the screening parades, they were often shipped directly to detention. If a Mau Mau suspect protested his rough handling, he would be hauled off and put in one of the "special police vehicles"; several of these suspects were never again seen.[8] Others remember the difficult separation of families—men being taken off in lorries for more screening at Langata, women and children sent to different lines for repatriation back to the reserves. "It was an unimaginable time," recalled one Kikuyu man. "I was standing inside the lorry holding on to the screen that surrounded the whole vehicle, designed to keep us from escaping. I could see my people being abused by the 'Johnnies.' Then a team of hooded screeners passed by the vehicle and hissed at us. When the lorry pulled away, I could see the 'Johnnies' looting the houses of those they had just picked up, taking the valuables left behind for themselves. The whole thing was just . . . God help me."[9]

Nairobi was the linchpin in Britain's military campaign against Mau Mau, and Erskine was determined to capture it once and for all. He firmly believed that "it had become the main Mau Mau supply base from which the terrorists obtained recruits, money, supplies and ammunition," and he was hardly alone in his sentiments.[10] There was an unusual consensus in the ranks of both the military and Baring's civilian government that the colony's capital was the nerve center for Mau Mau operations. Nearly three-quarters of the city's African male population of sixty thousand were Kikuyu, and most of these men, along with some twenty thousand Kikuyu women and children accompanying them, were allegedly either "active or passive supporters of Mau Mau."[11] According to British colonial officials, Nairobi was gripped by a "breakdown in respect for law and order," and Mau Mau adherents were murdering "loyal Kikuyu, Kikuyu-government-servants, suspected informers, and leading African personalities who were unsympathetic to the movement."[12] They were purported also to be perpetrating a host of other crimes, including armed robberies, the intimidation of potential witnesses, the levying of "protection money," and the organization of boycotts of government-run buses and European products. Worse, one of the British colonial government's greatest nightmares was becoming a reality: the Kikuyu were taking advantage of the tight living quarters of Africans in Nairobi to recruit members of other ethnic groups, particularly the Kamba, into the Mau Mau movement.[13]

Nearly two weeks later Erskine considered Operation Anvil largely finished. From the military's point of view, it was a complete success. A fortnight of relentless roundups, screenings, and deportations had cleansed Nairobi of all Kikuyu, except for those few who were considered "clean," had long-term contracts with European employers, and adequate housing within the city's limits. By the end of the operation and its mop-ups, Britain's security forces had sent over twenty thousand Mau Mau suspects for further screening at Langata Camp and deported nearly thirty thousand more back to the Kikuyu reserves, where the Administration would have to find some way of accommodating them.[14] Once the general's men had cleansed Nairobi and the surrounding areas of suspected Mau Mau supporters, their job was finished. The responsibility of detaining the Mau Mau suspects and somehow getting them to acquiesce to British colonial authority rested with Governor Baring and ultimately with the colonial secretary.

It would be difficult to argue that the colonial government envisioned its own version of a gulag when the Emergency first started. Colonial officials in Kenya and Britain all believed that Mau Mau would be over in less than three months. They were prepared to handle a few thousand of the political detainees who were being held under Governor's Detention Orders, but as yet had no plans to incarcerate the countless other "lesser Mau Maus." Yet when the movement did not collapse with the arrest of its presumed leadership, or shrink at Britain's initial show of force, the colonial government had to rethink its plan. As the situation worsened, the harsh Emergency directives already in place began to seem inadequate.

Long before Anvil, Governor Baring knew a major crisis was brewing in the Kikuyu reserves. Before 1953 they were already overcrowded and on the verge of ecological collapse, had been so for years, and were hardly capable of absorbing what would become a total influx of some 150,000 repatriates with no prospect of employment and no land on which to grow food. The repatriates alone constituted an administrative and fiscal nightmare for Baring, a nightmare only made worse by the steadily increasing number of Mau Mau suspects recommended for detention by the screening teams.

At no point did the British colonial government consider expanding the boundaries of the Kikuyu reserves. Time and again Baring strictly adhered to his edict that Mau Mau must not be rewarded with a concession to demands for more land.[15] There was, then, only one way around the population problems caused by repatriation. The governor had to find a way to make the reserves more agriculturally productive.

Adding to this seemingly unsolvable problem was the governor's inherent indecisiveness, which rendered him, at times, absolutely paralyzed by the complexities facing him. He needed an expert, and he turned to R. J. M. Swynnerton, Kenya's assistant director of agriculture, who in late 1953 drew up a five-year African land development plan. The Swynnerton Plan was intended not only for the agricultural reconstruction of Kikuyuland, the central Kikuyu homestead, but also for the improvement of all African farming and grazing areas throughout the colony. With Baring's leadership, Swynnerton secured a £5 million concession from the Colonial Development and Welfare Fund, and with it planned "intensified agricultural

Deportations of Mau Mau suspects from Nairobi

development in all African Areas of Kenya with due emphasis to the loyal tribes."[16]

The Swynnerton Plan began from the premise that Africans were destructive and ineffective custodians of their own land. Colonial officials assumed that Africans needed agricultural experts to show them how to cultivate and herd efficiently, despite the fact that they had successfully managed their land and livestock for centuries before the British arrived. The plan dovetailed neatly with the colonial government's intransigence on Mau Mau demands, and especially its refusal to expand the boundaries of the reserves. If the Kikuyu could only be shown how to make better use of their land, so the logic went, then its carrying capacity could be expanded and more people could subsist off of the small holdings. Swynnerton's plan described a variety of projects—like bench terracing, soil conservation, bracken clearing, and paddocking—that ostensibly would increase productivity in the Kikuyu reserves. Along with these measures were numerous agricultural projects designed to develop previously uninhabitable areas in Kikuyuland for future resettlement. Locales where no one could or wanted to live, some malaria-infested and others drought-plagued, would somehow be rendered fit for human habitation and would contribute further to easing overpopulation in the reserves.

The Swynnerton Plan did not stop there. The colony's leading agricultural expert also believed that the small landholdings that marked the Kikuyu landscape were inefficient, and that only through a process of landholding consolidation and legal deeding could agricultural productivity be maximized. The poorer Kikuyu—many of whom already formed the backbone of Mau Mau—had been fighting the colonial government on this issue for years, for they knew full well that such a policy would largely benefit their wealthier, loyalist neighbors and lead inevitably to their own further impoverishment. The dictatorial powers of the Emergency permitted Swynnerton to decide that "former Government policy will be reversed and able, energetic or rich Africans will be able to acquire more land and bad or poor farmers less, creating a landed and landless class. This is a normal step in the evolution of a country."[17] The colonial government was preparing to create permanent socioeconomic divisions within Kikuyu society based on access to land. In the future landed and landless (or land poor) Kikuyu would divide largely along the fault line between loyalist and Mau Mau. Most British colonial officials, Baring included, thought Swynnerton offered the panacea for all that ailed the colony. His unique brand of intense agricultural development, a veritable agrarian revolution, appeared to offer hope for solving the Kikuyu land crisis. It was also, however, a shameless reward scheme aimed at affirming the loyalists as effective, future instruments of colonial collaboration.[18]

How was Baring going to fund all of Swynnerton's proposals? As a result of the earlier forced removals from the White Highlands, there were already over eighty thousand repatriated Kikuyu in the reserves who were unemployed, had little if any land, and needed income from relief work. The provincial commissioner, Carruthers "Monkey" Johnston, made staggering cost estimates for funding even the barest measures needed to prevent starvation and ecological collapse.[19] Even the governor and his newly formed Reconstruction Committee—created specifically to address the crisis in the Kikuyu reserves—had arrived at their own, equally enormous cost projections. Over £2 million were needed simply to cover projected relief expenses for the coming two years. This amount exceeded Swynnerton's total budget for all Kikuyu agricultural reconstruction. Lack of money would continue to be a decisive issue, having devastating consequences for the Kikuyu.[20]

. . .

Repatriation was punctuated by daily tragedy: children separated from their parents, death from starvation and disease, suffering from exposure and dysentery, and the sheer chaos and uncertainty of the whole ordeal. Unable to ignore this growing catastrophe, Baring scrambled in the fall of 1953 and came up with another solution: the Four-Point Plan.[21]

First, the remainder of unwanted Kikuyu in the European settled areas would be parked in the transit camps until spaces could be made available in the reserves. Second, the basis for the flow of repatriates would henceforth be regulated by the results of screening. Priority for places in the reserves was given to those considered more cooperative, with no more than twenty families per month to be repatriated from any given transit camp. Third, a scheme for poor relief in the Kikuyu districts was outlined: Kikuyu labor would be directed only toward projects that were included in the Swynnerton Plan, and the repatriates would be paid on a sliding scale, based on age and gender.

But reality frustrated Baring's plans before they could even be put in place. The transit camps were already overflowing with repatriates and were completely ill equipped to handle thousands more of them for months on end. Moreover, whatever the labor schemes the Kikuyu were enrolled in, the governor still did not have the funds to pay for relief programs on any regular basis. Over the years, I've interviewed numerous Kikuyu who were forcibly removed from the Rift Valley and sent back to the reserves during the early years of the Emergency. To a person they worked on relief gangs, though few recollect ever receiving wages or rations for their labor. For nearly all of them their most enduring memory was scraping together enough money to pay the special or punitive tax that was levied by the colonial government against all Mau Mau suspects living in and returning to the reserves. Revenues from this tax were to be used to help fund the relief programs.[22] Baring's plan to reestablish colonial control—which included expanding the carrying capacity of Kikuyuland—was at this point cut loose from the purported objectives of the Four-Point Plan. Had the welfare of the repatriates been a consideration, if not a goal, then the governor would have stopped or at least slowed forced removals. Instead, the so-called relief programs were in fact designed to make use of cheap or free repatriate labor for Swynnerton's agricultural programs in the Kikuyu reserves.

The last item of the Four-Point Plan was the blueprint for the impending expansion of detention camps. It is in this regard that Baring made the decision to create works camps throughout the colony that would use detainees as a cheap labor source. As with the repatriates, he saw no problem in using the massive, captive workforce at his disposal. In fact, the governor was about to put thousands of beaten and half-starved Mau Mau suspects to work, not only on the agricultural redevelopment programs proposed by Swynnerton but also on numerous others suggested by the Public Works Department.

At first, there were ostensibly two types of works camps, though distinguishing between them would have been difficult. The first type were located within the Kikuyu districts and were intended for poor relief rather than punishment. They held dozens of homeless, repatriated families who were considered to have "soft" Mau Mau sympathies. The first three of these camps—Githunguri, Aguthi, and Fort Hall—were, within a matter of weeks, pushed beyond their combined capacity of two thousand people. Living conditions were makeshift, and the colonial government's complete disregard for sanitation or hygiene standards inevitably created much suffering for those forced into them.[23] Nevertheless, thousands of Kikuyu who languished in the squalor of the transit camps anxiously awaited vacancies in the new works camps in Central Province in a desperate hope for improved conditions.

Then there were the works camps located outside of the Kikuyu districts. These were designed for the thirty thousand Mau Mau suspects whom screening teams had already deemed unfit for return to the reserves. These camps were explicitly punitive. The camps housed alleged oath takers who fell somewhere between the extremes of the repatriate suspected of having "soft" Mau Mau sympathies and an internee who might qualify for transfer to the political or hard-core detention camps. This middling category of Mau Mau adherent was produced by the saturation crisis in the reserves. Because of limited space available in the Kikuyu areas, screening teams and the Administration were making more disciplined decisions about the numbers and nature of those who were to be repatriated.[24] Many Mau Mau suspects destined for works camps were no more committed to the movement, and some even less so, than those who had been repatriated to the Kikuyu reserves during the early months of the Emergency.

Forced labor was a constant in both types of camps. Although the colonial government had no difficulty forcing detainees to work, it risked the scrutiny of the international community. Whereas the European Convention on Human Rights could be derogated, in part, by citing the wartime and emergency clauses, the International Labour Organization (ILO) Forced Labour Convention caused the Colonial Office much greater concern. The ILO's position was crystal clear: when a person is incarcerated without trial, he or she cannot be made to work. The colonial secretary himself explicitly recognized that the "proposal [of detainee labor] was contrary to the letter of the International Convention on Forced Labour," and knew that his office would have to "refute any allegation that [the detainees] are being used as 'slave' or 'cheap labour' for the profit of Government."[25] The colonial government could easily have been accused of using forced labor for political and economic gain, an accusation which would of course have been true, but which Colonial Secretary Lyttelton needed to avoid.

To get around this problem, Governor Baring and the colonial secretary once again looked for help within Britain's own empire. It seemed that General Templer was already violating the ILO Convention in Malaya, though he managed to do it on a reduced scale by creating a two-tiered system of works camps. Templer sent his cooperative detainees to so-called ordinary works camps, where they volunteered to work on labor projects and were supposedly paid an appropriate wage. Those detainees who were uncooperative were sent instead to special detention camps, where they could be forced to work but were also paid. The logic behind this charade was that there were far more detainees working voluntarily—at least in theory—in the ordinary works camps than were being forcibly made to work in the special detention camps. In effect, the colonial government in Malaya was violating the ILO Convention only some of the time.[26] Lyttelton urged Baring to adopt a similar system, emphasizing that "the number subject to compulsory labour [would be] reduced accordingly."[27]

After Templer's system was exported to and implemented in Kenya, neither the ILO nor the United Nations Ad Hoc Committee on Forced Labour ever once charged the British colonial government with violating the Convention. Nonetheless, Lyttelton knew his government was "in technical breach of the forced labour conventions."[28] Even Kenya's minister for defense, Jake Cusack, plainly stated in reference to detainee labor, "We are *slave traders* and the employment of our slaves are, in this instance, by the Public Works Department" (emphasis in original).[29]

With Swynnerton's Four-Point Plan in place and with a green light for forced labor, a grand design was beginning to emerge. The works camps, though still in their formative stage, were going to fit into Governor Baring's broader strategy of overhauling the colony's African political economy and transforming it into the basis for continued British colonial rule. It almost sounds like a lofty colonial goal—except that there was a State of Emergency going on. The forced removal, repatriation, and detention of Mau Mau suspects would over time be integrated into the colonial government's broader plan of agricultural reconstruction, land reform, and overall modernization of Kenya. Emergency or not, the development of the colony was going to be carried out on the collective back of the suspected Mau Mau population.

. . .

It was at this juncture in the spring of 1954 that the fledgling Pipeline was impacted by Anvil's mass arrests. Forced by the momentum of the roundups to redirect temporarily his attention and resources away from the works camps, Baring and the Public Works Department began preparing vast "reception" facilities for the thousands of new Mau Mau suspects. Langata's capacity was expanded to over ten thousand, while two new reception centers, one at Manyani and the other at Mackinnon Road, were also established. Both of these camps were located in one of Kenya's most arid and desolate regions. Manyani was an enormous site, nearly three miles long by half a mile wide. It was, like most of the camps in the Pipeline, surrounded by barbed wire and watchtowers and patrolled by armed guards with police dogs. Farther toward the Indian Ocean coast stood Mackinnon Road, constructed from an old military airplane hangar remodeled for the new arrivals with dozens of separate compounds divided by thick barbed wire. With the addition of the two new reception centers, technically there was space for another fifteen thousand detainees.

But General Erskine grossly underestimated the number of Mau Mau suspects who would be slated for these camps. Initially projecting no more than a total of twenty thousand new detainees, by May of 1954 there were over twenty-four thousand Mau Mau suspects in the Langata, Manyani, and Mackinnon Road camps alone—a thirteenfold increase in the number of detainees held at the beginning of the year.[30] New intakes were coming in daily, by the lorryload, busload, and via railroad freight cars. Although these arriving hordes were largely a result of Erskine's military operations, the general and his forces were not to blame for all of them. Thousands were also being shipped in from the European settled areas and the Kikuyu reserves by Baring's men in the Administration.

At first, only the governor had the power to issue detention orders, but in time it became impossible for him to keep up with the numbers of pickups, while also managing the escalating crisis in the reserves. Thus he delegated the powers of detention, previously reserved solely for him, to members of the Administration. This meant that the provincial and district commissioners could issue the lesser detention orders, or Delegated Detention Orders (DDOs), to any African suspected of Mau Mau sympathies or any African they simply wanted out of their areas.[31] By the end of 1954 the British colonial government reported that the detainee population had risen to over fifty-two thousand—an increase of 2,500 percent from the beginning of the year.[32]

The growing population in the Pipeline included not only detainees held without trial in the camps but also those convicted of Mau Mau–related crimes and sent to prisons. In fact, the Pipeline would eventually process thousands who were tried and convicted of Mau Mau offenses in the colonial courts. The vast majority of these cases were brought in front of Emergency assizes, where the colonial prosecutors almost wholly abandoned evidentiary procedure. The suspects and their lawyers—if one were even present—were prohibited from mounting any reasonable defense, as the courts were created to enforce swift rather than impartial justice. Most of the attorneys representing Mau Mau defendants came from a small cadre of sympathetic Asians based in Nairobi. These were men like Fitz de Souza, who today recalls:

> [I had] no time to prepare a defense. These suspects were generally being brought up on trumped-up charges. Evidence was often planted, prosecution witnesses were brought in at the last minute, and we were not even allowed to cross-examine them when they did testify. There was no discovery at all. We just showed up to represent our clients, who were not even identified by name, but rather by a number. There was little we could do to help them, other than argue for lesser sentencing. These men were sentenced to prison—sometimes for a lifetime of hard labor—through a mockery of the legal system.[33]

With sentences ranging from a few months to life the convicts would be sent to one of the Mau Mau prisons within the Pipeline. The prisons were virtually indistinguishable from the system's detention camps, except that labor routines were reputedly harsher. The most notorious of these prisons was already in operation at the time of Anvil. Located at Embakasi, it held nearly two-thirds of the Mau Mau prisoners, all of whom were being forced to build the colony's new airport, still in use today and since renamed Jomo Kenyatta International Airport. Most people flying into Kenya today will land on its runway.

At the end of their sentences virtually none of these Mau Mau prisoners, whether at Embakasi or elsewhere, would be released. They were instead sent to the camps, or—in the language of the time—they were "Form C'ed." With the stroke of a pen, this administrative procedure transformed prisoners into detainees. Along with most of the Mau Mau suspects held without trial, they were destined for either Manyani or Mackinnon Road.[34]

The reception center set the tone for the rest of a detainee's Pipeline experience. In the case of Nelson Macharia it was filled with uncertainty and

Mau Mau suspects arriving at Langata Camp

personal degradation. After being picked up at the Asian garage, he spent three weeks at Langata. There detainees were strip-searched upon arrival. "The *askaris* and white officers took away all of our money and valuables, which they were searching for and removing from our clothes and bodies," Nelson later recalled. "We were being ordered to hand over our money and valuables voluntarily, but if you said that you did not have any, the white officer would order the *askaris* to search you and your things, even inside our boots and also in our mouths and anuses." From Langata, Macharia, along with several hundred other detainees, was loaded into an enclosed railcar for the overnight trip to Manyani. When they arrived they were greeted by "the *askaris*, who were arranged in two rows as far as the eye could see," Nelson remembered. "We then passed between them in a file. By then we had nothing but the clothes which we were wearing. The *askaris* on either side were beating us with batons as we passed between them, making us run faster." From there he was forced through a cattle dip full of disinfectant while the *askaris* pushed heads under the solution—sometimes for too long. "You know, many people couldn't swim," Nelson reminded me, "and the dip was very deep so they just didn't make it. Others were held under by the *askaris* and drowned."[35] After the detainees were thoroughly sanitized, the dehumanizing process continued as they were paraded into a large open area and ordered to strip and place their clothing in a collective pile. Each detainee was issued a single pair of yellow shorts and two blankets, which would be their only clothing, or covering, for the duration of their stay in Manyani, a location known for its hot days and very cool nights. In addition, each detainee was given a metal band, on which was etched a number, to be worn around the wrist. For the remainder of their time in the camps, this would be their official identification.

Nelson's experience was hardly unique. Dozens of other former detainees whom I interviewed recalled similar intake processes, as they were called, at Manyani. Karue Kibicho, who had been picked up earlier on River Road, was one of them. Like Nelson, he was transferred from Langata in an enclosed railcar that was "stifling from lack of fresh air and the fact that so many of us were crammed in the car." He remembered "Johnnies" on the train who would pass through the detainees, "stepping on [their] heads, hands, testicles—just anywhere they felt like."[36] They were ostensibly there for security but also managed to help themselves to whatever valuables the detainees still carried. In Karue's case:

> I had saved for several years for a very expensive watch that I had so admired and longed for in Nairobi, which was taken from me by one of the "Johnnies" who escorted us on the train. First he had wanted to buy it from me, but when I declined to sell it to him he took it by force, twisting my arm and yanking it off my wrist, then stuffing it in his pocket with the rest of the things he had stolen. But it was just as well he took it because even if I had sold it to him the money would have been taken from me during the searches at Manyani.[37]

Karue too arrived at the reception center to find two rows of *askaris*, the cattle dip, and a pervasive atmosphere of strict control and violence. The process was humiliating, but that was the point. "Before we were handed our yellow shorts we all stood there, young and old men alike, dripping wet from the dip and naked," he recollected. "They decided to search us again, for what reason I couldn't fathom because we had been searched so many times already. The white officers instructed the *askaris* to search every part of our naked bodies, to check every one of our orifices. It was sin enough to be standing there with our elders without our clothes, but then to have those kinds of things done to us."[38]

The reception center at Mackinnon Road was hardly better. Karega Njoroge was transferred there after he had been picked up in the Anvil sweep. He had been living in the Bahati area of Nairobi when the loud-speakers announced that everyone was to exit their homes and file into the nearby barbed-wire enclosure. After three days the screeners came, took one look at him, and pointed in the direction of a screened-in lorry. He was sent to the railway station, where he was handed a stale loaf of bread, herded into the car by several "Johnnies," and shipped off for the overnight journey to Mackinnon Road. The next morning, when the door rolled open, "I couldn't believe what was happening before us," Karega later told me. "There were hundreds and hundreds of *askaris*, and dozens of white officers shouting to them, '*Piga, piga sana*' [Beat them, keep beating them]. It was a very rough time. We were ordered to take off our clothes; we were searched thoroughly and then given a pair of yellow shorts and a blanket, but no shirts. The white officers then ordered all of our clothes and belongings to be put into an enormous pile. They then burned them all right in front of us."[39]

Karega stayed at Mackinnon Road for over a year, which was typical for most detainees held at the reception centers. This was not the British colonial government's intention. The initial plan had been to quickly screen and classify the detainees, issue them individual detention orders—as most had been arrested under communal detention orders, a violation of the Geneva Conventions—and transfer them either up or down the Pipeline.[40] But the screening teams were overwhelmed by the numbers detained during Anvil, and subsequent military and civilian operations, and could not keep up.

Screening teams—made up of Europeans and Africans from the Prisons Department, Special Branch, CID, the Community Development and Rehabilitation Department, as well as dozens of Kikuyu loyalists from the reserves—all converged on Langata, Manyani, and Mackinnon Road to classify the Mau Mau suspects using the white-grey-black system. The initial screening at the time of arrest was only an introductory interview. Now the screening teams conducted more thorough interrogations to determine how committed a suspect was to the Mau Mau cause. "Whites" were clean and repatriated back to the Kikuyu reserves, "greys" were considered more compliant oath takers and sent down the Pipeline to ordinary works camps in their home district, and "blacks" were the so-called hard core who went up the Pipeline for softening up in the special detention camps.

Even at this early stage, there was a definite logic to the planned organization of the Pipeline, which was predicated on the idea of detainee cooperation, and by cooperation the colonial government meant confession. Teams were constantly screening and rescreening detainees, hoping both to soften them up and to squeeze more intelligence from them. Detainees would be moved up or down the Pipeline, depending on their levels of cooperation, which would correspond with their classifications. When "blacks" began softening up, screening teams would reclassify them as "greys" and send them down the Pipeline, whereas any "greys" starting to express increased Mau Mau sympathy would be relabeled as "blacks" and transferred to harsher up-Pipeline camps. Theoretically, the colonial government's ultimate goal was to transform as many Mau Mau suspects into "whites" as possible and to exile the remainder to remote camps in the colony.

Detainees came to dread the constant screening to determine whether their Mau Mau sympathies had changed. The screening teams sought confessions and intelligence, and were willing to employ corrupt and brutal interrogation methods to get the answers they wanted. Baring knew of their objectives and described their techniques to the colonial secretary as being "a rough and ready method of interrogation."[41] Suspects were whipped, beaten, sodomized, burned, forced to eat feces and drink urine— all at the hands of the screening teams. "I was bent over the screening table at Manyani with my hands on my head," recalled one man who today lives in the Kariokor section of Nairobi. "I had lost sensation in my legs because of the beating with the rubber hose, and I was very weak. They were demanding that I tell them about Mau Mau activities in my home area in Kandara. I still refused, and the Ngombe [i.e., nickname for European settlers enlisted in the Kenya Regiment] ordered an African *askari* to take scorpions which were everywhere in the camp and force them into my back private part. I was soon writhing from the pain. I began telling them everything; I made up stories naming people. If I didn't, I was going to die."[42]

The screening teams at Manyani and Mackinnon Road could devote hours or days to a single suspect before finally issuing him an individual detention order and assigning him to a color category. One month after Anvil, only 10 percent of Mau Mau suspects at these two reception camps had as yet been screened and classified. It would take well over a year before the screening teams finished with those picked up during the sweep of Nairobi.[43] With very little movement out of the reception centers, there was no space for new intakes, a problem that could be solved only by further overpopulating the camps.

Extremely close quarters invariably created unhealthy conditions, and within a few months a major typhoid epidemic swept through Manyani Camp. The spread of infectious disease there and elsewhere in the Pipeline came as no surprise to the colony's chief medical officer, Colonel W. G. S. Foster. He had written a lengthy memorandum to Baring and the colonial secretary detailing the abhorrent sanitary conditions in the Manyani and Mackinnon Road camps, arguing that security and expediency had been given priority over health standards. Camp officials refused to allow detainees to dispose properly of human and other waste outside of the detention wires, and the quality and quantity of the camps' water supplies were not even close to acceptable standards.[44] Baring's chief secretary, Richard Turnbull, agreed with Foster's assessment of the "night soil problem," noting:

> The essence of this problem was that the buckets were brimming with urine as well as faeces—not even Blondin [French tightrope walker] himself could be expected to carry them without making an abominable mess. Once a proper system of keeping solid and liquid excrement apart has been instituted, the matter will be fairly easy to handle through . . . Night Soil trenches. The first trench we inspected was too near the camp, the second seemed sufficiently far away. In view of the very difficult nature of the soil and the lack of supervision available, it is unlikely that a manual working party could keep pace with the requirements.[45]

Health officials were also needed in the Pipeline, despite Baring's concern that such postings would be viewed by some as a reward to Mau Mau. The War Council concurred, calling the camps a "sanitary menace," though again offered very little in the way of financial or administrative resources to address the problem. Taxi Lewis knew his Prisons Department was not heeding Foster's warnings, conceding "the Medical Department cannot be answerable for the health of the inmates at either [Manyani or Mackinnon Road] Camp."[46]

When the first cases of typhoid appeared in May 1954, Governor Baring denied publicly the incidence of the disease and instead lauded the rise of Manyani Camp as "a million Sterling aluminium and steel 'town' . . . that stretch[ed] like some futuristic factory for three miles and is over half a mile wide."[47] But by September it was clear that the spread of typhoid in Manyani had reached epidemic proportions and that the entire camp would have to be quarantined. Publicly, official press releases from the colonial government maintained that the camp had state-of-the-art sanitation facilities, fresh water, and proper medical care. Nearly every internal assessment of the outbreak emphasized the opposite, with one memorandum clearly stating, "The camp was not completely finished when the detainees went in and some of the sanitary arrangements were incomplete."[48] Compounding this problem was the increase in Manyani's population, from a reported 6,600 immediately following Anvil, to over 16,000 at the time of the quarantine, well beyond its theoretical capacity of 10,000.[49]

The colonial government was inundated with hostile inquiries. Several members of the Labour Party blasted the Colonial Office, decrying the outbreak as "appalling" and demanding a thorough investigation.[50] Organizations on the left petitioned the colonial secretary, "In view of what happened in the Camps of this nature in Germany during the war ... [we insist] that emergency action be taken to end this system of detention, before the outbreak spreads and becomes completely out of control."[51] Mainstream and even relatively conservative newspapers like the *Times*, the *Daily Telegraph*, and the *Scotsman* also carried news of the outbreak and suggested strongly that remedial action was necessary.

Leading the charge to defend Britain's colonial image was Alan Lennox-Boyd. In July 1954 Lennox-Boyd took over from Oliver Lyttelton as head of the Colonial Office. He brought with him a High Tory imperialist attitude that impressed even the most conservative members of his party. An imposing man in every respect—standing nearly six and a half feet tall and with a penchant for fastidious self-grooming—Lennox-Boyd was a master of disinformation, as the Manyani outbreak would subsequently prove.

He and Governor Baring would quickly prove well-suited colleagues. They shared an aristocratic pedigree and ruling-class sense of duty, albeit one perverted by a high-minded sense of authoritarian righteousness. Lennox-Boyd was a descendant of the Napier family, was educated at the elite Sherborne School, and went on to read modern history at Christ Church, Oxford, where he forged friendships with numerous future politicians and high-level colonial officials, Baring among them. Intensely ambitious, after Oxford he moved into mainstream politics with the help of another friend he met during his university days, Winston Churchill. Churchill helped to position Lennox-Boyd within the Conservative Party and paved his way to an eventual seat in the House of Commons and later the Colonial Office. The future colonial secretary walked in lockstep with

Colonial Secretary Alan Lennox-Boyd inspecting the Home Guard

his mentor, embracing nearly every Churchillean view on empire, from the dislike of India's independence in 1947 to the prime minister's famous position that "he had not become the King's First Minister to preside over the liquidation of the British Empire."[52]

The new colonial secretary had no intention of facilitating self-government in any of Britain's colonial territories and instead considered himself a "brake" on the process of decolonization.[53] His open and unabashed ruling-class approach to empire led him to dismiss the ordinary Africans as backward and wholly unprepared in the 1950s for independent rule. From the perspective of this imperious man at the helm of the Colonial Office, the end of empire in Kenya was a least a generation away. His sentiments were shared by most in the Conservative government and of course by local colonial officials and settlers.[54] Critics considered him the epitome of the right wing, with Labour MPs like Barbara Castle commenting that Lennox-Boyd was "imbued with the conviction that the British ruling class, both at home and overseas, could do no wrong."[55] Politics aside, the new colonial secretary clearly held two standards in the empire: one for the civilized British and another for their imperial subjects. On this point his biographer, in an exhaustive review of Lennox-Boyd's political career, suggested that the seamy side of empire bothered the colonial secretary little: "If the maintenance of British control over people not yet ready to govern themselves occasionally necessitated use of force, this did not in itself disturb him. The methods of law-enforcement employed in the colonies sometimes appeared unacceptably harsh to the British public; but they were, he maintained, generally in accordance with the standards and expectations of the colonial peoples themselves."[56]

This ethos infused Lennox-Boyd's decision making and provides some context for his later political maneuverings. Time and again he would be forced to respond to allegations of brutality and cover-up in Kenya, and each time he would deftly navigate through the press and the House of Commons with responses that ranged from minor spins on the truth to outright lies. The colonial secretary was joined by Baring in their collective goal of maintaining British colonial rule in Kenya. Lennox-Boyd would routinely and unquestioningly back his governor and their men on the spot in the Pipeline, in the European settled areas, and in the Kikuyu districts. Until Lennox-Boyd left the Colonial Office in late 1959, he and Baring unhesitatingly shared a kind of "ends justifies the means" philosophy toward the some 1.5 million Kikuyu allegedly infected with Mau Mau.

Lennox-Boyd's version of the typhoid outbreak set the precedent for all of his future responses to allegations of negligence and brutality in Kenya. After a well-choreographed and highly publicized visit to East Africa—complete with a staged tour of Manyani—the colonial secretary stood on the floor of the House of Commons and announced that the outbreak "was not due to the camp water supplies or sanitation, or to any failure to take proper health measures."[57] The spread of the disease, he countered, was due to personal contact with detainees who were already infected prior to their transfer to the camp. In an outright misrepresentation of the medical and administrative reports he had received from Kenya, Lennox-Boyd implied that the camp was a model facility for maintaining the detainees' physical and mental well-being.

As Lennox-Boyd was appearing before Parliament, medical personnel were putting their limited resources to work to improve the camp's sanitation and drainage systems, such as existed, and its water supplies. The most important person in this whole operation, at least according to the detainees, was a European officer nicknamed Kihuga, or the Busy and Watchful One. "He was the most remarkable, humane man I met in the camps—he tried to save us from the typhoid and even the beatings," David Githigaita later remarked.[58] In the end, though, Kihuga's valiant efforts could not avert the pending disaster. Lennox-Boyd reported that 63 people had died of typhoid in Manyani and another 760 were infected with the disease.[59] These numbers seem low based on the observations of detainees who were in the camp at the time of the outbreak. Harun Kibe, in particular, had a unique vantage point as he was one of dozens of Mau Mau suspects who had medical experience prior to detention, and who as a result was conscripted by Kihuga in his effort to sanitize the camp and treat those infected. Harun recollected hundreds of detainees perishing from the disease: "Every few days there were a dozen, sometimes as much as two [dozen] taken to be buried or incinerated. We worked day and night to control the outbreak. I had never seen anything like it, and I haven't since."[60] Another former detainee, Phillip Macharia, was part of the burial working party and later recalled: "Our group alone buried over six hundred bodies. I lost count when we were around five hundred or so; I had just grown too tired. I'd say about two-thirds of these corpses were a result of the typhoid because they had no marks."[61]

The typhoid problems hardly ended with the epidemic in Manyani. Soon cases were being diagnosed in Mackinnon Road and Langata, though Baring, the final arbiter in Kenya, personally made the decision not to quarantine either of these facilities. He was anxious instead to move detainees, once they were classified, out of the reception centers to works camps in order to free up space for the continuous flow of new pickups. But the works camps were expanding only slowly prior to Anvil, and the rapid influx of new detainees meant Baring had to create dozens of new camps in order to accommodate the many "greys" and "blacks" coming out of Manyani, Mackinnon Road, and Langata.

To manage the crushing flow of human traffic, Baring established the Working Party, which included representatives from various departments with an interest in the camps—with the notable exception of Askwith and his Department of Community Development and Rehabilitation.[62] Chaired by Taxi Lewis, the prisons commissioner, the Working Party sought to maximize detainee labor by siting camps as near to agricultural or public works projects as possible but dismissed any camp plans requiring lengthy start-up times, regardless of their potential labor benefits. With some one thousand new pickups per week, there was simply no time to lose.[63] But there was little consensus in the Working Party, only compounding the human traffic problem; members of the Administration from Central Province were the most notably strident in some of their objections, largely because all the "grey" detainees were slated to filter through works camps in their districts before their final release. This meant, for example, that if a "grey" detainee originally came from Fort Hall, he would be sent to a works camp in Fort Hall District where he would labor and continue to confess before his final release. Initially, however, the district commissioners from Kiambu and Nyeri flatly refused to have any expanded system of works camps in their areas. The so-called poor relief camps that Baring had established earlier had proven an administrative disaster, and the DCs complained bitterly during the months before Anvil of the financial and staffing burdens that these camps were generating. The Nyeri DC hardly minced words when he wrote, "The establishment of Works Camps covering 'Operation Anvil' . . . has gone off at half cock and once again the Administration holds the baby. . . . Now it appears that all accounting, payment of salaries, acquisition of equipment, etc., etc. as well as the construction of the Camps falls to the lot of the Administration."[64]

Funding and administrative support were clearly the issue. Without additional financial assistance, the DCs from Kiambu and Nyeri refused to cooperate and rejected the creation of additional works camps in their districts—something that was well within their right given the administrative structure of the colony. Consequently, the Working Party was forced to create an elaborate system of works camps in nearby Embu District on the Mwea Plain for all the "grey" detainees originating from Kiambu and Nyeri districts. There these detainees would labor on the massive Mwea/Tebere irrigation scheme, a project that had been outlined by Swynnerton and that was aimed at developing rice cultivation in the previously uninhabitable and malarial region. In time, however, all the DCs in Central Province would agree to the works camps in their districts largely because it meant that they—along with local Kikuyu loyalists—would have the final say over whether a detainee would be released or sent into exile.[65]

The colony's Treasury, in charge of approving or more often declining requests for funds for the camps, wielded the greatest influence over the pace and scope of Pipeline expansion. The Ministry of Defence and its Prisons Department, which continued to bear the greatest administrative responsibility for the camps, and the Finance ministry had radically different opinions on the need to create additional works camps. On the one hand, Finance Minister Ernest Vasey, who was desperately trying to keep the colony solvent during the Emergency, asserted that the government was "planning too many 'Works' Camps in the Central Province."[66] Jake Cusack and Taxi Lewis, on the other hand, were watching the detainee population steadily grow and responded to Vasey, "It is clear that we are not planning too many 'Works' Camps in the Central Province and, in fact, . . . we should proceed with our examination of the extra . . . extensions."[67] But the Treasury had already granted over £1 million for Pipeline expansion, and nearly all of it had been exhausted within a matter of months. Additional camps had to be built, though the necessary funding simply was not there.[68]

In its attempts to solve the problem of inadequate financing, the Working Party cut nearly every corner possible. Cusack ordered labor gangs to be transferred from reception centers at Manyani and Mackinnon Road to locations around Kenya so that they could build most of the works camps from the ground up. These labor gangs worked under grueling conditions to complete more than twenty camps in less than three months. "When I was selected I thought I was going home," remembers one former detainee. "I had only taken one oath and knew I didn't belong with some of the others [i.e., hard-core Mau Mau]. Instead they took us to Embu, where they worked and beat us like dogs, from sunrise until dark. We built our own prison. Can you imagine?"[69] Only the bare necessities like barbed wire and perimeter trenches—proper sanitation and sleeping barracks were of secondary concern—were in place before the Prisons Department began moving large numbers of detainees out of the reception centers and into the works camps in Embu and elsewhere. Detainees sometimes arrived at a camp to find nothing. This seems to have been more the norm for the remote camps, like the one on Mageta Island in Lake Victoria. There, the first batch of detainees arrived in shackles in the cargo hold of a boat. When they were taken ashore, they spent days building perimeter trenches and watchtowers, uncoiling barbed wire, and digging isolation pits before their shackles were removed and they were allowed to walk freely within the confines of the new facility.[70]

Camps also became incubators for a variety of infectious diseases, despite warnings from local medical officials. Kenya's director of medical services, T. F. Anderson, issued recommendations ranging from proper sanitation facilities, water supplies, and construction materials to medical staffing, inoculations, and nutritional requirements.[71] Nearly all were ignored. In June 1954, Kenya's minister of local government, health, and housing, Wilfred Havelock, alerted the governor to public health risks resulting from the Pipeline's hasty expansion: "As can be imagined a number of matters to do with Health have been neglected . . . as the speed at which the camps have been erected and occupied have prevented any particular attention to this aspect. . . . In the Central Province, however, there seems to be little co-ordination, and there is no single person who is prepared to help to get the requisite work done on the health requirements in camps."[72]

Eventually, H. Stott, the medical adviser to Kenya's Labor Department, was appointed to coordinate the health and sanitation requirements in the Pipeline—hardly a one-man job. He found a myriad of problems and attributed them not just to a lack of resources but also to the refusal of many officers in the Administration to address the health issues. In his November 1954 "Report on Health and Hygiene in Emergency Camps," Stott wrote that members of the Administration held lower health and sanitation standards for Africans than they did for themselves.[73] Combined with their overall distaste for Mau Mau and the constraints of the Emergency, it is not surprising that the provincial and district commissioners, and their subordinates, ignored the medical recommendations. In place of the suggested corrugated iron, mud and wattle and recycled canvas became the building materials of choice for many of the camps. The camp compounds were routinely filled above capacity. Detainees slept on the ground, often one on top of the other. Stott was fully aware of the detainees' close quarters, constantly reminding Taxi Lewis "that a minimum of 20 square feet *floor area* be provided for each inmate" (emphasis in original).[74] Water supplies were also abysmal. Detainees remember drawing drinking water from drainage ditches, swamps, and muddy boreholes. On numerous occasions Stott himself noted that water "purity [was] not all that could be desired,"[75] and European camp commandants often concurred. At Waithaka Camp, for example, the officer in charge reported "the water [in this camp] is unfiltered and comes directly from a highly contaminated river."[76]

Despite Scott's efforts, infectious diseases continued to be ubiquitous in the Pipeline. Pulmonary tuberculosis was widely reported, with Kenya's director of medical services remarking, "The number of cases of pulmonary tuberculosis, which is being disclosed in Prison and Detention Camps is causing some embarrassment."[77] The overcrowded conditions, together with the detainees' weakened immune systems, exhaustion from forced labor, and poor access to proper clothing or blankets, facilitated its spread. To reduce the incidence of tuberculosis, camp officials needed to reduce the number of detainees in each compound. The Medical Department decided to adopt a policy of repatriating all infectious detainees back to the reserves. In effect, they were trading one public health crisis for another. Detainees suffering from not only tuberculosis but also typhoid, pneumonia, leprosy, and measles were repatriated to the overcrowded Kikuyu districts, where accommodations were arguably tighter than those in the camps.[78]

Waterborne infections—particularly dysentery, diarrhea, and other "epidemic intestinal diseases"—also ran through the camps.[79] So too did vitamin deficiency, with cases of scurvy, pellagra, kwashiorkor, and night blindness afflicting some detainees.[80] Adjustments to their rations and vitamin supplements would generally cure such ailments, though detainees typically suffered for weeks or months before camp authorities took action. Others were not so lucky, dying from the painful effects of these nutritional diseases, which could have been remedied with expedient and proper medical care.[81]

Detainees thus lived in infernal conditions. They often slept and ate in the same room where toilet buckets overflowed with urine and feces. With poor sanitation and worse ventilation, the air quality was wretched. Bedbugs infested the detainees' blankets, and lice their hair. Their rations generally consisted of maize meal, with an occasional piece of meat or vegetable thrown in—a diet that was often reduced or completely taken away as a form of punishment. In short, living conditions in many of these camps were unbearable, which was of course the point.

Already stretched thin, the colonial government recruited the vast majority of camp commandants from within the ranks of the European population in Kenya. Local settlers were more than eager to enlist in the fight against Mau Mau, alleviating Baring from the costly process of overseas recruitment. Many of these settlers were often officers in the Kenya Regiment and the Kenya Police Reserve, and brought with them an already hardened stereotype of Mau Mau savagery and varying degrees of the now typical eliminationist attitude that dominated settler opinion. Scores had also served their apprenticeship in the Kikuyu reserves, screening Mau Mau suspects and generally terrorizing the local population. For their part, British colonial officers, many of whom appeared to share the sentiments of their settler counterparts, took charge of those camps not under the control of the settler recruits.

Virtually all camp commandants carried guns, *viboko* (rhino whips), or clubs, or all three. Today former detainees still carry vivid memories of the commandants' weapons and their use during roll calls. Regardless of where they were in the Pipeline, roll call meant squatting in groups of five with their hands clasped over their heads. The European commandants would then walk through the lines, counting and beating the detainees with clubs or *viboko*. "The whole thing was just so ridiculous," recalled one former detainee from Lodwar. "Whitehouse [the European in charge] would just count us over and over again. We would be there in the hot sun, and our feet were burning from the sand and the heat. You couldn't move your hands to wipe your face, because that would just invite him to beat you. Every time [there was roll call] he liked to pick one or two of us, and just go crazy beating the person. But we never knew who it would be; you'd just pray it was someone else."[82]

Then there were the guards. Some were recruited from the European population in Kenya, others from Britain, and by all accounts they represented the "bottom of the barrel." Those drawn from the Kikuyu loyalists, or from other African ethnic groups within the colony and neighboring Tanganyika, were hardly paragons of efficiency or virtue. Most of these

Loyalist guard keeping watch over Mau Mau suspects
at Langata Camp from an observation tower

guards considered the camps the best of all possible bad employment options, even if they were underpaid, worked in dreadful circumstances, and were, they thought, surrounded by human waste in the form of the detainees. Many of the guards considered the camps revolting, even more so because they were isolated from the rest of the colony in some of Kenya's most remote and inhospitable places—locations that were "Conradesque," as one camp official called them.[83]

"The horror" of Kenya's heart of darkness was then hyperbolized by the specter of evil cast over the camps by the detainees themselves. Many guards seemed to fear the detainees greatly. Camp commandants repeatedly told them that the Mau Mau were cannibals and that unless they beat the detainees into submission, they would be eaten.[84] At once empowered and maddened by the confining atmosphere of the camps, many of the guards, not surprisingly, beat, tortured, and murdered the detainees without, it seemed, any remorse.

It would be wrong to view these men, along with the handful of female guards, merely as victims of an ugly system. Although they often complied with orders to beat or torture the detainees, guards also had options. They could choose to be brutal, or they could opt to be compassionate, or even kind. Some former detainees were adamant that guards from certain

African ethnic groups were notoriously harsh, but others said there was no consistent pattern. There is, however, one point of consensus: without exception, ex-detainees pointed to the Kikuyu loyalists as the most brutal. The vast majority of these loyalist guards were assigned to the works camps in the Kikuyu districts where they had immense power not just in the day-to-day operation of the camps but also in the final release decisions.

Like the guards, the moral fiber of the camp commandants also varied greatly. In contrast to those who were cruel or sadistic, there were other camp commandants who were singled out by former detainees for their kindness. Major James Breckenridge from Athi River Camp is legendary among the ex-detainees today, who still praise his humanity and concern for the well-being of the detainees in his camp. Echoing the sentiment of many other former detainees from Athi River, Eric Kamau recalls, "We all respected him very much. He and his wife, who was also at the camp, tried very hard to treat us like human beings—to them we weren't animals but humans like them."[85] Still others were cruel one minute and normal, as some of the detainees termed it, the next. Regardless, the fate of the detainees was in the camp commandants' hands. They could beat them, provide them with proper clothing, force them to work harder, give them five minutes' rest, torture them, or offer them rewards in return for their cooperation. In the end, the choices were left to the individual in charge.

For the Pipeline to function efficiently, it also needed the cooperation of some of the detainees themselves. The noted German sociologist Wolfgang Sofsky wrote about the establishment of absolute power in the Nazi concentration camps, emphasizing that it was not a simple matter of a minority of people establishing dominance over the lives of the majority. Instead, the Nazis needed help from within. In his work, Sofsky stressed that "by making a small number of victims into its accomplices, the regime blurred the boundary between personnel and inmates. . . . Had it not been for the self-administration and the collaboration of the prison-functionaries [i.e., detainees], discipline and social control would soon have buckled and collapsed."[86] This characteristic of camp life was notable not just in the Nazi system but also in that of the Soviets, and it later would be employed in Kenya's Pipeline as well.[87]

Some detainees were tempted to collaborate with colonial oppression and were offered in return rewards and privileges that elevated them above the other detainees. These detainees helped to keep the Pipeline going and enabled authorities to exert more efficient control over the camps. In some cases those who had not confessed were nevertheless relieved from their hard labor and given jobs cleaning commandants' offices, cooking for them, or, if literate, performing clerical duties such as organizing files and typing. Then there were those detainees who had admitted their Mau Mau sympathies to the screening teams and were now willing to cooperate. These men, and less frequently women, often underwent a complete meta-morphosis. As they changed from detainee to collaborator, their carriage, habits, and manner of communication also changed. Most refused to rec-ognize their former compound mates, perhaps from shame or self-loathing. They were often as cruel as their former captors, brutalizing detainees, demanding their confessions, and often informing on their Mau Mau activities both before and during detention. The most famous exam-ple of this was Peter Muigai Kenyatta—Jomo Kenyatta's own son—who af-ter his confession joined the ranks of the screening team in Athi River Camp and eventually traveled throughout the Pipeline interrogating other detainees.

One question about the Pipeline remains unanswered: where were Askwith's men in all of this? If the colonial government was implementing rehabilitation on a scale even close to its public proclamations, we should see its evidence in budgetary allocations and manpower on the ground. In reality, there was very little of either. In Kenya's Development Plan for 1954–57, Ernest Vasey allocated the Community Development and Rehabil-itation Department £103,000, or 0.5 percent of the colony's total budget. This amount was to be spent not only on Mau Mau rehabilitation but also on other community development projects throughout Kenya. This is in contrast to the allocation for the "maintenance of law and order," which to-taled over £2 million, or 20 percent of Kenya's budget.[88] The hypocrisy did not escape the notice of newspapers in Britain. The *Liverpool Post,* for ex-ample, commented, "For nearly one-fifth of a development programme to comprise expenditure on capital installations necessary for the preserva-tion of law and order is nothing less than tragic, but such are the realities of the contemporary situation."[89]

During his euphoric days drafting the rehabilitation plan, Askwith was looking for the "right type of man" for his staff—someone who was "Christian, idealistic, practical, with a keen desire to help Kikuyu to adjust themselves to the new conditions."[90] In time, he was happy to take whomever he could get on his limited budget. Askwith's so-called rehabili-tation team would number over five hundred, but more than half of these individuals were designated for the screening teams.[91] People like Peter Muigai Kenyatta and the notorious Isaiah Mwai Mathenge, David Waruhiu, and Jeremiah Kiereini would all technically be employees of the Community Development and Rehabilitation Department but hardly fit Askwith's profile of the "right type of man." To add to their burden,

Askwith's staff was theoretically responsible for the reform of not only the detainees in the Pipeline but the rest of the colony's suspected Mau Mau population as well.

There were few rehabilitation officers to carry out Askwith's program. Manyani, for example, had one rehabilitation officer for ten thousand detainees, and many camps had none at all.[92] In total, Askwith had some 250 men and women working on the rehabilitation of nearly 1.5 million Kikuyu, a ratio of 1 to 6,000. Without adequate funding for waste disposal and clean water supplies, allocations for even the most meager rehabilitation staffing, recreational materials, and educational supplies would have been unthinkable. But at the heart of the issue was the attitude that pervaded the Pipeline's conceptualization and implementation. Most of those people overseeing and executing the expansion of the camps and prisons simply did not believe in rewarding Mau Mau, and certainly not in offering them any kind of hearts-and-minds campaign. Many of them wanted the detainees to be absolutely miserable, and in extreme cases they wanted them to die.

Administratively, within the Pipeline Askwith and his rehabilitation officers were always subordinate to the Prisons Department and were relatively powerless when trying to alter the system.[93] On several occasions Askwith appealed to Jake Cusack, Kenya's defense minister, about the violence, stating in one instance: "The other worry is about the thug attitude of a number of Prison Officers. We have constantly had to make representations about the beating up of convicts and detainees in the past and our staff have made themselves pretty unpopular in the process. We claim that you cannot successfully rehabilitate a man in the evening if he is to be knocked about the next day."[94] Despite the colonial government's sunny depiction of detention camp life, the Pipeline was not oriented around any kind of hearts-and-minds campaign. Privately, Kenya's Defence Ministry emphasized this point when its secretary wrote, "There may be a [rehabilitation] programme, but I have never seen it."[95]

By the end of 1955 the Pipeline was fully in place. With its completion came a consolidation of the camps and prisons, characterized by standardization within the system. The centralized bureaucracy, located within the Prisons Department, was finally established and with it the stabilization of a formal camp structure. The Pipeline could now stand completely on its own.

We will never know exactly how many Mau Mau camps and prisons the colonial government constructed in Kenya. There is no single extant document that lists them all. Moreover, camps and prisons were constantly

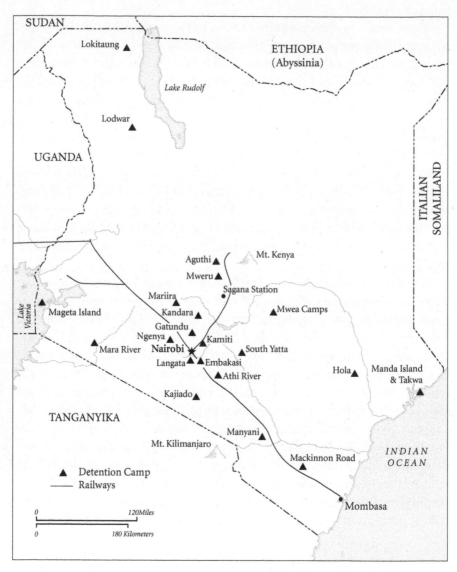

SUDAN

Lokitaung ▲

ETHIOPIA
(Abyssinia)

Lake Rudolf

Lodwar ▲

UGANDA

Lake Victoria

Mageta Island ▲

Aguthi ▲
Mweru ▲

Mt. Kenya

Mariira ▲
Sagana Station •
Kandara ▲
Mwea Camps ▲
Gatundu ▲
Ngenya ▲ Kamiti ▲
Mara River ▲ **Nairobi** ✦
Langata ▲ Embakasi ▲
South Yatta ▲
Athi River ▲
Hola ▲
Manda Island & Takwa ▲

Kajiado ▲

TANGANYIKA

Manyani ▲

Mt. Kilimanjaro

Mackinnon Road ▲

ITALIAN SOMALILAND

INDIAN OCEAN

Mombasa •

▲ Detention Camp
— Railways

0   120 Miles
0   180 Kilometers

Main Detention Camps

opened and closed—new ones often arising and old ones shutting down as works projects were finished, and as other projects in new locations were started. By carefully studying the remaining colonial files, and cross-referencing them with interview data and documents from private and missionary archives, I was able to compile what I believe to be a near-complete listing of the camps and prisons in the Pipeline.[96] There were over one hundred in all, not including the scores of camps run by loyalist chiefs, and others run by private settlers—technically illegal under international law—scattered throughout the Rift Valley and Central provinces.

Defining accurately each camp's particular function within the integrated Pipeline system presents a challenge. Some camps were up-Pipeline, or special detention camps only for "blacks," and others were down-Pipeline camps, or ordinary works camps, for "greys." There were also the reception centers, which Governor Baring later renamed holding camps to reflect the fact that detainees housed there often ended up staying for months or even years. There were also camps set aside for non-Kikuyu Mau Mau suspects—particularly Kamba and Maasai. Many of these oath takers either had married Kikuyu or had lived in close proximity to them in Nairobi. Finally, all the way up the Pipeline were the exile camps; at the other end were the chiefs' camps, or open camps, to which "grey" detainees were transferred from the ordinary works camps as a final step before their release.

Because each camp had a specific function within the Pipeline, detainees would not be moved about haphazardly, but rather according to their profiles, that is, according to their degree of demonstrated cooperation, their ethnicity, and their district of origin. For example, most "blacks" were sent to camps like Lodwar, Manda Island, Takwa, and Saiyusi, though Kamba and Maasai "blacks" were sent to Mara River, Kajiado, or South Yatta. By the end of 1955 a "grey" detainee from Fort Hall would never be sent to, for example, Aguthi or Mukurweini in Nyeri District, save by accident, because all "grey" detainees heralding from Fort Hall were sent to works camps in Fort Hall, those from Kiambu District to works camps in Kiambu, those from Nyeri District to works camps in Nyeri, and so forth. This is because the British colonial officers and local loyalists wanted to have the final say over whether a particular detainee from their district was ultimately released. Camp sequencing therefore had a very explicit rationale.

In general the Pipeline was a system for adult male suspects only. Exceptions were those women considered too "black" or hard core to be repatriated to the reserves. Instead, they were sent to the colony's only all-female detention camp at Kamiti, which, once built in late 1953, would be the place where the vast majority of women, totaling a few thousand in all, were detained in the Pipeline. Included in this number were countless girls under the age of puberty; not included were the dozens of babies born to the female detainees, many of whom had been in Kamiti for years.

In comparison to the number of girls, there were far more unaccompanied male children in the Pipeline, though there was only one camp set aside for them at Wamumu. The total number of boys detained went, not surprisingly, unrecorded, or at least the records are no longer available. Certainly, hundreds if not thousands of these children never saw Wamumu Camp. There simply was not enough room for them, and they instead lived and moved through the other camps with the adult population. (See appendix for diagram of the operating Pipeline circa January 1956.)

When fully assembled, the Pipeline came to embody British colonialism in Kenya, for it was the final step in a longue durée of increasing authoritarianism in the colony. For decades before the Emergency, British colonizers sought to control the African population through a complex, apartheidlike set of laws dictating among other things where Africans could live, where and when they could move, what crops they could grow, and what social places they could frequent. Virulent racism and European self-interest prejudiced the colonial justice system, and punishments typically included public floggings, stiff fines, and long prison terms. Indeed, Kenya had one of the most notoriously harsh penal systems in all of Britain's African colonies. When these repressive measures were not enough to thwart the growth of Mau Mau, the colonial government declared a State of Emergency, enacted dozens of draconian regulations, and began employing terror as a means to subdue the suspected Mau Mau population. In many ways, it was this exploitative and repressive system itself that had helped to fuel the growth of Mau Mau, and it would take the final consolidation and bureaucratization of absolute colonial power in the form of the Pipeline to break it.

Confession was the sine qua non for a detainee's release. The purpose of detention in Kenya was not necessarily to keep the Mau Mau suspects alive but to force them to confess through a punishing routine of forced labor and brutality. In terms of productivity this pattern ultimately revealed an inherent contradiction. A tension emerged between the need for ever greater supplies of labor, without which it would be impossible to continue the colony's infrastructure development, and the competing impulse to punish, debilitate, and even exterminate the Kikuyu population. Exhausting labor routines, beatings, torture, food deprivation, all used to force confession, could and often did render detainees incapable of working.

The British colonial government's works camps in Kenya were not wholly different from those in Nazi Germany or Stalinist Russia; they functioned on what Wolfgang Sofsky called "the economy of waste."[97]

The Pipeline was a microcosm where the contradictions and antagonisms between Kikuyu and European societies in Kenya were brought to a boiling intensity, and the world behind the barbed wire rendered utterly transparent, for the first time, the dark side of Britain's colonial project. The hypocrisies, the exploitations, the violence, and the suffering were all laid bare in the Pipeline. It was there that Britain finally revealed the true nature of its civilizing mission.

CHAPTER SIX

THE WORLD BEHIND
THE WIRE

Mau Mau suspects congregated around the gallows at Thomson's Falls Camp
before their final departure to the Pipeline

*The "state of nature," it turns out, is not natural. A war of everyone against everyone
must be imposed by force.* —TERENCE DES PRES, The Survivor

LIKE SCORES OF OTHERS WHO PRECEDED HIM, NDERI KAGOMBE STOOD
in front of the entrance to Compound 6 of Manyani's "A" Camp wearing
only a thin pair of yellow shorts and the reddish metal wristband that bore
his detention number, x21437. He felt nauseous from the insecticide he
swallowed in the cattle dip, or possibly from the public spectacle of cavity
searches he had endured. Or perhaps it was just the whole intake ordeal.
Forty-five years later, he could not quite remember which. "Besides, it
didn't really matter once I was hustled into the compound," he recalled,
"because Wagithundia was waiting there. It was as if Satan himself stood in
front of us, and everything else vanished from our minds."[1]

Wagithundia was one of the most notorious guards in Manyani Camp.[2]
He had been recruited to work in the Pipeline from neighboring Tanganyika, and, like many detainees, Nderi believed Wagithundia had been

selected in part because of his extraordinary physical appearance. "It was horrific just to look at him," Nderi remembered. "There was something wrong with his skin, some kind of disease that made you want to look the other way. He was the ugliest human being I have ever seen."[3] And for many who passed through Compound 6, it was difficult to disentangle Wagithundia's unsightliness from his behavior. "He was born with animal instincts," recalled one former detainee. "He was not a human being; he looked and behaved like a diseased animal."[4] He also seemed to possess a sixth sense, quietly stalking detainees when they were most vulnerable. In one instance he appeared, seemingly out of nowhere, when a detainee was relieving himself on a toilet bucket. "I felt a presence in front of me," the man remembered, "and the next thing I knew he took me by the shoulders and jammed me into the bucket. My entire bottom was folded inside and I couldn't get out. . . . I was stuck there in a bucket of human waste. That is why we called him Wagithundia—it means 'he who appears'—because he would appear just like that."[5]

Wagithundia was not a wholly independent operator, but rather the right-hand man to one of Manyani's British camp officers—a young settler who had a very personal stake in the Emergency. "This *Mzungu* [European] was a very bitter man," recalled Nderi. "He had come from the Rift Valley, where his mother had been killed by Mau Mau. That was why he was always mistreating us and giving Wagithundia orders to do the same. He used to call us 'bloody Mau Mau' and told us that we all deserved to die."[6] Nicknamed Mapiga, or the Beater, this young settler turned Compound 6 into the hazing site for hundreds of detainees who had been classified "black" and were considered by the screening teams to be the worst of Manyani's lot. He and Wagithundia devised countless ways to humiliate and torture.

Detainees were frog-marched around the compound and beaten until blood ran from their ears. On other occasions their ankles were shackled together and they were made to "hop up and down like bunnies" until their skin tore away, leaving their flesh hanging about the leg constraints. Detainees were awakened at all hours of the night; other times they were forced to stand endlessly, and any flinching or attempt to sit down was met with a rain of blows from the African guards.[7] There were denials of food that could last for several days, sometimes ending with forced consumptions. As Nderi later explained, "We would be starved for as many as six or seven days; then Mapiga would have the *askaris* bring in huge quantities of porridge and force us to eat it. Having not eaten for so long, it was very painful. Sometimes Wagithundia would have the other detainees hold a man down, and then he would start jumping on the man's stomach. It was

a terrible sight, because the person was screaming with pain and would often die from the ordeal."[8]

For those detainees labeled "black"—ostensibly the worst of the Mau
Mau "savages"—the rituals of the first intake procedure were not enough.
Special treatment was needed to complete the dehumanization process and
to transform them into social nonentities. It was within select compounds
like Compound 6 that the newest principle of the Pipeline was unmistakable. Its idiom was intense pain and degradation. Only through physical
suffering and humiliation would detainees, "blacks" in particular, achieve
their new socially dead status.[9]

The violence did not end with indoctrination. These tortures were a
kind of public spectacle, often conducted in the open barbed-wire areas for
all to see. For men like Pascasio Macharia, the only thing worse than being
in Compound 6 of Manyani was being assigned to Compound 1, where he
and the others had a clear view of what was taking place at the hands of the
camp officer and Wagithundia. Certainly, Compound 1 was not immune
from the usual beatings and deprivations, but for Pascasio, as for most detainees, mere floggings hardly merited mentioning. The routine violence
and brutality of Manyani, as in the rest of the Pipeline, had become banal.
It was the more outstanding forms of torture that stood out in their minds,
and in Pascasio's case what was happening just across the barbed wire in
Compound 6 was, in his words, "completely unimaginable."[10] It was there
that one particular incident left a lasting impression he later recounted in
great detail.

One day the *askaris* brought in a group of "black" detainees which included
Chief Peterson and his headman, Gathumbi. You see the Chief and his
headman had actually sided with Mau Mau, and from what we could tell
they had been discovered by the authorities and they were now in the
camps with the rest of us. When they were brought to Compound 6, that
was where I saw the worst kind of sadistic punishment being meted out to
detainees. Something happened in that compound that I had never seen before, and which I shall forever remember. When the whole group of detainees was herded inside, they were told to remove all their clothes and
leave them in the corner of the compound. . . . Then the *askaris* set on
them, beating them indiscriminately with clubs and mattock handles, chasing them around the compound. Those people were beaten and chased so
badly, we kept saying to each other that they would only survive through a
miracle. Then Peterson, who was a fat man because he had formerly been a
chief, became so dark in his complexion we thought he was going to die.
But then, the *askaris* brought in fire buckets full of water, and the detainees
were called one by one, Peterson first. The *askaris* then put his head in the
bucket of water and lifted his legs high in the air so he was upside down.

That's when Wagithundia, who was the painfully ugly guard from Tanganyika, started cramming sand in Peterson's anus and stuffed it in with a stick. Then the other *askaris* would put water in, and then more sand, and Wagithundia kept cramming it in with a stick. They kept doing this back and forth, alternating between the sand and the water, occasionally lifting Peterson so he could breath. Mapiga, the *Mzungu* officer in charge of the camp, was standing there the whole time, ordering them to keep shoving the sand and water and stick in his anus. Eventually, they finished with Peterson and carried him off, only to start on the next detainee in the compound.[11]

Other reception camp personnel lacked neither enthusiasm nor inventiveness in their own vocation of torture. At Mackinnon Road, for instance, Kenda Kenda took charge of indoctrinating the "black" detainees. Like Mapiga, Kenda Kenda was a young European settler whose nickname reflected his penchant for singling out the ninth in a line of detainees. "You see," explained one man from Nyeri District, "he would come into the compound for the 'blacks' and scream for a head count. Everyone would line up in rows of five, squatted with their hands on their heads. He would then count us—one, two, three, four, five, six, seven, eight—whacking us each on the head with a club. Then he would reach number nine, and whomever that ninth person was he would beat them mercilessly. He particularly liked stomping people, and there would be blood and sometimes brains splattered everywhere."[12] Kenda Kenda—or Nine Nine—rightly earned his name, though he was known for much more than his stomping prowess. "He really liked barbed wire," remembered one detainee who had spent several months in Mackinnon Road. "He would take the 'blacks' just after they came into the camp and start screaming for them to squat in fives, he would start counting, and then the unfortunate ninth man was sometimes rolled inside a coil of barbed wire by the *askaris* and Kenda Kenda would start kicking him around, screaming at the man, calling him a 'bloody Mau Mau.' "[13]

By the time detainees at Manyani, as well as Mackinnon Road, were transferred out of the hazing compounds, the Pipeline's language of force had been literally impressed upon them. Nderi left Compound 6 with only a faint memory of the world he had left behind but a few months earlier, when he had been living in the Bahati area of Nairobi. There he had owned two small shops that sold restaurant supplies, and supplemented his income with a lucrative subletting business. By the standards of the times he was successful, saving some money while also supporting his wife and children back in Nyeri. But after Compound 6 "it was as if my former world had left my mind," Nderi recollected. "Before my arrest I had taken the oath and was helping to organize some of the supplies for Mau Mau. I had reached a point in my life where I could not go any further. The white man was keeping me down, so I joined Mau Mau. . . . But then I was picked up, taken to Manyani, and after two months with Wagithundia and Mapiga, how can I put it? I was completely disoriented. My whole body was numb, and I was moving in this kind of fog. I could hardly remember my name or where I had come from. I just thought I was going to die, though I wasn't certain when or how it was going to happen."[14]

Like many who passed through Compound 6, Nderi survived, although he would spend his next five years in detention, ultimately moving through seven different camps. Nearly every mode of available transportation was used to move Nderi around the gulag. Always shackled, he was loaded into enclosed railcars, the hulls of cargo ships and old military planes, and the backs of caged-in lorries. The journeys often took days, with little or no food and seldom any sanitation facilities for detainees.[15] Regardless of what camp he was in, Nderi would always awaken to a piercing, predawn siren, or the shouts of the guards, after which he would take his breakfast of watery porridge before marching out for a day of forced labor. Over the years he would work on a trunk road, an airport, an irrigation scheme, and a hospital, as well as in various quarries and on bench terraces and other agricultural projects. At the end of each day he would march back to his compound, usually hustled along by the clubs of the camp guards and the vituperation of the British officers in charge. Night could be a relief, though often sleep was interrupted by unannounced inspections, or a camp loudspeaker blaring British colonial propaganda, or, on Mageta Island, a constant refrain of "God Save the Queen."[16]

Having survived Wagithundia and Compound 6, Nderi soon became expert in the internal order evolving in the Pipeline's compounds. The detainees' world had its own committees, codes of conduct, language, and networks—it was a virtual community created and run by the detainees themselves. This new social world fought against the onslaught of colonial power inside the Pipeline. A collective strategy of survival emerged from the brutality imposed upon the detainees; it was as if misery itself forged their collective will to resist the colonial government's demands for confession and cooperation.

Survival was not enough. Had it been, most would have confessed and submitted to colonial demands. Denouncing Mau Mau and kowtowing to the screening teams would obviously have helped avoid further torture or death. Detainees submitted themselves to the control and discipline of their Mau Mau peers not only because there was greater safety within a group but also because such organization afforded maximum resistance— the group being stronger than the sum of its members. Together, they could eventually exit the camps without having betrayed their own beliefs; they would outlast the colonial government and its infernal Pipeline. The detainees wished for more than mere survival. They demanded to live on their own terms.

That such a secret universe could evolve clearly signaled weakness in the Pipeline camp system. Despite brutal efforts by camp authorities to destroy their prior social existence, the detainees found maneuvering room within the camps that allowed them to organize. This was particularly true during the aftermath of Operation Anvil, when the colonial government struggled to consolidate the camp system. Compounds were overcrowded, forced labor systems not yet perfected, screening teams not fully coordinated, and the use of torture not yet systematized. This period lasted until late 1955, when the Pipeline became a fully operational, well-organized system. For the first three years there were greater opportunities for the Mau Mau adherents to try to negotiate and redefine their world behind the wire. The effects of this early detainee organization would persist right up to the dismantling of the Pipeline in 1960.

The detainees were attempting to turn colonial power against itself. A proliferation of detainee committees was at the heart of this subversion, and they evolved independently of, and in opposition to, the official structure of the camps. In many compounds there were dozens of committees, organizing and governing nearly every facet of the detainees' lives. There was the welcoming committee, the judicial committee, the rehabilitation committee, the debate committee, the mending committee, the medical committee; the list went on and on.

Overseeing all was the executive committee. Selected by the detainees, its members were often singled out because of their ability to arbitrate disputes, their knowledge of colonial and international law, and their understanding of the political scene in both Kenya and Britain. This generally meant that the head of the executive committee, the effective compound leader, was well educated and spoke English. In time, this person not only came to represent authority among his peers but also would be recognized by camp authorities as the unofficial spokesman for his fellow detainees. Complaints about the lack of food or soap or water, overflowing toilet buckets, particularly sadistic guards, unreasonable work quotas—all of these were channeled to the camp commandant through the compound leader.

Perhaps the most famous compound leader was Josiah Mwangi Kariuki, or J. M., as he was popularly known. In many ways J. M.'s beginnings

were similar to those of thousands of other detainees. The son of impoverished squatter parents, J. M. was born on a European settler's farm in the
Rift Valley in 1929. There he was destined for a life of sharecropping had it
not been for his mother's persistence and his own good fortune, in the
form of a winning sweepstakes ticket, which paid his school fees. By the
time of his arrest in October 1953, the now twenty-four-year-old J. M. had
had a secondary education, owned a hotel in Nakuru, and was actively involved in Kikuyu politics. It was, though, his seven years in detention that
would catapult him from the role of a political lightweight to that of a pop-
ulist politician on the national stage, an unmistakable man of his people.
His leadership among the detainees in the Pipeline earned him a reputation for fighting for the oppressed—something that would carry him into
Kenya's Parliament at independence.[17]

J. M. wrote a memoir, *Mau Mau Detaineee,* depicting life and survival
in Britain's gulag. It is one of the few autobiographical documents that give
us a vivid picture of the world behind the wire. The work includes a description of J. M.'s first stay in Manyani Camp in the summer of 1954,
where he was elected the leader of Compound 13. There he presented numerous requests to the camp commandant, reminding him in one face-to-
face meeting that the detainees regarded themselves "in the same way as
prisoners of war and [that] I . . . knew all about the Geneva Convention."[18]
In the wake of this appeal a visiting committee, which included the minister for local government, health, and housing, Wilfred Havelock, was sent
from Nairobi to inspect the camp. This was not an unusual response, as
Governor Baring had previously sent numerous deputations to the camps
to investigate conditions and to assess the progress being made in breaking
down the detainees' allegiance to Mau Mau. What was different this time,
according to J. M.'s account, was that he was allowed to present to the visiting committee, in quite candid terms, the detainees' complaints. J. M. told
them, among other things, how detainees "were made to cut the sticks with
which they were later beaten."[19] In the wake of his revelations, as he later
wrote, "I was left in little doubt that these criticisms were unwelcome to the
camp officers for on the next morning, lying on a bench, naked save for my
yellow shorts, I was given twenty-four strokes by a warder in the presence
of Marlow [pseudonym used by J. M.], one of the camp officers who
earned the nickname from us of *Mapiga*."[20] The public spectacle of this
punishment left a deep impression, particularly on other compound leaders. According to J. M., "many of [them] decided against being outspoken
after what had been done to me."[21] Others shared the sentiment. "We had to
stand up for ourselves," another detainee recalled, "but it was very danger-

ous. Depending on who was in charge, they might change things or they might beat you senseless for speaking out."[22]

For the detainees, controlling their own society also meant drafting and enforcing what they called "rules to live by." These were codes of conduct that guided social behavior and, wherever possible, replaced camp authority with detainee discipline. In so doing, the detainees were, curiously, mimicking some of the disciplinary tactics of the guards and British officers. Of course, the punishments meted out by the detainees were never as brutal or capricious as those of the camp personnel. Through self-policing and discipline the detainees sought to avoid, or at least minimize, the so-called justice of the guards and European officers, and the insecurity it created.

Detainee norms forbade everything from chastising the guards to stealing, physically fighting, and lying to their peers. While the men in large reception centers like Manyani generally had separate sets of rules in each compound, some of the smaller works camps instead had a single code of conduct that governed everyone. There were the famous Twelve Laws of Lodwar and the Ten Rules of Yatta. In the case of Mageta Island, the detainees had a rule book that they passed between the camp's two compounds, adding to and amending it over time. In the Mageta Manifesto, as some detainees called it, spitting was forbidden, as was urinating and defecating outside of the toilet bucket. Detainees were not permitted to malinger when walking to and from the camp worksite; nor could they circumvent the ration line.[23]

Overall there was not a lot of variation between the social norms in different camps, and those that did arise tended to reflect some unique condition in a particular camp. In several Manyani compounds, for example, where detainee after detainee recalled the unbearable heat and duststorms, drinking another man's "cool water" was specifically forbidden. Presumably, the prohibition of stealing did not sufficiently capture the seriousness of taking a person's water after he had cooled it down. "You see," explained Nderi,

the water that we received at Manyani was always hot. The whole place was just boiling—the dust and the sun were unbearable. You couldn't cool yourself down by drinking hot water, so a man would spend a very long time passing it between two tins. These were the same tins we were issued, and we ate our porridge and drank our water out of them, and used them to dig ballast on the work projects. . . . Sometimes a person would borrow another man's tin and pass the water back and forth using his own as well, and this would cool the water down. But when you were hot and tired, this was a very long process. . . . To take such water from someone was very, very serious.[24]

The punishment for stealing could take several forms. Each compound generally held its own court, presided over by the compound leader and several other judges. In some cases, specific laws were enforced with equally specific punishments. For example, any offender convicted of spitting or urinating in the compound was often made to clean the toilet bucket, sometimes for several days.[25] This could be particularly unpleasant, because camp authorities provided no water or soap for the toilet bucket brigades, the detainees having to clean out the human waste using their hands, sticks, and sand. There was also the dreaded knee march. This punishment was decreed by the courts to anyone starting a fight with another detainee, or who was insolent with one of the camp authorities. The offender was forced to shuffle bare-kneed back and forth across the compound, and, depending on the case, the march could go on for an hour or more. In particularly egregious circumstances the detainee was stripped of his clothing and had to carry a tin filled with stones on his head while crawling on his knees. This was always done in plain view for its humiliating effect.[26]

The harshest forms of justice were shunning and ostracism, punishments meted out after severe or repeated infractions. During a period of shunning all other detainees kept their distance from the offender, and at night he was forced to sleep alone in the corner, the toilet bucket his only companion. Already isolated from the group, the ostracized offender was then taunted unmercifully about any apparent physical or social weakness. In one case, a man was harassed incessantly for days about what another detainee called "his oddly shaped testicles." "It went on and on and on," this man continued. "It got to the point that you couldn't help but feel sorry for him. He had been caught stealing from our food rations so many times that the punishment was warranted, but we were all happy when it came to an end."[27]

To ensure their survival, the detainees needed to do more than create a camp self-government. They had to engage with camp personnel, particularly the guards. While the British officers administering the camps set the overall tone, the guards patrolled the compounds, escorted the detainees to labor sites, enforced the work pace, reported rule infractions, issued the food rations, and controlled the riot sirens. But engagement was difficult because the guards were taught and retaught to hate the detainees, told over and again that they were cannibals, and marched through parade drills that reinforced the colonial government's version of Mau Mau savagery. "We used to be forced to sit and observe their processions," recalled one detainee, "whereby the British officers in charge would march the guards through the camps and shout questions. 'Who is the enemy of government?' and the guards would respond in unison, 'The enemy of government is Mau Mau.' The white men would then shout, 'Who is your enemy?' and they would respond together, 'Our enemy is Mau Mau.' They would then be asked, 'Who eats the flesh of young children?' and they would shout, 'The flesh eater is Mau Mau.' "[28]

The guards had their own agendas, personalities, and beliefs. Despite brainwashing by their superiors, they were not the pure automatons their commandants hoped for. Individual personality had much to do with this, but so did the miserable circumstances in which the guards lived. It was one thing to be taught to hate the people you were holding in detention; it was quite another to live on such poor rations and meager earnings that your daily plight often resembled theirs. With morale low, the guards sought to improve their own conditions, and it is hardly surprising that, given the few available options, they turned to the detainees.

There were often immensely tangled relations between the two groups. Beating the detainees one minute, the guards might illicitly trade with them the next. Black markets were well established in the camps, and the commandants were virtually powerless to control them. Detainees exchanged their blankets, food rations, and homemade items, like wooden spoons and jewelry crafted from corrugated iron, for cigarettes, snuff, pens, paper, medicine, newspapers, and a host of other items. The black markets, said one former detainee, were like "the Burma market in Nairobi"[29]—one of the largest markets in the city.

Black markets operate through trust, nowhere more than in prison, but in the Pipeline duplicity was also par for the course. Double-dealings were common, with detainees ripping blankets in half and passing them off as whole, guards mixing snuff with animal manure, or substituting a bag of the much-hated red sorghum for maize meal. Cheating the guards became a kind of recreation for the detainees and was seen as honorable, whereas cheating mates in one's compound was an abomination. In spite of the deception, black market lore has become as much a part of the Pipeline's history as screening or forced labor. Whether a camp was for "blacks" or "greys," politicals or women, where there were guards and detainees there was a black market for almost anything.[30]

The black market extended to bribery, with detainees trading prized items like sugar or tea or cigarettes for favors from the guards. In some instances, the detainees purchased goods from the camp commissaries with "token money," or the wages they received for their labor. But not all detainees were paid; token money was the exception rather than the norm. Instead, many detainees relied on packages sent from home, which generally were permitted, containing censored items that would be put to wide use, often starting with a "postage fee" to the guard who delivered the package. Detainees caught speaking or singing would hand over some flour, or perhaps a pinch of snuff, to avert a beating or, worse, a report to the camp commandant. When recalling his perpetual need for cigarettes, an addiction shared by many other detainees, Phillip Macharia immediately recalled a moment when he was caught passing a note to the next compound: "The guard asked me if I wanted to be beaten or if there was something I might have to persuade him to change his mind. I liked to smoke, so I had several Jets [the brand of that time] in my pocket and handed them to him with some matches. He took them all but lit two, handing me one, and we smoked those two Jets together."[31]

Bribery could also be preemptive. In exchange for some flour, or a prized pair of socks, the guards might look the other way when compound meetings were convened or when detainees were too sick or weak to make it out to work. Sometimes detainees shared their rations with the guards, if only to curry favor with them. Some affirmed that such gestures made the guards less susceptible to raising the alarm when camp rules were broken. "In our compound at Mara River, we had the habit of singing our Mau Mau songs quietly in the evening," recalled one former detainee now living in Nairobi. "So we would give the Luo guard some cigarettes every few days, and he never told on us, except one time when the commandant was nearby and we knew he must've heard us as well."[32] Many detainees did their best to convert their African guards, telling them about the history of Kenya and the solidarity they ought to have in the fight against the British. In some instances there were guards who became, according to some detainees, notably sympathetic to their cause.[33]

How do we begin to untangle the complex relationships between these men? Some former Mau Mau adherents analyzed their interactions with guards the way they would with human relations generally: "Some people are friends, while others are not," or "Some men are good, others bad, and then there are lot of us who fall somewhere in between."[34] In his memoir, J. M. chose as an explanatory device a Kikuyu allegory about a dog and a jackal.

> We say that when a man takes a dog out hunting a jackal, the dog will run far ahead out of sight and start playing with the jackal in a hidden place because they are really the same kind. When the man catches up with them the dog will straightaway begin barking fiercely and chasing the jackal again for a safe distance. This is because it is the man who gives the dog food which it will not get if it disobeys his orders.[35]

The fable suggests only a partial explanation. In the Pipeline the guards and detainees were bound together by dependency and fear, antagonism and sympathy, and even by hatred. Both groups lived under extraordinary constraints that can never fully be appreciated. In the end, it was the guards who often determined the fate of the detainees. Both parties knew this, and both parties tried to use and manipulate this power to their own advantage.

Technically, most communication between detainees, including singing, shouting, and passing notes and messages, was forbidden within the Pipeline. Even talking was prohibited, except within the individual huts or barracks where the detainees slept. To circumvent this regulation the detainees usually bribed the guards. They also did something much more ingenious. They turned the stereotype of Mau Mau savagery and madness to their advantage, creating a message system they christened "speaking to the wire." "If they were going to consider us mad because we were demanding *ithaka na wiyathi* [land and freedom]," recalled one former detainee, "then we were going to give them our own form of madness."[36] This man then went on to explain how the detainees' communication system functioned.

> We used to speak as if we were speaking to the wire; that is, you did not face the person you were speaking to, but faced the other side. You would pretend that you were talking to yourself like a mad person, while you were actually talking to someone in the compound behind you. The *askaris* would dismiss one as mad—you know, infected with the oath. Words were spoken in a clever manner, and the person in the other compound would send the message to another detainee in another compound. Within a short time, the whole camp would receive the message or news. Even in a large camp like Manyani, which was many miles long, messages used to be received in this way up to the farthest compound.[37]

In some cases a detainee would stand just beside the wire of his compound and start "having fits," as one man called them, jerking his body and head while shouting what seemed to be nonsensical statements.[38] They were, in fact, perfectly rational expressions disguised in a language that was a curious mixture of slang, euphemisms, and parables, combining English, Kiswahili, and Kikuyu. New words or phrases were created that had specific meaning to the detainees in the Pipeline. There was "*chakula cha* Manyani," which meant porridge filled with dust and flies; "*kiboko cha* screening," which translates literally into "the whip of screening," but to the detainees it signified the intelligence being used by the screening teams. There was "*kazi ya* Embakasi," the phrase for any punishing labor routine, its meaning derived from the reputation of Embakasi airport's work regime. To the passive listener it sounded as if the detainees were speaking jibberish, their words, phrases, and camp-specific parables having little, if any, apparent meaning.

When detainees were caught communicating, the guards would often simply throw rocks at them to get them to shut up, or accepted a payoff. But on other occasions the consequences were more severe. Like J. M., some detainees were brought to the center of the compound, where they were publicly whipped or beaten, presumably to send a message to the others. In one instance in Saiyusi Camp a detainee was thrown up against the barbed wire and whipped; in another the camp commandant at Mara River ordered the guards to shackle a detainee's feet together, tie a rope around the middle of the restraint, and collectively drag him around the compound "until bits of him were all over."[39] It was not unusual for retribution to be meted out against everyone in the compound, or even the entire camp, rather than only the individual transgressor. In the case of Karue Kibicho, who had earlier been picked up during Operation Anvil and taken to Manyani Camp, the infamous riot squad was called in. (These squads were used in nearly every major camp in the Pipeline, and their job was to bring order when detainees got out of line.) Karue later described what happened when he was caught speaking to a detainee across the barbed wire of his compound.

> The guard on the watchtower blew his whistle, and the *askaris*, who we called *rioti* [riot squad], were set upon us all. They were using their hoe-handle clubs, clubbing us indiscriminately. Some of the detainees died from the beatings before we were all told to come out of our compound naked, holding our clothing and blankets in our hands. This was not done peacefully, because the *askaris* were inside the compound beating us, and as we hurried out there were others waiting for us, beating us some more. We rushed to squat in fives with our clothing beside us. Those who didn't move quickly enough were set upon by the *askaris* and beaten. Then we would be ordered to throw all of our clothing in a heap; again if we weren't fast enough we were beaten. Then we were ordered to go and retrieve our things. The *askaris* would set on us as we rushed to get our clothes and blankets, without any regard as to where they hit us. . . . It was total mayhem, and the white man in charge just stood there screaming, '*Piga, piga sana*' [hit them, hit them more].[40]

These public displays of discipline could not but deter communication, though by no means did they thwart the detainees' efforts to exchange messages and speak with one another. If speaking was impossible, notes were written and tied to rocks or stuffed inside cigarette butts, which were then tossed across the barbed wire into other compounds or dropped, apparently indiscriminately, during marches out to the camp work sites. In some camps detainees exchanged messages in designated "mailboxes." The so-called post office at Manyani was located under the main water container. In Athi River the detainees chose a book on Queen Victoria in the camp's library as their exchange site, leaving them to wonder later why camp officials never discovered the ruse. As one man candidly observed, "Can you imagine any of us caring that much about Queen Victoria?"[41]

When they "spoke to the wire" or wrote notes, the detainees' communications extended far beyond social norms or the election of compound leaders. They were hungry for information and news about almost anything. Eager to find out what was happening in the compound across the camp, they also wanted to know what was going on in other camps up and down the Pipeline. They sought news on their family members and friends, often housed in other camps, on the harshness of the up-Pipeline camps that might await them, and the questions and intelligence of the other screening teams. They wanted more than anything to know what was happening outside the wire. Who was winning the war in the forest? What was the British colonial government doing to the property it confiscated during Anvil? What was happening in the reserves to their wives and children—not to mention their land? Was there any news of Jomo Kenyatta and the rest of their leaders at Lokitaung?

Work provided the best and most legitimate opportunity for speaking with relative freedom. Brief moments were stolen in the quarries, fields, or public works projects. At Manyani, Mageta Island, Saiyusi, and Kajiado camps detainees would often be shackled together in twos for their march to the work sites and would sometimes remain chained together throughout the day. Curiously, they were often allowed to partner up themselves, so that in the morning hours there was often a mad scramble to find a shackle mate who could not only bear the day's workload but also provide a bit of news, or at the very least some conversation. "It was always such a scene when it was time to be shackled," recalled a former detainee from Kajiado Camp. "We would try to get the shackle with the longest chain, because it made walking and working easier, but we also wanted a good partner—someone who could work and talk and give us news on what else was happening in the camps."[42]

Some specific works projects, like the thirty-seven-mile-long irrigation furrow at South Yatta, facilitated the spread of news. Hundreds of detainees would work standing at various angles along the furrow, using picks and shovels to deepen it. The irrigation ditch was a hazardous work site, so guards kept their distance, enabling the detainees at times to rest a bit as

Forced labor at South Yatta irrigation furrow, circa December 1955

well as talk. "I remember standing in the irrigation furrow at South Yatta," recalled a man who labored there for two and a half years, "it was [many] meters deep in some places, much more in others. There was always the fear of it collapsing on us, which it did one time, killing a bunch of men. But there were so many of us laboring, and the ditch was so deep, that the *askaris* couldn't possibly listen to us all so we would talk and talk about what was going on in the camp, and of the news from elsewhere."[43]

Compound committees sought to place their literate detainees on the cleaning teams that did the janitorial work in the offices of the camp commandant and his staff. Once there, they would read newspapers and official memoranda, returning in the evenings to divulge their latest news. Sometimes they would pick up information by surreptitiously listening in to the wireless that played aloud in the camp commandant's office. In other instances, detainees would steal scraps of newspaper, or *tama*, during the cleaning details. Njari Githui was one of those on cleaning detail at Manyani Camp, where he and a few others were responsible for Mapiga's office. Together, he recalled,

we would fold a piece of newspaper and hide it neatly inside our clothes such that it was not found during the inspection which we had to undergo before we went into the camps. In the evening, the *tama* would be read, and interpreted for those who could not understand. . . . We wanted to know when Kenyatta would be released, and when we would get our independence. We wanted to know if anyone knew about our fight in the camps. . . . After reading the paper, we would pass it on to the next compound. To do that, someone from one compound would lie flat on the ground near the fence, and another from the other compound would lie flat on his side of the fence. With both our hands outstretched, we could manage to pass over the piece of paper. . . . Of course, we would do this at night so as not to be detected.[44]

Throughout the Pipeline, the detainees called this secret circulation of news the *Manyani Times*. There was, however, another grapevine, one literally invented by the detainees. It was generally called *By Way of the Wire*, though also the *Waya Times*, the *Kimongo Times*, or *Nyandarua*. Its content was utter propaganda or deliberately false rumor fabricated by detainees to encourage other detainees and compel them to go on or, more to the point, to help them resist any temptation to confess and cooperate with camp authorities. "News" circulated that those who confessed their oaths in the camps were not released but instead taken to court, convicted of Mau Mau crimes based on their own self-incrimination, and then sent to jail in South Africa. In other instances, it was rumored that the colonial government had deported those who had confessed to an island off the coast of India, where they were to live forever in unbearable heat and humidity.[45]

Most often, though, the detainee rumor mill was about what J. M. and others called "wishful thinking." Nearly every detainee recalled hearing at some point that independence was on the horizon, that the colonial government was about to capitulate and leave Kenya, and that such exciting news was "all over the papers."[46] Rumors of rebellions, escapes, and labor strikes also spread like bushfire in the Pipeline. *By Way of the Wire* circulated reports that the United Nations was going to intervene on their behalf, or that the Labour Party was coming to help them. Along with Jomo Kenyatta, Fenner Brockway and Barbara Castle were veritable legends in the Pipeline, and the detainees enjoyed reporting that Castle and Brockway were negotiating for their release or were going to convict the camp authorities for torturing them and forcing them to labor against their will.[47]

Generating false hope was not without its psychological benefit. Many men remember the rumors for what they were intended to be, "words of comfort." "They gave us something to hold on to," one former detainee explained. "When you looked into the eyes of another man and saw nothing, you knew that such words would help him."[48] Rumor could also take a more humorous line, though its ultimate goal was the same. Detainees roared with laughter when they heard that certain screeners had sent home for, say, a shirt, and their wives instead sent them a baby carrier, or they had asked for a pair of pants and were sent a pair of knickers.[49] For the Kikuyu, this was interpreted as an affront to the screeners' manhood, that their wives did not approve of them collaborating, that taking the side of the British colonial government had made them lesser men. It was the screeners who now had their masculinity challenged, and the detainees would revel in it.

The spread of knowledge and ideas also took another form, something the detainees called rehabilitation. Not to be confused with the rehabilitation program drafted by Askwith and touted by the governor and colonial secretary, this program was developed by the Mau Mau adherents themselves. It was intended to curtail the damaging effects of the Pipeline by turning the camps into impromptu schools. Dozens of literacy classes sprang up. Many detainees had been well educated in the missionary and independent African schools, some had advanced degrees from foreign universities, and together they taught the illiterate and semiliterate how to read, write, and do arithmetic. Despite obviously trying circumstances, the classes were well organized, with curricula and lessons modeled on the British system that had been introduced by the missionaries throughout Kenya. Some camps had virtual schools, with forms or grades starting at Standard I and going all the way up to Standard IX. There were also lectures and discussions on politics, history, law, geography, and religion—all were wildly popular with the detainees.[50]

Lessons extended into the practical as well, with many classes designed to impart survival skills to detainees, particularly the newcomers. Such wisdom had been accrued over time, often through trial and error. When transfers came into the compounds, they were apprised of which guards to avoid and which ones could be more easily bribed; they were also told about rationing their water supplies and how eating slowly would allow them to feel more satiated. They were instructed never to gorge after a long food-denial to avoid rupturing internal organs, something which nevertheless happened all too frequently. There were hygiene classes that instructed detainees to put ash over their waste in the toilet buckets, and to wash their hands using cooking fuel and ballast. There were lessons on how to treat scorpion bites using tobacco snuff, how to most effectively bathe using sand, and how to eat amid swarms of flies.

Teaching and learning were often conducted through the age-old method of "writing in the sand."[51] Using a stick in his hand and the dirt on the floor, Nderi Kagombe instructed his fellow detainees in Manyani's Compound 9 in the basics of Kiswahili grammar. He had been transferred there after his initiation by Wagithundia in Compound 6, and, once the welcoming committee painstakingly apprised him of all the compound rules, the rehabilitation committee stepped in and recruited him to teach a variety of courses ranging from reading and grammar to history and politics. "Everyone would be gathered around not wanting to miss a word of the lesson," he later reminisced. "It was quite inspiring to see how these weary men wanted to feed their minds."[52] This homegrown education system helped deflect attention from the abysmal conditions in the Pipeline and inspired more meaningful thought. "I forgot how exhausted and starved I was [while] learning with the other men in my compounds," recalled one man from Nyeri District. "It was when we tried to sleep that I was tormented by my life in detention and not knowing what was happening to my wife and family. You see, our classes and our teachers kept me alive. They were as important as our miserable food rations."[53]

To a certain degree the survival and resistance strategies adopted by the detainees are universal. One is struck by the similarities—across social organizations, communication networks, and camp personnel—between the Pipeline, the Nazi concentration camps, the Soviet gulag, and South Africa's Robben Island. But the world that evolved inside the Pipeline was also different. Kikuyu culture and religion, and the colonial government's response to the detainees' indigenous ways of interpreting and organizing their world, were carried into the camps and made life there unique from that in other systems of detention.

While recalling their years in the Pipeline, detainees invariably ruminate about their belief system. They are not referring to the Christianity that was proffered by the colonial authority, but rather to their indigenous religion, which focused on the Kikuyu creator god Ngai and to their mythical ancestors Gikuyu and Mumbi. They looked to their own Kikuyu belief system to help explain the circumstances in which they were living, and to strengthen them in their resistance. Clandestine prayer sessions, where detainees drew upon their traditional beliefs and practices, paying homage to their ancestral gods and looking to them for answers to the conditions that had befallen them in the camps, were common. Prior to the Emergency, however, many of the detainees were, to varying degrees, practicing Christians.[54] Most believed that the tenets of Mau Mau were not incompatible with the Christian faith as they interpreted it. This was particularly true for those who had been members of the Kikuyu independent churches that had broken away from the Western missionaries in the 1930s—churches which had been one of the hotbeds for the growth of Mau Mau. But in the camps there arose over time a resentment and even hatred of Christianity, particularly as it became associated more and more with British colonial oppression. For many detainees, Christianity was ineffective in explaining what was happening to them and was, in fact, partly responsible for their condition.

Missionaries were contributing directly to the detainees' cynicism about Christianity. On Sundays and some weekday evenings, missionaries would enter the compounds to preach cooperation with the government, the need to confess oaths, and, most important, that to become good Christians like the British, the Kikuyu had to reject Mau Mau. "They used to preach and preach and preach," one animated man said as he stood up in parody of a missionary. " 'Receive Christ's salvation and leave everything about the oath behind; become one with Him, and you will be redeemed.' These preachers would stand there for hours saying such things with their Bibles in their hands. We just sat there and listened to them and couldn't believe our ears. Hah, the hypocrisy of it all only made us more determined not to give in."[55]

On Sundays, when most detainees did not have to labor the whole day, the collective air of the Pipeline was filled with lessons from the Bible and Christian urgings to confess Mau Mau sins. Preachers took to the loudspeakers to broadcast their message throughout the camps. Some detainees logically viewed these men of the cloth as working hand in glove with the colonial government. They were seen as trying to oppress Mau Mau minds just as the camp authorities were attempting to do the same with their Mau Mau bodies. Many detainees had already recognized the insidious partnership between Christianity and Britain's civilizing mission, but in the camps it became utterly transparent. For Muraya Mutahi, who had spent several years fighting in the forests before his detention, it was "in the camps where we fully realized that Christianity had been used so as to make us blind to the injustices that were being done to us. We composed a song that we would sing at night that went, 'We were told to close our eyes, and we obeyed, and as we did so, all of our land was taken from us. Now, that is the reason why we are crying.' We realized that we had been fooled, and we weren't going to be fooled again."[56]

The detainees had nicknames for these men of God. One was renowned for starting every sermon with "Confess and believe in the Gospel," so the detainees christened him just that: "Confess and believe in the Gospel."[57] Then there was the elderly white preacher from the Africa Inland Mission who seemed to have made Manyani his second home. With a captive audience of over ten thousand detainees and a loudspeaker system at his disposal, Sundays were a bonanza for him as he went on for hours about the evils of Mau Mau and the need for Christian repentance. "He used to preach to us," recalled one man who had been held in the reception center for two and half years, "telling us how we would never be released unless we confessed the Mau Mau oath, how our quest for independence was futile. We tried not to listen to him, but he just went on and on."[58] Caught up in his own enthusiasm, the missionary would repeatedly sing his favorite hymnal verse: "We shall live forever with Jesus in Heaven." Without fail he would end with great inflection on the last word, earning him his nickname Matuini, or Heaven.[59]

There were also dozens of Africans, mostly Kikuyu, who would come to preach the Gospel and exhort detainees to confess and repent. There were Nyenjeri and Phillips, who used to accompany Matuini to Manyani Camp, there was Brooks in Mackinnon Road, Mwangi in South Yatta, and scores of others up and down the Pipeline. Perhaps the most famous was Obadiah Kariuki, who would later, after independence, become bishop of the Anglican Church of Kenya. Sporting his driving goggles—which made him look like a "bespectacled frog," according to one British camp officer— Reverend Kariuki traveled thousands of miles on his motorcycle as he journeyed to various sites in the Pipeline, preaching and observing the situation in the camps.[60] The detainees had mixed feelings about this specific group of African Christians. There were some, like the Presbyterian minister from Nyeri, Charles Muhoro, who would preach the Gospel but avoid any mention of the Mau Mau oath, or confession. According to many detainees, he was also Mau Mau, having taken the oath and now refusing to do anything actively to thwart the movement.[61] But the detainees called most of the others stooges. It was bad enough that they blasphemed Mau Mau, but several clergy were also known to be Home Guards—men actively fighting with the colonial government against Mau Mau and personally profiting from their colonial alliances. "Did the British think we didn't see this hypocrisy?" one former detainee asked. "These men preaching Christian brotherhood were some of the same ones fighting against us and benefiting from our losses."[62] Others were alleged to be working closely with the camp authorities in the more brutal approaches to forcing confessions. Detainees reported some of the preachers, both black and white, would sit in with the screening teams as they used a variety of techniques to get the detainees to cooperate. It appears as if most were providing only intelligence to the screening teams, rather than an additional rough hand in the softening-up process. This did not diminish the antipathy that the former detainees still feel toward the missionaries today. In fact, a sentiment expressed by one former Mau Mau adherent sums up the beliefs of others: "Even the preachers were also screeners. They would observe how people were receiving their preaching, and they would go and make reports about it to the screening teams. They were not just coming to preach. No, they had other reasons."[63] These suspicions were not ill-founded. There is written evidence that the missionaries were constantly providing the colonial government with information about the camps and the various levels of detainee cooperation.[64]

The Catholics impressed the detainees as being in a category all their own. Wearing their long robes, the Fathers would often preach with a gun holstered around their waist—or, in one case, "with a Bible in one hand and gun in the other."[65] The Catholics seemed to epitomize Christian hypocrisy. In the reserves they were known for preaching during the day and going out on active patrols at night to hunt down the Mau Mau, a point confirmed in colonial documents as well as in missionary records.[66] In the camps they endorsed a route to redemption that seemed off-limits to their Protestant counterparts. "We liked it when the Protestants came," remarked one former detainee. "Not because we agreed with what they said but because the guards would leave us alone. They would never beat us in their presence."[67] But the Catholics were different. In a kind of twentieth-century inquisition, some Fathers would preach and demand confessions of all Mau Mau sins while the African guards would chase and beat the detainees with clubs and whips. According to Elijah Gikuya, for one Sunday morning service in Manyani he and all of the men in his compound were taken to "attend a prayer session in a large hall which was in the camp. We were escorted there by the guards. While there, I don't know what provoked them, but the guards came inside and started beating people mercilessly. It was chaos, with people trying to cover themselves from the blows. The Catholic priest just stood there continuing to preach as if nothing was happening. Since then we never trusted another one of the Catholics."[68] Many of the camp officials seemed to prefer the fathers to the Protestant preachers despite the fact that few of them were themselves Catholics. As the British camp commandant at Tebere reported in early 1954, "My experience is that Roman Catholic Missions in East Africa inculcate into their flocks considerably more wholesome discipline than most other missions and cause less embarrassment to Government."[69]

Predictably, the effect of Christian preaching in the camps was often counterproductive. But it would be inaccurate to argue that missionaries were solely responsible for the detainees' rejection of Christianity and the resurgence of traditional Kikuyu worship. Certainly, many of the detainees came into the Pipeline with a renewed or strengthened belief in Ngai and their mythical creators, Gikuyu and Mumbi. These religious figures were often invoked in Mau Mau oathing ceremonies prior to the Emergency and were the source of much collective psychological strength during the early days of the war. Not surprisingly, it was the detainees' experiences in the camps that served to catalyze their religious transformation. When Nderi Kagombe later reflected on this spiritual shift, it made perfect sense to him.

> When you understand that you are being oppressed, then you make changes. We had taken the oath because we had realized that the leadership of the white man was only oppressing us more and more, and that we had a color bar which was as bad as that one which existed in South Africa. So we decided to take the oath and unite against the white man. In detention, we abandoned Christianity entirely, and we began praying in the traditional Kikuyu way. We used to raise our hands in the air, facing the direction of Mount Kenya, and prayed and praised Ngai saying, '*Thaai thathaiya Ngai thaai*' [Praise, Praise, God Praise].[70]

Like Nderi, many other detainees beseeched Ngai for guidance, asking Him for protection in the camps. They also invoked His protection of everything of importance—wives, children, livestock, and of course their land—while they were locked away. Together these were not just sources of material wealth but also the symbols of their Kikuyu manhood, perpetually under assault in the Pipeline.

Night was the greatest opportunity for group prayer in the compounds. Under the cover of darkness the detainees would kneel together side by side, facing Mount Kenya, holding each other's hands and raising their arms high in the air. "It was an amazing thing," recalled Nderi. "All of these men crouched on the floor with their heads up toward the sky and their hands linked and outstretched. . . . Sometimes I felt myself straining, trying to reach to Him with my hands and my mind."[71] He and the others would repeat various prayers, many of which had been scripted in the camps.

Hymns were also composed, and detainees would bribe the guards or calculate their comings and goings, strategically deciding the best moments to sing. But even with careful planning they were often caught, and the consequences could be devastating. Some guards did nothing for a cigarette or two; other times they only yelled at the detainees to be quiet. But they might set on the detainees and beat them or bring the infraction to the attention of the camp commandant. In the case of Wilson Njoroge, his entire compound at Mackinnon Road was caught singing:

> Ngai we beseech you to be the judge,
> If the white men defeat us it is you who will have been defeated
> We shall be full of joy
> When the House of Mumbi will be receiving her land back.

The next morning he was singled out as an example by Kenda Kenda. After being beaten with mattock handles by the *askaris*, Wilson was taken to the small cells and dumped into a pit, filled with water and animal carcasses. "I was there for four or five days, I can't really remember which," he said. "It was a very trying time because I had no food and the only water there was to drink was just what was there in the pit. I remember spending much of the time reciting prayers. Not Christian ones but the kind that our ancestors would have said and that we would say during Mau Mau, the ones to Ngai. There was one in particular that I repeated over and over again.

> I pray to you Ngai, with my eyes facing Kirinyaga [Mount Kenya]
> Where our forefathers used to face when praying for rains,
> and rains used to come.
> We pray that you grant us victory because we believe that if we win,
> You will have won.
> But if we lose, it is you who will have lost.[72]

For the detainees, it was virtually impossible to separate the Kikuyu belief system from the meaning and power of the Mau Mau oath. The oath, like their indigenous religion, was transformed and its importance heightened with every day spent in the Pipeline. The oath had united the adherents long before they were detained; its ritual, the ingestion of blood and goat meat, and the symbolic rebirth of Kikuyu into Mau Mau members were all critical to establishing cohesion in the movement. Yet when colonial authorities like Askwith, Leakey, and Governor Baring decided to make the oath the focal point of the struggle behind the wire, they infused it with yet new meaning, further elevating its importance to the Kikuyu and transforming it into the ultimate symbol of unity and resistance in the camps.

Like the clandestine prayer sessions, oathing ceremonies also took place in the Pipeline, though they were less common, for it was basically impossible for the detainees to obtain the necessary oathing paraphernalia. They especially needed banana leaves and a sacrificial goat. But in characteristic form, detainees improvised. Instead of leaves, blankets were tied together and held aloft in the shape of an arc. They bought animal blood and entrails on the black market, using them to replace the goat. There was also bribery, perhaps the biggest facilitator of the oathing ceremony in the camps. Guards demanded a huge honorarium to turn the other way; the equivalent could be as much as several packs of cigarettes or a few days' worth of the compound's rations. This alone was enough to keep oathing in the Pipeline at a minimum.

The oath was largely taken by the uninitiated entering the camps. Many of these innocent men were mistakenly swept up by the colonial government and thrust into the Pipeline. There they could either take the oath or face the wrath of their fellow detainees. In the compounds the non–oath takers could easily be identified because there were certain signs or phrases that were known only by those who had taken the oath. "If you held up two sticks to someone in the sign of the cross," one man recalled, "then the person who was a Mau Mau knew to say, 'I am a true Kikuyu.' If he didn't, then you knew he had not taken the oath."[73] There were apparently other ways of knowing. One man recounted that by scratching his head a certain way those around him who were Mau Mau would respond by rubbing their left earlobe. Once someone was aware that an uninitiated man was in their midst, he would declare, "There are fleas in this place!"[74]—a warning to others not to talk about the oath.

In the compounds the oathing ceremony was generally conducted in conjunction with a prayer session to Ngai, invoking Him to aid in their unity. "We would gather and pray in our Kikuyu way," said Nderi. "Then we would prepare those who were taking the oath, stripping them down and telling them about the ways of Gikuyu and Mumbi whose land it was that we were fighting for. We beseeched Ngai for the strength we needed. Then the oath was given, and it unified us; it made us one. In the camps it was an indescribable oneness that we were forbidden to break."[75] But there were those detainees, mostly devout Christians, who refused to take it, and their fate was similar to some of those who refused to accept the oath outside of the camps—they were often killed. The detainees would strangle them with their blankets or, using blades fashioned from the corrugated-iron roofs of some of the barracks, would slit their throats. "You see," Nderi went on, "we could not be in the company of those who were not bound together. They would betray us, and we would be defeated. The oath was the most important thing for us. Without it we were nothing."[76]

We should not romanticize the anticolonial struggle in the Pipeline. There was divisiveness of the kind that invariably arises in any resistance movement, particularly in those in the pressure cooker of such extreme conditions as existed in the camps. There undoubtedly was a kind of "us versus them" mentality, pitting the detainees against the many faces of British colonial authority. Creating committees, instituting social norms and discipline, working to educate fellow compound members—these were all attempts to protect the unified Mau Mau social body. But the history of the Pipeline is not only a story of collective resistance and survival. It is also one of disagreement, self-interest, and excruciatingly difficult moral choices. The poisonous reality of the detainees' everyday lives, the hunger, hard labor, torture, affected each person differently, as did their degree of belief in the purpose and strength of the Mau Mau movement. Some detainees broke down, even after years of resisting, confessing their oaths and cooperating with camp authorities.

What determined a person's breaking point? This is a question that perplexed many within the colonial government. Thousands upon thousands of Mau Mau suspects were deprived of their rights, sent to slave labor camps, stripped of every shred of human dignity, worked sometimes to death, beaten senseless, tortured, and murdered. Still, many refused to confess. Particularly during the first year after Operation Anvil camp officials had little success in forcing detainees to cooperate.

Part of the colonial authority's failure was self-inflicted. Screening, processing new intakes, and issuing individual detention orders required huge amounts of administrative manpower and financial resources. Camp officials simply could not keep pace with the roundups and intakes, let alone carry through with the much tougher challenge of forcing detainees to cooperate. Compounding these problems was the constant flow of new arrivals into the Pipeline—all of whom were being indoctrinated into the detainees' world. Many colonial officials believed that the camps were "saturated," and that some detainees were "going sour" and becoming "blacker" while others were "sitting behind barbed wire pondering the pros and cons of anti Government subversity."[77] In the summer of 1955—over a year after Anvil—Colonial Secretary Alan Lennox-Boyd assessed the situation and wrote, "I fear that the net figure of detainees may still be rising. If so, the outlook is grim."[78]

In time, though, officials in Kenya improved their efforts at making the Pipeline an unbearable experience. By the end of 1955 the colonial government was much better equipped to deal with the detainees and turned its full attention to breaking them. Colonial officials had managed to bring a measure of rational organization to the labyrinth of camps now fully in place. Intelligence was shared and coordinated, making screening far more effective, work quotas were clearly spelled out, transfers were tracked more effectively, and the Prisons Department successfully delegated some of its powers to the Administration in the district works camps.[79] With these changes detainees found less and less room to maneuver, and survival became increasingly more difficult. The collective will to resist gradually began to break down as individual survival instincts took over.

The well-oiled colonial propaganda machine fed on the detainees' fears and concerns. Pamphlets in the vernacular were circulated through the compounds, pointing out the fairness of the Carter Land Commission, as well as correcting the "misguided" belief that African land had been stolen by the British. At the same time, loudspeakers would blare warnings about ongoing land confiscations in the reserves, describing how land taken from Mau Mau sympathizers was being redistributed to those who were loyal to the British colonial cause. "Confess and Save Your Land" was one broadcast that the British colonial government played throughout the Pipeline, and is still bitterly remembered today by many of the former detainees.[80] So too are the news programs that constantly blared updates of Mau Mau losses in the forests, and the imprisonment of Jomo Kenyatta. Pictures of Her Majesty in full regalia were hung up throughout the compounds alongside images of Kenyatta in shackles, wild-haired and looking dazed and pathetic. Obviously, the implied contrast between civilization and savagery could not have been more stark. Home Guards who were imported from the reserves were used by camp authorities to relate local news over the public address system. These Kikuyu loyalists sliced straight to the detainees' manhood, announcing that their wives were suffering and needed their protection. "These Kikuyu scum would announce throughout the camp that so and so's wife had given birth to a child with loyalist blood," Nderi recalled, "or that his wife had left him for the comforts of the Home Guard post."[81]

The colonial government clearly had time on its side. Detention camps are a waiting game; given enough time, they will eventually transform human beings into something they never imagined possible. When reflecting on his experience in the Soviet gulag, Gustaw Herling concluded that "there is nothing . . . a man cannot be forced to do by hunger and pain."[82] Having spent months or years in the Pipeline, former detainees expressed sentiments that were strikingly similar. "There is only so much a man can bear," Phillip Macharia said when recalling why he confessed his oath. He had been detained for nearly two years, spending most of his time at Manyani making ballast at the work site, overcoming several bouts of pellagra, living in filthy clothes, and listening to British colonial propaganda day in and day out. "I felt as though I could no longer persevere with life. I had been beaten; I watched others being tortured and killed. I just couldn't take it any more."[83] For Phillip, the breaking point came when he and some other detainees were caught by the guards reading a scrap of newspaper. As punishment, they were forced to put toilet buckets on their heads and run to the site where they were to be dumped and cleaned. "We had excrement and urine running down our faces and backs; all the while the guards were beating us with their clubs to make us go faster. A few days later I was taken to screening, and this time I confessed my oath to get out of the hell I was living in."[84]

Though most stories of detention culminated with the moment of confession, each account was as much about a man's individual metamorphosis as it was about his ultimate decision to cooperate and save his own life. Hungry, more and more detainees began to steal rations from weaker men. Desperate to avoid punishment, they implicated others for camp violations that were, in fact, their own. Some tried to escape and were sometimes successful, while knowing full well that camp authorities would exact unimaginable retribution on the detainees left behind. Exhausted, individuals would feign illness and head to the camp infirmary—one of the true absurdities of the Pipeline. There, they would be examined and sometimes allowed to rest. Their comrades still marched off to hard labor but with the added burden of having to fill the work quotas of those left behind.[85]

Other detainees routinely compromised with their captors to secure a better life for themselves in the camps. Some collusions were more subtle than others. There were, for example, the *fundis*. These were men who had particular skills and who used them to angle for the relatively benign opportunities open to them in the camps. Prior to detention they were mechanics, agricultural assistants, carpenters, clerks, medical staff, and houseboys. Behind the wire, they built torture cells and fixed vehicles, typed transfer and screening documents, ran the infirmaries, and kept the British officers in their clean and neatly pressed khaki uniforms. In their relatively comfortable jobs these detainees avoided the harsh labor routines endured by the others, received favors in the form of extra food or cigarettes or even clothes, and at a very basic level were critical to the functioning of the Pipeline's oppressive system.[86] Over time many of their peers grew to dislike them, sharing the sentiments of Aleksandr Solzhenitsyn who asked in his *Gulag Archipelago*, "What trusty position did not in fact involve playing up to the bosses and participating in the general system of compulsion?"[87]

It was the *fundis* who were instrumental in creating hierarchies in the camps, based upon the privilege and wealth they derived from their soft jobs. Through favoritism or theft they amassed items like pens and paper, cigarettes, newspapers, and tea. With these they dominated the black market, routinely buying off guards, and ultimately increasing their chances of individual survival. It was not unusual for a *fundi* to be a compound leader, though any leadership role secured by popular acclamation would tend to evolve into a kind of despotic control. Just as a detainee's status in the compound determined where he slept, that is, his distance from the toilet bucket, the *fundis* and their coteries generally amassed for themselves such luxuries as were available to detainees. Unequal relationships were part of the Pipeline's fabric from its earliest days. The social cleavages between those detainees who cooperated and those who did not widened over time as the effects of sustained detention, hard labor, starvation, and torture broke down the collective efforts at unity.

Other detainees simply became the favorites of the camp officers, assuring them a special quality of protection. At one of the camps, one man recalled, "[I was caught] speaking to the camp commandant's 'wife,' as we called this particular detainee. The guard took me and beat me unconscious, but told the other man he [the guard] could not touch him by order of the commandant."[88] This does leave one wondering what exactly the relationship was between the camp's commandant and his favorite detainee, or "wife." In oral testimonies several men spoke elliptically about homosexuality—both among themselves and between camp personnel and the detainees. It certainly must have existed, but the extent of such sexual relations is unclear. One fact is certain: some detainees served the domestic needs of the camp officers, spending more than a night or two in their quarters. Others traded sex with guards to ensure their protection, and some—particularly the younger men—found both protection and affection by becoming the so-called junior wives of fellow detainees, particularly the *fundis*.[89]

There were others in the Pipeline for whom—in the words of Tzvetan Todorov, who wrote extensively on moral life in concentration camps— "staying human [was] more important than staying alive."[90] Random acts of kindness, or "ordinary virtues" as Todorov calls them, are found throughout the annals of Britain's gulag. There are recollections from former detainees of men giving their day's food ration and blankets to those who were so ill and weak they were near death. Detainees traded cigarettes for vitamins with the intention of giving them to their compound mates who were suffering from scurvy. In Mara River a man painstakingly hoarded and cooled water to bathe a fellow detainee whose body was covered with boils. Some detainees were crippled with pellagra and dependent on others to help them walk and work. In one case "there was this man called Mwangi who had come from the Rift Valley," recalled Phillip Macharia. "He spent every day for almost a month carrying this man with pellagra on his back, back and forth to the labor site at Mara River. Because of the pellagra this detainee had scabs all over his legs and could hardly walk, he was in so much pain. Once he arrived at the quarry, Mwangi would set him down, and we would allocate him the job of picking out the debris from our ballast loads. It is difficult to imagine the strength it took for Mwangi to bear the heavy load of another on his back. Mind you, the work site was a very long walk from the camp."[91]

Within the Pipeline's crucible, moral choices daily confronted the detainees. As some placed self-interest before everything, others put their own survival at risk to maintain what one detainee called "human dignity and friendship."[92] What is most striking in the oral testimonies is the degree to which detainees wrestled with their commitment to Mau Mau, on the one hand, and their desire to save themselves, on the other. Of course, the two were not necessarily mutually exclusive. The compound detainee organizations, codes of conduct, and oathing were all designed to protect collectively the detainees. There was safety in numbers, and together they could mount a more effective defense against the onslaught of British colonial authority.

Nevertheless, the extreme and sustained conditions of detention have a way of eroding social contracts at their very foundations. Camp committees became less effective and detainee norms harder to enforce as the proverbial "law of the jungle" began to eclipse ordinary virtues and collective solidarity. Although the decay was slow, and probably difficult to track, detention was nonetheless as unnatural a state for Mau Mau as for any other people struggling to prevent a social breakdown and the formation of unhealthy and destructive hierarchies and personal interests. What control the detainees had managed to establish was slipping, and the colonial government, quite opportunistically, took advantage, adding even more pressure designed to turn the detainees against themselves.

Variations on the divide-and-rule policy had been used for some time. Screening teams had routinely told detainees that compound mates had "sold them out" when in fact they had not. Camp commandants purposely put detainees of different ages and geographic backgrounds together in the same compounds, thinking their differences would create divisions. Some of these tactics were effective, but none yielded the kind of result that came when camp authorities started to make widespread use of those who had begun to break down and confess. Some were recruited into the system as compound informants; others became the notorious "surrenders"—those detainees who after confession joined the camp screening teams, providing vital intelligence as well as softening-up support. Already pushed to the brink, detainee cohesion faced its most difficult challenge from these two by-products of the camp divide-and-conquer strategy.

Today, former detainees recall informants and surrenders with disgust and despair. They are described as sellouts, traitors, CIDs—a play on the British colonial government's Criminal Investigation Department—and, perhaps worst of all, Home Guards. Some informants were passed off by camp authorities as new transfers, whereas others, after privately confessing to the screening teams, returned to their old compounds to spy. From wherever the threat came, the detainees did their best to try to detect "the rats in the compounds."[93] When they did, the result was always the same: informants were summarily executed by the detainees. "It was just like in the days before our detention," one detainee explained. "We did not have our own jails to hold an informant in, so we would strangle him and then cut his tongue out."[94] He pointed out that the law in the camps was the same, and the preferred method of execution was still strangulation. When reflecting on the murders of informants, this detainee, like many others, considered them moral acts that prevented the worsening of their already difficult conditions. Despite camp authorities often collectively punishing a compound for killing a spy, one detainee insisted that "it was better to be beaten than to let an informant live, because they were like a poison sure to kill us."[95]

Some informants did have great success in providing their superiors with detailed information about Mau Mau activities in the compounds. This information in turn strongly influenced the colonial government's camp policies. As early as 1954 Governor Baring had written to Lennox-Boyd about the "Mau Mau organization" in the camps with its "Chairman" and "Mau Mau rules," but neither he nor his subordinates had yet to appreciate fully the pervasiveness of the detainees' world.[96] This changed with the more effective use of the government's "eyes and ears," or "stool pigeons," as colonial officials called informants.[97] Once the Special Branch began reporting "sufficient evidence of Mau Mau activities within Detention Camps," screening requirements changed.[98] From the end of 1955 forward, all screening teams were ordered to "take into account not only whether the individual concerned has confessed to his or her Mau Mau activities before detention but also whether he or she has provided information about anything that took place during the period of detention."[99] Moreover, screeners were encouraged to abandon any "set forms of questions" because, as one official commented, "[they] would be useless as the Mau Mau Committees most certainly have their own set form of answers."[100] The commissioner of prisons, Taxi Lewis, also directed his men to take control of the "illicit oathing" problem that was far more widespread than anyone had initially thought.[101] In translating this directive, several of his camp commandants interpreted their order in the same way: they publicly hung suspected oath administrators in the camp compounds, leaving them to dangle on display for several days.[102]

The presence of informants predictably resulted in a climate of distrust among detainees, who started hiding their camp identities, that is, their detention numbers, from the others. The reason for doing this was, as David Githigaita explained, fairly obvious.

At Manyani, we would not leave our detention numbers uncovered, because if one of the secret informers whom we could not identify saw the numbers, he could use you to make himself look better by reporting that you were the one persuading other detainees not to confess or that you were the one leading prayers to Ngai. We had to keep those numbers covered using an aluminum metal plate which we made from the roofs. You see, a detainee's name without his detention number was useless, because even if one's name was called several times, without calling his number he would not answer. There were many detainees who shared names, but the numbers could not be the same.[103]

Oathing, prayer sessions, singing—all of these collective acts that helped to forge and maintain unity became less practiced as detainees feared being betrayed by one another. Mau Mau activities did not cease altogether, but the colonial government succeeded in separating the "weaker members from the herd."[104] In the language of the time, camp authorities targeted the "waverers."[105]

They also targeted the guards. Camp authorities more and more shuffled guards around the Pipeline, cutting short any relationships they might forge with the detainees.[106] They also introduced an effective system of reward and punishment intended to shut down black markets and the widespread bribery. The guards' quality of life improved when Askwith's rehabilitation officers redirected their limited funds and manpower away from the detainees and toward the guards. Memoranda ordering rehabilitation officers to organize classes, football matches, and the like exclusively for the guards became more common each year. There were special "fun days" with prizes and ribbons for the strongest and fastest warders. The Prisons Department also agreed to exempt all of its loyalist African staff working in the Pipeline from their hut taxes and gave them additional support for their dependents, some of whom were living with them in the camps.[107] However, not all attempts to improve the guards' loyalty to the Crown were quite as accommodating. The threat and use of punishment also went a long way toward building a self-policing culture among guards. For instance, a British officer at Waithaka Camp, tipped off by an informant, caught a guard trading cigarettes with some detainees through the wire of a compound. Rather than order the legal use of twelve strokes with a cane, the officer pulled out his gun and killed the guard and then did the same to one of the detainees. At Waithaka black market dealings reportedly receded for many months.[108] It would be ridiculous, of course, to suggest that illicit trading and bribery disappeared altogether in the Pipeline, but with the shift in policies and the help of the informants it did diminish over time.

Surrenders stepped in where the informants left off. Integrated as members of the camp screening teams, they provided their own vital knowledge and with their colleagues made use of the intelligence passed along by informants. "It became much more difficult to talk around the questions of the screening teams when more of the surrenders started joining them," recalled Nderi Kagombe. "We could no longer use the same kind of false confessions that we had once used; they knew when we were lying because they had accurate information on what we had been doing in the compounds and during the time before we were detained. The surrenders would just keep harassing us and harassing us."[109] The surrenders went well beyond verbal interrogation. They took to the loudspeakers where they named names, and gave their own long confessions about Mau Mau activities both before and during detention. The surrenders also zealously participated in beating and torturing the detainees—many of whom were their former compound mates or neighbors from the rural areas. Former detainees recall these so-called sellouts as being some of the worst among the Africans who tortured them. "They wanted to prove that they were really part of the government," one man pointed out. "But, you understand, don't you, that they were very ashamed at what they had done; they beat us because they hated themselves for what they were doing. They were also afraid that if they didn't force us to confess and give in, we would come back to kill them for having turned on us and on Mau Mau."[110]

When pondering why some men turn against others, Auschwitz survivor Primo Levi came to this conclusion: "If one offers a position of privilege to a few individuals in a state of slavery exacting in exchange the betrayal of a natural solidarity with their comrades, there will certainly be someone who will accept."[111] Levi's observation applies equally to the detention camps in Kenya. Informants and surrenders were both rewarded handsomely, and with more than just their survival. During the course of my research I identified several men who had decided to join ranks with the camp system once they had confessed, but only a few were willing to speak with me and only then on the condition of anonymity. When asked why he became an informant, one man replied simply, "Because the camp commandant made sure I was given things. Back at home I was assured that my land was protected, and I was also provided with two goats and a cow when I returned to my home. In return I had to report everything that was happening. . . . It was a very dangerous job, and I earned what was given to me. You know, I wasn't the only one who accepted these things in return for my help; there were many of us."[112]

When ordinary threats did not compel enough of them to join the ranks of the camp system, the colonial government also used extortion. "I was told that if I didn't cooperate they would take my land and kill my family," recalled another man from Kiambu District. "I conducted my work as a surrender, screening and beating people because I was trying to save myself and my family. Imagine, I had confessed to get out of Manyani, but that was just the start of my problems."[113] In some camps, in fact, there was an explicit policy: detainees who wanted to be released had to join the ranks of the Home Guard and fight actively against their former comrades either in the camps or back in the reserves.[114] Yet no matter how much these former detainees cooperated with the British colonial government, they would never ascend to the top of the loyalist hierarchy outside of the camps. Their status as former Mau Mau adherents would brand them forever in the eyes of their British colonizers.

Some men joined the screening teams because of their Christian conversion. Though many of the detainees could not bear to hear the missionaries preach, a few did listen and internalized their message. "These men became real Christian fanatics," explained a detainee from Nyeri Distict. "They accepted everything the preachers said and then joined the screening teams. They would generally not beat us, but they also did not stop the other people screening us from doing it. The whole time they would be saying things like 'accept the blood of Christ' and 'vomit the poison of Mau Mau.' "[115] The actions of these converted detainees betrayed an astonishing transformation. Perhaps some had been waverers from the start. Perhaps for them Ngai was impotent in explaining the wretched situation they were enduring. Others must have simply believed the missionaries' preachings, that Mau Mau had led them astray and only Christianity could rescue them from the hell in which they were living. To the other detainees their change was a total, Judas-like betrayal.

Ultimately, detainees confessed to save themselves, however broadly defined. Some would break down in front of the screening teams, others would raise their hands in the compounds to be escorted away by the guards, and some wrote their detention numbers down on a slip of paper and placed them in the camp's confession box. But such gestures of cooperation were the first step in the very long journey out of the Pipeline. One wonders if detainees might have reconsidered their decision to confess had they known what awaited them in the works camps in their home districts. "Confessed greys," as they were called by the colonial government, would be transferred to works camps to be worked over, once more, before their final release.

The works camps were erected to sift through the population yet again, searching for those with some shred of intelligence that could be used to further consolidate the Pipeline and obliterate whatever Mau Mau organization remained outside of it. Like everywhere else in the Pipeline, works camps were also dedicated to labor. There was, however, one critical difference. The torture, both physical and psychological, in the works camps was intimate, for these camps were located in a detainee's home district in the reserves. The colonial officers running the works camps and the guards, the vast majority of whom were local Kikuyu loyalists, all personally knew the detainees.

"It was not enough just to confess your oath," Hunja Njuki recalled when reflecting on his time at Aguthi Camp. "No, they worked us and beat us constantly to get more information out of us and to make certain we were clean of Mau Mau. I had spent so many years in detention it didn't matter anymore, but Aguthi . . . There the men beating us were the same Kikuyu who were our neighbors. They had taken our land and our women, but that wasn't enough."[116] Hunja had spent nearly five years in the Pipeline before he arrived in the works camp at Aguthi. Arrested in early 1953, when he was a single twenty-five-year-old working at a sawmill near the Mount Kenya forest, he was convicted by one of the local kangaroo courts of feeding the so-called terrorists and sentenced to three years in the Mau Mau prison at Embakasi.

Embakasi was one of the worst destinations in the Pipeline, according to Hunja and several others who had been imprisoned there. Colonial officials at the prison were under enormous pressure to complete the airport, a massive project that had a limitless need for labor, before the end of the Emergency.[117] Camp commandants—like Major Helo, Kabui (the White-Haired One), and Mlango wa Simba (the Entrance to the Lion)—seemed to consider it their duty to work the convicts to death. Production pressures combined with the pervasive exterminationist attitude toward Mau Mau to create a uniquely perverse environment, even for the Pipeline. Major Helo, for example, had a habit of forcing the convicts to kneel down every evening and pray to God that they would live another day. He called them all "bloody Mau Mau savages," while his comrade Mlango wa Simba preferred to inform the convicts, "You all will die a terrible death," often making good on his threat.[118] Many went mad at Embakasi, some committing suicide, others self-mutilating. Recalling his time there, Hunja broke down, regained his composure, and slowly described the place known as "Satan's Paradise."

> Let me assure you that no single group that arrived at Embakasi left with the same number. Many of them had to die; that was the order of the place. People used to be killed, not because of the sickness in other camps, though that happened sometimes, but because of the beatings. The *askaris* and the *Wazungu* [Europeans] did not need any good excuse in order to beat a Mau Mau to death. Some people used to go crazy in the morning during our porridge when they remembered that they would go to the field to do the backbreaking work. Some would go mad and pick up the toilet buckets and start splashing everybody while at the same time screaming. Some would place their hands on the *ndaba* [soil carriers that moved on rails] so as to sever their limbs and escape from the work. Because it did not matter whether one worked hard or not, or whether one carried hundreds of basins full of soil, because if the *askari* looked at him and decided to beat him, he would just set upon him with his club. The work and the beatings at Embakasi were incomparable with anything I had witnessed before or ever since.[119]

"Form C'ed," or transferred to detainee status, at the end of his sentence, Hunja was sent to Manyani, where he spent nearly two more years before he finally confessed. "I could not persevere with life any more," he later recalled. "I had worked too much. I had buried too many bodies. I felt defeated." The screening team reclassified him from "black" to "grey" and recommended his transfer down the Pipeline. With scores of other cooperative detainees, Hunja spent two days in an enclosed railcar en route to Sagana station—the Pipeline's hub for the works camps in the three Kikuyu districts of Kiambu, Murang'a, and Nyeri, as well as those in neighboring Embu and Meru. Once there, reception teams of British officers and guards separated the detainees according to their districts of origin and sent them on, via lorry or chain gang, to their final destination. Should any of these men have had the inclination to look up when they arrived at their destination, they would have seen the arch of the gate, on which would be emblazoned a slogan. At Aguthi Camp detainees were greeted with large letters that read, "He Who Helps Himself Will Also Be Helped." Fort Hall's main camp—which the detainees called Kwa Futi—bore the sign "Abandon Hope All Ye Who Enter Here." For a time at Ngenya Camp the gate was decorated with the command "Labor and Freedom."[120] These slogans hardly evoke images of the rehabilitation paradise being peddled by Governor Baring and the colonial secretary to the media and anticolonial critics; instead, they recollect the one at Solovetsky in the Soviet gulag that read, "Through Labor—Freedom!," and of course Auschwitz's infamous "Arbeit Macht Frei" (Work Makes You Free).

Hunja arrived at Aguthi Camp in the midst of an afternoon downpour. Along with other inductees, he was held down by the *askaris*, his head shaved and his clothes and shackles removed. They were then greeted by the camp commandant—a man the detainee's nicknamed Karuahu, or the Mongoose. Standing in front of his newest lot, he announced, "You have just entered a works camp, and you are going to learn the meaning of this term."[121] This forbidding welcome was an accurate introduction to an average works-camp day: building terraces up the steep ridges, marching long distances to break stones in a quarry, and at other times performing what one man called "nonsense work." "You know," Hunja said, "we would be ordered sometimes to take our basins to go and empty the river and would spend the whole day scooping water out and dumping it on the bank. Other times we would dig very large holes and then fill them up again. Karuahu just wanted to make us miserable, and he was very good at it."[122]

There was incentive in the works camps to comply and fully acquiesce. Karuahu and the other commandants could always send a detainee back up the Pipeline to the so-called hard-core camps. Unrepentant men also faced the risk of summary executions. To be released, detainees had to convince the local screening teams and the camp personnel that they were fully purged of their Mau Mau sympathies, and that they had divulged all of their knowledge of past Mau Mau activities. In practice, this was an incremental process. Even in the works camps many men tried their best to avoid naming names, providing as much false intelligence as possible. Camp authorities knew this and would move detainees through several compounds in a single works camp, each successive compound assigned to detainees who had evinced greater cooperation. Cooperation entailed not only working hard, singing Christian hymns enthusiastically, and shouting anti–Mau Mau propaganda, but also providing truthful and accurate intelligence.

In Hunja's case it took him nearly two years to reach the so-called release compound. But even then, he was still not headed straight for home. Instead, he was handed over to his chief, who himself operated a mini–detention camp—or, in British colonial parlance, an open camp. There detainees like

Aguthi Camp gate slogan: "He Who Helps Himself Will Also Be Helped."

Hunja would stay for several weeks, sometimes more, kept under the watchful eyes and loose clubs of the loyalists. As was the case everywhere in the Pipeline, detainees were a ready and free source of labor. From the open camps they were sent to the loyalists' farms—drawing water, tending livestock, and planting crops. They built miles of bench terraces and cleared bracken for the chiefs, often while being taunted by the Home Guards for their Mau Mau pasts and the uncertain economic and marital futures that awaited them when they returned home.

The Pipeline was based upon the principles of organized terror, violence, and degradation, all applied in an environment where space, time, and social exchange were completely organized and routinized. Mau Mau suspects were subjected to constant control: when they woke up, when they ate, when they were head-counted, when they went to work, how long they labored, when they urinated and defecated, when they went to sleep. Freedom was eliminated, and violence, or the threat of it, was part of every waking and sleeping moment.

Each camp or prison was a closed universe where Mau Mau suspects were confined and where those in command operated with a free hand. In fact, it was this free hand that led to enormous variation in experiences in the Pipeline world, with the personalities, antagonisms, and dependencies of the camp commandants, the guards, and the detainees shaping official policies to create closed societies that were, to varying degrees, unique to each camp. Nonetheless, the purpose of the camps was the same throughout the Pipeline: to force Mau Mau suspects together, to destroy their social ties outside of the camp, and to devastate their lives, all with the ultimate goal of breaking their resistance and forcing them to comply with British colonial rule.

Nevertheless, at the close of 1956 there were still tens of thousands of resolute detainees in the Pipeline continuing to stand up to torture, humiliation, deprivation, and harsh labor. They refused to break, their time in the Pipeline making them more resolute and determined in their commitment to Mau Mau. Increasingly embittered by the colonial government's treatment, they would not, in the words of one man, "give the camp authorities the satisfaction" of forcing them to confess.[123] Some like Nderi continued to pray to Ngai and to conspire against the screening teams, despite the increasing numbers of informants and worsening camp conditions. "We decided not to speak any longer," he later recalled, "after being beaten so much and seeing many of our comrades die. We decided nothing would change our minds; nothing mattered to us anymore. We were prepared to die."[124] Eventually, Nderi would move out of Manyani and up the Pipeline, only to break, as others would. Although the will of these men was strong, so was the grip of the colonial government.

CHAPTER SEVEN

THE HARD CORE

Letter from Mau Mau prisoners at Embakasi, December 1956

In the case of subversive leaders it is quite clear that steps must be taken in some way for their neutralization or liquidation. —ELECTORS' UNION, *August 1952*

Those who have not had the opportunity of interviewing the hard core Mau Mau to whom I refer, can have little conception of their mental attitude. They are, to say the least of it, homicidal lunatics and should be treated as such. It would be dangerous in the extreme to release, under any circumstances, men of this type, and the person who does so should be required to answer for those murdered, as victims there will surely be. To release these psychopathic, hard core lunatics would be tantamount to opening the doors of Broadmoor. — G.E.C. ROBERTSON,
community development officer in charge of screening
Mageta Island and Saiyusi camps, May 1955[1]

FROM THE START OF THE EMERGENCY THERE WAS NEVER A QUESTION in the minds of Governor Baring, the colonial secretary, their men on the spot, or the settlers that the Mau Mau leadership had at all costs to be eliminated. As the war stretched on, the impulse to eradicate the movement's leaders shifted to include permanently eliminating all hard-core detainees. Every individual Mau Mau who refused to cooperate with the colonial government in the Pipeline, and who therefore constituted a threat to the long-term viability of British rule and influence in Kenya, was ipso facto hard-core. This included the original Mau Mau intelligentsia who had been detained early in the Emergency during Operation Jock Scott, the presumed secondary and tertiary organizers whom the colonial government arrested in later operations, and the captured forest fighters and leaders of the passive wing. It also included those detainees who as a result of their experiences in the Pipeline had been hardened into strong unrepentance. As they were reclassified by the screening teams, these detainees were relabeled militants, politicals, or, in the introductory quotation from G. E. C. Robertson, one of the reformers from Askwith's Community Development and Rehabilitation Department, "homicidal lunatics."

There were various techniques for dealing with the hard core. Some, according to a former settler who was a member of the Kenya Regiment, "were handpicked out of the camps." He went on, "We would be given word that we were needed at, say, the camps out in Lake Victoria, and we would go and pick up a few of the filthy pigs and bring them to one of the interrogation centers set up by the CID. These were the hard-core scum, the ones who wouldn't listen to anyone and [were] causing trouble. So we would give them a good thrashing. It would be a bloody awful mess by the time we were done. . . . Never knew a Kuke had so many brains until we cracked open a few heads."[2] Former detainees also recall several of their compound mates in the up-Pipeline camps being led away and never returning. "At first we just thought they were taken to be screened," recalled Wilson Njoroge. "But when they failed to return, we asked if they had been transferred. [The British officer in charge] just smiled and said, 'Oh no, they have found their *wiyathi* [freedom], and you'll soon join them if you don't start cooperating.' "[3]

With incomplete documentation in the official archives, we will likely never know if targeted eliminations were part of the colonial government's policy. What is apparent, however, is the support and energy the colonial government invested in the plan to exile permanently twelve thousand of the hard core, or irreconcilables, as they were also called. Baring, in particular, obsessed over the exile policy, believing that future loyalist support and British control over the colony depended on it. In late 1954 he created the Resettlement Committee, one of whose responsibilities was overseeing the design and creation of exile camps. Soon plans were under way to deal with the "unrepentant hard-core Mau Mau detainees," as the committee called them. They were "evil" and destined to spend the rest of their lives in some inhospitable parts of Kenya. The largest exile settlement was slated for the area of Hola, located on the malarial Tana River, in Coast Province. There, detainees "of a less evil disposition" would be allowed to bring their families; the others would remain separated from their wives and children for the rest of their lives.[4]

Baring consistently reminded European settlers and Africans alike that exile camps and settlements would be lasting features of Kenya's landscape. In a widely publicized speech given in Nyeri District in January 1955, the governor announced to the crowd: "The Government's policy regarding irreconcilables has already been declared. On 8th September last year, the Secretary of State for the Colonies, Mr. Lennox-Boyd, stated in Nairobi that he could say on behalf of Her Majesty's Government that irreconcilables would not be allowed to return. He said 'there is no question whatsoever of irreconcilables being allowed to return to areas where loyal Kikuyu live.' "[5]

These high-level officials were making assurances about permanent exile knowing full well that such policies were in violation of international conventions. H. Steel, a legal adviser from Britain's Home Office, voiced concern to both the Colonial Office and Foreign Office that the long-term exile policies in force in Kenya were problematic.[6] The colonial government had managed to derogate the European Convention on Human Rights and to enforce its policy of detention without trial because there was a State of Emergency in place. Once Governor Baring were to lift the Emergency, however, the Convention could no longer be sidestepped. Moreover, if colonial officials were planning on forcing detainees in permanent exile to work, which was exactly the plan, then they would be in continued violation of the International Labour Organization (ILO) Convention. But "national security" was to take priority over any conventions to which Britain was a party. The colonial government believed it could not maintain power in Kenya if such arbitrary measures as detention without trial were not at its disposal. In the words of one of the Colonial Office's undersecretaries, William Gorell Barnes, "If we are to maintain our authority in Kenya . . . there can, I fear, be no doubt that in one way or another the Governor will need to be given these powers."[7]

The Hola exile plan was a massive undertaking. Even with an unlimited supply of detainee labor at its disposal, it was not until late 1955 that the colonial government could even break ground. The African Land Development Board, or ALDEV, had to survey and design engineering plans for irrigating some twenty thousand acres of previously uncultivated land. To start the development, hundreds of men were removed from their compounds at Manyani, shackled, and transferred to the banks of the Tana River, where they were forced to dig an eleven-mile canal by hand.[8] The plan was to develop a fully economic rice-growing scheme that would support up to seven thousand exiled detainees, along with as many as twenty thousand to twenty-five thousand of their dependents. To strike a preemptive blow at any future "public danger," as Governor Baring termed the potential release of these hard-core detainees, he and his men on the spot were creating a community for them and their families in the middle of nowhere.[9]

The colonial government's fears were justified. If the masses of Mau Mau detainees were empowering themselves through the spread of knowledge in the Pipeline, then the so-called politicals, especially those arrested during the early days of the Emergency, were turning the camps into classrooms for anticolonial organization and future action. Locked up together, they took advantage of their confinement to discuss the illegitimacy and inequities of colonial rule, the hypocrisies of loyalist support and reward schemes, and the need for a land reform system that was free from control by colonial self-interest.[10] In the words of Eric Kamau, a political detainee at Athi River, "We were planning for our release, when we would take over the country and implement the ideas we were putting together in the camps."[11] These men were clearly a threat to the future of Britain's trusteeship in Kenya, rendering them, a priori, subversive criminals. These troublemakers were viewed as preying on the inherent backwardness of the Kikuyu masses, who were, according to colonial officials, incapable of deciding between right and wrong. Baring and Lennox-Boyd were not, according to their own rhetoric, proposing exile camps for British political gain, but were instead merely protecting the majority of Africans from these allegedly manipulative, self-interested leaders. For Baring and Lennox-Boyd, it was simply one more regrettable and unavoidable consequence of the White Man's Burden.

In the wake of the Kapenguria trial those believed to be the most evil of the Mau Mau masterminds were safely locked away in the desert wilderness of Lokitaung. It was there that Jomo Kenyatta, Bildad Kaggia, Paul Ngei, and the three others, having been convicted by the corrupt Judge Thacker of using their "power and influence over the less educated Africans [to implement] this foul scheme of driving the Europeans from Kenya," lived in total isolation.[12] If the colonial government's objective was for these six men to dwell in utter discomfort, it was realized. Conditions at Lokitaung were bleak. It was a lifeless place of sandstorms and hellish heat.

The Mau Mau prisoners had no outside human contact other than with their warders and the British officers in charge, and possibly with an occasional nomadic Turkana herdsman.

Days were filled with work, generally of the nonsense sort. For months the men at Lokitaung labored on a purposeless trench, then moved to making ballast. During 1954 and 1955, they spent each day breaking rocks into tiny pieces, enough to fill six four-gallon tins a day. Exempt from this work was Kenyatta, whom camp officials had classified as "fit for light duties."[13] He became the designated cook for the group, a comparatively easy task, though as Bildad Kaggia later pointed out, "in such a hot climate [cooking] was more tormenting than hard labour."[14] Like thousands in the Pipeline, these so-called managers of Mau Mau also suffered variously from malaria, pellagra, dysentery, and dehydration. Just twenty miles south of the Sudanese border, Lokitaung had an average rainfall of less than one inch per year. There was a chronic shortage of water, and the prisoners found their rations constantly reduced, making bathing or washing clothes an occasional luxury. But, as Bildad Kaggia pointed out years later, "had the local district officer not had a swimming pool filled with clean water, maybe there would have been more for us to drink."[15]

The men of Lokitaung knew they were facing years of enforced isolation. Colonial officials seemed to delight in reminding them, over and over again, that they would be locked away "indefinitely." Strict discipline was enforced, and while the prisoners did not endure the extensive physical tortures suffered by other detainees, they were subjected to other kinds of abuse and deprivation. For this elite group of Africans, though, it was the radical shift in the quality of their lives that affected them most. As Jomo Kenyatta later reflected:

> There are more subtle ways of breaking a widely-traveled man whose life had been rich, and dedicated, and full of promise: the psychology of nothingness, the impeccable correctness of prison discipline and nomenclature, like a slap of contempt, the absence of human contact, slow passage of remorseless days of torridity and dust and meaningless surroundings. There was nothing green, nothing cool, nothing creative, nothing demanding, nothing at all.[16]

Kenyatta's prison experience began to differ from that of his fellow convicts at Lokitaung. It was not long before he was isolated socially and later physically from the other men. By 1954 the group included two new convicts, Kariuki Chotara and the famed General China, who had been wounded and captured by the British security forces in the forests of Mount

Kenya. It had also lost one of the original Kapenguria Six. Achieng' Oneko was sent to Manda Island Camp as a detainee after his Kapenguria conviction was overturned, the justices believing that as a Luo, Oneko was incapable of directing Mau Mau. Despite Oneko's departure, the character of the group changed little. The majority wanted to use their time in Lokitaung to discuss structures and articulate ideologies that would remake Kikuyu and Kenyan society once they were released. Despite all that was said to them, they held hope that they would one day be free, and that they would assume their roles as leaders of the country. They sought to transform their oppressive prison experience into an opportunity to plan the future challenge to the power of the colonial state. At Lokitaung they even created their own National Democratic Party with officers, a constitution, ministerial positions, and even a party slogan: Liberty, Equality, and Justice.[17]

Kenyatta, however, stayed out of prison politics. Paradoxically, at the same time that the "cult of Kenyatta" was spreading through the Pipeline, this presumed martyr to the Kikuyu cause was apparently jettisoning any anti-European or antiloyalist politics. In a situation where prisoners were desperate for human contact and spirited discussion, Kenyatta refused to join the prisoners' political party. He did not agree with their agenda. Lokitaung seemed to render transparent Kenyatta's true political leanings, which were, according to the other men, scarcely in line with Mau Mau doctrine. Kaggia, in particular, has been vocal about Kenyatta's conservative and even loyalist sympathies.

> Kenyatta was not one of us in prison. He had married a woman whose father was a chief, and because of that when we went to prison, he was often on the side of the conservatives and the government. I became the leader of the group in his place, though we were all disappointed. . . . The camp commandant later separated him from us because of our arguments. One day he and Chotara got into a fistfight, allegedly because Kenyatta was selling some of our food to the *askaris,* but it was also because we didn't agree with his politics.[18]

That Kenyatta needed to be separated, perhaps for his own safety, was a known fact in certain administrative circles in the British colonial government. Later reflecting on this, Askwith said simply, "Kenyatta was not a militant, and the other Mau Mau leaders knew this. . . . It just took government some time to come to terms with this when circumstances forced the governor and others, like myself, to radically alter their view of this man."[19]

.   .   .

It was the thousands of other hard-core men and women who posed the much larger problem for the colonial government. Regardless of their label—militants, fanatics, politicals, lunatics, irreconcilables, obdurate savages, hard-core scum—these detainees spent years in the Pipeline before Hola or any of the other proposed exile settlements were ready. Many men and even some women who entered the camps as ordinary Mau Mau were radicalized by their desperate conditions and by their fellow detainees. Rather than capitulating, they became more resolute. As one former detainee put it, "Even when I had been reduced to nothing, I knew I couldn't give in. To save myself for what? A life with no land. A life under the thumb of the *Wazungu* and those African stooges. In my mind, that was no life. For many years I thought there was nothing they could do to me that would make me cooperate. I thought for certain I would end up like so many others. Dead."[20]

Governor Baring personally signed the detention orders for the first wave of this hard-core group. They were arrested in the early days of the war and shipped to the outskirts of Nairobi, where Taxi Lewis's men had prepared two "internee camps," as they were then called—one at Kajiado and another, larger one at Athi River. Among those awaiting their arrival was S. H. La Fontaine, an officer in the Administration who was in charge of camp organization and discipline. At his side was David Waruhiu, the son of the recently assassinated Senior Chief Waruhiu. Young Waruhiu was becoming a favored loyalist, and Governor Baring eventually appointed him a temporary district officer. Throughout the Emergency he was in charge of all screening operations at Athi River Camp. In later years, he would take his father's place as the darling of the colonial government, a true exemplar of loyalism and British, Christian values.

The detainees christened Athi River the "Queen's Lodge" and its renowned screening officer Mtoto wa Waruhiu, or Waruhiu's Child.[21] For their part, the governor and his Resettlement Committee considered Athi River a "holding camp for the deeply indoctrinated Mau Mau" and pursued a policy of screening, segregating, and "reeducating" these detainees not because they foresaw releasing them but because they were viewed as excellent sources of intelligence.[22]

Mau Mau intelligentsia were not ordinary detainees. According to official reports, "a high percentage of them appeared well above the average in intelligence and education."[23] As in other camps in the Pipeline, they had developed their own committees and rules; they also became particularly adept at fabricating false information and then carefully coordinating their stories for the screening teams. La Fontaine would need to marshal all of the resources at his disposal to break these men, a point that hardly escaped him. Only "by hard work and discipline, by propaganda, by mass education and other means," he wrote, would the British colonial government succeed in its objectives at Athi River.[24]

The variety of forces that converged on the Queen's Lodge made it unique. There were dozens of Christian missionaries, including Reverend Howard Church, who eventually became the camp's ideological training officer, and Father Colleton, who assumed the post of educational officer. Most curiously, Alan Knight—the leader of Kenya's branch of Moral Rearmament, or MRA—became camp commandant at Athi River, answerable only to La Fontaine and the governor himself. MRA espoused a kind of ersatz Christian faith, pushing a doctrine of personal justification through works alone. The doctrine espoused four absolute standards: honesty, purity, unselfishness, and love. Typically, MRA focused its conversion efforts on a society's leaders. Under Knight's camp command it became one of several Christian messages deployed against the detainees at Athi River. Together the various missionaries pummeled the detainees with lectures, sermons, and nightly public broadcasts that blared the message of the Lord. Or, in the case of MRA, the message of Frank Buchman—the movement's founder and spiritual leader.[25]

Former detainees scarcely recall Athi River as a site of spiritual awakening, perhaps because they were cycled through an endless regime of physical and psychological coercion. Knight himself insisted, "Rigid discipline is the keynote of Athi, and hard work the basis of everything. . . . A man whose body is disciplined and subject to control, will be more open to subjecting his mind to control."[26] Detainees were forced to work, and if they refused, their rations were reduced. They might spend days with no food and then, half starved and dehydrated, they could be subjected to hours of preaching and lectures on Christian ethics and the virtues of Britain's civilizing mission. Camp officials also imported scores of Home Guards from the Kikuyu districts, who took to the camp broadcasting system, denouncing Mau Mau and publicly dividing detainees into "murderers, thugs, leaders, and fellow travelers," according to Father Colleton.[27] Screening teams, led by Mtoto wa Waruhiu, himself an ardent MRA convert, worked the detainees over as well, interrogating them incessantly. As one man who was held at Athi River for over a year recalled later:

> Waruhiu would stand outside of a compound and shout, "People who killed my father, you come with me." The person singled out would then be taken for screening. When my turn came, they beat me with kicks, a hose, and anything else they could get their hands on. They jumped on me, while Waruhiu would demand to know what I knew, telling me to confess. The

whole time making fun of me and laughing at my suffering. After that I urinated blood for several days. Because I refused to talk, I was again forced out to work, which I did so they would feed me.[28]

Following a detainee's willingness to work, he would be separated and put into a compound with others who were softening up. In total there were ten compounds at Athi River, nine of them holding one of three categories of political detainee. Camp officials and screening teams labeled them "A—Hard Core, B—Old & Stupid, and C—Reclaimable."[29] But even with constant shuffling of As, Bs, and Cs, there often appeared to be little difference in political attitude between the various compounds. As one colonial official reported, "They employed similar phrases and a common manner in denying any knowledge of Mau Mau," and went on to warn of "the clannishness of the detainees who have a common idea and ample time to work out their plans."[30] This, despite the fact that Knight and his men were bringing everything they could to bear on the Mau Mau suspects. They screened them, starved them, humiliated them, worked those they could, and inundated everyone with masses of Bibles, MRA literature, and Christian handouts that were passed out for "compound reflection time."[31]

Much of this material was put to use as toilet paper, but some of it was read. The story of the Israelites, beginning with Exodus, was a favorite among the Athi River detainees, as it was for other men in the Pipeline. It had a remarkable impact upon many of the Mau Mau suspects, one that could not have been intended by the missionaries. Many of the politicals were familiar with the Old Testament prior to being arrested, but their time in the camps prompted them to reinterpret the Bible within the context of their tightening repression. They created their own liberation theology, likening themselves to the children of Israel.[32] As one man later told me, "Sometimes we would be issued with Bibles, the Gideon Bibles. But we would only read the verses we liked, which we repeated over and over again. We particularly liked the verse in the book of Lamentations, chapter seven which talks of Prophet Jeremiah's lamentations because of the children of Israel. We liked it because it seemed to apply very well to our case, and the way we were being punished just like the Israelites."[33] Later in the Emergency many Athi River men were transferred to other hard-core camps, taking their Bibles with them. But at camps like Mageta, G. E. C. Robertson scarcely considered the "homicidal lunatics" under his charge capable of extracting political meaning from religious texts. Writing to Askwith in late 1956, he observed: "Another very interesting matter disclosed during the month [of September 1956] was the significant fact that many apparently hard-core Mau Mau possessed Bibles and used them solely for practising soothsaying."[34]

Though detainee cooperation was not widespread among the hard core, there were some notable confessors. At the top of the list was Peter Muigai Kenyatta, Jomo Kenyatta's son, who became an enthusiastic colonial supporter, joining forces with the screening teams and undergoing a transformation similar to that of other surrenders at Manyani, Mageta, Mara River, and elsewhere. In the case of the younger Kenyatta and some of the other politicals as well, one wonders how much they had actually changed. In other words, was Peter simply his father's son? He visited his father in detention to inform him of his screening activities at Athi River and to seek his approval.[35] The elder Kenyatta must have granted his blessing because Peter bore a red star on his breast pocket for nearly the entire Emergency, the colonial government's symbol for detainees at Athi River who surrendered and joined the screening teams. The other detainees ridiculed these political surrenders, derisively calling them the Wise Men of the Star and warning Peter in particular that his father, *Mzee* Kenyatta, would deal with him when the war was over. It was not until years after the Emergency that former detainees would realize how grossly they had miscalculated both father and son.

With scores of other Athi River detainees, Gakaara wa Wanjau was given no warning of his imminent transfer. He was headed for the worst of the hard-core camps on Manda Island, a place located in the Indian Ocean just off Kenya's northern coast, and notable for its overwhelming heat and humidity, voracious mosquitoes, and virulent strain of malaria. The journey took three days. The detainees traveled in a relay of different transports—lorries, enclosed boxcars, and a cargo ship, the latter two inadequately ventilated, with toilet buckets overflowing and food and water "considered luxuries by the British officers in charge," according to Gakaara.[36] When he and the others finally arrived, they found they were in prestigious company. After Lokitaung, Manda Island and nearby Takwa held the colony's most subversive and therefore elite politicals, men who created enormous problems for the colonial government not just outside of the camps but within them as well.

That Gakaara was shipped to "Mau Mau University," as colonial officials called Manda Island, was no surprise. He was among the 181 Mau Mau politicals originally arrested during Operation Jock Scott, and an intellectual driving force behind the rise of Kikuyu nationalism after the Second World War. He had been educated at the Tumutumu Presbyterian mission in Nyeri and went on to Alliance High School, an important training ground for other African politicians, like Paul Ngei and Achieng' Oneko. He then joined the British army.[37] Embittered by his wartime experience, he later wrote, "I knew that this war was not our war. I could not, however, stand aloof from the maltreatment of and discrimination against black servicemen practiced by the British imperialists. It is not possible to give an indication here of the magnitude of that maltreatment and discrimination."[38] When he returned, he channeled his energies into writing and became the first great homegrown intellectual living in rural Kenya. He wrote and published books, songs, pamphlets, and a monthly magazine in the Kikuyu vernacular, all with an anticolonial message.

Gakaara was not alone. In the years immediately before Mau Mau there was a proliferation of newspapers and magazines published by Kikuyu intellectuals—men like Henry Muoria Mwaniki, Bildad Kaggia, and John Cege.[39] Gakaara was gifted in his use of idiomatic forms, proverbial turns of speech, and analogy. To the ordinary reader, particularly a colonial censor, his writings would appear innocuous, though for Kikuyu they were politically charged. The government eventually banned Gakaara's writings as subversive. Catapulting him to the top of the "black list" was surely the publication in August 1952 of his *Creed of Gikuyu and Mumbi*. A glance at it reveals how closely Gakaara modeled it on the Christian creed, and how clever this intellectual was in integrating literary and biblical form with anticolonial politics.

> I believe in God the Almighty Father, Creator of Heaven and Earth. And I believe in Gikuyu and Mumbi our dear ancestral parents to whom God bequeathed this our land. Their children were persecuted in the era of Cege and Waiyaki by the clan of white people, they were robbed of their government and their land and relegated to the status of humiliated menials. Their children's children had their eyes opened, they achieved the light of a great awareness and they fought to restore their parents to their seats of glory. And I believe in the holy religious ceremonies of Gikuyu and Mumbi, and I believe in the good leadership of Kenyatta and Mbiyu and the unbreakable solidarity between the Mwangi and Irungu generations and the oneness of the nine full Gikuyu clans and the everlastingness of the Gikuyu Nation.[40]

Gakaara's writings have influenced generations of Kikuyu. Later postcolonial politics and culture would draw inspiration from his essays and poetry, books and songs. But in the context of this story, the diary that Gakaara kept during his years in the Pipeline is the most significant work in his otherwise remarkable literary production. That he was able to write, keep safe, and eventually publish this diary was extraordinary, given the conditions of the camps. During the first four years of his detention, he kept a small wooden box that contained a false bottom. In it he hid several sixteen-page exercise books into which he recorded his experiences and those of the other detainees, first at Athi River and then at Manda Island. In 1956, when he was transferred back to Athi River, Gakaara feared the box would be confiscated. He bribed a warder to take it to his shop at Karatina, where he planned for his wife to recover it once she was released from detention. The plan worked. Many years later he added a recollection of his final four years of detention to the original diary, making his completed account, titled *Mau Mau Author in Detention*, vital historical evidence.

In it, Gakaara describes Manda Island as a hotbed of conflict. The detainees were well aware of their rights as defined under international law and refused initially to cooperate in any way. The colonial government had listed the site as a special detention camp and could therefore, based upon its earlier exercise in legal gymnastics, force the detainees to work. When the men refused, food rations were cut. When they still refused, water was eliminated. Camp officers would order beatings and a trip to the punishment cells for the most minor or even imagined infractions. Men like La Fontaine and Dr. Alfred Becker, the camp's community development officer, or Askwith's man on the spot, wanted compliance, not just with work orders but with their demands for intelligence. The idea was that the one begat the other. A degree of cooperation in the fields or the local public work project would lead, so the theory went, to an eventual breakdown in resistance and finally to the divulgence of vital information.

Camp officials were successful. Some men buckled under the pressure and deprivations and agreed to work. In return, they were separated from the other "noncooperators"—as the government labeled them—in Compound 1 and transferred to Compound 2, or the "cooperator" compound. There, they were provided with adequate rations, allowed to take a limited number of correspondence classes with universities in England and South Africa, and enjoyed more freedom to move about the island. As at Athi River, this policy reflected a divide-and-rule strategy tailored to conditions in the camp. Still, colonial officials constantly searched for new ways to drive a wedge between detainees. One favored approach was to call in David Waruhiu and his screening teams from Athi River, who were later praised endlessly by Alan Knight for their ability to "break those evil men at Manda Island."[41]

There was also the "Becker Touch." Officials in the Colonial Office used this phrase to describe Dr. Becker's unorthodox methods of persuasion and overall dealings with the detainees.[42] In early 1954, for instance, he launched his Operation Bibi. As the community development officer, he was ostensibly responsible for the rehabilitation and moral uplift of the detainees in Britain's "concentration camps," as Becker liked to call them.[43] In fact, Becker and several men from the CID were in charge of the interrogation center on nearby Lamu Island. Detainees would be brought in from Manda, and, along with the usual strong-arm tactics, Becker would tell them that their wives and children were starving in the reserves, living in poverty, and being physically and sexually abused by the Home Guards. Their Mau Mau politics and obstinacy were at the root of this suffering, he would tell them. If they cooperated, they could go home and protect their loved ones. Such ploys, combined with other, more traditional methods of persuasion, sometimes worked. Several of the politicals began confessing and were moved along to Compound 2. Of course, none were released. They were still destined for permanent exile.[44]

Gakaara was among those in Compound 1 who would not cooperate. Along with others, he devised various strategies to defend against the colonial offensive. Over and over again they refused to participate in any labor project, incensing the British officer in charge, Commandant Martin. The situation came to a head when the commandant stood outside the compound and declared:

> You are great fools because you have failed to realize that you were isolated in this remote island because the Government had given up on you, and you were now being left to your fate; it was your business if all of you died. Look on every side: you are surrounded by the sea. Where could you escape to? We need not even keep a substantial number of guards on this island. A guard manning the watchtower would suffice—to pass on information when any one of you drops dead so that his body could be collected for dumping into the sea.[45]

Turning on his heels, Martin departed, telling the noncooperators that their food and water would be left for them outside the compound gate and could be picked up only on the way back from a full day's work. The detainees refused. For days they went without food rations, but it was the lack of water in the extraordinary heat of Kenya's tropical coast that soon became unbearable. Under the cover of darkness, the men decided to dig a well. With the injured and weak standing watch, the rest used their hands and tin cups to scoop down twelve feet until they hit muddy water. At daybreak, blankets covered the well sufficiently to dupe the guards during their many inspections. It was not long, however, before the men of Compound 1 became seriously ill from their unclean water supply. Hunger also took its toll, and the few pieces of meat and loaves of bread smuggled in from Compound 2 were not enough to keep them alive. Many were too weak to stand; some were urinating and defecating blood; others became delirious. In the end they broke, agreeing in return for food and water to work on a new addition to Britain's gulag to be built on the other side of the island.[46]

The detainees' most powerful weapon at Manda was their political know-how. This political sophistication was what made them so dangerous to the colonial government in the first place, and this did not change in the camps. It was there, inside the wire, that Gakaara and many of the others continued doing what they did best. They wrote. More specifically, they wrote letters, dozens and dozens of letters. These men were clearly aware that external attention was imperative if their situation stood any chance of being improved. They chronicled conditions in the camps and smuggled the correspondence out through a variety of methods. They bribed guards, folded letters into the pages of the educational correspondence books, and even stuffed notes into bottles that were then tossed into the sea. They targeted British colonial politicians of any persuasion. Pleas for a reprieve in work routines, an end to coercion, increased rations, and greater access to reading material were all posted to Governor Baring and the colonial secretary, ministers in the local government and members of Kenya's Legislative Council, Labour MPs and members of the Kenya Committee living in Britain, as well as Queen Elizabeth herself.

Letter writing was not limited to Manda Island. Though many of the most sophisticated politicals were confined in that camp, scores of lesser Mau Maus were scattered throughout the Pipeline. Men like J. M. Kariuki, whom the British colonial government considered to be less politically dangerous, were shipped off to Manyani with tens of thousands of other detainees. There J. M. assumed the role of compound leader, presenting collective complaints to the camp commandant and apprising the other detainees of their rights. He and others like him also began letter-writing campaigns. When these men were transferred up and down the Pipeline, along with them went their knowledge of anticolonial politics and the art of correspondence. Soon, detainees all over Kenya were writing. By the end of the Emergency hundreds of these letters had reached virtually every high-level colonial official and many in Parliament as well.

Several files of these letters managed to escape the official purge. The Kenya National Archives in Nairobi contains hundreds of letters written by detainees, their contents ranging from indignation over detention without trial, to absolute desperation when chronicling camp conditions, forced

Letter signed "Yours Black African Detainees in Manyani Camp"

labor, torture, starvation, and murder. These letters are key pieces of historical documentation from this period. Many offer rich details about life in the camps and validate later oral testimonies and the handful of existing memoirs. But their significance is greater. With these letters the colonial government, including the governor and colonial secretary in London, could never credibly claim to have been in the dark about the tragedy of the Pipeline. Colonial officials at the highest level were intimately aware of its brutal details.

"What is the meaning of the word emergency? Is emergency inhuman deeds?"[47] "Is it the British law that when they have got the captives not to get enough food?"[48] "Where does custration [*sic*] come from? Is that the democrat law?"[49] "Is this the British system or the Nazi system?"[50] These are just a few of the questions detainees posed in their letters. They wanted the governor, the colonial secretary, and others to explain the meaning of

British colonial law and democratic civilization, because the Pipeline world in which they were living seemed to them a travesty of these ideals. It was a universe where rehabilitation was synonymous with brutality and British colonial rule an abrogation of basic human rights. These letters reveal that within the camps British hypocrisy had nowhere to hide; human action and colonial rhetoric were clearly understood by detainees for what they were.

Detainees did not write abstractly about torture. They gave colonial officials detailed accounts of what was being done to them, and who was doing it. According to their illicit correspondence, detainees were beaten by warders, camp commandants, officers in charge, rehabilitation teams, and screening teams. Among their weapons of choice were "permabox handles and rifle buts [*sic*]," rhino whips, batons, and chains. At Athi River the men from Compounds 5 and 10 wrote to Taxi Lewis, the commissioner of prisons, "We hope the time is ripe when everyone in this country is prepared to make friendship amongst all races in Kenya. We therefore ask the government to safe [*sic*] us in this Camp of Athi River Detention Camp, from the practice which is going on since last week." They then went on to describe the new practice of "night screening." Interrogation teams would enter the compounds late at night and

> persons to be screened are handcuffed with their hands on their backs, then water starts to be poured on them 4 debes at a time in every hour's time. Then at 12 midnight soap is smeared on the head and by pouring water it gets to eyes of the detainees punished paining as anything when it gets into the eyes. At the same time pliers is also applied to work as the apparatus of castrating the testicles, and also at the ears. All these is done so as to make everyone attended to confess whether true or not to oblige him (them) to agree to what has been alleged against someone whether is true or not true as a result that none can resist these deeds some do confess and say yes so as to safe themselves from the troubles and hardships.[51]

Letters document that torture was not unique to Athi River but was commonplace up and down the Pipeline, and conditions were abysmal nearly everywhere. In Mageta Island Camp, which colonial officials used as one of the destinations for the worst hard core, detainees wrote often to the governor and to Kenya's attorney general, Eric Griffith-Jones, reporting on one occasion:

> An officer of the Special Branch who is now at Mageta is now badly beating detainees when interrogating them. . . . Heavy beatings take place and even

some of detainees have their testicles pulled. . . . It seems to us that he was sent here for torturing us and that is against the British Government laws. When detainees are taken to the Screening Officer far apart from the camp they are punished and beaten badly. Instead of their being taken to the Hospital, their put in cell and denied food for several days. These beatings are not done secretly as it led by Camp Commandant and he himself plays a great part in it, who ought to act against beatings, instead he is encouraging these beatings.[52]

In one letter a detainee in the holding camp at Manyani related some of the methods employed by the camp commandant and his chief warder. "I have been beaten badly," he wrote, "and tortured terribly in Manyani Camp. I was tortured in Compound No 6 and the mode of torture used was being beaten while necked [sic] climbing on each others back, sand and water being put into the rectum and other methods only fit to be done to animals and not to human beings; besides, I was suffering from amebic dysentery during those years."[53] This account is strikingly similar to more recent oral testimonies chronicling life in Compound 6, and the work of Wagithundia and Mapiga.[54]

Sexual violence was clearly a recurring theme in the detainee letters, much as it would be in later oral testimonies. Sexually abusing the detainees—whether through sodomy with foreign objects, animals, and insects, cavity searches, the imposition of a filthy toilet-bucket system, or forced penetrative sex—was one part of the broader dehumanization process that struck at the core of white fear. Throughout European colonial rule in Africa white men were terrified of the black man's purported sexuality. According to European myth, all black men had gargantuan-sized penises, and given the chance, these well-endowed "savages" would rape white women. Called the black peril, the African man's alleged sexual prowess was certainly a threat to European male sexuality and, by extension, to Europe's ability to establish and maintain dominance over their African colonies. Land was also at the heart of European domination. It was not just a critical material resource for the colonizers, but as with the Kikuyu, land was one of the fundamental bases of manhood for the European settlers in Kenya and elsewhere. Because land had held both economic and social meaning for the settlers, when Mau Mau adherents demanded it be returned they were not just threatening the material well-being of the British; they were affronting their masculinity as well. It's hardly shocking, then, that within the context of Mau Mau British colonial agents targeted the symbols of Kikuyu manhood: their land, their women, their children, and their bodies.

Whether conscious or not, sexual violence was a method of regaining masculine control. Indeed, how better to assert British male domination than to emasculate, literally, the enemy? The most grotesque form of this tactic was castration. Accounts of men's testicles being forcibly removed are widespread in various written and oral sources. J. M. Kariuki discussed castrations in his memoir, as did detainees in their illicit letters.[55] Men like those at Athi River referred to the castration pliers that were used throughout the Pipeline, as well as in the Kikuyu reserves. Apparently, this was an instrument devised to crush the men's testicles before they were eventually ripped off. In their oral accounts, other detainees also discussed castration pliers, along with other methods of beating and mutilating men's testicles. Colonial officials knew this was an ongoing practice, not only from the detainee letters but also from reports sent to them by the missionaries who were preaching in the camps. In one memorandum delivered to Governor Baring, the Christian Council of Kenya stated that British colonial agents were castrating Mau Mau suspects, and that on one occasion a man "had his private parts laid on a table and beaten till the scrotum burst because he would not speak."[56]

Detainee letters refer often to their "naked" conditions. In one account sent to "the Honourable Secretary of the States for the Colonies," John Gitiri wrote, "When we reached the camps, they robbed the money we had and our shoes and clothes. We were left nacked [*sic*] as we were born. Some of those things were given to the Home Guards and Askaris and they burnt the rest."[57] In another letter, signed "Black African Detainees in Manyani Camp," colonial officials were asked to "please urge them [the Manyani officers] not to take our clothes. . . . We are detainees. We are not animals to remain naked."[58] In Gatundu works camp, one of the down-Pipeline camps in Kiambu District, camp warders were notorious for stripping the detainees while they went out to work on the agricultural projects, for all of the locals to see.[59]

Reduced rations, forced starvations, lack of meat and vegetables, and the countless diseases caused by these deprivations were also the subjects of many letters.[60] Detainees wrote asking colonial officials to "go and urge the man who is supplyer [*sic*] of meat here [at Manyani] that we do not want him to supply us with heads and feet and stomachs of cattle nor we do not want the feet, heads and stomachs of pigs, we want meat itself to avoid bad diseases. They are very horrible meat."[61] Another letter, addressed to Kenya's chief secretary, Richard Turnbull, stated: "The food we are getting can not supply the energy required for a day's work. . . . Recently detainees have been punished by forced fast and work without break for lunch. This leads to the deterioration of the already poor health of poor detainees and should be discontinued."[62] But a reduction of food rations to the point of enforced starvation was one of the coercive tactics most favored by camp officials. It was never abandoned in the Pipeline. Instead, as the Emergency wore on, the British colonial government took deliberate steps to expand its use.

"CAMP CLEANLINESS is the worst nature since detainees use same buckets for lavatory uses and for bathing uses."[63] This was one of several issues voiced by "All the detainees from Aguthi Works Camp" in their letter to Governor Baring. The problem of hygiene, disease, and the lack of medical treatment was foremost in many detainee letters. On Mageta Island several men wrote, "We are very amazed to see ourselves being kept in a very dirty and entirely anti-hygiene Camp. The camp contains no water, we are to draw water from the lake, the same place we draw drinking and cooking water, the same place we wash our latrine buckets."[64] Detainees from all over the Pipeline asked for insecticide to help control the flies breeding around the drains and the toilet buckets, for shoes to prevent the spread of disease when they walked over human waste in their barracks, for a removal of the rats infesting their compounds, and for a modicum of medical care to address the "dangerous diseases" that were afflicting many of them.[65] In another letter, from Mageta Camp, the men wrote: "More than thirty (30) detainees are bloodly [sic] suffering diarrhoea, dysentery, which afterwards turns to Typhoid. Those with such sort of disease are kept in Compounds without treatments. This sounds in our mind as if we were brought here to be tortured, and if not we are kindly crying on you. Those diseases were mainly increased by lock-up and denial of food for eighty-six hours (86 hours) as from 21st to 25th of June, 1956. We have reported all these occurrences to both Commissioner and Deputy Commissioner of Prisons during visits to Mageta last month."[66]

Many detainees wondered how much longer they were going to survive. Some simply asked that they be shot rather than hung in the camps. Others requested that their leg irons be removed when they were shipped by boat to the island camps, to prevent any further "accidental" drownings. They begged colonial officials "to tell the Commandant to remove the hard labour he has planned to keep us in pain and misery" and to end the deadly cycle of starvation and forced labor.[67] They wanted relief from the small cells or the "dirty holes," as the men at Langata called them; according to other letters, such as one from Thiba Camp, detainees were punished and tortured in these cells for weeks on end.[68] From the reception camps, they asked that the commandants' guard dogs be restrained from biting and thrashing them. This was a problem in other camps as well, something noted not just by the detainees but by the community development officer at Mara River Camp, J. Bischoff. In a letter to Askwith, Bischoff wrote: "On their arrival at Mara River they [the detainees] were taken in front of the Officer in Charge who not only beat them badly but also had his Alsatian dog biting them on their legs. I would like to know whether the Officer in Charge is allowed to do this without the Commissioner's approval and also without having the detainees medically examined by the Station Medical Officer so as to see if they are fit to receive such treatment."[69]

Death was a fact of life in the Pipeline, something the detainees conveyed repeatedly to colonial officials. Lennox-Boyd was informed in one letter that "most of us are sick and people are dying daily and we are badly treated."[70] According to other detainees, men were dying from "head injuries," beatings, and the combined effects of torture, overwork, disease, and exhaustion.[71] At South Yatta Camp the irrigation furrow claimed numerous lives, including that of Karumbi Mugenda, also known as detainee number 2017. One man in his labor gang wrote to Taxi Lewis apprising him of the situation.

I should mention to you that, the entrusted people to chase people from the camp to work are warders who often send out very sick detainees to work. I remember it was on the 23rd January, 1957 when a detainee by name of Karumbi s/o Mugenda no. 2017 of Kiambu District was forced to go to furrow digging and was very sick. After having knocked off, this man was in a serious condition. He was sent to Thika N.G.H. [Native General Hospital] and admitted. He then died the following day. I am certain that, if you sympathetically trouble yourself and visit the mentioned Hospital, you will undoubtedly be satisfied and agree with me.[72]

Clearly, some camps were worse than others. Oral testimonies from former detainees, when compared to detainee letters, suggest that death rates were higher in the hard-core up-Pipeline camps, where, as the Emergency continued, the colonial government would officially endorse rationing further, as well as the use of more force and violence. But death was a reality everywhere.

What did the colonial government do about these letters and the information they contained? First, colonial officials went to extreme lengths to try to stop the illicit letters. In fact, the volume of letters arriving directly to Jake Cusack and various members of his Defence Ministry was so heavy that he ordered Taxi Lewis to get control of the problem, writing, "This office is being inundated with a number of petitions from inmates of various detention camps. I fully realize the difficulties involved in controlling this illegal flow of correspondence, but wonder whether tighter measures could

not be introduced—if not to stop it, at least to reduce it."[73] Colonial officials also took it upon themselves to alter unofficially the Emergency Regulation that permitted detainees to both write and receive one censored
letter per month by revoking this privilege in many camps. According to
Askwith, detainees were managing to slip coded messages past camp censors. In the case of the politicals at Mageta Island, the camp library was dis-
banded, and all correspondence courses ended in the spring of 1956.
Lennox-Boyd was informed that these actions were necessary not just as a
punishment for the "generally uncooperative attitude" of the hard-core detainees but because the Mau Mau suspects were using the books as conduits for posting letters.[74]

African warders were also targeted. It was well known that they were
the linchpin in letter-smuggling operations, offering their services in return for a bribe or, in other instances, because they were sympathetic to the
detainees' plight. Increasingly, these warders were also subjected to frequent and unannounced searches and were punished and threatened with
immediate dismissal and prosecution if found shepherding a letter out of
the camps.[75] Several former detainees recalled camp officials making an
example of those warders who were caught sneaking out mail. In Manyani
Camp, a man living today in Nairobi recalled, "There was this Luo warder
who was helping us. He had been caught several times and finally the
commandant took him and buried him in a hole up to his neck. The soldier ants and scorpions crawled on his head and face biting him. It was
very terrible to see this. . . . After that our correspondence stopped for a
while."[76]

The first priority for the colonial government was obvious. Yet despite
the efforts to prevent letters from coming out of the Pipeline, detainees
managed to keep circumventing the tighter restrictions and the "illegal
flow of correspondence" continued. Of course, had these letters reached
only colonial officials, perhaps there would have been less cause for British
concern. But the letters came to a host of other recipients beyond the
purview of Lennox-Boyd and Governor Baring. Among them was Barbara
Castle. In one instance she would have received a letter postmarked
Manyani Camp, and upon opening it the first thing the Labour MP would
have seen was "S.O.S." printed boldly across the top. Six men from the
camp stated, "Prison and rehabilitation officers are ferocious and treat detainees indecently." They went on:

> The record shows that many of our detainees who were physically fit by the
> time of their arrest have already been maimed for life by both prison and
> rehabilitation officers. To induce self-incrimination, the ministry of de-

fence and ministry of community development resort to, (a) Hanging detainees head downwards and vice versa and inflicting pains of any nature ranges from putting soap lather, snuff, salt, D.D.T. and soil in the eyes. (b) To scare detainees completely some detainees are hanged and killed. . . . (c) Incessant pouring of the water on the face thus preventing a person from breathing in and out, e.g. the recent case of KARIUKI s/o MURITHI who was killed with these process in the night of 17th July 1957 by confessed detainees under instructions of camp commandant and rehabilitation officers. (d) Medical treatment is hardly given unless one confesses, (e) Starving and giving insufficient meal one time daily. (f) Organise riot squad to make unreasonable onslaught on detainees. (g) Forcing detainees to co-operate and to work under duress. (h) Trials of ordeal. (i) Running gauntlet. (j) Regular letting detainees survive without food or water for a complete fortnight.[77]

Many such letters reached Castle and other members of the Labour Opposition. Labour MPs took to the floor of the Commons and demanded impartial inquiries into their government's conduct in Kenya. For the most part, they got nowhere. At every turn the Opposition was stonewalled and misled by Lennox-Boyd and his Colonial Office, compelling Castle, years later, to comment, "The number of letters we received was really heart rending. I always sent it to the Secretary of State, of course for verification, but what was so infuriating was that he always had an administrative enquiry which meant that the very people who were in charge of the security forces who were committing these atrocities were the ones who sat in judgment on the case and the whole instinct of the Europeans and those in charge was to cover up, always cover up."[78]

The colonial government dismissed the majority of these letters out of hand, claiming their stories were made up. In response to one posted from Aguthi Camp, the officer in charge wrote to Taxi Lewis, "The anonymous letter appears to me to be the usual attempt at complete distortion of the facts of detention camp routine, for the purpose of eliciting unwarranted sympathy. I have no reason to believe that any of the complaints in the letter have any substance."[79] The key word in this colonial officer's statement is "anonymous." The letter in question, like countless others, went uninvestigated because Governor Baring and the colonial secretary insisted upon "identifiable details" if allegations were to be investigated.[80] Colonial officials demanded that the detainees provide their names, the date and time of specific claims of abuse, and the person or persons responsible for perpetrating the alleged brutalities or deprivations.

But at the same time, the colonial government enacted regulations punishing detainees who smuggled letters out of the camps. In January 1954, according to a government decree, it became a major offense if "a detainee was found guilty of communicating with people outside of the detention camps by unauthorized means."[81] Thus if a detainee provided all of the details necessary for an investigation, including his name, by law he could be punished with up to fourteen days of solitary confinement with reduced rations and twelve strokes with a cane. In fact, there were actually reported cases of this happening. In one instance a delegation went to investigate the specific claims of a detainee at Aguthi Camp, and in a subsequent meeting with Lennox-Boyd one of its members. T. George Thomas, told the colonial secretary:

> It had come to his notice that at Aguthi camp the detainee who had smuggled out a letter to Mrs. Castle about the death of Kabui had been awarded 12 strokes for a breach of Prisons Rules. He [the member of the investigation team] had not told any of his colleagues about this since he returned, but he wished to point out that in these circumstances it was not very surprising that so many complaints emerging from the camps were anonymous.[82]

Time and again camp officials broadly interpreted the punishment for many so-called infractions in the Pipeline, including letter smuggling. In one oral account a detainee from Mara River reported the camp commandant making an example of one of their scribes. The letter writer was paraded in front of the other detainees and his fingers cut off by the *askaris* with a *panga*, or machete, before he was taken to the makeshift gallows in the middle of the camp and hung.[83] In his memoir J.M. discusses several instances of being tortured as a direct result of his letter-writing campaign. In one case his "buttocks swelled considerably" after Mapiga ordered an *askari* to give him sixty strokes with a cane. The following morning, according to J.M.,

> [Mapiga] took me outside "C" Camp to a place near the Forest and said that he would shoot me unless I wrote down on a piece of paper that I would not send any more letters to England, that I would co-operate with the Government and that I would help to type in the screeners' office. Although the thought of death was still not wholly desirable, I refused. He then took from his car a piece of three-ply wood about three feet by two feet and told me to hold it up above my head at arm's length. He walked five yards away and said that he was going to kill me if I did not agree to write the sentences. Still, not imagining he could be serious, I refused. To my horror he raised his gun and shot at me.

Mapiga did this three times. On the first two attempts he missed, though not without sending J. M. to the ground in fear. The third time he hit the detainee's right hand. Freshly wounded, J. M. was taken back to the camp and put into solitary confinement in a small cell. Several days later the camp commandant brought him in front of the rest of the detainees and shouted in Kiswahili, "Here is your leader. He wants to show you he is God. You follow him because he writes letters to the Colonial Office. Do not follow him any more. If you do you will get into the same trouble as he is in today. [J. M.] take off your clothes and lie down on the bench." At that point J. M. received another twelve cane strokes, and when he still refused to stop writing letters, he was taken to the notorious Compound 6 for some more roughing up. It was there, according to J. M., that "the Riot Squad was always coming in and they would make everyone take off their clothes and beat them all round the compound, young and old naked together, which is shameful to my people. But they did not disturb me in my isolation, although I could feel that the place was becoming like a mental home."[84]

There were several inquiries made into detainee allegations similar to the one at Aguthi. Governor Baring, Jake Cusack, Taxi Lewis, and Thomas Askwith took the lead, often personally touring the camp in question. After their inspections there were instances, according to detainees, where life for them improved, albeit temporarily. More often than not, nothing was done, perhaps because few members of the inspection committees actually bothered to speak with detainees. Camp officials were prone to hiding the most outspoken detainees in small cells, which were apparently beyond the view of the investigating teams. Nonetheless, there were other men who wanted to present their grievances, but they were never heard. In one letter the men held in Fort Hall Camp stated, "We do not see any officer entering into the compound to investigate our troubles," while those at Aguthi Camp remarked in a section of their letter titled "Visitings of Officials in Camps," "It is a curious thing to acknowledge to you that when the Mother Govt or the Kenya Govt. depute members for sifting rights of laws, they do not see the opposing side [i.e, the detainees]."[85] In the case of Manyani Camp several detainees wrote to Baring asking him the purpose of his visit since it was clearly not to investigate the allegations of brutality that they had previously sent to him. In a letter to the governor following one of his tours of the camp the detainees had several questions for him.

We have to inform you that we detainees of Manyani we are very much disappointed of you because you came here [to] Manyani you did not see us. . . . Therefore we want to ask you, did you come to see the barbed wire

that [is] surrounding us or did you come to see us? You have already come
here two times and you never get any chance to tell us anything nor you
never let us to tell you our difficulties. . . . Our hearts were quite angry and
much pained when you was here and you did not spoke to us, you saw the
barbed wire then you turned back to your home. We saw you, when you entered the camp at about 100 yds. We were ready to tell you our wishes and
our difficulties, our minds were ready, but you did not entered in the compounds. . . . When you prepared yourself journey to Manyani and report to
the Government that you are going to Manyani Camp, what did you report
to Govt.? Did you tell them that you are going to see the detainees who are
over 5,400 or you told the Government that you are going to see the officers
in Manyani who are over 10 or over 20? We are sure that you saw Detainees
near the camp-gate where they were sitting waiting to go to working parties, and actually you saw how they were weakest because of eating too little
food that does not sufficient them. . . . You saw like this how people are
very thinnest and the same [time] you saw good number of detainees were
naked without clothes like wild animals, that is what you saw with your
eyes. Your eyes are witness of all that.[86]

Technically, inspection committees were required to visit the camps on
a regular basis, regardless of detainees' complaints. Made up of local missionaries, low-level colonial officers, and notably any settlers interested in
touring the camps, these committees' visits were irregular, and their reporting was, based upon what remains in the archives, haphazard at best.
Many of these committees provided Askwith, Lewis, and the governor with
verbal rather than written reports, ostensibly because they were under
pressure and did not have the time to commit their observations to writing.[87] This may well have been the case, but Cusack's office held a much
more cynical opinion. In late 1956 the colonial government discovered an
"oversight" at Saiyusi, an up-Pipeline destination for the hard core.[88] One
of the Opposition party members received a letter from the detainees held
at this island camp, detailing conditions as well as the fact that there was no
inspection committee, something the detainees knew was required by law.
Cusack and his Defence Ministry were hardly alarmed by this news. Instead, the ministry's deputy dispatched a telegram to the Colonial Office,
emphasizing that the whole inspection procedure was really a farcical
waste of time.

I fully agree that it should have been appointed sooner, and I only discovered by accident a few months ago that several of the detention camps still
had not been provided with Inspection Committees, apparently through
oversight, and put this right as soon as I could. You will appreciate however
that it is far from easy to find public spirited people willing to visit these

camps in out of the way places, partly no doubt because they feel not without some justification that the whole thing is window dressing anyway.[89]

The degree to which the detainees were aware of their rights, as defined under Emergency Regulations and international law, is impressive. Their requests went well beyond visiting committees, more often addressing issues that dealt with forced labor and detention without trial. Writing to the colony's chief secretary in 1955, the men at Athi River pointed out:

> Referring to the Government Notice No 729 which appeared in the Kenya Official Gazette Supplement No 33 of 5th May 1953, in Paragraph 8. The Commandant has only power to make detainees to do only the work which concerns camp cleanliness and tidiness. Contrary to this regulation he has forced detainees to work in gardens, in a dam, and in ways leading to them thus violating Government Regulations and his actions has therefore been unconstitution. Actually we shall not take this lightly, it is a very serious matter. As the result of malnutrition detainees have been so weak that they cannot do hard work. Our demand is for you to abolish it as we honestly ask you.[90]

The detainees were correct about the colonial regulation, at least as it read in the spring of 1953. However, the government had anticipated the need for forced labor at a camp like Athi River. So, as with many other camps in the Pipeline, Governor Baring designated it a special detention camp, sidestepping the earlier regulation to which the Athi River detainees were referring. Still, there remained the issue of due process. Detainees repeatedly demanded that they be given a fair trial, that they be able to defend themselves against charges that they were savages, infected with the Mau Mau spell, and misleading the masses of ordinary Kikuyu. It was not just the hard-core detainees who demanded due process. Men in camps like Aguthi, a works camp for the "grey" detainees, demanded that they too be allowed their day in court. They wrote to Taxi Lewis stating, "Corv'ee [*sic*] labours are forced hard to all detainees after the arrival of the destination camps. It is curious to say that castigation by beatings and by hunger is imposed on us. If the Govt wishes Corv'ee [*sic*] labour to be accepted by the detainees, according to the law of the British Govt, it should pass through the courts all detainees for sentences."[91]

Some of the men behind the wire wanted their cases heard by the Advisory Committee on Detainees. Headed by Justice C. P. Connell, this committee traveled to various camps in the Pipeline, where they listened to Mau Mau suspects appeal their detention orders. Typically, two kinds of cases were brought to the Advisory Committee. First there were those detainees held under Delegated Detention Orders, some of whom were devout practicing Christians at the time of arrest. These unfortunate converts had been swept up with the Mau Mau suspects because they refused to fight actively on the side of the colonial government during the war. The second type, and larger number of cases, were those detainees held under Governor's Detention Orders, or GDOs. The majority were classified as politicals, who, being aware of Emergency Regulations, knew full well that the Advisory Committee existed and that they were guaranteed access to it. This was no small matter. In fact, today most former detainees who were not politicals recall nothing about such an appeals process. The colonial government made little effort to inform the detainees of this appeals avenue, explaining why out of several hundred thousand detainees the Advisory Committee adjudicated only a few thousand cases.[92]

When preparing and making their appeals, detainees had no right to legal help or representation. They were entitled to only the slimmest explanation of why they were detained. Governor Baring justified this procedure by stating that he did not want the committee "compromising the individual sources of information regarding [the detainee in question]."[93] One would presume from this statement that Baring wished to protect the government's informants. In certain instances this may well have been the case, but there was another motive as well. Some colonial officers were ordered to fabricate charges to include in the GDOs. One young district officer, for example, was handed a stack of detention orders by the colonial administrator in charge of his district. This would not have been unusual, except that they were largely blank. Only the name of the Mau Mau suspect appeared at the top and Governor Baring's signature at the bottom. At this point the district officer, a recent Oxford graduate on his first assignment in Britain's empire, was, in his words, "told to fill in the reasons for these men's detention. So there I was in the local *boma* filling these things with everything I could think of, trying not to make them the same. I didn't know any of these people, I had just recently arrived. And this was one of my first lessons in how we ruled Kenya."[94]

With no attorney a detainee was nevertheless expected to appeal and attempt to refute charges left unspecified, because any revelation of the specific allegations leveled against him by informants would constitute a breach in colonial security regulations. The colonial government's real fear, of course, was that the detainees would have reasonable explanations for some of these charges, particularly since many were fabricated. This included not just those made up by colonial officers but those created by African informants as well. In all, the Advisory Committee recommended the release of fewer than 250 men who appealed their detention orders. The list of those denied is a veritable who's who of Kenyan nationalist politics—men like Gakaara wa Wanjau, John Cege, James Beauttah, Achieng' Oneko, and Frederick and James Koinange. Most were detained at the Manda Island and nearby Takwa camps and realistically had no chance of their detention orders being overturned. The appeals process was, for most detainees, an exercise in futility. It was, indeed, "window dressing."[95]

The question of what to do with the hundreds of thousands of women who took the Mau Mau oath plagued the colonial government from the Emergency's inception. Colonial officials would eventually detain the vast majority of them in some eight hundred Emergency villages scattered throughout the Kikuyu countryside. However, several thousand of these women were classified as hard core and, in the words of Askwith, "had to be separated from the rest of those who had been misguided by the Mau Mau doctrine."[96] Some were arrested at the start of the Emergency, already having been identified as people who helped to organize the Mau Mau movement at the grassroots level. Others were later arrested at their homes—accused by their loyalist neighbors, local colonial administrators, or security forces of directing the passive-wing operations that supplied forest fighters with intelligence, food, ammunition, clothing, and other supplies. Included in this hard-core sorority were Shifra Wametumi and Helen Macharia. The two sisters were arrested together in Fort Hall District, along with more than a dozen men, on suspicion that they functioned as the backbone of the Mau Mau organization in their local area. Screened thoroughly in a makeshift camp at Kahuro, the two women managed to escape the fate of the men who were arrested and detained with them. The British officer in charge ordered that they all be herded together, shot, and buried in a large pit.[97] Spared their lives, Shifra and Helen would spend the next five years detained without trial.

By their own later admission, the sisters were helping to direct the movement's activities in their area. Of the two, the elder, Shifra, likely raised the suspicions of local authorities because of the broad scale of her involvement. She was a leader in one of the local African independent churches and, according to her later account, "knew just about everyone who was Mau Mau in our location, because our independent church was the center of Mau Mau activity. We directed the oathing, collected funds, and prepared ourselves for our war. We wanted our land back; we wanted the Europeans out. They had caused many problems in our country, and we wanted our freedom so we could organize our lives and our communities as we saw fit."[98] Such resolute commitment had its consequences. The two sisters left several young children behind when they were taken away. In Helen's case, she kept her nursing infant with her until the time of her deportation to Kajiado Camp. At this point she decided to hand the young child to her husband, who was standing beneath the lorry, rather than take the infant with her to the camp. But a few months later her husband would also be detained. Helen and her widowed sister Shifra, like so many other women in the Pipeline, would rely upon the goodwill of their Mau Mau family members and neighbors to feed and protect their children during their detention.

Throughout their years in detention Shifra and Helen would be known by their numbers, 98 and 99, respectively. At the co-ed Kajiado Camp they joined thirty-two other women, and together, according to Shifra, they "were being referred to as condemned people by the *Mzungu* in charge, to be killed at any time he saw fit."[99] After a year they were transferred to Athi River Camp, making them the first women to occupy the new all-female compound, Compound 1. Though separated from the men, they too experienced daily the Pipeline's same idiom of violence, as well as its hard labor and deprivations. Their days consisted of siren wake-up calls, inspections, and marches out to the labor site, where they dug by hand an eight-foot-deep security trench encircling the camp. When now recalling this forced labor, former detainees of Compound 1 cannot separate the work from the heat and the beatings. They would voluntarily strip down to their underclothes to contend with "scorching sun," as Shifra recollected. There was no clean water, and, according to Helen:

> We had to do with the water coming down the drainages, after dishes had been washed and toilets and bathrooms cleaned. . . . I remember being asked by women to use my big foot to stop the draining water flowing, so as to make a small pool where others could be able to scoop the water with their hands. This was because the thirst was so much, and the digging was like a punishment. And we couldn't complain. That was a punishment. Nobody would listen to our complaints. They used to call us the bloody Mau Mau and abuse us more.[100]

Women at Athi River did, however, voice their grievances. Literate detainees like Helen and the legendary one-eyed detainee named Nyaguthii, from Nyeri District, drafted and wrote letters detailing the forced labor, the beatings, and the screenings. Without fail Fridays at Athi River meant screening, and the women hardly escaped the usual tactics of the government's interrogators. They were beaten, whipped, and sexually violated with bottles, hot eggs, and other foreign objects, all in an effort to force them to talk. Alsatian shepherd dogs were also brought into the screening huts, where they would growl at and eventually maul those women who refused to cooperate.[101] Compound 1 sent numerous letters to the governor, who, on occasion, responded personally by inspecting the camp. According to Shifra, Baring would "sometimes come and see us being screened. Other times we would be ordered to squat, and he would come around looking at us. He never asked us anything; he would just walk around glancing at us like we were animals."[102]

Governor Baring's impression was not so far off the mark. The women's hair was matted, they had not bathed properly since their arrests, toilet bucket waste was encrusted in their scalps and backs, their skin was often covered with scabs and boils, and they walked around—in Helen's words—"like paranoid creatures, always jerking our heads from side to side for fear of being hit with a club or whip."[103] The camp experience had fully transformed their physical appearance, to the point that they had become the feral-looking Mau Mau savages that Baring and the colonial secretary were peddling in their propaganda to Britain and the international community.

For most of the Emergency, women were detained primarily at Kamiti Camp. Kamiti had previously been a maximum security prison for criminals, but the circumstances of the war forced its transformation into a multipurpose facility. It was an overflow site for Embakasi prison and held several thousand men convicted of Mau Mau–related crimes. Behind its walls and barbed wire was also one of the largest known burial sites for Mau Mau adherents killed in the forests, on the reserves, and in detention camps, as well as those executed under Emergency Regulations. In the spring of 1954 the colonial government decided to open the gates of Kamiti to accommodate a surge of female Mau Mau convicts and detainees. Once fully operational, Kamiti would be unique in that it functioned as a self-contained Pipeline. In it women of all classifications—from the blackest of "black" to "white," and various shades of "grey" in between—were detained and moved to different compounds based on their level of cooperation. Female Mau Mau convicts were fully integrated with the detainees, living in the same compounds and laboring together. At the end of their sentences they too became detainees, little altering their lives.

Kamiti was also unique in that the colonial government envisioned eventually releasing some of its hard core back into the Kikuyu reserves. This exception to an otherwise hard-and-fast exile policy was a reflection of the challenge that these female Mau Mau adherents posed to the British colonial stereotype of African women, who were supposedly intellectually

weak and easily manipulated. In the case of Mau Mau they were presumed
to have joined the movement because their husbands, fathers, and sons had
coerced them into taking the oath.[104] But women like Shifra and Helen exploded this myth. Colonial officials were left struggling to reconcile female
Mau Mau militancy and solidarity with their simplistic notions of a passive and compliant African womanhood.

Askwith, however, turned this colonial stereotype on its head. In a report to the Colonial Office in early 1954 he wrote, "There is evidence that
wives have in many cases persuaded their husbands to take the oath and
are often very militant. They are also said to be bringing up their children
to follow the Mau Mau creed. It is therefore more important to rehabilitate
the women than the men if the next generation is to be saved."[105] Despite
evidence from intelligence reports that women were the "eyes and ears of
Mau Mau" and that "the part played by women to aid the terrorists is considerable," old British gender stereotypes would not fade away.[106] At Kamiti
the gender stereotype curiously seemed to render some of the hard-core
women redeemable. Some female detainees may have been among the
most militant of the Mau Mau adherents, but most colonial officials simply
could not attribute this behavior to any kind of independent thought or
agency, as they did the men of the movement. If these women had simply
been manipulated by their menfolk, they could also be reoriented, as
British logic went, toward the colonial way of thinking. In other words, if
women like Helen and Shifra had been manipulated once, under the right
conditions they could be manipulated again.

Their reorientation began with Kamiti's intake procedure. They were
strip-searched, scrubbed down, fingerprinted, and photographed. From
there they were sent for screening, where they often encountered Mahuru,
or the Eagle, for the first time. This was the nickname given to Katherine
Warren-Gash—the officer in charge of screening at Kamiti Camp—because of her piercing eyes and the way she preyed upon them in the screening huts like "defenseless mice," according to one woman.[107] Mahuru was,
in fact, the daughter of a settler who reportedly lived near the Delamere Estate. She spoke fluent Kikuyu, told the detainees to call her Gathoni (a typical Kikuyu name), and like Louis Leakey prided herself on her knowledge
of Kikuyu traditions and presumed superstitions. Her screening tactics
ranged from ordering beatings and ration reductions to threatening the
lives of those children accompanying, as well as those born to, their mothers in the camp. She even requested and received from Askwith several
"lions' claws as a bit of hoodoo in connection with her screening of Mau
Mau women."[108]

Metal bracelets etched with detention numbers were standard issue in

Kamiti. Some women had as many as three identical bands affixed to their wrists. In a camp where different categories of Mau Mau detainees were held altogether, multiple banding was an important identification system. Women with one metal band were classified as "black," those with two were various shades of "grey," and those with three were designated as "white." The detainees were dispatched to one of five separate compounds within the camp, each corresponding to the screening classifications as well as to a different and symbolic animal, a personal touch bestowed by Warren-Gash herself. Wearing their single bracelets, "blacks" were sent to the *hiti*, or hyena, compound, which consisted of seventy-five *nyumba ndogo*, or small individual cells where women were kept individually or in small groups of up to four or five. Then there was the *mburi*, or goat, compound for the "dark greys." The names of the three remaining compounds corresponded to the life cycle of the cow: "greys" were passed along to the compound labeled *njau*, which is the Kikuyu word for a calf too young to determine its sex; "light greys" were promoted to the *mori* compound, named for a cow that has just entered its milking stage; and finally the "whites" went to the *ng'ombe* compound, that is, the compound named for the fully mature cow.[109]

Such symbolism was not lost on the women of Kamiti. They disliked Warren-Gash's appropriation of their culture. As one woman from Kiambu District later described, "Our cooperation was being equated to different animals that had important meaning to us as Kikuyu. This only irritated us, because we knew Mahuru was trying to be clever. She pretended like she was one of us, but no true Kikuyu woman would behave as she did."[110] In time, Mahuru's tactics would become more coercive, perhaps in response to the subsequent intake of the hardest of the hard core. Shifra, Helen, and the other so-called hardened women from Athi River were among the last to be sent to Kamiti. They were left with their single metal bracelets, etched 98 and 99, and sent to one of the individual cells of the hyena compound, where they would spend the next two years alongside several notables like Shifra Wairire Gakaara, the wife of Kikuyu intellectual Gakaara wa Wanjau.

Secured to the waist of every woman at Kamiti was a tin mug. It was their most precious possession, because without it they could not eat or drink. Most detainees were issued their mug at intake, but some found themselves without one and spent their first disorienting days in the camp trying to procure one. As at other camps, there was a black market at Kamiti, and a tin mug would fetch a high price. New arrivals were left with little choice but to trade one of their two issued blankets, exchanging warmth and comfort for food. The nearby male convicts were also active in this black market. Messages would be sent to them through the guards, in Kamiti both male and female, or tossed into their work brigades as they passed by. Using metal sheeting from the roofs of their barracks, the convicts created mugs that were highly coveted, because they were larger than those issued by the prison administration.

As elsewhere in the Pipeline, porridge was the basis of the Kamiti diet. Detainees received a mugful at breakfast and another at dinner. Bean stew was sometimes a supplement, though it generally contained insect larvae.[111] Most of the women suffered from nutritional-related ailments, with night blindness, boils, and other painful skin ailments the most common symptoms.[112] So, too, were hard, bloody stools. During colder months exposure was also a serious problem. Many women slept together; in fact, Helen and Shifra huddled together under their combined four blankets every night they spent in the camps. From their first Pipeline stop at Kajiado to Athi River to Kamiti they never spent a night apart. Today, they are convinced that this was the key to their survival.

Everyone worked at Kamiti. The camp had four different work details: digging and moving murram (hardened asphaltlike earth), toilet bucket cleaning, cutting grass and tending the vegetable garden, and off-loading and burying dead bodies. Camp officials assigned the majority of detainees to the murram project, by all accounts grueling work. The warders marched the women out to the digging site, where they were divided up into a kind of assembly-line production. A third of the women were given mattocks for breaking up the hard encrusted soil, another third shovels to dig it out, and the remainder large metal basins that were filled with the murram. This last group was expected to carry the heavy loads on their heads, while running, in order to dump the murram at a site about a quarter of a mile away. The sisters from Fort Hall both worked on this gang, later remembering vividly their years of labor. In her animated oral testimony, Shifra recalled their work, while simultaneously dramatizing it.

> We would start work in the morning with no rest. Stopping would mean a thorough beating, and no one cared whether a detainee was killed by beating. One would start carrying the murram in a tin basin, and it had to be filled properly until the guard was satisfied. Then one would be ordered to run, all the way to the field, pour it out and run back to the quarry without stopping, the whole day. When we could, we would sing songs to ourselves about the hard work, and when singing we would momentarily forget how tired we were. One used to go like this. 'We used to carry murram in basins, We used to carry murram in basins, Until our necks got bent, And then we carried it in our dresses.'[113]

Her recollection was similar to countless other women, all of whom recalled the enormous difficulty they had raising the murram-filled basins above their heads and the beatings they received while struggling to do it.

Detainees and convicts did strategize to minimize some of the labor, even if they could not avoid it entirely. One favored tactic was to jump on top of the tin basins, creating a dent in the bottom. This made for easier head portage as well as a lighter load. Winnie Mahinda, who had been arrested at her home in Nyeri District, recalled: "To reduce the number of trips which we made carrying the murram, we would decide to try to slow down our pace. Someone in the gang would call out, 'Walk like a chameleon,' and we would all start walking like a chameleon. Of course, the *askaris* would eventually start beating us to move us along, but we managed to get some rest."[114] There was also something that Winnie and others called "goat droppings." Using this tactic, they would reach into the basins that they were holding on their heads and scoop some of the murram out to lessen their load. "Looking back on the road we had taken," Winnie went on to say, "it would be full of murram, which looked like goat droppings. We would arrive with only a little murram to our destination. Sometimes the *askaris* beat us for it; other times they didn't. They would also discover sometimes that we had bent the undersides of our basins. They would inspect them—or we would say they were screening the basins, because they would beat them to repair the dents with the mattocks handles, though not without a few blows for us as well. But we would still bend them again, and the whole thing would start all over."[115]

The toilet bucket and garden duties were the most coveted at Kamiti. Despite the foul nature of the work, cleaning human waste was a far better assignment than bearing the heavy murram loads, which left many crippled, some permanently. Women jockeyed for the toilet bucket and garden jobs, knowing full well that success could mean survival. For many months Winnie had been part of the waste brigade, going from compound to compound with forty other women gathering the buckets and carrying them on their heads to the disposal site. "We would start by draining the urine from the solid feces," Winnie recalled. "We would use brooms to prevent the feces from pouring over." Then, she continued,

we would combine the solid waste into the buckets, lift them onto our heads again, and carry them out to the dumping area, which was a considerable distance from the camp. The guards would often be chasing us and whipping our legs, which made the runny waste go down our faces. The gang which was involved with cutting grass used to heap it like four walls made of grass, resembling a room. A lot of grass would be heaped to a height of about five feet, and into the area enclosed therein was where we dumped the contents of the buckets. . . . The whole time we used our bare hands and the ends of the brooms to clean out the feces.[116]

After a few months, the grass-cutting and garden workers would take the composted human waste and use it as fertilizer for the camp's vegetable garden. The women on this brigade were generally the cooperative "light greys" and "whites," their job a reward for good behavior. "It was quite incredible," recalled one former detainee who was responsible for digging the human manure. "We would lift it with our shovels, and this steam would rise, and the stench was unbearable. But it made for very good fertilizer. We grew many vegetables, though they were not for us. They were eaten by the warders, and some were sent outside of the camp."[117]

The burial gang was considered the worst punishment at Kamiti. Truckloads of bodies would be brought to the camp, sometimes once or twice a day, other times every other day or every few days. The high stacks of bodies were either dumped on-site or left in a pile in the back of the truck, forcing the women to climb on top for off-loading. The dead were men and women, old and young. Some had been shot, others visibly tortured, and some emaciated from starvation. Male convicts held at Kamiti dug large burial pits, both within and outside of the complex, into which the women deposited the bodies.[118] As Mary Nyambura, a convict and later detainee from Kiambu District, recalled, "Some of these bodies were heavy for us women, and we would have to lift them, sometimes three or four of us at a time. It was terrible; sometimes a woman would recognize someone she knew, and she couldn't do anything. If she started weeping, the *askaris* would just starting beating her."[119]

Punishment took other forms as well. Mahuru and other white officers were known for physically abusing the detainees, but more often than not they ordered the African warders to do the work for them. "The whites were very cunning," Helen insisted. "They generally did not carry out such acts but gave orders to the Africans to do it. Even when people were being killed, a white man would stand there watching."[120] There was Ngindira (the Stuffer), an African male guard who was renowned for forcing women into their compound by kicking them between the shoulders with his spiked boots. He was often accompanied by Nyagaki, so nicknamed because of her cleanly pressed Khaki uniform. This female Kamba guard had a distinct penchant for beating women on the head until they fell unconscious. Sexual torture was widespread, particularly in screening sessions, where women would have various foreign objects thrust into their vaginas, and their breasts squeezed and mutilated with pliers.[121] It is hardly surprising that many former detainees and convicts from Kamiti expressed sentiments similar to those of Gakaara wa Wanjau's wife, Shifra. "Detention was hell," she said. "It was meant to kill us. We only came out by the grace of God."[122]

Many women brought their young children with them to the camp, and others gave birth there. After completing a day's work on the toilet bucket brigade, Lucy Mugwe delivered a son in the barracks of the goat compound. In retrospect, Lucy found it incredible she carried full term considering the weight of the buckets she had been carrying and the whippings she endured during screening. After her delivery "the women contributed pieces of their old dresses," she later recalled. "I also cut pieces of canvas from the tent windows. We had to survive somehow. I had to be very careful not to get caught stealing the canvas because if I had it would have meant severe punishment."[123] In 1955 camp officials estimated that about 15 percent of the four thousand female detainees and convicts had at least one child in the camp with them.[124] If these estimates are correct, nearly six hundred children were in Kamiti. Their mothers had to find some way of clothing, feeding, and protecting them from the host of communicable and nutritional diseases that periodically swept through the camp.

It was the rare child who survived Kamiti. Camp officials occasionally allocated lighter work duties to mothers, while the old and infirm women—or the *kuba kuba*, as the other detainees called them—were put in charge of minding the children remaining in the compounds while their mothers were digging murram, burying dead bodies, or cleaning out waste buckets. Askwith's men inspected the camp from time to time, compiled alarming reports about the state of these children, and scrambled to come up with the funds simply to clothe them. They were mostly unsuccessful, leading one official to report, "We really do need these cloths for the children as it is impossible to keep them clean and tidy while dressed in dirty pieces of sacking and blanket. I have successfully clothed several of the children but I am now very short of material."[125] Infants especially succumbed to disease and starvation, as their mothers were incapable of producing enough breast milk because of poor rations and strenuous work. In Mary Nyumbura's case her young child died while strapped to her back. Other mothers would return from their day's work to find their child dead.[126]

Many surviving women from Kamiti are convinced that camp officials were intent on killing their children. Colonial officials did little to provide for their welfare, but many former detainees feel the children's deaths were not solely from neglect. They recalled infants and young children being lined up for inoculations, as camp officials called them. But within twenty-four hours some of these children were dead. "They would be given medicine one day," Shifra Gakaara later insisted, "and the next day you would hear that three, four, or five of them were dead. Every morning, when the barracks were unlocked, the *askaris* would ask, 'How many children have died?' That was what made many women shed tears. A lot of children were buried at Kamiti."[127] In fact, camp officials singled out the most recalcitrant Mau Mau adherents assigned to the burial brigade to take charge of disposing of these children's corpses. "They would be tied in bundles of six babies," Helen recalled, "and each of us selected was ordered to take the bundle and bury it with the rest of the bodies in the big graves."[128]

The sisters from Fort Hall and the other women at Kamiti wrote letters. They petitioned all of the usual characters, including the governor, the colonial secretary, Taxi Lewis, as well as Barbara Castle, whose reputation for helping detainees was widespread in the Pipeline. They petitioned for fair trials, an end to the screening sessions, and the return of their stolen land. "We wanted our freedom," Lucy Mugwe later remembered. "Our experience in detention made us hate the British even more, and we wrote to officials telling them that."[129] In their correspondence the women of Kamiti also made very specific complaints and charges about their condition and the fate of their children. In one letter, for example, a woman from the camp wrote:

> Infants and young children [are] underfed. They are not given enough milk, and are fed on unbalanced diet. They cry all the day long. Women are made to cook for themselves but they are not given enough food. Some women die because of brutal treatment in the prison. There are many diseases amongst the prisoners now. T.B. and typhoid are the commonest. Many women have died of these diseases. The officers torture our women and force them to confess things they don't know. We start work at 6 a.m. and come back at 6 p.m. or even at 7 p.m. We are constantly beaten while working. We are sent to work in European farms many miles from the camp and we have to go there on foot, and we have to run, and those who walk slowly because of bad health are beaten up. Children are neglected when they are ill, and they just die like animals.[130]

If press reports and government handouts are to be believed, Warren-Gash was spearheading an emotional and physical revolution in the camp. In April 1956 the *Sunday Post* ran a story championing the alleged success of Kamiti, stating:

> Mrs. Gash said that confession and rehabilitation of woman detainees at Kamiti was proving "better than a course of beauty treatment." The women arrived at the prison "sullen, sour, unpleasant, and downright ugly." But af-

ter confession and rehabilitation they lifted their heads, and many of them became "really pretty." . . . The final screening was done by [Mrs. Gash] herself, with questioning, done indirectly but based on confidential individual dossiers.[131]

By all accounts the screening officer was obsessed with her own power. Warren-Gash was the ultimate gatekeeper, insisting that she have the final say over any detainee's downgrading in classification as well as her ultimate release. Despite her official title Warren-Gash also took control of all rehabilitation activities in the camp, such as they were. Much later, when recollecting his subordinate's work, Askwith expressed considerable dismay. "Warren-Gash at first appeared to be the ideal person to run things at Kamiti, but she would prove otherwise. But she wanted the job, and with so few even partly qualified people I kept her there and hoped to influence activities in the camp as best as I could."[132]

Mind bending was also a Kamiti tactic. Anti–Mau Mau propaganda blared through the loudspeakers, posters of a deranged-looking Kenyatta hung throughout the camp, and pamphlets touting the virtues of confession and the benefits of British colonial rule were distributed to the various compounds. Films demonstrating the greatness of Britain were also shown, with one camp official reporting that "the Coronation film [has big reactions], showing the Might and Majesty of the Commonwealth."[133] Chiefs and district officers from the Kikuyu reserves paid visits to the camp, urging the women to confess so they could return home to "save their families from the hardships of the Emergency."[134] Warren-Gash even took to the road, traveling to Kikuyu country to track down the family members of her detainees, urging them to write letters to their recalcitrant mothers, daughters, sisters, and aunts telling them to denounce Mau Mau so they could be released. On many occasions she was successful.[135] "[These letters] were," one woman recalled, "terribly difficult for us. They were sometimes much worse than the beatings and tortures. You see, beating was how they were reforming us in Kamiti. But the words of our children and mothers and fathers who needed us because most of our husbands were also detained . . . many women broke down because of them and confessed so they would be released."[136]

All women, confessed or not, were also barraged with Christian preaching. Missionaries seeking to save Mau Mau souls made their pilgrimages to Kamiti, where their captive audience had no choice but to listen to the words of the Lord. Many women liked when the preachers came, if only because they were relieved of a few hours' worth of work. Like the men, many preferred to use their complimentary Bibles as a toilet paper supply, and to pray in what they called the traditional Kikuyu manner. "We used to pray in the form of songs, praying to the God of Kirinyaga to help us triumph in the struggle," Helen Macharia recalled. "We prayed that we had full trust in Him, Ngai, the God of the Kikuyu, and that if we triumphed it was He who would have triumphed, and if we lost our loss would be His."[137] During Christian hymn services, the women also sometimes altered words and verses, rendering the songs "subversive," according to one government report. It went on to declare "this practice is extremely dangerous to the maintenance of good order and discipline. . . . The singing of hymns in Kikuyu is prohibited in this prison and detention camp."[138]

Thereafter, singing became a major offense. This is not to say that women ceased composing and singing their songs. Guards were bribed, others were sympathetic, and still others were too lazy to enforce camp rules. Singing was an expressive form of empowerment that was both inspirational and soothing. There was also a collective component to their musical composition that encouraged group solidarity and commitment to the Mau Mau cause. Generally, the songs were composed ad hoc in the compounds and in the labor gangs, and today they are still remembered by the women from Kamiti. In one of the most widely recalled verses, the women provide a window into the conditions of the camp and the goals of their struggle. Today, they can still sing:

> There is no fun in detention
> It eliminated our firstborns.
> Children of elders stay at home,
> Ngai is great, we shall go home.
> Even if you looked around from the door,
> You would not see a white person.
> It is only the children of Mumbi who are crying,
> Ngai is great, we shall go home.
> When we are in jail the warders say,
> Let the years be more.
> And we say it shouldn't be that way,
> And we pray to our God to deliver us so that we may go home.
> Ngai is great, we shall go home.[139]

Eventually, many of the women at Kamiti would go home, though not before they had been thoroughly cleansed. Once a woman had been broken by the endless cycle of physical and mental torture, and then confessed, she began her journey to the *ng'ombe*, or "white," compound, in part by attending classes taught by a handful of rehabilitation officers. Ironically, instruction largely focused on developing good domestic skills, like proper hygiene, nutrition, and mending clothes. But even these courses were limited. In 1955 Kenya's Treasury cut by half the meager rehabilitation funding for the camp, affecting significantly the work of Askwith's men and women.[140]

All reform in Kamiti seemed an afterthought, with the notable exception of Christian conversion. Confessed detainees were required to attend missionary-led courses in Bible study before their release. This Christian rehabilitation culminated in an actual cleansing ceremony organized by the Christian Council of Kenya. Three large ceremonies of this kind were held at Kamiti, with the inaugural a kind of Christian jamboree presided over by the archbishop of Mombasa, the Reverend Leonard Beecher. Held in September 1955, this cleansing ceremony apparently rid nearly one hundred confessed female detainees of their Mau Mau sins once and for all. Wearing his full Anglican regalia, Archbishop Beecher stood in front of the repentant women and engaged them in the following dialogue.

> ARCHBISHOP: Do you confess that you have taken the Mau Mau oath (or oaths)?
> RESPONDENTS: I do.
> ARCHBISHOP: Do you truly repent of this sin (or these sins)?
> RESPONDENTS: I do.
> ARCHBISHOP: Do you renounce these oaths and put them from you forever?
> RESPONDENTS: I do.
> ARCHBISHOP: Do you seek forgiveness through the blood of Christ our Saviour?
> RESPONDENTS: I do.
> ARCHBISHOP: Will you now stand firm with the people of Christ in worship and witness?
> RESPONDENTS: I will.
> ARCHBISHOP: Do you affirm that, by the help and grace of God, you will confess the faith of Christ, and fight against the world, the flesh and the devil?
> RESPONDENTS: I do.
> ARCHBISHOP: Do you promise to attend regularly further instruction in the Christian faith?
> RESPONDENTS: I do.[141]

With these affirmations and the blessings of the archbishop as well as Mrs. Warren-Gash, the women would be transferred to the custody of their local chiefs and eventually sent home.

Some detainees, like the sisters from Fort Hall, refused to confess. Like the hard-core men, these so-called obdurate and irreconcilable women were slated for permanent exile in remote places like Hola. In retrospect, though, there was very little difference between the prospect of Hola and a return to a Kikuyu reserve, because under Emergency Regulations release from the Pipeline hardly spelled freedom. When the confessed and cleansed women returned to Central Province, they found their homes destroyed and their families, along with hundreds of thousands of other Kikuyu, rounded up and detained in the Emergency villages. These former detainees would live like the rest of the Mau Mau population in the reserves, that is, behind barbed wire and under the strict control of the Administration and local loyalists. Long days would be spent on forced communal labor projects. There was extreme overcrowding in the huts, little food, a host of diseases, and still torture and death. Many wondered why they had bothered to cooperate at Kamiti, for when they returned home they realized that they had simply traded one form of detention for another.

CHAPTER EIGHT

DOMESTIC TERROR

Emergency village guarded by Home Guard, Nyeri District

DRIVING NORTH OUT OF NAIROBI IN THE DIRECTION OF MOUNT
Kenya is by any standard a remarkable journey. The contrast between the
urban congestion of the country's capital and the scenic beauty of Central
Province, the heart of Kikuyuland, is stunning. Within a few miles from the
city, the hubbub gives way to a serenity punctuated by a rural landscape of
lush banana trees, maize crops, and modest mud-and-wattle homesteads.
Looking up from the main road, one cannot help but marvel at the men
and women cultivating their small plots on the steep ridges that carve
through the countryside. After passing through Kiambu District, the road
turns to Murang'a and then to Nyeri and the foothills of Mount Kenya.
There are indications of poverty, particularly when passing through some
of the smaller towns like Karatina. But nowhere does the beauty and
rhythm of rural life in Kikuyuland betray the devastation that ravaged its
people some fifty years ago.

It is hard not to marvel at nature's ability to conceal the past. At once it
can rejuvenate a war-torn society while disguising the physical scars of
conflict. As a result, searching for evidence of the Mau Mau era in Kenya's

Central Province is challenging—that is, if one chooses not to get out of one's car to speak to the people living there. From the southern reaches of Kiambu to the northernmost region of Nyeri, most Kikuyu people, particularly women, recall the Emergency years in Kikuyuland as a period of total destruction. The colonial government ordered their homes destroyed and detained them and their children in barbed-wire villages that dotted the countryside, where they were forced to labor under deplorable conditions. By the end of the war torture, exhaustion, disease, and starvation would claim the lives of tens of thousands of these rural people.

When giving their oral testimonies, many Kikuyu women struggled while searching for a vocabulary capable of describing the brutalities of the Emergency. In most Kikuyu survivor testimonies the problem of vocabulary, of being able to summon the right words to describe the past, frustrates efforts to document personal tragedy.[1] Those women who had been detained in the villages, and who now sought to convey their bitter memories to an outsider, were faced with a great challenge. In their oral accounts, they had to transport the listener back in time to re-create a war-torn world that was now completely absent from the bucolic landscape. "Look around you," one woman implored. "Even if you closed your eyes—how can I explain?—you cannot imagine what we lived through. How can I possibly explain it to you? All you know of this place is what you see today—the *shambas* [farms] and the vegetation, our homes, and our livestock. I have to take you to places that no longer exist to explain their meaning. . . . How can I make you understand what the British and their Home Guards did to us? I cannot begin to tell you what we experienced in those villages."[2]

The war in the Kikuyu reserves was bitter from the start yet became worse over time. From the beginning of the Emergency the colonial government followed an explicit policy of dividing the Kikuyu people into one of two camps: either one supported the colonial authority, or one fought against it. One was either a loyalist, fighting actively on the side of the forces of British law and order, or a Mau Mau. Civil tensions seethed in Kikuyu country long before the start of the war, and in many ways these tensions were a wellspring of Mau Mau. The oath takers were enraged by the privileges of the colonial-appointed chiefs and their retainers, linking them directly to the injustices of British colonial rule and to the presence of white settlers. But as war unfolded, the chasm between Mau Mau and loyalists widened, and civil anger took on a violent dimension never before seen.

In June 1954 the War Council took the extraordinary action of mandat-

Emergency village with loyalist compound visible on hillside,
Nyeri District, circa January 1956

ing forced villagization throughout the Kikuyu reserves.[3] By the end of
1955, less than eighteen months after the measure's introduction, 1,050,899
Kikuyu were removed from their scattered homesteads throughout Central
Province and herded into 804 villages, consisting of some 230,000 huts.[4] As
with so many other control policies in Kenya, General Templer's use of
barbed-wire villages to suppress the communist threat in Malaya in the
early 1950s had inspired Baring and his officers. In Britain's Asian colony,
hundreds of thousands of civilians were removed from their homes and
forced into barbed-wire villages, effectively cutting off their supply lines
to the communist guerrillas. Of course, Malaya was not the first place
where the British had employed such tactics. Alfred Milner had used them
in his campaign against the Afrikaners during the Boer War at the turn of
the century, directly causing the deaths of tens of thousands of women
and children from disease and starvation. Somehow Templer's approach
was perceived as kinder and gentler, if only because he claimed to be introducing reform measures that would "win the hearts and minds of the
people."[5]

The policy was adopted in the Kenyan villages as well. As Labour critics
questioned the fate of the detainees' dependents in the reserves, and rumors of terror in the Kikuyu countryside, public relations officer Granville

Roberts trumpeted the colonial government's role as benevolent trustee. The Colonial Office repeatedly justified the use of enforced villagization by emphasizing the supposed long-term benefits of rehabilitation.[6] The Kenya Information Office publicized speeches by comparatively liberal settler representatives like Michael Blundell in which it was suggested that villagization was an unprecedented opportunity for the introduction of liberal reform and British civilizing values.[7] For his part, Askwith believed that the rehabilitation of the women and children was critical to the success of the social counterrevolution that he envisioned. By early 1955 he began shifting his focus away from the Pipeline and toward the Kikuyu reserves. When Askwith wrote that "more and more the department is changing over from rehabilitation in the camps to rehabilitation in the villages which is in fact community development," the subtext of his message was clear.[8] By returning to his department's roots in the rural areas, he hoped to wield more influence over at least one facet of the war. He soon began lobbying Baring and the colonial secretary for additional funding and manpower, stressing, "There has been a shift of emphasis from camps and prisons to districts where increasing pressure is being applied to the passive wing by Community Development Officers carrying out an intensive programme of education, construction, and recreation in the villages."[9] Nothing came of his requests. By the middle of 1955 there were only six full-time community development officers for women in all of Central Province. Together with four part-time officers and one voluntary officer, as well as eight African assistants, these community development officers were expected to carry out the rehabilitation of the entire population of "Mau Mau–infected" women in the reserves.[10]

For the colonial government to tout this effort as a far-reaching hearts-and-minds campaign was duplicity at its finest. Granted the slimmest of staff and virtually no funding, Askwith lobbied not just his own government but also international donors for assistance. Still, there was barely enough funding to cover salary costs, let alone supplies. Both frustrated and dismayed, he wrote to Kenya's Treasury in late 1954, "I beg to apply for £2,500 to enable basic grants of £500 to be allocated to each of the districts of Central Province for the fostering of women's homecrafts as a means of rehabilitating the large numbers of women and girls on the fringes of Mau Mau. These grants will not meet all the requirements of District Commissioners, and must be supplemented from African District Council funds."[11] But such pleas for the barest of allocations most often were left unmet. Without additional loans from the Colonial Office the money simply was not there, at least based upon allocations from Nairobi. Indeed, Kenya's minister of finance, Ernest Vasey, was one of the most forward-looking thinkers in Baring's administration, and a personal friend of Askwith's who had helped establish the multiracial United Kenya Club, the only dining and social club in Kenya free of the color bar. If there was money to be had in the Treasury, chances were good that Vasey would have found it and allocated some to rehabilitation.

But Vasey was not in charge, nor was Askwith. In the forest war Erskine was largely calling the shots. As for the Pipeline, Jake Cusack and Taxi Lewis had full control under Baring. In the reserves the Administration was in charge, in the persons of the provincial and district commissioners, who saw Askwith's attempts at rehabilitation in the villages as misguided and threatening to their own power. Askwith's men found themselves on the margins of decision making, serving as mere advisers to the provincial and district commissioners. Askwith's immediate superior, Beniah Ohanga, the minister for community development and rehabilitation, observed the unfolding power play between the Administration and the rehabilitation officers in the villages, and repeatedly told Baring and others, "With our [Rehabilitation] Officers in the field we cannot be regarded as complete aliens there."[12] He proposed the creation of an interdepartmental rehabilitation advisory committee, but the Ministry of African Affairs, which oversaw the work of the provincial and district commissioners, was not interested. Within the Kikuyu reserves and behind the wires of the villages, the British colonial officers in the Administration wanted to maintain full control over Mau Mau adherents and their future. Frank Loyd, a high-ranking colonial officer, summed up the general sentiment of many of his peers and subordinates: "Only we [the Administration] understood what was happening out there. First things first, we had to break Mau Mau and keep the support of those loyal to us. It's not like I was against rehabilitation in principle, but the Emergency wasn't the time for such things. It would have its place, but much later."[13] With neither the funding nor the support of the Administration, Askwith and his skeleton staff had no hope of implementing rehabilitation in the newly created villages.

Certainly, the villages helped to sever supply lines to the forests, but that was only one aspect of their broader function. Surrounded by barbed wire and spiked trenches, heavily guarded by armed Home Guards and watchtowers, and routinized by sirens and daily forced labor, these villages were also detention camps in all but name. They came to serve a dual purpose for the colonial government at a time when its men on the spot wondered how they were going to break the hundreds of thousands of so-called lesser Mau Mau adherents, mostly women, children, and the elderly. As one district commissioner observed during the early years of the Emergency, "It is obviously not practical politics to incarcerate a million and a half Kikuyu who are admitting freely to having taken the illegal oath."[14] Villagization became another form of detention, one that solved the practical and financial problems that would have been associated with a further, massive expansion of the Pipeline. The colonial government adopted a policy of sending most men, and hard-core women, to the Pipeline, leaving the remainder of the Kikuyu population in the reserves. In the villages detainment of over a million Mau Mau adherents was left largely to the same agents who had been responsible for carrying out the earlier screening campaign.

When Gathoni Mutahi saw smoke billowing from the homesteads on the ridge next to hers, she knew that villagization had begun in her location of Nyeri District. The sight and smell of burning wattle and roof thatching hung thickly over Kenya's Central Province throughout the second half of 1954. Neither Gathoni nor any of the other women living in the reserves were given explicit warning of their impending forced removal. "It all happened so quickly," Gathoni later remembered. "All the homes and cattle *bomas* in our area were wiped out in a matter of hours. When I saw the smoke in the next ridge I started burying pots and other items under the floor, and I bundled my children and took what I could."[15] British officers from the Administration and patrolling security forces directed the operations, though the Home Guards were largely responsible for the actual removal of the Kikuyu from their homesteads—torching the thatched-roof huts as they moved through the reserves. The huge scope of the forced removals generated a wave of confusion and terror throughout Kikuyuland. Inhabitants fled the infernos, carrying children and household items; others were trapped inside and perished in the flames. Beds, cooking items, bicycles, clothing, and livestock were all confiscated by the Home Guards for their own use. Later many loyalists returned to the smoldering homesteads, poking the ground with their spears to unearth items like those Gathoni Mutahi had cached away.

Amid the chaos and smoke families were often separated, and many young children were never recovered. Prior to villagization, Ruth Ndegwa was living several ridges away from Gathoni. Her husband had already been arrested and detained, and she was left alone to take care of her children and elderly relatives. Ruth later recalled the moment of forced removal.

> We had not been given any warning beforehand that our houses were going to be burned. No one in the whole ridge knew that we were to move. The

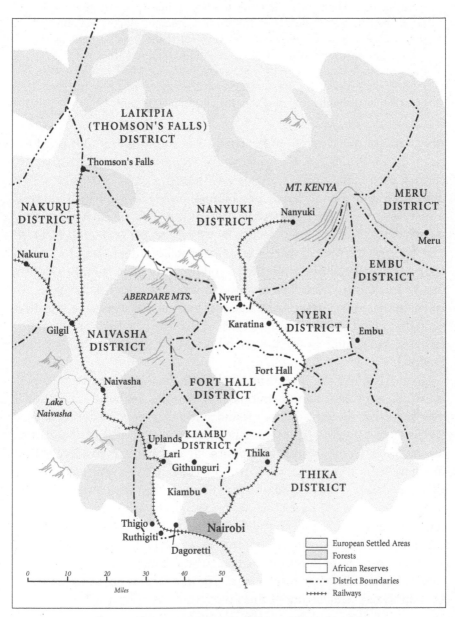

Areas of Central Kenya Affected by Mau Mau

police just came one day, and drove everybody out of their homes, while the Home Guards burned the houses right behind us. Our household goods were burned down, including the foodstuffs like maize, potatoes, and beans, which were in our stores. Everything, even our clothes were burned down. One only saved what one was wearing at the time! . . . During the move I got separated from my children, and I could not trace them. They had been in front, leading our remaining cattle, but I failed to find them. During the whole night I could hear a lot of shooting and screaming. I cried the whole night, knowing that my children were gone.[16]

At sunrise she found herself in Kiamariga, one of the several "protected villages," as the British colonial government called them, in her district. According to colonial officials, the new villages in Central Province were a proud physical manifestation of colonial progress. As British colonial forces were razing the homesteads, various ministers in Baring's government had gathered in Nairobi, where they filed a report stating, "It is agreed that amongst the Kikuyu there is a fundamental craving to acquire knowledge on European lines. Whilst they could not be expected to take kindly at first to a departure from their traditional way of life, such as living in villages, they need and desire to be told just what to do." The same ministers went on to laud the process, emphasizing that the new Kikuyu communities were being built along "the same lines as the villages in the North of England."[17]

Kiamariga, like the other Emergency villages, hardly evoked the pastoral images of the English countryside. When the women arrived at their new collective homesteads, they found nothing, save a cordon of armed loyalists and a nearby Home Guard post. There was no shelter, food, water, sanitation facilities, or medical supplies. "It was a site of absolute suffering," recalled one woman from Kiambu District. "It was very cold, and we slept just there on the ground. If we had known then what awaited us, I'm not certain we would have gone on."[18] Despite the self-satisfied and optimistic rhetoric of Britain's colonial planners, villagization was intended as a punitive strategy to contain, control, and discipline Mau Mau women. They had refused to cooperate with British colonial authority, and they were going to suffer the consequences. The district commissioner of Nyeri, Oswald "Ozzie" Hughes, made this point clear when he wrote:

At the end of 1953, the Administration were faced with the serious problem of the concealment of terrorists and supply of food to them. This was widespread and, owing to the scattered nature of the homesteads, fear of detection was negligible; so, in the first instance, the inhabitants of those areas were made to build and live in concentrated villages. This first step had to be taken speedily, somewhat to the detriment of usual health measures and was definitely a punitive short-term measure.[19]

A routine of forced communal labor dominated the day-to-day lives of the villagers. They spent the first several months living outdoors or in makeshift lean-to structures while they built hundreds of huts. With Home Guards chasing them about with whips and clubs, the work was done at breakneck speed. From dawn until dusk women and the handful of men, mostly the elderly and infirm, cut wood, thatched roofs, and plastered walls with mud and then white clay, giving the structures a whitewashed look. Wandia wa Muriithi, one of Ruth Ndegwa's fellow villagers from Kiamariga, described her enforced labor.

> Sometime in 1954 we were ordered to move from where our home was, and everything was burned. Our cattle were also confiscated. I was then heavily pregnant and gave birth three days after the move. The people were many and could not possibly fit into the few homes that had been made. We were ordered to go into the forest to get logs and cut reeds, to construct more houses. Even me, with my tiny two-day-old baby, had to carry thatching reeds. The construction of the village began, and everybody was involved. There was no discrimination in the work. Whenever a house was complete, ten or more women would occupy it, together with their families. All the houses were constructed in the same circular style, with conical roofs. Every day we would leave early, to start getting construction material. In one day we could construct about ten houses. The whole location was accommodated in a few large villages.[20]

Today women throughout Central Province recall the mad rush whenever a hut was ready to be occupied. Several women and their children would occupy a single hut of approximately one hundred square feet. In it they would cook on small hearths that were cleared away at night so as to use every square inch for sleeping space. Even then, the quarters were unbearably tight, leaving the villagers little choice but to sleep virtually on top of one another.

Once the huts were finished, the women began to dig trenches to encircle the villages. About ten feet deep and fifteen feet wide, they were lined with *nyambo*, or thick sharpened sticks. The trench perimeters were then surrounded with barbed wire. The intent was to keep villagers in and to prevent them from supplying any of the remaining forest fighters. All access to a village was through a single gate and bridge that were kept under round-the-clock Home Guard surveillance. The loyalists and their families lived in nearby Home Guard posts, which were sites of comparative luxury.

They enjoyed ample living space and food, largely provided by confiscated livestock and food stores, and the free labor of the thousands of imprisoned villagers living nearby. Initially their labor was used to build trenches surrounding the Home Guard posts, similar to those constructed around the villages. Later the villagers would become personal servants to the loyalists, sent to the Home Guard posts to draw water, fetch firewood, cultivate farms, and tend to loyalist livestock. Loyalist women were not required to work on the forced communal projects or even on the basic domestic upkeep of their own homes. Their special status earned them the derisive label of *thata*, or barren. In a society where reproduction defined womanhood, such a label was the ultimate insult.

The hard labor began when the villages were finally completed. In Kiamariga and the other villages of Nyeri District the days began before dawn with the sound of a siren or the shrill of a whistle blown from the Home Guard watchtower. Women scurried to prepare the usual meager morning meal for the children. They often made *ugali*, a polentalike meal, and gave their children one small piece each; the remainder was then mixed with warm salted water to be consumed as a kind of porridge. Other times breakfast was simply warm salted water. But the children's hunger was not so easily deceived, and the early morning air would be filled with their cacophonous wails and later, when exhausted, whimpers for more food. For women like Ruth Ndegwa, the realities of village life quickly sobered the elation she felt after reuniting with some of her children. She later recalled how they, like all of the other children, would be left behind in the village while she worked—the younger ones, including infants, being tended to by the older children, as well as by the elderly and crippled, some of whom were family, others barely acquaintances. Today, the sound of a whistle brings to mind those mornings, when, she said,

> I prepared whatever food I had from the previous night, and the porridge I made before going to work was what I gave them to eat for breakfast. Then I left them alone in the village. If we had nothing to eat the previous night, the children would have to remain without eating the whole day. . . . If you delayed in the hut after the whistle to report outside the village for work had been blown, maybe because you were preparing the porridge to leave for your children, the Home Guards would come kicking doors down, and if you were found inside, they would kick and overturn the porridge and you would be beaten because of being late.[21]

With hoes, shovels, and *viondo*, or baskets, the villagers would then march in the morning darkness for two to three hours, guided by the light of hurricane lamps hung from long poles. Their destination was the forest edge on Mount Kenya, several miles away, where they were constructing yet another trench, this one to separate the forest from the reserves. Their warders in the villages, the Home Guards, were also their escorts. Already exhausted and battered from their march, the women spent the remainder of the day filling their individual work quotas at the trench site. The work brigades were divided between those digging the ten-foot-deep trench and those lifting the baskets of soil from below and hauling them away. This assembly-line process continued without pause throughout the day. The colonial officers overseeing the projects would often survey the vast labor site from their Land Rovers, shouting orders to the Home Guards: "*Kazi, kazi*" (Work, work). The Home Guards were more than happy to impress their white superiors. "While [you were] digging the trench," one woman from Kiganjo village later recalled, "the Home Guards would be standing on either side, in front and behind, such that if you raised your head to take a break, you were hit on the head or back. It was a reminder that you should be working."[22]

Singing, talking, eating, and drinking were all forbidden during forced labor. This is not to say that women did not compose songs late at night, in the relative safety of their huts. They sung verses that disparaged the Home Guards, pointed to colonial injustices, and begged for humane treatment. In Nyeri's Gatung'ang'a village one song asked that

> Women tell Kariuki [the headman],
> So that Kariuki may tell Gatoto [the subchief],
> And Gatoto may tell Karangi [the chief],
> And Karangi may inform the DO
> That this trench digging is going to kill the women.[23]

In Gaikuyu village the women decided to take their chances, breaking the rules with the hope that their condition would change. "When the DO came to inspect the progress of the trench," one villager later recalled, "we composed a song for him in desperation, asking him why he had detained our husbands at Manyani and left us to die from digging the trenches."[24] Not surprisingly, many women did die from the deadly combination of exhaustion, brutality, and hunger. Miles from the villages, the Home Guards would order several of their laborers to dig a grave, sometimes inside the trench and other times outside of it near the forest edge. Unceremoniously, the dead would be buried, and the work would continue.

· · ·

Violence in the Emergency villages was not confined to the hours of forced labor. Women and their dependents lived in constant anxiety, not knowing when they would be singled out for the most minor infraction or, more often than not, for no reason at all. If any logic is to be construed from the violence, the perpetual atmosphere of fear and uncertainty was intended to break the villagers of their Mau Mau support. As in the Pipeline, Mau Mau suspects in the reserves were expected to provide full confessions of their oaths as well as their knowledge of all subversive activities. There was also a kind of frenzy to violence in the Emergency villages, similar to that in the camps. Colonial agents, white and black alike, were not seeking simply to extract confessions and intelligence. They clearly also wanted the villagers to suffer or die.

The Home Guard posts were the epicenters of torture. The contrast between the idleness of the loyalist women living there and the brutality inflicted upon the villagers in courtyards of the posts or in the *ndaki*, the interior subterranean holding cells, could not have been more stark. If a woman was late to communal labor roll call, if she walked too slowly or failed to fulfill her daily work quota, if she was suspected of harboring Mau Mau sympathies—or worse, if she was caught trying to supply the remaining forest fighters, which was not unusual—she could be sent to the Home Guard post. "I was tending to my sick child when the final morning whistle blew," recalled one villager from Kiamariga. "Before I knew it, the Home Guards broke the door down and hauled me off to the post. I grabbed on to an old lady, who held me tightly, but it was no use. They hit her in the face with a rifle butt and dragged me away."[25] After a thorough beating outside of her hut, this woman was taken to the *ndaki*. As in other villages, the *ndaki* at Kiamariga was about four feet deep, halfway filled with water, and covered with a thick matting of sisal and branches—forcing those inside to crouch and fumble their way around in the darkness. The hole itself was many feet long, and there were generally a dozen or more captives inside at any given time. They often huddled together for warmth and for protection against the snakes and vermin that infested the cell.

After being released from the *ndaki*, a woman might be sent back to the village and more forced labor, or she might suffer additional torture at the post. Sometimes the Home Guards took the initiative, squeezing and mutilating women's breasts with pliers, pushing vermin and rifles into their vaginas, and forcing them to run naked around the inside of the post while carrying buckets of excrement on their heads. The women were also raped, oftentimes repeatedly by several men. Resistance could lead to summary execution or further torture before reconsideration of a life or death judgment. Simon Rutho—one of the few men left in Nyeri District's

Gatung'ang'a village—later recalled the screams that would come from the Home Guard post. He had a unique vantage point, having been screened as "white" and serving as the teacher for the local loyalist children. But Simon was, by all accounts, a Mau Mau supporter even if he could do nothing to help those being tortured other than drop food into the *ndaki* when he found the opportunity. Otherwise, he later said, he tried not to watch the public displays of brutality no matter how difficult they were to avoid.

> I remember in our village there was a headman who had come from Kiamariga. He was a very cruel man. Whenever that headman desired a woman, and she refused him, he would take a beer bottle, then order an *askari* to hold one of the woman's legs, and another to hold the other, wide apart. Then he would insert the bottle into the woman's private parts and punch it up to the stomach. Many women died after having been treated that way. First he beat them with sticks and kicks, but if they still resisted his advances he used the beer bottle. . . . Nobody cared about them. The village men would be told to go and bury them in the village [when they died]. . . . So many people died. I remember a few years ago a farmer who was digging in his *shamba* [farm] exhumed a human skull into which a sweet potato had grown. The skull was taken to the local school, for the young children to see how people had been buried. The area around where the skull was found had been the village graveyard, and if you tried digging there you would unearth skeletons of the people who were buried at that time. Nobody cared about the village people.[26]

The Home Guards were following the example of those in charge, but they also had choices, albeit those that were incredibly constrained by their bosses in the colonial government. They could have chosen not to rape, beat, and torture, but if they had, it could have meant running the risk of being labeled Mau Mau, and thus on the receiving end of British colonial justice. Men like Simon Rutho toed a very dangerous line and were, in fact, beaten by local district officers for not reporting Mau Mau activities. When double agents like Simon were caught, they were relieved of their duties and sent to the Pipeline or summarily executed as an example to the rest.[27] Other Home Guards were ordered by their white commanding officers to beat and torture the local villagers, and failure to comply would mean a beating identical to that which they could not bring themselves to administer. In the face of this pressure, and considering the rewards that accompanied compliance, it is easy to understand why many loyalists were willing participants in the torture of villagers, demonstrating their active support for the colonial government.

The handful of former Home Guards who offered their recollections of the Emergency invariably used language similar to that of colonial officials and local settlers. In their words, Mau Mau adherents were "scum," "filthy pigs," and "savage animals" who had to be wiped out.[28] How much this eliminationist mentality was the result of intense exposure to British colonial discourse and how much was independently conceived by the loyalists themselves we will never know for certain. Today, many former Mau Mau share the sentiment of Wachehu Magayu, who lived in the North Tetu Division of Nyeri District during the Emergency. "The Home Guards behaved with such hatred and cruelty because they were being paid by the government to do it," she explained. "They had agreed to become sellouts of their people, and the government was rewarding them for it. They had put money and personal gain before everything else. That coupled with the fact that they did not believe that Kenya would ever be free, that we would ever be independent. So they thought they chose the winner's side by supporting the colonialists."[29]

The behavior of the Home Guards cannot be analyzed without understanding the origins of their training and their inculcation into the philosophy and procedures of the British security forces. The women detained in the villages called Britain's security forces *haraka*, "the fast ones," because of the speed with which they could inflict damage on the local population. "Whenever those groups came into the villages," recalled Shelmith Njeri, "they would wreak havoc within no time. They would be everywhere within a short period, turning houses inside out, burning houses, and raping women. It was so fast that a person in one house would have no time to know what was happening in another. As soon as she heard the screams, they had already burst into her house and began tearing it apart."[30] Some women like Shelmith distinguished between the British soldiers who were members of the military and paramilitary units, and the whites who belonged to the Kenya Police Reserve, the King's African Rifles, and the Kenya Regiment. Others simply referred to all of these men as "Johnnies," or, in the words of several women, "British savages."

Women suspected of continuing to feed the Mau Mau guerrillas were sometimes brought into the village square and shot or hung as an example to the rest. Sometimes they were beaten first with clubs and rifle butts, and sometimes raped. On other occasions members of the security forces would take captured Mau Mau fighters, rope them to the back of Land Rovers, and drive them around the villages, leaving bits of body parts in their wake. Young children were slaughtered and their remains skewered on spears and paraded around the village squares by the Home Guards. Excrement-based torture was also widespread.[31] "The Johnnies would make us run around with toilet buckets on our heads," recalled one woman. "The contents would be running down our faces, and we would have to wipe it off and eat it, or else we were shot. Even then, some people were killed anyway."[32] There were also public executions of captured forest fighters, like this one described by Milka Muriuki, who was a teenager at the time.

> When we were still living in Hombe village . . . the British soldiers shot dead a man named Stephano and another. Many of these soldiers came, and the villagers were herded out into the square, and soon there were British soldiers everywhere. I do not know where the two Mau Mau fighters had been caught, but they were tied with ropes and hung onto a tree branch and then shot one after the other, in full view of all the villagers. That day, all of the remaining men were rounded up and taken to Nyeri, and only the women were left behind. The soldiers raped many of us.[33]

It did not matter whether they were young or old, all women in the villages lived in fear of sexual assault. Some, like Milka, connived to avoid the fate of so many other women.

> The white officers had no shame. They would rape women in full view of everyone. They would take whomever they wanted at one corner and just do it right there. Whenever those soldiers came into the village, I remember I used to sneak into our house and smear ashes all over my body so they would not fancy me. Then, when they saw me, they would say, "Now look at this one, what is wrong with her?"[34]

Many women were not so fortunate. Mothers and daughters were sometimes raped together in the same hut by white and black members of the security forces. At gunpoint others were given the choice between death and rape. Margaret Nyaruai explained why many chose rape: "We felt that we would rather allow them to rape us than get killed, especially those who had small children depending on them."[35] Some women were assaulted on their way to or from forced communal labor, others while they worked. "We would be digging the trench," recalled one woman, "being whipped if we worked too slowly or looked lethargic. And then a security force patrol would come by and just start dragging women into the forests and raping them. Then when they were finished with us we had to go back to work, and if we didn't fill our quotas we would be beaten some more or sent to the Home Guard post, where we would be beaten and raped again."[36] Oftentimes the security forces were demanding intelligence at the same time they were brutalizing the women. If the Mau Mau guerrillas had launched a successful attack, the Johnnies would often exact their revenge on the villagers while simultaneously interrogating them. "They would sometimes squeeze women's breasts with pliers," recalled Njeri Wamai, "or swing women by their long hair. Other times, one would be interrogated while lying on the ground, with a soldier stepping on her neck, while others would beat her all over her body. Then one would be allowed to sit upright and tell everything. If she still refused, she would be beaten again. Many died this way."[37]

The capriciousness of these raids was complemented by the certainty of confessional *barazas*. After returning in the late afternoon from forced labor, the women often would be led into the village squares, where they would be forced to listen to anti–Mau Mau propaganda and endure more screening. The Home Guards and local district officers were present, as were various members of the security forces, depending on who was patrolling the area or who wanted to participate in the action. The *barazas* were clearly intended to elicit confessions of oaths as well as of all knowledge of Mau Mau activities, past and present. By the time the villagers made it into the square, they had been, to put it mildly, worked over. They were exhausted, beaten, violated, and famished, and, once the *baraza* was finished, they would have a similar routine to look forward to the following day, as well as every day thereafter. Nothing they said or did would change their status. Confession did not mean an end to forced labor, a relief from hunger, or improved care for their children. It meant only that they were spared from death, for the time being.

Lined up in the village square, women would be singled out one by one. The haphazard method of selection infused the unfolding drama with anxiety, with each person fearing they would be the center of the public spectacle. Those taken to the front of the crowd were often stripped naked and forced to lead the rest of the village in rounds of anti–Mau Mau songs. When the music stopped and the questioning began, those who refused to confess were beaten, often unconscious. The British officers would order villagers to bring buckets of water—the same water they were forbidden from drinking—to douse the unconscious victim. Once she was revived, the questioning resumed, and if she still refused to cooperate, the British officers and Home Guards used other methods. Many of the village detainees in Nyeri later recalled what would happen next. According to Margaret Nyaruai:

At that time, some people who had refused to confess were being put in sacks, one covering the lower part of their bodies while the other covered the upper part. Then petrol or paraffin would be poured over the sacks, and those in charge would order them to be lit. The people inside would die writhing in the flames. Many people were dying every day. And it was the people who refused to confess, even after all the bad things that were being done to them; they were always killed in order to instill fear into others who might think of concealing the truth.[38]

There were many variations on this form of public terror. In the village near Othaya British security forces often brought in the bodies of the dead forest fighters and forced the women to carry them around the village square while chanting, "This is independence." Other times, the same women repeated the drill carrying the bodies of dead villagers of all ages, including children. British officers burned women with cigarette butts and ordered them to walk barefoot on beds of hot coals. Home Guards pulled the villagers' hair out in fistfuls, while screaming at them to confess their Mau Mau sins.[39] There were also other, less physically brutal tactics that were no less harrowing for those involved. Throughout Central Province various colonial officers had their own versions of counteroathing ceremonies.[40] In Kiamariga village women were forced to denounce Mau Mau while sticking their finger in a gourd filled with blood—which was, according to the local district officer, the blood of dead Mau Mau forest fighters who had found their *wiyathi*, or independence.[41] On other occasions torture took on a specific Kikuyu meaning, with one woman from Nyeri District recalling:

At one point, all the villagers were ordered to remove every article of clothing and remain stark naked. You cannot start to imagine the shame and embarrassment we felt when, without any consideration for the small children, we were told to arrange ourselves in two rows, one for the men and the other for the women, old and young alike. To everyone's horror we were ordered at gunpoint to embrace each other, man with a woman, regardless of whether the man happened to be your father, father-in-law, or brother. It was all so humiliating that one woman hanged herself later, as she felt that she could not continue to live with the humiliating experience of having been forced to embrace her son-in-law while both of them were naked. In our custom that is a curse.[42]

Torture was also highly personalized. Home Guards were often neighbors or even relatives of the villagers they were brutalizing. There were also local British officers whom the women knew by name, or rather by nickname. By far the most notorious of these men in Nyeri District was YY. As a member of the Kenya Police Reserve, this young British settler and Napoleonic-like figure had acted with particularly cruel abandon during the early days of the war, screening Mau Mau suspects with a perverse enthusiasm. With the formation of the Emergency villages, YY and others like him, along with their minions, perpetrated daily acts of brutality. They took no pity on those suffering around them. Rather than revolting these young British officers, the gruesomeness of their behavior only aroused their eliminationist mentality. Or perhaps over time their repeated tortures and killing anesthetized them, wiping out any inhibitions they may have had, thus making their murderous deeds a form of daily labor. Still, many of these men hardly seemed like automatons. Some joked and laughed while perpetrating tortures; others casually smoked cigarettes or ate snacks. Even through the prism of Mau Mau their behavior was extraordinary, only partly explainable by the moral approbation that belied it.

By early 1955 General Erskine had seized the initiative over the Mau Mau guerrillas, and there were at most a few thousand of them remaining in the vast tracts of forest around Mount Kenya and the nearby Aberdares. The general's success in rooting out Mau Mau was partly attributable to villagization, disrupting as it did the supply line between the women and the forest fighters. The spiked trenches, barbed wires, and armed guards were all deterrents, as were the demarcated zones called special areas, or the territory that stretched between the villages and the forest edges (usually known as the "one-mile strip"). They were a kind of no-man's-land where villagers, unaccompanied by Home Guard escorts, would be shot on sight. It was also where many women tended what remained of their farms. Once a week, those living in the villages were given permission to go into the special areas to gather what little there was growing in their abandoned plots. The Home Guards would lead them out of the villages en masse, and the women would hurry about collecting what they could in the few hours allotted to them. But there was increasingly little to be found, because villagers had been given no time to plant or cultivate their crops. The women would fill their skirts or blankets with roots and wild vegetables, or, when they were lucky, with sweet potatoes or maize that had germinated on their own. Still, there was only enough time to collect food for three or four days, even though they were permitted into the special areas just once a week. If a woman was confined in the *ndaki*, she missed her opportunity for weekly food collection. If sick or lame from the day's beating or forced labor, she did what she could to make it to the food collection roll call.

When reflecting on their weekly food brigades, former villagers remember the desperation they felt scavenging the decimated countryside or, worse, their fear of hunger when the opportunity was missed altogether. "If a woman happened to miss the chance to go to her farm," Grace Kaharika later recalled, "for whatever reason, her family would have to beg for food the whole week from the neighbors, who barely had enough for themselves in the first place." She went on to say:

> No amount of pleading would arouse the sympathy of the headman and his Home Guards to agree to allow the poor woman to go to the farm. Even if her failure might have been occasioned by illness, as was often the case, she would have to wait until the set day on the following week. Even if it was a child who had been very sick and could not be left alone, they still would not understand. Sometimes the other women, if they knew of her problem before going to the farm, would contribute some food each to the woman, and she would be able to survive the week.[43]

Some women took their chances and snuck out of the villages and into the special areas. It was then that YY, lying in wait, would shoot them dead. The no-man's-land was his personal domain. Often he would patrol the area on food collection day, and when the whistle blew for the villagers to return, he would start shooting. Many of the women fled, dropping some or all of the food they had gathered as they ran to the relative safety of the Home Guards. "You never knew when YY would be there," recalled one Kiamariga villager. "When the shooting started, it was total mayhem. Here we were, exhausted trying to gather the pitiful food that was left, and even then we had no peace. If someone was shot and killed, we just left them there. If you stopped to help them or grieve, you ran the risk of being shot yourself."[44] Or, in the words of Milka Muriuki, "It was like he was hunting wild game, only we were the animals."[45]

YY also ventured inside the villages and Home Guard posts. He tortured countless women without provocation, squeezing their breasts with pliers, beating them with his riding whip, clubs, or the butt of one of the several pistols that hung from his waist. It was not unusual for villagers to die during such episodes, their bodies later strapped to YY's Land Rover and driven around for all to see. Any reluctance on the part of the women to look at the corpses was met with a rain of blows from the Home Guards.[46] In several Nyeri villages YY traveled with another British district officer, known by the locals as the One with the Crooked Nose. Like YY, this man was young, though he was not a settler but a member of the Administration. Together they were a physical study of contrast—YY, a diminutive figure, and the One with the Crooked Nose, an extremely tall, muscular man. Sometimes with his confrere, other times alone, YY would single out women, men, and some of the older children from the village square and take them to Kwa Wood—the name of the execution site not far from YY's police post at Gaikuyu. There, those selected would dig their own graves and line up in front of them. YY or his accomplice would shoot them dead, and their bodies would be covered up by the Home Guards.

Despite their death march to Kwa Wood, some villagers were spared. "I remember the day when I was chosen," one woman later recalled. "I was taken with five others to Kwa Wood, where we were ordered to begin digging our way to our *wiyathi* [independence]. As we dug, YY and the other white man just stood there talking casually, though I could not understand them. We finished digging, and YY shot the others and kicked the ones into their graves who did not fall in. Then he came to me, and he paused. I was a young woman at the time, and he decided to rape me instead. He took me back to the village, and until my husband returned from detention he raped me whenever he had the chance."[47] As did other members of the security forces, YY raped women in their huts, during forced labor, and in the Home Guard posts. In a gesture of bravado, he also had the habit of removing his shirt while perpetrating acts of sexual violence, earning him another nickname, Gathiiutheri, or the One Who Walked Naked. He also appeared more than willing to help out his fellow officers. On one occasion, "YY stood there holding a gun to a woman's head," recalled a former Hombe villager. "I then saw her being made to do something that I had not imagined possible. She was made to put the penis of the other white man who was with YY in her mouth and ordered to suck it. This lady only died recently as an old woman."[48]

To suggest that YY was a rogue operator, or that the villages of Nyeri District were somehow unique, would be a mischaracterization of the war in the Kikuyu countryside. There may have been degrees of difference between some of the villages, just as there were between the camps in the Pipeline. Nonetheless, the point of villagization was to make the suspected population of Mau Mau adherents suffer, and many white and black members of the British forces of law and order were masters at their vocation. Today, whether one travels through Nyeri, Murang'a, or Kiambu District, former Mau Mau adherents will share similar stories of destruction. "It became clear to us very quickly," recalled one woman living in the Kiharu Division of Murang'a, some twenty-five miles south of YY's territory in Nyeri, "that the British wanted to kill us, and those that were not killed were going to suffer. That was what those times were like. They just thought we were animals."[49]

Farther south another thirty miles or so toward Nairobi is the region of southern Kiambu, which during Mau Mau was the domain of Kiboroboro, or the Killer, and his fellow members of the Kenya Regiment. A young settler who was known by many of the locals prior to the Emergency, Kiboroboro launched his operations from the Kenya Regiment post at Thigio. From there he often traveled along the southern Kiambu road that stretched from the Nairobi suburb of Dagoretti in the east, westward toward Makutano village. The villagers along this stretch of highway even had a nickname for Kiboroboro's Land Rover. They called it Gitune, or the Big Red. When asked if it was because the truck was painted red, villagers provided a response similar to Njuhi Gachau's. "Oh no," she said, "it was not red. It had a greenish blue color. We used to call it Gitune because it was always bloody."[50] On the dashboard of this Land Rover Kiboroboro had affixed an automatic rifle, which he used to hunt down local villagers—men, women, and children—as he made his rounds. "He mostly used to pass along this route, going from Gikambura, Kamangu, Thigio, to and fro," Stanley Wainaina, a former villager, later recalled. "If he happened to see anyone crossing the road ahead, he would not hesitate to shoot them. . . . People came to fear him so much."[51]

In fact, anyone standing near the roadside, outside of a hut, working on communal labor—they were all targets. On any given day two, five, ten, or several dozen unsuspecting villagers would be mowed down.[52] Some were picked up and tossed into the back of Kiboroboro's Land Rover by the local Home Guards; others were picked up later in a kind of flatbed truck— described by one villager as "a bus whose body had been cut off, leaving only the cab and a back without sides."[53] Like Kiboroboro's vehicle, this one also had a nickname. It was called Warurungana, or the Gatherer. Bodies were sometimes picked up immediately; other times they were left for several days decomposing and attracting wild animals and dogs, who fed on the rotting flesh. There were also other forms of postmortem humiliation. "This lady and her father were shot by Kiboroboro one morning," Rahab Wakibunja recalled. "They were both shot right there by the roadside. But what shocked and infuriated the locals here was that after the shooting the killers laid the lady's body facing upwards while they laid that of the father on top of the lady, in a manner suggestive of copulation. The two bodies were then left lying like that, by the roadside, to be collected later."[54]

Kiboroboro also operated with the British military forces. Like other members of the Kenya Regiment, he would have been expected to act as an adviser to any of the British units deployed to Kenya, be they the paramilitary, the King's African Rifles, or the British regiments. "At night Kiboroboro would come to our homes accompanied by the young soldiers we called Johnnies," recalled Esther Muchiri. She went on to say:

> They would walk around the village, knocking down the doors of our huts, and nobody dared to complain. Sometimes Kiboroboro would just empty his Bren gun inside the room without caring about who or what was hit. Other times they would enter a house, and on finding a young man inside, they would take him away with them. The following morning we would get reports from those detained at [Thigio] post that so and so's body was lying there. That was the way things were at this place. Most people were taken to detention, while the others were killed. We had no peace. We couldn't even go out to our farms to get food for fear of getting caught. If you were found with cooked food in your hut, you would be punished because you would be said to have prepared the food for Mau Mau, which they referred to as our husbands. It was real persecution. We cried until our tears ran dry. Sometimes during their patrols some would deliberately be left behind to rape you. If you happened to have a nasty one, he would force a bottle inside your private parts. It was painful, my child.[55]

Young women, pregnant women, and old women were raped, often repeatedly, during such raids. The Johnnies would generally rape them first, then leave the women for the Home Guards, who also took their turns. Other times women were divided up, the Johnnies and locals like Kiboroboro getting first pick—preferring the adolescent girls whom they called "unplucked chickens."[56] There was no way to resist, though many adopted tactics similar to the women in Nyeri District, smearing their hair and bodies with soot and excrement. Sometimes this tactic worked; other times it meant they were violated by the younger Home Guards who occupied the lowest rung on the raping hierarchy. Regardless of who raped them "we could not utter a word because that would mean instant death," one woman from Mung'etho village in Ndeiya later recalled. "Can you imagine living in the same room with your father-in-law [a taboo for the Kikuyu]? That was how we lived, because there was no room to live separately. When the Johnnies and Home Guards came, they would rape you, in full sight of your father-in-law, and he would not say a word of protest. He would just watch quietly and bear the pain patiently. Even your own daughters could be raped in your sight, and you wouldn't protest or prevent it."[57]

Still, these women considered themselves lucky to be alive. As the Emergency wore on, they were increasingly terrorized by Kiboroboro and other members of the security forces, who dressed in blackface, pretending to be Africans. The metamorphosis of these white men was now complete: no longer were they simply behaving like the so-called savages they were allegedly pacifying; they looked like them as well. Disguised, they would move into the villages undetected, before the locals had an opportunity to run. In Kiboroboro's case "people would not know that it was him and bolt away," recalled Njuhi Gachau. "They would only realize the truth when it was too late to run away. He would then spray them with bullets 'ta, ta, ta, ta, ta,' killing everyone."[58]

Many corpses were eventually taken to the post at Thigio, located along the southern Kiambu road. It was there that the Kenya Regiment had established its area headquarters. At the start of the Emergency, the local Mau Mau population was forced to turn the post into a fortresslike structure, surrounded by the customary deep trench, barbed wire, and a watchtower. Hundreds of villagers were called out for the project. As one woman later recalled:

> Our first assignment as communal work was to dig a trench which went all around the post. The trench was the first obstacle that any unauthorized visitor to the post would encounter before reaching the high barbed-wire fence. As we were digging the trench, the old men were engaged in cutting and sharpening sticks into spikes, which would then be planted inside the trench, both on the floor and on the sides, in a crisscrossing way, so that it would be impossible for anyone falling into that trench to come out alive, or without sustaining fatal injuries. The post was also where the white man we called Kiboroboro lived with the other British soldiers and their Home Guards. It was also used as a temporary detention camp for all those arrested during the frequent raids inside the village.[59]

Not far beyond Thigio's spiked trench was a massive burial site. Dozens of villagers confirm today that this was one of the area's largest mass graves, smaller by only a little than the one at the Ruthigiti Home Guard post, farther down the road in the direction of Nairobi. The men and women arrested and later held at Thigio were responsible for burying the bodies. Villagers would off-load the corpses from the Big Red and the Gatherer and bury them in pits deep enough to hold a dozen bodies or so. Beatrice Gatonye was one of the many women assigned this task, and she later remembered her work: "In Thigio, trenchlike graves were dug in rows, and dead bodies would be laid in them. When one was full, it would be covered, and we would go on to the next."[60] Villagers like Beatrice insisted that many of these corpses were not from the local area. Thigio was apparently one of the dumping spots for bodies as far north as Limuru. The grave site was active for most of 1954 and 1955, though it was used intermittently until the end of the war. "I don't think anybody can say for sure how many people are buried here," Rahab Mungai later stated, "owing to the fact that [the corpses] were also brought from surrounding areas and at different times. At a guess I would say more than two thousand. Probably three. But no one can say for sure."[61]

The gruesome scene outside of the Thigio post was rivaled only by what was happening inside. There, alongside the barracks of the Kenya Regiment, were interrogation rooms where local villagers were brought in for torture. Men and women were questioned incessantly about their knowledge of Mau Mau and told to confess their oaths if they wanted to live. Hung upside down from rafters, they were beaten with whips, clubs, and rifle butts. Women were often held for days and raped repeatedly by white and black alike. Some were gang-raped, others molested by individuals. They were raped at gunpoint, at knifepoint, or were tied up or held down by the force of a boot or the butt of a gun. Men were also sexually assaulted, sodomized with bottles and rifle barrels, and castrated. For many taken to the Thigio post, the struggle was not to avoid the beating or sexual torture but simply to survive. "Even the men who were being arrested and taken to this post," Rachel Kiruku later recalled, "would only believe that they were alive when they awoke in the morning. This was because the same people who would bury their dead colleagues today would be corpses tomorrow, to be buried by the others."[62]

Several miles down the road at the Ruthigiti Home Guard post the situation was much the same. Kiboroboro made his usual appearances there, but most of the operations were directed by another young member of the Kenya Regiment who took the liberty of nicknaming himself Major wa Wanjiru, or the Major, Son of Wanjiru. Proudly bearing the image of an African buffalo, the regiment's symbol, on his hat, this sadist joined the ranks of Kiboroboro, YY, and others when it came to the cruelty of his torture and killing. He would select villagers at random, line them up in the post, and then shoot them in the back. Presumably, if ever questioned, he could claim they were shot while trying to escape. Others were killed after they were told to leave the post—a few steps outside the gate, and they were shot dead.

Major wa Wanjiru and his comrades often tortured their victims before executing them. Not long after villagization, they rounded up Esther Muchiri and several dozen women and men early one morning, marching them off to the Ruthigiti Home Guard post. There Major wa Wanjiru began his work. The Home Guards were ordered to strip all of the victims naked, and then, according to Esther:

We were beaten the whole day until evening, when we were separated from the men, who were ordered to sit a distance away with their hands cuffed together. Then the interrogators started to squeeze their private parts with a pair of pliers. There was only a short distance between where they were and ourselves. I even saw one of them being hit on his face, a blow that sent him sprawling down unconscious. A whole bucket of water had to be poured on his body to revive him. The same evening, the men were loaded onto a vehicle and driven away. We were to learn the following morning that all of them had been executed. That night all of the women including myself were divided amongst the Home Guards and raped. Even this lady who was eight months pregnant was not spared. We were raped throughout the night. The following morning we were anxious to know the fate of the men. I remember asking the same pregnant woman what happened to our men after they were castrated. She pointed to a vehicle which was a short distance away. The bodies of our men lay inside. They had already been killed.[63]

It was the women who were later forced to bury the bodies of those murdered. Many corpses were taken to the forest edge and dumped, but others were put into pits. "We would lift them one by one, one person holding the wrists while the other held the ankles," recalled Njuhi Gachau, who underwent a similar ordeal at the Ruthigiti post. "It was one experience I will never forget."[64] Unlike the graves around Thigio, those in the vicinity of Ruthigiti were reportedly much larger, containing scores of bodies that were, according to one woman "lying on each other like heaps of maize cobs. And the graves were not very deep, but they were wide," she continued. "They were heaped on top of each other like pieces of wood."[65]

The sites would often be left open for several days until filled. Some of the dead were local villagers, but many were being brought in by Land Rovers from elsewhere, "reversing near the graves and dumping the bodies in," according to one man.[66] Both at Thigio and Ruthigiti women were selected to fingerprint the bodies, a task that served no other purpose than to punish. The identification process was nearly always done days after a body or batch of bodies had been thrown into a burial pit. By the time the women began their work the flesh of the corpses was rotting. Amid the stench, the flies, and the errant dogs, they would start fingerprinting. But the decomposing skin was sticky, often adhering to the women's hands. "The job we were told to do was just to torture us," Beatrice Gatonye later recalled. "The flesh would come off in our hands, and you couldn't get it off of you. For days you would have this sticky substance attached to your skin, knowing that it was the skin of someone else. We never managed to get many fingerprints. Anyway, those white men in charge would just stand near us with their guns, joking and laughing with each other and at us, smoking their cigarettes."[67]

As was true elsewhere in Central Province, the cruelty perpetrated by the colonial forces just went on and on, knowing no bounds other than the sadistic imagination of its perpetrators. The demand for intelligence or confessions was often a mere pretext, if one was even needed, to torture and murder the Mau Mau population. Women in Kiambu with husbands or relatives fighting in the forest were also assured of being singled out. Salome Maina was picked up with another woman and two adolescent boys, all of whom were accused of supplying arms to their husbands and fathers, who were allegedly still alive and fighting in the forests. Major wa Wanjiru ordered they be taken to the Ruthigiti post. There, according to Salome,

> he made the two young men strip naked and then commenced to beat them mercilessly. Then he came and started kicking me with his boots all over my body. The other lady was said to be the one who used to accommodate gangs in her home. He would hold us by our necks and bang our heads together. Then we were beaten until we fell unconscious. [When I awoke] I saw the two young men were beaten so badly until blood was coming down their faces and bodies, but we could still hear them pleading with those who were beating us. . . . When they still couldn't get information from me they decided to put paprika pepper inside my private parts. We were ordered to lie down on the open area inside the Ruthigiti post. No one held us down, but guards stood over us with guns. We were ordered to separate our legs with our knees raised. Failure to comply invited ruthless beating. Then a bottle full of a mixture of pepper and water was inserted into my birth canal and the contents emptied inside me. As the bottle was being emptied, it was held in place with the heel of a booted foot. After the pepper was inside of me, it is impossible for anyone to imagine the torment. The burning could be felt everywhere, in the eyes, ears, nose, mouth, and all over. It happened that the previous day, the day we were arrested, a lady named Watiri had been given the same treatment, only her mixture had been made from pepper and petrol. It was fortunate that the vehicle had left by the time my mixture was being prepared. After this treatment I was later carried to where Watiri was still lying groaning in agony and vomiting.

Several days later, Watiri was dead. Salome recovered, only to be subject to more torture. "It was the first time electric shock was used on us," she later recalled. "The small conductor was either placed on the tongue, on the arm, or anywhere else they desired. At first, I was made to hold it in my hands, and it swirled me around until I found myself hitting the wall. When it was placed on your tongue, held in place with some kind of wire, it would shake you until you wouldn't even realize when it was removed. . . . This was after we had been subjected to such terrible things already. The stories of that time are difficult to recount. But some of us still survived."[68]

Farther down the road in the direction of Nairobi was Dagoretti, the domain of Muru wa Itina, or the Son of the Buttocks. Like YY in Nyeri District, he was a member of the Kenya Police Reserve, running his operations from the Dagoretti police station and the nearby Home Guard post. Muru wa Itina, in fact, had a notable pedigree; his father was the infamous local settler known as Itina, or the Ass, and two of his brothers were also eliminating the Mau Mau threat, one in Fort Hall District, the other in Nairobi. Muru wa Itina patrolled the villages of Dagoretti Division, shooting people at random and parading the locals past the corpses before they were taken off for burial. "We were used to such mockery," recalled one woman. "It was usual for us to be collected and made to view dead bodies before they were buried. . . . It was a way of scaring us. Once there were many who had been killed inside a hut, which had been set ablaze by the security forces. Some were shot as they tried to escape, while others were burnt. Then there were other times when they just tossed grenades inside, blowing up everyone."[69] It was the murderous cruelty of Muru wa Itina's campaign that was so striking; no effort was expended to spare the victims unnecessary suffering. "He would just single people out and shoot them," recalled one man who today lives in the Mutuini Ward of Dagoretti. "There were also the rampages of burning of people's houses and the confiscation of their livestock which was used to feed the Home Guards. Those were punishments whose deliberate aim was to cause people pain. He also used to order the merciless beatings of the villagers while interrogating them about the oath. Those are just a few of the things he did here."[70]

It is not the random selections, the sexual assaults, the forced labor, or the torture that the Kikuyu women of Central Province remember most about the years of the Emergency. It was the lack of food. Today many former Mau Mau adherents are convinced that the colonial government was trying to starve them to death. In the words of one villager from Nyeri District:

> Hunger was the worst problem; that's what was killing most of the people. They were starving us on purpose, hoping we would give in. The little time we were allowed to go to the *shamba* was too short to allow for any meaningful food gathering. Also, the area we were allowed to use was too small, because the largest areas had been declared Special Areas and were off-limits. So the allowed areas had been overharvested, but that was what we had.[71]

The colonial government did virtually nothing to avert the food crisis. Despite reports from the districts beginning in early 1955 that starvation and malnutrition were widespread, Baring refused to confirm any serious scarcity of food. What malnutrition did exist was blamed on the Kikuyu themselves. According to A. C. C. Swann, the acting provincial commissioner for Central Province, "In many cases the parents have adequate food supplies, but do not make them available to their children. The intelligent Kikuyu are adept at leaving Government to feed their children, and are also fully aware of the propaganda value of apparent malnutrition among the young."[72] By November, however, the East African Standard detailed the starvation-related deaths of forty-five villagers in the Kiambaa Location of Kiambu. This district, containing some of the most densely populated areas in the Kikuyu reserves, suffered from the worst food shortages. There the Red Cross intervened with soup kitchens and supplies of dried milk, while Kenya's Medical Department dispatched several assistants. Missionaries also actively assisted such relief efforts, drawing largely upon private funds from international donors.[73] Still, British colonial officials denied any responsibility, the minister for local government, health, and housing, Wilfred Havelock, recognizing there were "undoubtedly bad spots in the Central Province" but insisting "one of the main factors was the ignorance of mothers in the feeding of their children. They did not realise the great importance of proteins."[74]

By denying the mounting crisis and blaming the victims of the incipient famine, the colonial government managed to deflect most of the criticism of its villagization policy. It did not address, however, the hardship in the reserves. It refused to allocate more funds and, instead, relied upon the efforts mainly of the Red Cross to assist the Emergency villages.[75] Baring turned to Malaya for help, approving the transfer of a handful of volunteer workers from the Malaya Federation to Kenya. By mid-1955, eleven Red Cross workers were in Central Province distributing food, along with a handful of missionaries. Everywhere, the collective efforts of these relief workers were under Baring's direct control, with him and his men on the spot insisting that the Red Cross and missionaries target their operations not to the areas of greatest need but to the locations where loyalists were demanding more government support.[76] The colony's own Medical Department issued scathing reports highlighting the "alarming number of deaths occurring amongst children in the 'punitive' villages" and the "political considerations" that were blocking the Red Cross relief efforts.[77] Indeed, throughout the Emergency the Medical Department would criticize the colonial government for its failure to address the causes and the effects of the food shortages in Kikuyuland. Moreover, reports issued by the Red Cross underscored the need for more concentrated and well-funded efforts in the villages. The director of the Overseas Branch of the British Red

Cross, during her tour through Central Province, commented that "women frequently have to feed a family in addition to themselves and that cases had been brought to her notice of women who, from progressive under-nourishment, had been unable to carry on with their work."[78]

In the path of this worsening famine lay Askwith's Community Development and Rehabilitation Department. With whatever meager funds he was granted, Askwith soon redirected his efforts away from rehabilitation, such as existed, and toward famine relief. Milk and soup distribution, together with orphan care, accounted for most of his officers' work in the Kikuyu reserves. Some home-craft classes and leisure-time activities were introduced, but hardly on the scale proposed by Askwith or advertised by the governor and colonial secretary. By far the most significant measure undertaken by Askwith's department was the establishment of Maendeleo ya Wanawake, or Progress among Women Clubs, which were essentially self-help organizations for women.[79] With additional input from voluntary organizations like the Red Cross and the East African Women's League, these clubs became centers for expanding home-craft training. But like other community development efforts undertaken in the context of the war, Maendeleo had little financial support and could not be separated from the colonial government's preeminent objective of punishing Mau Mau and rewarding loyalism. In March 1955 the two British women in charge of Maendeleo—Mary Beecher, the wife of Archbishop Leonard Beecher, and Nancy Shepherd, the assistant commissioner for community development and rehabilitation and chairwoman of Maendeleo—drafted a resolution condemning the effects of villagization.

> The Headquarters Committee of the Maendeleo ya Wanawake Organisation deprecate the excessive use of communal labour for women as it leaves too little time for the care of homes and children, causes great suffering, creates anti-Government feeling, and makes the teaching given in the Maendeleo Clubs very largely useless. . . . Where the communal labour is essential, this Committee feels that at least the women should be paid so that money is available to buy food for the children.[80]

The response was predictable. The acting provincial commissioner insisted that Kikuyu women in the districts labored for no more than two days per week, and that Maendeleo sewing and knitting classes were well attended.[81] In other words, the villagers weren't dying from the combined effects of forced labor, torture, and famine; they were sewing and weaving and learning the virtues of British hygiene. If there was any truth in these statements, it applied to the lives of loyalist women, not to the villagers who often attended to the loyalists as maids or houseboys might. The wives and daughters of the Home Guard were regular members of Maendeleo throughout the Emergency. Even Nancy Shepherd, the organization's chairwoman, insisted that no one could join Maendeleo unless "she has forsworn Mau Mau" and that the clubs were being used as "a way of breaking the bonds of Mau Mau amongst the women."[82] This implied that women who confessed and cooperated benefited from Maendeleo, but for the most part this simply was not the case, at least not until the last years of the war. Moreover, many European women directing local club efforts, particularly those from the settler-dominated East African Women's League, strictly enforced a loyalist-first policy. That is, regardless of a woman's level of cooperation, priority would always be given to those Kikuyu who had remained faithful servants to the British Crown throughout the Emergency.[83] Even with the effects of famine devastating the Mau Mau population, the well-fed loyalists were generally the first to queue up for Maendeleo's relief efforts. Not until 1957 did the extent of famine-related deaths compel some within the Administration to rethink villagization and to demand assistance from Nairobi.[84] Even then, the colonial government dismissed the reports as alarmist, continuing to rely largely on international donors and voluntary organizations for assistance.[85]

Thus there may be some plausibility in the villagers' contention of enforced starvation. What other explanation could there be for actively contriving to starve hundreds of thousands of Mau Mau adherents? The same people who were purportedly being rehabilitated, an educational effort that requires a certain degree of free time, were scavenging at every opportunity for food. They fed their children what little could be found: boiled roots, garbage from the Home Guard rubbish piles, vermin, wild berries, and as a last resort warm salted water, just to survive. In time, death tolls in the villages were enormous, according to various eyewitnesses. "This was because the sickness always found bodies which were weak from hunger, in an environment where cleanliness was impossible due to lack of water and there were no health facilities," one woman from Kiambu later deduced.[86] In Nyeri District, one former missionary reported, "It was terribly pitiful how many of the children and the older Kikuyu were dying. They were so emaciated and so very susceptible to any kind of disease that came along."[87] There was hardly a woman of childbearing age during the Emergency who did not lose a son or daughter, or elderly relative, to the combined effects of famine and disease. The overcrowded huts were incubators for tuberculosis, typhoid, pneumonia, and whooping cough—just a few of the illnesses that swept through the villages. Malnutrition also manifested itself in the form of scurvy, kwashiorkor, and pellagra. Diarrhea too was endemic, particularly among the children. "You would not have wished to see them when they woke up," Mary wa Kuria later recalled, "with their dirty faces and their clothes unwashed for months. . . . Even our own bodies, we had no time to bathe or to wash our clothes."[88] The lack of hygiene was compounded by curfew orders that forbade the villagers to leave their huts between nightfall and the morning siren. This meant that everyone had to use the interior toilet bucket, though even this was a luxury. At night, the villagers often had to urinate and defecate on the same floor where they cooked and slept.

The colonial officers in the Administration were fully aware of the health consequences of their policies. In Meru, the district commissioner summed up the general sentiment held by some of his counterparts when he stated, "From the health point of view, I regard villagisation as being exceedingly dangerous and we are already starting to reap the benefits. We are, in fact, trying to effect in a few months a major social revolution which took 500 years or more to achieve in England."[89] In spite of these warnings, Baring refused to do anything to alleviate the crisis. He never altered his policy of continued repatriations from the White Highlands and the urban areas. Many illnesses that incubated in the transit camps, where repatriates would wait for months in overcrowded and unsanitary conditions, were later expressed as epidemics in the villages. While the colonial government eventually condemned Gilgil and Langata camps because "they were unfit to hold Kikuyu . . . for medical epidemiological reasons," thousands passed through these locations en route to the Kikuyu reserves before they were finally closed.[90] All chronically ill detainees, provided they were not classified as hard-core Mau Mau, were sent back to the Kikuyu districts. In fact, in 1955 the director of medical services reminded all camp commandants, "It is accepted policy that cases of pulmonary tuberculosis . . . be returned to their reserve to avail themselves of the routine medical control and treatment within their areas."[91] But there was virtually no medical treatment to be found in the reserves. Baring himself was aware of this when he made a tour of the Emergency villages in Central Province in June 1956, during which he had to have witnessed the hardships and human destruction caused by village life; this perception was wholly unavoidable by any but the blind. Rather than endorse a policy to alter these destructive conditions, he instead decided to do nothing. Writing his follow-up report to his visit, the governor noted that "there have been a number of discussions about the expenditure of money on villages. The financial position has now worsened. It is therefore necessary strictly to justify this expenditure on Emergency grounds. . . . Schemes of medical help, however desirable and however high their medical priority, could not in [these] circumstances be approved."[92]

As Baring took deliberate steps not to intervene, the villagers in Central Province continued to bury the dead. "Whenever anybody fell ill or a child fell sick," recalled Margaret Nyaruai, "the only thing was to look after them until they died, as there was no help forthcoming from anybody."[93] Returning from a day of forced labor, women were often greeted with the news that a child or elderly relative had died. The local Home Guards would hand them shovels and lead them to the special areas or other designated spots for burial. Other times, women tied their dying infants to their backs, carrying them along to communal work. Some did so with the hope of being able to beg for help from a sympathetic Home Guard or British officer, others because they did not want their child to die alone. "When you carried your child with you to work," Wamahiga Wahugo later recalled, "if the Home Guard in charge of you disliked you, you would not be allowed even some time to sit down and feed the sick child." She went on to say:

> The sick child would be strapped to your back while you worked, being burnt by the hot sun. It was like we were in slavery. You would dig like everybody else the whole day. . . . You would be so busy at work, trying to finish your task, and go home to look for food with which to feed your other children that by the time you realized that the child hadn't cried for some time and decided to bring it to your front from your back to check its condition, you would find that the child had been dead awhile. You would start screaming in shock and anguish. Only then would the Home Guards order some others to come and help you bury the child.[94]

Throughout Central Province former villagers related countless stories like Wamahiga's. Children were dying on their mothers' backs, in the huts, or on the roadside when their mothers were granted permission by a sympathetic Home Guard to go to one of the few local mission hospitals. Even for those fortunate few who reached medical assistance, their efforts were often in vain. The missionaries or their African assistants generally demanded a few shillings for treatment, and the women had no money. In other cases the medical staff simply turned them away, fearing—not without some justification—that they would be arrested for assisting Mau Mau.[95]

Today, many of these women think of the entire Central Province as a kind of mass unmarked grave. There were bodies that had been left out exposed to the elements and the animals. Some were buried alone and others together, all in unmarked graves. After independence some were exhumed when the locals began tilling their farms again, unearthing skeletons from shallow graves as they planted maize or sweet potatoes. But according to many former Mau Mau, the majority still remain in unmarked locations throughout the countryside. "They are just everywhere," one man summed up. "When we walk through our land, we know that those who died are near to us. It is a very painful thought and something we live with every day of our lives."[96]

Then came the day when detainees began returning from the Pipeline. By the end of 1955 nearly one thousand were being released every month, a figure that would climb to as high as two thousand by the end of 1957.[97] The cumulative effect of forced labor and torture had compelled them to confess and cooperate, with the ultimate hope that life would improve once they were released to their wives and families. For the colonial government, this mass movement of detainees down the Pipeline was no small feat. Baring and the colonial secretary, first Lyttelton and then Lennox-Boyd, had spent nearly two years constructing and consolidating the camp system. But before they could release thousands of detainees en masse, the colonial officials had to solve one last vexing problem, which they called reabsorption.

There was no more room in the reserves. Of course, the colonial government had itself to thank for the problem. Overcrowded conditions in Kikuyuland, exacerbated by continuous forced repatriations, completely saturated the reserves by December 1954, at least according to the official standard-of-living index.[98] For a time, returns slowed as the Prisons Department diverted many Mau Mau suspects, mostly women, children, and the elderly, to the Langata Camp. But Langata was condemned for its atrocious conditions in April 1955, and the repatriates who had been awaiting their return now flooded back to the Kikuyu districts.[99] As a consequence, detainees who were beginning to confess their Mau Mau oaths and cooperate were not immediately released until space could be found for them in the reserves.

To solve the reabsorption problem, the colonial government had to address the dilemma of agricultural reform. In the context of the Emergency, agrarian reform and suppression of the Mau Mau uprising were intimately related. Despite the fact that colonial officials refused to acknowledge Kikuyu land grievances as legitimate, they knew they had to, at the very least, find a way to make the overcrowded reserves more agriculturally productive. They were not going to reward Mau Mau with more land, but they still needed to find a long-term solution to feeding the Kikuyu people.

Governor Baring needed a seasoned veteran to take charge and plan exactly how to do this. In September 1955 he created the new position of special commissioner for Central Province and appointed Carruthers
"Monkey" Johnston to take the helm. In time, Johnston would also take
over from Edward Windley as the head of the Ministry of African Affairs
and Beniah Ohanga at the Ministry of Community Development and Rehabilitation. With this unprecedented triple role, he would emerge as the
most powerful person in Kenya overseeing the colonial government's suppression of Mau Mau in the reserves, with the obvious exception of Baring
himself. Like so many other colonial officials, Monkey Johnston came from
a formidable upper-class background. He was educated at one of Britain's
finest public schools before heading off to Oxford and a career in the colonial service. Among his subordinates in Central Province, he was
renowned for his English civility and fine manners, hosting drinks and
dinner parties that are remembered to this day for their flawless execution
in the middle of the African bush. Despite his unfortunate physical appearance, which some said was almost primatelike, Monkey Johnston was
an unmistakable leader who, according to one colonial officer, remained
"gracefully unchanged by his Gilbertian status."[100]

Johnston's first order of business was to take over Kenya's Resettlement
Committee and force a rethinking of the Swynnerton Plan. Initially, the
colonial government thought this far-reaching agricultural agenda, which
had been adopted as official policy in late 1954, would provide the solution
to its dilemma of resettlement and overpopulation in the reserves. Swynnerton introduced several measures—including land consolidation, improved farming techniques, and land reclamation and antierosion
schemes—that would in theory expand the carrying capacity of the reserves, creating room for the vast influx of Kikuyu returns.[101] Under the
plan the government would also over time lift restrictions placed on
African coffee, tea, and pyrethrum production. Swynnerton projected that
the average family income would rise from eight to twelve pounds to one
hundred pounds per annum. An agricultural revolution would sweep
through the Kikuyu countryside, transforming it into a progressive and efficient model of production and, significantly, render it capable of accommodating tens of thousands more people.

Like all colonial policies during the Emergency, agricultural reform was
highly politicized. The Emergency ushered in a state-directed class revolution in Central Province, one that was intimately linked to land access and
loyalism. The Kikuyuland of the post–Mau Mau future would be a model
of agricultural production, with former loyalists living on the large efficient parcels of land, and many former Mau Mau adherents serving as the

landless laborers either on the loyalist farms or in some as yet to be defined industry. For their part, the loyalists took an active role in ensuring their own aggrandizement. In fact, colonial officials put their loyalist supporters in charge of the demarcation committees for land consolidation throughout the Kikuyu reserves. Practically, this meant that the loyalists were empowered to decide not only who got land in the Kikuyu reserves but also how much. The subsequent fraud was shameless, so much so that consolidation had to be completely redone in Fort Hall in the early 1960s.[102]

Those held in detention routinely lost out in the consolidation process, despite the best efforts of their wives who remained in the villages to protect their land. It was not unusual for former detainees to return to the reserves to find that loyalist kinsmen or neighbors had expropriated their land. In light of ongoing reward policies in the reserves, it would have been surprising to find that such land theft had not taken place.[103] In his groundbreaking work on land reform in Kikuyuland, M. P. K. Sorrenson asserts that land consolidation for the colonial government "was regarded as a means of establishing a politically reliable, anti–Mau Mau force in the Kikuyu countryside, perhaps on the analogy that such classes in Britain and Europe were nicely conservative."[104] There is no ambiguity, therefore, in the results of the land consolidation process. The classes of "haves" and "have-nots" split fairly evenly along the line of British colonial versus Mau Mau supporters. The agricultural consolidation legally codified the land tenure inequalities of the pre-Emergency era and exacerbated the crisis of land access in the reserves.

Monkey Johnston had no intention of deviating from Swynnerton's course. Land consolidation and other concurrent agrarian "reforms" would guarantee the long-term ascendancy of the loyalist supporters. But the problem of reabsorption still loomed, and Johnston made two critical decisions. At the top of his agenda was the acceleration of two detainee labor projects that were turning once desolate areas into settlements for some of the surplus Kikuyu population. The first was the Mwea project in Embu District, where a massive rice production scheme was intended to transform the area and eventually feed some fifty thousand people.[105] In addition, there were settlement schemes for the high-forest zones of Kiambu, Fort Hall, and Nyeri districts, projected to reabsorb another estimated five thousand Kikuyu.[106] The settlement of these locations by landless Kikuyu was secondary to satisfying loyalists seeking to improve their living conditions. Commenting on the projects under his direction, the minister for forest development emphasized, "The scheme is essentially one of 'reward' for loyal Kikuyu, Meru, and Embu and not for the reclamation of doubtful Mau Mau."[107]

Johnston's second decision was staggering in its cynicism and simplicity. Rather than expanding the boundaries of the reserves, or deviating from the government's position of rewarding loyalists, either of which would have opened up more land for former Mau Mau adherents, Johnston and the Resettlement Committee chose instead to reword the Swynnerton Plan. Clearly, in the long term the proletariat Swynnerton aimed to create would come from the ex-detainee community. But in the near term, Johnston realized he had to alter some of Swynnerton's assumptions if he was going to make room in the Kikuyu reserves for returning detainees. Prior to Johnston's appointment the committee had asserted:

> Over the greater part of the three Kikuyu Districts . . . no significant increase in production, relative to the present problem, can be expected in less than 8 to 10 years. However, the extent to which the Kikuyu districts can absorb displaced persons may be considered independently of this gradual improvement. Here the answer is governed largely by another variable factor, namely, *what standard of living is aimed at* [emphasis in original]? . . . As regards standard of living, while the relatively high standard of surplus income of 100 pounds p.a. is a proper target for Government long-term policy to aim at, it is impractical to plan short-term action on such a high target. The fact is that the 1954 population . . . was, and is, living in the three Kikuyu Districts at a standard of living, which may be low, but which the people are used to. There are strong reasons why, for the next few years at least, the Government should let these people go on living at this standard, and make its plans on that basis.[108]

By tinkering with the official numbers and readjusting the originally targeted standard of African living downward, the committee was able to magically render the reserves, on paper, fully capable of accommodating the surplus population of 150,000 additional Kikuyu.[109] When Johnston took over the committee, he fully believed the district commissioners should be "able to absorb the bulk of those released into the reserves."[110] He then explained that the remainder of the former detainees would be resettled in those locales that either the loyalists had declined or that exceeded their needs. With a stroke of the pen, the problem of reabsorption was suddenly solved. Within the stale corridors of the colonial government the Kikuyu reserves were in a moment transformed, now capable of absorbing well over one hundred thousand more people. In effect, at the same time that the vast majority of Kikuyu were starving, the colonial government reconciled its population balance sheet, simply by reducing a standard of living that was already wholly fictitious.

. . .

Immediately after Johnston's maneuver the Pipeline began to empty. Many detainees already had an intimation of the chaos that awaited, having witnessed and worked on the changing landscape while at district works camps. Few were prepared, however, for what they found when they were finally released. Often they had to be directed to their families, as the new villages were foreign to them, having been created while most were in the Pipeline. "It was completely disorienting," one former detainee from Kiambu recalled. "I wandered around the wired village knocking on doors looking for my wife, but I never found her. I was told she had been killed during one of the Johnnies' raids and only my eldest child was left alive, being tended to by my mother, who somehow managed to survive."[111] Detainee after detainee recounted similar homecoming stories. "When I returned," another man from Nyeri stated, "I learned those who had been killed were being buried in random spots outside the village. . . . No one can be able to say for certain where his father, mother, wife, or children were buried. They were all large, unmarked graves."[112] Those they did find alive lived in horrendous conditions, leading many detainees to conclude that life in the villages had, in fact, been worse than in the Pipeline.

Most women recalled the bittersweet moment of joy and shame when their husbands returned to them. "I wept when I first saw my husband walk into the village," remembered one woman from Nyeri. "At first I did not recognize him, but once I did I knew how lucky I was because so many women were widowed, their men never came home."[113] But some women, having given birth to children during their detention in the villages, reluctantly welcomed their husbands. Sometimes called *nusu-nusu* or *chotara*, meaning half-caste, these children were physical reminders of the repeated rapes they had endured. Some were clearly fathered by men from other African ethnic groups; others were most definitely mixed race. "A lot of half-white children were born at that time," Lucy Ngima later recalled. "In fact there is one on the other ridge not far from here. There is another lady [who is] named Nyawira wife of Zakayo, [one man named] John son of Nyambere, [a woman called] Wangari daughter of Milka, and even the mother of Migwi gave birth to such a child at the Consolata Hospital, Nyeri, where the sisters offered to adopt him. The mother refused, but the sisters forcefully took the baby, arguing that they were in a position to look after the child and give him a better life than the mother."[114] Detainees also returned to find their wives rearing children that bore a striking resemblance to their Home Guard neighbors. Often, though, they found that women in the villages were amenorrheic, or incapable of reproducing because of their emaciated and exhausted condition. Some, like Rachel Kiruku, attributed this temporary infertile state to the anxiety of village life. "The constant fear of death and guns had frozen the women's wombs," she said.[115] There were countless women for whom infertility would be a lifelong problem, the damage caused by sexual violence, contraction of venereal disease, or both, irreparable.[116]

Silence was a widespread remedy for coping with the difficulties of family reunification. Generally women would not provide their husbands with accounts of their sufferings, though the former detainees could often deduce what they were, particularly after local boastful loyalists and colonial officers filled them in on some of the details. Similarly, many men also chose not to speak about the Pipeline. "One could not talk to the people about his experiences in detention," Karega Njoroge later said. "That was not allowed. We used to warn each other not to take our detention days to the people. How could it have helped them?"[117] There were also several thousand women who would eventually return from Kamiti, and they too chose simply to move on as best they could. Of course, what other choice did any of these men and women have? The Emergency was ongoing, and the repressive policies were still in place. The colonial government was certainly not going to help them; if they had any hope of surviving and piecing their lives back together, they simply had to move forward. For some, like Mary wa Kuria, this was the only possible way of coping.

> While our men were detained, we had to learn to live like widows. A lot of things had happened during the time they had been detained, but we never even once gave up hope that they would come home one day. Even after we were raped, we still kept on hoping that life would one day be normal again. When the men came back, we picked up life where we had left. Even those men who found their wives with children born while they were away did not blame them, but just accepted the children as their own. Everybody understood that we had been forcefully separated, that whatever happened could not be blamed on anybody, because all of us had been living in our separate hells, where none had any certainty that the other would survive—that a reunion would ever be possible. This was another divine chance we had been given for a normal life, and we couldn't allow the lost time to interfere with the future.[118]

But there were many instances where men and women simply could not go on, or could not accept the circumstances in which they were living. Throughout Central Province former villagers recall men who spent years in the Pipeline, only to commit suicide when they returned, after finding their families dead or their wives raising half-caste children. Marriages, too, did not always survive. Some men rejected wives who had been raped, particularly those who had borne children from such encounters. Their anger and masculine shame was too much to bear. They had failed in their roles as Kikuyu men, as guardians of production and reproduction. "You can imagine it yourself," one man opined, "a woman who was accustomed to having someone to rely on, someone earning the daily bread for her, who had now been left alone amongst enemies while we men were away. Most of the people who were Home Guards used to mistreat women by forcing them to do what they did not want; even some of them were being raped by those people. By imagining it, you can understand how life was. It was a very harsh life for the women, and we men could do nothing. I was so ashamed of myself when I returned, and am sometimes now when I think about it all."[119]

The elation of some women also gave way to anger, anger at their husbands and fathers. They resented the absence of their men and the consequent hardships they had to endure, though in spite of their resentment few left the reserves.[120] Restrictions on movement were still in place, but later, when these restrictions were finally relaxed, most women still chose to remain and rebuild their lives, living with pain and bitterness. Others, however, left their husbands and went to work in Nairobi, where they became part of an expanding class of entrepreneurial women whose existence presented a challenge to Kikuyu men struggling to reestablish their manhood after the war.

Few loyalists were enthusiastic about the detainees' returning. There was the fear of revenge, although with Emergency Regulations still in place, and support from the colonial government continuing, the loyalists were still well empowered. Their greatest weapon was their right to determine whether an individual was ultimately released from the Pipeline or exiled. Loyalists used their power to deny former detainees the right to return to the reserves, often banishing them instead to a lifetime in settlements like Hola. Such abuses made yet another mockery of the rehabilitation system and of the colonial government's ability to reintegrate the Kikuyu population. In a speech to Kenya's Legislative Council, Beniah Ohanga, Monkey Johnston's predecessor as minister of community development and rehabilitation, implored his peers and the loyalists in the reserves. "The time has come," he said, "when the attitude of the country generally should bend slightly towards released rehabilitated detainees." He went on, arguing:

> I am a firm believer in the gospel of the second chance. All down history individuals and nations have fallen by following wrong ideals and by taking the wrong steps. If their wrong-doing is to be continuously remembered as

long as they live and no opportunity given them to reform we can be nowhere in this world. I should, therefore, like to make a general appeal to the loyal Kikuyu, Embu and Meru who have supported the Government during the dark days of terrorism and stood firmly by their convictions that terrorism and Mau Mau did not pay, to open their doors wider to give their fellows who have fallen a second chance to make good.[121]

But second chances were few in the Kikuyu reserves. The continuing policies of the colonial government made certain of that. For Baring and the Colonial Office, the whole point of launching a total war against Mau Mau had been to cement control over Kenya for the future. This lust for control did not stop with the mass confessions in the Pipeline or the Emergency villages but was continued with a series of policies designed to lock in permanently the socioeconomic divisions in Kikuyu society. It was here that the impact in the Kikuyu reserves of the newly modified Swynnerton Plan was critically important. When finally released, the former detainees quickly realized that their economic futures were being manipulated by the colonial government, and there was little that they could do about it. Many had already lost what material possessions and livestock they had during their detention, and often part or all of their land. Throughout the Emergency, countless appeals were made to the Administration and to the governor, like that filed by several former detainees from the Othaya Division of Nyeri District.

In general on land, we wish to make the point that there is great and growing land hunger in the Central Province. Many people are landless and many have very small pieces of land which are uneconomic to work. In addition there is the young generation which is growing to adulthood without any land or any means of earning a living. . . . We do not support the methods which were used and are being used to implement the Land Consolidation programme. There is an element of force in it. At the same time most of the programme was implemented, at least in this District, when thousands of people were still in detention camps or in Gaol. They were not given facilities to take care of their land in the general transactions which took place. Consequently they harbour many grievances because in many cases they were unjustly treated by their more fortunate neighbours who were on the spot. When they were released, they were brusquely treated by the Land Consolidation officers and the demarcation committees if they raised any question on demarcation or the measurement of land. They were told by these committees that the government had left them to do as they pleased. They were even threatened by the local administration with imprisonment or detention if they persisted with their requests.[122]

With the introduction of the Loyalty Certificate the colonial government created a legal distinction between loyalist supporters and former Mau Mau adherents. This document was issued only to men whom members of the Administration considered to be steadfast loyalists. No Mau Mau adherent, regardless of how much he confessed and cooperated, was ever to be issued one of these crucial, and coveted, certificates. Carrying this document, loyalists were not subject to movement restriction orders, meaning they could engage in private and government employment outside of the reserves, where there were countless more opportunities to find good-paying jobs. Certificate holders were exempt from paying the Kikuyu, Embu, and Meru special taxes, a tax all former detainees had to pay, despite the fact that they had no source of income. Loyalists were also given special consideration for various commercial licenses, and they were the first to be granted permission to plant and sell coveted cash crops like coffee and tea.[123] With a Loyalty Certificate a man was also given the right to vote; without it he had no political voice in elections.

Ex-detainees did not emerge from the Pipeline as rehabilitated citizens with equal rights. This inequality was the precise intention of the colonial government. With the future net effects of Swynnerton's agricultural overhaul at least another decade off, and the immediate discriminating effects of that plan all too apparent, even a subsistence income was beyond the reach of many former detainees and their families. Those released from the Pipeline were also expected to labor for part of the week on unpaid communal works projects such as terracing, bracken clearing, and cultivating the *shambas* of the local loyalists. Many men were forced to violate pass laws and movement restrictions in order to search for employment outside of the reserves. By the end of 1956 nearly three thousand Kikuyu were being arrested monthly under Emergency Regulations, which when compared to the Pipeline release-rate figure of one thousand per month dramatizes the predicament. Of these arrests, over two-thirds were pass book and curfew offenses. Ex-detainees were breaking the law in order to search for work in urban centers. Even Lennox-Boyd reluctantly admitted that the movement and curfew violations reflected the overcrowding and unemployment problems that plagued the Kikuyu reserves. While those arrested were generally not returned to the Pipeline, they were imprisoned and then fined before eventually being repatriated back to the reserves, where the cycle started again.[124]

Clearly, there were perpetrators of violence both in the Pipeline and in the Emergency villages, men like Kiboroboro, Mapiga, YY, and Kenda Kenda.

There were other brutal elements as well: members of the Kenya Regiment, the King's African Rifles, the Kenya Police, battalions from Britain, and colonial officers in the Administration. And there were the local loyalists who contributed enormously to the violence, though their choices were generally more constrained than those of their white superiors. There were also degrees of participation. Some chose to murder and rape, others to engage only in beatings and humiliation. In the reserves some dutifully carried out orders to favor loyalists over Mau Mau when dispensing rations, and in the Pipeline others carried out only the punishments allowable by Emergency decree. Still others chose to observe but remain silent.

Not all of those responsible for the destruction of the Kikuyu people chose to exert their power physically. The agricultural redevelopment policies of the colonial government fit hand in glove with the ongoing enforcement of mass detention without trial; in fact, these policies were arguably as destructive as the physical brutality against the detainees and villagers, ensuring as they did the Mau Mau population's continued economic marginalization in the post-Emergency future. In the end, outright violence and bureaucratic manipulation cannot be divorced. They worked in concert toward the ultimate goal of restoring and strengthening British colonial control in Kenya.

Critics like Barbara Castle soon came to realize this, as did many others. Much of the protest came from the ranks of the Labour Party, some from within the British colonial government itself. Some came from missionaries, others from the press. Together, the critics marshaled forth a stream and then a flood of evidence and decried the continued use of detention without trial, torture, famine, abuse of Emergency Regulations, and summary executions, leaving little doubt that officials at the highest level—the prime minister, the colonial secretary, and the governor—had detailed knowledge about the ongoing brutality in Kenya.

CHAPTER NINE

OUTRAGE, SUPPRESSION, AND SILENCE

Barbara Castle

In the heart of the British Empire there is a police state where the rule of law has broken down, where the murder and torture of Africans by Europeans goes unpunished and where the authorities pledged to enforce justice regularly connive at its violation. And at last the Labour Party has declared war on this state of affairs.

—BARBARA CASTLE, Tribune, *September 30, 1955*[1]

BY THE FALL OF 1955 THE SITUATION IN KENYA HAD DETERIORATED TO its worst level, and the British Labour Party's outrage had exploded. Reports of atrocities continued to make it back to Britain, directly contradicting Lennox-Boyd's repeated protests that the situation was improving. On the floor of the Commons the Opposition continually pressed the colonial secretary on allegations of atrocities, as well as the numbers of those detained without trial, those forcibly removed, the legal defense of the politicals, the rate of release of those still detained, and the day-to-day operations and conditions of the camps and villages.[2] Never wavering, Lennox-Boyd fought off accusations of brutality, neglect, and widespread suffering with regard to the Kikuyu. When specific incidents of violence were brought to light, he condemned them as deplorable but argued vociferously that they were isolated. Lennox-Boyd was stonewalling, and Labour Party members like Barbara Castle knew it. "You were chasing a sense of complacency and cover up by the government in Kenya and at home," she later recalled, "that made one realize there was something very wrong."[3] And so Castle made her party's very public declaration of war against the Conservative government on the front page of the *Tribune*. The headline read "Labour to Fight Kenya Thugs," but the thugs in this case were not the Mau Mau insurgents; they were the leaders of the British colonial government and their men on the spot.

Colonel Arthur Young's resignation as commissioner of police in Kenya incited Labour outrage. In February 1954, Young had been posted to the colony from his position as the City of London's police commissioner with the express purpose of cleaning up Kenya's police force and transforming it into an impartial instrument of the rule of law. His appointment came after a bipartisan parliamentary delegation traveled to Kenya earlier in 1954 and reported that the best way to address the allegations of brutality was through a reorganization of the police, which did not operate as an independent unit in Kenya, but rather came under the direct control of the Administration and ultimately the governor himself.[4] Young's task was to establish the police force as an autonomous and incorruptible division within the colony's government in Kenya, one that not only would transcend the local Emergency mentality but also bring cases of brutality and torture to the attention of the attorney general for prosecution. In the context of the times this would be a monumental task, but if anyone were to succeed it would be Young. The colonel brought with him a proven record of success, having recently returned from Malaya, where he had overseen a similar housecleaning. There was every expectation that he would at the very least help to establish some control over the chaotic law enforcement situation in Kenya.

It was not long, however, before Young was thoroughly disgusted with colonial officials in Kenya and, most specifically, with the governor himself. "I felt it my unpleasant duty," the colonel later recalled, "to pursue with Baring my apprehensions that members of the civilian security forces were uncontrolled and were committing crimes of violence and brutality upon their alleged enemies, which were unjustified and abhorrent."[5] But the governor did nothing. In fact, he seems to have done everything within his power to stymie Young's work. On later reflection, Young recalled:

I addressed an official report to H.E. [His Excellency] expressing my apprehensions in writing, with the belief that supporting evidence would soon be

forthcoming. I also requested that he should take an initiative in administrative action which would indicate his own repugnance of brutality committed by security forces and do what he could to bring this to an end. I
received no acknowledgment of this appreciation, far less an answer to it,
in spite of a number of reminders.[6]

Less than a year after his arrival the colonel handed Baring his letter of
resignation, which stood as a personal indictment of the governor's refusal to rein in the colony's forces of law and order. In the letter Young detailed the reasons for his "anxiety at the continuance of the rule of fear
rather than that of impartial justice."[7] The first of his complaints was
about Baring's refusal to allow the Police Department, and its ancillary
Criminal Investigation Department, to operate independently from the
Administration. Young had repeatedly demanded "impartial status" for
the police, insisting that it was essential to Kenya's law enforcement. But
neither Baring nor his men on the spot were about to relinquish their control over police investigations or investigations into brutality by the civilian security forces.

For his part, Baring insisted that prosecuting any of his men, black or
white, would undermine morale and damage whatever inroads they had
made against the so-called Mau Mau savages. In correspondence with the
Colonial Office the governor insisted, "If we have a weak Police force we
have a strong Administrative service; and I am convinced that we cannot
and should not weaken the position of our Administrative officers."[8] In
other words, Baring knew a strong independent police force and a powerful cadre of colonial officers in the reserves were mutually exclusive, as an
independent police force would surely have weakened the Administration
by exposing its corruption and brutality. In fact, Young had provided Baring with exhaustive details of the "many serious and revolting crimes [that]
were being perpetrated both by 'loyal' Africans and by Europeans, not in-
frequently with the tacit approval of the Administration, concerning which
no reports were being received at Police Headquarters."[9] Many members of
the police force were, of course, also complicit in these "revolting crimes,"
making Young's job of creating an impartial investigation unit all the more
challenging. Indeed, it was commonplace for the police force to act in concert with some members of the Administration, as well as with camp officials and the Home Guard.

Even more disturbing was the governor's deliberate intrusions into ongoing police investigations. In September 1954, for example, Chief Mundia
in the Mathira Division of Nyeri District, and a handful of his Home
Guards, were accused of beating several detainees in their charge, one of

whom died. The corpse was allegedly transported in the chief's car, then buried, only to be exhumed later by the police. According to Young and K. P. Hadingham, the assistant police commissioner in Nyeri, both Ozzie Hughes and Monkey Johnston, then the district commissioner of Nyeri and the provincial commissioner of Central Province, respectively, actively sought to thwart any investigation. Most astounding was Hadingham's report that the governor had also become involved. According to Nyeri's assistant commissioner of police, "On the occasion of a recent visit of the Secretary of State for the Colonies accompanied by His Excellency the Governor to South Nyeri, HE drew me aside for some ten minutes to discuss the Chief Mundia case." Hadingham then went on to describe the nature of His Excellency's request.

> HE said that his discussion with me was "off the record," and while he would not give me any directions in the matter he considered it would be politically most inexpedient to prosecute a loyal chief who had taken a leading part in the fight against Mau Mau. He said that a loyal Kikuyu would find it difficult to differentiate between killing Mau Mau in the heat of battle and killing the government's enemies out of battle. He said that one should take into account the difference of mentality between loyal Kikuyu and, say, European security force personnel who were well able to realize the wrong of taking the law into their own hands.[10]

Young was outraged by this turn of events. Later both Baring and Monkey Johnston called the young Hadingham to Nairobi, apologized for their heavy-handed tactics, and gave him the green light to continue with the investigation. Eventually, Mundia and his underlings were tried for the murder and acquitted, but convicted of the lesser charge of assault.[11]

When Young returned to London in January 1955, his reception at the Colonial Office was decidedly chilly. Lennox-Boyd had been friends with Baring since their days at Oxford, and they shared a ruling-class conviction and vision of empire. The colonial secretary had every intention of supporting the governor, which meant he first had to silence Young as best he could. If the commissioner's letter of resignation were published or otherwise made its way to the press, the ensuing political damage would have been irreparable, both for Baring and for Lennox-Boyd. In a later statement Young hardly equivocated on this point. "In retrospect," he wrote, "it is clear that if my report had been published to Parliament, the Governor in the very least would have been recalled and the Colonial Secretary himself would have been in a very hazardous position."[12] Young, like all others who served in the colonial government during the Emergency, had signed the Official Secrets Act, binding him to confidentiality under penalty of law. But his departure still had to be explained—a delicate task. Together he and Lennox-Boyd drafted a carefully scripted press release that was wholly devoid of any of the particulars contained in the colonel's original resignation letter. Nevertheless, its implications were clear, even shrouded in the studied language of the Colonial Office.

> There was . . . a difference of opinion between the Kenya Government and Colonel Young on the functions of the Police Force in the Emergency. It was their common aim that the Kenya Police should be regarded as impartial custodians of the law and should command the trust and confidence of the public. Colonel Young explained to the Secretary of State that in his view no progress towards this aim could be made unless the Police were given a greater measure of independence in the performance of their functions than they at present possessed in the Emergency areas and unless it was recognized that the respect of the public for the impartial administration of the law was seriously jeopardised by the activities of the Home Guard whose powers were liable to abuse owing to their lack of discipline. The Kenya Government for their part were determined to eradicate abuses among members of Kikuyu Guard. But they considered that for as long as the present violent phase of the Emergency lasted it was essential that the Administration, the Police and the military should jointly concentrate all their efforts on bringing terrorism to an early end and that for this purpose there must be the highest degree of integration and co-ordination between the three bodies at all levels.[13]

Absent from the statement was any reference to crimes by Europeans, which Young had described in his earlier internal memoranda. Despite the release of this joint statement, there were still other matters outstanding, not the least of which was some internal reshuffling. During his ten months in Kenya, Young had managed to secure a handful of allies, most notably John Whyatt, the colony's attorney general, and Duncan McPherson, Kenya's assistant commissioner of police. Whyatt had supported the prosecution of brutalities perpetrated during screening and detention operations, going as far as assuring Young that he would move forward with cases even if it meant doing so without the governor's prior knowledge.[14] On the heels of Young's departure Whyatt was shipped out of Kenya, promoted to chief justice of Singapore. He was soon replaced by Eric Griffith-Jones, whose views on the prosecution of crimes perpetrated by the civilian security forces, and on the use of force more generally, could not have been farther from those of his predecessor. McPherson, who had been transferred to Kenya from Hong Kong expressly to assist Young, was virtually powerless without an attorney general willing to prosecute cases. More-over, his new boss, Richard Catling, had been transferred from Malaya and was clearly cut from the same cloth as Baring and Griffith-Jones.

The coup de grâce was the colonial government's decision to issue an amnesty for all crimes committed prior to January 1955. This amnesty also applied to those Mau Mau insurgents still in the forests, though surrender meant only that they would not be prosecuted for a capital offense. In other words, amnesty for Mau Mau adherents translated into detention without trial and Emergency justice in the Pipeline. For white and black members of the security forces amnesty meant they would remain wholly unaccountable for any torture, rape, or murder they had committed against Mau Mau people in the reserves or in detention camps. Of course, this had been the British colonial government's de facto policy for years. But the blanket pardon left little doubt that the colonial government, in-cluding Churchill and his cabinet, who discussed and approved the amnesty, were wholly willing to abandon the enforcement of law and order and to subordinate the basic human rights of Mau Mau adherents in order to maintain the support of the security forces and, ultimately, uphold British colonial rule in Kenya.[15]

Criticism in London over the Young affair came from several corners and built to a maelstrom of outrage. The first round of public censure came not from the Labour Opposition but from the Anglican Church. The Executive Committee of the Church Missionary Society, the Anglican Church's over-sight committee for its missionary work around the world, launched its first round of censure with a letter to the editor at the *Times*. The commit-tee targeted Baring's amnesty declaration, stating, "[The] appeal to the se-curity forces in the Governor's speech not to maltreat people held in captivity and warnings to the effect that 'any of you, or any other person, who commits any offence [in the postamnesty period] will be prosecuted with the full strength of the law' are welcome, but they are not new. Hith-erto they have not led to a cessation of malpractices by members of the se-curity forces."[16] The Anglican Church had been hearing for years that the British colonial government was going to rein in its men and prosecute perpetrators of brutality. Yet nothing new had been introduced into Kenya's system of policing to herald a dramatic change in policy. In fact, with Young's departure the situation appeared to worsen rather than im-prove.

It was the Church Missionary Society's publication of the pamphlet *Kenya—time for Action* that first signaled serious skepticism over the standards of colonial rule in Britain's empire. Anglican leaders labeled the brutality and breakdown of law and order "the Government's Mau Mau," an especially insulting analogy given Mau Mau's presumed savagery. They pointed to Canon T. F. C. Bewes's initial report about colonial violence during the early days of the Emergency, accusations that the Colonial Office had characterized as relating to widely isolated events. At the time Bewes and the Church were assured that "vigorous steps" were being taken against any abuses, though subsequent events rendered these official promises hollow. The pamphlet decried the official amnesty, stating, "An amnesty does not itself make bad men good," and went on to point out "that under Colonel Young's direction, an increasingly vigilant police force had uncovered an alarming number of contraventions of the law and of elementary standards of decency and reasonable restraint by some whose duty it was to be upholders of civilized standards against barbarism; but that Colonel Young found reluctance in some official quarters to support the taking of proceedings against these offenders."[17]

The debate quickly moved to the floor of the House of Lords, where Lord Jowitt, who had been solicitor general and then attorney general in the postwar Labour government, teamed up with the archbishop of Canterbury to launch an exhaustive review of the events surrounding Young's resignation, highlighting several known atrocities that had been perpetrated by Britain's forces of law and order. "We must paint these events in their true colours," Jowitt urged his fellow Lords. "There is nothing whatever to be said for massacring disarmed prisoners or for employing torture to exact confessions. These things are repellent to the Christian ideal and repellent to the British system of justice. He who tries to gloss them over as a mere excess of loyalty, or to make light of them, is doing no good service to our good name."[18] In response Lord Lloyd, the parliamentary undersecretary of state for the colonies, agreed that "the ultimate responsibility for affairs in Kenya—including the surrender offer—rests with Her Majesty's Government," but went on to add, "I do not dispute that it would be impossible to deny that serious malpractices have taken place, though here again I cannot entirely forget the circumstances in which such malpractices have arisen."[19]

The government insisted that these instances of brutality had to be understood in the context of Mau Mau. It was a brutal war in Kenya, so the government's logic went, and the local British forces were doing their best considering the bloodthirsty savagery of the enemy. Lennox-Boyd offered this reasoning when faced with a similar assault on the floor of the Commons less than a week later. Labour MPs were demanding explanations along with the publication of Young's resignation letter in full. But, as Castle later recalled, "[Lennox-Boyd] brushed us aside. There had been some abuses, he admitted, but the Governor of Kenya was correcting them. We must not forget the horrors of Mau Mau and so on. There was no need for him to publish Colonel Young's report."[20]

Hardly satisfied, Castle began her own independent investigation into Kenyan atrocities and discovered a small article in the British press about the flogging to death of a Mau Mau suspect named Kamau Kichina. She continued to dig and soon discovered that "the legal records revealed a picture of behaviour so horrifying that one could not imagine it happening in a British colony."[21] Kamau had been employed at a police station, and when the two British officers in charge, Fuller and Waters, discovered some money had disappeared, they suspected Kamau of stealing it to fund Mau Mau. After several days of torture Kamau allegedly confessed to the crime, and on the fifth day he died. Remarkably, the case was prosecuted and brought to trial. During the preliminary hearing, the resident magistrate, Mr. Harrison, offered the following evidence.

> Throughout Kamau's captivity no effort was spared to force him to admit his guilt. He was flogged, kicked, handcuffed with his arms between his legs and fastened behind his neck, made to eat earth, pushed into a river, denied food for a period and left out for at least two nights, tied to a pole in a shed not surrounded by walls with only a roof overhead and wearing merely a blanket to keep out the cold. . . . He was never brought before a magistrate in the proper manner and he received no trial whatever, the right of all British subjects.[22]

Castle was stunned to learn that Harrison, rather than fully prosecuting Fuller and Waters, actually reduced their murder charge to one of "causing grievous bodily harm." Ultimately, the magistrate did convict the two British officers, sentencing them each to eighteen months in prison, a sentence so light that the Supreme Court intervened and increased their sentences to three and a half years.

It was the case of Kamau Kichina, coming so soon after the Young affair, that prompted Castle and the Labour Party's National Executive Committee to declare war on the Conservative government because of its dereliction of rule in Kenya. Lennox-Boyd was furious, and in another round of debate in the House of Commons he again deflected charges that there was a massive cover-up ongoing in Kenya. According to Castle, the colonial secretary insisted, "I was wrong in suggesting that Colonel Young's resignation had anything to do with cases like this [i.e., Kamau Kichina's] and, no he could not publish his resignation report. The charges against Fuller and Waters had been reduced 'in consequence of the medical evidence,' but he

would not put that evidence in the [House] library."[23] Lennox-Boyd knew
that Young's resignation and the Kamau Kichina case were but the tip of an
iceberg, as did Castle and other members of the Labour Party. But the Opposition needed more hard evidence, which meant someone had to go to
Kenya. Within weeks Castle had her bags packed, and on November 1, 1955,
she boarded a plane to Nairobi.

Not surprisingly, Castle's informant in Kenya was Duncan McPherson,
the assistant police commissioner who had served under Young. Like his
former boss, McPherson was "another prototype of the British policeman
at his best—a sturdy Scot, frank, open and direct."[24] But like the handful of
others willing to challenge the colonial government, McPherson was cau-
tious, taking Castle to the middle of Kenya's National Park where the only
audience for their first conversation were the herds of zebra and wilde-
beest. There he confirmed that evidence in the Kamau Kichina case had
been covered up, and insisted there were plenty of others just like it that
were still ongoing. In fact, on the eve of Young's resignation, McPherson
had drafted two lengthy memoranda outlining dozens of screening and detention camp abuses, cases where Mau Mau suspects were "battered to
death" and "summarily shot," and numerous instances where colonial officers either were directly involved with the torture and murder or had actively participated in the cover-ups, including exhuming corpses and
dumping them into the forest.[25] At least one of these memoranda had been
sent to Governor Baring.[26] He went on to tell Castle about the Pipeline, a
situation that particularly disturbed him given his own internment during
the Second World War. "The conditions in these camps were worse than he
himself had ever experienced in the Japanese prisoner of war camps,"
McPherson told her. "The diet was appalling, there was a lack of medical attention, there were illegal beatings, and above all else . . . many of these detainees were just rounded up by detention happy clerks without any real
evidence of participation."[27]

Castle then made her rounds through Kenya, where the rest of Lennox-
Boyd's underlings were just as she expected, tight-lipped and evasive.
Many of them despised the Labour MP, who in their eyes was a liberal
busybody, an outsider who did not understand how Kenya had to be ruled,
and, worst of all, a woman. The new attorney general, Eric Griffith-Jones,
took the liberty of bestowing upon her the nickname That Castellated
Bitch.[28] But not everyone in Kenya disliked her. There were several Asian
attorneys who greatly facilitated Castle's investigation, as did her translator,
Jean Wanjiru, who traveled with the MP throughout the colony. "She was
the most remarkable woman I have ever met," Jean later recalled. "I can still
see her with her bright red hair telling Mr. [Monkey] Johnston that she

would not stand for me, her Kikuyu translator, being fed and housed in different quarters. She hated the color bar, and Mr. Johnston was less than pleased when I sat at the dinner table with him. You must understand that the British officers did their best to intimidate her just like they did the Africans. Mrs. Castle never backed down, though. She wanted to know the truth, and they did their best to hide it from her. But you see, my dear, at that time in Kenya the government couldn't hide everything, and despite their best efforts someone like Mrs. Castle was going to find out."[29] Indeed, by the time she returned to Britain Castle had in fact amassed enough evidence to prove that the Kamau Kichina case was not an isolated one, and that the situation was worse than even Young and McPherson had described.[30]

The Labour MP also had the power of the press behind her. After her trip she contributed articles to the *Daily Mirror* and the *New Statesman and Nation* with headlines like "The Truth About the Secret Police" and "Justice in Kenya."[31] In fact, the *Daily Mirror* had sponsored Castle's tour, ensuring that her findings would make their way not just to a narrow group of concerned anticolonial critics but to a mass, largely working-class readership. Lennox-Boyd was less than pleased, snapping at Castle in the first round of House of Commons questioning after her return, "Ministers have not the privilege of being able to write regular articles for the *Mirror*," and accusing her of "monstrous slanders."[32] But then the colonial secretary went too far, attacking Castle personally and sparking a great partisan row that ended with Irene Ward, a Tory backbencher, declaring, "Is my Rt Hon. Friend [Lennox-Boyd] aware with what contempt responsible public opinion in Kenya will regard the conduct of the hon. Lady the Member for Blackburn [Mrs. Castle]?"[33] As Castle's biographer later pointed out, "Defending the rights of the untried against the Fleet Street lynch mob who were determined that all black Kenyans were implicated in the indiscriminate brutality of the Mau Mau, was of course guaranteeing [the Labour MP] fame and abuse in almost equal measure."[34] Lennox-Boyd eventually did put the full report of Kamau Kichina's case in the House of Commons library and promised that he would "look into" the other cases that Castle had brought to light. In the end, though, little was done. Castle later wrote, "[Lennox-Boyd] gave no sign whatsoever of a fundamental change of attitude. It was clear to me that the old complacent cover-ups were still going on."[35]

In Kenya Governor Baring and his men on the spot were engaged in an effort to stem the flow of damaging information out of the colony. Despite the Official Secrets Act and shared loyalty to empire, there was a concern on the part of the colonial government that some of its officers in the field would leak details to the press or members of the Labour Party. These concerns had a basis as news did make its way out of Kenya, passed on deliberately or unwittingly by some of Britain's local officers. In early 1953 Tony Cross had sent his account of police operations to the boys back home in London, prompting the *Daily Worker* to publish one of its many articles denouncing the government's brutal behavior, this one titled "Gestapo Way in Kenya."[36] In response, Kenya's chief secretary, Henry Potter, reminded the local colonial servants of their expected code of conduct, issuing the first of several "Security of Information" memos in April of 1953. In it he rebuked his men, writing, "Leakages of information have already occurred, some of them being of a nature which might well have caused considerable embarrassment to Government."[37]

Apparently, this directive was not enough. In late 1954 Taxi Lewis's office sent out another memorandum, "Security of Information," this time to all camp commandants in the Pipeline. The memo began by stating, "It is reported that some officers on leave in Nairobi and Mombasa are apt to air opinions and make statements in public places about the health, management and conditions of detainees at Manyani and Mackinnon Road camps which, being overheard by or repeated to reporters, are subsequently printed in the United Kingdom press and elsewhere." Lewis then went on to remind his men of the consequences of such reckless behavior.

> The attention of all officers is drawn to the Code of Regulations, Paragraphs 270 (1) and (2) and 271 (1) which state most clearly that an officer may not contribute to the publishing of anything which may properly be regarded as of a political or administrative nature and should not allow himself to be interviewed on questions of public policy. The Commissioner directs that this instruction shall be brought to the notice of all officers and shall be strictly adhered to. It will be necessary to take disciplinary action against any officer contravening this order.[38]

But the leaks continued and would have been even more difficult to deflect had photographic evidence accompanied them. Rumors circulated in the corridors of the Governor's House in Nairobi that some colonial officers were compiling personal photo albums of the camps, with images of deprivation and torture that, if put in the wrong hands, would be devastating.[39] Lewis again responded with a stern reminder: "Under no circumstances—except as provided by special exception, Section 22 of the Prisons Ordinance of 1948—will the photographs in or at any Prison building or installation or of any person or persons in the custody of the Prisons Department be

ONE SHILLING

TRUTH about KENYA

— an eye witness account by

Eileen Fletcher

FORMER REHABILITATION OFFICER KENYA GOVERNMENT

Foreword by

LESLIE HALE

Member of Parliament for Oldham West

- **Concentration Camps**
- **White Supremacy**
- **Children Starved**
- **Tortured to Death**
- **Government Statement**

"Suffer the little children . . . . ."

allowed."[40] This did not stop unauthorized information from finding its way into the press, both in Kenya and in Britain. Locally the *East African Standard* covered the camps, along with the wider war, on a daily basis. Back home the *Manchester Guardian*, the *Observer*, the *Daily Mirror*, the *Daily Worker*, and the *New Statesman and Nation* printed stories of colonial brutality and government evasiveness, while the more conservative papers like the *Daily Telegraph* and the *Daily Mail* hewed to the government line, evoking images of Mau Mau savagery and a benevolent if battered settler community that was entitled to the protection of Her Majesty's forces.

The colonial government was fighting the battle of information on two fronts. First, it sought to cut accusations of wrongdoing off at the source; without detailed reports or photographs Labour critics had only suggestive hearsay on which to base their accusations. Generally, Baring and his ministers were effective at controlling news leakages from their men on the spot. Of course, in many instances these were the same men who were perpetrating crimes against the Kikuyu population or who tacitly condoned the behavior of their public school and Oxbridge-trained colleagues. But a few officials did break ranks, anonymously or even publicly. Some were no doubt provoked by their own moral sense, others by the ostracism and retribution they suffered after lobbying internally to stop the ongoing brutality. Regardless, they sent uncensored information on to the Colonial Office, Labour MPs, and the British press, providing specific details on brutality and wrongdoing that continued to fuel bitter public debate over Kenya. With the publication of these reports Lennox-Boyd had to turn his attention to the other front in information management. That is, he had to control the damage.

Still under pressure from the Young affair, the colonial secretary was assaulted by more accusations in May of 1956, this time from a former rehabilitation officer by the name of Eileen Fletcher. The charges she leveled concerning brutalities and breaches of law in the camps were more specific and extensive than those in previous reports. What made the situation particularly problematic for the colonial government was Fletcher's credibility. A devout Quaker from Middlesex, England, Fletcher had been hired personally by Askwith because of her unusual credentials. "So many of my recruits were really the bottom of the barrel," Askwith later recalled, "which made Ms. Fletcher and her abilities all the more impressive."[41] Fletcher had twenty years of social welfare experience, including work in Europe's postwar reeducation efforts. Convinced that she had a significant role to play in Kenya, Fletcher signed a four-year contract in 1954 to design and oversee the rehabilitation program for women and girls at Kamiti. Less than a year later she resigned from her post in protest against "the redefinition and distribution of functions of herself and the officers at Kamiti."[42] Instead of spearheading reform work in the camp, she found herself taking orders from Katherine Warren-Gash, who had much different ideas about the nature of rehabilitation in the Pipeline. Fletcher had come to Kenya believing in Askwith's vision of the camps and the role of reform in winning the war against Mau Mau, only to leave completely disillusioned.

When Fletcher's three-part series, titled "Kenya's Concentration

Camps—An Eyewitness Account," was published in the Quaker periodical
Peace News, the revelations electrified all sides of the political divide.[43] As
part of her rehabilitation post, Fletcher had traveled throughout the colony
from the transit camp at Gilgil, the holding camps at Langata and
Manyani, to Narok and Athi River camps, as well as to the Mau Mau
prison at Embakasi and to various screening centers and Emergency villages. It was from these experiences, together with her day-to-day observations at Kamiti, that Fletcher leveled her extensive list of allegations. At
Langata she "found that all the males in the camp (many hundreds) including small boys, were wearing nothing but a blanket," and orphaned
children, as young as four years old, were malnourished and had little
chance of leaving the camp since no one was stepping forward to claim
them.[44] One prison officer told her that some women were banished to
"single corrugated iron cells" for as long as a year, at which point, he
boasted, "even the blackest will give in."[45] Fletcher's account emphasized
the capricious justice of the screening camps, the relentless labor routines
in the works camps, the sexual abuse of female detainees, the unsanitary
conditions of most of the camps, and the undernourishment and general
poor health of many of the detainees.

Her allegations describing the treatment of juveniles were some of the
most disturbing, at least for the Opposition. Fletcher reported that numerous girls under the age of fourteen, some as young as eleven, were incarcerated in Kamiti Prison for Mau Mau crimes. Several of these girls were
reportedly lifers. In effect, they had been convicted of capital crimes, like
consorting with terrorists, but because they were under the age of eighteen
they were sentenced to life imprisonment, rather than to death.[46] This was
a violation of Section 12(1) of Kenya's Juveniles Ordinance, which declared
it illegal to imprison any child under the age of fourteen. In theory the
courts were supposed to remand such juveniles to an approved school, but
no such institutions for girls even existed prior to Mau Mau. With
nowhere to incarcerate young convicts, the judges sent them to the
Pipeline, where they were detained with the adult population. According to
Fletcher, many boys under the age of fourteen were similarly imprisoned.
In fact, she recounted how Askwith himself would comment upon those
held at Embakasi. "It will break your heart," he said, "to see them shackled,
nothing to do, in a very small dormitory and with a very small space for
exercise. They have been there for a year and are just rotting."[47]

Today, what remains of the evidence on juvenile detention strongly
supports Fletcher's allegations. Prior to the Emergency, the colonial government did very little in response to its own internally generated recommendations regarding the need for juvenile delinquency facilities

throughout the colony.[48] With the notable exception of the approved schools for boys at Kabete and Dagoretti, nothing was being done to address the mounting problem of juvenile crime. With the outbreak of Mau Mau, there was simply nowhere to put juveniles either convicted or detained without trial for Emergency-related offenses. By the time Fletcher arrived, there were officially some sixteen hundred juveniles in Manyani Camp and at least two thousand being held throughout the Pipeline.[49] In theory, three departments had a degree of responsibility for these youths—the Prisons Department, the Community Development and Rehabilitation Department, and the Probation Department—but as with the adult population, it was the Prisons Department that had the decisive say over their treatment in the detention camps and prisons.

There was, however, one promising development. In July 1955 Wamumu Approved School and Youth Camp was opened for male juveniles convicted and detained for Mau Mau offenses. This camp was arguably the only rehabilitation success story in Kenya, largely because it was under the sole control of Askwith and the liberal Probation Department. This made it the only facility in the Pipeline, aside from Perkerra Open Camp, that was wholly devoid of Prisons Department personnel and influence.[50] A comprehensive hearts-and-minds program—including physical recreation, Kiswahili and English classes, literacy courses, skill training, civics instruction, Boy Scout troops, and Empire Day parades—was implemented in Wamumu to great success. There were, nevertheless, some juveniles who did not cooperate, and like the adults they were slated for permanent exile. But in comparison to the rest of the camps in the Pipeline, Wamumu, with its proclaimed ethos of "Truth and Loyalty," was a paradise for young Mau Mau suspects. Many of them went on after release to be employed in the Community Development and Rehabilitation Department or with settlers who were impressed with the success of the camp and the skills and discipline it imparted.[51]

It was not long before the reputation of Wamumu spread to the other camps in the Pipeline. When the principal probation officer, Colin Owen, came to assess the youths being held in places like Manyani, young detainees clamored to be selected for transfer to Askwith's camp, though there clearly was not enough room in Wamumu for all of the boys being held at Manyani and elsewhere. Hundreds of those who were arrested and either imprisoned or detained as teenagers remained in the camps for several years, by which time they were too old to be transferred to Wamumu because they appeared to be over eighteen and were thus classified as adults.[52] Some young detainees, in an attempt to get around this, did their best to appear even younger than they were. "When the teams were identifying

those who were young enough to be transferred to Wamumu," Samuel
Gakuru later recalled, "they checked for the presence of beards, pubic and
armpit hairs. I was lucky since I had no beard. As for the other hairs, we
had devised a way of getting rid of them by applying hot ash to these spots,
and the hairs would just come off."[53] In Samuel's case, he was successful.
Twenty-three years old at the time of the transfer inspection, he passed for
a teenager and was sent to Wamumu, a move which brought an enormous
change to his life not just in the Pipeline but well after his release, as he was
later hired as a clerk in the Community Development and Rehabilitation
Department.

Samuel was one of the lucky ones. Most of the boys in the Pipeline
would remain in the adult camps, and all of the girls would be sent to
Kamiti Camp as there was no female equivalent of Wamumu. Aside from
those boys and girls detained or imprisoned, there were also thousands of
others who were lumped into the colonial government's orphan, waif, and
stray problem. Many had lost their parents to the war or had become separated from them during the upheavals of the forced removals, leaving them
"wandering about" the White Highlands and Nairobi, according to official
reports.[54] Juvenile delinquency and child prostitution skyrocketed as these
children did what they could in order to survive. Young girls worked in
the Nairobi brothels or traveled with the help of local taxi drivers to the
African servants' quarters in the European and Asian areas of Kenya, where
they sold their services for roughly two shillings, or the equivalent of a
meal.[55] No single party within the government wanted to, or could, assume
the fiscal or administrative responsibility for these unclaimed children and
instead looked to voluntary associations and the missionaries to take care
of them. Beniah Ohanga, the minister of community development and rehabilitation, voiced his outrage over this state of affairs: "The lack of remand homes [i.e., facilities for juveniles] is nothing short of a scandal, and
the Judiciary has on many occasions expressed its grave disquiet at the failure of Government to fulfill its statutory obligation to provide remand
homes."[56] Simply put, the situation was hell for the children, and no one
wanted to deal with it. Rather than improving, it only worsened when
camps like Langata were condemned and youngsters either were released
with nowhere to go or were sent to the arguably worse conditions in places
like Manyani. Most colonial officials refused to accept responsibility for
the juvenile crisis, instead adopting the same line as the district commissioner of Fort Hall, who blamed Kikuyu parents for not "looking after their
own children in the traditional manner."[57]

· · ·

The crisis of the incarceration of juveniles, along with the spike in delinquency and prostitution, was occurring at the very time that Fletcher leveled her allegations. Labour MPs, though unaware of many of these details that supported Fletcher's claims, still held up the former rehabilitation officer's account as unimpeachable proof that all was not right in Kenya. This time it was Labour MP Leslie Hale who took the lead in demanding a full explanation from Lennox-Boyd. From the start, Hale became Fletcher's chief liaison with the Colonial Office, assisted her with press conferences, and wrote a foreword to her much-referenced pamphlet *Truth about Kenya—an eye witness account by Eileen Fletcher*.[58] In the days leading up to the first showdown on the floor of the Commons over Fletcher's allegations, Lennox-Boyd and Baring fired secret memoranda back and forth, trying to get their stories straight.[59] There was, of course, no reasonable explanation for Fletcher's account, but there would be no mea culpa. Lennox-Boyd and Baring never deviated from their script, instead conceding that perhaps there were one or two incidents in the Pipeline, but that these should be evaluated not just in the context of Mau Mau but also in the light of the progressive reforms they were introducing through their massive rehabilitation campaign in the camps and villages.

But what to do about Fletcher? If the colonial government could not credibly contradict each of her charges, Lennox-Boyd had to somehow discredit the character of an abundantly well-qualified woman, one who had earlier received a glowing review by Askwith. Colonial officials did their best to besmirch her character, alleging she was hysterical in temper and had a "catty manner."[60] After her allegations were revealed, Fletcher was suddenly found to be disliked by her fellow officers and detainees, her work was substandard, and her knowledge of the Pipeline, despite her numerous and detailed safari reports, deemed superficial. But even during this assault, Lennox-Boyd knew he needed to minimize his public exchange with Labour. When the first Commons debate began in early June 1956, the colonial secretary announced he would provide no response to the Opposition until it had introduced all of its charges. The Labour MPs would then have little opportunity to redirect after he provided the government's defense against Fletcher's allegations. By the end of the six-and-a-half-hour session the colonial secretary had refuted some of Fletcher's charges, stating, for example, that errors had been made in prison and court documents relating to the ages of the alleged juveniles. Once those errors were corrected, it turned out that every single juvenile detained in the Pipeline was, in fact, over the legal age for imprisonment. As for the remainder of Fletcher's charges, he did not seek to refute them directly but dismissed them obliquely by questioning the integrity and judgment of Fletcher herself.[61]

In light of the private evidence in front of the Colonial Office pertaining to delinquency, prostitution, and abhorrent detention conditions for the Mau Mau juveniles, Lennox-Boyd's deceptions and outright lies were, and remain today, stunning. During the debate Labour MPs like Barbara Castle, Leslie Hale, Aneurin Bevan, and Fenner Brockway refused to accept the colonial government's spin on the situation, demanding an independent judicial investigation into Kenya. When their calls fell on deaf ears, the debate nevertheless played out in the press. The *Observer* led the liberal media with its headline "No More Whitewash." Its article plainly stated that Lennox-Boyd had failed in his efforts to shake the public's confidence in Fletcher's testimony, and that the "mysterious alteration in prison records of the ages of Kikuyu girls . . . is in itself disturbing." The *Observer* also called upon the colonial secretary to introduce an independent investigation, declaring, "If we tolerate such practices in British territories, on what grounds do we criticise Russian prison camps?"[62]

Had Lennox-Boyd acceded to the investigation, Young, Fletcher, Castle, and the rest of the government's anticolonial critics would have been vindicated. Instead, the colonial secretary stood his ground. That thousands of men, women, and children were living under abhorrent conditions, enduring torture, and being murdered was of secondary importance to maintaining the image of colonial trusteeship as well as British rule over Kenya. Personal and political reputations were also obviously at stake. But as the level of cover-up became more blatant with each passing month, there emerged the sense that Lennox-Boyd and those around him must have actually believed their public representations of the facts. In a later debate over Fletcher in the fall of 1956 he implored the public to look at the evidence as he did: "I am quite satisfied that Miss Fletcher's charges are based in the main on hearsay, on partisan opinion and personal prejudice. The negligible amount of criticism which could be levelled has proved to be wholly disproportionate to the impression that she has contrived to create. I would ask all fair-minded people to read carefully the documents in the Library of this House and to make up their own minds."[63] Lennox-Boyd's Labour critics would have none of it. Aneurin Bevan leveled one of the most bitter responses during the ongoing Fletcher debates, shooting back:

Is not that a most monstrous statement to make, to accuse a person of telling lies—a person who is very respected indeed? Is it not the fact that both the Government of Kenya and the right hon. Gentleman [Lennox-Boyd] are now seeking to be judges in their own cause? Accusations have been made against the Administration there; is it not a fact that no one can have any confidence in what the right hon. Gentleman says unless he allows an impartial investigation to take place into the allegations? So far, all he has said is that he is satisfied, and he is satisfied, but we are not satisfied . . . What we want to know is: as charges of the gravest possible kind have been made against the administration of justice in Kenya and against the prison administration, is it not the right hon. Gentleman's proper course now to justify his own charges by having an investigation into the whole case, and not call people "liars" in the way he has?[64]

A little over two months after Bevan's attack, another British officer stepped forward with allegations of atrocities. This time they came from Captain Philip Meldon, who had spent from March 1954 to May 1955 working in the Pipeline, first as a temporary officer in the Kenya Police Reserve and then as a rehabilitation officer in Askwith's department. During his service Meldon worked in five camps and received positive evaluations from all his superiors. One came from James Breckenridge, the senior rehabilitation officer in the Rift Valley camps, who stated, "Meldon is extremely good with Africans and if he learns Kiswahili or Kikuyu, he will make an excellent Rehabilitation Officer."[65] By the end of May 1955, however, Askwith had terminated Meldon's contract "owing to absence without leave." Nearly a year and a half after his return to Britain, Meldon came forward with a series of detailed accounts that alleged brutalities, poor administration, and cover-ups. Perhaps prompted by Fletcher's revelations, Meldon broke the code of silence, writing to Breckenridge in December 1956, "I have given this matter a lot of consideration but my conscience will not let me keep quiet any longer."[66] Meldon first published his allegations in *Peace News* and *Reynolds News* in January 1957 and followed them up with a personal letter to Lennox-Boyd that provided further details of his observations and offered names of specific British officers who had perpetrated crimes in Kenya's camps.[67]

Like Fletcher, Meldon revealed a picture of widespread torture and suffering in Britain's East African colony. "The plight of detainees . . . during 1954 and 1955, except for those in Marigat Camp," he wrote, "included short rations, overwork, brutality, humiliating and disgusting treatment and flogging—all in violation of the United Nations Universal Declaration of Human Rights."[68] Meldon described "lavatories [at the Gilgil transit camp that] were merely large pits in the ground, about 20' by 14' by 12' with the excreta lapping over the top," as well as a security officer at Tebere Camp in Embu District who "kicked one detainee head-first into a large container of boiling maize meal which a Kikuyu detainee was stirring."[69] In his letter to Lennox-Boyd the former officer provided a table that listed the "most flagrant irregularities" under various headings with titles like "Torture,"

"Floggings," "Beatings," "Assault," and "Overwork." The same catalog also attached the camps and the names of the officers associated with the offenses.[70] In his account "My Two Years in Kenya" Meldon emphasized, as Fletcher and Askwith also had, the poor quality of the British officers in the camps, as well as the absence of any kind of systematic rehabilitation program. He went on to add, "The rehabilitation of these people and offering them a more hopeful outlook on life and future was a problem of vital importance to the future of Kenya, as the Kikuyu are the largest, most intelligent and hardwoking of all the peoples of Kenya, and are absolutely essential to the economy of the country. Tragically, this responsibility was not met and the opportunity was lost."[71]

By the time Meldon made his allegations the Colonial Office was better prepared to take the offensive. Having learned from their experiences with Fletcher, Lennox-Boyd and Baring sought to control the political agenda immediately, which meant foremost questioning the character of the former British officer. With Meldon's first suggestion of exposing the Pipeline in December 1956, the governor sent a secret telegram to the colonial secretary, stating, "[The] letter may be bluff or blackmail but I am inclined to take it seriously. It may have the makings of another Eileen Fletcher affair."[72] The governor went on to note that his office was "collecting all possible further information which may be of use in discrediting him if necessary," and in fact labeled Meldon as "quarrelsome," "indebted," and "pugnacious" even before any investigation into his character had been launched.[73] For his part, Lennox-Boyd had to manage the political damage that would inevitably follow Meldon's revelations. To this end, he stressed to Baring the importance of trying to keep press coverage to a minimum.

> Fletcher campaign had shown how much heat and little constructive action was occasioned by launching of allegations through Press which neither the Governor of Kenya nor the Secretary of State had been given prior opportunity to investigate. While no one could or would attempt to stop publication by Press of what they considered it was in the public interest to publish, nevertheless the political encouragement of such campaigns might be unproductive.[74]

The colonial secretary was now going as far as to meddle with the Opposition, inveigling Labour MP James Griffiths to do what he could to limit his party's negative publicity of the Meldon case. But even with this behind-the-scenes scheming, Lennox-Boyd only hoped to weaken the coming storm. As he later telegrammed Baring, "[The] maximum results we can hope for from this approach is moderation and control of political exploitation of any disclosures made."[75]

That Meldon waited two years to come forward with his revelations was to the advantage of the Colonial Office. Together, the colonial secretary and the governor pointed to this lapse, to Meldon's questionable character, and to the alleged success of rehabilitation to dismiss the former officer's charges. Internally, the colonial government was fully aware that many of Meldon's accusations were true. Gilgil Camp, for instance, was known for its wretched conditions and had been condemned by Kenya's Medical Department in 1955. Similarly, Manyani Camp was overcrowded, lacked a rehabilitation program, and was plagued by violence and neglect, facts which Meldon had pointed out several times both publicly and privately to the colonial secretary.[76] Nevertheless, in correspondence with the Opposition and in written responses in the House of Commons, Lennox-Boyd rejected any credibility in Meldon's claims. In one of several letters to Meldon's leading supporter in the Labour Party, Fenner Brockway, the colonial secretary wrote:

> I do not think it is necessary to go too deeply into Mr. Meldon's general allegations. That "the opportunity was lost" to rehabilitate detainees is of course patently absurd. As you know, over 40,000 have already found their way to freedom and well under 30,000 now remain. . . . I think I should add, for your private information, that Mr. Meldon, as is obvious from his statement, spent a relatively short time in most of the camps with which he was concerned, and that the reason for this was that he was not considered suitable for rehabilitation work. . . . He was personally at odds with several officers, including the Staff Officer of the Rift Valley Works Camps. I would not wish you to infer from this that we have treated his allegations with any less care than we would otherwise have done or that because he has this background it is to be inferred that they are to be treated a priori as a complete fabrication. Nevertheless I cannot agree that on examination of the allegations, particularly as they are made after a lapse of two years and do not refer to conditions in detention camps today, reveal any grounds whatsoever for appointing a judicial commission of enquiry into these matters.[77]

Meldon's revelations never resulted in an independent judicial inquiry.

While witnesses were being discredited, Lennox-Boyd bolstered his defenses with the many positive reports coming in from government-sponsored evaluation committees. The colonial secretary certainly emphasized that regular inspection committees, as provided for under Emergency Regulations, toured the Pipeline. Of course, he had to have been aware that these committees did not visit the Pipeline on a regular basis. Moreover, the few reports that were issued were perfunctory and biased, or, in the words of Kenya's Defence Ministry, "the whole thing is window dressing anyway."[78] There were also the visits conducted by the missionaries' liaison officers, Father Colleton, Reverend Howard Church, and Canon Eric Webster. All three of these men toured the camps on a regular basis, filing reports that assessed the Christian progress being made in the Pipeline. Several of the reports bemoaned the lack of proper religious facilities in the camps, the limited access enjoyed by Colleton, Church, and Webster to the detainees, the absence of rehabilitation programs, and the relentless labor routines and prolonged shackling of Mau Mau suspects.[79] Quite notably, in July 1956, Church was released from his duties, largely because he protested internally over the conditions of some of the camps, while attributing some of Mau Mau's influence and demands to the harsh actions of the colonial government. At the time of Church's sacking, both Baring and the colonial secretary feared he would go public, so they issued a memorandum stating, "For information—a 'warning note' in order, in the words of the Department, that a latter-day Fletcher may not strike without warning. The Minister of State has seen and minuted that Mr. Church may well be difficult."[80]

For validation, the colonial government relied heavily on the Commonwealth Parliamentary Association (CPA) delegations that traveled to Kenya to observe and report on the Emergency conditions. These delegations were composed of MPs from Britain, though the selection process was dictated by the CPA with influence from the Colonial Office rather than by independent nomination by each political party. With painstakingly choreographed itineraries, colonial officials would escort the MPs through the colony and introduce them to various members of the local government responsible for overseeing Emergency policies. The first of these two-man CPA delegations set off in 1956 and was made up of Hugh Fraser, the same Conservative MP who earlier directed Baring to emphasize "rehabilitation," and R. W. Williams. When they completed their work, Fraser and Williams followed the stated rules of the CPA and filed their report for the association's private review only.

In 1957, with the outcries about the Fletcher and Meldon allegations reaching a crescendo, Lennox-Boyd needed a positive report on Kenya. More to the point, he saw the CPA delegation as a way to sidestep an all-out independent investigation. In place of a two-person envoy, Lennox-Boyd lobbied the United Kingdom branch of the CPA to send a larger committee, presumably because with more people its report would carry more credibility. If the colonial secretary's intentions were not transparent, the head of the Colonial Office's East Africa Department, Will Mathieson, plainly spelled them out when he wrote, "A CPA delegation was a goodwill delegation and by this definition could not be as searching as a delegation chosen by the 'Shadow Cabinet.' "[81] Another one of Lennox-Boyd's men, Gorell Barnes, went on to underscore the political importance of the situation: "If the delegation can be brought to recognize and endorse the principles on which our policies rest, the visit will clearly pay important dividends here for Kenya."[82]

The CPA did move forward with an expanded delegation, but one which hardly represented all sides of the political spectrum. None of the Labour MPs who were most knowledgeable, and critical, of the Emergency were included in the delegation, a point which hardly escaped members of the Labour Party. One of its MPs, James Johnson, bluntly told Mathieson that "had Parliament been sending a delegation to produce a report which would represent the views of both parties on the situation in Kenya, the delegation from the Labour side would have been very differently composed and would have been led by a Privy Councillor and contain at least one Q.C. probably Mr. Elwyn Jones." The Labour MP went on to add that "what Kenya needed was a thorough going over not a pat on the back."[83] In the end, there were three Labour MPs and four Conservatives in the delegation, including Thomas Dugdale, who was appointed as leader. Granville Roberts, the public relations officer for Kenya, conveniently served as the delegation's secretary when it toured the colony during the month of January 1957.

Not surprisingly, when the CPA delegation returned to Britain it issued a positive report. An issue remained, however. CPA reports were not supposed to be published. Lennox-Boyd relentlessly lobbied the association to take exception in this instance and to allow the findings to be circulated. In light of the biased composition of the delegation, the Opposition protested vehemently. An agreement was eventually reached whereby the delegation would publish a report for "Private Circulation Only." A few weeks after the report was privately circulated, an anonymous source leaked it to the *Times*. Lennox-Boyd seized on this turn of events by pressing the CPA to reconsider the association's policy of not publishing delegation reports. He said that "he felt bound to raise [the issue of publication] because the Report's wider distribution would be helpful not least to the Kenya Government."[84] The CPA capitulated, and in July 1957 the delegation's report was offered in full to the public. In turn, the Colonial Office used this allegedly bipartisan document as unimpeachable evidence that the system of detention without trial, the conditions in the Emergency villages, and the suppression of Mau Mau generally were all devoid of the alleged brutalities and injustices.

The colonial government benefited greatly from the relative silence and outright support of many of the local Christian missionaries. At one extreme, the Catholics largely threw their weight behind the British forces of law and order, some going so far as to serve on armed patrols.[85] The response of the Protestant churches to the Emergency, however, was much less clear-cut. Most believed Mau Mau had cast a specter of evil over Kenya and that it had to be eradicated. But when it came to the increasing allegations of colonial injustice, their reactions were complicated by a host of competing loyalties and interests.

The most controversial church figure by far was Leonard Beecher, the Anglican Church's archbishop of Mombasa. In response to the Church Missionary Society's earlier publication of *Kenya—time for Action*, the archbishop quite astonishingly expressed his "embarrassment and bewilderment" at the pamphlet.[86] This despite the fact that he had befriended Police Commissioner Young and had promised him that the story behind his resignation would not be buried.[87] At first Beecher kept his word, issuing a joint statement with other Christian leaders in Kenya, notably the Reverend David Steel, the colony's moderator of the Church of Scotland, declaring, "It is important that a full explanation of the reasons for the difference between Government and Colonel Young should be given to the public."[88] For his part, Steel followed up the joint release with a scathing broadcast sermon in Nairobi, where he stated, "A judicial commission of experts in constitutional law is called for to pronounce on the legality of much of our emergency legislation. . . . [They] give the appearance of legality to practices not only unjust in the eyes of God but illegal by the accepted law of man." He went on to say, "During the emergency we have taken some very dangerous steps along the road [to tyranny]. It is time to retrace."[89] But when Anglican Church representatives in Britain stepped forward to denounce the actions of Kenya's colonial police force, the archbishop balked. Virtually overnight he became the star witness for the Conservative government's defense against the onslaught of allegations. In his sparring with Lord Jowitt in the House of Lords, for instance, the parliamentary undersecretary of state for the colonies declared:

> I am very sorry that a Society [i.e., Church Missionary Society] for which I have such great respect, a society which has co-operated with us in the Colonial Office in so many fields and which has done such wonderful work

in Africa and elsewhere, should have published this document. My own views on this pamphlet were well expressed by the Bishop of Mombasa, Bishop Beecher, a man of the highest reputation in Africa, with deep knowledge and experience of its problems and an acknowledged expert on the Kikuyu tribe. The Bishop, after making it clear that the document was published without his knowledge, criticised it as being "one-sided and particularly unfortunate." I do not want to question for one moment the sincerity of those who wrote this pamphlet, but I cannot help feeling that in a delicate situation of this kind those concerned might have come to the Colonial Office before publication, to hear the other side of the story, or that at any rate they might have consulted the Bishop on the spot.[90]

What explains this apparent about-face by the Anglican archbishop? Certainly, he had sufficient accurate information about the brutalities and deprivations not only from Young but from his missionaries in the field, as well as from other Protestant church leaders in Kenya. Within months after the Declaration of Emergency the Christian Council of Kenya (CCK), the umbrella organization for Protestant churches in the colony, began privately lobbying Governor Baring to stop the abuses and the breakdown of the rule of law, as well as to reconsider his government's position on loyalty. Countless numbers of devout Kikuyu converts were being rounded up and detained, despite repeated protests from the missionaries that these Africans constituted the most loyal foundation of a future Christian community in Central Province.[91] Indeed, just prior to Beecher's denunciation of the CMS pamphlet he wrote to Baring's office on this very issue, stating, "I have repeatedly made it clear that the Church desire[s] to co-operate wholeheartedly and to offer its fullest support to the Government. I should hope that there might be sufficient reciprocity."[92]

Deputation after deputation of missionaries went to express their growing concern to the governor over the abuses being perpetrated against the Mau Mau population, demanding that he take action to stop them. This strategy, however, proved ineffective, and in November 1953 the CCK struggled with "whether to continue to urge Government privately to correct abuses or to take direct action through the press." Ultimately, the council agreed "to continue to press privately for the correction of abuses," and if that did not succeed, appeals would be made to the Colonial Office through the missionary societies at home. Surely, the council reasoned, they "could count on [the Colonial Office's] good will."[93] Less than a fortnight later the various Protestant church leaders in Kenya, including Beecher, published a joint petition titled "An Open Letter from Leaders of Christian Churches in Kenya." The publication was a clear indication that the Colonial Office had fallen short in its "good will." The letter expressed dismay over the general breakdown of law and order in Kenya and urged all Africans and Europeans in the colony, "In spite of seeming provocation or even in face of apparent encouragement to indulge in cruel abuse of power, do not do so. You are Christians, and such action is un-Christian."[94] A month later the churches published a second letter clarifying their position, in part because of the widely published court-martial case of Captain Gerald Griffiths. This settler and army officer reputedly mutilated prisoners, kept a scoreboard of Mau Mau kills, and took a liking to shooting them with an automatic weapon until, according to one witness, bullets "practically poured out of the man's stomach."[95] In light of this case, the church leaders now declared:

> In our [first] statement we referred to repeated representations at the highest level concerning abuses of power by certain members of the Forces of Law and Order. These were based on incidents adequate in number and sufficiently well authenticated to warrant such representations. It was only after certain aspects of abuse had been publicised as a result of recent trials and courts-martial that the public statement became, in our view, necessary. The Churches have a particular responsibility in that in the African areas they are the only independent observers of the situation.[96]

But it was over two years before the CCK and Archbishop Beecher would issue another statement that questioned the conduct of the colonial government in Kenya, and even then it would be framed in careful language.[97] Clearly, the missionaries were struggling between their moral obligation to step in and put a stop to the atrocities and their need to maintain the goodwill of the local colonial government. Beecher, Steel, the CCK, and all of their local missionaries were in Kenya at the pleasure of the governor. Although the likelihood of Baring actually sending all of the missionaries packing was slim, he could make their jobs exceedingly difficult, and, if he chose, he could further reduce the already minimal access that the churches had to the camps and Emergency villages. Moreover, if the missionaries were one of the few relatively impartial observers in the field, who would be left behind to hold the already beleaguered moral compass in Kenya if they were dismissed? There was also the self-interest of these men of God to consider. While Mau Mau, with its anti-Christian message, was certainly an indictment of previous missionary activity in Kenya, its suppression also offered the churches an unprecedented opportunity for conversions, something upon which they were all eager to capitalize. Furthermore, Christian salvation during the Emergency was not just a means for redeeming Mau Mau sinners; it was also a form of personal and institutional redemption for the missionaries themselves, who clearly saw in Mau Mau a reflection of their own past failures. Undoubtedly, all of these considerations weighed on Beecher when he expressed his "embarrassment and bewilderment" in early 1955. A heavy burden too was his widely acknowledged close personal friendship with Governor Baring, as well as their privileged religious relationship—Beecher gave Baring communion daily before breakfast.[98]

Despite these public ambiguities, private deputations to the governor continued in earnest, and each one reflected more clearly the missionaries' inside knowledge. At the same time that Beecher denounced the CMS pamphlet, he, along with several other church leaders, filed a petition with Baring condemning the continued detention without trial of Christians, the violence in the camps, the absence of police reform, and the inability of the government to ensure that its stated policies were carried out on the ground.[99] Three months later the missionaries issued another private petition, declaring, "The disquiet expressed in our earlier memorandum and at our interview [with the governor] has not been removed or allayed by subsequent events."[100] They went on to list yet again their concerns over Emergency abuses, as well as to alert Baring to the fact that "starvation, with its consequences of malnutrition and crime, is on the increase; a spirit of apathy, frustration and hopelessness prevails; there is utter perplexity as to government's policy."[101] Rehabilitation, or the lack of it, was also a focal point of their complaints, as well as the need to extend Christian reform to the agents of British colonialism.

> It has been admitted to us on more than one occasion that a major impediment in the way of a constructive policy in Kenya is the difficulty experienced in ensuring its implementation by the executive officers, European or African, at the local level. Some, at least, of these openly adopt an attitude toward Africans or towards Christianity, which runs counter to government's declared policy. Others, by their habits of life, show a deplorable example to the African population.[102]

Other than the local realities that these deputations brought to light, their most striking feature was their utter futility. Like Lennox-Boyd, Baring had pat answers for every charge, either declaring them unfounded or assuring that every effort was being made to look into them. Despite this stonewalling, the missionaries did not change their approach. Despite the fact that nothing was being done, despite the fact that the church leaders continued to hear of new incidences of abuses, and despite the fact that one of their own independent deputations "said that there was good evidence of distress, sickness and even death from lack of food" in the Emergency villages, the missionaries continued to stay their course.[103] This despite the fact that various internal reports indicated that the missionaries' knowledge of atrocities was overwhelming. "Evil seems firmly entrenched," began one letter by Reverend Peter Bostock to the Church Missionary Society in London. He went on, "Europeans on the spot back one another up, don't report things, lie readily to cover up investigations, and there seems no way of breaking through this. . . . The European lies and says the African was trying to escape, but reports are too numerous and too varied for us to be able to give credence to the bona fides of the European in many cases."[104] Anglican Church officials in Kenya later compiled a compendium of some of the atrocities in the camps and reserves.

> Africans have been beaten to extract information.
>
> Africans have been shot and left to die in agony without any semblance of trial and on mere suspicion.
>
> Africans have been arrested and taken to the Forest and shot there in cold blood. In one case their arrest had been ordered and not their death. In another case they were driven into the Forest so that they could be shot. Shooting in the forests is "legal."
>
> Men have been known to boast of "scores" and of taking no prisoners and asking no questions.
>
> The hands of men shot have been cut off and used not merely to identify the victim but also to extract information from their relatives. Is mutilation of the dead permissible?
>
> Men have been tortured to reveal what they knew often only on the merest suspicion:
>
> > A. had his legs broken with a stone because he would not speak
> > B. had his private parts laid on a table and beaten till the scrotum burst because he would not speak.
> > C. was beaten on the soles of his feet till he could not walk because he would not speak.
> > D. Was arrested on a Saturday night and by Sunday night or Monday was dead. True the cause of death has not yet been established but he was buried at once without his relatives being informed and without his property being returned to them.
> > E. Has been castrated and claims it was the work of the police.[105]

The archbishop of Mombasa knew some of these details, for they were contained in the private petitions that he and other members of the Christian Council of Kenya sent to Baring. Even after the Young affair passed without sufficient answer from the British colonial governor, and after Fletcher and Meldon stepped forward with their allegations, these Christian leaders continued to believe, in the words of one missionary, that "the Churches and Missionary Societies in Kenya must exercise the greatest care in not bringing unnecessary embarrassment to the Government, since in fact the British Press is well able to take care now of unlawful happenings by police or military."[106] This statement was made in early 1954. Had the British press enough empirical evidence to mount an effective challenge against the Conservative government, presumably the brutalities and the starvation would have at least abated, and presumably Young, Fletcher, Meldon, and the Labour MPs would have had very little to report in subsequent years. Instead, the situation only became worse, and when Anglican Church leaders in London decided to step in, their own missionaries on the spot did not support them. Had they wanted to intervene and put an end to the horrors, the local church leaders could have gone public with precise details, or they could have provided information to a public figure like Barbara Castle. This the CCK in fact considered in late 1954, though it ultimately decided—according to its general secretary, Sam Morrison— that "before the help of Members of Parliament is invoked representations should first be made to responsible authorities in Kenya, whose difficulties deserve the most sympathetic understanding."[107] The Protestant churches never reconsidered this position. Instead, in July 1956, the Protestant Church leaders in Kenya decided, rather than stepping forward with specific allegations, to issue yet another of their carefully worded statements that contained almost as much praise as criticism.

In the course of all this work the Church has from time to time become aware of certain abuses and of other matters needing correction and as leaders of Churches with our loyalty to the Kingdom of God and its standards of righteousness we have not hesitated to make representations to the Government. We have sought to do this in the spirit of our Master who directed as a first step "if thy brother shall trespass against thee go and tell him his fault between thee and him alone." As a result of representations made at various levels action has been taken on most matters and there has been improvement. In some cases progress has been slow, and the Government has not always agreed to our suggestions to the degree that we would have wished.[108]

. . .

By early 1957 it was clear that officials at the highest level of the British government knew about the destruction unleashed in Kenya by colonial forces. In addition to the public revelations and debates, Lennox-Boyd had had lengthy private correspondences and meetings with Colonel Young, church leaders, Meldon, and various Labour MPs. Like Castle, he received letters from detainees in the Pipeline asking him to intervene to stop the ongoing abuses.[109] Throughout the war against Mau Mau, various members of his Colonial Office staff repeatedly commented upon the "bloody-mindedness" of both the British settlers and members of the Administration, as well as their African loyalist supporters.[110] Years later the head of the East Africa Department, Will Mathieson, publicly revealed some of the thoughts and concerns of the colonial secretary and his staff. He stated that both the Colonial Office and Lennox-Boyd realized that there was an "infringement of basic legal rights going on in one of Her Majesty's colonies" and that they were all very unhappy about it. But he went on to say that the Colonial Office "also regarded it as a really inevitable casualty of the situation." Moreover, according to Mathieson, "there was evidence that there were incidences [of violence against individuals practiced illegally], probably there were more that didn't come to light than actually did come to light. . . . I think we all realize that there must be a lot; if there was one or two things going on, there was probably a whole lot more."[111]

It was inevitable that these issues would come up in cabinet discussions. Churchill's ministers had met on numerous occasions to review various aspects of their ongoing war in Kenya and specifically addressed issues related to detention without trial and forced labor. In one meeting in February of 1954, for example, the cabinet minutes recorded that Churchill and his men realized, "This course [i.e., detention without trial and forced labor] had been recommended despite the fact that it was thought to involve a technical breach of the Forced Labour Convention of 1930 and of the Convention on Human Rights adopted by the Council of Europe."[112] They then went on to recommend finding legal-appearing means for circumventing the constraints of these treaties. Nearly a year later Churchill's cabinet would discuss the public relations problems caused by the blanket amnesty, ultimately agreeing to it despite its implications.

That insiders in both official and unofficial circles knew about British crimes in Kenya was an open secret, as a 1953 row between Churchill and Lord and Lady Mountbatten would illustrate. During a precoronation reception at Buckingham Palace the flamboyant Edwina Mountbatten was conversing about the Emergency with India's prime minister, Jawaharlal Nehru, and the then colonial secretary, Oliver Lyttelton. When Lyttelton commented on the "terrible savagery" of Mau Mau, Lady Mountbatten infuriated him by firing back "on both sides." Word of the exchange quickly made it to Churchill, and the colonial secretary told him, "Nehru afterwards said to me that Africans were being shot down and that we should not solve anything by these means. He was barely civil and turned on his heel and went away. I am thinking of sending Edwina the photographs of some of the atrocities so she cannot repeat her disgraceful remarks." Presumably, Lyttelton was speaking of Mau Mau atrocities, not those dispensed by the hands of Britain's forces. Angered by the incident, Churchill retaliated, refusing to allow Lord Mountbatten to take his wife with him on an official visit to Turkey.[113] Though Edwina eventually did travel with her husband on the tour—the official invitation had already been accepted—a clear message had been sent not just to the Mountbattens but to everyone else who traveled in their circle. Indiscretions would not be tolerated by the prime minister.

As charge after charge was leveled at the colonial government, neither of the colonial secretaries nor Governor Baring nor Churchill nor his successors Anthony Eden and Harold Macmillan ever wavered from their course. The situation in Kenya had created a very partisan, bitter, and often personal debate, particularly between Lennox-Boyd and Castle. But there were alternatives. In retrospect, the most obvious was immediate decolonization. At any point Britain's prime minister and colonial secretary could have put an end to the violence by pulling out of the colony altogether and granting Kenya its independence. There would have been angry repercussions to this decision, to be sure, most especially from the still intractable settlers. There would have also remained the question of what to do with the politicals who were still locked away. Moreover, the precedent that such a decision would set—that is, that the British gave in to or, worse, were defeated by an African uprising—remained unthinkable. Officials in the British colonial government also believed they were fighting a moral war for Western civilization over the forces of dark savagery. There would be no contemplation of an imperial retreat from Kenya before Mau Mau had been crushed. In their minds, the colony had to be rendered governable, if only to protect long-term British interests. Yet, paradoxically, Britain's very presence in Kenya and the brutality of its forces were the real root of the turmoil. Withdrawing was never considered, though, at least not until the end of the Emergency when Mau Mau had been destroyed and with it much of the Kikuyu population. Even then, there were colonial officials, particularly in Kenya, who believed the colony would remain part of the empire for at least another generation.

Ultimately, hanging in the balance was the whole rationale, both past and present, for the British Empire. Decades had been spent constructing Britain's imperial image, and that image contrasted sharply with the brutal behavior of other European empires in Africa. King Leopold's bloody rule in the Congo, the German-directed genocide of the Herero in South West Africa, and France's disgrace in Algeria—the British reputedly avoided all of those excesses because, simply, it was British to do so. That is what the civilizing mission led much of the Western world to believe, and it was certainly believed by the British public at home. For many years the White Man's Burden was accepted on all sides of the political divide because it was understood to be a reformist endeavor that would nurture Africans, and others in the empire, for future responsible citizenship. Both liberals and conservatives in Britain believed in the superiority of British colonial rule. Unlike other European nations, so it was thought, Britain avoided the corrupting effects of absolute power in its colonies because of its higher, Christian moral principles and economic know-how. It also had a uniquely professional, elite cadre of overseas civil servants, who led with their ruling-class sense of obligation and duty, honor and discipline. In places like Kenya the "paramountcy of native interests" had been declared in the early 1920s. At face value, this notion meant that the colonial government and its men on the spot were protecting the feckless Africans from settler greed and international capitalism while developing African resources and minds for future self-rule.

Mau Mau threatened to blow apart this charade of colonial trusteeship. For years the British had employed their own brand of violence in the colony to extract resources and maintain rule, but the Emergency brought an intensification and spread of white anger and brutality that converted racial exploitation and hatred into something far more lethal. Kenya was not the first time, nor would it be the last, in which the British used violence and repression to maintain rule over its twentieth-century empire. At the start of the century there was the Boer War in South Africa, and later there were the brutal tactics deployed in Palestine and Malaya. These cases are significant not because they represent other instances where colonial violence was widespread but because each one had an impact, through the sharing of policy or manpower, or both, on the implementation of Emergency powers in Kenya. Further, in the history of the transfer of ideas and people around the British Empire, Kenya would later provide models for interrogation and dentention used in colonies like Northern Ireland.

It is in this light that the government's refusal to end the bloodshed in Kenya must be at least partly understood. Pulling out of Kenya because of Britain's bad behavior would shatter a carefully cultivated colonial image.

So too would have the findings of any independent judicial inquiry into the Pipeline and Emergency villages. The rationale for empire had been built around the civilizing mission. If British colonialism's superficial, and deceptive, nature had been exposed in Kenya, what possible justification would be left for the anachronism of British colonial rule in a post–World War II world community? If the truth about Kenya were to become known, British colonial rule would be comparable to that of the Germans, the French, and even King Leopold of Belgium.

Hindsight about high politics is easier than analyzing popular opinion. The real dilemma, some fifty years later, is comprehending why the British public was so silent on the issue of colonial atrocities during Mau Mau. By virtue of the debates in the Houses of Commons and Lords, and the popular press, Mau Mau and the colonial atrocities it inspired were very much a part of British public discourse. In fact, press coverage reached a vast readership, which included not just the white-collar middle and upper classes but the lower-middle and working classes as well, thanks in large part to the British tabloids. Both the *Daily Mirror*, which routinely backed the Labour Party, and the Conservative-leaning *Daily Mail* found much to report in Kenya, filling their pages with lurid atrocities and breaking scandals. For all their sensationalism, however, these tabloids also brought hard news about Britain's empire, news like Castle's tour of Kenya, to its combined daily readership of some 15 million people. Then there were the *Observer*, the *Times*, the *Daily Worker*, the *Manchester Guardian*, the *New Statesman and Nation*, and the *Daily Telegraph*, as well as pamphlets from missionaries and extra-Parliamentary interest groups, which each covered the outbreak of Mau Mau, the reported savagery of the oath takers, and atrocities by the British colonial forces. It was the press that helped to turn *Mau Mau* into a British household word, and indeed into a term that continues to have common currency. In fact, not since the phrase "the Black Hole of Calcutta" became part of everyday British discourse over a century earlier had empire entered popular language and culture with so much impact.[114]

The stereotype of Mau Mau helps us understand British silence. From the moment Britons first heard of Mau Mau's beginnings, the movement and its name became synonymous with the worst kind of savage terror.[115] Except for the *Daily Worker*, every newspaper in Britain, and around the world for that matter, gave its readers lurid accounts of Mau Mau bestiality, accounts that ranged from the relatively straightforward to the utterly sensational.[116] Before the *New Statesman and Nation* began criticizing the colonial government and demanding independent inquiries into the camps and villages, it labeled the Mau Mau oath as "nasty mumbo-jumbo" and declared that "people are being murdered in their beds and children hacked to pieces [by Mau Mau]."[117] So too did the *Manchester Guardian* condemn the "filthy poison of Mau Mau" and its "barbarous" oath, while supporting the settlers and the understandable panic that gripped their community.[118] Even Fenner Brockway was quoted in the liberal paper, describing Mau Mau as "an ugly and brutal form of extreme nationalism. It is based on frustration. Frustration brings bitterness and bitterness brings viciousness."[119] If such accounts of Mau Mau terror were coming from papers representing the views of the left, the same publications that would soon rip into British colonial excesses, it is not difficult to imagine what was being printed in the conservative newspapers, particularly tabloids like the *Daily Mail*. Grisly photographs of alleged oathing ceremonies and murderous Mau Mau activities were splashed alongside headlines decrying the movement's "terrorism" and bloody cannibalistic rituals. The coverage had a patina of the occult, a kind of incomprehensible African black magic that had preyed in the recesses of racist minds for years. Everyone's worst black African nightmare had become a reality.

To the British public, it seemed that civilization itself was at stake in Kenya. The British government and the press had the nation convinced that Mau Mau was slaughtering Europeans in vast numbers, and that its terror was undermining any sense of law and order in the colony. Also, the African loyalists, the representation of British colonial success, needed British protection and understanding. "How can we treat these people who have thrown in their lot with us and with the future of Kenya," Lennox-Boyd publicly reasoned, "in precisely the same legalistic manner as we are obliged to treat those who are convinced Mau Mau?"[120] With the perception that countless settlers and British supporters were dying at the hands of the bloodthirsty Mau Mau, with the very roots of civilization threatened by unspeakable terror, it becomes easier to contextualize the lack of public support for the mounting allegations of cruelty and human rights violations against the colonial government.

The British public was misled. Government rhetoric had British citizens believing that their boys in Kenya were fighting a war for human progress and against godless savages bent on destroying Christian values. It might have been a little bloody at times, but, so went the rationale, think about all of the hearts and minds the benevolent colonial officials were saving. There was Lennox-Boyd, standing in the well of the House of Commons, declaring that no independent inquiry was needed, that the offenses were one-offs, and that British crimes were not really crimes anyway. Lending an air of credibility to this version of events was the public ambivalence of Archbishop Beecher, as well as the local missionaries, all of whom, regardless of any personal allegiances, were much more interested in the prospect of re-deeming lost Mau Mau souls than they were in ameliorating the brutal conditions under which their future converts were living.

Nevertheless, the evidence kept coming in, and still nothing was done. The British became distracted by other pressing issues, most especially postwar reconstruction. Rationing continued until 1953, and economic re-covery was slow. There was also great sympathy for "our boys" overseas, many of whom had won enormous respect for their gallantry in Korea. Many of the Labour MPs' allegations must be considered in the context of the Cold War. Although Mau Mau was not a communist movement, the fact that the conservative press often labeled Castle, Brockway, and other members of the Labour Party as socialists lent a suspiciously Red air to the crisis in Kenya.

In the post–World War II era few Britons were interested in human rights abuses occurring in the empire. The knowledge of brutalities in Kenya simply did not have much of an impact on the daily concerns of the average British citizen. For Labour Party activists the violence, murders, and detention without trial in Kenya were important; indeed, for many Labour leaders the issues were moral ones that went to the heart of their party's values. But their belief ran against the popular understanding of empire, particularly in Africa, where in the 1950s any discussions of race and social development still inspired nineteenth-century reactions. People were much less inclined to care about colonial atrocities when African lives were at stake, and particularly when those lives had been corrupted by the Mau Mau oath. Thus it is easier to understand why the leaders of the Labour Party, men like Hugh Gaitskell and Harold Wilson, were never front and center in the campaign against the Conservative government's actions in Kenya. Instead, the Labour MPs leading the charge, with the ex-ception of Aneurin Bevan, were relative lightweights. For her part, Castle would not be at the forefront of Labour politics until 1964, when Harold Wilson appointed her to his cabinet as minister of overseas development. Until then, she was never in a position to strike any political bargains in the government; nor was she taken seriously by her fellow Labour MPs, who viewed her causes as self-promotional. In the end, despite shared Labour outrage, no one in the leadership of the party really wanted to rock the boat over Mau Mau, particularly in view of the widespread public apathy about Kenyan affairs.[121]

This silence around Mau Mau in the mid-1950s would send a dangerous signal to the British colonial government. Because of the public's failure to act, Lennox-Boyd, Baring, and others assumed an endorsement of their policies and a belief in their justifications for harshly suppressing Mau

Mau. Emboldened by the public's apathy, they analyzed the situation in early 1957 and decided to break the remaining detainees in the Pipeline once and for all by using the most extreme form of officially sanctioned violence ever seen in colonial Kenya. This new assault would be called, ironically, Operation Progress.

· CHAPTER TEN ·

DETENTION EXPOSED

Hola Exile Camp

*There was no other way [than to use force]. The men were obdurate and very
dangerous. . . . You had to knock the evil out of a person.*
— JOHN COWAN, *senior prisons officer in charge of Mwea camps*

*Emergency powers, mass detention, violence unleashed and suppressed were not good
arguments for political evolution, nor indeed the outward sign of good stewardship.*
— TERENCE GAVAGHAN, *district officer in charge of rehabilitation, Mwea camps*[1]

STAGGERING TO HIS FEET WITH BLOOD OOZING FROM HIS NOSE AND
mouth, Nderi Kagombe saw a double image of Isaiah Mwai Mathenge
standing over him, his club ready to strike another blow. In front of Nderi
lay the heavy metal bucket that he had been carrying on his head for
nearly the entire morning. Much of the sand, urine, and feces mixture was
still inside; some was caked on Nderi's face. Exhaustion and a final blow
to his nose had sent him tumbling to the ground, headfirst into the splat-
tering excrement. "Mathenge was shouting at me to get up," Nderi later

remembered, "but I couldn't. I was on my knees, but everything was moving and I couldn't see Mathenge properly because my vision had been affected from carrying the bucket for so long and for being beaten with the clubs."[2]

After the warm-up of "bucket fatigue," as camp authorities called it, Nderi was kicked along toward one of the cement-blocked screening rooms that were scattered throughout the five detention camps that made up Mwea. There he saw two men strung up by their ankles, hanging from the rafters. They were naked and dripping wet from the cold water that was being poured over their bodies. The man hanging nearest the door had blood and puss running from his nose, his face swollen and distorted. "The white man in charge was yelling at him," Nderi later recalled. "He was shouting to confess, but there was no way this man could have spoken even if he had wanted to. To see the torture like this . . . I had become so used to it during my time in the Pipeline, but Mwea was different. They never stopped. It was day and night until we gave in. Those people running Mwea were like animals. Either you confessed, or you died."[3]

But Nderi was a survivor. It had been nearly three years since he had been sanitized, numbered, and subjected to the tortures of Wagithundia in Manyani's Compound 6. In the interim he had been shackled, loaded onto a railcar and then into a ship's cargo for transfer to the hard-core camp on Mageta Island. There his home was Compound 2—located on a high ridge above the water—where he was among the "blackest of the filthy pigs," as one of the camp officials, nicknamed Gosma, called them.[4] Gosma was a British officer as notorious as Manyani's Mapiga or Mackinnon Road's Kenda Kenda, beating detainees mercilessly and meting out special treatment to those who refused to work. Whips, rubber hoses, truncheons, and sticks were all used, as were more inventive forms of torture. The swamp surrounding Mageta filled the island with mosquitoes. "A few times I saw the white man in charge order the *askaris* to take the sap from a certain leaf and rub it all over a detainee who had been shackled to a post," recalled another former detainee from the Lake Victoria island. "Within no time the man would be covered with these mosquitoes, and it was such a terrible scene. If you saw these people afterwards, you would never have recognized them; their bodies had been devoured."[5] In Nderi's case the camp commandant "used to order two *askaris* to pin us down on our backs, facing the sun, and we were not allowed to even blink let alone shade our eyes."[6] This would go on for several hours, though Nderi and others recalled how they could not control themselves; they had to close their eyes from time to time even if it meant a beating.

In return for his uncooperative behavior Nderi was sent to the dry heat and dust of Lodwar, not far from where Kenyatta and the other so-called masterminds were imprisoned. There Leslie Whitehouse, a British officer, was in charge, and the torture he handed out "convinced me to go and work," Nderi remembered. "It didn't mean I confessed," he went on. "Many of us had agreed that working didn't mean we were giving in." For over a year Nderi labored building the local hospital, where, as the cement was drying on the floor inside, he took a stick and scratched in the words *Icua Hospital* (Hell Hospital) because, he said, "it was so unbearably hot there." Taxi Lewis made frequent visits to the camp, and on one occasion not long after arriving he ordered the detainees to go to the dry riverbed to dig for water. "When we refused because we were not prisoners," Nderi recalled, "we were beaten thoroughly after the white man named Lewis, who was then the commissioner of prisons, ordered that we be beaten for refusing to work. The *askaris* were let into our compounds and beat us indiscriminately with their batons. A lot of detainees were seriously injured after that."[7]

Nderi and several others were loaded into lorries for their journey to the Mwea camps. Bouncing along the unpaved roads, the detainees, many of whom had broken limbs and open wounds, were enveloped in choking dust for nearly two days before they reached Embu District. "We could see hundreds of detainees bent over the rice fields," Nderi said. "The guards were all around just beating anyone who paused or stood up from their work. We had heard this was a very bad place, but I don't think even we knew how bad it would be. It was the place where I was worn down." When Nderi and the others were hustled off the lorries, dozens of armed guards as well as white officers were waiting for them. They were told to take off their clothes. They refused. They were told again, and again they refused. "The next thing we knew they set on us," Nderi told me. "Several of them would just start beating us, and when some of us screamed they shoved dirt in our months. They beat one man, who was very injured already, unconscious. They ripped off my clothes and shaved off all of my hair. Then they put a uniform on me and then pushed me into one of the cages. That was my reception into Mwea. I was in Hell."[8]

Violence and torture had for years dominated life in Kenya's camps. A pornography of terror, including public brutality, rape, and starvation, swept through the villages as well, and thousands died there. Yet Nderi, a man who lived through seven of the worst camps in the Pipeline, described Mwea as the nadir. Other survivors have similar memories. "It was Hell on Earth," one man from Kiambu recalled. "It was where men were being killed," another man from Nyeri went on. "It was where they finally broke us, where Satan defeated our God."[9] All of these men arrived in the Mwea camps in the late 1950s and recall receptions similar to Nderi's, relentless torture and work, and deaths. Little did they know either at the time or even today that the colonial government had singled them out. The governor and the colonial secretary decided in early 1957 that they had to break the remaining thirty thousand or so hard-core Mau Mau, and to do it they had to reverse their policy on permanent exile or drastically modify it. This was a radical step, and to understand it, and its ferocity, we need to look closely at decisions being made at the highest levels of British colonial governance.

At issue was the European Convention on Human Rights. For nearly five years the British had disregarded this treaty, believing that it did not apply to their African subjects in the empire, people whose level of social, cultural, and economic development left them decades if not generations away from the rights of international citizenship. But, as we have seen, rather than articulate these racist ideas publicly, the colonial government decided early on to derogate the Convention's article prohibiting detention without trial by arguing that an Emergency was in place. This activated a loophole in the European Convention that permitted such human rights violations during periods of national emergency. The language of its Article 15 is startling, given that the accord was drawn up only shortly after the gross human rights violations of the Second World War. "In time of war or other public emergency threatening the life of the nation," the article states, "any High Contracting Party may take measures derogating from its obligations under this Convention."[10] Nations could detain without trial during wartime or in defense of national security. In Kenya's case, were Baring to have lifted the Emergency, such a derogation would no longer have been possible, and the colonial government would have had no legal justification for indefinitely detaining the so-called hard core.[11]

"How long can we hope to keep 12,000 people locked up?" Will Mathieson at the Colonial Office's East Africa Department wrote in the summer of 1955. Further assessing the situation, he went on, "If we are not to be driven step by step to revocation of our statement that they will never return we must reconcile the bulk of them very quickly."[12] His colleague Gorell Barnes concurred: "My own feeling is that, after a great deal of further effort and correspondence, we might be able to agree on provisions which it might be possible to keep in force for a very long time, provided that the number of 'exiles' were very much fewer than at present contemplated."[13] Clearly, the question dogging the Colonial Office was not the basic human rights of those men and women still in detention. Lennox-Boyd and his men had already decided to violate the European Convention after the Emergency ended. At issue was to what degree the international treaty could be violated without resulting in a censure.

Baring was no less involved in the collusion going on behind the scene. He and the other colonial policy makers viewed the European Convention as an irritant, something that was not immutable, but rather open to political negotiation. Apparently, this sentiment was shared by other signatories as well. Baring said as much when he wrote, "Her Majesty's Government could only in the first instance be expected to justify a breach of the Convention to the other signatories if the numbers concerned were not too large."[14] Both he and Lennox-Boyd were keenly aware that Britain's future rule over Kenya turned on keeping the political detainees in exile. The grand design for breaking Mau Mau, forcing its supporters to cooperate and submit to British colonial authority, and installing the loyalists as the Kikuyu leaders of the future would surely come undone were the politicals to be released. By early 1957 the Colonial Office decided to throw its support behind the permanent banishment of the most politically threatening hard core, a few thousand in all, provided the rest of the detainees were let go. The agenda was clear: empty the Pipeline of most of the hard core, and new legislation authorizing permanent exile would take care of the rest.[15]

This mandate was no small challenge to the colonial government's men on the spot. For over two years Baring and Lennox-Boyd had anxiously labored under pressure to get the remaining tens of thousands of detainees out of the Pipeline. They had to contend with the steadily mounting criticism in Britain from the left as well as the allegations of brutality and murder, not to mention the staggering costs of the war. There was every reason to accelerate the rate of release, and Monkey Johnston was the point man overseeing this vexing challenge. His primary job as special commissioner was to get the detainees out of the Pipeline, and from the start he approached this task with a calculated bureaucratic ruthlessness. As noted earlier, first he adjusted downward the standard-of-living estimates for the entire Kikuyu population, thereby creating space in the reserves for the future release of tens of thousands of detainees. This was accomplished with the stroke of a pen. The problem of forcing confessions from the remaining group of Mau Mau adherents in the Pipeline, which remained their only ticket out, was another matter.[16]

When Johnston took up his post in late 1955, thousands of detainees like Nderi Kagombe were still refusing to confess. Some would eventually be worn down by the sheer cumulative effects of labor and torture; others would submit after falling prey to informants and surrenders. A year later, there remained over thirty thousand men and women who would still not give in. To make matters worse, they began to resist collectively. Several months after Nderi left Mageta Island the men in Compound 2 decided to fight back. In one former detainee's words, "We rioted to show the commandant that we would not die like cowards, even if some of us had had our manhood taken."[17] The mayhem began when the *askaris* attempted to haul off several men accused of causing trouble. Under newly revised Emergency Regulations, even the most minor of infractions were deemed "major offences."[18] Camp authorities could legally put a detainee in solitary confinement for two weeks with little or no food. "There was no way we were going to let them take our brothers," Wilson Ndirangu later recalled. "We attacked the guards, and then all hell broke loose."[19] For four days the detainees and the guards, reinforced by the General Service Unit and the Kenya Police Reserve, fought for control of the compound. Then, as Wilson later related, Major Mwangi—one of the prison officers in charge—organized a final crackdown. "We could see from our compounds that the whole camp was surrounded by the GSU, the regular police, and the KPR," Wilson said. He then went on to describe what happened next.

> We knew that we were to prepare for battle. . . . Those in the kitchen split as many firewood planks as they could. Then, Major Mwangi climbed onto the guard's tower, ready to give orders to his troops. He gave an order, and all the white officers came. We were ordered out of our cage and told to squat outside. We obeyed. They came and surrounded us, surveying us. The officer on the tower, Major Mwangi, raised a red flag, meaning that we should be beaten, and if anyone got killed there would be no case, because we had disobeyed. He gave the order, and the white officers and their *askaris* started beating us. . . . As per our plan, I stood up and started screaming. I screamed three times, and that was meant to alert the other cages in the compound. By the end of my three screams, none of the cages had any doors because the detainees had ripped them off. Other detainees started distributing the pieces of firewood to the others. The *askaris* had shields, clubs, and metal helmets on their heads. Major Mwangi put up the white flag to signal a stop of the beating, but the battle went on that way for many days, until they began to starve us.[20]

It was the food denial that finally ended the standoff. Government reports suggest that the detainees engaged in a hunger strike voluntarily, but those who were there in the camp, men like Muraya Mutahi, remember otherwise. "[We] were denied food for about six or seven days. By the end of six days the room in which we slept—because we could not summon enough strength to go outside—was stinking so badly. . . . We did not stay much longer at Mageta because we fought with the *askaris* there and refused to work. After we recovered from the imposed starvation we were split into two groups. One was taken to Hola, and the other was Lodwar. I was taken to Lodwar."[21] In some ways Muraya was lucky. Camp authorities singled out nearly nine hundred of the rioters at random, tried them in a makeshift court, and sent them on to Embakasi Prison—or "Satan's Paradise," as some former Mau Mau adherents call it.

Riots were now also breaking out in other Pipeline camps, at the same time that Johnston and his colleagues were trying to accelerate the rate of release. The camps had succeeded in further embittering many of the detainees, numbers of whom had become hard core only because of their treatment in the Pipeline. Feeding the detainees' anger was the perennial issue of land. Numerous camp officials commented on this, including one of Askwith's men in the Rift Valley, who wrote:

> The principle underlying idea of all detainees is still that their fathers' land was stolen by "Government" and that no compensation has ever been paid. This doctrine is so prevalent that I suggest it would be worth while for a booklet in the vernacular to be produced giving the true history of the Carter Commission and its awards. I have been unable to borrow a copy of the Report for use but something of this sort is much needed.[22]

But many detainees had already been bombarded with government propaganda declaring the fairness of colonial land policies and the illegitimacy of Mau Mau's battle cry for "a return of stolen land." The absurdity of attempts to convince the Kikuyu of the impartiality and equitability of land expropriation was not lost on Askwith. At the time he wrote, "Whatever you say the Kikuyu will not be satisfied that they have been treated justly."[23] Later, when reflecting on this issue at the heart of Mau Mau, Askwith said, "If you wanted to solve the bigger problem, you had to give these people land, you had to accord them a degree of humanity, which meant you had to understand their grievances. You had to understand that you weren't going to win this thing by putting them all back in the reserves, where there was no way they could live with the amount of land that they had."[24]

But forcing the Kikuyu to cooperate and sending them back to the overcrowded, famine-stricken reserves was exactly what Johnston and the governor planned. First, the special commissioner attempted to increase the rate of release by fine-tuning the established colonial policy of divide and rule. He decided to introduce a new classification system, one that replaced the color system of "black," "grey," and "white" with a much more complex letter-based system. "Blacks" were separated into "Z1s" and "Z2s," "greys" into "Ys," and "whites" became either "Xs" or "Cs."[25] By separating the most recalcitrant "blacks" from those who were at least agreeing to work, Johnston thought he would have better luck at breaking the hard core. The maneuver was an administrative nightmare and scarcely complied with the governor's new quotas; he was now demanding, in the spring of 1956, a doubling in the rate of release, from one thousand per month to two thousand.[26] A few months later, Johnston learned that the twelve thousand spots for permanent exile had been reduced to a few thousand, leaving him with the responsibility for breaking an additional eight or nine thousand detainees who were considered to be among the most truculent in the Pipeline, but for whom exile could no longer be justified. Johnston again tried to refine the classification system with the idea that more discrete categories would separate the waverers from the true hard core, theoretically freeing them from contact with the worst Mau Mau dogma and thus removing any hesitation they might have had in confessing the oath. There were now "Zs" and "Y1s," "YYs" and "XRs." The whole exercise seemed like a parody of bureaucratic procedure.[27] Johnston, hardly a fool, quickly realized the futility of his changes. Throwing away his pen, he looked instead for someone with a heavy hand to do his dirty work.

In early 1957 Monkey Johnston sat in the tranquillity of the Cottage Hospital in the foothills of Mount Kenya. He came with a gift in hand, a copy of Philip Mason's *The Men Who Ruled India*, for the man lying in the bed next to him. The patient was in a cast that extended from his foot to his thigh—a victim of an unfortunate squash accident on the court at the nearby European-only Outspan Hotel. He was one of the British colonial government's young district officers serving in Kenya, and his name was Terence Gavaghan.

Gavaghan was by all accounts, particularly his own, a formidable human being. When not nursing a torn Achilles tendon, he was an imposing figure. His height—well over six feet—his short cropped hair, solid physique, piercing blue eyes, and bent nose all gave him an air of masculine toughness. Prior to Monkey Johnston's unannounced bedside visit, Gavaghan had served the Crown for nearly thirteen years, most recently in the camps and villages of Nyeri District. But the thirty-four-year-old was by no means a prototypical British colonial officer. Instead, as Gavaghan recounts in his first autobiography, *Corridors of Wire*, he was "a loner and a maverick." He also elaborates on his own outsider status and alludes to the purpose of Johnston's hospital visit, writing under the pseudonym Corrigan:

Corrigan [Gavaghan] is, by background and self-esteem, in the service but not of it and he knows it. It riles him, so he takes a perverse pride in being different. . . . [He] himself was not one of "us" although no one quite knew why. There was always surrounding him a sense of instinctive restiveness as at the presence of a different species of animal at the waterhole. Here he saw an advantage. Colville [Johnston] had said that the detention camps were a "no-go" area for the others so he would be effectively among them but not of them. No one was going to envy him the task itself. They needed its success, but did not want the responsibility for its performance. . . . Corrigan [Gavaghan] was no paragon of gentleness. He knew his temper and the usually suppressed urge to violence when thwarted. It overtook him more strongly when he lacked for sex too long.[28]

It was only Gavaghan who did not know why he was "not one of 'us.' " Other British colonial officers were irritated by his renegade mentality and insatiable sexual appetite. There was also the matter of Gavaghan's ethnic background. He was of Irish descent, something that was hardly unimportant to the public-school and Oxbridge crowd around him. Gavaghan did not enjoy the ruling-class pedigree shared by his peers. He was indeed an outsider and therefore someone who, in an embarrassing situation, could be sacrificed, making him the perfect person to spearhead a new campaign in the Pipeline. Johnston had secured his heavy hand.

There remained at least thirty thousand detainees who required breaking, and Johnston was prepared to give Gavaghan free license to do whatever was necessary to force them to confess. Gavaghan was appointed to the newly created position of district officer in charge of rehabilitation and was answerable only to Johnston and the governor. When later reflecting on this new position, Gavaghan emphasized, "There was no way in which I could assess the magnitude and nature of what was being asked of me since there was no precedent for it and no guide book to the way out of the impasse. . . . I had only that most dangerous thing, an irrational and unjustified belief in my ability to face the challenge of the impossible."[29] Johnston did point Gavaghan in the direction of a solution. At Gathigiriri Camp, which was one of the five camps on the Mwea plain, a prisons staff officer by the name of John Cowan was working on a new method for breaking the hard core. It was something called the *dilution technique,* and its impact in the camps would be unparalleled.

The dilution technique was straightforward. Under Cowan's direction, camp officials would take fifty detainees in leg irons from one of the other four Mwea camps and send them to Gathigiriri. According to Cowan's carefully worded recollection, once the lorryload arrived, [the European officers] isolated a small number of uncooperative detainees who were surrounded by prison staff. [The detainees] were ordered, and refused, to carry out some simple task, and were then forced physically to comply by the preponderance of warders, thus submitting, however symbolically, to hitherto resisted discipline. They were then harangued without respite, by rehabilitation staff and selected detainees working together, until finally they confessed their oaths.[30]

Two related strategies upheld Cowan's dilution technique. First, camp officials had to separate detainees from the other hard core and arrange them into small, manageable groups. Then they had to use unbridled brute force to overpower the Mau Mau adherents, using fists, clubs, truncheons, whips, and any other weapons at their disposal. This brutality would continue until the detainees cooperated by listening to orders, working, and ultimately confessing.

In the dilution technique colonial officials believed they had discovered the beginnings of a systematic approach to brutalizing detainees and forcing them to confess. Countless other forms of torture were employed in the Pipeline, but they were disorganized and inefficient in comparison, and none held the promise of dilution, a quick and complete repudiation of Mau Mau. Reports were sent to Nairobi detailing the technique's success in breaking the hard core. New batches were being dispatched regularly to Gathigiriri, where each detainee was individually overpowered by Cowan, other officers, African warders, and former Mau Mau adherents, or the surrenders. It was clear that the majority of the detainees, most of whom had been uncooperative for years, were finally cooperating and even confessing. The minister for defense, Jake Cusack, went to witness dilution personally and was so impressed by the results that he immediately recommended the tactic be exported to other camps. At a moment when everyone in the government was under enormous pressure to empty the Pipeline, Cowan offered a tangible and proven solution to the release dilemma.[31]

But there was one small problem. Detainees were dying, something Johnston knew well when he paid Gavaghan his bedside visit. In one case Baring sent a secret telegraph to the colonial secretary in early 1957, reporting that a Gathigiriri detainee undergoing dilution, one Muchiri Githuma, was "severely beaten and died as a result."[32] The governor planned to blame the murder on the African rehabilitation assistant and the surrenders working with him, noting that "no Europeans were involved."[33] Meanwhile Baring put a temporary stop to the dilution technique, although neither he nor Lennox-Boyd had any intention of abandoning it altogether. An internal visiting committee was sent out to tour the Mwea camps and later reported, "It soon became apparent to us that there has been a marked deterioration in the advance of rehabilitation in the Camp, which we were told was attributed to the strict withdrawal of any form of 'physical persuasion.' "[34] By now there was no doubt that to break the hard core there had to be systematic and relentless brute force. "If we abandon the 'dilution' method," the governor wrote, "a severe check would be given to a process which is not only working well now but also offers hope of bringing down a 'pipeline' towards release many Mau Mau detainees who a few months ago we all considered would remain irreconcilable for years."[35] Baring, Lennox-Boyd, and Johnston all knew that the dilution technique had to be reintroduced, but this time they needed someone on the ground who could oversee the operation, someone who could do what needed to be done.

It was at this juncture that a now healed Gavaghan stepped in, proclaiming his new mission Operation Progress. He would resurrect the dilution technique into a systematized and well-executed program of brutality. To do this, he enlisted the help of the prisons and rehabilitation officers posted at the Mwea camps. Without question, Gavaghan's right-hand man was Cowan, and they proved a study in contrasts: Gavaghan, the physically imposing and emotionally passionate man, juxtaposed with the diminutive Cowan, whose coldhearted detachment from his work was stunning, given the level of brutality he was overseeing. Among those working alongside them were Ivan Hook, Emile Hawley, and David Blair, all still technically under Askwith's authority, and the most notorious African rehabilitation assistants at Mwea, Isaiah Mwai Mathenge and Jeremiah Kiereini.

Under Gavaghan's command, these British officers and their African assistants began preparing a force of African warders capable of launching Operation Progress. The first step was to break the detainees already being held in Mwea, which meant an all-out blitz inside the compounds. Gavaghan's own description of this initial "show of force," as he later called it, gives some sense of the atmosphere he was creating.

We . . . decided to apply the first control operation to the subdivision of the Thiba camp compound containing 1,000 men into four of 250, leaving a fenced cruciform access corridor between. This required advance preparation of tall posts, deep holes and rolls of barbed wire, with implements. We also recruited from eager volunteers a "Praetorian Guard" of over 100 educated young Kikuyu of good physique and address. They were quickly drilled in simple unarmed combat and equipped with short wooden truncheons slung from leather belts binding judo style heavy cotton tunics over

calf length trousers. Their heads were shaven for effect as well as protection. . . . Outnumbered by five to one, we had prepared against resistance
of some kind, but did not expect any concerted attack. The options open to
either side were limited by space and weapons to hand, if not by hours of
daylight. The front lines and outer fringes did not so much crumble as con-
certina, scrambling awkwardly into each other until no inch was left. We
could not have imagined the hysterical crescendo of a convulsion which
imploded within their ranks. Limb intertwined with limb in a tangle of
bodies, squirming upwards into a living mound. . . . Fists, nails, feet and
teeth were engaged. Truncheons were not drawn except in defence. How
long it lasted I could not tell, but in about two hours, singly or in clusters,
frog-marched or stumbling loose, the whole thousand sat and slumped on
the grass outside in several large rings.[36]

The new intake procedure came next, something Gavaghan later described as "a kind of rape."[37] Small batches of detainees from Manyani,
home to some twenty thousand hard-core detainees, were shackled and
transferred to Mwea by rail. Upon arrival, they were faced by a mob of European officers, African assistants, *askaris,* and surrenders. During the intake, Gavaghan's men used raw physical power to force the detainees to
change from their Manyani clothes into a new camp uniform and submit
to a shaving. The whole operation, or the "rape," hinged on the use of brutality, something Gavaghan recounts in his second memoir.

At first it seemed that . . . persuasive voices and the familiar faces through
the wire had taken effect and the shaving of heads began without fuss or resistance. Suddenly a remembered howl sounded from the rear and a man
was thrown to the ground thrashing about wildly, followed instantly by
several more, and a general melee took place. The warders had been trained
for just such an outbreak. One took their man in an armlock, tripped and
forced him to the ground, head pressed sideways against the angle of the
body, astride which the other sat while the barber did his work.[38]

Other compounds holding already cooperative detainees awaited them.
The new intakes were under strict orders: follow all commands, labor on
the irrigation scheme, attend the propaganda lectures, and confess. But
many detainees, like Nderi, would refuse to submit and so would quickly
learn why Mwea was called "Hell on Earth."

At the same time that Lennox-Boyd was publicly discrediting Fletcher and
Meldon as his way of denying allegations of brutality in Kenya's camps and

of refusing any independent investigation, he was poised to endorse Gavaghan's Operation Progress. Just as he had received plenty of information about the true conditions in the Pipeline, so too had Lennox-Boyd been fully briefed on the dilution technique. Baring and his attorney general, Eric Griffith-Jones, sent numerous secret memoranda to the Colonial Office, outlining the plan for systematic use of brute force and asking for official approval from the colonial secretary. "Gavaghan has been perfectly open with us," the governor secretly wrote to Lennox-Boyd. "He has said that he can cope with a regular flow in of Manyani 'Zs' and turn them out later to the district camps. We believe that he will be able to go on doing this a very long way down the list of the worst detainees. But he can only do it if the hard cases are dealt with on their first arrival in a rough way . . . there must be with some a phase of violent shock."[39] In a separate memorandum sent to the colonial secretary, Griffith-Jones provided extensive details of Mwea, details that he and several other high-level colonial officials in Kenya witnessed firsthand when they went to observe Gavaghan's work. The attorney general, Jake Cusack, Thomas Askwith, Taxi Lewis, and others had seen detainees who refused to change their clothes "hit with fists and/or slapped with the open hand," according to Griffith-Jones. He went on to write that in some cases "defiance was more obstinate, and on the first indication of such obstinacy three or four of the European officers immediately converged on the man and 'rough-housed' him, stripping his clothes off him, hitting him, on occasion kicking him, and, if necessary, putting him on the ground. Blows struck were solid, hard ones, mostly with closed fists and about the head, stomach, sides and back."[40] Apparently, the colonial officials did not see some of the more brutal methods of persuasion, as the attorney general went on to suggest.

> Gavaghan explained, however, that there had, in past intakes, been more persistent resistors, who had had to be forcibly changed into the camp clothing; that some of them had started the "Mau Mau moan," a familiar cry which was promptly taken up by the rest of the camp, representing a concerted and symbolic defiance of the camp authorities; that in such cases it was essential to prevent the infection of this "moan" spreading through the camp, and that accordingly a resistor who started it was promptly put on the ground, a foot placed on his throat and mud stuffed in his mouth; and that a man whose resistance could not be broken down was in the last resort knocked unconscious.[41]

At first Lennox-Boyd balked when he learned of Gavaghan's methods. It was one thing to endorse unofficially the violence and torture that was

ongoing in the camps and villages; it was another to make it officially sanctioned policy. The colonial secretary was clearly on the verge of adopting
systematized brutality as a way of breaking down the tens of thousands of
detainees who remained in the Pipeline, and his rationalization was the
protection of the British colony. Sensing the questionable logic of this
proposition, Griffith-Jones took charge, drafting a series of codes written
in legal doublespeak, differentiating between something he termed legal
compelling force from the otherwise illegal *punitive force. Compelling force*
could be used "when immediately necessary to restrain or overpower a re-
fractory detained person, or to compel compliance with a lawful order to
prevent disorder."[42] *Punitive force* was apparently used to describe any kind
of unlawful physical punishment. This rhetorical hairsplitting provided
some comfort to the colonial secretary, and he approved Regulation 17 of
the Emergency (Detained Persons) Regulations, which gave license to all of
his men on the spot to employ systematized violence in order to break
down remaining detainees.[43]

The colonial secretary understood what was going on in Kenya, and this
knowledge further inspired his efforts to protect his government with legal
mumbo jumbo. Nevertheless, he turned his head and hoped it would all
soon be over. Gavaghan certainly knew this, later writing, "The gap between the supreme policy makers with their grave political concerns, and
the actions of location functionaries in a small remote place was too wide
for mutual comprehension or proper control."[44] This was all too true in
late colonial Kenya, though certainly if Lennox-Boyd or the governor had
wanted to assert "proper control," they could have. Instead they vested men
like Gavaghan with carte blanche to extract confessions, by whatever
means necessary. "Punishment was being meted out which clearly skirted
the edges of the quasi-legal concept of 'compelling force,'" Gavaghan later
conceded, describing it in this way:

> A dozen or so men in their twenties and thirties were half running at the
> level bent-kneed gait of rickshaw pullers, following an elliptical path in a
> single file around the hump [in the grass]. They carried galvanized iron
> buckets filled with mud and stones on woven grass circlets placed on their
> shaven heads, gripped at the rim by each hand in turn, or by both if the
> bucket started to slip. Under the mud and sweat which streaked their faces,
> they were expressionless and made no attempt to cast down their buckets
> or run out of the ring in which they were enclosed. . . . This [was a] long
> practiced form of punishment, accurately known as "bucket fatigue." . . . It
> was visually "brutal and degrading," but was held to be both necessary and
> effective.[45]

It was not long before detainees at the Mwea camps, like others before them, began sneaking out letters of protest to British colonial officials, Labour MPs, and even the queen. But colonial officials in Nairobi and London did nothing. They instead forwarded the letters to Gavaghan, who had set up his own form of complaints department. First, he subjected several letter-writing detainees to what he called "a 'square bashing' exercise." That is, a kind of bucket fatigue, with some extra brutality added in. Then, in his words, "the same day [as a 'square bashing'], I brought a number of letters of complaint which had been returned through the Government to such varied addresses as 'Queen Elizabeth' or 'Lake Success' (United Nations). I read them aloud inside the full compound, explaining that they had been delivered, taken into account and sent back. I then tore them up publicly saying that, if they felt that they had scores to settle with me, I promised that after 'freedom' and Independence they would find my name board outside my house in Nairobi, which I would buy with my Kenya earnings."[46]

The detainees nicknamed Gavaghan Karuga Ndua, or the Big Troublemaker.[47] They feared him not just because of "his enormous body and eyes that would stare through you," as one man recalled, "but because of the terror he directed."[48] Samson Karanja was particularly well placed to observe the British officer, having served as his personal launderer. It was a job that Samson, in his own words, coveted as it "saved me from the brutal labor in the rice fields." Today he remembers washing and pressing Gavaghan's clothes and the "neat creases that the Big Troublemaker so liked." He then went on to say, "Gavaghan evoked in me the idea of a dog in someone's home. The way the owner of a house can order the dog to attack someone. That was the same way Gavaghan used to use the sergeants and corporals under his charge. He used to order them to beat the Mau Mau detainees, though he himself did not beat anyone. But it was according to his orders that detainees were beaten."[49]

Gavaghan seldom admitted to losing control but did on occasion come close. Detainees like Maingi Waweru, who had been captured in the forest by the pseudogangsters and was known by his alias, General Kamwamba, would "play dumb" in order to avoid the relentless physical and psychological pressure to confess. Kamwamba recalled the forced starvations at Mwea, the rancid meat, and the upside-down tortures when men would be beaten on the testicles with "special instruments." "I decided to play dumb," he said. "I even refused to walk, pretending I was lame, and the guards used to have to carry me everywhere. This worked for a time, but then they just started beating me more knowing that I was tricking them. They meted out their anger on me during the screening."[50] Detainees like

General Kamwamba brought out the worst in Gavaghan. The British officer described such men as "hypnotized," with one detainee in particular refusing to respond even after he was struck several times. It was at this point that Gavaghan could not help himself. He decided to have a go and, in his own words, "drove his open hand backwards across the slack mouth face in an overpowering urge to force entry into the locked mind and evoke some response—any response."[51] Still unresponsive, the "uninhabited husk" was then, according to Gavaghan, just left alone. Perhaps this case was an exception, because more often than not, according to former detainees who were under his authority, uncooperative behavior of any kind meant a trip to the screening cell or, worse, a ride behind the Land Rover. "There was this one detainee who kept stealing food even though he would be punished severely for it," recalled Charles Mwai. "Finally one of the white men in charge tied his foot with a rope, and then tied the other end to the Land Rover vehicle he was driving. Then he drove off, dragging the poor detainee along."[52]

Public torture was not unusual at Mwea. Sometimes after refusing to confess, "a detainee would have all his clothes removed," according to Wachira Murage. "Then [he] was taken to a field, where he would have a wet cloth sprinkled with salt placed on his wet and naked body, and then whipped. The whipping would tear off pieces of flesh after every stroke. Mwea was a terrible pace during [Gavaghan's] time. He and Mr. Isaiah Mathenge were very cruel to the detainees. They always walked together. . . . Mathenge was a very bad man, but his commandant was even worse, because he used to order everything that Mathenge was doing."[53] Many recall the rafter technique, hanging upside down until blood ran from their eyes, ears, noses, and mouths. "Mathenge would be standing there with the man we called the Big Troublemaker," recalled another man now living in Nairobi. "They would be yelling at us as we hung from our feet to confess, but I just couldn't. It seems impossible to understand now, I know, but I had been beaten for so long that I was steeled to anything. I preferred to die rather than give in, and eventually they got tired of me and sent me to Hola. But some men died from such ordeals, and there were several who committed suicide because they couldn't take the endless punishment but still didn't want to confess."[54]

The majority of hard-core detainees did confess in Mwea. For many the relentless assaults and tortures came after years of forced labor and brutality, and Mwea simply became their breaking point. Each detainee caught in Operation Progress had his own story of confession. For some it came during castration, for others when they were being whipped or hung upside down for hours. Still others broke during Mwea's version of rehabilitation.

"It was compulsory that every detainee had to go out and join in those activities," Nderi later recalled. "But since some of us had been so badly beaten that we could not sing or dance to the music, we would only sit and nod our heads to the music as one had to show that he was participating. If one failed to do that, he would be beaten again." It was not unusual, according to Nderi, for men to raise their hands for confession during the song and dance of rehabilitation. "I think it was because they had been so abused, and sitting there unable to sing and being beaten for it, they just couldn't take it anymore."[55]

One distinct voice of protest during this period was Thomas Askwith. Along with Griffith-Jones, Cusack, and others, he had gone to observe Gavaghan and his version of the dilution technique. Askwith witnessed the militialike operation and the beatings incredulously.[56] He saw Gavaghan's men, many of whom were technically part of his own department, beat detainees senseless with clubs and truncheons, shove mud into their mouths, and, to finish off the "kind of rape," strip them naked, shave them down, and throw them into the barbed-wire compounds.[57] This was directly witnessed by the man who had championed liberal reform, and who had been publicly promised by the governor that his hearts-and-minds campaign would be the centerpiece in redeeming Mau Mau adherents and brokering a future, peaceful Kenya. For years Askwith was blinded by his idealistic liberalism, but Mwea would shake him out of his naive stupor. He complained bitterly that Gavaghan's appointment as district officer in charge of rehabilitation, directly reporting to Johnston and thus circumventing the chain of command, "was not only invidious but irregular."[58] Askwith's own rehabilitation staff was removed from his direct control in Mwea and was now answerable only to Gavaghan. But Johnston was hardly sympathetic; bypassing Askwith was exactly what he wanted. By the end of 1957 Askwith had submitted several reports to Johnston and the chief secretary, Richard Turnbull, "the gist of which was [he] considered that the violent treatment to which the detainees were subjected to obtain their obedience and submission might well by misfortune lead to death or serious injury."[59]

For his troubles, Askwith was sacked in late December 1957. He appealed to the colonial secretary, who rejected his representations—"so I was dismissed from my [rehabilitation] post."[60] The governor then transferred all responsibility for the detainees and their so-called rehabilitation to Monkey Johnston, and through him to Gavaghan. It was the characteristically unreflective Cowan who later summed up events behind the shake-up: "Askwith left a disgruntled man—got no honor—most people of his rank get one—he was a nuisance at the end. The government had their hands full with the Emergency, and he went on with rehabilitation and the brutal methods at Mwea. Government was hard-pressed and didn't need pressure from within . . . though I admire him for sticking to his guns the way he did."[61]

After his dismissal, Askwith remained as the commissioner for community development, arguably one of the most impotent positions in the colony. Even today, Gavaghan revels in Askwith's sacking. In interviews and discussions over the years, Gavaghan rarely failed to express his "deep dislike of this pathetic man who needed some good sex and who had this ridiculous idea that you could solve the problem with land."[62] The animosity was mutual, though Askwith refrained from discussing Gavaghan's sex life. Just prior to his death Askwith recalled his "unending need to convince this man [Gavaghan] that what he was doing was wrong, that this ran against everything the British colonial service was built upon. You couldn't just beat people up and call it a success."[63]

But it was Askwith who was wrong about the character of British colonial rule in Kenya. Once he and his liberal conscience were out of the picture, the entire Pipeline was redesigned around Gavaghan's version of the dilution technique. Strictly from the standpoint of expediency, this made perfect sense. Systematized brutality had already been proven to do the trick, breaking down the hard core and making possible release figures of up to seventeen hundred detainees per month.[64] By the summer of 1957 Aguthi and Mweru camps in Nyeri District, Mariira Camp in Fort Hall, as well as Athi River Camp were all practicing dilution and had accordingly been renamed filter camps, the colonial government's code name for those places using officially sanctioned violence. Manyani continued to hold most of the hard core who were slated for dilution, and Gavaghan recommended that a softening-up policy be instituted there, prepping the detainees for what was to come. "It must be considered," he wrote at the time, "that the Officer in Charge [of Manyani] must have at his disposal until the end a trained and powerful force sufficient to ensure continuing obedience, that this force must have a high morale and be suited to local conditions, and that it must be followed up by sustained propaganda, supporting a policy laid down in writing that Manyani should be a 'conditioning' camp for movement [down] the Pipeline."[65]

Not all rehabilitation officers were willing to join Operation Progress. At Athi River, Askwith described how "the Minister [Johnston] had instructed [Breckenridge] personally to use a certain amount of violence to induce the detainees to confess to the screening teams."[66] Breckenridge had flatly refused, according to Askwith. Indeed, to have agreed with systematized brutality would have been out of character for Askwith's point man at Athi River. In interview after interview with detainees held at this camp, "Breckenridge's humanity" is mentioned time and again. He "was the one person in my five years in the Pipeline who tried to treat us like human beings, though he couldn't always stop the beatings," one former detainee insisted.[67] Johnston must have thought Breckenridge would come around, because he soon started sending scores of hard core from Mageta Island and Lodwar to Athi River. But without systematized force the detainees refused to cooperate. Instead, they launched a riot in August 1957.[68] The target of their anger was Robert Harrison, the camp commandant and assistant prisons superintendent, who as prisons officer in charge had the upper hand over Breckenridge, a senior rehabilitation officer. Apparently, Harrison and his prisons staff were known to have "severely beaten a number of detainees for refusing to work"; at least that is what is said in Colonial Office files. Nevertheless, neither Harrison nor any other officer at Athi River was ever convicted of abusing detainees. In contrast, the detainees at Athi River who attacked the camp commandant were executed, and their fellow rioters were sent to Embakasi prison.[69]

It was not long before Breckenridge was pushed aside. Johnston brought in Hugh Galton-Fenzi, who had worked with Gavaghan and the dilution technique in Nyeri District and therefore knew what had to be done. Like Gavaghan, he was given a new title, administrative district officer in charge of rehabilitation, and reported directly to Johnston. He too was given a free hand to use systematized violence to break the hard core. In practice, this translated into torture techniques similar to those being used in the other filter camps throughout the Pipeline.[70] Paul Mahehu, one of hundreds of detainees who had been transferred into Athi River from Mageta Island, recalled what happened after his initial intake.

The day after our arrival, some of us were sent for. We had all been mentioned by some people who had confessed. The intention was to take us to Compound No. 9, where detainees were subjected to the worst punishment to make them confess. There, detainees were hung by their feet, with their heads facing downwards. The rafters where detainees were hung were high, and one detainee would need about five people to lift him up there. Bad things would be done to the detainees. Some detainees would start bleeding from their noses and ears after a prolonged stay in that hanging position. It was during the cold month of July, and cold water would be poured on the hanging detainee to worsen the punishment. . . . When the *askaris* came to get us, we resisted, and the other detainees in the compound joined in to prevent the *askaris* from dragging us out, and that was when the *askaris* were sent to beat us. We fought back, and fortunately, despite having been in chains, no one was killed.[71]

In other cases detainees were not so fortunate. Munyinyi Githiriga was one of several former detainees who later described yet other instances of torture and death. "People were being beaten," he said. "I remember that three people in our group died from beatings at Athi River after we had come from Kisumu. Athi River is sometimes a very cold place. One of those who died had been badly beaten during screening and was later thrown into a cell full of water. He died from the cold. It was the screening team and rehabilitation officers [who were doing this]. . . . We knew other things like this were happening because we could hear the screaming [from the other cells], but we could do nothing about it." When asked if anything was done about these deaths, Munyinyi replied, "Nothing. That was nothing to the white officers."[72] He also recalled sending out letters, which he called "help cries." Today, a few of these remain in the British colonial files—letters like the one sent on August 7, 1957, which began, "We detainees from Mageta and Kisumu are harshly treated [at Athi River Camp]. From 9th July 1957 it was arranged a special compound whereby eight or seven detainees from other compound are sent to be tortured till he says he has taken the oath whether he has or not. Some detainees have made false statements as far as one detainee died there called Kariuki Murithi on 18th July 1957 the very day another detainee was sent to hospital unable to speak, he died later."[73]

Internal visiting committees did come to observe, though often they wrote glowing reports about the successful run-down rates, mentioning little about the tactics used to achieve them. After one visit to Athi River, for instance, the committee recorded: "Mr. Galton Fenzi described the present methods briefly as 'hustle generally, demonstrate strength and immediate and strict discipline on first arrival of new batches . . . ' To sum up, we were considerably impressed by the astonishing improvement in every respect in this camp which appears to coincide with the take-over of Rehabilitation by 'African Affairs.' "[74] Exactly how much these committees actually saw is unclear. It is unlikely that they would have been taken into screening huts or through detainees' compounds. There were other reports of filter camps, in one case Thiba, where members of the visiting committees expressed their approval of the intake procedure but concern over its potential consequences. "I witnessed all the trouble which . . . [District Officer Gavaghan] undertook to persuade these people to enter the camp," wrote David Wanguhu, "but to no avail." The visiting observer then went on to say:

However, persuasion having failed, there was no alternative but to resort to force, and this was exactly what was done. When an attempt was made to have them wear the camp's uniform, they resisted it, and they eventually had to change into the uniform by force. I happened to know a few of these people, and I succeeded in persuading some to take the uniform but still a number of them refused completely. I believe that those concerned were quite justified to employ force. However, I think if this has to continue as being the only way of dealing with such people, it appears as if eventually some incidents will end tragically.[75]

There were also the observations of Henri Junod, an old friend of Baring's from his South Africa days, and a delegate to the International Committee for the Red Cross. In February 1957 Junod came to Kenya for an official, two-month tour of the detention camps and Emergency villages. The governor apparently sought counsel from the delegate on the issue of dilution, writing to the colonial secretary, "I privately discussed this question [a phase of violent shock] with Dr. Junod of the International Red Cross, who I knew well in South Africa and who has spent his whole life working with Africans and most of it with African prisoners. He has no doubt in his own mind that if the violent shock was the price to be paid for pushing detainees out . . . we should pay it."[76] After touring the Mwea camps and witnessing dilution firsthand, Junod turned to Gavaghan and said, "Ne vous inquietez pas [Do not distress yourself]. Compared to the French in Algeria, you are angels of mercy."[77] Interestingly, in Junod's final report for the International Committee for the Red Cross dilution is nowhere to be found, despite the fact that he obviously witnessed the technique in practice and counseled the governor on its merits.[78]

Dilution was also brought to the Mau Mau prisons, starting with Embakasi. For years, the prison held thousands of men tried and convicted of Mau Mau offenses in one of the many kangaroo courts set up under Emergency Regulations. On the backs of the convicts the Embakasi airport had been built, and it was not until the project was nearly completed in the summer of 1958 that the Public Works Department was prepared to send them to the Pipeline for eventual release.[79] Those who were cooperative were Form C'ed and issued Delegated Detention Orders, or DDOs, and sent on to South Yatta Camp and eventually to a works camp in their districts. As for the hard core, they were first sent to Mara River and Ngulot camps before being forwarded to Gavaghan at Mwea.[80] Then, in order to step up the rate of release from prisons like Embakasi, the Review Committee of Mau Mau Prison Sentences, chaired by S. H. La Fontaine, began for the first time to hear hundreds of parole cases, recommending nearly 95 percent of them for eventual release. All of these former prisoners were also Form C'ed and sent to works camps in their districts for final softening up before they were handed over to the chiefs in their home locations.[81]

The rapid pace at which the detainees and former Mau Mau prisoners were being broken down and released was astounding. Governor Baring was ecstatic, attributing to Gavaghan this success in breaking down the hard core and forcing confessions. As the governor wrote to Lennox-Boyd in the spring of 1958, "I recently visited the Mwea camps and was enormously impressed by the remarkable work done during the period of exactly one year by Mr. Gavaghan. It is his work in these camps that has been the key to the flow out of detainees. It is due to this work above all else that we are no longer faced with the danger of having tens of thousands of people on our hands, who would be dangerous to release but whose retention would gradually become a political impossibility."[82] Not long after, Gavaghan left his post and later noted, "In March 1958 we came to the point where the Special Commissioner, Monkey Johnston, declared the job sufficiently done to cope with the remaining few hundred [in the Mwea camps]."[83] For his efforts, Gavaghan took over as district commissioner of Kiambu, a prestigious position for a young man of thirty-five. One of his first duties would be to break the remaining 120 or so women from Kamiti Camp who, impervious to Warren-Gash's order to confess, also seemed to need a heavier hand.[84] As for the Mwea camps, Cowan stayed on, overseeing the continuation of dilution for the several thousand hard core remaining in the Pipeline. Finding a replacement for Gavaghan, however, was not so easy. Johnston first approached John Nottingham, then posted as district officer in Nandi. Nottingham later recalled, "[I flatly refused] to be involved in such a despicable and unlawful procedure, whose notoriety throughout the colony for its brutality was unprecedented. I told him this, and he told me in not so many words to be quiet."[85] Eventually, there was a taker; Denis Lakin, who had been implementing the dilution technique along with Galton-Fenzi at Athi River, stepped in to fill Gavaghan's large void. And later Hugh Galton-Fenzi himself was brought in from Athi River to mop up what remained of Operation Progress.

To defend the dilution technique to his critics in the House of Commons, Lennox-Boyd did what he did best: he obfuscated the facts, skirted the issues, and lied. He shrouded violence and torture in the camps inside the garment of Britain's civilizing mission and the alleged success of liberal reform. The colonial secretary may have convinced himself and his supporters that this policy of legalized brutality was for the best, that they were saving civilization from Mau Mau savagery, but Barbara Castle, Fenner Brockway, and a growing list of MPs from the Labour Party would have none of it.

When news of Muchiri Githuma's murder in Gathigiriri Camp made its way to London in early 1957, Castle was again snapping at Lennox-Boyd's heels. She wanted to know "how many convictions there have been for assault on prisoners at Gathigiriri Works Camp ... [and] how many prisoners have died as a consequence of ill-treatment?"[86] Her ire had been raised not simply by the beating to death of Muchiri Githuma but also by the farcical nature of the subsequent inquiry. One of the African rehabilitation assistants and several surrenders were eventually charged with murder and the case was heard by Justice Pelly Murphy in a Nairobi court. Despite evidence showing Muchiri Githuma had been "hung by the wrists" and beaten with "lengths of rubber or pieces of sisal," the judge decided to acquit all of the accused of murder because he could not determine who actually dealt the blow that caused the prisoner's cerebral hemorrhage. He did, however, find the defendants guilty of the lesser charge of assault causing bodily harm, and sentenced them to less than a year of hard labor. Neither Cowan nor any of the other Europeans in charge of the camp were held responsible for the crime, despite the fact that the judge "suspected strongly the orders were given and carried out with the tacit approval of the assistant's superior officer."[87]

Castle refused to let go of this cover-up, only one of many, she believed.[88] She pushed Lennox-Boyd for an explanation of the evidence coming from the trial, arguing that the record showed there were at least twenty-seven other known cases of assault at Gathigiriri. Why had he not made the Commons aware of this? The colonial secretary shot back, with his usual aristocratic confidence, "I cannot agree with what the hon. Lady has said. If she cares to give us those details or come and see the Governor of Kenya, who is now in London, and give him personally the details, I shall be only too anxious, as is the Governor, that nothing should be covered up."[89] Apparently, Lennox-Boyd must have gone back and had a clarifying word with Baring, because less than a fortnight later he admitted not to twenty-seven but to thirty-seven other cases of assault occurring at Gathigiriri. The colonial secretary assured the House of Commons that the incidents were appropriately taken care of in Kenya's local courts of justice, and that those accused of beating the detainees, all of whom were African loyalists, had been sentenced to a few weeks in prison.[90]

"Does not this reveal that there has been the most unsatisfactory state of affairs in this camp for a very long time?" Castle demanded. In light of his own candid revelations of thirty-seven assaults, it would have been

laughable for the colonial secretary to argue that as usual these were isolated incidents. Instead he deftly shifted gears, imploring her to "see this in
perspective," that these were only "very minor cases of assault." He went on
to say, "The hon. Lady knows enough about the conditions and the type of
men who are detained not to regard this very, very serious. She asked about
the disciplinary inquiry. . . . The report is made to the Governor-in-
Council, and I do not propose to publish it." The Opposition was outraged,
and another Labour MP cut in, demanding, "When the right hon. Gentleman [Lennox-Boyd] says that these were minor offences, is he aware that
the offence was that hard-core detainees in this camp who did not confess
were tied by their hands some three feet from the ground and flogged with
strips of rubber cut from tyres until they did confess? Is this a minor assault?" "I was dealing with minor injuries," he protested. "Only minor injuries were inflicted. The hon. Lady [Castle] should not draw from that the
belief that there was widespread violence and cruelty at this camp."[91]

At the same time the colonial secretary was digging himself out of a
hole on the Commons floor, he was authorizing the use of systematic violence and brutality in the Mwea camps. Moreover, the hard-core detainees
were fighting back, even rioting, and the Opposition wanted to know why.
In fact, MPs on both sides pressed Lennox-Boyd for explanations about the
Mageta Island standoff, as well as riots at Manyani, Langata Prison, and the
small-scale uprising at Mwea around the time of Gavaghan's takeover.
Their suspicions were justified. Lord Balniel and others questioned the
colonial secretary as to whether "he can give an assurance that no pressure
is being brought to bear on the Kenya Government to accelerate the pace
[of release] beyond what they regard as desirable." Lennox-Boyd, knowing
full well that an all-out campaign had been launched to run down the
Pipeline, replied, "I can certainly give that assurance. We all knew that
when the Kenya government introduced the dilution technique it was
bound to be followed by an increased security risk." He then added, "No
pressure of any kind is being imposed."[92]

The colonial secretary had clearly amassed an artful repertoire of responses to the allegations of abuse, misconduct, and obstruction leveled at
him in the Commons. He would soon have to draw on all of them to defuse the bombshell that next landed on the colonial government. It came in
the form of a letter from the political prisoners held at Lokitaung. On June
8, 1958, the *Observer* published a laundry list of allegations contained in a
letter signed by all those detained there, with the notable exception of
Kenyatta. In it, the political prisoners like Bildad Kaggia and Paul Ngei
wrote they had "suffered a great deal" during their five years at Lokitaung.
They were permitted no visitors, they were beaten, and "owing to insuffi-

cient and unbalanced diet . . . [they] bec[a]me prone to many kinds of diseases." They went on to report, "Most of us have been ill many times, and some for long periods. Some have almost lost their eyesight."[93] The motivation for the letter was not the food deprivation and illnesses, but rather a complete embargo of potable water instituted in late April by the camp commandant. In their publicly circulated letter the prisoners spelled out clearly what was happening.

> On April 23 the District Officer, Mr. C.L. Ryland, who is in charge of our prison, curtailed our water ration to two gallons per person. We appealed to him but he refused to listen to us. The following day the D.O. said we were not to get any water at all. We demanded to see him, but he refused. On the twenty-fifth we went to the well for our share of water. The D.O. came to the well and told us to draw our water from a nearby old and discarded well which had long ago been condemned by doctors and in which dogs' carcases and filth have been thrown for years. Vehicles are also washed on the top of the well, the dirty and oily water and petrol returning into the well. The well has no lid and when it rains the flood collects rubbish and excrement into it. The D.O. told us the clean well is for Europeans only. Knowing very well that the water is unfit for human beings, we refused, and demanded the clean water which we have been drinking the past five years and which is now reserved for six Europeans only [officers and warders]. The D.O. maintains that we cannot get any water from the clean well. Now as we write this letter we are entering our fourth day without water in a desert while the now "European" well is full of clean water.

The detainees concluded their letter, "We consider this the most brutal and inhuman treatment ever compared to the Nazi concentration camp. As we have nowhere to appeal we now appeal to the High Court of World Public Opinion."[94]

Immediately Lennox-Boyd telegrammed Baring, assuring him, "We will now do our best to kill the allegations here."[95] But with dozens of newspapers in Britain covering the story and demanding explanations, the colonial secretary was not going to be able to sweep these newest allegations under the rug so easily. The press awaited a response from the colonial government, which came on June 11 from Kenya's Legislative Council. The colony's new chief secretary, Walter Coutts, summarily dispatched all of the allegations made in the Lokitaung letter, and concluded by reminding the members of Kenya's parliament that

> these allegations have been made by convicts who include the principal leaders of Mau Mau, men who were responsible for the collapse of law and

order in the Kikuyu country, which resulted in the need for the Emergency to be declared. These were the men who inspired superstitions and fear among the mass of the Kikuyu. . . . It is clear from the allegations which have been made that these men succeeded in illegally smuggling a letter out of prison; it is equally clear that had they been held nearer the Kikuyu country, they might have tried to smuggle out more letters, letters which might well have caused further outbreaks of violence.[96]

Nevertheless, several members of the Legislative Council could not contain their outrage. They were not white members, but rather the handful of African members. These men, including Luo members Tom Mboya and Oginga Odinga, were brought into the Legislative Council when the first limited African elections were held in early 1957, a concession to placate African demands for elected representation. This change, though, was by no means a move toward majority representation, and certainly not one that provided the Mau Mau adherents a say in government, as only those Kikuyu holding Loyalty Certificates could run for office and vote in elections. Mboya and Odinga pushed hard for fair treatment and release of political detainees, and refused to accept Coutts's and the colonial government's self-serving explanation of the Lokitaung letter. Mboya pressed the chief secretary, "Would not, Sir, the Government consider that in view of the fact that this is not the only allegation of its kind that has been made, that it is time we had an independent enquiry into the allegations that have been made because, Sir, I find it difficult to believe that all these allegations could have been invented."[97] Coutts certainly thought—or at least expressed publicly—that the Lokitaung prisoners, and every other detainee in the Pipeline, had made up their stories of abuse and deprivation. He finally cut Mboya off, saying, "I have given a full reply, Sir, to all the points which were raised. I consider, myself, that the enquiry was full, and that we have done our best in this particular matter. I cannot agree with the hon. Gentleman that another enquiry is needed."[98]

Barbara Castle picked up the scent and demanded to know why members of Kenya's Legislative Council, the colony's highest legislative body, could not go to investigate Lokitaung for themselves. Colonial Undersecretary John Profumo brushed her aside, saying local ordinances dealt with issues of access to the camps. These were hardly the answers the press was looking for, and journalists joined in the demand for access to the prisoners being held at Lokitaung. They too were summarily denied, a practice the colonial government had observed with the press for years. Potentially unsympathetic correspondents were almost always denied access to the camps, and on the rare occasions they were allowed in, they were forbidden to speak with detainees, could not deviate from the guided tour, and could not question camp officials. In spite of the furor over the Lokitaung letter, the government certainly was not about to change its policies.[99] A resounding chorus of dissent soon followed, with publications like the *New Statesman and Nation* calling for, yet again, an end to the evasiveness and a thorough review of the detention camp system in Kenya.[100] "The case for regular inspection and supervision of prison and detention camps in Kenya by independent persons who are outside the government service seems overwhelming," the *New Statesman and Nation* proclaimed. The editorial then continued:

> This and other journals have published many allegations about these remote camps, particularly about conditions in Mageta Island. The matter has now been brought to a head by the *Observer*'s publication of a letter signed by five prisoners in Lokitaung gaol in the northern province of Kenya. . . . Mr Lennox-Boyd has been often questioned about similar allegations and has now reached the point of merely replying that he is assured by senior officials in Kenya that all such charges are baseless. Such answers, which are based on a Minister's natural loyalty to his officials, can never satisfy either African opinion or thoughtful people anywhere; it is obvious that in these isolated camps shocking conditions and occasional atrocities are likely to occur and that when they are found by senior officials the Old Pals Protection Society is likely to come into operation.[101]

Behind the scenes, the Old Pals Protection Society included some most unlikely members. Just weeks after the uproar over the Lokitaung letter Colin Legum, the *Observer*'s most celebrated African correspondent, received a letter from the detainees at Mariira Camp in Fort Hall. The paper's editor, David Astor, quickly informed the colonial secretary of the illicit correspondence by personal letter. "You will recall your reproach when we published a letter from a Kenya gaol [i.e., Lokitaung] without having first sought the opinion or advice of your Department," Astor reminded Lennox-Boyd. He went on to offer the colonial secretary the opportunity to respond privately to the Mariira letter's contents, suggesting that he might hold off on publishing the illicit correspondence should he be satisfied with the Colonial Office's findings.[102] The contents of the letter hardly presented new revelations to the colonial secretary or his staff. In it, the detainees offer specific details about their confinement, all of which are sadly familiar.

> This Camp . . . is a place where many wonderful tortures and maltreatment are meted to us by a South African born European, D.E. Hardy. . . . The Camp is hidden in a deep valley covered by a forest of wattle trees. No

outsider or people around locally can notice what is going on there. Here is a camp comparable to none—perhaps the Nazi Concentration camps could be better. The Government pays no heed whatsoever, although deaths after severe beatings have been reported by us. The first death was of a detainee who on 23rd January 1958 was beaten by warders to death. On the 9th June a convict was battered to death. His name is Mwaura Gathirwa, and 3 others Kariuki s/o Mwangi, Githutha s/o Wahoga, and Irungu s/o Kariuki, were seriously injured and were rushed to Fort Hall Hospital unconsciously.

So far, we have written several letters to the Kenya Government about these cases and none of our letters has been answered. Nor do we see any improvement of the situation or action to stop these atrocities. For the first time in the history of our detention we [have] been denied water, bathing or washing. Here bathing and washing is restricted to once a week (Saturday). We do not have lights in our huts. We are issued with one shirt and one pair of shorts, and two blankets. The camp being very cold as it lies within the Kenya highlands, we find the life very hard. We receive very little medical care. A detainee is not to attend hospital treatment unless he is on the brim of dying. We get inadequate and very badly cooked food. . . .

The only work we do, which is breaking stones in the quarry, is supervised very harshly. Everyone is forced to shout songs as he works. The day's work commences at 6am. till 6pm., and in the evening everyone's voice is completely gone.

In this camp about 50 detainees are cripples, having been beaten, and others suffering from asthma and poliomyelitis are forced to do heavy duties in the quarry. They must be carried by their friends if they cannot walk to the quarry where they remain the whole day. Their complaints are not considered. . . .

We write this article to you so that the public in the United Kingdom and the Commonwealth may know how we are treated. Your paper is esteemed and impartial and is well known all over the world. We therefore hope that you will kindly implore all your readers to pray for us in our difficult times in our lives.[103]

In response to Lennox-Boyd's sneak preview of the letter, the colonial government's spin team shifted into overdrive. Kenya's chief secretary, Walter Coutts, led the internal investigation, at the same time fending off demands from Colin Legum for a full, unescorted tour of Mariira Camp. According to the local district commissioner, Commandant Hardy was a sound chap from Derbyshire, not from South Africa, who believed in "strict discipline and hard work" and whose attitude was that of a "headmaster of a preparatory school." The DC then refuted and explained away every allegation made in the letter.[104] Uncritically, the colonial secretary accepted these excuses and justifications and sent them along to Astor, though conveniently failing to mention that other similar letters from Mariira detainees already packed the government's files in Kenya. Lennox-Boyd wrote the *Observer*'s editor a lengthy letter about the success of rehabilitation and the continuing releases of the hard core, dismissing all of the allegations as unfounded and addressing the issue of the two deaths. One detainee reportedly died of "natural causes," while the other, after a brief skirmish with the guards, simply "collapsed and died." The colonial secretary went on to describe exactly why this man had "collapsed and died": "His body was sent to Fort Hall Hospital for a post mortem examination, and it was discovered that he had received a bruise on the head, but that his skull was not fractured. This was his only injury. The Medical Officer reported that the deceased had an abnormally thin lining of the brain, and that had he been a normally healthy person the blow he had received would not have been sufficient to cause death. An inquest was held in open court at Fort Hall by the Resident Magistrate, Thika, a professional member of the judiciary, who also visited the scene of the disturbance. His finding was 'death by misadventure.' "[105] Remarkably, Astor seemed satisfied with the response, and much to the Colonial Office's relief he published neither the Mariira letter nor Lennox-Boyd's.

No sooner was this bomb defused than another was lobbed into the arena. A detainee named Kabebe Macharia was beaten to death at Gathigiriri Camp. According to internal secret memoranda exchanged between the Colonial Office and officials in Nairobi, "he had been beaten with rubber strips cut from motor-car tyres." It was argued that those responsible for his murder were not among the European officers in charge of the camp. The explanation given for the death of this "Fort Hall terrorist," as Baring termed the murdered detainee, was that he provided inconsistent responses during screening, and eventually his truculence got the better of two African interrogators, who then beat him to death. Allegedly, the senior African rehabilitation officer had given repeated warnings not to use violence during screening, though systematized brutality with its compelling force was already official policy in the Pipeline. The prisons officer in charge, Daniel Derek Luies, was reportedly absent from the camp at the time of the murder, an argument the governor not only accepted but explained away: "I have little doubt that the Prison Officer in question at the end of a long, successful and arduous period of service forgot the danger of beating and that advantage was taken of his absence. It is therefore most unlikely that the circumstances which led to the beating will recur." Finally, Baring argued that there was no connection between this beating to death and the earlier beating to death of Muchiri Githuma that had occurred at Gathigiriri in 1957. Despite the unmistakable similarities between the two murders, they were maintained to be isolated and unrelated incidents.[106]

When Senior Crown Counsel Jack Webber conducted an internal disciplinary investigation into Prison Officer Luies's role in Kabebe Macharia's murder, his findings were similar to those from previous such probes. Webber merely reprimanded Luies for taking a day off, and was inclined to agree with John Cowan, who told the Crown's senior counsel "that whilst one would hope that a warder seeing or hearing brutality used towards detainees would report it to his superior officer, in practice, it is extremely unlikely that this would happen."[107] In other words, if beatings and tortures took place, it was the still uncivilized African assistants who were responsible. From the investigation transcripts it is clear that Webber had no problem agreeing. He believed that British officers could have in no way been involved in such acts, and, moreover, if and when they occurred the only way any of the officers could know of such torture was if their African underlings were to report it. This in spite of the fact that systematized brutality had already been made official British policy. No independent investigation into any British officer's role in Kabebe Macharia's murder followed Webber's report. Two African assistants, however, were later tried for murder, convicted on the lesser charge of manslaughter and sentenced to three years in prison. That Kabebe Macharia was "savagely beaten," and that "evidence shewed that the deceased's screams could be heard in the compound," was not enough to convince the presiding judge, Justice Rudd, that any particular person, including the officer in charge, Hugh Galton-Fenzi, had actually heard the screams.[108]

By the close of 1958 the colonial government had seemingly argued away a mountain of evidence pointing to brutality, murders, cover-ups, breaches of international conventions, and an overall dereliction of trusteeship in Kenya. The Opposition had brought numerous cases of wrongdoing into public light; the press likewise had published letters from detainees and issued calls for independent inquiries. There were the reports by Fletcher and Meldon, censures by various church leaders in Britain, and numerous unpublished accounts of brutality in the Colonial Office files, including additional letters from detainees detailing abuses and asking for help. It is a testament to Alan Lennox-Boyd's power of persuasion and political cleverness that he successfully held at bay independent judicial investigations.

But additional accounts of brutality soon came to light. Victor Shuter, a former prisons officer in Manyani and later Fort Hall and Mariira camps, presented the colonial government in early 1959 with a fifteen-page sworn affidavit, listing charge after charge of brutal abuse and cover-up. He named more than a dozen British officers, serving in the Prisons Department, the Community Development and Rehabilitation Department, and on the police force, who had perpetrated acts of cruelty, and he provided specific details of each offense. According to Shuter, many of these officers "carried home-made weapons of various kinds, with which they frequently and arbitrarily assaulted the detainees. . . . These weapons were pieces of rubber hose filled with sand and tied at both ends, and short rhino whips known as 'kibokos.'" He went on to say, "I saw . . . W. Cumberland force a detainee's head into a latrine bucket, which contained excreta," and that European officers routinely took detainees into a "small room" and collectively beat them. He described the Manyani intake procedure with the cattle dip and "detainees [who] could not swim, and had to struggle through the water holding onto the edge of the tank"—though many nearly drowned when the African chief warder put "his foot on the heads of detainees and push[ed] them under water in the aforementioned dipping tank." Over evening drinks, officers would discuss the next day's torture techniques, which included unleashing the riot squad in the compounds, singling out detainees for public beatings, collective punishments, kicking the crutches out from beneath amputees, and yanking men along by their shackle chains.[109]

Shuter also provided a list describing the "welcome" system at Kamaguta Camp whereby the officer in charge would personally screen each new intake by beating him. At the same camp, a detainee named Macharia was "deaf and paralyzed" as a result of having been "beaten daily over a period of about three weeks" by D. Hartley, the camp's commandant. Shuter wrote of the assaults at Fort Hall Camp and the "new batches of detainees [who were] 'beaten up' as a matter of course" during their dilution at Mariira. Detainees with broken limbs and visible welts and bruises were the ones who "were concealed from the Inspecting Committee on the orders of [the officer in charge]." Moreover, he said, "before inspections by visiting committees, the [other] detainees were threatened with beatings if they made any complaints." As for Shuter himself, he had written numerous complaint letters to his superior officers and to the superintendent of prisons but had gotten nowhere. Responses had ranged from "the camp was being run efficiently" to "some of us were being too lenient with the detainees." In response to his criticisms, Shuter had been "subjected to considerable open ridicule."[110]

On the heels of Shuter's allegations came another round of accusations, this time from Captain Ernest Law. In an interview with the *Daily Mail* Law said, "I knew too much" and went on to claim that he "lost his job as a

chief officer at Main Prison, Nairobi after protesting about sadistic treatment of African prisoners by some English prison officers and their
African assistants."[111] Out of work, Law found himself in debt and took the
unusual step of turning himself in to the local police as a vagrant in hopes
that the government would pay for his return to Britain. Instead he was
sent to Kamiti Prison. There, according to his statement, he saw African
warders "frog-marching two women convicts" inside an office, and once
"they got outside the beating started. The Chief Warder Cha-Cha and his
askaris started hitting and kicking the women. . . . [He] hit with the flat
hands each side of the head with enough force to burst their eardrums and
during the beating I saw the women pass their motions with fright. I was
soon to learn this was a daily occurrence. During my first two months at
Kamiti there were beatings every day." He described the riot squads beating
entire compounds with truncheons and sticks, and one British officer—
after severely beating a convict—telling his *askaris*, "Give him some more.
He is not dead yet." Outside of Kamiti's tuberculosis ward, "4 convicts were
dragged, kicked and beaten towards our compound," Law wrote. "One of
the convicts had crutches, one had no use of his body from the waist down,
one had his right leg in plaster of Paris and the other was too old to do anything. They had been brought out because they refused to have their hair
cut. The barbers arrived with Mr. 'H' who was carrying a walking stick. He
began to beat all four with his stick until it broke then he began to kick
them, the convicts collapsed too weak to speak or ask for mercy. Then Mr.
'H' put his face close to the one who had no use of his legs and shouted . . .
'who is the boss now?' "[112]

    After Shuter and Law came two other European eyewitnesses who had
unique vantage points on the Pipeline abuses. Unusual among the European population in Kenya, Leonard Bird and Anthony Williams-Meyrick
were petty criminals, convicted of theft and sent to Kisumu Prison and
later Kamiti. Their backgrounds would provide easy ammunition for the
credibility assaults that awaited them. Nonetheless, their statements, when
considered together with those of Law and Shuter, clearly merited attention, or at least the Opposition thought so. During his time at Kamiti, Bird
was the clerk in the prisons office, where he "witnessed a number of incidents involving brutality towards African prisoners." He saw transfers from
Embakasi being brutalized, men in leg irons tortured, and a general "sadistic attitude of the European prison officer."[113] Likewise, Williams-Meyrick
offered up accounts of daily beatings with truncheons, batons, concealed
daggers, and "pick handles," detainees being forced to eat contraband like
tobacco until they were "violently ill," and a British officer who routinely

knocked "African prisoners over the head with a heavy swagger cane which he carried . . . without provocation."[114]

A frenzy ensued in the Commons and in the press, as well as along the wires connecting the colonial secretary to Governor Baring. Now it was not just Castle, Brockway, and other predictable left-wingers demanding explanations; rather it was the entire Labour Party, with nearly two hundred MPs signing a motion urging "the Secretary of State for the Colonies to institute an independent inquiry into the conditions and administration of prisons and detention camps in Kenya, including Lokitaung Prison, Northern Province, in view of allegations of ill treatment received from prisoners and detainees in Kenya and allegations about the conditions made by former officers of the Kenya Prison Service."[115] A showdown debate was set for the Commons on February 24, and the colonial government's political wheels were spinning.

An independent investigation had to be avoided. Lennox-Boyd and Baring were now so close to emptying the camps, and to succeeding with their plan to cement British control over the colony, that the governor insisted, "We must not fall for this gambit in the war of nerves being conducted by those trying to undo us in Kenya."[116] By early 1959 Baring and his men on the spot were putting the finishing touches on the main exile camp at Hola. Remarkably, the number of hard core slated for permanent detention was down to a few thousand, and with systematic brutality still in place the numbers were still dropping. "An enquiry disorganises rehabilitation work," the governor went on to reason, "and demoralises rehabilitation workers. Therefore I think that in the interests of detainees who should be released as soon as possible an enquiry without a *prima facie* case should be avoided. At present the 'pipeline' is still running very well. . . ."[117] Baring also sent other cables expressly to discredit the new round of accusers. Shuter was "probably a forger" and "certainly in heavy debt," Law was a "vagrant" and "his medical reports suggest he was an alcoholic," and as for Bird and Williams-Meyrick, they were child's play— summarily dismissed as thieves and convicts.[118]

Insults continued to fly in Parliament in the days leading up to the debate over the motion for an independent inquiry. Time and again Lennox-Boyd stonewalled on questions, and the Opposition voiced its anger. Labour MPs wanted to know what was being done about the allegations, why thousands were still in the camps, and when would political detainees— men like Achieng' Oneko, whose conviction at Kapenguria had been overturned years before—be released. "Why cannot the Minister do some homework for a change," one Opposition member barked, "and consult his

Civil Service and give this House some decent and factual Answers? On about six occasions today there has been no answer to perfectly simple Questions." To this, the colonial secretary had no answer, and another Labour MP chimed in, "There are still thousands detained. It is monstrous."[119]

It was a bitter partisan fight, and in the end politics vanquished morality. The vote on the motion to authorize an independent inquiry split along party lines, with 232 in favor and 288 opposed. The morning after the debate, conservative papers like the *Daily Telegraph* portrayed the defeat of the motion as a vindication for the British colonial government and yet another failed ploy by the "Socialists."[120] The liberal media took their usual stand, with the *New Statesman and Nation* declaring, "It is characteristic of the present political set-up in the Colonial Office that the refusal to set up an independent inquiry into the Kenya prisons is carried beyond the point of reason."[121] But it was the conservative-leaning *Economist* that offered the most reflective conclusion to this latest drama over an independent inquiry. "All the same," its article said in closing, "the one overriding consideration in treating any present-day colonial question must be what last memories of the British way of doing things are to be left behind before the connections with Westminster are severed."[122]

Had the story of detention, violence, murder, deceit, and abuse of power in Kenya ended with the February vote, it still would have been one of the great stains on Britain's already blemished record of twentieth-century imperial rule. Nonetheless, one must wonder: had Lennox-Boyd and Baring taken the groundswell of Labour outrage, the relatively close call on the independent inquiry motion, and the dogged questioning in the press as signs to moderate the abuses in Kenya, there might have been a very narrow opening still left for them to escape at least some of the critical judgment they have earned. This was not to be. Instead, British colonial officials saw the motion's defeat not just as an endorsement of their behavior but as a kind of green light to proceed with even more institutionalized violence. But this time the scenario would play out differently, and they would be caught red-handed.

On March 4, 1959, a news report came over the wires that ten detainees died at Hola Camp and that "the deaths occurred after they had drunk water from a water cart."[123] The clear implication was that these men had died from contaminated water they had consumed. At first, everyone seemed to accept the explanation, even Barbara Castle. "I might have been forced to accept this innocent version like everyone else," she later recalled, "if I had not received a telephone call at the Commons from D. N. Pritt, the left-wing QC who was in Kenya representing the African detainees."[124] Using his own connections, Pritt had learned of the initial autopsy findings, which told a much different story. "He said, 'Barbara, this is the worst cover up in the whole history of colonial government,'" Castle later told an interviewer. "'These men were beaten to death—they were clubbed to death—they did not die of drinking water. Please pursue this in the House.' So of course what I did then was to ask the Secretary of State of the time please put the documents in the House of Commons library—the documents of the inquest, the documents of the enquiry. There we had the evidence and I was able to go through those documents to prove to the House of Commons that these men had in fact been clubbed to death by illegal behaviour in the running of the camp."[125]

Still, neither Lennox-Boyd nor Baring were prepared to fully admit the facts. "The medical reports indicate," a second press release on March 12 announced, "that there were injuries on the bodies which may have been due to violence."[126] These were the same bodies that had broken teeth and extensive facial bruisings, not to mention multiple other blunt-force injuries that had been duly recorded by the coroner.

"The Hola Massacre," as it was termed in the press, would finally validate years of allegations. It would expose the evasions and refusals for what they were: politically motivated cover-ups. Baring and Lennox-Boyd above everything protected their men on the spot, at all costs. No one was going to go down for this, not the local British officers, not the governor, not the colonial secretary, and certainly not Prime Minister Harold Macmillan. Elections were coming in October, and Hola was exactly the kind of scandal that could bring a government down. At the time Macmillan understood that the situation was dire, writing in his diary that his government was "in a real jam."[127] He and Lennox-Boyd were prepared to pull out all of the stops to make certain this tragedy was whitewashed and, most important, to ensure that no one was forced to accept direct responsibility. They knew that once blame was apportioned, it would be impossible to control how far up the ladder it might go.

The colonial government tried to massage the facts by arranging an internal investigation. Senior Resident Magistrate W. H. Goudie took charge, opening an inquest into the Hola deaths on March 18. His investigation focused on one of the top camp officials from the original Operation Progress, Gavaghan's right-hand man, John Cowan. In early February Cowan had been sent to Hola by Taxi Lewis to deal with the hard core who were still refusing to cooperate. When Cowan arrived, he found that the camp was divided into two sections. There was the open camp for detainees who were cooperating and willing to work, among them Gakaara wa Wanjau, the famed Kikuyu intellectual. After being released from the Pipeline, Gakaara had been rejected by the loyalists in his home area and was sent to Hola, where he was later joined by his recently released wife, Shifra. Together, they set up housekeeping in the insufferable heat and mosquito-infested new settlement scheme, a place they believed they would have to endure for the rest of their lives.[128]

It was the hard core in the nearby closed camp that was the motive for Cowan's new assignment. Whatever tactics he tried, the camp commandant, G. M. Sullivan, could not force these men to cooperate, let alone work. Cowan arrived on the scene, assessed the situation, and subsequently drew up what was to be the famous Cowan Plan. In it he directed Sullivan to take out small batches of twenty or so detainees to the irrigation project and order them to work. "Should they refuse to work," Cowan went on to direct, "they would be manhandled to the site of work and forced to carry out the task."[129] The Cowan Plan was a departure from the earlier tactics used at Mwea only in one sense: it was written for internal distribution. The plan was reviewed by Johnston, Cusack, and Taxi Lewis, all of whom were determined to show the hard core who was in command. Still, they all knew the Cowan Plan could be a recipe for disaster, with Lewis later conceding, "It would mean the use of a certain degree of force in which operation someone might get hurt or even killed."[130] For his part, Sullivan was wary about the scheme, knowing that the solidarity and intractability of the detainees in his camp made it an incredibly risky venture.

Permission to implement the Cowan Plan was given a day after the House of Commons voted to defeat the motion to establish an independent inquiry into the camps. A week later Sullivan moved ahead, and what happened next more than fulfilled Taxi Lewis's worst fear. Even the sanitized government reports issued by the internal investigation would reveal clearly that the detainees were beaten severely by the guards. At specific issue, however, was whether Sullivan tried to put a stop to the beatings once they got out of hand. British officers said he did. Detainees like Paul Mahehu, though, had a different story to tell.[131] After refusing to buckle at Athi River, Paul had been shipped to Hola, where he would join the ill-fated group of detainees assigned to the working party on March 3, 1959. "We were selected a hundred people from the closed camp, which housed about four hundred detainees," Paul began. He then went on to relate what happened next.

> We were told that we would go to work. The *askaris* were all armed with heavy sticks. We were taken to the trench, which was being used to bring water for the whole Hola irrigation system. . . . What we were required to work

on was the enlargement of the experimental garden. The most surprising thing was that for each detainee there were about five *askaris*—that is, for one hundred detainees there were well over five hundred *askaris* there. It was something that had been planned in advance, and any observer could have seen that it was a prepared attack. The shovels had been put a short distance away, but they were very well guarded. When the officer in charge [Sullivan] informed us that we would be required to work, we hesitated. But a fellow detainee named Munyi Mutahi advised us to agree to work, as it was clear that the officer was only hoping for an excuse to set the armed *askaris* on us. We agreed and asked to be given our tasks, but they were impossible ones. We were each to dig about one hundred cubic feet of earth in two hours. We complained, and the white officer said that we would have to do it, but we maintained that the task was too much. When he ordered us to do the tasks a third time, he blew his whistle and ordered the *askaris* on to us. It was as if the *askaris* had been coached about it. The dust that was there cannot be described. Even today, whenever I remember about Hola, I shed tears. I cannot understand how I escaped death on that day. The *askaris* were so many, their clubs would hit against each other as several *askaris* tried to hit the same detainee. I was hit, and I fell down. The detainee who fell over me had his skull broken, and I was covered in his brains and blood. I pretended to be dead. Other detainees continued to be beaten long after they had died. The first time the six detainees died. The white officer blew his whistle to stop the beating and then asked, "How many detainees have been killed?"[132]

Rather than stop the beatings, Sullivan ordered the six bodies dragged away and then blew his whistle again. The mayhem started up once more until another shrill of the whistle. Sullivan again asked how many had died; this time the number had reached ten, at which point, according to Paul, he ordered the beatings to stop. The survivors were later taken to the camp clinic, including Paul, who was in his own words "full of blood and brains but still alive." Along with scores of others he stayed there for several weeks, and together they watched when the eleventh man died from the compelling force that had been imprinted all over him.[133]

When it came time for Goudie's report, there was only so much the senior magistrate could do to obscure the actual causes of death. Given that Castle had exposed the truth about the "water cart" incident, Goudie had little choice but to reveal, albeit with scant detail, how the detainees died. "In each case death was found to have been caused by shock and haemorrhage *due to multiple bruising caused by violence*" (emphasis in original), Goudie summarized in his report. "There was no serious combined attempt [by the detainees] to attack warders . . . [and] there was a very considerable amount of beating by warders with batons solely for the purpose of compelling them to work or punishing them for refusing to work."[134]

When the senior magistrate went on to apportion blame for the murders, he ultimately found that no one could be held accountable. Surely Goudie was not about to be the one to bring down the British colonial government in Kenya; nor was he going to offer any findings that would derail Lennox-Boyd's or Baring's desperate attempts to protect their men on the spot, not to mention themselves and Prime Minister Macmillan. "At first sight it might be considered extraordinary that such opinions should be recorded in view of my finds of illegal beatings having taken place at the work site," Goudie prefaced his summary remarks. He then continued:

> The following factors, however, in my view clearly justify such opinions. It is impossible to determine beyond reasonable doubt which injuries on the deceased were caused by justifiable and which by unjustifiable blows, and which injury or combination of injuries resulted in the shock and haemorrhage causing death. It is impossible to say on the evidence with any degree of certainty which particular person struck the blows, whether justifiable or unjustifiable. . . . The Cowan Plan, which apparently had government approval and backing, gave, intentionally or unintentionally carte blanche in "forcing detainees to carry out the task." If criminal offences were committed which were clearly illegal, the defence of "superior orders" would be of no avail, but I do not consider that the orders were so clearly illegal on the face of the orders as to justify my recommending the preferment of charges. That is, however, ultimately a question of policy, which is a matter for the Attorney General and not for me to decide.[135]

But little could be expected of Kenya's attorney general, Eric Griffith-Jones, as he had been the chief legal strategist for officially sanctioned violence in the Pipeline. Griffith-Jones was not about to prosecute anyone, in spite of the fact that he had himself been a Japanese prisoner during the Second World War. In fact, he led the charge in pushing Gavaghan's Operation Progress, offering up his brainchild of compelling versus punitive force to persuade the Colonial Office to move forward with institutionalized violence.

Lennox-Boyd and Baring were left to deal with the political fallout back in London. As soon as Goudie's findings were made public, the Opposition issued a motion condemning Hola and demanding a full public investigation into the incident. A first debate was set for mid-June in the Commons, and in the interim the prime minister and his men worked overtime to control the damage and to calculate how they might avoid an independent investigation. Baring began by inviting a host of newspaper reporters to a choreographed tour of Hola Camp. Many left with a favorable impression, printing dispatches that helped mitigate the earlier, damaging newspaper accounts of the camp.[136] The government then launched an internal disciplinary proceeding against Hola's commandant, Sullivan, and a handful of his lieutenants. Macmillan now stepped in to sort out the bigger issue of how in the weeks to come to handle Castle and the rest of the Opposition.

In a cabinet meeting, several of the prime minister's men, though divided on the issue of an independent inquiry, felt strongly that responsibility for Hola should be assigned to Baring and his colonial government in Kenya.[137] Baring flew to London to insist that he would not allow his men, particularly Cowan and Cusack, to be made into "scape-goats."[138] Policies endorsing the use of systematized violence had been approved at the highest levels, starting with Gavaghan's Operation Progress, and he was not about to let his boys, or himself, take the blame. After a private session with his chief whip and Lennox-Boyd, Macmillan agreed. The prime minister then set down a clear course of action, and neither he nor anyone in his government would deviate from it in the weeks and months to come. First, they would refuse any independent inquiry into the past events in the Pipeline; rather, they would establish an internal review, called the Fairn Commission, that would offer guidelines for the future administration of the camps only.[139] Macmillan, Lennox-Boyd, and Lord Perth (minister of state for the colonies) would take the lead in stressing their government's success in winning the war against terrorism in Kenya, and with it concede that one or two unfortunate incidents may have occurred but that they needed to be understood in light of the extraordinary achievement of rehabilitation in the face of unimaginable Mau Mau savagery.[140]

There was strong resistance by some in Macmillan's cabinet to this course of action. The most strident calls for censure came from his own attorney general, Reginald Manningham-Buller. Behind the scenes, the prime minister was tenuously pulling his dissenters along when a most incredible announcement was made by the Colonial Office. In the middle of the gathering storm centered largely on the Cowan Plan, Lennox-Boyd bestowed upon Cowan the honor of Member of the British Empire (M.B.E.). It was an extraordinary bungle, one that prompted Macmillan to write in his diary, not for the first time, that the colonial secretary's shop was "a badly run office."[141] Nonetheless, in an election year of all times, there was dogged resolve that no one was going to be sacrificed.

After squaring off for the first debate in the Commons in June 1959, Harold Macmillan wrote in his diary that "the debate has gone as 'well as could be expected' but it has been an anxious day."[142] In hindsight, the drama was predictable, with the Opposition demanding straight answers and calling for an inquiry and a well-prepared Lennox-Boyd dodging and weaving in remarkable and typical form. It was, though, just a preview of what was to come in the next debate on the massacre. MPs on both sides of the political divide postured, threw "barbed personal criticisms," and gave indications, both strong and subtle, of their positions, not just on Hola but on the question of Britian's colonial mission more broadly. Ultimately, Macmillan's greatest challenge came not from Labour but from onetime Tory MP Enoch Powell. Powell had left the Conservatives six months earlier after a falling-out occasioned by the prime minister's fiscal policies, and so was preparing to use Hola as a pretext for launching a vigorous attack against the government's colonial policies. "The Tory Party," he believed, "must be cured of the British Empire, of the pitiful yearning to cling to the relics of a bygone system. . . . The courage to act rationally will follow from the courage to see other things as they are."[143]

For Powell, colonial heads would have to roll. "A large slice of responsibility for this administrative disaster lies at a high level in Kenya," he told Macmillan, "and I trust that it is going to be accepted publicly and in the only way possible."[144] If by this he meant the colonial secretary had to step down, he was not alone. Labour MPs were calling for his immediate resignation, and Lennox-Boyd himself even pressed Macmillan to let him leave the helm of the Colonial Office. But the prime minister would hear none of it. His mind was made up, reasoning that Lennox-Boyd's resignation would lead to irreparable damage to his government, suggesting as it would culpability for Hola, not to mention the scores of other alleged atrocities. Moreover, Macmillan said, it "might make the more extreme Africans feel that they had now got the white man on the run."[145]

Closing ranks only stoked the political fires. Certainly, outrage was expected from the Opposition, but it was Lord Lambton's break from the Tory party line that sent a clear message to Macmillan: his handling of the Hola massacre was proving disastrous. In early July the Conservative MP felt compelled to publish a scathing article in the *Evening Standard*. The headline "When Loyalty Is Not Enough" made his message clear. His concern was less about the human rights violations in and of themselves, but rather their geopolitical implications, as well as the mockery that Hola was making of Britain's formidable and otherwise successful civilizing mission. "We are in Kenya in the process of making the tragic mistake of handing to the Communists and anti-British elements in the whole of the African continent a propaganda stick with which they will beat us for years," he wrote. He went on to tell the public that he was not alone in his sentiments. "Hola has caused deep concern to many Tory MPs. . . . Responsibility must be accepted whatever the cost."[146] After the internal disciplinary hearing, Sullivan was merely told to retire, suffering no loss of income and with his subordinate fully exonerated. As for Taxi Lewis, Lennox-Boyd asked that he take a six-month leave of absence until his retirement—which he gladly did.

With the House of Commons showdown looming at the end of July, the government was hardly out of the woods. Macmillan retreated to Chequers, accompanied by Lennox-Boyd and a handful of other colonial policy makers, all of whom went directly to work concocting their final plan of action, with help from the government's resident expert on public relations. No doubt the situation must have seemed dire, particularly since the Hola debate was scheduled for the same day as the debate over Nyasaland, where another State of Emergency had been in effect for several months. As with Kenya, there were also allegations of Britain's misuse of power, as well as of brutality and murder in this southern African colony. In fact, Britain's own commission had found that "illegal force" had been used and that the government had greatly exaggerated the alleged savagery of Nyasaland's African National Congress. In spite of Lennox-Boyd's successful insistence that the commission's report—the Devlin Report—be sanitized before its publication, the Colonial Office's censors missed what would become the most famous and embarrassing passage of the whole report: "Nyasaland is—no doubt temporarily—a police state, where it is not safe for anyone to express approval of the policies of the Congress party, to which the vast majority of politically-minded Africans belonged, and where it is unwise to express any but the most restrained criticism of government policy."[147]

Kenya was clearly no exception in British colonial Africa. The mass murder and torture of unrecorded numbers of Mau Mau suspects was the extreme, but it was becoming abundantly clear that there was blood on the hands of Britain's so-called civilizers in other parts of the continent as well. The outcome of the two colonial debates in the Commons would be perceived as a referendum not just on Hola and the Nyasaland Emergency but on Britain's colonial mission more broadly and, ultimately, on confidence in Macmillan's government.

Hola was first on the docket, and Barbara Castle among the first to speak. In her own account, she recalled "trembling so much from anger I could barely get out my facts."[148] For nearly three-quarters of an hour, Castle cataloged several atrocities that had occurred prior to Hola, the deceptions and stonewalling that followed them all, demanded again that an independent inquiry be held, and ended with an attack on Lennox-Boyd. "When this terrible shame comes upon the Colonial Secretary, whether he willed it or not, and he does not act, he shows he does not deserve to hold his office."[149] It was then Enoch Powell's turn. With calculating, surgical skill the onetime Tory MP dissected the British colonial government, leaving it exposed on the table for all to see. He called the whole debacle "a great administrative disaster" and insisted the colonial secretary "ensure that the responsibility is recognized and carried where it belongs, and is seen to belong."[150]

Powell's concluding remarks were the most damning. In his final bit of grandstanding he declared, "We cannot say, 'We will have African standards in Africa, Asian standards in Asia and perhaps British standards here at home'. . . . We cannot, we dare not, in Africa of all places, fall below our own highest standards in the acceptance of responsibility."[151] But was it not precisely the double standard condemned by Powell that had guided British colonial policy? Baring had taken his direction from General Templer in Malaya, and certainly there were other instances of such a double standard throughout Africa, Nyasaland being only one example. The colonial government had squandered numerous occasions to apply the so-called British principles of law in Kenya, the posting of Sir Arthur Young to overhaul the police force being one such instance. Rather than supporting Young, Baring refused to endorse British standards of policing and ultimately drove the police commissioner out of the colony. Together with Lennox-Boyd, the governor covered up the whole affair and went on to pack Young's supporter, Attorney General Whyatt, off to Singapore. In the end, few of the high-ranking officials in the British colonial government actually believed that the standards of British law applied to Africa, or most parts of Asia for that matter, and particularly not while they were fighting a war against savagery.

Alongside the high-minded, imperial reasoning used to construct a defense for the failures at Hola came a still darker side of colonial logic. Prime Minister Churchill, and later Eden and Macmillan, as well as the colonial secretary and his men on the spot, were willing to accept the use of brute force and systematized violence to save civilization in Britain's far-flung corners of the world. A powerful critique of this convoluted and ultimately counterproductive reasoning was the message that Barbara Castle and other outspoken Labour critics had been sending for years, though it had fallen on deaf ears. By the time the Hola investigations surfaced, some Conservatives had begun to listen, though it cannot be known how far they might have been willing to go in opposing their own government's policies. After Lennox-Boyd's predictable defense of his department's good administration in Kenya, and his lauding of the success of rehabilitation, no vote was entered in the Commons. In what must stand as perhaps one of their gravest tactical errors, the Labour Party MPs had arranged for the debate on Hola to be appended to an appropriation bill, which meant that the issue could not be put to a vote. "There might well have been quite a number of Conservatives voting against the Government or abstaining," Macmillan later conceded, knowing the Opposition's error most likely saved him and his government from what should have been a disaster.[152]

In the end, an independent investigation into Kenya's detention camps was never conducted. Nor was there one for Nyasaland. The day after the Hola debate, Lennox-Boyd again defended his government's actions, sidestepping the Devlin Report and instead holding up what he bragged were the countless success stories of British colonial performance around the globe under his five-year stewardship. British rule had not been "squalid," as the Opposition charged; rather, it was a triumph. Lennox-Boyd offered the examples of newly independent Ghana and Malaya as illustrations of British success, indeed tangible evidence of Britain's civilizing mission. Even his harshest critics like Enoch Powell were convinced, at least enough to vote against a further probe into Nyasaland.

For Lennox-Boyd, the nightmare was coming to an end. The skeletons left over from the repression of Mau Mau, and the other colonial scandals, would remain in the closet, and he would soon quietly retire from the Colonial Office. But the future of British colonial rule in Kenya would not be given such a storied ending. The colonial secretary and Governor Baring escaped the final chapter, only to see the loss of the one prize to which they had so desperately tried to cling. In the aftermath of Hola it was simply impossible for the British to remain any longer in Kenya, and Lennox-Boyd's successor, Iain Macleod, undertook the measures needed to decolonize. The British had won a long, costly, and bloody battle against Mau Mau, only to lose the war for Kenya. The devastation they left in their wake would be inherited by Jomo Kenyatta and Kenya's first independent government.

EPILOGUE

Survivors at grave site in Dagoretti, August 2003

IN THE FALL OF 1965 SIR EVELYN BARING STOOD INSIDE WHAT HAD once been his office. Since leaving Kenya and the governor's post nearly six years earlier, when the country was still under British rule and the Mau Mau politicals remained safely locked away, the country had changed. Kenya was now an independent nation, Government House had become State House, and what had been the former governor's command site throughout the Emergency now belonged to Kenya's first president, Jomo Kenyatta.

It seems remarkable that until that October afternoon in 1965 Baring and Kenyatta had neither met nor spoken. In fact, the last time the two men had been in the same room was at Senior Chief Waruhiu's funeral thirteen years earlier. Baring was uncharacteristically nervous as he visited his old office, especially because Kenyatta was standing just opposite him. Indeed, what do you possibly say to a man whose trial you rigged and who, because of your signature, spent years of his life banished to a desert wasteland? There was no avoiding the subject, so after some initial pleasantries the former jailor turned to his onetime captive, gestured, and said, "By the way,

I was sitting at that actual desk when I signed your detention order twenty years ago." "I know," Kenyatta told him. "If I had been in your shoes at the time I would have done exactly the same." The nervousness evaporated, and the room erupted in relieved laughter. With everyone still chuckling, the new president chimed in, "And I have myself signed a number of detention orders sitting right there too."[1] As the two later strolled through the gardens admiring the Naivasha thorns that Baring's wife, Mary, had planted years before, Kenya's jails were already beginning to fill up with detainees whom the new independent government deemed threats to the country's young democracy.

It was by no means foreordained that Kenyatta would walk out of detention in August 1961. When it happened, neither the local settlers nor the Kikuyu loyalists could believe it. Neither group had been particularly disturbed by what had happened at Hola, and certainly never believed that as a result of that final tragedy the British would take rapid steps toward decolonization. To the surprise and dismay of both groups, Hola proved to be the point of no return.

The world was changing, but the settlers were impervious, living as they did in their bunker of white privilege. They were certain Harold Macmillan's and the Conservative Party's victory in October 1959 was cause for celebration. As they were dancing on the tables of the Muthaiga Club, Macmillan was studying the rest of Africa and catching an ugly glimpse of what the future of Kenya might look like should he decide to cast his lot with white settler rule. There was the French disaster in Algeria, where by the end of 1959 a reported 20,000 Frenchmen and 150,000 Algerians had died—largely as a result of France's draconian tactics of quelling dissent, eerily similar to those the British had employed in Kenya and elsewhere in their empire. In neighboring Congo the Belgians in 1959 were moving quickly toward decolonization, though it would prove unsuccessful in staving off a brutal African backlash against the local Belgian settlers—nearly fifteen thousand of whom were forced to flee the colony with nothing but the clothes on their backs. In South Africa television cameras would soon capture the brutal racism of the apartheid government, which allowed white policemen to open fire on a crowd of African demonstrators in Sharpeville, killing close to one hundred people and injuring countless others. Farther to the north Britain, along with France, was still suffering from the earlier embarrassment of the Suez debacle, where in 1956 the United States and the Soviet Union forced them both to pull out.

The Cold War was clearly under way and bearing heavily on Africa. The administration of John F. Kennedy was becoming increasingly intolerant of anticolonial conflicts—not necessarily because colonialism was, in and of itself, a bad thing but because these wars were perceived as hotbeds for communist recruitment. Harold Macmillan knew he could no longer justify bloodshed in Africa and that without Britain's age-old weapons of force and oppression he could no longer hold on to Kenya or Nyasaland, nor for that matter any of Britain's other African colonies. Moreover, the romantic and fraternal attachment to the settlers was disappearing, only to be replaced with a cold indifference that bordered on outright hostility. The "prevailing mood" after Hola, the onetime settler leader Michael Blundell later wrote, was best captured by the remarks of a young Conservative MP who proclaimed, "What do I care about the f . . . cking settlers, let them bloody well look after themselves."[2] Rather than functioning as a referendum for empire, the general election in 1959 was its death knell.

But the history of Britain's empire is not just about the decision making in London. If this story has revealed anything, it is that African colonial subjects and their resistance shaped power just as much as British power shaped their resistance. It was a two-way street, and one the colonial government was going to find increasingly difficult to navigate as it moved toward decolonization in Kenya. While the British had managed to defeat Mau Mau, the drawn-out and bloody struggle against the detainees and villagers together with the irrepressible demands of the more radical African nationalists forced them to abandon any gradualist approach toward decolonization in Kenya.[3] Driving the African high-political agenda were the Luo leaders Tom Mboya and Oginga Odinga, both of whom had been resoundingly critical of the British government during the final days of the Emergency. Together they helped forge a Kikuyu-Luo alliance that was poised to undo the careful, measured pace of decolonization laid out at the first constitutional talks held at Lancaster House in January 1960. It was there that Macleod announced his plans for Kenya's future: it would become a parliamentary democracy based on universal franchise. The Europeans, including Michael Blundell and members of his moderate New Kenya Group, were stunned. Many settlers, particularly the conservative diehards, saw the announcement as the ultimate betrayal—that the new colonial secretary had "sold them down the river."[4] Nonetheless, they all felt that they had at least ten years before independence, plenty of time to prepare the colony's sixty thousand whites for African rule.[5]

The settlers were also convinced that Kenyatta would never be released. There was scarcely a single European—even Baring, whose moral righteousness prevented him from ever admitting that Kenyatta might have been innocent of the crimes he had been unjustly convicted of—who doubted that Kenyatta was the mastermind who had brewed the evil poison of Mau Mau.[6] To add an official stamp on this British colonial version of the truth, the government released its report on Mau Mau in early 1960. Its author, F. D. Corfield, relied solely on British and loyalist sources when drafting the so-called definitive history of the movement. He employed the usual terms, speaking of British enlightenment and African darkness, and declared Mau Mau to have been "wholly evil" and Kenyatta its chief protagonist.[7]

This line was echoed by Kenya's new governor, Sir Patrick Renison, who had replaced Baring during the closing days of 1959. Renison was notably sympathetic to the settler plight and was determined to cut down Kenyatta at every turn. When the new governor returned from London and the Lancaster House talks in May 1960, he delivered what would become one of the most famous denunciations of Mau Mau and its alleged mastermind. Perhaps the rest of Kenya's Africans could be civilized, but not Kenyatta. Renison minced no words. "Jomo Kenyatta was the recognized leader of the non-co-operation movement which organised Mau Mau," he said in a widely circulated speech. "Mau Mau, with its foul oathing and violent aims, had been declared an unlawful society. He was convicted of managing that unlawful society and being a member of it. He appealed to the Supreme Court and the Privy Council. In these three courts his guilt was established and confirmed. Here was the African leader to darkness and death."[8]

Renison conveniently forgot to mention the small technicality that Kenyatta's trial had been rigged, something that was up for public debate by this time, for the Crown's star witness, Rawson Macharia, had stepped forward and admitted to both perjury and accepting a bribe.[9] There was undoubtedly a genuine fear on the part of the settlers and some British colonial officials that Kenyatta, if released, would start up the whole bloody mess all over again. At the very least, they thought he was unpredictable and held an almost hypnotic sway over the ordinary African, particularly the easily misled Kikuyu. Even Macleod, who was vehemently opposed to Renison's "darkness and death" speech, was doing his best to save from the ruins the earlier postcolonial vision espoused by Lennox-Boyd and Baring. Macleod, like his predecessors, wanted no part of nationalists like Mboya and Odinga. Rather, he had every intention of seeing moderate Africans, men like the Kikuyu loyalists who would safeguard Britain's commercial and strategic interests, firmly installed in power before handing over the colony to majority rule.

Eventually, the British would get their way, but few would have ever predicted the path they would take to get there. The world was poised to witness a dramatic reinvention of Kenyatta, one that would transform him from a Machiavellian, satanic figure into a conservative, civilized man who

embraced the so-called enemies of his past. Of course, this transformation
was hardly one at all, except in the minds of the British and those they had
hoodwinked into accepting their version of Mau Mau. Kenyatta had never
been the oath-taking revolutionary he was purported to be. He was instead
a mission-educated politician who had preached moderate reform. Kenyatta wanted a piece of the colonial pie and to be accepted like the rest of
the African colonial elite, and he sought the social and economic privileges
that went along with that acceptance.

Kenyatta's reinvention was never planned. Instead his release, and subsequent transformation, were foisted upon the British colonial establishment by the Africans in Kenya, who were demanding their rightful leader
be set free. When the first colony-wide elections were scheduled for February 1961, Kenyatta's release was practically the only issue that mattered to
many ordinary Africans, particularly the Kikuyu. At this point, everyone in
Kenya, regardless of whether they held a Loyalty Certificate or not, had
been enfranchised. For their part, Mboya, Odinga, and their Luo-Kikuyu
coalition party—the Kenya African National Union, or KANU—knew
how to win the vote. They campaigned on the pledge that they would not
take their seats in office unless Kenyatta was released. The opposition, the
Kenya African Democratic Union (KADU), which was secretly supported
by the British colonial government, championed minority ethnic rights,
including the rights of the European settlers, and had no desire to see
Kenyatta freed. When the election results were in, KANU had won a resounding victory and, as promised, its members refused to join the government unless Kenyatta was released.

News of KANU's victory was broadcast all over the world, reaching
even the remotest part of northern Kenya where Kenyatta sat listening to
the results on his small transistor radio. He was no longer living in the
desert wilderness of Lokitaung, but rather ninety miles south in the arid
wasteland of Lodwar, where he had been moved after the completion of his
prison sentence. Lodwar was thought to be his final resting place. But
Mboya, Odinga, and the rest of the newly elected KANU MPs backed the
British colonial government into a corner, and for the first time the African
majority had the upper hand, leaving Macleod no choice. Kenyatta had to
be released.

After eight years of desert seclusion the Mau Mau mastermind was
reintroduced to the world in April 1961. A press conference was called, and
Kenyatta stood in front of the cameras wearing his trademark leather
jacket. His seventy-year-old face was gaunt and his eyes were sunken, but
his voice and mind were robust. He told the phalanx of reporters, officials,
and curiosity seekers, "I have been greatly misrepresented by some of you,

but today I hope you will stick to the truth and refrain from writing sensationalist stories about me." He then went on to reject the Corfield Report as "a pack of lies," before turning his attention to the issue of vengeance. Much like Nelson Mandela would do some thirty years later, Kenyatta emerged from detention preaching forgiveness. Here, the presumed leader of "darkness and death" borrowed from the words of Jesus, "Father forgive them, for they know not what they do." He went on to say, "I have never been a violent man. My whole life has been anti-violence. If I am free I will continue to do so."[10] Then Kenyatta imparted one last unforgettable message before stepping down. *"Uhuru,"* he declared. *"Uhuru."* The Kiswahili word *uhuru* would become the slogan for all Africans in Kenya in the weeks and months to come. It would become the greeting on the streets, the closing word in conversations, and the lyrical base for children's songs. *"Uhuru,"* they would sing. *"Uhuru na* Kenyatta." That is, "Freedom . . . Freedom and Kenyatta."

For hundreds of thousands of Kikuyu, Kenyatta's final liberation in August 1961 was as sweet, if not sweeter, than their own. "I wept, I wept with joy," recalled one former detainee. "Word got around very quickly when he was released, and we danced and celebrated into the morning. Our leader was free, and he was going to save us from the colonial oppressors. Ngai had answered our prayers."[11] Triumphal appearances soon followed, with Kenyatta touring the country for the first time in nearly a decade. He also made a remarkable, if enigmatic, impression upon the British public when he gripped millions of viewers in their living rooms during a forty-five-minute interview on the BBC's television series *Face to Face.* No one knew quite what to make of this man who spoke eloquently, wore a Western-style suit, and had no horns coming out of his head. It was becoming apparent to everyone, though, that once the countless details had been worked through, this "leader to darkness and death," or great African statesman, no one at the time was entirely sure which, was going to become Kenya's first president.

In fact, less than two years after he was reintroduced to the world, Kenyatta stood on the podium of Nairobi's Uhuru Stadium. "This is the greatest day in Kenya's history and the happiest day in my life," he told a crowd of some forty thousand ecstatic Africans. As always, Kenyatta was a spellbinding speaker, refusing to read his prepared address in English. Dramatically, he tossed his speech aside and spoke extemporaneously to his people in Kiswahili, and the crowd was virtually uncontrollable. Looking down with him on the scene were dignitaries from around the world who had all come to Kenya on that eleventh day of December 1963, to witness Africa's thirty-fourth country achieve its independence from European rule. Then at midnight, after hours of ceremonies and dancing, a spotlight zeroed in on the Union Jack being lowered, and Kenya's new flag was raised for the first time. For a moment it refused to unfurl, and the Duke of Edinburgh, the queen's representative for the affair, leaned over and whispered to Kenyatta, "Do you want to change your mind?" In his moment of glory Kenyatta only grinned and watched as the wind finally picked up his country's flag, and the crowd again roared.

Hidden beneath this euphoric moment, however, was another much less triumphant picture of cover-up and betrayal, self-interest and greed. Time and again, Kenyatta would declare that "we all fought for freedom," and that his new nation must "forgive and forget the past." Less than a year after independence, the country celebrated its first Kenyatta Day—which, not coincidentally, took place on October 20, the same day as the declaration of the State of Emergency. In a broadcast speech to another massive crowd, the country's president declared, "Let this be the day on which all of us commit ourselves to erase from our minds all the hatreds and the difficulties of those years which now belong to history. Let us agree that we shall never refer to the past. Let us instead unite, in all our utterances and activities, in concern for the reconstruction of our country and the vitality of Kenya's future."[12] In other words, there would be no day of reckoning for the crimes committed during Mau Mau, no memorializing of those Mau Mau men and women who had fought in the forests and died in the camps and villages. There would be no prosecutions against former loyalists, and certainly not against any of the British colonial officers or settlers, many of whom continued to live a very privileged life in Kenya.

On one level, it could be argued that Kenyatta was sacrificing the past for the future. He was, in the only way he knew how, trying to prevent his country from descending into a civil backlash. In Kikuyuland, former Mau Mau adherents despised their loyalist neighbors for taking their land, raping their wives, killing their children, and murdering their husbands. Worst of all, they saw the same loyalists profiting from their losses. For the former Mau Mau adherents, the Home Guard and their leaders were being rewarded for their crimes, with nearly all of them living in comparative luxury. Calls for vengeance were universal, and only Kenyatta had the moral authority to contain the anger, even if he could not eliminate it.

Another problem was the issue of the non-Kikuyu people of Kenya.

There were millions of Africans who were wholly uninvolved with Mau Mau, and who were deeply suspicious of a Kikuyu oligarchy taking over the country. Had Kenyatta recognized Mau Mau as a legitimate nationalist uprising that drove the British out of Kenya, where would this have left all of Kenya's other ethnic groups when it came time to parcel out the fruits of independence? One way around this potentially explosive issue was to erase Mau Mau from the public's memory and replace it with the politically correct and widely embracing message: "We all fought for freedom." With Kenyatta's politicized spin on the truth, every Kenyan had a claim to make on the past and therefore the right to share in the benefits of independence.

Kenyatta the great reconciler was also Kenyatta the conservative politician who had never supported Mau Mau's oathing or guerrilla tactics. Hardly the mastermind of the movement, he instead did everything in his power both before and after independence to marginalize those who had fought and been detained in the war. After their release, many former hard-core detainees banned together to form the Land and Freedom Army, administering once again an oath of unity. They demanded the return of their land, pledging to fight if Kenya's new government betrayed their cause. But Kenyatta would have none of it. He told the veterans and former detainees again and again that "nothing is free." If they wanted their land back, Kenyatta insisted, they would have to purchase it like everyone else. He denounced those demanding compensation and recognition, admonishing a crowd in Kiambu, "We are determined to have independence in peace, and we shall not allow hooligans to rule Kenya. We must have no hatred towards one another. Mau Mau was a disease which had been eradicated, and must never be remembered again."[13] In fact, some of those "hooligans," or former Mau Mau supporters, who refused to listen would soon find themselves locked up, with Kenyatta signing their detention orders at the same desk that had once belonged to Sir Evelyn Baring.

In the end, the fruits of freedom were going to be divided up between Kenyatta's emerging oligarchy, the loyalists, and those settlers who remained in Kenya. It was a scenario that the British colonial government had fantasized about for years, albeit with a slight twist. No longer would Kenyatta be the lifelong captive but instead, over time, would become the darling of the British political establishment. From the moment he stepped out of detention, Kenyatta did his best to allay the fears of the British government and the settler population, assuring them that an independent Kenya would forgive the past and, most important, would not take their land. In one of the most revealing confrontations during the run-up to decolonization, Kenyatta went to the heart of the settler nation in Nakuru, where he won over the white, hostile crowd. "We are going to forget the past and look forward to the future," he told them. "I have suffered imprisonment and detention, but that is gone and I am not going to remember it. . . . Let us join hands and work for the benefit of Kenya, not for the benefit of one particular community. We want you to stay and farm well in this country: that is the policy of this government."[14] By the end of the meeting the settlers—the same ones who had for years condemned Kenyatta—were patting him on the back, laughing at his jokes, and shouting, "Harambee," or "Let's All Pull Together," which had become Kenyatta's preferred rally cry.

Not all settlers endorsed the reinvention of Kenyatta or his vision for the country's future. Thousands packed their bags, sold their farms, and left—many fleeing to the warm embrace of apartheid South Africa, others going back to a Britain that in many ways must have been completely foreign to them. But unlike their counterparts in the Belgian Congo, the Kenyan settlers departed with much more than the clothes on their backs. The newly independent Kenyan government bought their land at market rates, using nearly £12.5 million in loans from the British government to finance the buyout. In total, nearly twenty thousand European settlers left Kenya and with them went an enormous outflow of foreign investment capital. Nonetheless, Kenyatta successfully convinced well over thirty thousand of them to stay, along with their investments, and to this day many of these former settlers and their descendants continue to live a life of racial privilege, complete with houseboys and gardeners, cooks and nannies, frequent visits to the Muthaiga Club, and countless reminiscences of the good old days when the "natives" knew their place.

Much of the land that was sold to the Kenya government was resold to European investors and to wealthy Kikuyu, many of whom had been loyalists during the Emergency. These Africans certainly had the means to purchase this property. During British colonial rule they had enjoyed years of economic privilege, amassing wealth from their enormous and oftentimes illegally gotten plots of land, the cash crops that colonial officials had allowed them to grow first, the trading licenses, and their extortion and bribery.

During the run-up to independence and in the years that followed, former loyalists also wielded political clout to consolidate their own interests and power. Under Kenyatta many became influential members of the new government, people like Isaiah Mwai Mathenge and Jeremiah Kiereini, both of whom had worked in the Pipeline for years and who had proved instrumental to Gavaghan's success in the Mwea camps. This system of loyalist patronage percolated all the way down to the local level of government, with former Home Guards dominating bureaucracies that had once been the preserve of the young British colonial officers in the African districts. Of the numerous vacancies created by decolonization—powerful posts like provincial commissioner and district commissioner—the vast majority were filled by onetime loyalists. As a result, the nature of governance in the Kikuyu countryside did not change much with independence. The loyalists still wielded a great deal of day-to-day power over the former Mau Mau detainees and villagers.

Back in Britain there would be no soul-searching or public accounting for the crimes perpetrated against the hundreds of thousands of men and women in Kenya. When Iain Macleod took over the Colonial Office in the months after Hola, he wrote to Kenya's new governor, Patrick Renison, assuring him that he had "decided to draw a veil over the past."[15] The final lasting image of Britain's moral war in the empire was not going to be revealed by thorough investigation into the torture, murder, and starvation of Kikuyu men, women, and children. Instead, there was a great deal of sympathy, if not admiration, for the professional soldiers, British colonial officers, and ordinary settlers who fought the terror of Mau Mau, even if that terror pushed them into casual brutality and violence. In the end, it was these representatives of the British colonial government who would be remembered as the victims of the battle to save civilization, not the savage Mau Mau adherents, not the Kikuyu people.

Nonetheless, the new colonial secretary did some of his own internal probing. Though he had picked up the baton from his predecessor and continued denying publicly any systematic abuse or official culpability for the atrocities in Kenya, his report to the Colonial Policy Committee in November 1959 told a different story.

Separate allegations of ill-treatment in some of the Mwea "pipeline" camps have revealed signs that widespread irregularities took place there up to December 1958. The responsibility for these irregularities, which took place mainly during the intake of recalcitrant detainees into the camps and involved a certain amount of unauthorised corporal punishment and some physical violence, has been investigated personally by the Acting Chief Secretary (who is substantively the Attorney-General). The investigation indicates that the principal responsibility lies with the then Provincial Commissioner and the Minister for African Affairs . . . who have virtually admitted that, at the very least, they ignored the previous Governor's personal directives and the Kenya Government's policy, and condoned illegal methods of "persuading" detainees to confess and co-operate.[16]

Macleod's assessment was accurate, except that he did not go far enough up the ladder in apportioning blame. In the Colonial Office's own files were several documents suggesting that Monkey Johnston and Gavaghan were not out there beating detainees into submission without approval from above. From Lennox-Boyd at the top to Governor Baring and his attorney general Griffith-Jones, British colonial officials knew what was happening, endorsed the policy, and later even commended Gavaghan for his extraordinary success.

In spite of these investigations, there was never a single internal reprimand issued, nor any sign of a housecleaning. Sir Evelyn Baring left Kenya in the fall of 1959 and returned to the luxury of his family estate at Howick, where he pursued his passion for bird-watching. Shortly thereafter he accepted an offer to head up the government's Colonial Development Corporation (CDC), another arm of British colonialism that offered loans and management to developing countries provided they followed the rules that Baring and his men set out for them. John Cowan, the former prisons officer and author of the Cowan Plan, retired to the Bank of England.[17] As for Monkey Johnston, he left Kenya to work for MI8 back in Britain, while Gavaghan stayed in Kenya overseeing the country's Africanization program, or the transitioning of loyalists into the Administration. For all of his hard work and success during the Emergency, Gavaghan was ultimately awarded the prestigious Order of the British Empire (O.B.E.). Askwith, by contrast, received no gong, as the former British colonial officers called these coveted honors, and instead left for Afghanistan after his posting in Kenya. Even after his death, Askwith continues to be ostracized by many of his former colleagues from the colonial service.

Once Britain began moving toward decolonization in Kenya, the demands for an independent investigation began to subside. Enoch Powell, who both at the time and years later insisted that either Governor Baring or Lennox-Boyd, or both, should have assumed responsibility, never again pursued the matter in the political arena.[18] As for Labour MPs like Barbara Castle, their wish was to see colonies like Kenya gain their freedom. With the Conservatives retaining power in the fall of 1959, and Macleod's subsequent concessions at Lancaster House, there was not much to be gained politically by pursuing the atrocities and cover-ups in Kenya. For the Opposition, there were still battles to be fought, but empire in Africa would no longer be one of them. The Conservatives too were already looking beyond their African colonies. In early 1960 Harold Macmillan had gone on a tour of Africa, where he made his position on the future of British colonialism abundantly clear. "The wind of change is blowing through this continent," Macmillan told the South African Parliament, "and, whether we like it or not, this growth of national consciousness is a political fact. We must all accept it as a fact, and our national policies must take account of it."[19]

All that remained were the guilty consciences of those who perpetrated the atrocities, and those who witnessed the tortures and murders and did little or nothing to stop them. During the course of my work, I certainly met or learned about a wide range of people who perpetrated or witnessed terrible crimes, and all displayed or professed varying degrees of guilt and denial. I also interviewed a number of former settlers who some fifty years later still seemed to take delight in their handiwork during Mau Mau. They spoke of heinous tortures as if they were describing yesterday's weather; for them the brutality they perpetrated during the Emergency is as banal today as it was some fifty years ago. At the other extreme were those like Cowan, who later described his work as simply that, work. "I didn't feel guilty, I don't think," he said when later asked about Hola. "I don't think that's quite the word. . . . I felt extremely sorry that it had gone wrong, but not actually guilty."[20] For his part, Gavaghan is much more perplexing. I have spoken with him in person and by phone perhaps several dozen times over the years and was often struck by the moral weight he seemed to be carrying. I was therefore surprised when he later told another interviewer that, with regard to guilt, he felt "none whatever."[21]

One is then left to wonder about the others. Why didn't Askwith say anything outside of official circles? He knew that detainees "had been illegally assaulted and even killed," and he had protested vehemently over Gavaghan and the dilution technique, yet he never broke ranks.[22] In the end, Askwith upheld the unwritten rules of British colonial conduct, though he later reflected, "I wished I had done more, but I'm not certain even today what I could have done because no one was listening."[23] As for the others—the "good commandants," as some detainees called them, and the missionaries—certainly many lobbied behind the scenes, perhaps thinking they were doing the best they could given the constraints under which they were operating. But, still, when allegation after allegation kept coming, right up to Hola, it is at the very least puzzling to understand why nothing more was done. Perhaps these men and others like them ultimately believed that Mau Mau was savage, that they were fighting a moral war, and that the ends justified the means. Perhaps they did not want to appear weak, or perhaps they were too weak to confront authority. Or perhaps they just did not think much at all about what was happening around them.[24]

.   .   .

How is it possible to evaluate the impact that this war had on the hundreds of thousands of men and women who were detained in the camps and villages of British colonial Kenya? There is no record of how many people died as a result of torture, hard labor, sexual abuse, malnutrition, and starvation. If the British did keep records of these deaths, they were destroyed long ago. We can make an informed evaluation of the official statistic of eleven thousand Mau Mau killed by reviewing the historical evidence we now know. Former detainees and villagers recall thousands dying; others remember being assigned to burial parties that disposed of hundreds of corpses in any given day; missionaries wrote of widespread famine; Kenya's medical officers described deaths from contagious diseases and malnutrition. There were countless letters written by detainees during the Emergency, describing tortures and deaths, and there were the independent findings by people like Arthur Young, his assistant, Duncan McPherson, and Barbara Castle—all of which revealed unspeakable brutalities and murders. There are also the recollections of Asian advocates, men like Fitz de Souza, who remember representing thousands of detainees, none of whom they ever saw again. "By the end I would say there were several hundred thousand killed," de Souza later reflected. "One hundred easily, though more like two to three hundred thousand. All these people just never came back when it was over."[25]

There are the demographic figures. The British colonial government undertook a census of the Africans in Kenya in 1948 and 1962, years on either end of the Emergency. The population figures reveal that the growth rate of the Kikuyu was notably below that of the neighboring Kamba, Luo, and Luhya populations, something that should not have been the case. If the Kikuyu population figure in 1962 is adjusted using growth rates comparable to the other Africans, we find that somewhere between 130,000 and 300,000 Kikuyu are unaccounted for.[26] I believe the lower growth rate was likely due to two factors: actual deaths and a slower birthrate due to lower female fertility. This lower fertility would have been caused by such factors as malnourishment, disease, miscarriage, the absence of regular male partners, and the psychological stress resulting from war trauma. I would argue that at the very least it is safe to assume that the official figure of some eleven thousand Mau Mau killed is implausible given all that has been uncovered.[27]

Of course, we will never know exactly how many Kikuyu died during the last years of British colonial rule in Kenya. But does this matter? The impact of the detention camps and villages goes well beyond statistics. Hundreds of thousands of men and women have quietly lived with the damage—physical, psychological, and economic—that was inflicted upon them during the Mau Mau war. In the aftermath of independence they had their advocates in Kenyatta's new government—MPs like Bildad Kaggia, Paul Ngei, and J. M. Kariuki who demanded the detainees be remembered and who insisted they be given compensation or at least consideration for their contributions and losses during the Mau Mau struggle. But over time these protagonists for the Mau Mau past were either pushed aside or, in the case of J. M. Kariuki, assassinated. For Kenyatta and his successor, Daniel T. arap Moi, Mau Mau was to remain buried—it was a moment in Kenya's past that would divide more than it would unite.

To this day there has never been any form of official reconciliation in Kenya. There are no monuments for Mau Mau, children are not taught about this part of their nation's past in school, few speak about it in the privacy of their own homes, and, with the exception of the relatives of the Hola massacre victims, there has never been any kind of financial consideration given to those who lost family members in the camps and villages, or property to the local loyalists. Some men and women lost the use of their limbs, others their minds, as a result of the years they spent behind the wire, though neither the former colonial government nor the new independent government did anything to help them piece their lives back together. Insofar as there has been any successful social rebuilding, the burden has been shouldered by local Christian churches. But they too have insisted that bygones remain bygones. If you ask former Mau Mau adherents today if they get along with their loyalist neighbors, the response is generally the same as Mary Mbote's. "We are Christians, and I do not hate them," she told me. When I probed a bit further, she expressed a sentiment shared by many other former villagers and detainees. "I hate them; I hate them for what they did to us," she said. "We all hate them and will not speak to them if we see them outside of church. We even refuse to go to their funerals, which is against the church, but they didn't go to the funerals of our husbands and children and parents when they killed them. Aye, I despise them." She then paused before continuing. "You know," she finally said to me, "this will only change when everyone knows what happened to us. Maybe then there will be some peace once our people are able to mourn in public and our children and our grandchildren will know how hard we fought and how much we lost to make Kenya free for them."[28]

APPENDIX:

THE OPERATING PIPELINE CIRCA JANUARY 1956, MAIN CAMPS

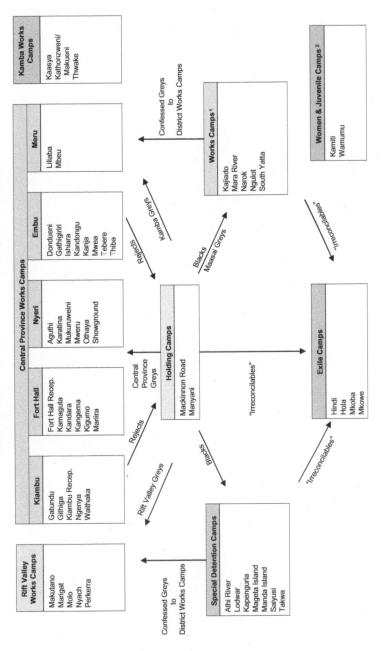

1. Note that all Maasai suspects—both "blacks" and "greys"—were sent to Kajiado, Mara River, Narok, and Ngulot camps. In addition, other Kikuyu "blacks" were also sent to these camps. In effect, while not gazetted as such, they were being used as special detention camps. Similarly, South Yatta was being used for Kikuyu "blacks" as well as self-confessed murderers.

2. Kamiti was the only all-female camp and was used for both women and juvenile girls. However, Athi River Camp also held female detainees. Similarly, Wamumu was the only all-juvenile camp for boys, though many camps throughout the Pipeline also contained males under the age of eighteen.

NOTE ON METHODS

TO CREATE THE EVIDENTIARY LATTICE FOR THIS BOOK, I DREW UPON a wide range of written and oral source materials. It is therefore important to outline the considerations of method that shaped my research agenda and analyses.

Three sets of questions drove my inquiry. I first wanted to re-create and explain the structure of the Pipeline and the Emergency villages: how this detention system functioned, how many were detained, who was in charge, the chain of command, and finally the logic behind the transfer of detainees between different camps.[1] Second, I sought to move beyond a mere reconstruction of the Pipeline by going behind the wire to explore life inside the camps and villages. The relationships among the detainees and the camp personnel remained for years largely unexplored, as did the role of rehabilitation and labor in detainee "reform." By opening up a window into the day-to-day world of the camps and villages, I could understand why the Pipeline took the form that it did. Finally, I wanted to know why the British were introducing a policy of mass detention in the aftermath of World War II and the various declarations on human rights passed in its wake, including no detention without trial. It was not enough to explain the structure and the world of the camps; I sought to understand how the Pipeline and the Emergency villages fit into Britain's broader colonial policy and its long-term plans in Kenya.

When I began this project, the scope of what remained unknown or undisclosed about the detention camps and Emergency villages was enormous. This was largely a result of the British colonial government's concerted effort to purge most of its detention and villagization files prior to decolonization in 1963.[2] It was also due to independent Kenya's state-imposed amnesia, introduced initially by Kenya's first president, Jomo Kenyatta, and then advocated by his successor, Daniel T. arap Moi. Consequently, I began my research by carefully sorting through what remains in the official archives at the Public Record Office in London and the Kenya National Archives in Nairobi. Despite the earlier destruction and continued censorship of files, my research in both places yielded a wealth of information. I first went through every official document I could locate that pertained to Mau Mau. I then moved on to cabinet minutes, premier files, and the records of several ancillary departments like the Medical Department and the Labour Department. I soon found that some of the documents missing from the Prisons Department and the Ministry of African Affairs had been copied to other departments, like Medical or Labour, and had been overlooked by those who purged the files. I also found hundreds of unexcised letters and memos relating to the camps, rehabilitation, and works projects that were small pieces of the complex puzzle. With them I was able for the first time to compile a list of the camps in the Pipeline, and to start to understand how and why these camps functioned.

The official record was not enough to understand fully the origin, structure, and purpose of the Pipeline. I traveled to some twenty archives and libraries on three different continents to amass the research necessary to write this book. Missionary data were extremely important as were private paper collections, including those from settlers, British colonial officials, British MPs, and missionaries, primarily located at the Rhodes House Library, Oxford. I also went through newspaper collections in Kenya, Britain, and the United States, as well as numerous private, public, and commercial photograph collections. The fragmented remains of official documentation from colonial government sources, when read alongside materials from private collections and missionary archives, began to reveal a clearer picture of how and why the Pipeline functioned.

Nevertheless, understanding what life was like inside the camps was difficult to ascertain solely from official and private archives. Certainly, the missionary reports provided some firsthand insights. So, too, did the papers of the men and women directly involved with the day-to-day administration of the camps, as did the detainee letters sent to British colonial officials, Labour MPs, and others in Kenya and Britain. But to get behind the wire and capture the intimate details of detention life, I needed to use two other sources.

First, there is the handful of memoirs written by former Mau Mau detainees chronicling their lives in the camps. Like the massive literature produced by the survivors of the Nazi concentration camps and the Soviet gulag, the Mau Mau texts offer an unmediated voice of those detained. These highly personalized historical accounts provide a counterbalance to the biases and silences inherent in any official archival source; however, to be useful as historical sources, memoirs, like other texts, must be read with and against other evidence.[3]

Because few survivors of the detention camps in Kenya wrote and published their memoirs, I needed a much larger source of data to re-create the world behind the wire.[4] With this in mind I began collecting survivor testimonies in 1998. I am certainly aware that oral histories, like written memoirs, represent a person's subjective remembering of past events.[5] Memories are, as cognitive psychologist Daniel Schacter points out, "complex constructions—not literal recordings of reality."[6] There is a constant interaction between the past and the present in all human memory such that oral testimonies, like memoirs, tell us as much about a person's current state of mind and the society in which he or she lives as they do about a particular historical moment.

When one considers testimonies from those who have experienced traumatic events, the use of memory can be challenging. At issue is the degree to which violence affects a person's ability to remember. Put another way, all memories are fallible to some extent, but memories of traumatic events are often perceived as being more fallible than memories of mundane episodes. There is certainly plenty of evidence to support the notion that people who have experienced violent pasts would often prefer to forget them, and in extreme cases they simply cannot remember them.[7] But, interestingly, some of the same evidence suggests that, when recalled, traumatic events are actually better and more accurately remembered than ordinary experiences.[8]

Nevertheless, issues of accuracy and believability are often present when using survivor testimony. No one senses this more than the survivors themselves. In nearly all of the interviews that I conducted with former detainees there emerged a shared concern that I, their audience, would have a hard time believing the events they were recalling. It became clear to me as well that any problem in believing and using oral testimonies also resided with me, the listener. Occasionally, there was the problem of language as survivors struggled to find words to capture the events and meanings of their pasts. But there was also my limited ability to understand these brutal and traumatic moments within the mental framework of my comparatively normal world, a fact several former detainees were able to sense. One man, when recalling forced sodomy at Manyani Camp, asked me, "How do I explain this to you, how can I make you understand this? The white man in charge ripped our shorts off and then made us do terrible things. . . . Do you understand me?"[9] In another instance a woman stated simply, "How can I possibly tell you what it's like to bury lorryloads of dead bodies? How can I make you understand?"[10]

But what struck me the most about these oral testimonies were the consistencies between them. It was not just that survivor memories when taken together evoked a general period of brutality; it was that they provided recollections of events, processes, relationships, and individuals that were very similar. Take, for example, the detainees' reception at Manyani Camp. Without prompting, nearly every man recalling his time in this camp described to me the two rows of *askaris,* the beatings, the cattle dip, the stripping, and the body searches. Notorious guards, struggles over food, mending clothes, walking when shackled, trying to communicate with each other and the outside world, and the moral dilemmas they faced were all commonalities in the oral testimonies of life in Manyani Camp. Today, many of these former detainees live many miles apart, have poor access to transportation and communication, and many have not left the general area around their homes for decades. This is one of the countless instances in my research whereby the men and women of rural Kenya recalled very similar traumatic experiences that occurred some fifty years ago.[11]

Yet it was not just the consistency of the oral testimonies over time and space that I found striking; it was also the degree to which the oral data correlated with what remains in the written record. I was able to cross-reference many of the survivor accounts with details contained in detainee letters written at the time of Mau Mau. Additionally, the court proceedings from various screening and detention abuse cases, the internal memoranda from missionaries, newspaper accounts, demographic data, as well as eye-witness testimonies from former colonial officials, settlers, politicians, and lawyers, all provide similar details to those offered by the detainees in their oral testimonies. In effect, the arguments that I make in this book are derived not from any one historical source but from the combined weight of a wide variety of sources. Within this methodological framework, survivor accounts give a face to the otherwise bureaucratic structure and procedure of the camps. Without these testimonies, we would be unable to see fully into the world behind the wire or understand what day-to-day life was like for the detainees in the camps and villages. Nonetheless, we would still have to explain why the myriad of other sources, when read together, present a picture of destruction leveled against the Kikuyu population by the British colonial government.

The version of history for which I found little corroborating evidence is that which depicts the camps as a benign system, and colonial officials, camp commandants, and guards as paternalistic reformers. In the official written record as well as in later interviews the testimonies of British colonial agents are littered with omissions, half-truths, and lies. Powerful motivations existed for them to evade and conceal the truth; but to believe many of their testimonies, those offered either at the time or in subsequent years, would require dismissing all other historical evidence. Except for a few writers such as Ngugi wa Thiong'o, these self-exonerations were for years largely accepted.[12] My research sought to avoid the path laid out by those directing and executing the policies of detention and villagization and to offer instead a comprehensive account of Britain's last desperate efforts to maintain colonial rule in Kenya.

NOTES

ONE: PAX BRITANNICA

1. Kenya National Archives (KNA), MAC/KEN 34/9, Colonel Meinertzhagen, "Mau Mau," 1956.
2. Charles Miller, *The Lunatic Express: An Entertainment in Imperialism* (New York: Macmillan, 1971).
3. Sir Charles Eliot, *The East Africa Protectorate* (London: Edward Arnold, 1905).
4. Godfrey Muriuki, *A History of the Kikuyu, 1500–1900* (Nairobi: Oxford University Press, 1974), 15, as quoted in Robert B. Edgerton, *Mau Mau: An African Crucible* (London: I. B. Tauris, 1990), 4.
5. Richard Meinertzhagen, *Kenya Diary, 1902–1906* (London: Oliver and Boyd, 1957), 51–52.
6. Robert L. Tignor, *The Colonial Transformation of Kenya: The Kamba, Kikuyu, and Maasai from 1900 to 1939* (Princeton: Princeton University Press, 1976), chapter 2; and John Lonsdale, "The Conquest State of Kenya 1895–1905," in *Unhappy Valley: Conflict in Kenya and Africa*, ed. Bruce Berman and John Lonsdale, Book 1 (London: James Currey, 1992), 13–39. See also Greet Kershaw, *Mau Mau from Below* (Oxford: James Currey, 1997), 70–76, for a discussion of the demographic impact of the drought and famine on the Kikuyu population.
7. Robert Weisbord, *African Zion: The Attempt to Establish a Jewish Colony in the East Africa Protectorate, 1903–1905* (Philadelphia: Jewish Publication Society of America, 1968); and M. P. K. Sorrenson, *Origins of European Settlement in Kenya* (Nairobi: Oxford University Press, 1968), parts 1 and 2.
8. David Koff and Anthony Howarth, *Black Man's Land: Images of Colonialism and Independence in Kenya* (Van Nuys, Calif.: Bellweather Group, 1979).
9. This term was commonly used to describe Kenya after the establishment of British settlement. It was popularized by the famed author and Kenyan settler Elspeth Huxley in her two-volume work titled *White Man's Country: Lord Delamere and the Making of Kenya* (London: Macmillan, 1935).
10. John Gallagher and Ronald Robinson, "The Imperialism of Free Trade," *Economic History Review* 6, no. 1 (1953): 1–15.
11. Thomas Pakenham, *The Scramble for Africa, 1876–1912* (London: Weidenfeld and Nicholson, 1991); and Raymond Betts, ed., *The "Scramble" for Africa: Causes and Dimensions of Empire* (Boston: Heath, 1966).
12. Numerous books chronicle Britain's empire, including William Roger Louis, ed., *The Oxford History of the British Empire*, 5 vols. (Oxford: Oxford University Press, 1998–99); Lawrence James, *The Rise and Fall of the British Empire* (New York: St. Martin's Press, 1996); Trevor Lloyd, *Empire: The History of the British Empire* (London: Hambledon and London, 2001); Andrew Porter, ed., *Atlas of British Overseas Expansion* (London: Routledge, 1991); and Niall Ferguson, *Empire: The Rise and Demise of the British World Order and the Lessons for Global Power* (New York: Basic Books, 2002).
13. "Victorian aspirations," or the civilizing mission, has been rather uncritically accepted by various authors writing on the British Empire. The most notable and recent is Niall Ferguson in his work *Empire*, chapter 3.
14. Kenya was never capable of paying its railway debt, and the British government finally wrote it off in the 1930s.

15. Bruce Berman, *Control and Crisis in Colonial Kenya: The Dialectic of Domination* (London: James Currey, 1990), esp. 73–75.

16. Note that while the Colonial Office was responsible for the vast majority of colonies in Africa and elsewhere in the empire, the Foreign Office had jurisdiction over a sizable portion of Britain's imperial holdings (including Kenya until 1905), and the India Office had responsibility for the colony of India until its independence in 1947.

17. Bruce Berman's in-depth analysis of the Kenya Administration in *Control and Crisis* demonstrates that despite the governing hierarchy from the center, the Administration wielded great local influence, to the point of dictating some policies in the districts, as would particularly be the case during Mau Mau.

18. As quoted in Berman, *Control and Crisis*, 103.

19. There are numerous published and unpublished manuscripts from various members of the Kenya Administration, including Charles Chenevix-Trench's useful book, which chronicles the history of the men who served in Kenya, titled *Men Who Ruled Kenya: The Kenya Administration, 1892–1963* (London: Radcliffe Press, 1993). In addition, various files in the Rhodes House Library contain the unpublished work of numerous men who served in Kenya, such as T. C. Colchester, O. E. B. Hughes, T. G. Askwith, T. H. R. Cashmore, and A. D. Galton-Fenzi. The importance of a shared pedigree and aristocratic ideology is not limited to Kenya, but instead knit together the entire empire of colonial servants with London, as well argued in Robert Heussler, *Yesterday's Rulers: The Making of the British Colonial Service* (London: Oxford University Press, 1963); and Richard Symonds, *Oxford and Empire: The Last Lost Cause?* (Oxford: Clarendon Press, 1986).

20. Errol Trzebinski, *Kenya Pioneers* (London: Heinemann, 1985); V. M. Carnegie, *A Kenyan Farm Diary* (Edinburgh: William Blackwood and Sons, 1930); Baron Bertram Francis Gordon Cranworth, *A Colony in the Making: Sport and Profit in British East Africa* (London: Macmillan, 1912) and *Kenya Chronicles* (London: Macmillan, 1939); Elspeth Huxley and Arnold Curtis, eds., *Pioneers' Scrapbook: Reminiscences of Kenya, 1890–1968* (London: Evans Brothers, 1980); Elspeth Huxley, *Nine Faces of Kenya* (London: Harvill Press, 1990), part 3; and Edgerton, *Mau Mau*, chapter 1.

21. Huxley, *White Man's Country*; and Dane Kennedy, *Islands of White: Settler Society and Culture in Kenya and Southern Rhodesia, 1890–1939* (Durham, N.C.: Duke University Press, 1987), 44–47.

22. Karen Blixen, *Out of Africa* (London: Putnam, 1937).

23. I interviewed several Kenyan settlers who regaled me with endlessly amusing stories about the "good old days," though I would not say that the "good old days" are entirely over in Kenya. Spouse swapping was rampant, particularly in the "Happy Valley," as were hard-core drugs. For a published account see James Fox, *White Mischief* (London: Jonathan Cape, 1982).

24. Though race had provided a category for exclusion since the Enlightenment, Europeans systematized racial hierarchies and used them to subjugate the African population in an unprecedented manner in the twentieth century. Ivan Hannaford, *Race: The History of an Idea in the West* (Baltimore: Johns Hopkins University Press, 1996); George L. Moss, *Toward the Final Solution: A History of European Racism* (Madison: University of Wisconsin Press, 1985); Albert Memmi, *Racism* (Minneapolis: University of Minnesota Press, 2000); and Crawford Young, *The African Colonial State in Comparative Perspective* (New Haven: Yale University Press, 1994).

25. The notion of the "black peril"—or black men sexually violating the purity of white women—has intrigued many authors writing on empire and Africa. For example, Jock McCulloch, *Black Peril, White Virtue: Sexual Crime in Southern Rhodesia, 1902–1935* (Bloomington: Indiana University Press, 2000); and Norman Etherington, "Natal's Black Rape Scare of the 1870s," *Journal of Southern African Studies* 15, no. 1 (1988): 36–53.

26. The pastoralist groups in Kenya, particularly the Maasai, had more land alienated than did the Kikuyu, but the Kikuyu, with their expanding population and practice of settled farming, were affected more by the alienation and the consequent overcrowding and depletion of resources.

27. M. G. Redley, "The Politics of Predicament: The White Community in Kenya, 1918–1932" (Ph.D. diss., Cambridge University, 1976). The land was expropriated from the Nandi and Kipsigis, though the loss left all Africans feeling less secure about their land.

28. R. M. A. Van Zwanenberg, "Kenya's Primitive Colonial Capitalism: The Economic Weakness of Kenya's Settlers up to 1940," *Canadian Journal of African Historical Studies* 9, no. 2 (1975): 277–92.

29. Note that the African reserves in Kenya were de facto ones until the establishment of administrative boundaries in 1926. It was at this point that the Administration officially gazetted, after several earlier lobbying efforts by the settlers, twenty-four so-called tribal reserves covering some 50,000 square miles. At the time, an observer noted that the population density in the reserves closest to the White Highlands already exceeded that of many South African reserves, and predicted that there would be a land shortage within twenty-five years. As Bruce Berman points out, because the African population sizes were underestimated, the density pressures were felt much sooner. See Berman, *Control and Crisis*, 150–151; and Christopher Leo, *Land and Class in Kenya* (Toronto: University of Toronto Press, 1984), chapter 1.

30. Magayu Kiama, interview, Aguthi, North Tetu, Nyeri District, 25 February 1999.

31. Robert H. Bates, *Beyond the Miracle of the Market: The Political Economy of Agrarian Development in Kenya* (Cambridge: Cambridge University Press, 1989); and Berman *Control and Crisis*, 168–70, 267–68.

32. Tabitha Kanogo, *Squatters and the Roots of Mau Mau* (London: James Currey, 1987).

33. Ibid.

34. Lord Frederick Lugard developed this policy of indirect rule and articulated it in his book, *The Dual Mandate in British Tropical Africa* (Edinburgh: Blackwood and Sons, 1922).

35. Robert L. Tignor, *The Colonial Transformation of Kenya: The Kamba, Kikuyu and Maasai from 1900 to 1939* (Princeton: Princeton University Press, 1976); and David P. Sandgren, *Christianity and the Kikuyu: Religious Divisions and Social Conflict* (New York: P. Lang, 1989).

36. Lynn M. Thomas, *Politics of the Womb: Women, Reproduction, and the State in Kenya* (Berkeley: University of California Press, 2003), 24–26; Jocelyn Murray, "The Church Missionary Society and the 'Female Circumcision' Issue in Kenya, 1919–1932," *Journal of Religion in Africa* 8, no. 2 (1976): 92–104; and Tignor, *Colonial Transformation of Kenya*, 235–49.

37. Berman, *Control and Crisis*, 256–74.

38. This period of time when the British colonial government introduced its so-called development policy into the Kikuyu reserves with its accompanied disruption of local economic and social life has been coined the "Second Colonial Occupation," by D. A. Low and John Lonsdale, in "Introduction: Towards the New Order 1945–1963," in *History of East Africa*, ed. D. A. Low and Alison Smith (Oxford: Clarendon, 1976), 3:12–16.

39. From 1932 to 1934, the Kenya Land Commission (Carter Commission) heard land disputes, nearly one-third of which were brought by Kikuyu. The commission considered it impossible to investigate each claim, and ultimately decided to grant the Kikuyu 30.5 additional square miles of territory for their losses, and 350 square miles for future needs. After the Kenya Land Commission's ruling, there would be no further land grants made to the Kikuyu. See *Report of the Kenya Land Commission*, Cmnd. 4556 (1934), 71–77, 129–44.

40. Timothy Parsons, *The African Rank-and-File: Social Implications of Colonial Military Service in the King's African Rifles, 1902–1964* (Portsmouth, N.H.: Heinemann, 1999), 25–35, 70–91.

41. Jomo Kenyatta, *Facing Mount Kenya: The Tribal Life of the Gikuyu* (Nairobi: Heinemann, 1978 [1939]).

42. Kanogo, *Squatters*, 105–20.

43. KNA, African Affairs Department, *Annual Report, 1950*, 2.

44. There is no consensus on the etymology of the term *Mau Mau*. The first appearance of the word in a British colonial government source occurred in 1948. *Mau Mau*, however, was not originally used by the Kikuyu to refer to their movement. Louis Leakey, the government's expert on the Kikuyu, could find no indigenous origin and wrote, "Most of the Kikuyu that I have asked say it is just a 'name without meaning'" (L. S. B. Leakey, *Mau Mau and the Kikuyu* [London: Methuen, 1953], 95). Several explanations have been offered as to the possible origin of the term. Some believe that it was derived from a distortion by Europeans of *muma*, the Kikuyu word for oath. Others hold that it is a type of Kiswahili play on words.

45. This analysis of the growth of African discontent out of socioeconomic conditions during the post–World War II period is derived from the phase of Mau Mau historiography that began in the mid-1980s. Whereas the three earlier phases of historiography—which include the first phase of the early 1960s, punctuated by F. D. Corfield's *Historical Survey of the Origins and Growth of Mau Mau*, Cmnd. 1030 (London: HMSO, 1960); the second phase of the late 1960s as defined by Carl Rosberg and John Nottingham's *The Myth of "Mau Mau": Nationalism in Kenya* (Nairobi: East African Publishing House, 1966); and the third phase of the 1970s and early 1980s as highlighted by the works of Robert Buijtenhuijs and B. Kipkorir—presumed there was a single point of origin for the movement, the work that began in the mid-1980s presents three distinct fronts of Mau Mau. No longer a narrow movement directed by the political elite, Mau Mau is seen as emerging from three focal points: the settler estates in the White Highlands of the Rift Valley and Central provinces; the urban slums of Nairobi; and the African reserves of the Kikuyu. For the most comprehensive accounts, see David Throup, *Economic and Social Origins of Mau Mau, 1945–53* (London: James Currey, 1987); John Spencer, *The Kenya African Union* (London: KPI, 1985); Kanogo, *Squatters;* and Frank Furedi, *The Mau Mau War in Perspective* (London: James Currey, 1989).

46. Njama s/o Ireri, interview, Ruguru, Mathira, Nyeri District, 31 January 1999.

47. Ibid.

48. I heard various kinds of language used in the oath during my interviews, though they would all end with the phrase "may this oath kill me." For further details written by the British colonial government at the time, see *Report to the Secretary of State for the Colonies by the Parliamentary Delegation to Kenya, 1954*, Cmnd. 9081 (London: HMSO, 1954), appendix 2; and KNA, MAC/KEN 30/5, "Mau Mau Oaths," 28 February 1955.

49. Nelson Macharia Gathigi, interview, Murarandia, Kiharu, Murang'a District, 20 February 1999.

50. Lucy Ngima Mugwe, interview, Ruguru, Mathira, Nyeri District, 10 March 2002.

51. Note that this figure includes the closely related Embu and Meru ethnic groups; oftentimes the British colonial government referred to the Kikuyu, Embu, and Meru as simply the Kikuyu.

52. Patrick Gaitho Kihuria, interview, Ruguru, Mathira, Nyeri District, 24 January 1999.

53. Shadrack Ndibui Kang'ee, interview, Mugoiri, Kahuro, Murang'a District, 17 January 1999; and Samson Karanja, interview, Ngecha, Limuru, Kiambu District, 28 February 1999.

54. Hunja Njuki, Ngorano, Mathira, Nyeri District, 23 January 1999; and Samuel Gathuu Njoroge, interview, Ruguru, Mathira, Nyeri District, 10 February 1999.

55. Susanna Gathoni Kibaara, interview, Ruguru, Mathira, Nyeri District, 22 March 1999; and Gladys Wairimu, interview, Ruguru, Mathira, Nyeri District, 21 March 1999.

56. Esther Wangari, interview, Ngecha, Limuru, Kiambu District, 28 March 1999; and Helen Njari Macharia, interview, Mugoiri, Kahuro, Murang'a District, 16 January 1999.

57. Berman makes a similar point in *Control and Crisis*, 138.

58. Throup, *Economic and Social Origins*, 11–12, 54–56.

Two: Britain's Assault on Mau Mau

1. I am indebted to Sam Waruhiu, son of the late senior chief, who provided me with details of the assassination and subsequent false arrests. Note that his father had been summoned to hear a land case in Gachie by the DC, which was contrary to procedure by that time. Sam Waruhiu, interview, Nairobi, Kenya, 7 September 2004.

2. Charles Douglas-Home, *Evelyn Baring: The Last Proconsul* (London: Collins, 1978), 221–25.

3. David Throup, *Economic and Social Origins of Mau Mau, 1945–53* (London: James Currey, 1988), 54–56; and Douglas-Home, *Evelyn Baring*, 223–24.

4. *Historical Survey of the Origins and Growth of Mau Mau*, Cmnd. 1030 (London: HMSO, 1960), chapter 20.

5. Rhodes House (RH), Mss. Afr. s. 1574, Lord Howick (Sir Evelyn Baring) and Dame Margery Perham, interview, 19 October 1969.

6. Ibid.

7. For a full biographical account on Sir Evelyn Baring, see Douglas-Home, *Evelyn Baring*.

8. The most detailed descriptions of Baring's dietary restrictions were given to me by Terence Gavaghan in various conversations between 1998 and 2000. According to Gavaghan, Baring's stomach was so sensitive that he would pick out the small slivers of orange peel from his marmalade before spreading it on his morning toast.

9. "Mau Mau Shoot Africa's Churchill," *Daily Mail*, 8 October 1952.

10. I heard this song sung several times in the Mathira Division of Nyeri District, in Kahuro in Murang'a, and throughout the Kikuyu Division of Kiambu District.

11. Baring (Howick of Glendale) Papers, University of Durham, GRE/1/19/150–164. This file contains correspondence between Evelyn Baring and Oliver Lyttelton detailing the decision-making processes they went through prior to declaring the State of Emergency. See also the Public Record Office (PRO), CO 822/450, "Correspondence with Sir Evelyn Baring concerning the situation in Kenya." This file includes numerous memoranda between the governor and the Colonial Office reviewing the situation both before and after the declaration.

12. Jomo Kenyatta, *Suffering without Bitterness, The founding of the Kenya Nation* (Nairobi: East African Publishing House, 1968), 340.

13. Mary Nyambura, interview, Banana Hill, Kiambu District, 16 December 1998; Hunja Njuki, interview, Ngorano, Mathira, Nyeri District, 23 January 1999; and Magayu Kiama, interview, Aguthi, North Tetu, Nyeri District, 25 February 1999.

14. For the generalship in the forests, see John Lonsdale, "Authority, Gender and Violence: the war within Mau Mau's fight for land and freedom," in *Mau Mau and Nationhood: Arms, Authority and Narration*, ed. E. S. Atieno Odhiambo and John Lonsdale (Oxford: James Currey, 2003), 46–75; and Caroline Elkins and John Lonsdale, "Memories of Mau Mau in Kenya: Public Crises and Private Shame," in *Memoria e Violenza*, ed. Alessandro Triulzi (Napoli: L'Ancora del Mediterraneo, forthcoming, 2005). For accounts from former forest fighters on their organization, see Karari Njama, *Mau Mau from Within: Autobiography and Analysis of Kenya's Peasant Revolt* (New York: Modern Reader, 1966); Waruhiu Itote, *"Mau Mau" General* (Nairobi: East African Publishing House, 1967); and H. K. Wachanga, *The Swords of Kirinyaga* (Nairobi: East African Literature Bureau, 1975).

15. One woman who participated in the attack on the Meiklejohns described the incident in detail to me, as well as the utter amazement of the attackers that Dr. Meiklejohn, the wife, survived her injuries. Anonymous, interview, Ruguru, Mathira, Nyeri District, 22 March 1999.

16. Jeremy Murray-Brown, *Kenyatta* (London: George Allen and Unwin, 1972), 255–56; Robert B. Edgerton, *Mau Mau: An African Crucible* (London: I. B. Tauris, 1990), 71; and KNA, MAC/KEN 33/6, memorandum, "Shooting of innocent people, confiscation and destruction of property," no date.

17. As cited in Anthony Clayton, *Counter-insurgency in Kenya, 1952–60: A Study of Military Operations against Mau Mau* (Nairobi: Transafrica Publishers, 1976), 51.
18. PRO, CO 822/450/10, letter from Baring to Lyttelton, 24 November 1952.
19. All of Kenyatta's codefendants were members of Kenya African Union's Executive Committee.
20. Douglas-Home, *Evelyn Baring*, 246.
21. For the most authoritative account of the Kapenguria trial and its meanings, see John Lonsdale, "Kenyatta's Trials: Breaking and Making an African Nationalist," in *The Moral World of the Law*, ed. Peter Cross (Cambridge: Cambridge University Press, 2000), 196–239.
22. Douglas-Home, *Evelyn Baring*, 246.
23. Douglas-Home, *Evelyn Baring*, 247–48; and Edgerton, *Mau Mau*, 145.
24. Montagu Slater, *The Trial of Jomo Kenyatta* (London: Mercury Books, 1965), 34.
25. Murray-Brown, *Kenyatta*, 262–63.
26. Ibid., 264.
27. RH, Mss. Brit. Emp. s. 527/528, *End of Empire, Kenya*, vol. 1, Sir Michael Blundell, interview, 55.
28. For example, RH, Mss. Brit. Emp. s. 527/528, *End of Empire, Kenya*, vol. 3, Maurice Randall, interview; Fitz de Souza, interview, Nairobi, Kenya, 11 August 2003; and Edgerton, *Mau Mau*, 148.
29. "A Small-Scale African Hitler," *Daily Telegraph*, 1 November 1952.
30. KNA, DC/NVA 1/1, *Naivasha District Annual Report*, 1953, 1–2.
31. Slater, *Trial of Jomo Kenyatta*, 240–41.
32. Ibid., 242–43.
33. Murray-Brown, *Kenyatta*, 278–80.
34. Granville Roberts, foreword, *The Mau Mau in Kenya* (London: Hutchinson, 1954), 7–9.
35. Ibid. Such adjectives are found throughout official files from the British colonial government in both Kenya and London.
36. Such accounts were most likely to be seen in conservative British papers like the *Daily Mail*, which ran numerous accounts of Mau Mau atrocities. For the most recent study on the British press and Mau Mau, see Joanna Lewis, " 'Daddy Wouldn't Buy Me a Mau Mau': The British Popular Press and the Demoralization of Empire," in *Mau Mau and Nationhood*, ed. Odhiambo and Lonsdale, 227–50.
37. For details on early forms of settler justice, see *Correspondence Relating to the Flogging of Natives by Certain Europeans in Nairobi*, Cmnd. 3256 (London: HMSO, 1907); *Report of the Native Labour Commission, 1912–13* (Nairobi: Government Printer, 1914); Dane Kennedy, *Islands of White: Settler Society and Culture in Kenya and Southern Rhodesia, 1890–1939* (Durham, N.C.: Duke University Press, 1987), 142–44; and David M. Anderson, "Master and Servant in Colonial Kenya, 1895–1939," *Journal of African History* 41, 3 (2000): 459–85.
38. RH, Mss. Brit. Emp. s. 527/528, *End of Empire, Kenya*, vol. 2, Sir Frank Loyd, interview.
39. Sir Frank Loyd, interview, Aldeburgh, England, 13 July 1999.
40. Terence Gavaghan, interview, London, England, 29 July 1998.
41. John Nottingham, interview, Nairobi, Kenya, 29 January 1999.
42. Anthony Sampson, telephone interview, 12 May 2004; and copies of Anthony Sampson's diary extracts (seen courtesy of Sampson).
43. See, for example, PRO, CO 822/489/20, secret memorandum from Frederick Crawford to E. B. David, 16 March 1953; and RH, Mss. Brit. Emp. s. 527/528, *End of Empire, Kenya*, vols. 1 and 2.
44. For accounts of genocidal killings and the dehumanization of targeted ethnic groups, see Frank Chalk and Kurt Jonassohn, *The History and Sociology of Genocide: Analyses and Case Studies* (New Haven: Yale University Press, 1990); and Samantha Power, *"A Problem From Hell": America and the Age of Genocide* (New York: Basic Books, 2002). For the best case of Jewish and Nazi exceptionalism, see Daniel Jonas Goldhagen, *Hitler's Willing Executioners: Ordinary Germans and the Holocaust* (New York: Vintage,

1997), 412, where he argues that "almost all other large-scale mass slaughters occurred in the context of some preexisting realistic conflict (territorial, class, ethnic, or religious)"; whereas, he goes on to state, in the case of the Nazis and the Jewish population, such a preexisting conflict did not exist.

45. For example PRO, CO 822/1337/10, draft memorandum by secretary of state for the colonies, "Colonial Policy Committee, Kenya: Proposed Amnesty," November 1959.

46. For a transcript of the European Elected Members' discussions with Lyttelton, including the quotes from Blundell, Keyser, and Slade, see PRO, CO 822/460/B, "Verbatim Report Meeting of Secretary of State and European Elected Members," 30 October 1952. Note that "White Mau Mau" was another phrase used at the time to describe settler extremists. See, for example, RH, Mss. Afr. s. 1580, Major General Sir Robert Hinde, papers, box 1, file 1, letter from Lieutenant Colonel MacKay to Hinde, 27 September 1953. For reference to extremist opinion gaining control over the local population, see Granville Roberts's comments in PRO, CO 822/459/7, handwritten memo by Granville Roberts, 4 November 1952.

47. Oliver Lyttelton [Lord Chandos], *The Memoirs of Lord Chandos: An Unexpected View from the Summit* (New York: New American Library, 1963), 380.

48. RH, Mss. Afr. s. 1574, Lord Howick (Sir Evelyn Baring) and Dame Margery Perham, interview, 19 November 1969.

49. PRO, CO 822/460/B, "Verbatim Report Meeting between Secretary of State and European Elected Members," 30 October 1952.

50. See, for example, PRO, CO 822/489/20, secret memorandum from Frederick Crawford to E. B. David, 16 March 1953.

51. PRO, CO 822/486/1, letter from Robertson, commander in chief, Middle East Land Forces, to Harding, 12 January 1963.

52. W. Robert Foran, *The Kenya Police, 1887–1960* (London: Robert Hale, 1962), 183.

53. Naftaly Kanino Mang'ara, interview, Kiruara, Gatanga, Murang'a District, 5 August 2003.

54. On 5 October 2003, I conducted interviews in the Kiruara sublocation of Gatanga, Murang'a District, with the following survivors of the Kiruara massacre: Paul Kimani Gatuha, Naftaly Kanino Mang'ara, Njuguna Njoroge, Mary Wangui Mungai, Kinuthia wa Ndirangu, Julia Wachu, Mburu Gichung'wa, and Francis Chege Kabiru.

55. "Police Fire on Crowd: 15 Die," *East African Standard*, 24 November 1952; "Police Stations in Kikuyuland," *East African Standard*, 26 November 1952; and Foran, *The Kenya Police*, 183.

56. Reprinted in Clayton, *Counter-insurgency in Kenya*, 38–39.

57. As quoted in Ibid., fn 21.

58. As quoted in Edgerton, *Mau Mau*, 84.

59. Erskine's famous Churchill letter and the snapping of his glasses case is another well-known story of the Emergency in Kenya. The most interesting rendition told to me was provided by Petal Erskine Allen, a young settler at the time of Mau Mau and niece of General Erskine. Petal Erskine Allen, interview, Nairobi, Kenya, 12 January 1999.

60. There are several books on Mau Mau's guerrilla war and Britain's counterinsurgency campaign in Kenya. Some of the best contributions include Clayton, *Counter-insurgency in Kenya*; Frank Kitson, *Gangs and Counter-Gangs* (London: Barrie and Rockliffe, 1960); Wunyabari O. Maloba, *Mau Mau and Kenya: An Analysis of a Peasant Revolt* (Bloomington: Indiana University Press, 1993), part 2; and Randall Heather, "Intelligence and Counter-insurgency in Kenya, 1952–56" (Ph.D. diss, Cambridge University, 1993).

61. Mwaria Juma, interview, Kiamariga, Mathira, Nyeri District, 10 February 1999; and George Maingi Waweru (General Kamwamba), interview, Muhito, Mukuruweini, Nyeri District, 1 March 1999.

62. "Britain's Klaus Barbie Still Walks Free," *New Statesman*, 29 November 1999. For further details on Henderson and the pseudogangs, see Ian Henderson, *Man Hunt in Kenya* (New York: Doubleday, 1958); Ian Henderson and Philip Goodhart, *The Hunt for Kimathi* (London: Hamish Hamilton, 1958); and Kitson, *Gangs and Counter-Gangs*. Note that Henderson was deported from Kenya by the independent government in

1964 after the protest of several of Kenyatta's cabinet ministers who insisted that the onetime leader of the pseudogangs should not be allowed to remain in the country.

63. I am suggesting that the British colonial government could not assert morally legitimate rule over the entire African population in Kenya, and that any inroads the government may have been able to make in regard to its lack of moral legitimacy came undone with the draconian Emergency Regulations and the subsequent colonial violence perpetrated during Mau Mau. For further discussion of the colonial government's legitimacy, see Berman, *Control and Crisis*; John Lonsdale, "KAU's Cultures: Imaginations of Community and Constructions of Leadership in Kenya after the Second World War," *Journal of African Cultural Studies* 13, 1 (2000): 107–24; and Lonsdale, "Kenyatta's Trials."

64. For details on specific Emergency Regulations, see Colony and Protectorate of Kenya, *Emergency Regulations made under the Emergency Powers Order in Council, 1939* (Nairobi: Government Printer, 1954). The *Kenya Official Gazette* also published the Emergency Regulations and the amendments as they were enacted by Governor Baring.

65. For a convincing argument about the efforts of Ernest Vasey to keep Kenya financially solvent during the Emergency, see Robert L. Tignor, *Capitalism and Nationalism at the End of Empire: State and Business in Decolonizing Egypt, Nigeria, and Kenya, 1945–1963* (Princeton: Princeton University Press, 1998).

66. The initial power to move individual Kikuyu was granted under the original Emergency Regulation 2, 1952. Three subsequent regulations were enacted in 1953 providing the necessary powers to remove and transit any Kikuyu from one area to another, regardless of circumstances. These regulations were: Emergency (Movement of Kikuyu) Regulations, 1953; Emergency (Amendment No. 4) Regulations, 1953; Emergency (Control of Kikuyu Labour) Regulations, 1953.

67. Ndiritu Kibira, interview, Kirimukuyu, Mathira, Nyeri District, 9 February 1999.

68. Ibid.

69. KNA, MAA 7/786/10/1, memorandum from O. E. B. Hughes to Desmond O'Hagan, "Action Against Mau Mau in Nairobi," 8 April 1953; KNA, DC/MSA 1/6, *Mombasa District Annual Report, 1953*, 1–2 and 12–13; KNA, OP/EST 1/361, "Repatriation of Kikuyu from Tanganyika"; and PRO, CO 822/502/14, memorandum from Governor Twining, "An Appreciation of the Kikuyu Situation in the Northern Province on 27 October 1952," 30 October 1952.

70. The phrase "the trickle became a stream" was used often by Legislative Council members during debates over the movement of Kikuyu, and indicated the shift in the volume of Kikuyu repatriates from the Rift Valley to the Kikuyu reserves that occurred between late 1952 and January 1953. See *Kenya Legislative Council Debates*, vol. 54, 19 February 1953, 128–85; and *Kenya Legislative Council Debates*, vol. 55, 7 May 1953, 74–117.

71. John Nottingham, interview, Nairobi, Kenya, 7 August 2003.

72. KNA, MAA 8/163, "Advisory Committee on Kikuyu Movement." This file contains the minutes from the Advisory Committee that met four times to attempt to coordinate the Kikuyu forced removals. The minutes provide details on the movements, the opening of the transit camps, and commentary on the volume of deportations.

73. KNA, AH 9/31/40 and KNA, JZ 8/8/108, memorandum from K. M. Cowley, "Repatriation of Kikuyu, Embu and Meru who have not been Detained in Central Province," 10 December 1954; and KNA, AH 9/31/65, memorandum from Wainwright, "Repatriation of Kikuyu by Magistrates," 25 February 1955.

74. KNA, MAA 9/939/10, memorandum from Desmond O'Hagan to chief native commissioner, "Future Administration of the Kikuyu Districts," 31 July 1953.

75. *Kenya Legislative Council Debates*, vol. 55, 7 May 1953, 96.

76. Ibid., 80.

77. Ibid., 108.

78. In the early 1950s, the Churchill government was notably concerned about white minority interests in its East and Central African colonies. There was a determination at this point not to let these colonies go the way of African majority rule; rather the

British government wanted to promote multiracialism and the creation of federations (ultimately rejected for Kenya) to safeguard white interests. There was a uniformity between the Churchill, Eden, and Macmillan governments, at least until 1959–60, that this move toward multiracialism would be very slow and significantly different from the relatively rapid retreat in West Africa. For a comprehensive account of the gradualist approach toward decolonization in Britain's settler colonies in Africa, see Frank Heinlein, *British Government Policy and Decolonisation, 1945–1963—Scrutinising the Official Mind* (London: Frank Cass, 2002), 119–23, 177–78, 189–91, 237–38, 243–63. Also note that while the settlers and the British government had different visions of Kenya in the long term (the former demanding white minority rule in perpetuity, while the latter conceding that some form of multiracialism would be necessary, albeit one that would protect white interests and temper African majority rule), both parties shared a short-term commitment to stamping out Mau Mau in order to make the country governable. Of course, restoring order could have been achieved by granting the Kikuyu more land and socioeconomic opportunities, though the British government believed its own rhetoric about Mau Mau savagery and illegitimacy and would never step back to reevaluate its perception of Mau Mau or its policies, even in the face of rapidly worsening colonial violence.

79. RH, Mss. Afr. s. 596, Electors' Union and the European Elected Members Organisation, papers, box 38(A), East Africa Women's League, newsletter no. 2, February 1953. This sentiment is expressed repeatedly in the writings of Baring, the colonial secretary, and various members of the Administration and settler community. For the creation of a moderate African political class in Britain's own image, see Berman, *Control and Crisis*, 309–14.

THREE: SCREENING

1. D. H. Rawcliffe, *The Struggle for Kenya* (London: Victor Gollancz, 1954), 68.
2. Records of the Anglican Church, Imani House, Nairobi, "Mau Mau" files, box 2, Christian Council of Kenya, "The Forces of Law and Order," c. January 1954.
3. RH, Mss. Afr. s. 917, memoirs of Christopher Todd, 55–56.
4. Ibid., 240–41.
5. Ibid., 263.
6. Anonymous, interview, Naivasha, Kenya, 14 January 1999.
7. Njama Ireri, interview, Ruguru, Mathira, Nyeri District, Kenya, 31 January 1999.
8. RH, Mss. Brit. Emp. s. 527/528, *End of Empire, Kenya*, vol. 2, Kirigumi Kagunda, interview, 52.
9. RH, Mss. Afr. s. 917, memoirs of Christopher Todd, 263.
10. Margery Perham, foreword to Josiah Mwangi Kariuki, *"Mau Mau" Detainee: The Account by a Kenya African of His Experience in Detention Camps, 1953–1960* (London: Oxford University Press, 1963), xii.
11. KNA, MAA 7/206/1, memorandum, "Screening Camps and Centres," c. December 1954; and KNA, MAA 7/206/2, memorandum from E. G. Eggins, "Screening Centres," 15 December 1954. For details on the relationship between the CID and the settlers in screening operations that oscillated between European farms and screening centers like that at Mweiga in Nanyuki, see KNA, DC/NKY 3/15/4, "CID Nyeri—Confession—R. Nelson Ngodit"; and KNA, DC/NKY 3/9/24, "Screened Mweiga"; KNA, DC/NKY 3/15/5, "CID Nyeri—Mweiga S/Camp—Confessions."
12. KNA, DC/NKU 1/6, *Annual Report—Nakuru District, 1953*, 9.
13. Anonymous, interview, Nairobi, Kenya, 12 January 1999.
14. Alan Knight, interview, Nairobi, Kenya, 21 January 1999.
15. Margaret Nyaruai, interview, Ruguru, Mathira, Nyeri District, 21 March 1999.
16. Ibid.
17. Kamau Githiriji, interview, Ruguru, Mathira, Nyeri District, 24 February 1999.
18. Anonymous, interview, Kiambaa, Kiambu District, Kenya, 11 August 2003.

19. Interviews with Hunja Njuki, Ngorano, Mathira, Nyeri District, 23 January 1999; Lucy Ngima Mugwe, Ruguru, Mathira, Nyeri District, 31 January 1999; and Jean Wanjiru Cliffe, Tigoni, Limuru, Kiambu District, 10 August 2003.

20. Douglas Kariuki Njuguna, interview, Mugoiri, Kahuro, Murang'a District, 17 January 1999.

21. RH, Mss. Afr. s. 424, J. A. Rutherford, *History of the Kikuyu Guard*, 169.

22. Ibid.; and RH, Mss. Afr. s. 1579, S. H. Fazan, "A Tribute to the Tribal Police, African Guards and All Loyalists of the Kikuyu, Embu and Meru Tribes Who Resisted the Mau Mau Revolt," 1956.

23. RH, Mss. Afr. s. 424, Rutherford, *History of the Kikuyu Guard*, 178–79.

24. Ibid., 178–79.

25. Ibid., 337.

26. Muthoni Waciuma, interview, Limuru, Kenya, 10 August 2003.

27. The *Times*, 11 March 1954; and PRO, WO 32/15834, "Court of Enquiry into conduct of troops in Kenya during operations against Mau Mau, 1953–1954," closed for sixty years. See also Michael Chege, "Mau Mau Rebellion Fifty Years On," *African Affairs* 103 (2004): 134.

28. Molly Wairimu, interview, Ruguru, Mathira, Nyeri District, 3 October 2002.

29. Joseph Karuanji, interview, Thigio, Ndeiya, Kiambu District, 9 August 2003. A similar account was provided by Rachel Mwihaki Kiruku, interview, Thigio, Ndeiya, Kiambu District, 12 August 2003.

30. Samuel Kamau, interview, Ngorano, Mathira, Nyeri District, 20 March 1999.

31. Muringo Njooro, interview, Kirimukuyu, Mathira, Nyeri District, 23 February 1999.

32. Nesiphorus Muragu Nganga, interview, Mugoiri, Kahuro, Murang'a District, 20 February 1999.

33. Mwaria Juma, interview, Kiamariga, Mathira, Nyeri District, 10 February 1999.

34. Frederick Waweru Kinyanjui, interview, Ruthigiti, Kurai, Kiambu District, 12 August 2003.

35. See the *Kenya Official Gazette* and its supplements for the years 1953 to 1959 for extensive lists of Africans against whom the Kenya government ordered the confiscation of land, livestock, or material property such a bicycles. For example, *Kenya Official Gazette, Supplement No. 4*, 26 January 1954, 29–32, "The Emergency Regulations, 1952—Forfeiture Order," provides an example of a government order that officially supported the district officer of the Muthuaini Itura in the Tetu Location of South Nyeri District to exercise the powers vested in him by Regulation 4A of the Emergency Regulations, 1952. In this case the DO seized several thousand heads of cattle, goats, and sheep.

36. Wachehu Magayu, interview, Aguthi, North Tetu, Nyeri District, 25 February 1999.

37. Magayu Kiama, interview, Aguthi, North Tetu, Nyeri District, 25 February 1999.

38. Ndiritu Goro, interview, Kirimukuyu, Mathira, Nyeri District, 22 February 1999.

39. Sir Frank Loyd, interview, Aldeburgh, England, 13 July 1999.

40. Njuguna Karatu Robinson Mwangi, interview, Kinyona, Mununga, Murang'a District, 6 August 2003.

41. Karuma Karumi, interview, Kinyona, Mununga, Murang'a District, 6 August 2003; and Paul Mwangi Kimanja, interview, Kinyona, Mununga, Murang'a District, 6 August 2003.

42. Mwangi, interview, 6 August 2003.

43. Waciuma, interview, 10 August 2003.

44. Ibid.

45. RH, Mss. Afr. s. 486, Sir Arthur Young, papers, box 5, file 3, Her Majesty's Supreme Court of Kenya, Nyeri, criminal case no. 240 of 1954.

46. Ibid.

47. Ibid., box 5, file 3, memorandum from G. Hill, district officer in charge, Nyeri, 4 December 1954.

48. Ibid.

49. PRO, CO 822/499/7, secret telegram from Governor Twining to W. L. Gorell Barnes, 25 November 1953.

50. PRO, CO 822/697, "Reports on the Kenya Situation by the Secretary to the Emergency Council and Emergency Committee, Nairobi, 1953."

51. For additional accounts of torture against Mau Mau suspects see Anthony Clayton, *Counter-insurgency in Kenya: A Study of Military Operations against Mau Mau* (Nairobi: Transafrica Publishers, 1976), 44–45, where he discusses, among other incidents, two KPR officers "torturing a prisoner over a slow fire," and another "setting a fierce dog on a prisoner." See also Peter Evans, *Law and Disorder or Scenes of Life in Kenya* (London: Secker and Warburg, 1956), chapter 31.

52. Kiama, interview, 25 February 1999.

53. Pascasio Macharia, interview, Mugoiri, Kahuro, Murang'a District, 17 January 1999.

54. Ibid.

55. Anonymous, interview, Naivasha, Kenya, 14 January 1999.

56. "Law and the People," *East African Standard*, 2 December 1953.

57. Records of the Anglican Church, Imani House, Nairobi, "Mau Mau" files, box 2, Christian Council of Kenya, "The Forces of Law and Order," c. January 1954.

58. W. W. Baldwin, *Mau Mau Manhunt: The Adventures of the Only American Who Fought the Terrorists in Kenya* (New York: E. P. Dutton, 1957).

59. RH, Mss. Brit. Emp. s. 527/528, *End of Empire, Kenya,* vol. 2, John Nottingham, interview, 180. For an example of Nottingham's outspokenness during the Emergency, see PRO, CO 822/1911/260, telegram from R. E. Wainwright to F. D. Webber, 14 April 1961.

60. PRO, CO 822/489/1, letter from Inspector H. A. Cross, 1 March 1953.

61. KNA, MAC/KEN 33/6, *The People,* 7 February 1954.

62. Clayton, *Counter-insurgency in Kenya* 45, n. 89.

63. RH, Mss. Brit. Emp. s. 527/528, *End of Empire, Kenya,* vol. 2, John Nottingham, interview, 180.

64. Anonymous, interview, Naivasha, Kenya, 14 January 1999. For a similar account of police brutality involving testicle mutilation, see Robert Edgerton, *Mau Mau: An African Crucible* (London: I. B. Tauris, 1990), 160.

65. RH, Mss. Brit. Emp. s. 527/528, *End of Empire, Kenya,* vol. 2, Rhoderick Macleod, interview, 118

66. Ibid., vol. 1, Fitz de Souza, interview, 131.

67. Cyril Dunn, "Justice in Kenya," *Observer,* 12 December 1954.

68. Richard Meinertzhagen, *Kenya Diary, 1902–1906* (London: Oliver and Boyd, 1957), 51–52.

69. Fitz de Souza, interview, Muthaiga, Kenya, 11 August 2003. For a similar statement by de Souza made in the late 1980s, see RH, Mss. Brit Emp. s. 527/528, *End of Empire, Kenya,* vol. 1, Fitz de Souza, interview, 134.

70. Jan Philipp Reemtsma, "On War Crimes," in *Crimes of War: Guilt and Denial in the Twentieth Century,* ed. Omer Bartov, Atina Grossman, and Mary Nolan (New York: New Press, 2002), 10.

Four: Rehabilitation

1. PRO, CO 822/471/5, "Canon T. F. C. Bewes, African Secretary of the CMS on his special mission to the 'Mau Mau' area of Kenya," 9 February 1953; and PRO, CO 822/471/7, cable from Granville Roberts to Potter, 10 February 1953.

2. PRO, CO 822/471/5, "Canon T. F. C. Bewes, African Secretary of the CMS on his special mission to the 'Mau Mau' area of Kenya," 9 February 1953.

3. PRO, CO 822/471/6, "Private and Confidential" letter from T. F. C. Bewes to Governor Baring, 28 January 1953.

4. Ibid.

5. Ibid.

6. PRO, CO 822/471/7, cable from Granville Roberts to Potter, 10 February 1953.

7. PRO, CO 822/471/12, telegram no. 282 to the secretary of state for the colonies from Governor Baring, 9 March 1953.

8. Ibid.

9. PRO, CO 822/471, "Finding of R. A. Wilkinson, 1st Class Magistrate at Embu who was in charge of enquiring into the death of Elijah Gideon Njeru at Embu on the 29th January, 1953."

10. PRO, CO 822/471/25, Reuters report on the verdict in the Elijah Njeru manslaughter case, 30 September 1953.

11. "African's Death after Beating—Two Europeans Fined," *Times*, 1 October 1953.

12. PRO, CO 822/471/36, letter from Canon T. F. C Bewes to Colonial Secretary Oliver Lyttelton, 22 October 1953.

13. PRO, CO 822/451/53, telegram from Governor Baring to Secretary of State Lyttelton, 15 November 1952.

14. PRO, CO 822/489/40, letter from eighteen detainees at Lamu to Fenner Brockway, c. October 1953.

15. Interviews with Gakaara wa Wanjau, Kirimukuyu, Mathira, Nyeri District, 23 February 1999; Wilson Ruhoni, Kirimukuyu, Mathira, Nyeri District, 1 February 1999; and Muthuita Zakayo, Mugoiri, Kahuro, Murang'a District, 17 January 1999.

16. *European Convention on Human Rights and its Five Protocols*, Articles 5 and 15, signed in Rome on 4 November 1950 and put into force in September 1953.

17. *European Convention on Human Rights and its Five Protocols*, Articles 3 and 15 (for the nonpermissible derogations), signed in Rome on 4 November 1950 and put into force in September 1953.

18. *Fourth Geneva Convention Relative to the Protection of Civilian Persons in Time of War*, Article 3, adopted on 12 August 1949 and put into force 21 October 1950.

19. PRO, CO 822/692/3, letter from Governor Baring to the secretary of state for the colonies, 17 July 1953.

20. Barbara Castle, *Fighting All the Way* (London: Macmillan, 1993), xi.

21. RH, Mss. Brit Emp. s. 527/528, *End of Empire, Kenya*, vol. 1, Barbara Castle, interview, 116.

22. PRO, CO 822/485/2, telegram no. 515 from Governor Baring to the secretary of state for the colonies, 29 April 1953.

23. Fenner Brockway, *African Journeys* (London: Victor Gollancz, 1955), 87–88.

24. PRO, CO 822/489/125, letter from several detainees to officer in charge, Kilimani Police Station, 25 April 1953; PRO, CO 822/485/4, letter from Fenner Brockway to Colonial Secretary Lyttelton, 20 July 1953; PRO, CO 822/485/6, savingram no. 994 from the secretary of state for the colonies to Governor Baring, 21 July 1953; and PRO, CO 822/485/7, savingram no. 1259/53 from Governor Baring to the secretary of state for the colonies, 29 August 1953.

25. For further details on the formation of the Movement for Colonial Freedom, see Stephen Howe, *Anticolonialism in British Politics—the Left and the End of Empire, 1918–1964* (Oxford: Clarendon Press, 1993), 231–67; and Fenner Brockway, *Towards Tomorrow: The Autobiography of Fenner Brockway* (London: Hart-Davis, MacGibbon, 1977), 160–67. See also Partha Sarathi Gupta, *Imperialism and the British Labour Movement, 1914–1964* (New York: Holmes and Meier, 1975), 360–61. Gupta, however, points to the British Guiana crisis as the sole reason for the congress's foundation and neglects to look at the anticolonial issues in Africa that were prompting Brockway and others to form a new organization. See Howe for a more accurate account of the genesis of the congress.

26. The birth of the Fabian Colonial Bureau coincided directly with the passage of the Colonial Development and Welfare Act in 1940. The bureau emerged more as an advisory organization, as opposed to a source for anticolonial criticism. A hallmark of the bureau was a policy of gradualism; this policy drew heavy criticism from indigenous leaders throughout the empire. By 1950 the influence of the bureau was in decline. Many of its members lost their seats in the general election of 1950, and when the Conservatives came to power in 1951 the bureau's ability to work with the Colonial Office came to a near standstill. The bureau did continue to publish its journal,

Empire, which after 1949 was renamed *Venture*. *Venture* provided the left with a twice-monthly source for expressing its opinion on colonial policy throughout the empire; during Mau Mau there were several pieces questioning the conduct of the Emergency, though more often addressing issues of future development and political participation in the colony. In 1958 the bureau changed its name to the Fabian Commonwealth Bureau to reflect the transformation in imperial relations that had taken place since its founding. Finally, in 1963 the bureau merged with the Fabian International Bureau to "avoid overlapping interests." The anticolonial organizations founded after the war were clearly less interested in influencing the nature of development policy and geared more toward criticizing the Conservative government and demanding an end to the colonial anachronism. For complete details on the work of the Fabian Colonial Bureau, see RH, Mss. Brit. Emp. s. 365, Fabian Colonial Bureau, papers. See also David Goldsworthy, *Colonial Issues in British Politics, 1945–1961* (Oxford: Clarendon Press, 1971), 123–44; and Gupta, *Imperialism and the British Labour Movement*, 301–48.

27. The Reverend Guthrie Michael Scott formed the Africa Bureau to pursue a twofold scheme: to raise and disburse funds; and to educate public opinion, to provide a platform for Africans, and to obtain guidance for them through the political and legal complications that they would face in their anticolonial endeavors. The members of the executive and advisory committees were a "who's who" of notables in the anticolonial movement for Africa. They included Dingle Foot; Arthur Creech Jones; David Astor and Colin Legum, the editor and the East African correspondent, respectively, for the *Observer*; Charles W. W. Greenidge, secretary of the Anti-Slavery Society; Rita Hinden, former secretary of the Fabian Colonial Bureau; W. Arthur Lewis; and Margery Perham, fellow of Nuffield College, Oxford. In May 1956 the Africa Bureau organized the first Kenya Conference, which collected a wide range of nearly one hundred organizations interested in the issues and events of the Kenya Emergency, including the Mother's Union, representatives from the Gold Coast Office and the Edinburgh House, Rotary International, and the YMCA. The Africa Bureau continued its operations until the end of the 1970s, though its directive changed from that of a political organization advocating the interests of the Africans to a more charitable one. For further details on the Africa Bureau, see RH, Mss. Afr. s. 1681, Africa Bureau, records.

28. Mbiyu Koinange and Joseph Murumbi, along with several other Kenyan exiles in Britain, formed the Kenya Committee in 1952, shortly before the State of Emergency. In 1953 the committee issued a statement of its aims, which included: "Because we believe that the causes of the present unrest in Kenya lie in the intolerable poverty and land hunger of the vast majority of the African people, and their complete denial of any democratic rights, we aim—1. To put before the British people the true facts concerning the present situation in Kenya. . . . 2. To arouse the British people to their direct responsibility for the conduct of the affairs in Kenya, and to enlist their sympathy and support to ensure that justice is done in Kenya. 3. To win the support of the British people for the just demands of the Africans in Kenya for elementary democratic rights, the right to have their own trade union and political organisations, and against all forms of racial discrimination." See KNA, MAC/KEN 34/1, Kenya Committee, *Kenya Report*, 1953.

29. RH, Mss. Brit. Emp. s. 365, Fabian Colonial Bureau, papers, box 117, file 4, item 13, National Council for Civil Liberties, "Civil Liberties in Kenya," 1953.

30. PRO, CO 822/479/3, Hugh Fraser, MP, "Report of Visit to Kenya," 6 October 1953.

31. For details on the formation of the United Kenya Club as an institution "to change people's attitudes on racial matters," see RH, Mss. Afr. s. 1770, Thomas Askwith, papers, T. G. Askwith, *Memoirs of Kenya, 1936–61*, 1: 25.

32. T. G. Askwith, interview, Cirencester, England, 9 June 1998.

33. T. G. Askwith, interview, Cirencester, England, 8 June 1998.

34. Petal Erskine Allen, interview, Nairobi, Kenya, 12 January 1999. Petal Erskine Allen occupied an interesting position within Kenya's settler community. Her father, Derek Erskine,

was one of the more liberal-minded settlers in the colony, having founded the United Kenya Club with Thomas Askwith and others. Her uncle was General George Erskine, the commander in chief of the British security forces in the colony, and her brother was the notorious Francis Erskine, a member of the Kenya Regiment and participant in the pseudogang operations in the forests.

35. Note that throughout Askwith's writings he stresses that he was particularly drawn to Templer's "repeated insistence that in order to overcome the uprising it [was] necessary to win over the hearts and minds of the people." See RH, Mss. Afr. s. 1770, Thomas Askwith, papers, T. G. Askwith, *Memoirs of Kenya, 1936–61*, 1: 49.

36. KNA, MAA 8/154/2 and KNA, AB 4/133/11, *Detention and Rehabilitation*, a report submitted by T. G. Askwith to Henry Potter, chief secretary, 27 August 1953, 2–3. See also KNA, CS 2/8/211, memorandum from T. G. Askwith to Potter, 28 August 1953.

37. KNA, MAA 8/154/2 and KNA, AB 4/133/11, *Detention and Rehabilitation*, a report submitted by T. G. Askwith to Henry Potter, chief secretary, 27 August 1953, 3.

38. Ibid.

39. PRO, CO 822/479/3, Hugh Fraser, MP, "Report of Visit to Kenya," 6 October 1953.

40. Note that Askwith was also the permanent secretary to the minister of community development, who was Beniah Ohanga. In most of the documentation, however, Askwith is referred to by his title of commissioner.

41. PRO, CO 822/703/14, record of a meeting held on Friday, 2 October 1953, at Government House, 5 October 1953.

42. T. G. Askwith, "Address Given to the African Affairs Sub-Committee of the Electors Union on November 16th, 1953," 1 (seen courtesy of Askwith). The text of this address is also reprinted in Askwith's *From Mau Mau to Harambee* (Cambridge: African Studies Centre, 1995), 100–09.

43. The repatriation of Chinese nationals was policy throughout the Malayan Emergency, and one that facilitated the rehabilitation process. In October 1949, however, Chinese communist armies refused to receive the repatriates. As a result, special detention camps—like those eventually instituted in Kenya—were created for the internment of the hard core. By September 1950, the Chinese government reopened deportation channels and welcomed them. With deportation reinstated, the numbers of special detention camps instituted in Malaya were minimal compared to the numbers eventually established in Kenya. See PRO, CO 1022/132/33, White Paper No. 24 of 1953, Federation of Malaya, "Detention and Deportation during the Emergency in the Federation of Malaya," 14 March 1953; and "Rehabilitation in Singapore," *Times*, 3 March 1953.

44. PRO, CO 822/794, minute from Bruce, 25 November 1955.

45. See PRO, CO 968/510, "Deportation," cabinet paper, 1954.

46. Askwith, "Address Given to the African Affairs Sub-Committee," 1.

47. Note that the Carter Land Commission conducted its hearings from 1932 to 1934, during which time it granted the Kikuyu 30.5 additional square miles of territory for their losses and 350 square miles for future needs. With its ruling, the commission deemed the Kikuyu to have ample territory, a view upheld by the British colonial government throughout the Emergency. See *Report of the Kenya Land Commission*, Cmnd. 4556 (1934), 71–77, 129–44.

48. Askwith, interview, 9 June 1998. For further details on Askwith's view of the Mau Mau oath, see KNA, MAA 8/154/2 and KNA, AB 4/133/11, *Detention and Rehabilitation*, a report submitted by T. G. Askwith to Henry Potter, chief secretary, 27 August 1953, 3; KNA, MAA 8/154/1, Askwith to Potter, 28 August 1953; and KNA, AH 14/26/61, Askwith to Potter, 1 September 1953.

49. Ibid.

50. Michael Blundell, *So Rough a Wind* (London: Weidenfeld and Nicholson, 1964), 171.

51. T. G. Askwith, *The Story of Kenya's Progress* (Nairobi: Eagle Press, 1957), 77.

52. J. C. Carothers, *The Psychology of Mau Mau* (Nairobi: Government Printer, 1954).

53. Askwith, interview, 8 June 1998; also see Leakey's *Defeating Mau Mau* in which he describes the benefits of a "full and free confession followed either by a traditional

cleansing ceremony, or by a genuine return to Christianity." L. S. B. Leakey, *Defeating Mau Mau* (London: Methuen, 1954), 85–86.

54. RH, Mss. Afr. 1770, Thomas Askwith, papers, T. G. Askwith, *Memoirs of Kenya, 1936–61*, 1:55; and PRO, CO 822/794/1, "Rehabilitation," 6 January 1954, 2.

55. Memorandum, "African Vagrancy," 12 January 1950; memorandum, "Some Observations on the Growth of Unrest in Kenya," 24 October 1952; and memorandum, "Remedies for Unrest," 30 October 1952 (seen courtesy of Askwith).

56. PRO, CO 822/576, W. H. Chinn, "Tour of Kenya," 1951, 7.

57. KNA, AB 4/112/5 and PRO, CO 822/655/8, memorandum from T. G. Askwith, "Purpose of the Community Development Organization," 26 February 1953, 19.

58. Askwith, interview, 8 June 1998.

59. PRO, CO 822/794/1, "Rehabilitation," 6 January 1954.

60. T. G. Askwith, personal correspondence with author, 12 August 1998. Note that Askwith expressed the same concept throughout his writings, both in memoranda and correspondence during the late colonial period and in subsequent memoirs.

61. PRO, CO 822/794/1, "Rehabilitation," 6 January 1954, 3.

62. Askwith, interview, 9 June 1998.

63. For example, in his speech to the Legislative Council on the first anniversary of the declaration of the State of Emergency, Baring stressed the government's commitment to the principles of rehabilitation and its importance to reconstructing the socio-economic landscape of the Kikuyu, and of the colony more generally. Moreover, the colonial government's adoption of Askwith's rehabilitation plan—together with its public statements—were certainly indicators of Britain's endorsement of liberal reform as a cornerstone of the counterinsurgency measures. See *Kenya Legislative Council Debates*, vol. 58, 20 October 1953, 2–17.

64. For example, Wunyabari O. Maloba, *Mau Mau and Kenya: An Analysis of a Peasant Revolt* (Bloomington: Indiana University Press, 1993), chapter 7.

65. RH, Mss. Afr. s. 746, Sir Michael Blundell, papers, box 12, file 3, letter from Blundell to Hugh Fraser, MP, 2 May 1953.

66. RH, Mss. Afr. s. 596, EU and EEMO, papers, box 38(A), East African Women's League newsletter no. 2, February 1953. Note that the EU and EEMO commented extensively on this point, stating, for example, that there was "considerable difference of opinion as to the speed of progress and the lines along which it is most desirable." RH, Mss. Afr. s. 596, EU and EEMO, papers, box 41, file 1, Joint EEMO/Electors' Union African Affairs Committee, 5 January 1954.

67. *Kenya Legislative Council Debates*, vol. 57, 8 October 1953, 112–13.

68. RH, Mss. Afr. s. 2154, Elspeth Huxley, papers, box 26, file 3, "The Kenya Scene—I," *Time and Tide*, 28 November 1953, 1539–40.

69. RH, Mss. Afr. s. 486, Sir Arthur Young, papers, box 6, file 6, 1–4, Ronald Sherbrooke-Walker, "Visitor to Mau Mau Kenya," March 1953.

70. John Nottingham, interview, Nairobi, Kenya, 21 January 1999.

71. KNA, VQ 1/32/29, memorandum from F. D. Homan, 31 October 1953, 2.

72. See, for example, KNA, AB 1/91/21, memorandum from A. F. Holford-Walker to T. G. Askwith, 30 December, 1953.

73. In the mid-1950s colonial officials in Kenya and Whitehall spoke of at least another generation, if not more, before any type of self-government would be considered. See, for example, Viscount Boyd, "Opening Address," in *The Transfer of Power: The Colonial Administrator in the Age of Decolonisation*, ed. Anthony Kirk-Greene (Oxford: Committee for African Studies, 1979), 8; and Blundell, *So Rough a Wind*, 261–62.

74. For the most comprehensive analysis of the colonial state's ongoing struggle to maintain its authoritarian position in Kenya, see Bruce Berman, *Control and Crisis in Colonial Kenya: The Dialectic of Domination* (London: James Currey, 1990).

75. See *Kenya Official Gazette, Supplement No. 33*, 5 May 1953, Government Notice No. 727, 399–404; and *Kenya Official Gazette, Supplement No. 36*, 19 May 1953, Government Notice No. 796, 443–44.

76. PRO, CO 822/1273/E/5, *Report of the Committee on Emergency Detention Camps* (Fairn Report), July 1959, 7.

77. *Kenya Official Gazette, Supplement No. 36*, 19 May 1953, Government Notice No. 796, 443–44.

78. For example, Muringo Njooro, interview, Kirimukuyu, Mathira, Nyeri District, 22 February 1999; Marion Wambui Mwai, interview, Ruguru, Mathira, Nyeri District, 21 March 1999; and Josephine Nduta Kariuki, interview, Ngecha, Limuru, Kiambu District, 28 March 1999.

79. Mwai, interviews, 20 and 21 March 1999.

80. RH, Mss. Brit Emp. s. 365, Fabian Colonial Bureau, papers, box 117, file 4, item 10, Fenner Brockway, *Why Mau Mau?—An Analysis and a Remedy*, March 1953, 10.

81. KNA, OP/EST 1/985/25, minute to file, 26 October 1953.

82. PRO, CO 822/498/2, petition signed by Chief Muhoya Kagumba, Chief William Mathangani et al., c. May 1953. For details on demands for the confiscation of Mau Mau land and property, see PRO, CO 822/498/2, petition signed by Senior Chief Njiiri Karanja, Harry Thuku, Meshak M. Kamwaro, Chief Eliud Mugo, Chief Ignatio M. Kariuki et al., c. May 1953.

83. PRO, CO 822/794, minute from Bruce, 25 November 1955.

84. There is extensive archival documentation on the Kenya government's preoccupation with and drafting of post-Emergency legislation. As with its plans for permanent exile, Nairobi was focused on the issue of continuation of arbitrary powers from the very start of the insurgency. The attorney general's office recognized that any ability to derogate international conventions would be lost once the government lifted the Emergency. Kenya's legal counsel—as well as the governor—therefore spent several years negotiating with Whitehall over the nature of the post-Emergency regulations and their scope of control. For details on early negotiation of post-Emergency legislation, see PRO, CO 968/296/6, memorandum from Oliver Lyttelton, "Emergency Powers Order-in-Council, 1939," 2 January 1953; and PRO, CO 968/296/21, letter from J. Whyatt, attorney general, to Roberts-Wray, 11 May 1953. For reference on the negotiations that took place between the Kenya government and the Colonial Office and the Home Office legal counsel, see, for example, PRO, CO 822/1334, "Maintenance of Law and Order in Kenya"; PRO, CO 822/1337, "Maintenance of Law and Order in Kenya, Detained and Restricted Persons (Special Provisions) Legislation"; PRO, CO 822/1420, "The Detention Legislation, Kenya"; and PRO, CO 822/2095, "The Preservation of Public Security 1960 Legislation in Kenya." For the colonial government's justification of the continuation of sweeping, arbitrary powers, see PRO, CO 822/1230/8, telegram from Commonwealth Relations Office to various high commissioners, 6 November 1959; PRO, CO 822/1230/13, statement made by the secretary of state for the colonies, Iain Macleod, to the House of Commons, "Revocation of the Emergency Regulations in Kenya," 10 November 1959; and PRO, CO 822/1230/14, statement made by Patrick Renison to the Kenya Legislative Council, "Revocation of the Emergency Regulations in Kenya," 10 November 1959.

85. RH, Mss. Brit. Emp. s. 365, Fabian Colonial Bureau, papers, box 117, file 4, item 10, Fenner Brockway, *Why Mau Mau?—An Analysis and a Remedy*, March 1953, 14.

FIVE: THE BIRTH OF BRITAIN'S GULAG

1. PRO, WO 236/18, General Sir George Erskine, "The Kenya Emergency," 25 April 1955, 18. For the size and composition of the security forces, see Fred Majdalany, *State of Emergency: The Full Story of the Mau Mau* (Boston: Houghton Mifflin, 1963), 203.

2. T. G. Askwith, interview, Cirencester, England, 9 June 1998; and Peter Evans, *Law and Disorder or Scenes in Life of Kenya* (London: Secker and Warburg, 1956), 270.

3. For a more detailed discussion of Operation Anvil, see Randall Heather, "Intelligence and Counter-insurgency in Kenya, 1952–56" (Ph.D. diss, Cambridge University, 1993); and Anthony Clayton, *Counter-insurgency in Kenya: A Study of Military Operations against Mau Mau* (Nairobi: Transafrica Publishers, 1976), 25–26.

4. Nelson Macharia Gathigi, interview, Murarandia, Kiharu, Murang'a District, 20 February 1999.
5. Ibid.
6. Karue Kibicho, interview, Kirimukuyu, Mathira, Nyeri District, 8 February 1999.
7. Ibid.
8. Examples were provided in interviews with Shadrack Ndibui Kang'ee, Mugoiri, Kahuro, Murang'a District, 17 January 1999; Kahuthu Kamiri, Kirimukuyu, Mathira, Nyeri District, 2 February 1999; Gachomo Gikuya, Murarandia, Kiharu, Murang'a District, 20 February 1999; Mwangi Maithori, Kirimukuyu, Mathira, Nyeri District, 22 February 1999; Nderi Kagombe, Ruguru, Mathira, Nyeri District, 24 February 1999; and Kaharika Gachugi, Ngorano, Mathira, Nyeri District, 21 March 1999.
9. Kariuki Karanja, interview, Ngecha, Limuru, Kiambu District, 27 March 1999.
10. PRO, WO 236/18, General Sir George Erskine, "The Kenya Emergency," 25 April 1955.
11. PRO, CO 822/796 and PRO, WO 276/214, "Outline Plan for Operation ANVIL," 22 February 1954, 6.
12. Ibid., 4.
13. Ibid., 3–4.
14. PRO, CO 822/796/32, telegram from acting governor to secretary of state for the colonies, 9 May 1954.
15. Note that the Kenya Land Commission's recommendations from the 1930s would not be overturned during the course of the Emergency.
16. KNA, VQ 1/32/18, memorandum from R. J. M. Swynnerton, "Agricultural Development: Central Province," c. October 1953. For further details on Swynnerton's project, see R. J. M. Swynnerton, *A Plan to Intensify the Development of African Agriculture in Kenya* (Nairobi: Government Printer, 1954).
17. Swynnerton, *A Plan to Intensify the Development of African Agriculture*, 10.
18. Bruce Berman provides an excellent assessment of the Swynnerton Plan in *Control and Crisis in Colonial Kenya: The Dialectic of Domination* (London: James Currey, 1990), 369–71. M. P. K. Sorrenson also assesses fully the Swynnerton Plan in his book *Land Reform in the Kikuyu Country: A Study in Government Policy* (London: Oxford University Press, 1967). See Sorrenson, page 118, for an example of the creation of landed and landless classes of Kikuyu.
19. Based upon the assumption that the repatriates would have some access to subsistence farming, Johnston projected that twenty-seven months of relief employment would cost a total of £1.2 million, or £15 per head. This did not include estimates for another thirty thousand Kikuyu whom the civilian authorities did not want returned to the reserves. See KNA, VQ 1/32/1, memorandum from Carruthers Johnston, "Employment of Kikuyu Repatriates," with enclosures, "Interim Measures for Employment of Kikuyu," 28 September 1953.
20. KNA, VQ 1/32/23, memorandum from R. J. M. Swynnerton, "Reemployment Schemes for Kikuyu Repatriates," 26 October 1953.
21. KNA, VQ 1/32/4, memorandum from Governor Baring, "Movement of Kikuyu," 28 September 1953; and KNA, VQ 1/32/23, memorandum from R. J. M. Swynnerton, "Reemployment Schemes for Kikuyu Repatriates," 26 October 1953.
22. Such recollections reflected, in part, the Kenya government's Emergency Regulation that provided for the special or punitive taxation of all Kikuyu, with the exception of the loyalists. It could be argued that Nairobi envisaged a type of self-financing relief system whereby it paid the destitute Kikuyu for their labor on local projects but then recouped these monies through ongoing taxation programs. The problem, of course, was that there was not enough initial start-up money to remunerate the laborers in the first place. Instead, they received little if any pay or rations but were still required, somehow, to pay the Emergency tax. Not surprisingly, a host of abuses arose out of this process, particularly with regard to the local loyalists demanding material and sexual favors from the oath-taking women, in return for relief from taxation requirements. Joshuah Murakaru, interview, Kirimukuyu, Mathira, Nyeri District, 22 February 1999;

and Mwaria Juma, interview, Kiamariga, Mathira, Nyeri District, 10 February 1999. For details on the Kenya government's view of the Kikuyu special tax financing the Swynnerton schemes in the Emergency areas, see KNA, VQ 1/32/23, memorandum from Swynnerton, "Reemployment Schemes for Kikuyu Repatriates," 26 October 1953.

23. KNA, AH 9/13/7/1, memorandum from the director of medical services, "Medical Estimates: Works Camps," 11 May 1954.

24. See, for example, PRO, CO 822/703/13, directive from Governor Baring, "African Agricultural Development and Reconstruction," 2 November 1953, where Baring writes, "For operational reasons, it has been found necessary to control the repatriation of further Kikuyu, Embu and Meru of certain classes to their Native Land Unit, since disgruntled repatriates without the means of subsistence form ready recruits for the gangs. . . . It has been decided to employ the persons, and probably also part of the surplus Kikuyu population in Nairobi, on Government projects in organized camps. It is the intention that these projects should as far as possible form part of the programme of African agricultural development and resettlement."

25. PRO, CO 822/728/31, telegram from Lyttelton to Baring, 12 March 1953.

26. *Federation of Malaya Government Gazette, Supplement,* 23 July 1948, no. 13, vol. 1, notification federal no. 2032.

27. PRO, CO 822/728/31, telegram from Lyttelton to Baring, 12 March 1953.

28. PRO, CAB 128/27, 9 (8), "17 February, 1954—Kenya, Detention of Mau Mau Supporters."

29. KNA, AH 9/36/59, minute from Cusack to Tatton-Brown, 20 November 1954.

30. It is difficult to adjust figures on a month-to-month basis prior to the end of 1954 as the Kenya government did not begin publishing monthly figures until December of that year. In this instance, the numbers provided by Nairobi at the time of Askwith's "Rehabilitation" memorandum in early January 1954 are compared with the Kenya government's reported figures to the Colonial Office in the wake of Operation Anvil. See PRO, CO 822/794/1, memorandum from Thomas Askwith, "Rehabilitation," 6 January 1954; and PRO, CO 822/796/36, telegram from R. G. Turnbull to secretary of state for the colonies, 11 May 1954. Included in the post-Anvil detainee figures are all those picked up during the sweep of Nairobi, along with those picked up in the "Pepper-pots," or post-Anvil mopups (see PRO, WO 236/18, General Sir George Erskine, "The Kenya Emergency," 25 April 1955). They also include all of the Kikuyu government employees who were sent directly to Langata from Nairobi (see, for example, PRO, CO 822/796/48, minister of African affairs, "Control of the African Population in Nairobi," 11 August 1954), as well as the numerous female domestic servants who were, because of their close proximity to potential supplies, rounded up and sent to Langata as well. Eventually, over seven thousand of these women would be rounded up and sent either to detention or back to the reserves, despite the fact that they had valid employment contracts. See PRO, WO 236/18, General Sir George Erskine, "The Kenya Emergency," 25 April 1955; PRO, CO 822/796/59, War Council extract of minutes of eighty-seventh meeting, 1 March 1955; and PRO, CO 822/796/61, Nairobi Extra-Provincial District Emergency Committee, "Security of Nairobi—Selective Pick-up of KEM Domestics," 6 April 1955.

31. KNA, VQ 1/32/4, memorandum from Governor Baring, "Movement of Kikuyu," 28 September 1953.

32. These numbers are government figures and are not adjusted for intake and release rates as those that are extant are not reliable enough to make the adjustment.

33. Fitz de Souza, interview, Nairobi, Kenya, 11 August 2003.

34. PRO, WO 428/276/110, memorandum from Lieutenant Colonel Hope, "Mau Mau Convicts," 20 October 1955; and PRO, WO 428/276/111, memorandum from Major General W. R. N. Hinde, "Mau Mau Convicts," 21 October 1955. For a commentary on the numbers of prisoners being "Form C'ed," see the Rehabilitation Advisory Committee, which queried in 1955, "Have *any* Mau Mau convicts been completely released at the end of their sentences?" (emphasis in original). KNA, JZ 2/26/44, "Notes from Rehabilitation Advisory Committee Meeting held on 10 September, 1955."

35. Gathigi, interview, 20 February 1999.
36. Kibicho, interview, 8 February 1999.
37. Ibid.
38. Ibid.
39. Karega Njoroge, interview, Mugoiri, Kahuro, Murang'a District, 16 January 1999.
40. Communal detention without trial—regardless of the State of Emergency—was a violation of the Third Geneva Convention, Article 87. In an attempt to get around this issue, the Colonial Office allowed Baring to issue the Emergency (Control of Nairobi) Regulation, 1954, which permitted him to round up Mau Mau suspects without individual detention orders, though only for the purposes of the operation. In the wake of Anvil, the Colonial Office had no alternative—other than releasing those held under communal orders—but to grant an extension of the Emergency (Control of Nairobi) Regulation, 1954 until such time as individual orders could be drafted for all those in the Pipeline. See PRO, CO 822/796/57, telegram from secretary of state for the colonies to Governor Baring, 19 February 1955; KNA, JZ 8/8/188 and JZ 8/12, memorandum from N. A. Cameron, "Expiry of Anvil Order," 31 May 1955. For an example of detainees yet to be issued individual detention orders over a year and a half after their arrests, see KNA, AB 1/87/12, letter from Martin to Lewis, 9 February 1954. In Manyani Camp, there were still detainees without individual orders two years after Operation Anvil; they were labeled, "U-Anvil Greys." See KNA, ARC MAA 2/5/222II/340, memorandum from Ministry of Defence, "Movement of Detainees," 27 April 1956.
41. PRO, CO 822/794/42, letter from Governor Baring to Lennox-Boyd, 27 September 1955.
42. Anonymous, interview, Kariokor, Nairobi, 14 December 1998. Note that this former detainee consented to my interview on the basis of anonymity, in large part because of his "continued embarrassment" over his experience in Manyani.
43. PRO, WO 276/428, "Minutes of a Meeting at the Secretariat to Consider the Disposal of Certain Kikuyu, Embu, and Meru males arrested during Operation Anvil and Subsequent Operations," 22 May 1954.
44. PRO, CO 822/801, Colonel W. G. S. Foster, director of medical services, "Manyani and Mackinnon Road Camps," 25 May 1954.
45. KNA, AH 9/5/5 minute from Turnbull, "Notes on Public Health and Public Works at Manyani," 15 May 1954.
46. KNA, AH 9/5/16, memorandum from Lewis to minister of defense, "Prisons Department Emergency Expenditure Sanitation Mackinnon Road and Manyani," 21 May 1954.
47. PRO, CO 822/801/2, Press Office, handout no. 568—"Medical Arrangements at Detention Camps," 10 May 1954; and PRO CO 822/801/6, Reuters report, 16 August 1954.
48. PRO, CO 822/801, internal memorandum, "Points made in discussion at Manyani," no date. For an example of a government press release on the typhoid outbreak and sanitary conditions of the camps, see PRO, CO 822/801/17, Granville Roberts, "Typhoid at Manyani," 29 September 1954.
49. PRO, CO 822/801/35, War Council brief, "Numbers of Detainees," 15 October 1954.
50. PRO, CO 822/801/15, letter from Fenner Brockway to Alan Lennox-Boyd, 28 September 1954.
51. PRO, CO 822/801/18, letter from Socialist Medical Association to Lennox-Boyd, 28 September 1954.
52. Winston Churchill speech at the Lord Mayor's Day Luncheon, London, November 10, 1942.
53. Viscount Boyd [Alan Lennox-Boyd], "Opening Address," in *The Transfer of Power: The Colonial Administrator in the Age of Decolonisation*, ed. Anthony Kirk-Greene (Oxford: Committee for African Studies, 1979), 5; see also Frank Heinlein, *British Government Policy and Decolonisation, 1945–1963—Scrutinising the Official Mind* (London: Frank Cass, 2002), passim. Askwith was an exception to this, as were some of his supporters.
54. Kirk-Greene, *The Transfer of Power*, 5, 8; and Michael Blundell, *So Rough a Wind* (London: Weidenfeld and Nicolson, 1964), 261–62.

55. Barbara Castle, *Fighting All the Way* (London: Macmillan, 1993), 262.

56. Philip Murphy, *Alan Lennox-Boyd, a Biography* (London: I. B. Tauris, 1999), 102.

57. *House of Commons Debates* (*HCD*), vol. 531, col. 1192, 20 October 1954.

58. David Githigaita, interview, Kirimukuyu, Mathira, Nyeri District, 1 February 1999.

59. *HCD*, vol. 531, col. 1192, 20 October 1954.

60. Harun Kibe, interview, Murarandia, Kahuro, Murang'a District, 31 January 1999.

61. Phillip Macharia, interview, Kariokor, Nairobi, 25 January 1999.

62. Members of the Working Party included representatives from the Treasury, the Medical Department, the African Land Development Board, the Administration, and the Ministry for Defence.

63. Note that this figure of approximately one thousand new pickups per week is based upon estimates provided by the Kenya government. In August 1954 the Defence Ministry reported that these estimated pickup figures had been recorded for the months of May through July; it projected a continuation of these pickup numbers through mid-November. See KNA, AH 9/32/79, memorandum from the minister of defense for the Resettlement Committee, "Works Projects for Detainees Screened 'Grey,'" 9 August 1954.

64. KNA, VQ 1/49/42, memorandum from district commissioner, Nyeri, to provincial commissioner, Central Province, "Supervision of Works Camps," 26 March 1954.

65. Note that the district commissioner of Fort Hall, J. Pinney, opted to have the works camps in his district right from the start. Though he assumed a great deal of the fiscal and administrative responsibility, he was also able to dictate the nature and pace of the detainee releases and their reabsorption back into his district. He developed what was called the "Fort Hall Pipeline," whereby all "grey" detainees returning to Fort Hall were first sent to Fort Hall Reception Camp, where they would be rescreened and then dispatched to a works camp closer to their home location, where screening teams of loyalists and members of the Administration would presumably be more familiar with their histories, including their past involvement in Mau Mau. In time, the Fort Hall Pipeline would serve as the model for Kiambu and Nyeri districts. See KNA, AH 9/20, "Works Camps–Fort Hall"; KNA, VQ 1/49/14, memorandum from district commissioner, Fort Hall, "Repatriation Policy 1 March, 1954"; and Fort Hall District, *Annual Report, 1958*, 28–31. For reference to the Fort Hall Pipeline providing the later model for Kiambu and Nyeri districts, see, for example, KNA, AH 9/25/21, Lewis, "Proposed Detainees Works Camps at Gitwe in Kiambu District," 19 October 1954. See also Berman, *Control and Crisis*, for an outline of the Administration's increased influence in Kenya's colonial bureaucracy during Mau Mau, of which the works camps in their districts are one example.

66. KNA, AH 9/32/56, minute from E. C. Eggins to minister of defense, 19 July 1954. Robert L. Tignor provides an excellent analysis of Ernest Vasey's successful struggle to keep Kenya fiscally afloat during Mau Mau in his *Capitalism and Nationalism at the End of Empire: State and Business in Decolonizing Egypt, Nigeria, and Kenya, 1945–1963* (Princeton: Princeton University Press, 1998).

67. Ibid.

68. KNA, AH 9/32/88, memorandum, "Emergency Expenditure—Works Camps," 17 August 1954.

69. Anonymous, interview, Murarandia, Kahuro, Murang'a District, 31 January 1999.

70. Kang'ee, interview, 16 January 1999.

71. For example, KNA, AH 9/13/7/1, memorandum from the director of medical services, "Medical Estimates: Works Camps," 11 May 1954.

72. KNA, MAA 7/813/49/3, letter from Wilfred Havelock to Governor Baring, 7 June 1954.

73. KNA, AH 9/13/43, H. Stott, "Report on Health and Hygiene in Emergency Camps," 9 November 1954, 1.

74. KNA, AH 9/19/22, memorandum from H. Stott to Lewis, "Central Province Works Camps," 4 September 1954.

75. KNA, MAA 7/813/39, memorandum from the hydraulic engineer, Public Works

Department, to Johnston, "Emergency Camps—Water Supplies," 28 May 1954; and KNA, AH 9/13/43, H. Stott, "Report on Health and Hygiene in Emergency Camps," 9 November 1954, 5.

76. KNA, JZ 18/7/29, A. L. Brown, officer in charge, Waithaka Works Camp, to commissioner of prisons, *Annual Report, 1955*, 13 January 1956.

77. KNA, MAA 7/813/36/1, memorandum from T. F. Anderson, director of medical services, to the commissioner of prisons, "Pulmonary Tuberculosis in Prison and Detention Camps," 18 May 1954.

78. For details on the repatriation of detainees with infectious diseases or other chronic illness, see KNA, AB 9/4/110, memorandum from the director of medical services, "Disposal of Chronic Sick," 9 June 1955; KNA, AH 9/8/63, J.J. Delmege to the district commissioners of Fort Hall, Kiambu, Meru, and Nyeri, "Chronically Sick Detainees," 9 June 1956; and KNA, OP/EST 1/1391, memorandum from the secretary of defense to the district commissioner, Kipini, 6 March 1956.

79. KNA, AH 9/13/43, H. Stott, "Report on Health and Hygiene in Emergency Camps," 9 November 1954, 33.

80. Pellagra results from niacin deficiency, which is common in grain-dominated diets. Symptoms include diarrhea, inflamed mucous membranes, mental confusion, and delusion. Kwashiorkor results from protein malnutrition. Its most visible symptom is a protracted belly. Skin conditions like dermatitis, changes in pigmentation, and thinning of hair occur frequently. Fatigue and lethargy are also common. Death is often the result if left untreated.

81. Note that the effects of scurvy, and its impact on the spread of infectious diseases, was also a concern of Dr. Stott's. He noted, "It is my opinion that the Vitamin 'C' level of detainees in many Works and Transit camps is likely to be low, and that this is likely to reflect itself in a reduction in the general health level of the inmate of these camps and particularly to an increased susceptibility of the inmates to infection." (KNA, AH 9/27/31, H. Stott, medical adviser, Labor Department, "Scurvey at Yatta Camp," 4 June 1954.) See also KNA, AH 9/10/55/3, John D. Russell, officer in charge, Manda Island Special Detention Camp, "Health-Detainees," 16 September 1955; KNA, AH 9/27/240, memorandum from the secretary of defense, "Camps on the Yatta Furrow," 28 May 1956; and KNA, AH 9/27/252, minute from Cusack to Baring, 11 June 1956.

82. Pascasio Macharia, interview, Mugoiri, Kahuro, Murang'a District, 17 January 1999.

83. Alan Knight, interview, Nairobi, Kenya, 21 January 1999.

84. In numerous interviews former detainees recall hearing the European commandants in charge of their camps saying this to the guards.

85. Eric Kamau, interview, Mugoiri, Kahuro, Murang'a District, 16 January 1999.

86. Wolfgang Sofsky, *The Order of Terror: The Concentration Camp,* translated by William Templer (Princeton: Princeton University Press, 1997), 130.

87. Aleksandr Solzhenitsyn discusses this in *The Gulag Archipelago, 1918–1956,* translated by Thomas P. Whitney and Harry Willetts (New York: HarperCollins, 1985). For a comparative analysis of collaboration within the Soviet gulag, see Anne Applebaum, *Gulag, A History* (New York: Doubleday, 2003), 360–69.

88. PRO, CO 822/970/3, memorandum from Governor Baring to secretary of state for the colonies, "The Development Programme, 1954–57," 5 April 1955.

89. "New Development Plan for Kenya—Keeping Law and Order," *Liverpool Post,* 6 April 1955.

90. KNA, AB 17/7/6, letter from Askwith to the Right Reverend the Lord Bishop of Mombasa, 12 November 1953.

91. *Annual Report of the Ministry of Community Development, 1956,* 2.

92. KNA, AB 4/120/23, Jos Dames, "Report of Rehabilitation Manyani Special Camp," 9 August 1956.

93. For example, Dr. Alfred Becker—one of the more conservative rehabilitation officers—reported from Manda Island Camp, "It is obvious that as we start rehabilitation in earnest we will become increasingly a nuisance to the prison-authorities. . . . I

have come to the conclusion that serious rehabilitation can only be successful if and when the place [i.e., detention camp] is under our department." KNA, AB 1/87/60, memorandum from Becker to the commissioner of community development and rehabilitation, 2 August 1954. Note that the files from the Prisons Department and the Department of Community Development and Rehabilitation are filled with notations outlining the interdepartmental conflicts and rivalries. This also extended to the Administration, which was operating for the Prisons Department by proxy in the district works camps. While not always advocating the same form of "rehabilitation" as other members of the Prisons Department, the Administration jealously guarded its ascendancy in the districts and did not welcome any encroachments made by the rehabilitation and community development officers. See, for example, KNA, JZ 6/26, "Rehabilitation Advisory Committee, 1954–57"; KNA, AB 1/90, "Rehabilitation, Administration, Prisons, Embakasi, 8/6/54–17/1/58"; KNA, AH 9/19/17, memorandum from J. H. Lewis, "Procedure for the General Administration of Works and Transit Camps (Revised)," 6 August 1954; and KNA, JZ 18/7, *Reports Annual—Works Camps, 1955–1956.*

94. KNA, AH 9/17/83, memorandum from T. G. Askwith to W. Magor, 2 May 1956.
95. KNA, AH 9/19/16, minute from Secretary of Defence Magor to Minister of Defence Cusack, 10 August 1954.
96. The most useful sources from the British colonial files in determining the number and names of the camps and prisons in the Pipeline were KNA, JZ 2/16/48, memorandum from commissioner of prisons, "Headquarters and Provincial Organisation," 3 February 1956; KNA, AB 9/5/53, "Note Community Development Conference," 14 January 1957; KNA, JZ 6/26/45, "Minutes of the 17th Meeting of the Rehabilitation Advisory Committee held on Monday, 10th September, 1956"; KNA, AB 2/49/33, memorandum from commissioner of prisons, "List of Prison Establishments," 30 June 1956; and PRO, CO 822/801/75, "Review of Works Camps and Reception Centers," 24 February 1956.
97. Sofsky, *The Order of Terror*, 21. Daniel Jonas Goldhagen makes a similar argument in *Hitler's Willing Executioners: Ordinary Germans and the Holocaust* (New York: Knopf, 1997), part 4.

Six: The World behind the Wire

1. Nderi Kagombe, interview, Ruguru, Mathira, Nyeri District, 24 February 1999.
2. Numerous detainees discussed Wagithundia during their oral testimonies. The most detailed descriptions of this camp guard came from interviews with Pascasio Macharia, Mugoiri, Kahuro, Murang'a District, 17 January 1999; Hunja Njuki, Ngorano, Mathira, Nyeri District, 23 January 1999; Paul Mahehu, Kirimukuyu, Mathira, Nyeri District, 23 January 1999; Phillip Macharia, Kariokor, Nairobi, 25 January 1999; Wilson Ruhoni, Kirimukuyu, Mathira, Nyeri District, 1 February 1999; David Githigaita, Kirimukuyu, Mathira, Nyeri District, 1 February 1999; Nelson Macharia Gathigi, Murarandia, Kiharu Murang'a District, 20 February 1999; Kagombe, 24 February 1999; and Muraya Mutahi, Aguthi, North Tetu, Nyeri District, 25 February 1999.
3. Kagombe, interview, 24 February 1999.
4. Mahehu, interview, 23 January 1999.
5. Njuki, interview, 23 January 1999.
6. Kagombe, interview, 24 February 1999.
7. Mutahi, interview, 25 February 1999.
8. Kagombe, interview, 24 February 1999.
9. The ritual indoctrination of the detainees into the Pipeline is reminiscent of that accompanying the transformation of free men into slaves, rendering them into what Orlando Patterson calls "socially dead beings." See Orlando Patterson, *Slavery and Social Death: A Comparative Study* (Cambridge: Harvard University Press, 1982). This also bears a striking resemblance to the ritual dehumanization and transformation of Jews in the Nazi system. Daniel Jonas Goldhagen presents a similar discussion and elaborates more fully on the idiom of pain as introduced by the Nazis into their system of concentration camps

in *Hitler's Willing Executioners: Ordinary Germans and the Holocaust* (New York: Knopf, 1997), 298–99. How much the camp personnel in Kenya were aware of these historical precedents is a matter for speculation, though variations of these earlier ritual forms of subjugation and transformations into "socially dead beings" were recurring themes in the Pipeline, particularly in the large reception camps like Manyani. So too were the attempts of the Mau Mau detainees to resist or otherwise alter these dehumanization processes. The degree to which the detainees were successful in their efforts to reshape the coding of the intake processes will be discussed throughout this chapter.

10. Macharia, interview, 17 January 1999.
11. Ibid.
12. Mahehu, interview, 23 January 1999.
13. Charles Kariuki, interview, Ngecha, Limuru, Kiambu District, 10 April 1999.
14. Kagombe, interview, 24 February 1999.
15. British colonial health officers commented extensively on the unsanitary conditions of the Manyani Railway Station, where many detainees relieved themselves just before embarking or after their disembarkment from the *gari ya waya*, or detainee train. In one instance the local hygiene officer wrote, "Quantities of human faeces were found to be scattered in open trenches, some distance from latrines; human faeces also found on the ground outside of the latrines." KNA, AH 9/8/19/2, memorandum from A. A. Phillips, hygiene officer, to W. E. Terry, officer in charge, Manyani Camp, "Manyani Railway Station," 16 March 1956. See also KNA, AH 9/8/19/1, memorandum from W. E. Terry to Lewis, "Conditions at Manyani Railway Station," 20 March 1956. For reports on the lack of food and water during the rail transfers, see KNA, AH 9/31/108/1, memorandum from the district commissioner, Nyeri, "Complaints by Detained Transferred from Nyeri to Manyani," 2 November 1955.
16. Kagombe, interview, 24 February 1999. Several other detainees who spent time on Mageta Island also recalled awakening to endless replays of "God Save the Queen." For example, Paul Karanja, interview, Ngecha, Limuru, Kiambu District, 12 April 1999; and Mahehu, interview, 23 January 1999.
17. Josiah Mwangi Kariuki, *"Mau Mau" Detainee: The Account by a Kenya African of His Experiences in Detention Camps, 1953–1960* (Oxford: Oxford University Press, 1963).
18. Ibid., 67.
19. Ibid.
20. Ibid.
21. Ibid.
22. Gakaara wa Wanjau, interview, Karatina, Nyeri District, 23 February 1999.
23. These various "rules to live by" were discussed to varying degrees by nearly all of the former detainees whom I interviewed. In addition, they are mentioned in Kariuki's *"Mau Mau" Detainee*, 111–12; and Karigo Muchai and Daniel Barnett, *The Hardcore: The Story of Karigo Muchai* (Richmond: Liberation Support Movement, 1973), 43–44.
24. Kagombe, interview, 24 February 1999.
25. Eric Kamau Mithiori, interview, Mugoiri, Kahuro, Murang'a District, 16 January 1999; and Kagombe, interview, 24 February 1999.
26. Shadrack Ndibui Kang'ee, interview, Mugoiri, Kahuro, Murang'a District, 17 January 1999; Wanjau, interview, 23 February 1999; Charles Karuihu, interview, Ngecha, Limuru, Kiambu District, 10 April 1999; and Kariuki, *"Mau Mau" Detainee*, 113.
27. Karanja, interview, 12 April 1999.
28. Njari Githui, interview, Kirimukuyu, Mathira, Nyeri District, 22 February 1999. The constant "brainwashing"—as many detainees called it—of the guards by the British officers in charge of the camps was a recurring theme in the oral testimonies, particularly the emphasis on Mau Mau cannibalism. This is also discussed in some of the memoirs. See Gakaara wa Wanjau, *Mau Mau Author in Detention* (Nairobi: Heinemann, 1988), 29–31, with regard to the locals on Lamu; and Kariuki, *"Mau Mau" Detainee*, 62.
29. Gideon Muiyuro Kiamani, interview, Mugoiri, Kiharu, Murang'a District, 21 February 1999.

30. Nearly all of the detainees whom I interviewed discussed the black market, including Stephen Kinyanjui, Kariokor, Nairobi, 16 December 1998; Githui, 22 February 1999; Douglas Kariuki Njuguna, Mugoiri, Kahuro, Murang'a District, 17 January 1999; and Kaharika Gachugi, Ngorano, Mathira, Nyeri District, 21 March 1999.

31. Macharia, interview, 25 January 1999.

32. Wilson Njoroge, interview, Kariokor, Nairobi, 10 December 1998.

33. Detainees provided several descriptions of guards befriending them not necessarily—at least in their opinion—because of the illicit trading but because they sympathized with the detainees' condition in the camps and their struggle against the British colonial government. Gakaara wa Wanjau also discusses this extensively in his *Mau Mau Author in Detention*.

34. Mwaria Juma, interview, Kirimukuyu, Mathira, Nyeri District, 9 February 1999; and Githui, interview, 22 February 1999.

35. Kariuki, *"Mau Mau" Detainee*, 73.

36. Kinyanjui, interview, 16 December 1998.

37. Ibid.

38. Charles Mwai, interview, Ngorano, Mathira, Nyeri District, 21 March 1999.

39. Kariuki, interview, 10 April 1999; and Njoroge, interview, 10 December 1998.

40. Karue Kibicho, interview, Kirimukuyu, Mathira, Nyeri District, 8 February 1999. For the British colonial government's use of the riot or Emergency squads to enforce "strict discipline and control" in the camps and prisons, see, for example, KNA, JZ 4/51, memorandum from J. H. Lewis, "Emergency Squads," 19 February 1955; and KNA, JZ 8/7, memorandum from Lewis, "Draft of Orders to Officers i/c Prison Establishments on the Use of Emergency Squads," 7 January, 1955.

41. Stephen Kinyanjui, interview, Kariokor, Nairobi, 13 January 1999.

42. Paul Karanja, interview, Ngecha, Limuru, Kiambu District, 12 April 1999.

43. Joseph Wahome Gakuru, interview, Ruguru, Mathira, Nyeri District, 22 March 1999.

44. Githui, interview, 22 February 1999.

45. Several detainees discussed the secret circulation of news, including Macharia, interview, 17 January 1999; Harun Kibe, interview, Murarandia, Kiharu, Murang'a District, 30 January 1999; and Lawrence Mbugua Nduni, interview, Riruta Ward, Dagoretti Division, Nairobi, 13 August 2003. See also Kariuki, *"Mau Mau" Detainee*, 74; and for reference to *Kimongo Times*, see KNA, AB 1/94/38, memorandom from G. E. C. Robinson, "Report from the Sakwa/Saiyusi/Mageta and Kisumu Classification and Rehabilitation," 3 July 1956.

46. This phrase was used by Kang'ee, interview, 17 January 1999.

47. For example, Kinyanjui, interview, 16 December 1998; and Mithiori, interview, 16 January 1999.

48. Samuel Gathura, interview, Murarandia, Kiharu, Murang'a District, 20 February 1999.

49. J. M. Kariuki recounts this story in *"Mau Mau" Detainee*, 74. Several detainees who had been at Manyani Camp also recounted it to me, with some variation. They included Njuki, interview, 23 January 1999; and Kariuki Karanja, interview, Ngecha, Limuru, Kiambu District, 27 March 1999.

50. Many ex-detainees discussed their own rehabilitation classes in great detail, including Kariuki, *"Mau Mau" Detainee*, 110–11; Muthuita Zakayo, interview, Mugoiri, Kahuro, Murang'a District, 17 January 1999; Njuki, interview, 23 January 1999; Gathura, interview, 20 February 1999; and Kagombe, interview, 24 February 1999.

51. Zakayo, interview, 17 January 1999; and Gathura, interview, 20 February 1999.

52. Kagombe, interview, 24 February 1999.

53. Magayu Kiama, interview, Aguthi, North Tetu, Nyeri District, 25 February 1999.

54. In their oral interviews several former detainees attested to this. Also, the colonial government estimated in the early days of the Emergency that as many as half of the detainees were practicing Christians. KNA, AB 1/85/30, memorandum from Alan Knight, "Analysis of Religions of Detainees," 30 November 1953.

55. Mathu Mwangi, interview, Mugoiri, Kahuro, Murang'a District, 21 February 1999.

56. Mutahi, interview, 25 February 1999.

57. Mwangi Maithori, interview, Kirimukuyu, Mathira, Nyeri District, 22 February 1999.

58. Munyinyi Githiriga, interview, Murarandia, Kiharu, Murang'a District, 20 February 1999.

59. Matuini's preachings and constant presence in Manyani was discussed by nearly every detainee who recalled passing through the camp. He is also discussed at length in Kariuki, *"Mau Mau" Detainee.*

60. Terence Gavaghan, interview, London, England, 28 July 1998. In his book *Of Lions and Dung Beetles: A "Man in the Middle" of Colonial Administration in Kenya* (Devon: Arthur H. Stockwell, 1999), 236, Gavaghan uses a slightly different phrase to describe the Reverend Kariuki, writing he was "goggled like Mr Toad."

61. Maruga Maithori, interview, Kirimukuyu, Mathira, Nyeri District, 9 February 1999.

62. Joshuah Muvakavu, interview, Kirimukuyu, Mathira, Nyeri District, 22 February 1999.

63. Maithori, interview, 9 February 1999.

64. Detailed memoranda by missionaries are numerous and include KNA, AB 2/41/44, Father J. Scarcella, "Some notes on Screening and Rehabilitation," May 1957; and KNA, AB 4/121, "CCK Reports—Inspection of Camps, 1956–58."

65. Anonymous, interview, Kariokor, Nairobi, 14 December 1998.

66. RH, Mss. Brit. Emp. s. 365, Fabian Colonial Bureau, papers, box 117, file 4, 21–29, letter from anonymous CMS missionary to B. Nicholls, and forwarded to the Fabian Colonial Bureau, 23 November 1953; KNA, MAA 9/930/1, minute from the secretary of African affairs, K. M. Cowley, to E. H. Windley, 8 June 1954; and KNA, MAA 9/930/5, memorandum from Ernest Bastin, general superintendent of the Methodist mission, to E. H. Windley, 20 June 1954. Several detainees discussed Catholic anti–Mau Mau patrols in the reserves, including Kinyanjui, interview, 13 January 1999; and Mwai, interview, 21 March 1999.

67. Gathigi, interview, 20 February 1999.

68. Elijah Ndegwa Gikuya, interview, Murarandia, Kiharu, Murang'a District, 20 February 1999.

69. KNA, AB 1/106/2, memorandum from camp commandant, Tebere Works Camp, "Rehabilitation: Religious Services," 12 March 1954.

70. Kagombe, interview, 24 February 1999.

71. Ibid.

72. Njoroge, interview, 10 December 1998.

73. Mwaria Juma, interview, Kiamariga, Mathira, Nyeri District, 10 February 1999.

74. Gathigi, interview, 20 February 1999.

75. Kagombe, interview, 24 February 1999.

76. Ibid.

77. KNA, JZ 8/8/74, memorandum from officer in charge Molo Camp, "Greys and Whites," 17 August 1954. For the British colonial government's concern and response to the "saturation" of the camps, see, for example, KNA, AH 9/19/12, memorandum from E. C. Eggins, "Works Camps," 4 August 1954; and KNA, AH 9/1/90/1, memorandum from the minister of defense, "Detainees and Detention Camps," 27 November 1954, 7. For British colonial officials commenting on detainees "going sour" and becoming "blacker," see, for example, PRO, CO 822/794, minute from Buist, 16 March 1954; and PRO, WO 276/428/108, memorandum from Hope to Heyman, 8 October 1955.

78. PRO, CO 822/801/55, minute to file from Lennox-Boyd, "Confidential—Kenya," 23 August 1955.

79. Numerous official memoranda illustrate the streamlining of the Pipeline by the end of 1955. They include KNA, AB 2/41/34, memorandum from the secretary of defense to the secretaries of African affairs and treasury, 6 April 1956; KNA, AB 2/44/7, memorandum from Lewis, "Identification of Mau Mau and other convicted Prisoners on Reception into Prison or Approved School, and of Male Persons Detained under the Emergency Regulations on Reception into a Detention Camp"; KNA, AB 18/27/25, memorandum from the secretary of defense, "Movement of Detainees," 6 October 1955; KNA, AB 1/89/8, memorandum from G. Bennet to officer in charge, Nairobi area

rehabilitation, 31 October 1955; and KNA, AH 9/32/184, extract from the Official Committee on Resettlement, 7 December 1954.

80. Kinyanjui, interview, 16 December 1998; Henry Huthu, interview, Waithaka Ward, Dagoretti Division, Nairobi, 12 August 2003; and Michael Matindi Kariabe, interview, Ruthigiti, Karai, Kiambu, 9 August 2003.

81. Kagombe, interview, 24 February 1999. In their oral testimonies several other former Mau Mau adherents shared similar stories of Home Guards coming to the camps and announcing that the wives of the detainees were bearing their children.

82. Gustaw Herling, *A World Apart*, translated by Andrzej Ciozkosz (New York: Arbor House, 1986), 131

83. Macharia, interview, 25 January 1999.

84. Ibid. For a similar account of bucket fatigue and human waste, see RH, Mss. Brit. Emp. s. 527/528, *End of Empire, Kenya*, vol. 3, Sam Thebere, interview, 176.

85. Gathigi, interview, 20 February 1999; Mutahi, interview, 25 February 1999; and Mwai, interview, 21 March 1999.

86. Kibe, interview, 30 January 1999; Maithori, interview, 22 February 1999; and Gakuru, interview, 22 March, 1999.

87. As quoted in Anne Applebaum, *Gulag: A History* (New York: Doubleday, 2003), 368.

88. Anonymous, interview, Ngecha, Limuru, Kiambu District, 16 April 1999. In their oral testimonies, other detainees also discussed camp "wives," as they called them. They included Njoroge, interview, 10 December 1998; and Paul Mwangi, interview, Westlands, Nairobi, 7 August 2003.

89. Kinyanjui, interview, 16 December 1998; Njoroge, interview, 10 December 1998; and Mwangi, interview, 7 August 2003.

90. Tzvetan Todorov, *Facing the Extreme: Moral Life in the Concentration Camps*, translated by Arthur Denner and Abigail Pollak (New York: Henry Holt, 1996), 40.

91. Njoroge, interview, 10 December 1998.

92. Macharia, interview, 25 January 1999.

93. Kagombe, interview, 24 February 1999.

94. Anonymous, interview, 20 February 1999.

95. Ibid.

96. PRO, CO 822/794/27, "Progress Report—Rehabilitation," 30 December 1954.

97. KNA, JZ 8/8/102, memorandum from G. E. C. Robertson to Askwith, 6 December 1954.

98. KNA, JZ 8/1, memorandum from G. P. Lloyd for the acting secretary for African affairs to all PCs, Central and Rift Valley provinces, "Releases of Detainees," 24 February 1956.

99. Ibid.

100. KNA, AB 2/41/44, minute to file from Tatton-Brown, 19 July 1956.

101. KNA, JZ 8/12, memorandum from Cameron for Lewis, "Oathing in Camps," 26 September 1955.

102. KNA, OP/EST 1/527/2, memorandum from Askwith to provincial commissioner, Central Province, "Rehabilitation," 10 May 1955. This trend of public hangings in the camps increased over time with the use of informants, according to Askwith. T. G. Askwith, interview, Cirencester, England, 8 June 1998.

103. Githigaita, interview, 1 February 1999.

104. Askwith, interview, 8 June 1998.

105. This term is used throughout British colonial files to describe those detainees who were on the proverbial fence—"wavering" between Mau Mau and cooperation with the British colonial government. See, for example, KNA, MAA 9/930/41, memorandum from the provincial commissioner, Central Province, to the minister of African affairs, 22 February 1955.

106. For example, KNA, JZ 8/1, memorandum from W. E. Knowlden, staff officer, Kiambu Works Camp, "Movement of Warders," 7 July 1955. Numerous documents detail the increase in warder discipline, including KNA, JZ 18/7/39H, officer in charge, Mariira Works Camp, *Annual Report, 1956*; KNA, JZ 18/7/39F, officer in charge, Kamaguta

Works Camp, *Annual Report, 1956;* and KNA, JZ 18/7/39D, officer in charge, Kandara Works Camp, *Annual Report, 1956.*

107. KNA, JZ 4/51, memorandum from J. H. Lewis, "Welfare—Warder Staff and European Officers below the Rank of Assistant Superintendent," 19 February 1955; and KNA, AB 1/90/23, "Re: Exemption Certificates for KEM Special Tax," 1 April 1955.

108. Anonymous, interview, Ngecha, Limuru, Kiambu District, 12 April 1999.

109. Kagombe, interview, 24 February 1999.

110. Gachugi, interview, 21 March 1999.

111. Primo Levi, *If This Is a Man,* translated by Stuart Woolf (New York: Vintage, 1996), 97.

112. Anonymous, interview, Westlands, Nairobi, 8 August 2003.

113. Anonymous, interview, Ngecha, Limuru, Kiambu District, 16 April 1999.

114. KNA, AB 18/27/6, D. J. MacInnes, "Brief on White Detainees Undergoing Rehabilitation at Marigat Camp," February 1955.

115. Mutahi, interview, 25 February 1999.

116. Hunja Njuki, interview, Ngorano, Mathira, Nyeri District, 23 January 1999.

117. KNA, AB 1/90/64, minister of works and minister of commerce and industry, "Embakasi Airport—Progress Report," 18 December 1956; KNA, AB 1/90/65, memorandum from Secretary of Defence Magor, "Supply of Prison Labour for the Embakasi Airport," 27 December 1956; KNA, AB 2/44/23, telegram from W. M. Campbell, acting commissioner of prisons, "Labour: Embakasi Airport and Langata Quarry," 6 August 1955; and KNA, AB 2/44/27, telegram from secretary of defense, "Labour: Embakasi Airport and Langata Quarry," 20 August 1955.

118. Mlango wa Simba's directive is a quote from Kinyanjui, interview, 16 December 1998. The details on Embakasi are drawn from several interviews, including those with Njuki, 23 January 1999; Kinyanjui, 16 December 1998; Patrick Gaitho Kihuria, Ruguru, Mathira, Nyeri District, 24 January 1999; Githigaita, 1 February 1999; and George Maingi Waweru (General Kamwamba), Muhito, Mukurweini, Nyeri District, 25 February and 1 March 1999. Note that threats similar to those made by the officers in charge of Embakasi were made at several detention camps. For instance, in his memoir Karigo Muchai reflected at length on his years in detention and wrote that the "European in charge" of Mackinnon Road welcomed all new detainees by announcing, "This camp is called Kufa na Kupona, which means in English, 'Life and Death.' It is well named. Those who cooperate with the screening team and the rehab officers leave here alive. Those who faile to cooperate usually die at Mackinnon Road." (Muchai and Barnett, *The Hardcore,* 50).

119. Njuki, interview, 23 January 1999.

120. The detainees nicknamed Kwa Futi after the district officer in charge, Keith Foot. For a reference to Kwa Futi, see PRO, CO 822/1272, Jack Report on the Shuter allegations, statement of Aaron Irwin. For sign above Aguthi Camp, see Kenya National Archives, Mau Mau photograph collection; and for Ngenya Camp, Samson Karanja, interview, Ngecha, Limuru, Kiambu District, 28 February 1999; and Gilbert Kamau Muroki, interview, Kihara, Kiambaa, Kiambu District, 11 August 2003.

121. Njuki, interview, 23 January 1999.

122. Ibid.

123. Mahehu, interview, 23 January 1999.

124. Kagombe, interview, 24 February 1999.

Seven: The Hard Core

1. Letter from Kendall Ward, executive officer of the Electors' Union, to chairman, Elected Members' Organisation, 7 August, 1952, reprinted in Anthony Howarth, *Kenyatta: A Photographic Biography* (Nairobi: East African Publishing House, 1967), 86. KNA, AB 1/94/54/1, memorandum from G. E. C. Robertson, "Monthly Report from the Mageta and Saiyusi Classification Centres," 10 September 1956.

2. Anonymous, interview, Naivasha, Kenya, 14 January 1999.

3. Wilson Njoroge, interview, Kariokor, Nairobi, 10 December 1998.

4. PRO, CO 822/797/2, Resettlement Committee, "Resettlement of Kikuyu Embu and Meru," 4 October 1954; and KNA, JZ 8/7/90, "Machinery for Reconstruction," November 1954.

5. PRO, CO 822/1075/14, Kenya Colony and Protectorate, public relations officer, "Governor's Speech at Nyeri," 19 January 1955. Colonial officials made numerous public statements about their plan for the future exile of the Mau Mau hard core. See, for example, PRO, CO 801/822/51, Reuters report, "Exile," July 1955.

6. PRO, CO 822/1334/7, letter from H. Steel to F. A. Vallat, 24 April 1957.

7. PRO, CO 822/1334, minute to file from Gorell Barnes, 26 May 1959.

8. Charles Karumi, interview, Westlands, Nairobi, 9 August 2003. Defence Minister Jake Cusack ordered the first movement of detainees out of Manyani to begin constructing Hola in October 1955. PRO, CO 822/801/59A, *Detention Camps—Progress Report No. 21*, 13 October 1955.

9. The reference to the hard core, especially the politicals, posing a future "public danger" to Kenya is discussed in numerous memoranda and minutes in PRO, CO 822/1334, "Maintenance of Law and Order in Kenya." The most comprehensive account of the creation of the Galole Irrigation Scheme, otherwise known as Hola, is contained in *African Land Development in Kenya* (Nairobi: English Press, 1962), 216–17.

10. Many detainees recalled such discussions, the content of which was forwarded to the Colonial Office through petitions smuggled out of the camps. See, for example, that written by James Koinange from Manda Island Camp in PRO, CO 822/1234/76/1, C. M. Johnston, memorandum on James Koinange, with attached petition from Koinange, 12 November 1958.

11. Eric Kamau Mithiori, interview, Mugoiri, Kahuro, Murang'a District, 16 January 1999.

12. As quoted in Bildad Kaggia, *Roots of Freedom, 1921–1963: The Autobiography of Bildad Kaggia* (Nairobi: East African Publishing House, 1975), 134.

13. Jomo Kenyatta, *Suffering without Bitterness: The Founding of the Kenya Nation* (Nairobi: East African Publishing House, 1968), 67.

14. Kaggia, *Roots of Freedom,* 139.

15. Bildad Kaggia, interview, Makutano, Kandara, Murang'a District, 24 March 1999.

16. Kenyatta, *Suffering without Bitterness,* 68.

17. Kaggia, *Roots of Freedom,* 145–47.

18. Kaggia, interview, 24 March 1999.

19. T. G. Askwith, interview, Cirencester, England, 9 June 1998.

20. Njoroge, interview, 10 December 1998.

21. KNA, AB 1/85/1, memorandum from Howard Church, September 1953.

22. PRO, CO 822/794/39, "Resettlement Committee—Future of Athi River Detention Camp," 19 July 1955.

23. KNA, AH 14/26/1/1, P. S Foss, "Memorandum on a Visit to Kajiado," 18 March 1953.

24. KNA, AB 1/85/4A, memorandum from S. H. La Fontaine, "Establishment Athi River Internment Camp," 8 September 1953.

25. KNA, AH 14/26/24, memorandum from Lewis, "Supplementary Provision 1953—Rehabilitation of Internees," 29 June 1953; KNA, AH 14/26/36, memorandum from Lewis, "Athi River Internment Camp," 8 July 1953; KNA, AB 4/18/1, *Annual Report, Athi River Detention Camp,* 23 March 1954; PRO, CO 822/1742/1, Kenya Special Branch report—*Moral Re-Armament Movement in Kenya,* 2 March 1957; and "Rehabilitating the Kikuyu, Work of the Athi River Detention Camp," *East Africa and Rhodesia,* 22 April 1954.

26. "What Makes a Man Co-Operate?" *Kenya Weekly News,* 9 July 1954.

27. Letter to editor from Father Colleton, *Kenya Weekly News,* 15 August 1954.

28. Phillip Njoroge Mwangi, interview, Mugoiri, Kahuro, Murang'a District, 30 January 1999.

29. KNA, AH 14/26/36, memorandum from Lewis, "Athi River Internment Camp," 8 July 1953. The fourth category was "D-Women." Until Kamiti Camp was opened in the spring of 1954, most female detainees were held in compound 1 at Athi River.

30. KNA, AH 14/26/1/1, P. S Foss, "Memorandum on a Visit to Kajiado," 18 March 1953.

31. Alan Knight, interview, Nairobi, Kenya, 21 January 1999.
32. This is certainly not the only instance historically when liberation theology embraced the story of the Israelites. See Gustavo Gutierrez, *A Theology of Liberation: History, Politics and Salvation* (New York: Orbis Books, 1973); and Kofi Appiah-Kubi and Sergio Torres, eds., *African Theology en Route* (New York: Orbis Books, 1983).
33. David Githigaita, interview, Kirimukuyu, Mathira, Nyeri District, 1 February 1999.
34. KNA, AB 1/94/61/1, G. E. C Robertson, *Report from the Saiyusi/Mageta/Kisumu Classification Centres for the Month of September, 1956*.
35. Letter from James Breckenridge to John Lonsdale, 16 August 2003 (seen courtesy of Lonsdale).
36. Gakaara wa Wanjau, interview, Karatina, Nyeri District, 22 February 1999.
37. Ibid. Gakaara wa Wanjau attributes the participation of some Kamba, like Paul Ngei, and Luo, like Achieng' Oneko, in the predominantly Kikuyu movement of Mau Mau to their days of political indoctrination at Alliance High School. It was there that many future African nationalists studied and exchanged ideas, which they would later disseminate to members of their own ethnic groups.
38. Gakaara wa Wanjau, *Mau Mau Author in Detention* (Nairobi: Heinemann, 1988), x.
39. The first Kikuyu vernacular newspaper, *Muigwithania* (the Reconciler), was started in 1928 by the KCA. Edited by Jomo Kenyatta, it was banned by the colonial government in 1940, though it was clearly the precursor to many of the publications that proliferated after the Second World War. In 1945 Henry Muoria Mwaniki started the weekly *Mumenyereri* (the Guardian), and not long thereafter there emerged the KAU's *Sauti ya Mwafrika* (Voice of Africa), John Cege's *Wiyathi* (Freedom), and *Muthamaki* (the Statesman), among others. It was during this intense period of publication that Gakaara wa Wanjau published his monthly *Waigua Atia* (What's Up?), along with his 1948 political treatise in Kiswahili, *Roho ya Kiume na Bidii kwa Mwafrika* (The Spirit of Manhood and Hard Work for the African).
40. Wanjau, *Mau Mau Author in Detention*, 250.
41. Knight, interview, 21 January 1999.
42. For example, PRO CO 822/1233/96, secret memorandum from J. L. F. Buist to L. F. G. Pritchard, 27 June 1958.
43. "Over My Name, by Trial and Error," *Kenya Comment*, 29 November 1957.
44. KNA, AB 1/87/70, letter from district commissioner, Lamu to Askwith, 7 September 1954; and KNA, AB 1/87/106/1, internal memorandum from Becker, February 1954.
45. Wanjau, *Mau Mau Author in Detention*, 64–65.
46. This account is recorded in ibid., 64–74; it was also recounted to me by Gakaara wa Wanjau during several discussions, including 23 February 1999, in his office in Karatina, Nyeri District.
47. KNA, JZ 7/4/131, Albert Mbogo Njoroge, Gatundu Works Camp, Kiambu, no date.
48. KNA, JZ 7/4/79A and KNA, AH 9/17/172, "The black people of Kenya in Manyani Detention Camps and others who are in Detention Camps as we are," no date.
49. KNA, AH 9/17/169, Muhongo Kimani, Gathere Njehia, Njau Karingu, Gicuna Kuiri, Mburu Kimani, and Kihara Wangaru to governor of Kenya, 31 December 1956.
50. KNA, MAC/KEN 33/10, J. M. Njoroge, K. Kigo, W. Muhoro, M. Kamau, E. Kamau, "Re: Detainees Complaints," 15 February 1958.
51. KNA, JZ 7/4/89A, detainees in nos. 5 and 10 to commissioner of HM prisons, Kenya, 10 January 1957.
52. KNA, AH 9/17/106/1, Mageta Detention Camp "to the Attorney General," 8 July 1956; for the British colonial government's listing of the worst hard-core camps, see KNA, JZ 6/26/50A, "Ministry of Community Development—Community Development Conference," January 1957.
53. KNA, JZ 7/4/96A, Nganga Munyua to the secretary, parliamentary delegation in Kenya, 14 January 1957.
54. Pascasio Macharia, interview, Mugoiri, Kahuro, Murang'a District, 17 January 1999.
55. Josiah Mwangi Kariuki, *"Mau Mau" Detainee: The Account by a Kenya African of His*

Experiences in Detention Camps, 1953–1960 (London: Oxford University Press, 1963), 41, 131; KNA, JZ 9/17/169, Muhongo Kimani, Gathere Njehia, Njau Karingu, Gicuna Kuiri, Mburu Kimau, and Kihara Wangaru to governor of Kenya, 31 December 1956; KNA, JZ 7/4/89A, detainees in nos. 5 and 10 to commissioner of HM prisons, Kenya, 10 January 1957; and KNA, AH 9/17/106/1, Mageta Detention Camp "to the Attorney General," 8 July 1956.

56. Records of the Anglican Church, Imani House, Nairobi, "Mau Mau" files, box 2, Christian Council of Kenya, "The Forces of Law and Order," c. January 1954.

57. KNA, JZ 7/4/24A, letter from LX 52045 John s/o Gitiri "to the Honourable Secretary of the States for the Colonies," 5 September 1954.

58. KNA, JZ 7/4/97, "Black African Detainees in Manyani Camp," no date.

59. KNA, JZ 7/4/131, Albert Mbogo Njoroge, Gatundu Works Camp, Kiambu, no date.

60. Note that camp commandants also wrote of such dietary deprivations and their effects on the detainees' health. See KNA, AH 9/10/55/3, John D. Russell, officer in charge, Manda Island Special Detention Camp, "Health-Detainees," 16 September 1955.

61. KNA, JZ 7/4/97, "Black African Detainees in Manyani Camp," no date.

62. KNA, AH 9/17/49C/2, Athi River detainees to the chief secretary, 9 April, 1955.

63. KNA, JZ 7/4/142, letter from "All Detainees from Aguthi Works Camp" to "Sir" [referenced in KNA, JZ 7/4/142A as Governor Baring], May 1957.

64. KNA, AH 9/17/106/1, Mageta Detention Camp "to the Attorney General," 8 July 1956.

65. Many of the detainee letters address these issues. They include KNA, JZ 7/4/85, "Detainee, S. Yatta Works Camp to Commissioner of Prisons," 2 February 1957.

66. KNA, AH 9/17/106/1, Mageta Detention Camp "to the Attorney General," 8 July 1956.

67. KNA, AH 9/17/49C/2, Athi River detainees to the chief secretary, 9 April 1955.

68. KNA, JZ 7/4/26A, "Your obedient detainees" to "The Chief Secretary of Kenya," 19 October 1954; and KNA, AH 9/17/131/1, letter from Thiba Works Camp, "Complints of Dention," 30 September 1956.

69. KNA, AB 1/83/87, letter from J. Bischoff, community development officer, Mara River, to Askwith, 28 April 1956.

70. KNA, JZ 7/4/24A, letter from LX 52045 John s/o Gitiri "to the Honourable Secretary of the States for the Colonies," 5 September 1954.

71. For "head injuries" reference, see KNA, JZ 7/4/26A, "Your obedient detainees" to "The Chief Secretary of Kenya," 19 October 1954.

72. KNA, JZ 7/4/85, "Detainee, S. Yatta Works Camp to Commissioner of Prisons," 2 February 1957.

73. KNA, AH 9/17/159, memorandum from A. B. Simpson for the secretary of defense to Lewis, "Complaints by Detainees," 11 December 1956.

74. PRO, CO 822/801/88, telegram from deputy governor to secretary of state for the colonies, 26 June 1956.

75. KNA, JZ 8/1, memorandum from district officer, Kikuyu District, to district commissioner, Kiambu, 2 February 1956.

76. Anonymous, interview, Kariokor, Nairobi, 14 December 1998.

77. KNA, MAC/KEN 33/10, letter from J. M. Njoroge, S. A. Kamau, W. Muhoro, G. Githiri, G. N. Kamani, and K. Kigo to Barbara Castle, 8 March 1958.

78. RH, Mss. Brit. Emp. s. 527/528, *End of Empire, Kenya*, vol. 1, Barbara Castle, interview, 115. For reference to the volume of letters received by Fenner Brockway from detainees, see PRO, CO 822/489/104, letter from Brockway to Lyttelton, 30 April 1953.

79. KNA, JZ 7/4/120, H. Durant, officer in charge, Nyeri camps, to Lewis, "Detained Persons—Anonymous Letter dated March 1957—Aguthi Works Camp," 18 April 1957.

80. PRO, CO 822/489/42, "Atrocities," c. July 1953.

81. "New Regulation for Detention Camps," *East African Standard*, 26 January 1954; and KNA, AH 9/5/3, minute to file from Lewis to minister of defense, 14 May 1954.

82. PRO, CO 822/1789/26, "Record of Meeting with the 1959 CPA Delegation to Kenya and secretary of state for the colonies," 21 April 1959.

83. Kamau Mwangi, interview, Kariokor, Nairobi, 15 December 1998.

84. Kariuki, *"Mau Mau" Detainee*, 76–78.
85. KNA, AH 9/17/173/1, "Mwangi Makeri and Muriu Ngoroge and the rest [of the] detainees" to "Members of Kenya Ligislative Council," 1 January 1957; and KNA, JZ 7/4/144B, "all detainees" stamped received by commissioner of prisons, March 1957.
86. KNA, JZ 7/4/97, "Black African Detainees in Manyani Camp," no date. Note that other detainees make similar queries about Governor Baring and the purpose of his inspections. For example, KNA, JZ 7/4/79A and KNA, AH 9/17/172, "The black people of Kenya in Manyani Detention Camps and others who are in Detention Camps as we are," no date; and KNA, JZ 7/4/24A, letter from LX 52045 John s/o Gitiri "to the Honourable Secretary of the States for the Colonies," 5 September 1954.
87. T. G. Askwith, interview, Cirencester, England, 8 June 1998
88. KNA, JZ 7/4/73B, copy of letter to the Right Honorable Sir Thomas Dugdale, MP, from the secretary of state for the colonies, 7 December 1956; and KNA, JZ 6/26/50A, "Ministry of Community Development—Community Development Conference," January 1957.
89. PRO, CO 822/802/141, telegram from E. W. M. Magor to Buist, 19 December 1956.
90. KNA, AH 9/17/49C/2, Athi River detainees to the chief secretary, 9 April 1955.
91. KNA, JZ 7/4/144B, "all detainees" stamped received by commissioner of prisons, March 1957.
92. PRO, CO 822/1234/9, savingram from governor's deputy to the secretary of state for the colonies, 25 April 1957.
93. PRO, CO 822/1234/51, letter from Governor Baring to W. A. C. Mathieson, 16 August 1958, with enclosure of letter from Baring to the Honorable Sir Ronald Sinclair, chief justice of Kenya, 17 June 1958.
94. Anonymous, telephone interview, 12 March 2004.
95. PRO, CO 822/1234, "Advisory Committee set up to deal with appeals submitted by persons detained under Emergency Regulations in Kenya."
96. Askwith, interview, 8 June 1998.
97. Helen Njari Macharia interview, Mugoiri, Kahuro, Murang'a District, 16 January 1999; Shifra Wametumi, interview, Mugoiri, Kahuro, Murang'a District, 30 January 1999; and Susanna Wanjiku, interview, Ngecha, Limuru, Kiambu District, 29 March 1999.
98. Wametumi, interview, 30 January 1999.
99. Ibid.
100. Macharia, interview, 16 January 1999.
101. Many former detainees from Kamiti described such acts of violence and torture in their interviews with me, including Macharia, 16 January 1999; Susanna Wanjuku, Ruguru, Mathira, Nyeri District, 22 March 1999; Maritha Wanjiru Kanja, Ruguru, Mathira, Nyeri District, 22 March 1999; Molly Wairimu, Ruguru, Mathira, Nyeri District, 3 October 2003; Mary Nyambura, Banana Hill, Kiambu District, 16 December 1998; Winnie Njoki Mahinda, Ruguru, Mathira, Nyeri District, 24 January 1999; and Wametumi, 30 January 1999.
102. Wametumi, interview, 30 January 1999.
103. Macharia, interview, 16 January 1999.
104. PRO, CO 822/437, "Intimidation of and Attacks on Government Servants, Crown Witnesses, Women and Children by Mau Mau."
105. PRO, CO 822/794/1, "Rehabilitation," 6 January 1954, 3.
106. KNA, DC/KBU 1/44, *Kiambu District Annual Report*, 1953; and KNA, MAA/ARC 2/3/36, *Central Province Annual Report*, 1953.
107. Lucy Ngima Mugwe, interview, Ruguru, Mathira, Nyeri District, 31 January 1999.
108. KNA, AB/1/92/90, memorandum from Askwith to W. Hale, game warden, Coryndon Museum, 19 October 1955; and KNA, AB 1/92/93, memorandum from W. Hale to Askwith, 21 October 1955, in which the game warden writes that he is sending "Four Lion claws, Two large, Two small. I hope they do the trick."
109. KNA, AB 1/92/92, memorandum from Alison, officer in charge, Kamiti, "Rehabilitation and Screening—Kamiti Prison and Detention Camp—Monthly Report, September, 1955," 19 October 1955; and KNA, AB 1/92/106, memorandum from Paul Gathii,

"Rehabilitation and Screening—Kamiti Prison and Detention Camp—Monthly Report, December 1955," 10 January 1956. Numerous former detainees and convicts from Kamiti Camp also discussed these classifications and animal terms, noting consistently that Warren-Gash was the one who coined terminology in the camp.

110. Wanjiku, interview, 29 March 1999.
111. Mahinda, interview, 24 January 1999.
112. Shifra Wairire Gakaara, interview, Ngorano, Mathira, Nyeri District, 23 January 1999.
113. Wametumi, interview, 30 January 1999.
114. Mahinda, interview, 24 January 1999.
115. Ibid.
116. Ibid.
117. Wanjuku, interview, 22 March 1999.
118. BBC interview, "Kenya: White Terror," Wanyiri Gitatha, Othaya, Nyeri District, 1 October 2002.
119. Nyambura, interview, 16 December 1998. Molly Wairimu also provided vivid recollections of the burial brigade, as did Helen Macharia. Wairimu, interview, 3 October 2002; and Macharia, interview, 16 January 1999.
120. Macharia, interview, 16 January 1999.
121. Gakaara, interview, 23 January 1999; Mahinda, interview, 24 January 1999; Wanjuku, interview, 22 March 1999; Nyambura, interview, 16 December 1998; Wanjiku, interview, 29 March 1999; Kanja, interview, 22 March 1999.
122. Gakaara, interview, 23 January 1999.
123. Mugwe, interview, 31 January 1999.
124. KNA, AB 1/112/8, letter from Fletcher to Sam Morrison, 8 September 1955. For an estimate of 450 children, see also KNA, AB 1/92/106, memorandum from Paul Gathii, "Rehabilitation and Screening—Kamiti Prison and Detention Camp—Monthly Report, December 1955," 10 January 1956.
125. KNA, AB 1/84/3, memorandum from Burke-Collis to Askwith, "Clothing—Children of Detainees," 26 October 1956.
126. Nyambura, interview, 16 December 1998; Mugwe, interview, 31 January 1999; and Liberata Wanjiru, interview, Mugoiri, Kahuro, Murang'a District, 30 January 1999.
127. Gakaara, interview, 23 January 1999.
128. Macharia, interview, 16 January 1999.
129. Mugwe, interview, 31 January 1999
130. KNA, MAC/KEN 33/10, letter written by a woman from the Kamiti prison, no date.
131. "The Mau Mau Women at Kamiti," *Sunday Post*, 1 April 1956.
132. Askwith, interview, 9 June 1998. For Warren-Gash being in charge of rehabilitation activities in Kamiti, see KNA, AB 1/92/86, minute from Askwith to file, 19 November 1955. The two extant files in the Department of Community Development and Rehabilitation's deposit at the Kenya National Archives reference constantly Warren-Gash's control over the screening and rehabilitation in Kamiti, as well as her pervasive influence over the rest of the camp's operations, including the labor schemes and living arrangements. See KNA, AB 1/92, "Kamiti Rehabilitation, 12/5/54–11/7/58"; and KNA, AB 1/112, "Administration Women's Camps Kamiti, 1954–57."
133. KNA, AB 1/92/42, memorandum from S. H. La Fontaine, "Propaganda Literature," 20 November 1954; and KNA, AB 1/112/37, memorandum from Gathii to Askwith, "Re—Monthly Report—June, 1955," 27 June 1955.
134. KNA, AB 1/92/120, *Monthly Report, Kamiti Camp, March 1956*; and Nyambura, interview, 16 December 1998.
135. KNA, AB 1/92/140, memorandum from Warren-Gash, "Monthly Report for March 1957."
136. Nyambura, interview, 16 December 1998.
137. Macharia, interview, 16 January 1999.
138. KNA, AB 1/92/56, memorandum from Alison, officer in charge, "Singing of Kikuyu Hymns," 17 January 1955.

139. Nyambura, interview, 16 December 1998.
140. KNA, AB 1/112/44, minute from J. B. S. Lockhart, 28 September 1955; and Askwith, interview, 8 June 1998.
141. KNA, AB 1/92/87, memorandum from Bennett to Askwith, "Mau Mau Detainees Cleansing Ceremony," 13 September 1955.

Eight: Domestic Terror

1. Lawrence Langer confronted similar issues when collecting and analyzing testimonies from "former victims," as he calls them, of the Nazi Holocaust. See Lawrence Langer, *Holocaust Testimonies: The Ruins of Memory* (New Haven: Yale University Press, 1991).
2. Muringo Njooro, interview, Kirimukuyu, Mathira, Nyeri District, 23 February 1999.
3. Villagization took place throughout Kiambu, Fort Hall, Nyeri, and Embu districts. The Kenya government did not pursue a widescale policy in Meru District, largely because the district commissioner argued against it. In Meru, because of the sparser population density, the DC believed that it was a security benefit not to concentrate the indigenous population into villages. In total, fifty villages were officially created in Meru. See KNA, OP/EST 1/986/21/1, memorandum from the district commissioner, Meru, "Villagisation," 6 November 1954. Also note that villagization had been introduced as an ad hoc measure in various locations throughout the Kikuyu reserves beginning in March 1953, though it was not until the War Council's decision in June 1954 that it became a full-scale policy. See KNA, AB 2/53/1, "Memorandum on the Aggregation of the Population into Villages in Rural Areas," 12 April 1954; and PRO, CO 822/481/1, Press Office, handout no. 28, 19 March 1953.
4. KNA, VQ 16/103, Central Province, *Annual Report*, 1956.
5. PRO, CO 822/481/2, savingram no. 585 from the secretary of state to Baring, 5 May 1953; KNA, CS 2/8/211, memorandum from Askwith to Potter, 28 August 1953; KNA, MAA 7/788/1/5, memorandum, "Oulong New Village—Taiping," no date; KNA, MAA 7/788/1, memorandum from Askwith, "Resettlement and Rural Development," August 1953.
6. PRO, CO 822/794/8, brief for secretary of state for the colonies, "Rehabilitation Programmes in Kenya," c. July 1954.
7. RH, Mss. Brit. Emp. s. 365, Fabian Colonial Bureau, papers, box 118, file 2B, item 26, Colony and Protectorate of Kenya, Public Relations Office, "Michael Blundell Press Conference," 11 November 1954.
8. KNA, AB 2/13, minute from Askwith to Ohanga, 21 May 1955.
9. KNA, AB 2/5/110, letter from Askwith to the secretary of the Civil Service Commission, "Vacancies from Community Development Officers," 8 July 1955.
10. KNA, AB 2/51/32, memorandum from Askwith to the secretary of local government, health, and housing, "Emergency Work among Women—Central Province," 25 May 1955.
11. KNA, AB 2/72/29, memorandum from Askwith to the secretary of the treasury, "Rehabilitation—Women and Girls," 26 November 1954.
12. KNA, AB 2/12/1, memorandum from B. A. Ohanga, "Development in the Field," 1 September 1954.
13. Sir Frank Loyd, interview, Aldeburgh, England, 13 July 1999.
14. KNA, BZ 16/1/14, memorandum from the district commissioner, Nakuru to Colin Owen, 1 July 1953.
15. Gathoni Mutahi, interview, Kirimukuyu, Mathira, Nyeri District, 22 February 1999.
16. Ruth Wanjugu Ndegwa, interview, Ruguru, Mathira, Nyeri District, 22 March 1999.
17. KNA, AB 8/78/1/1, "Minutes of a Meeting of a Sub-Committee of the Council of Ministers set up to examine the Carothers Report in Accordance with Minute 63 of the Council of Ministers," July 1954. This committee included the ministers of African affairs; local government, health, and housing; community development and rehabilitation; and education, labor, and lands. Michael Blundell, the European minister without portfolio, was also a member of the committee.

18. Beatrice Nduta wa Gatonye, interview, Ruthigiti, Karai, Kiambu District, 9 August 2003.
19. African Affairs Department, *Annual Report, 1954,* 33.
20. Wandia wa Muriithi, interview, Ruguru, Mathira, Nyeri District, 22 March 1999.
21. Ndegwa, interview, 22 March 1999.
22. Njooro, interview, 23 February 1999.
23. Simon Kihara, interview, Ngorano, Mathira, Nyeri District, 20 March 1999.
24. Marion Wambui Mwai, interview, Ruguru, Mathira, Nyeri District, 21 March 1999.
25. Gathoni Mwaria, interview, Ruguru, Mathira, Nyeri District, 24 February 1999.
26. Simon Rutho, interview, Ngorano, Mathira, Nyeri District, 20 March 1999.
27. Ibid.; also John Mariga, interview, Kihara, Kiambaa, Kiambu District, 11 August 2003.
28. These quotes are from anonymous interviews conducted with loyalists in Kihara, Kiambaa, Kiambu District, 14 August 2003.
29. Wachehu Magayu, interview, Aguthi, North Tetu, Nyeri District, 25 February 1999.
30. Shelmith Njeri, interview, Ruguru, Mathira, Nyeri District, 4 October 2002.
31. Milka Wangui Muriuki, interview, Ruguru, Mathira, Nyeri District, 22 March 1999; Njeri, interview, 4 October 2002; Margaret Nyaruai, interview, Ruguru, Mathira, Nyeri District, 21 March 1999; Mary Waruguru wa Kuria, interview, Thigio, Ndeiya, Kiambu District, 13 August 2003; Rachel Mwihaki Kiruku, interview, Thigio, Ndeiya, Kiambu District, 13 August 2003; Hannah Njoki Kinuthia, interview, Waithaka, Dagoretti, Kiambu District, 12 August 2003; and Wambui Ndegwa, interview, Murarandia, Kiharu, Murang'a District, 21 February 1999.
32. Susanna Wanjuku, interview, Ruguru, Mathira, Nyeri District, 22 March 1999.
33. Muriuki, interview, 22 March 1999; I also interviewed Muriuki on 4 October 2002 when she recalled the same story nearly verbatim.
34. Muriuki, interview, 4 October 2002.
35. Nyaruai, interview, 21 March 1999.
36. Muriuki, interview, 4 October 2002.
37. Njeri Wamai, interview, Ruguru, Mathira, Nyeri District, 22 March 1999.
38. Nyaruai, interview, 21 March 1999.
39. Gladys Wairimu, interview, Ruguru, Mathira, Nyeri District, 21 March 1999; and Maritha Wanjiru Kanja, interview, Ruguru, Mathira, Nyeri District, 22 March 1999.
40. Some counteroathing ceremonies did involve physical brutality. For instance, one ceremony involved the detainees repeating a counteroath in which they pledged, among other things, never to say "the lands in Kenya do not belong to Europeans." At the end of the ceremony they were, according to several men who took the counteroath, "branded (with a hot steel) on the shoulder." See KNA, MAC/KEN 33/9, "Maltreatment of Kikuyus in Central and Rift Valley Provinces in Kenya," no date.
41. Njooro, interview, 23 February 1999. Ndegwa, interview, 21 February 1999, told of a similar kind of counteroathing ceremony in Murang'a District.
42. Nyaruai, interview, 21 March 1999.
43. Grace Wangui Kaharika, interview, Ngorano, Mathira, Nyeri District, 21 March 1999.
44. Wamai, interview, 22 March 1999.
45. Muriuki, interview, 22 March 1999.
46. Ibid.; Njeri, interview, 4 October 2002; Mwaria, interview, 24 February 1999; and Mwai, interview, 21 March 1999.
47. Anonymous, interview, Aguthi, North Tetu, Nyeri District, 25 February 1999.
48. Muriuki, interview, 22 March 1999 and 4 October 2002.
49. Ndegwa, interview, 21 February 1999; similar sentiments were shared with me by women from Kandara (August 2003) and Gacoce (August 2004), as well as from other areas of Murang'a District between 1999 and 2004.
50. Njuhi Gachau, interview, Thigio, Ndeiya, Kiambu District, 13 August 2003.
51. Stanley Njogu Wainaina, interview, Ruthigiti, Karia, Kiambu District, 9 August 1999.
52. Rahabu Wairimu Kibunja, interview, Thigio, Kikuyu, Kiambu District, 13 August 2003;

Gatonye, interview, 9 August 2003; and Mary Wambui Wambote, interview, Thigio, Kikuyu, Kiambu District, 13 August 2003.

53. Gatonye, interview, 9 August 2003.

54. Rahab Wakibunja, interview, Thigio, Ndeiya, Kiambu District, 13 August 2003.

55. Esther Kabura Muchiri, interview, Thigio, Ndeiya, Kiambu District, 13 August 2003. Also note that a Bren gun is a kind of gas-operated, air-cooled submachine gun adopted by the British army during World War II.

56. Salome Njoki Maina, interview, Thigio, Ndeiya, Kiambu District, 13 August 2003.

57. Kuria, interview, 13 August 2003.

58. Gachau, interview, 13 August 2003.

59. Ibid.

60. Gatonye, interview, 9 August 2003.

61. Rahab Wambui Mungai, interview, Kerua, Ndeiya, Kiambu District, 13 August 2003.

62. Kiruku, interview, 13 August 2003.

63. Muchiri, interview, 13 August 2003.

64. Gachau, interview, 13 August 2003.

65. Grace Njambi, interview, Thigio, Ndeiya, Kiambu District, 13 August 2003.

66. Hosewell Gichuhi Ng'anga'a, interview, Ruthigiti, Karai, Kiambu District, 9 August 2003.

67. Gatonye, interview, 9 August 2003.

68. Maina, interview, 13 August 2003.

69. Kinuthia, interview, 12 August 2003.

70. Evanson Mungai Kaburugu, interview, Mutuini, Dagoretti, Kiambu District, 12 August 2003.

71. Muriithi, interview, 22 March 1999.

72. KNA, OP/EST 1/627/1, memorandum from A. C. C. Swann to Havelock, "Malnutrition," 7 July 1955.

73. The two primary sources of international aid for the Christian Council of Kenya were the British Council of Churches and Inter-Church Aid. See KNA, AB 4/10, Christian Council of Kenya, *Annual Report, 1955/56,* 9 February 1956.

74. "45 Deaths in Kiambu Village," *East African Standard,* 17 November 1955.

75. There are several examples of the British colonial government's blatant refusal to allocate money for relief programs. For instance, by 1955 the African Land and Development Board (ALDEV) as well as the Resettlement Committee realized there would be no more funds allocated to the relief efforts established during the days of forced repatriation early on in the war. The Swynnerton Plan's £5 million Development Fund, as administered through ALDEV, was the only source for relief works. Despite the estimated need for well over £1 million, the plan provided only £300,000 for fourteen thousand Kikuyu needing relief. This allocation was intended to fund the 1954 to 1956 period. By October of 1954, however, more funding was needed as ALDEV projections indicated that they would deplete all relief monies by early 1955. As it was, only twenty-five thousand Kikuyu were receiving assistance, the remainder denied relief entirely. R. O. Hennings, who was directing the ALDEV programs, appealed to the Treasury, though to no avail. The War Council had directed the finance minister, Ernest Vasey, not to allocate any more funds. In turn, he told Hennings "[to] consider the obtaining of further funds for Kikuyu Relief Works—if they are to continue—from some more appropriate source." KNA, OP/EST 1/190/13, memorandum from G. J. Ellerton to R. O. Hennings, "Swynnerton Plan Estimates 1954–55," 26 October 1954. See also KNA, OP/EST 190/5, memorandum from G. J. Ellerton to K. M. Cowley, "Kikuyu Relief Works—Central Province," 1 October 1954; KNA, OP/EST 190/10, memorandum from Low to Cowley, "Kikuyu Relief Gangs," 18 October 1954; KNA, OP/EST 190/22, memorandum from R. O. Hennings to Baron, "Kikuyu Relief Works," 16 December 1954; and KNA, OP/EST 190/14, "Extract from 3rd Meeting of the Resettlement Committee of 28 October, 1954."

76. The Red Cross workers were divided—two in each Kikuyu district, with the exception of Kiambu and Nairobi, where there were three and one posted, respectively. KNA, AB

2/51/34, memorandum from the secretary of local government, health, and housing to Askwith, "Emergency Work among Women—Central Province," 6 June 1955. The missionaries' perspectives are drawn, in part, from Archdeacon Peter Bostock, interview, Oxford, England, 20 March 1998; and Reverend Alan Page, interview, Bath, England, 14 June 1999.

77. KNA, AB 17/11/46, memorandum from the provincial medical officer, Central Province, to the director of medical services, "Commentary on Work of Red Cross Team in Nyeri," 8 July 1954.

78. KNA, OP/EST 1/190/25, memorandum from the acting secretary of local government, health, and housing to Cowley, "Kikuyu Relief Workers," 23 May 1955. For monthly reports from Red Cross workers throughout Central Province, see KNA, VQ 1/33, "Red Cross Welfare Workers and CD&R, Monthly Reports," 1955.

79. The concept for Maendeleo ya Wanawake was born in the Jeanes School prior to the Emergency, though the villages were purported to be an ideal opportunity to expand the clubs into a larger, self-help network. See KNA, AB 2/13/44A, memorandum from the Community Development Department, "A Guide to all Welfare Workers in Kenya," c. December 1954; and KNA, OP/EST 1/688/5, memorandum from Askwith to the secretary for African affairs, 25 April 1955. See also Audrey Wipper, "The Maendeleo ya Wanawake Movement in the Colonial Period," *Rural Africana* 29 (1975–76): 195–214; Audrey Wipper, "The Maendeleo ya Wanawake Movement: Some Paradoxes and Contradictions," *African Studies Review* 18, no. 3 (1975): 99–120; and Thomas Askwith, *From Mau Mau to Harambee* (Cambridge: African Studies Centre, 1995), 142–46.

80. KNA, OP/EST 1/688/1/2, memorandum from Mrs. Beecher, "Resolution," 4 March 1955.

81. KNA, OP/EST 1/688/3, memorandum from A. C. C. Swann, "Communal Labour," 7 April 1955.

82. KNA, OP/EST 1/688/5, memorandum from Askwith to the secretary of African affairs, 25 April 1955.

83. KNA, JZ 6/26/30, memorandum from Gillian Solly, "Interim Report of the Joint Sub-Committee of the EAWL and the Women's Section, European Union," April 1955; and KNA, JZ 6/26/31, memorandum from Gillian Solly, "Final Report of the Joint Sub-Committee of the EAWL and the Women's Section, European Union," September 1955.

84. See, for example, KNA, OP/EST 1/190/43, memorandum from D. C. Penwill to Frank Loyd, "Famine Relief and Welfare Food Supplies," 18 June 1957; and KNA, OP/EST 1/627/21, memorandum from F. P. B. Derrick to Frank Loyd, "Malnutrition—Kiambu District," 31 December 1959.

85. KNA, OP/EST 1/627/9, memorandum from N. R. E. Fendall to the permanent secretary for the Ministry of African Affairs, "Malnutrition and Starvation," 9 November 1959.

86. Mary Wambui Wambote, interview, Thigio, Ndeiya, Kiambu District, 13 August 2003.

87. Anonymous, interview, 14 June 1999.

88. Kuria, interview, 13 August 2003.

89. KNA, OP/EST 1/986/21/1, memorandum from the district commissioner, Meru, J. A. Cumber, "Villagisation," 6 November 1954.

90. KNA, MAA 7/813/26/4, memorandum from E. H. Risley to C. M. Johnston, quoting the director of medical services, "Screening—Nanyuki," 11 January 1954; and KNA, MAA 7/813/165, memorandum from the director of medical services to the secretary of defense, "Movements of Repatriates and Langata Camp," 10 March 1955.

91. KNA, AH 9/4/110, memorandum from the director of medical services to the medical officers in charge of Manyani and Mackinnon Road camps, "Disposal of Chronic Sick," 9 June 1955. See also KNA, MAA 7/753/18, confidential memorandum from Cusack to Havelock, 27 July 1954, which details the government policy of repatriating those "grey" detainees back to the reserves who were diagnosed with an infectious disease.

92. KNA, OP/EST 1/988/14, minute from Baring to the ministers of African affairs and

local government, health, and housing, 9 August 1956. For details on Baring's tour through the Kikuyu reserves in June 1956, see KNA, OP/EST 1/988, minute from Baring to the ministers of the treasury and local government, health, and housing, June 1956.

93. Nyaruai, interview, 21 March 1999.

94. Wamahiga Wahugo, interview, Chinga, Othaya, Nyeri District, 26 February 1999.

95. Gathoni Mutahi, interview, Kirimukuyu, Mathira, Nyeri District, 22 February 1999; and anonymous, Westlands, Nairobi, 8 August 2003.

96. Mwaria Juma, interview, Kiamariga, Mathira, Nyeri District, 10 February 1999.

97. KNA, AH 9/32/251, memorandum from Cusack to the Resettlement Committee, "Movement of Detainees from Reception Centres to Works Camps," 4 May 1955; and PRO, CO/822/795/86, memorandum from Gorell Barnes, "Factors Affecting the Release of Detainees," June 1956. Note that the total rundown of detainees was offset by an intake figure of approximately seven hundred new detainees per month. This intake number remained constant through 1956.

98. KNA, AH 9/31/40 and KNA, JZ 8/8/108, memorandum from K. M. Cowley, "Repatriation of Kikuyu, Embu and Meru who have not been Detained to the Central Province," 10 December 1954; and KNA, AH/9/31/65, memorandum from Wainwright, "Repatriation of Kikuyu by Magistrates," 25 February 1955.

99. KNA, MAA (ARC) 2/5/222I/151, memorandum from Magor, "Co-ordination of Movement, Kikuyu, Embu and Meru," 15 April 1955.

100. Terence Gavaghan, *Of Lions and Dung Beetles: A "Man in the Middle" of Colonial Administration in Kenya* (Devon: Arthur H. Stockwell, 1999), 212.

101. R. J. M. Swynnerton, *A Plan to Intensify the Development of African Agriculture in Kenya* (Nairobi: Government Printer, 1954). See also M. P. K. Sorrenson, *Land Reform in the Kikuyu Country: A Study in Government Policy* (London: Oxford University Press, 1967), parts 2 and 3.

102. Note that after independence, a government commission investigated the claims of injustice. Though it denied any corruption or exclusionary tactics in the demarcation and consolidation process, it did state, "It should not be thought that enclosure is necessarily of benefit to every member of the community. In practice it is invariably the more influential members of the community who are the first to enclose." *Report of the Commission on Land Consolidation and Registration in Kenya, 1965–66* (Nairobi: Government Printer, 1966), paragraph 67, as quoted in Bruce Berman, *Control and Crisis in Colonial Kenya: The Dialectic of Domination* (London: James Currey, 1990), 368. The report provides full details on the results of land consolidation and attempts to exculpate the loyalist crowd from any wrongdoing during the Emergency and from charges of corruption during the postindependence period.

103. Note that for years the British colonial government had sought to introduce land consolidation but was met with strong resistance from much of the local Kikuyu population—many of whom would later join the Mau Mau movement. The local Administration was very keen to, in the words of J. M. Golds and Frank Loyd, "strike while the iron is hot"—that is, to push land consolidation through while the dissenters were locked away, unable to challenge the so-called land reform. See Sorrenson, *Land Reform*, 115.

104. Sorrenson, *Land Reform*, 232.

105. PRO, CO 822/794/12, Alastair Matheson, "Re-educating Mau Mau Detainees—Progress of Rehabilitation Work in Kenya," 25 October 1954; and PRO, 822/794/37, memorandum from Cusack, "Progress Report on the Rehabilitation of Mau Mau in Detention Camps," 13 April 1955.

106. PRO, CO 822/797/6, minister for forest development, "Scheme for Reabsorption of Kikuyu, Embu, and Meru," 8 December 1954. M. P. K. Sorrenson asserts that the resettlement of Kikuyu in the high bracken areas was also an official part of the government's resettlement program (see Sorrenson, *Land Reform*, 220). Nairobi, however, did not pursue this potential, as Carruthers Johnston, along with others in the Administration,

believed that "the land is already owned and, in many areas, by loyalists. To dispossess the loyalists for the benefit of Mau-Mau sympathisers would be a fatal error." See PRO, CO 822/794/45, memorandum from Carruthers Johnston to the Resettlement Committee, "Absorptive Capacity in Kikuyu Districts," 7 May 1955.

107. PRO, CO 822/797/6, minister for forest development, "Scheme for Reabsorption of Kikuyu, Embu, and Meru," 8 December 1954.

108. PRO, CO 822/797/8, Resettlement Committee, "Long Term Absorption of Displaced Kikuyu—Absorption in Kikuyu Districts," 15 February 1955.

109. The breakdown by district for the surplus population in Kiambu, Fort Hall, and Nyeri:

District	Total	Number of Families
Kiambu	50,000	6,000
Fort Hall	60,000	10,000
Nyeri	40,000	4,000
Total	150,000	20,000

Source: PRO, CO 822/797/8, memorandum from the Resettlement Committee, "Long Term Absorption of Displaced Kikuyu—Absorption in Kikuyu Districts," 15 February 1955.

110. PRO, CO 822/798/34, minutes of the Council of Ministers, Resettlement Committee, seventeenth meeting, 27 April 1956.

111. Stanley Njuguna, interview, Ruthigiti, Karai, Kiambu District, 9 August 2003.

112. Joshuah Murakaru, interview, Kirimukuyu, Mathira, Nyeri District, 22 February 1999.

113. Nyaruai, interview, 21 March 1999.

114. Lucy Ngima, interview, Ruguru, Mathira, Nyeri District, 3 October 2002. I also interviewed Lucy several times in January and February 1999 when she shared similar accounts of half-caste children being born in her location of Nyeri District during the Emergency.

115. Kiruku, interview, 13 August 2003.

116. Several women I spoke to discussed barrenness as a result of sexual violence, as did H. K. Wachanga in his autobiography, *The Swords of Kirinyaga* (Nairobi: East African Literature Bureau, 1975), 163.

117. Karega Njoroge, interview, Mugoiri, Kahuro, Murang'a District, 16 January 1999.

118. Kuria, interview, 13 August 2003.

119. Murakaru, interview, 22 February 1999.

120. Some feminist scholars depict the Kikuyu women from this period as assertive and completely independent of men. Kikuyu women, however, often take a different view—one that is clearly manifested when they discuss their anger with their husbands and fathers for not fulfilling their roles as guardians of the homesteads, or *riigi*. This gendered shame was expressed explicitly by the men themselves, though it can also be found in the silences or absence of women in most of the male-scripted Mau Mau memoirs. That there are few women in these male narratives reveals much about the nature of the war and the gendered shame the authors felt both during the conflict and in its aftermath. I explore the issue of gendered shame more fully with John Lonsdale in "Memories of Mau Mau in Kenya: Public Crises and Private Shame," in *Memoria e Violenza*, ed. Alessandro Triulzi (Naples: L'Ancora del Mediterraneo, forthcoming, 2005). For feminist perspectives on Mau Mau and women's participation, see Kathy Santilli, "Kikuyu Women in the Mau Mau Revolt," *Ufahamu* 8, no. 1 (1977–78): 143–59; Jean O'Barr, "Introductory Essay," in *Passbook Number F.47927* by Muthoni Likimani (London: Macmillan, 1985), 1–37; Tabitha Kanogo, "Kikuyu Women and the Politics of Protest: Mau Mau," in *Images of Women in Peace and War, Cross-Cultural and Historical Perspectives*, ed. Sharon Macdonald et al. (Madison: University of Wisconsin Press, 1988), 78–96; and Cora Ann Presley, *Kikuyu Women, the Mau Mau Rebellion, and Social Change in Kenya* (Boulder: Westview Press, 1992).

121. KNA, AB 2/41/25, speech made by the minister of community development, B. Ohanga, to the Legislative Council on 16 November 1956.

122. KNA, MAC/KEN 31/7, James Maina Wachira (on behalf of the people of Mahiga, Othaya, Nyeri), "Memorandum. Nyeri District. Our Grievances and our Requests to the Kenya Government," 30 October 1959.

123. PRO, CO 822/1421/30, Inward telegram from Pritchard to Buist, 3 April 1957; and memorandum from J. Pinney, district commissioner, Fort Hall, 7 June 1954, to Chief Ignatio Morai in Sorrenson, *Land Reform*, 114.

124. Editorial, *New Statesman and Nation*, 23 March 1957. For further details on the correlation between the increased rate of release, the unemployment and overcrowding crisis in the reserves, and the increase in movement and curfew violations, see "Castle Arrest Debates," in *House of Commons Debates*, March and April 1957.

NINE: OUTRAGE, SUPPRESSION, AND SILENCE

1. "Labour to Fight Kenya Thugs," *Tribune*, 30 September 1955.

2. See, for example, *House of Commons Debates (HCD)*, vol. 508, cols. 1551–53, 3 December 1952; *HCD*, vol. 512, cols. 359–60 and cols. 363–64, 4 March 1953; *HCD*, vol. 514, col. 2121, 29 April 1953; and *HCD*, vol. 528, cols. 193–99, 16 June 1954. For direct inquiries to the Colonial Office regarding the detainees' knowledge of their right to appeal, see PRO, CO 822/451/16, letter from E. M. David to Baring, 13 July 1953; and PRO, CO 822/451/17, letter from Crawford to E. M. David, 28 August 1953. For early inquiries regarding the "starvation" of the repatriates in the reserves, see, for example, PRO, CO 822/476/5, telegram from Baring to secretary of state for the colonies, 16 November 1953. For Labour MPs bringing detainee allegations and requests directly to the floor of the Commons, see, for example, PRO, CO 822/912/18/15, parliamentary questions, 22 February 1956. In this instance, Barbara Castle was raising concerns of several Manyani detainees who had written to her from within the Pipeline. By 1953 the Opposition also became much more detail-oriented in its requests from the Conservative government regarding the camps. For instance, the Labour MPs demanded arrest, screening, detention, and release statistics on a near fortnightly basis; posed questions regarding the nature and duration of labor in the camps and villages; demanded to know the extent and treatment of disease and malnutrition in both the Pipeline and reserves; sought death figures for both the camps and villages; and requested the list of detention camps that offered rehabilitation programs. See, for example, *HCD*, vol. 512, cols. 359–60, 4 March 1953; *HCD*, vol. 514, col. 2121, 29 April 1953; *HCD*, vol. 526, col. 1130, 14 April 1954; *HCD*, vol. 531, cols. 485–88, 28 July 1954, and col. 163, 20 October 1954; *HCD*, vol. 535, col. 139, 15 December 1954; *HCD*, vol. 537, cols. 1272–73, 23 February 1955; *HCD*, vol. 540, cols. 169–71, 20 April 1955; *HCD*, vol. 545, cols. 185–86, 26 October 1955; and *HCD*, vol. 549, col. 374, 22 February 1956.

3. RH, Mss. Brit Emp. s. 527/528, *End of Empire, Kenya*, vol. 1, Barbara Castle, Interview, 116.

4. This delegation, known more widely as the Elliot-Bottomley delegation, visited Kenya from 8 to 26 January 1954. During this time the delegation visited one detention camp, Athi River, and, in fact, spent almost half of its time either in Nairobi or in Mombasa—an area of Kenya almost wholly unaffected by the Emergency. The delegation's itinerary was planned by the British colonial government with the help of the chief public relations officer, Granville Roberts. For further details, see *Report to the Secretary of State for the Colonies by the Parliamentary Delegation to Kenya, 1954*, Cmnd. 9081 (London: HMSO, 1954).

5. RH, Mss. Afr. s. 486, Sir Arthur Young, papers, box 5, file 1, Arthur Young, "Introduction to Sir Arthur Young," no date, 18.

6. Ibid., 14.

7. Ibid., box 5, file 3, 84–89, letter from Arthur Young to Governor Baring, 14 December 1954.

8. PRO, CO 822/1037/7, memorandum from Governor Baring to Gorell Barnes, 6 November 1954.

9. RH, Mss. Afr. s. 486, Sir Arthur Young, papers, box 5, file 1, Arthur Young, "Introduction to Sir Arthur Young," no date, 13.

10. Ibid., box 5, file 6, memorandum from assistant commissioner of police, Nyeri, to Young, 22 November 1954, 1.

11. Peter Evans, *Law and Disorder or Scenes of Life in Kenya* (London: Secker and Warburg, 1956), 275–76.

12. RH, Mss. Afr. s. 486, Sir Arthur Young, papers, box 5, file 1, Arthur Young, "Introduction to Sir Arthur Young," no date, 29–30.

13. PRO, CO 822/1293/1, official statement of Colonel Young's resignation, February 1955; *HCD*, written answers, 2 February 1955, col. 119.

14. RH, Mss. Afr. s. 486, Sir Arthur Young, papers, box 5, file 1, Arthur Young, "Introduction to Sir Arthur Young," no date, 15.

15. PRO, CAB 128/28, CC (55) 3, minute 1, 13 January 1955; and PRO, CAB 128/28, CC (55) 4, 13 January 1955.

16. Kenneth Grubb, president, CMS, H. S. Mance, chairman, Executive Committee, CMS, and H. B. Thomas, chairman, African Committee, CMS, letter to the editor, *Times*, 22 January 1955. Note that Governor Baring's declaration of the 18 January amnesty was also published in the *Times* on 19 January 1955.

17. Church Missionary Society, *Kenya—time for Action*, 28 January 1955.

18. *House of Lords Debates (HLD)*, vol. 190, no. 19, col. 1139, 10 February 1955.

19. Ibid., cols. 1149 and 1157, 10 February 1955.

20. Barbara Castle, *Fighting All the Way* (London: Macmillan, 1993), 263–64.

21. Ibid., 264.

22. Ibid.

23. Ibid., 265.

24. Ibid., 269.

25. RH, Mss. Afr. s. 486, Sir Arthur Young, papers, box 5, file 3, 36–38, top-secret memorandum from Duncan McPherson to Colonel A. Young, 10 December 1954; and RH, Mss. Afr. s. 486, box 5, file 3, 101–07, top-secret memorandum from Duncan McPherson to commissioner of police, 23 December 1954.

26. In at least one instance six pages of detailed incident reports—which provide specific accounts of torture and murder—were sent to Governor Baring by Colonel Young with a cover letter that read: "I [Young] therefore suggest that a copy of this letter, together with a copy of the report attached, be forwarded to the Colonial Secretary in order that these facts, which provide the main reason for my departure from Kenya, should be made known to those who will be concerned in the debate." See RH, Mss. Afr. s. 486, Sir Arthur Young, papers, box 5, file 3, 100–107, confidential letter from A. E. Young to Sir Evelyn Baring, 28 December 1954.

27. RH, Mss. Brit. Emp. s. 527/528, *End of Empire, Kenya*, vol. 1, Barbara Castle, interview, 117.

28. Letter from Michael Evans to Terence Gavaghan, 11 May 1995 (seen courtesy of Gavaghan).

29. Jean Wanjiru Cliffe, interview, Tigoni, Limuru, Kiambu District, 10 August 2003.

30. Castle, *Fighting All the Way*, 269–73.

31. "The Truth About the Secret Police," *Daily Mirror*, 9 December 1955; and "Justice in Kenya," *New Statesman and Nation*, 17 December 1955.

32. *HCD*, vol. 547, col. 1177, 14 December 1955.

33. Ibid., col. 1181, 14 December 1955.

34. Anne Perkins, *Red Queen: The Authorized Biography of Barbara Castle* (London: Macmillan, 2003), 140.

35. Castle, *Fighting All the Way*, 274.

36. "Gestapo Way in Kenya," *Daily Worker*, 18 March 1953.

37. KNA, JZ 8/8/85, H. F. Potter, secretariat circular no. 13, "Security of Information," 15 April 1953.

38. KNA, JZ 8/8/86, B. W. Hemsley, for commissioner of prisons, memorandum, "Security of Information," 4 October 1954.

39. T. G. Askwith, interview, Cirencester, England, 8 June 1998; anonymous, interview, Nairobi, Kenya, 11 November 1998; and anonymous, telephone interview, 4 May 2004.
40. KNA, AB 2/49/30, memorandum from J. Lewis, "Photographs," 11 May 1956.
41. Askwith, interview, 8 June 1998. See also KNA, AB 25/211, personnel file, "Miss E. Fletcher, 1954–56."
42. PRO, CO 822/1239, "Memorandum on Allegations published by Miss Eileen Fletcher on conditions in prisons and camps," June 1956.
43. "Kenya's Concentration Camps—An Eyewitness Account," *Peace News—the International Pacifist Weekly*, 4 May 1956, 11 May 1956, and 18 May 1956. See also "Eileen Fletcher answers Mr. Lennox Boyd" and "Kenya: Inquiry Demanded—House debates Peace News exposures," *Peace News—the International Pacifist Weekly*, 15 June 1956.
44. PRO, CO 822/1239, Eileen Fletcher, *Report on My Period of Employment in the Community Development Department of the Kenya Government*, July 1956, 6.
45. Ibid., 8.
46. "Kenya's Concentration Camps," *Peace News—the International Pacifist Weekly*, 4 May 1956; PRO, CO 822/1239, Eileen Fletcher, *Report on My Period of Employment in the Community Development Department of the Kenya Government*, July 1956, 8–10.
47. PRO, CO 822/1239, Eileen Fletcher, *Report on My Period of Employment in the Community Development Department of the Kenya Government*, July 1956, 8; RH, Mss. Brit. Emp. s. 332, Arthur Creech Jones, papers, box 21, file 4, 33–42, Eileen Fletcher, "My comments on the Government Memorandum concerning my charges about Kenya," 8 January 1957; and Movement for Colonial Freedom, *Truth about Kenya—an eye witness account by Eileen Fletcher*, 1956.
48. *Report of the Committee on Juvenile Crime and Kabete Reformatory* (Nairobi: Kenya Government Printer, 1934); and *Annual Report on Native Affairs*, 1934, 140–42.
49. Note, for example, the observations made by Colin Owen, the principal probation officer during the initial months of the Emergency, whereupon he remarked, "I have been approached by Magistrates in the difficult problem of sentence when dealing with Juvenile Mau Mau cases and considerable anxiety has been shown by the lack of any alternative to imprisonment or detention." KNA, BZ 16/1/11, memorandum from Colin Owen to provincial commissioner, Rift Valley Province, "Juvenile Mau Mau Cases," 21 April 1953. Also, under Prisons Standing Order No. 177, juveniles were defined as either (a) child—under fourteen, or (b) young person—fourteen to eighteen. For further details on the number of juveniles in Emergency camps and prisons, see KNA, AB 2/43, minute to file, February 1955. The majority of those not being held in the holding camps were located at Langata Prison. Additionally, many juveniles arrived in Manyani and Mackinnon Road as a result of Special Branch operations. The Special Branch targeted young Mau Mau suspects, took them to local screening centers, where they interrogated them at length, and then deposited them in the camps. See KNA, BZ 16/1/51, memorandum from S. I. Moore to Owen, "Re: Surrendered Terrorists," 14 June 1954.
50. Perkerra Camp was an open camp located in the Rift Valley for the few thousand squatters who did not go to works camps in their home reserves, but rather remained in the settled areas. Askwith's department took over this camp, in part because it became a virtual community as thousands of detainees were parked there sometimes for years as they awaited the ban on Kikuyu labor to be lifted on the European farms. See KNA, AB 2/48/41, memo from community development officer in charge, Perkerra, to permanent secretary of community development, 29 October 1957.
51. For extensive details on the foundation and operation of Wamumu Camp, see KNA, AB 1/116, "Administration Youth Camps—Wamumu, 1955–56"; KNA, AB 1/117, "Wamumu, 1957–58"; and KNA, AB 1/118, "Wamumu—Youth Camp Approved School, 1956–57."
52. See, for example, KNA, AB 2/44/14, memorandum from Lewis to officer in charge, Manyani Camp, "Classification—Disposal of Juvenile Detainees," 30 April 1955.
53. Samuel Kariuki Gakuru, interview, Nyeri District, 21 March 1999.

54. KNA, PC/NKU 2/17/32/100, memorandum from A. C. C. Swann to the ministers of local government, health, and housing and community development, "Care of Kikuyu Children Left Without Guardians as a Result of the Emergency," 30 November 1954; KNA, PC/NKU 2/1/17/32/101, memorandum from the acting secretary of local government, health, and housing to Wainwright, 7 December 1954; and KNA, PC/NKU 2/17/32/102, memorandum from T. Askwith to A. C. C. Swann, "Care of Kikuyu Children Left Without Guardians as a Result of the Emergency," 17 December 1954. For the views of missionaries and voluntary associations like the Salvation Army and the Red Cross on the orphan and waif and stray problem, see, for example, KNA, AB 4/10, Christian Council of Kenya, "Annual Report 1955–56," 9 February 1956; and KNA, AB 4/10/1, The Federation of Social Services in Kenya, "Annual Report 1954," March 1955.

55. KNA, AB 2/69/18/1, memorandum from R. B. Lambe, "Girl Children beyond Control," 22 March 1957; and KNA, AB 2/69/46, memorandum from Colin Owen, "Place of Safety for Females," 25 June 1957. Note that some of these juvenile prostitutes, as well as those boys and girls who took to petty thieving in Nairobi, were generally arrested for vagrancy or pass-law violations and repatriated to the reserves. Many, though, were shrewd enough to claim Kiambu as their home district, thus easily making their way back to Nairobi. A cyclical process emerged whereby thousands of juveniles were arrested and repatriated, only to return to Nairobi and a life of petty crime or prostitution. See KNA, BZ 16/3/10, memorandum from G. M. Kimani, African probation officer, "Langata: Ending Report for February & March 1955," 31 March 1955; KNA, AB 2/75/16/1, memorandum, "Juvenile Reception Groups," 25 November 1957; and KNA, AB 2/4/37, memoranda from the Community Development Department, "The Problem of Juveniles in Nairobi" and "Juveniles in Nairobi," 26 April 1955.

56. KNA, AB 2/64/17, memorandum from Ohanga, "Juvenile Remand Homes," 31 August 1955.

57. KNA, AB 17/14/138, memorandum from district commissioner, Fort Hall, to E. H. Windley, 24 June 1955.

58. Movement for Colonial Freedom, *Truth About Kenya—an eye witness account by Eileen Fletcher*, 1956.

59. For example, the telegrams and savingrams in PRO, CO 822/1239, "Detention of Juvenile Delinquents in Kenya."

60. See, for example, PRO, CO 822/1236, Eileen Fletcher, "My Comments on the Government Memorandum concerning my charges about Kenya," 8 January 1957.

61. *HCD*, vol. 553, cols. 1087–1213, 6 June 1956. See also the colonial secretary's brief for the debate, PRO, CO 822/1239, "Memorandum on Allegations published by Miss Eileen Fletcher on conditions in prisons and camps," no date.

62. "No More Whitewash," *Observer*, 17 June 1956.

63. *HCD*, vol. 558, col. 1419, 31 October 1956.

64. Ibid., col. 1420, 31 October 1956.

65. PRO, CO 822/1237/6, enclosure 1, Philip Meldon, 2 January 1957, 1.

66. PRO, CO 822/1237, letter from Philip Meldon to Major James Breckenridge, 22 December 1956.

67. *Peace News—the International Pacifist Weekly*, 11 January 1957; *Reynolds News*, "I Saw Men Tortured," Philip Meldon, 13 January 1957; and PRO, CO 822/1237/30, letter from Philip Meldon to Alan Lennox-Boyd, 4 February 1957.

68. PRO, CO 822/1237, Philip Meldon, "My Two Years in Kenya," no date, 4–5.

69. Ibid., 5, 7.

70. PRO, CO 822/1237/30, letter from Philip Meldon to Alan Lennox-Boyd, 4 February 1957.

71. PRO, CO 822/1237, Philip Meldon, "My Two Years in Kenya," no date, 2.

72. PRO, CO 822/1237/1, secret telegram from Baring to secretary of state for the colonies, 31 December 1956.

73. Ibid.

74. PRO, CO 822/1237/3, telegram no. 9 from secretary of state for the colonies to Baring, 3 January 1957.

75. Ibid.

76. Baring and Lennox-Boyd corresponded directly on the conditions of Manyani Camp; the colonial secretary was trying to determine if the continued use of the riot squad in Manyani Camp constituted a breakdown of government control and a pervasion of indiscriminate violence. Ultimately, the Colonial Office denied any problems at Manyani, but this correspondence reveals otherwise. See PRO, CO 822/1237/19, savingram no. 499/57 from Baring to secretary of state for the colonies, 20 February 1957. In addition to the Medical Department condemning Gilgil, Nairobi received numerous reports about the camp's conditions. See, for example, Father Colleton's report whereupon visiting Gilgil he commented, "I must confess that I was appalled by the conditions prevailing in this camp," KNA, AB 17/14/95, memorandum from Colleton to Askwith, 26 March 1955.

77. PRO, CO 822/1237, letter from Lennox-Boyd to Fenner Brockway, 6 March 1957.

78. PRO, CO 822/802/141, telegram from E. W. M. Magor to Buist, 19 December 1956.

79. For details on the liaison officers' reports, see KNA, AB 4/121, "CCK Reports—Inspection of Camps, 1956–58"; and KNA, AB 17/14, "Christian Council of Kenya and Roman Catholic Mission, 1954–56."

80. PRO, CO 822/795/96, brief for secretary of state for the colonies "The Moral Rearmament Movement at Athi River Camp," c. July 1956. For details on the liaison officers' reports, see KNA, AB 4/121, "CCK Reports—Inspection of Camps, 1956–58"; and KNA, AB 17/14, "Christian Council of Kenya and Roman Catholic Mission, 1954–56." At Kisumu Prison, for example, Father Colleton made the following observations: "All the Mau Mau convicts are in chains continually. It is quite understandable and reasonable that an individual convict who attempts to escape or is guilty of a serious breach of discipline should be chained for a limited period. But I doubt the wisdom of subjecting a whole section of men—numbering some hundred—to the same drastic treatment for an indefinite space of time. . . . When I mentioned the matter to the Superintendent, he informed me that it is a Government Order made for security reasons. It appears to me that it would be preferable that ten convicts should escape—and probably be captured—than that hundreds should be perpetually degraded and tortured and thus embittered for the rest of their lives. This may appear an exaggeration but I suggest that anyone who thinks so should visit Kisumu Prison and form his own opinion. . . . The response of the convicts to my address was exactly as I expected under the circumstances—sneers and political questions and obvious hatred for anyone with a white face." KNA, AB 17/14/106B, memorandum from Colleton to Askwith, "Kisumu Central Prison," 28 April 1955. In addition, Canon Webster—who often filled in for Church, even before his dismissal—constantly emphasized the lack of support for spiritual rehabilitation—in both manpower and material needs. Moreover, he commented upon his inability to access the detainees and Mau Mau prisoners, mainly due to "security grounds." See KNA, AB 4/121/21, Eric Webster, "Report on Spiritual Welfare—Prisons, Prison Camps, Detention Camps and Works Camps," March 1956; and KNA, AB 4/121/87, Eric Webster, "Spiritual Welfare—Chaplain's Report to Commissioner of Prisons, October 1956," 5 January 1957. Commentary was also provided on the conditions of the camps themselves.

81. PRO, CO 822/1787/14, minute to file from Mathieson to Buist, 11 March 1957.

82. PRO, CO 822/1199/48, letter from Gorell Barnes to Baring, 29 October 1956.

83. Mathieson not only agreed with this statement but in fact had a hand as a Colonial Office representative in influencing the composition of the CPA delegation. See PRO, CO 822/1787/14, minute to file from Mathieson to Buist, 11 March 1957.

84. PRO, CO 822/1787/31, extract from minutes of a meeting of the Executive Committee of the UK branch of the CPA, 2 April 1957.

85. For details on the active support of some Catholic missionaries, see KNA, MAA 9/930/1, minute from the secretary of African affairs, K. M. Cowley, to E. H. Windley, 8 June 1954; and MAA 9/930/5, memorandum from Ernest Bastin, general superintendent of the Methodist mission, to E. H. Windley, 20 June 1954.

86. "Bishop Protests at C.M.S. Pamphlet," *East African Standard*, 24 January 1955.

87. RH, Mss. Afr. s. 486, Sir Arthur Young, papers, box 5, file 1, Arthur Young, "Introduction to Sir Arthur Young," no date.

88. As quoted in "Church Missionary Society's Concern About Kenya," *East Africa and Rhodesia*, 3 February 1955.

89. As quoted in ibid.

90. *HLD*, vol. 190, no. 19, cols. 1153–54, 10 February 1955.

91. See, for example, KNA, AB 17/14/100B, letter from S. A. Morrison to Governor Baring, "Comments by Church Leaders on the Present Situation in Kenya," 29 March 1955; KNA, MAA 9/930/41, memo from provincial commissioner, Central Province, to minister for African affairs, 22 February 1955; and RH, Mss. Brit. Emp. s. 365, Fabian Colonial Bureau, papers, box 117, file 4, 21–29, letter from anonymous CMS missionary to B. Nicholls, and forwarded to the Fabian Colonial Bureau, 23 November 1953.

92. KNA, MAA 9/930/11, memorandum from Archbishop Beecher to Turnbull, 15 December 1954.

93. KNA, AB 8/34/85, "The Christian Council of Kenya—Minutes of the Meeting of the Standing Committee," 27 November 1953.

94. RH, Mss. Brit. Emp. s. 365, Fabian Colonial Bureau, papers, box 117, file 4, 33–35, "An Open Letter from Leaders of Christian Churches in Kenya," 7 December 1953. The letter was published through the Church Missionary Society in London, with the assistance of B. D. Nicholls, the CMS information officer. The signatories to this letter included Archbishop Leonard Beecher; David Steel, the moderator of the Church of Scotland in East Africa; R. Macpherson, clerk of synod, PCEA and CSM; E. Bigwood, territorial commander, the Salvation Army; E. A. Bastin, district chairman of the Methodist Church in Kenya; and W. Scott Dickson, general secretary, CCK.

95. *Time*, 7 December 1953. The case of Captain Griffiths was covered by numerous papers at the time. See, for example, the *Daily Worker*, "Kenya: Sack The Guilty," 28 December 1953; and the *Times*, "Capt. Griffiths in the Box," 11 March 1954. See also Evans, *Law and Disorder*, 262–64.

96. RH, Mss. Brit. Emp. s. 365, Fabian Colonial Bureau, papers, box 188, file 2B, item 30, "Kenya Church Leaders' Second Statement on Abuses of Power by Certain Members of the Forces of Law and Order," 8 January 1954.

97. Note the churches made many statements about the rehabilitation efforts as well as the Christian conversions of former Mau Mau adherents throughout the Emergency. See, for example, RH, Mss. Afr. s. 1681, Africa Bureau, papers, box 291, file 9, 3–24, press conference by the bishop of Mombasa, 1 April 1954; and box 291, file 9, 30, "Report of the Bishop of Mombasa's Address to Members of Parliament and others in the House of Lords," 26 May 1954.

98. Askwith, interview, 8 June 1998; John Lonsdale, personal correspondence with author, 20 July 2004.

99. KNA, CS 1/16/19, memorandum from church leaders to Governor Baring, 18 January 1955; and minutes of the meeting between the acting governor and church leaders, 2 February 1955.

100. KNA, MA 9/930/52, letter from S. A. Morrison to Sir Evelyn Baring, 29 March 1955.

101. KNA, MAA 9/930/60, memorandum "Affirmations of Church Leaders," May 1955.

102. KNA, MAA 9/930/57, memorandum "Representations by Christian Council of Kenya on Emergency and Post-Emergency Planning," 13 April 1955.

103. KNA, MAA 9/930/62, memorandum "Christian Council of Kenya—Complaints against Public Officers," 10 May 1955.

104. KNA, MAA 129/27, letter from Reverend Peter Bostock to Reverend Canon M. A. C. Warren, 30 November 1953.

105. Records of the Anglican Church, Imani House, Nairobi, "Mau Mau" files, box 2, Christian Council of Kenya, "The Forces of Law and Order," c. January 1954.

106. Records of the Anglican Church, Imani House, Nairobi, "Mau Mau" files, box 1, letter

from W. Carey to Reverend Canon M. A. C. Warren, 12 January 1954. In his biography of Carey Francis, L. B. Greaves quotes the Anglican missionary as saying "the Security forces, and particularly the Police, have been involved in many acts of brutality to prisoners (sometimes amounting to deliberate and despicable torture)." Greaves went on to note that Francis "did in fact draft letters to the *Times* and the *Manchester Guardian*, but did not post them [not wanting to] aggravate still further the immense difficulties that faced the Administration." L. B. Greaves, *Carey Francis of Kenya* (London: Rex Collings, 1969), 116, 120.

107. Records of the Anglican Church, Imani House, Nairobi, "Mau Mau" files, box 1, Sam Morrison, "Kenya Survey and the Christian Council of Kenya," September 1954.

108. RH, Mss. Afr. s. 1681, Africa Bureau, papers, box 291, file 3, "Press Release—Statement by Church Leaders in Kenya," 8 July, 1956."

109. See, for example, PRO, CO 822/802/131, letter from detainees, Kisumu, to secretary of state for the colonies, 7 June 1956. For an example of detainees asking for a return of stolen property, see PRO, CO 822/131/113, "Re: Grievances: Loss of Property at Mackinnon Road Camp," 14 February 1956.

110. See, for example, PRO, CO 822/729, minute from Sir S. Abrahams, 15 October 1953.

111. RH, Mss. Brit. Emp. s. 527/528, *End of Empire, Kenya*, vol. 2, Will Mathieson, interview, 157.

112. PRO, CAB 128/27, 9 (8), 17 February 1954—Kenya, detention of Mau Mau supporters.

113. PRO, PREM 11/339, "Admiral Mountbatten's courtesy visit to Turkey," 1953; PRO, PREM 11/340, "Decision to omit Egypt from itinerary of visits made by Lord Mountbatten," 1952–53; and "Mountbatten's Wife Enraged Churchill," *Daily Telegraph*, 3 January 2004.

114. Joanna Lewis argues this point well in " 'Daddy Wouldn't Buy Me a Mau Mau': The British Popular Press and the Demoralization of Empire," in *Mau Mau and Nationhood: Arms, Authority and Narration*, ed. E. S. Atieno Odhiambo and John Lonsdale (Oxford: James Currey, 2002), 227. Additionally, Lewis offers here an excellent account of the importance and influence of the tabloid press on the popular understanding of Mau Mau.

115. The most important analyses of the Europeans' perceptions of Mau Mau come from John Lonsdale, "Mau Maus of the Mind: Making Mau Mau and Remaking Kenya," *Journal of African History* 31 (1990): 393–421; and Dane Kennedy, "Constructing the Colonial Myth of Mau Mau," *International Journal of African Historical Studies* 25, no. 2 (1992): 241–60.

116. David Maughan-Brown presents the evidence for the *Daily Worker* and its unique position on Mau Mau in *Land, Freedom, and Fiction: History and Ideology in Kenya* (London: Zed, 1985), 159–60.

117. "Report on Kenya," *New Statesman and Nation*, 6 December 1952; and "Imperialism in Our Time," *New Statesman and Nation*, 14 February 1953.

118. *Manchester Guardian*, 17 February 1953.

119. Ibid., 14 November 1952.

120. As quoted in Barbara Castle, "Police and Administration in Kenya," *Socialists and the Colonies Venture, Journal of the Fabian Colonial Bureau* 7, no. 9 (1956).

121. I am grateful to Anne Perkins and Anthony Sampson for sharing their insights with me regarding the place of anticolonial politics within the Labour movement during the postwar period.

Ten: Detention Exposed

1. John Cowan, interview, London, England, 24 July 1998; and RH, Mss. Afr. s. 2095, Terence Gavaghan, *Corridors of Wire*, 2.

2. Nderi Kagombe, interview, Ruguru, Mathira, Nyeri District, 24 February, 1999.

3. Ibid.

4. Ibid.

5. Anonymous, interview, Kariokor, Nairobi, 14 December 1998.

6. Kagombe, interview, 24 February 1999.

7. Ibid.

8. Ibid.

9. Anonymous, interview, Westlands, Nairobi, 8 August 2003; Maingi Waweru, interview, Muhito, Mukurweini, Nyeri District, 25 February 1999; and Wachira Murage, interview, Aguthi, North Tetu, Nyeri District, 25 February 1999.

10. *The European Convention on Human Rights and Its Five Protocols*, Section 1, Article 15, paragraph 1.

11. For further details regarding the derogation clause of the European Convention, see PRO, CO 822/1334/52, memorandum, "Security Powers of Colonial Governors," June 1959.

12. PRO, CO 822/888, minute from Mathieson to Gorell Barnes, 23 July 1955.

13. Ibid., minute from Gorell Barnes to Lloyd, 27 July 1955.

14. PRO, CO 822/798/34, minutes of the Council of Ministers, Resettlement Committee, seventeenth meeting, 27 April 1956.

15. PRO, CO 822/1229/1, brief for the secretary of state for the colonies for visit to Kenya, "The Continuation of the Emergency," 1957.

16. For a detailed description of Johnston's responsibilities, see PRO, CO 822/794/43, memorandum from Edward Windley, "The Council of Ministers—Special Administrative Organisation: Central Province," 17 September 1955; and PRO, CO 822/794/44, letter from Baring to C. M. Johnston, 4 October 1955.

17. Muraya Mutahi, interview, Aguthi, North Tetu, Nyeri District, 25 February 1999.

18. See KNA, JZ 7/4/73B, copy of letter to the Right Honorable Sir Thomas Dugdale, MP, from the secretary of state for the colonies, 7 December 1956.

19. Wilson Ndirangu, interview, Ruguru, Mathira, Nyeri District, 24 January 1999.

20. Ibid.; see also, "Police Stand by after Prison Disorders," *East African Standard*, 28 November 1956; and "Warders Quell Mutiny," *East African Standard*, 29 November, 1956.

21. Mutahi, interview, 25 February 1999.

22. KNA, AB 1/119/149, memorandum from Greaves to Askwith, "Perkerra Rehabilitation Camp/Marigat Works Camp—Monthly Report by Community Development Officer in Charge," 31 January 1957.

23. KNA, AB 1/119/150, memorandum from Askwith to Greaves, 11 February 1957.

24. T. G. Askwith, interview, Circencester, England, 8 June 1998.

25. KNA, JZ 4/20, "Classification of Detainees," 4 March 1955.

26. PRO, CO 822/798/32, Resettlement Committee, "Releases from Custody and Rate of Absorption of Landless K.E.M.," 25 April 1956.

27. Note that the detainees, once reclassified, would then move up and down the Pipeline to camps that corresponded with their new classification. The special commissioner also designated certain camps as "special rehabilitation camps," where prisons and rehabilitation staff were supposed to convince the newly segregated "Y1s"—or lesser hard cores—of the benefits of confession. For a reconstruction of this system, see KNA, JZ 2/17, A. B. Simpson, memorandum, "Classification of Detainees," 12 October 1956; KNA, AB 2/23/2, R. Tatton-Brown, memorandum, "Classification," 9 October 1956; KNA, AB 1/84/2, "Movement of Detainees," 20 October 1956; KNA, JZ 6/26/50A, Ministry of Community Development, Community Development Conference, 14–17 January 1957; and KNA, JZ 6/26/48, "Minutes of the 18th meeting of the Rehabilitation Advisory Committee," 12 November 1956.

28. RH, Mss. Afr. s. 2095, Terence Gavaghan, *Corridors of Wire*, 26, 32–33.

29. Terence Gavaghan, *Of Lions and Dung Beetles: A "Man in the Middle" of Colonial Administration in Kenya* (Devon: Arthur H. Stockwell, 1999), 217.

30. John Cowan, "The Mwea Camps and Hola," no date (seen courtesy of Cowan); and KNA, AH 9/21/215, J. Cowan to J. H. Lewis, "Transfer of Detainees Ex Manyani," 7 December 1956.

31. PRO, CO 822/802/148, memorandum from Cusack, "Detention Camps— Progress Report No. 34," 12 December 1956; KNA, JZ 6/26/51, "Minutes of the Nineteenth Meeting of the Rehabilitation Advisory Committee—11 March, 1957"; KNA, JZ 18/7/41A, *Annual Report 1956—Aguthi Works Camp,* 20 January 1957; KNA, JZ 18/7/54A, E. C. V. Kelsall, officer in charge, Gatundu Works Camp, *Annual Report,* 25 January 1957; and KNA, JZ 18/7/39A, R. J. Rowe, officer in charge, "Subject: Annual Report: 1956," 7 January 1957.

32. PRO, CO 822/1249/1, telegram no. 104 from Baring to secretary of state for the colonies, 5 February 1957.

33. Ibid.

34. KNA, JZ 6/26/54, "Report of a Visit of Members of the Rehabilitation Advisory Committee to Thiba Camp on 8th April, 1957."

35. PRO, CO 822/1249/3, telegram no. 144 from Baring to secretary of state for the colonies, 16 February 1957.

36. Gavaghan, *Of Lions and Dung Beetles,* 226–27. Gavaghan also described to me the recorded scene on several occasions and with great zeal.

37. Terence Gavaghan, interview, BBC Correspondent, "Kenya: White Terror," 17 November 2002.

38. Gavaghan, *Of Lions and Dung Beetles,* 231.

39. PRO, CO 822/1251/1, secret letter from Baring to secretary of state for the colonies, 25 June 1957.

40. PRO, CO 822/1251/E/1, memorandum from Eric Griffith-Jones, " 'Dilution' Detention Camps—Use of Force in Enforcing Discipline," June 1957.

41. Ibid.

42. Ibid.

43. PRO, CO 822/1251/7, telegram no. 53 from secretary of state for the colonies for Baring, 16 July 1957; and PRO, CO 822/1251/8, telegram no. 597 from Baring to secretary of state for the colonies, 17 July 1957.

44. RH, Mss. Afr. s. 2095, Terence Gavaghan, *Corridors of Wire,* 143.

45. Ibid., 90.

46. Gavaghan, *Of Lions and Dung Beetles,* 233–34.

47. The literal translation of Karuga Ndua is "one who jumps over a beer brewing pot." This nickname has an idiomatic meaning in Kikuyu because a *ndua,* or beer-brewing pot, was a very precious commodity. Therefore, if one jumped over it then he or she was considered willing to risk or make big trouble. Karuga Ndua is, therefore, translated here as the Big Troublemaker.

48. Anonymous, interview, 14 December 1998.

49. Samson Karanja, interview, Ngecha, Limuru, Kiambu District, 28 February 1999.

50. George Maingi Waweru (General Kamwamba), interview, Muhito, Mukurweini, Nyeri District, 1 March 1999.

51. RH, Mss. Afr. s. 2095, Terence Gavaghan, *Corridors of Wire,* 92.

52. Charles Mwai, interview, Ngorano, Mathira, Nyeri District, 21 March 1999.

53. Wachira Murage (General Mwangi wa Kirira), interview, Aguthi, North Tetu, Nyeri District, 1 March 1999.

54. Anonymous, interview, 14 December 1998.

55. Kagombe, interview, 24 February 1999.

56. Askwith, interview, Cirencester, England, 9 June 1998; and personal correspondence with the author, 31 July 1998.

57. Murage, interview, 1 March 1999; Kagombe, interview, 24 February 1999; anonymous, interview, 14 December 1998; Karanja, interview, 28 February 1999; and Waweru, interview, 1 March 1999.

58. Memorandum from T. G. Askwith to the chief secretary, "Rehabilitation," 16 December 1957 (seen courtesy of Askwith).

59. Ibid.

60. T. G. Askwith, personal correspondence with the author, 31 July 1998.

61. Cowan, interview, 24 July 1998. Note here that when Cowan states Askwith "got no

honor," he is referring to an Order of the British Empire (OBE) and a Member of the British Empire (MBE). For those in the colonial service, such distinctions were of greatest importance. That Askwith received neither an OBE nor an MBE was a deliberate oversight by the British colonial government.

62. Terence Gavaghan, interview, London, England, 29 July 1998.

63. Askwith, interview, 9 June 1998.

64. KNA, AH 6/5/53, monthly report of the Ministry of Defence, July 1957. Also note that Gavaghan, as of the summer of 1957, was taking in on average two hundred new detainees into the five Mwea camps each week. At one point, however, he and his staff received as many as five hundred detainees at once, though this resulted in the use of a "significant amount of force." Gavaghan, interview, 29 July 1998; and PRO, CO 822/1249/24, Colonial Office memorandum, "Detention Camps," October 1957.

65. KNA, AB 1/108/21, memorandum from T. Gavaghan to provincial commissioner, Central Province, "Manyani Special Detention Camp," 20 August 1957.

66. Memorandum from T. G. Askwith to the chief secretary, "Rehabilitation," 16 December 1957 (seen courtesy of Askwith).

67. Eric Kamau Mithiori, interview, Mugoiri, Kahuro, Murang'a District, 16 January 1999.

68. "Bren Gun Used to Quell Riot," *East African Standard*, 24 August 1957.

69. The Colonial Office became aware of Harrison's treatment of detainees at Athi River through the minutes of the chief secretary's Complaints Co-Ordinating Committee that were forwarded to London. When the Athi River riots occurred in April, London surmised that there was a causal connection between Harrison's alleged behavior and the furor of the riot. Later, in November 1957, Harrison and the others were "honourably acquitted" of any wrongdoing in Athi River Camp. See PRO, CO 822/1253, "Minute No. 745 (Kajiado SD.3/57)—Alleged assault of Athi River detainees," 10 June 1957; and "Minute No. 866 (Kajiado SD.3/57)—Alleged assault of Athi River detainees," 20 November 1957. Also PRO, CO 822/1253, minute to file, Hull, 28 June 1957.

70. For details on Hugh Galton-Fenzi's appointment and the adoption of the dilution technique at Athi River, see KNA, AB 1/86, "Rehabilitation Athi River, 16/5/58–15/3/59."

71. Paul Mahehu, interview, Kirimukuyu, Mathira, Nyeri District, 23 January 1999.

72. Munyinyi Githiriga, interview, Murarandia, Kiharu, Murang'a District, 20 February 1999.

73. KNA, JZ 7/4/193, letter from Athi River Detention Camp to the Ministry for Defence, 7 August 1957.

74. KNA, AB 1/86/5/1 and KNA, JZ 6/25/206A, "Report of a Visit to Athi River Detention Camp," 23 April 1958.

75. KNA, JZ 6/26/55, David Wanguhu, "A Report on a Visit to Embu Work Camps," May 1957.

76. PRO, CO 822/1251/1, letter from Governor Baring to the secretary for state for the colonies, 25 June 1957.

77. Gavaghan, *Of Lions and Dung Beetles*, 235.

78. PRO, CO 822/1258/E/27, "General Report on the Mission of the International Committee of the Red Cross," no date.

79. Note that in April 1957 nearly 5,000 of the reported 6,817 Mau Mau prisoners were held in Embakasi. See KNA, AB 1/89/39, Seaward—community development officer in charge of Nairobi Area, *Annual Report—Nairobi Area*, 3 April 1957. For Public Works Department and prison labor in Embakasi, see KNA, AB 1/90/64, minister for works and minister for commerce and industry, memorandum "Embakasi Airport—Progress Report," 18 December 1956; and KNA, AB 1/90/65, Magor to Lewis, "Supply of Prison Labour for the Embakasi Airport," 27 December 1956.

80. Nearly 90 percent of those ex-convicts sent to Mara River and Ngulot camps—which were adjoining—were classified as "Z," and sent to the Mwea camps (KNA, AB 1/96/22, message via prison radio 12/7/57, 2:20 p.m., Gavaghan to Ministry of Defence). Note

that the Prisons Department took over all so-called rehabilitation responsibilities in the prisons as of July 1957. Prior to this takeover there were some trial attempts to run-down the prisons. These attempts coincided with the beginning of the dilution technique. Those convicts remitted to DDOs under the Form C procedure and classified as "Y2" were sent to Kamiti Downs Prison, for eventual release to the district camps. "Y1s" were sent to Mara River, where cooperative detainees (i.e., those reclassified as "Y2s") were sent to district camps, and those deemed uncooperative (i.e., those reclassified as "Y1" or "Z") were sent to Mageta Island. Finally, all "Zs" were sent to Ngulot Camp, where those reclassified as "Y2" were sent to district camps, and all those reclassified as "Y1" or remaining "Z" were sent to Mageta Island. This movement policy was abandoned when it was decided to run-down Mageta Island Camp. Instead, Mara River and Ngulot camps were used for all Form C releases from the Mau Mau prisons. All "Zs" were eventually transferred to the Mwea camps for dilution. KNA AB 1/89/39, Seaward—community development officer in charge, Nairobi Area, *Annual Report—Nairobi Area,* 3 April 1957. Also, for reference to the hard-core "Zs" being sent to Karaba Camp, see PRO, CO 822/1252/25, letter from Baring to secretary of state for the colonies, 4 September 1958.

81. KNA, AB 4/21/1/1, S. H. La Fontaine, "Report of Work of Review Committee of Mau Mau Prison Sentences from 1955 to 1957," March 1958. Note that prior to the move to increase the Review Committee's approval rate, those convicts recommended for release were not transferred to district camps but to Kamiti Downs Prison. There, all those ex-convicts who were not from Fort Hall or Meru were sent to Gathigiriri Camp for further softening up before they were sent back to their districts. All ex-convicts who hailed from Fort Hall or Meru were sent directly to a district camp. KNA, AB 18/12, memorandum, "Movement of Detainees," 20 October, 1956.

82. PRO, CO 822/1252, letter from Baring to secretary of state for the colonies, April 1958.

83. Gavaghan, *Of Lions and Dung Beetles,* 238.

84. PRO, CO 822/1234/49, letter from Baring to Lennox-Boyd, 24 June 1958.

85. John Nottingham, interview, Nairobi, Kenya, 7 August 2003.

86. PRO, CO 912/19/30, Parliamentary Questions, 16 July 1957.

87. For the screening clerk's testimony, see *East African Standard,* "Camp beatings alleged," 6 July 1957. For the judge's verdict, see *East African Standard,* "Five Acquitted of Works Camp Murder—Jail for Assault," 11 July 1957.

88. *East African Standard,* "Camp Officials Facing Inquiry, Commons Reply," 18 July 1957. While there was no criminal investigation into the culpability of the European officers in charge of Gathigiriri Camp, Lennox-Boyd stated that an internal disciplinary inquiry was taking place under the chairmanship of the Kenya solicitor general, Mr. D. W. Conroy, QC. Conroy would eventually find there was no wrongdoing on the part of the European officers responsible for the camp. Throughout the Emergency, Conroy would play an important role in investigating internally allegations of wrongdoing in the Pipeline. He would later help to direct Nairobi's investigation into the Hola massacre.

89. PRO, CO 912/19/30, Parliamentary Questions, 16 July 1957.

90. Ibid., 29 July 1957.

91. Ibid.

92. Ibid., 18 April 1957.

93. *Observer,* 8 June 1958.

94. Ibid.

95. PRO, CO 822/1701/13, telegram no. 397 from secretary of state for the colonies to Baring, 10 June 1958.

96. *Kenya Legislative Council Debates,* vol. 76, 11 June 1958, 1701–2.

97. Ibid., 1703.

98. Ibid.

99. PRO, CO 822/1701/30, memorandum, "UK Policy of excluding/restricting journalists access to Prisons," 16 June 1958.

100. Note that the newspapers covering the Lokitaung allegations included the *Liverpool Post, Yorkshire Post, Daily Herald, Daily Worker, Daily Telegraph, Manchester Guardian, Times, Glasgow Herald, Birmingham Post,* and *News Chronicle.* Not surprisingly, those issuing demands for an independent investigation were those typically representing the views of the left.

101. "London Diary," *New Statesman and Nation,* 21 June 1958.

102. PRO, CO 822/1705/7, letter from David Astor to secretary of state for the colonies, 4 July 1958.

103. PRO, CO 822/1705/7, enclosure to letter from David Astor to secretary of state for the colonies, 4 July 1958. Copy of article from "383 Detainees and 25 long sentenced Convicts, situated at Mariira Works Camp," 16 June 1958.

104. PRO, CO 822/1705/10, letter to Sir Evelyn Baring from Walter Coutts, 5 July 1958, with enclosure "Report Telephoned by D.C. Fort Hall, 4th July, 1958."

105. PRO, CO 822/1705/12, letter from Alan Lennox-Boyd to David Astor, 14 July 1958.

106. PRO, CO 822/1276/3, secret savingram from Governor Baring to secretary of state for the colonies, 26 September 1958; and PRO, CO 822/1276/6, secret savingram from Governor Baring to secretary of state for the colonies, 7 October 1958.

107. PRO, CO 822/1276/11, report on Disciplinary Investigation into Assistant Superintendent D. D. Luies, officer in charge, Gathigiriri, 21 October 1958.

108. PRO, CO 822/1276/16, letter from D. W. Conroy to F. D. Webber, 25 November 1958; and Reuters, "Report on Verdict in Macharia Case," 20 November 1958.

109. PRO, CO 822/1271, "In the Matter of the Mau Mau Detention Camps in Kenya—Affidavit of Victor Charles Shuter," 10 January 1959.

110. Ibid.

111. "I Was Jailed Without Trial," *Daily Mail,* 2 February 1959.

112. PRO, CO 822/1270, statement by Captain E. Law, no date.

113. PRO, CO 822/1276/35, sworn affidavit of Leonard Bird, 11 February 1959.

114. PRO, CO 822/1276/34, sworn affidavit of Anthony Julian Stuart Williams-Meyrick, 9 February 1959.

115. Motion quoted in PRO, CO 822/1269/1, "House of Commons Extracts from Official Order of Papers," 3 February 1959.

116. PRO, CO 822/1269/7A, telegram no. 153 from secretary of state for the colonies to Amery, 22 February 1959.

117. PRO, CO 822/1269/3, secret telegram no. 133 from Baring to Amery, 9 February 1959.

118. PRO, CO 822/1269/8, secret telegram from Baring to secretary of state for the colonies, 22 February 1959; and PRO, CO 822/1269, "Background of Those Europeans Who Have Made Allegations," no date.

119. PRO, CO 912/21/20, parliamentary questions, 12 February 1959. See also PRO, CO 822/1242 and CO 822/1243, "Detention of Richard Achieng Oneko under emergency regulations in Kenya"; PRO, CO 822/1244, "Detention of Antonio Rudolfo Jose Pio Pinto under emergency regulations in Kenya"; and PRO, CO 822/1245 and CO 822/1246, "Detention of former Senior Chief Koinange under emergency regulations in Kenya."

120. "Kenya Inquiry Refused," *Daily Telegraph,* 25 February 1959.

121. "No Inquiry in Kenya," *New Statesman and Nation,* 28 February 1959.

122. "Fair Play for Mau Mau," *Economist,* 28 February 1959.

123. KNA, MSS 115/51, Press Office, Handout no. 142, "Death of Ten Detainees at Hola," 4 March 1959.

124. Barbara Castle, *Fighting All the Way,* (London: Macmillan, 1993), 288.

125. RH, Mss. Brit. Emp. s. 527/528, *End of Empire, Kenya,* vol. 1, Barbara Castle, interview, 118.

126. Cmnd. 778, *Documents relating to the deaths of eleven Mau Mau detainees at Hola Camp in Kenya* (London: HMSO, 1959), 18.

127. Alistair Horne, *Macmillan, 1957–1986* (London: Macmillan, 1989), 174.

128. Gakaara wa Wanjau, interview, Karatina, Nyeri District, 22 February 1999; and Gakaara wa Wanjau, *Mau Mau Author in Detention* (Nairobi: Heinemann, 1988), 198–205.

129. Cmnd. 816, *Further Documents relating to the deaths of eleven Mau Mau detainees at Hola Camp* (London: HMSO, 1959), 18.

130. Ibid., 23.

131. For a thorough assessment of the government's findings into the sequencing of events at Hola, see *Record of Proceedings and Evidence in the Inquiry into the deaths of eleven Mau Mau detainees at Hola Camp in Kenya*, Cmnd. 795 (London: HMSO, 1959); *Documents relating to the deaths of eleven Mau Mau detainees at Hola Camp in Kenya*, Cmnd. 778 (London: HMSO, 1959); and *Further Documents relating to the deaths of eleven Mau Mau detainees at Hola Camp*, Cmnd. 816 (London: HSMO, 1959).

132. Paul Mahehu, interview, Kirimukuyu, Mathira, Nyeri District, 23 January 1999.

133. Ibid. Note the number of dead and injured are confirmed in the British colonial government's inquest reports.

134. *Documents relating to the deaths of eleven Mau Mau detainees at Hola Camp in Kenya*, Cmnd. 778, 4, 14.

135. Ibid., 16–17.

136. For example, "Hola Shown to be neither a 'Horror' nor 'Holiday Camp,'" *East African Standard*, 5 June 1959.

137. PRO, CAB 128/33, cabinet minutes, 4 June 1959. For further discussions by the cabinet ministers over the Hola massacre and the future control over British colonial rule in Kenya, see PRO, CAB 128/33, 34 (3), cabinet minutes, 11 June 1959; PRO, CAB 128/33, 42 (3), cabinet minutes, 16 July 1959; and PRO, CAB 128/33, 43(2), cabinet minutes, 20 July 1959.

138. PRO, CO 822/1261, minute to file from Gorell Barnes, 4 June 1959.

139. The Fairn Commission was comprised of R. D. Fairn, Sir George Beresford-Stooke, and Canon T. F. C. Bewes, who had taken his concerns about brutality to the British public in the early years of the Emergency. Though the commission's mandate was only to make recommendations into the future of detention in Kenya, it nonetheless reported on several facets of the Pipeline's history. For example, the committee members expressed their alarm over the use of " 'shock' treatment" in the camps as a way of forcing detainees to confess, and their insistence that "in no circumstances should ['shock treatment'] be employed in the future." See *Report on the Committee on Emergency Detention Camps* (Nairobi: Government Printer, 1959), paragraphs 59–61.

140. PRO, CO 822/1261/211, secret memorandum by Harold Macmillan, *Africa*, 8 June 1959. The prime minister and his men were helped along by the final report of the internal investigation into Shuter's allegations, conducted by A. P. Jack. Though former Manyani camp commandant, H. F. H. Durant, admitted that many of his officers "ill-treated" the detainees, and medical officers confirmed several of Shuter's allegations, Jack concluded that brutality was due to a few "bad" officers and was not endemic to the camps. He also finished off the character assassination on Shuter, and asserted that he misrepresented the truth. In the end, he dismissed all charges. See *Administrative Enquiry into Allegations of Ill-treatment and Irregular Practices Against Detainees at Manyani Detention Camp and Fort Hall District Works Camp* (Nairobi: Government Printer, 1959).

141. Horne, *Macmillan*, 175.

142. Harold Macmillan, *Riding the Storm, 1956–59* (London: Macmillan, 1971), 734.

143. As quoted in Philip Murphy, *Party Politics and Decolonization: The Conservative Party and British Colonial Policy in Tropical Africa, 1951–1964* (Oxford: Clarendon Press, 1995), 164.

144. As quoted in Philip Murphy, *Alan Lennox-Boyd, a Biography* (London: I. B. Tauris, 1999), 215.

145. As quoted in ibid., 216.

146. Lord Lambton, MP, "When Loyalty Is Not Enough," *Evening Standard*, 9 June 1959.

147. *Report on the Nyasaland Commission of Inquiry*, Cmnd. 814 (1959).

148. Castle, *Fighting All the Way*, 288.

149. *HCD*, vol 610, col. 231, 27 July 1959.

150. Ibid., col. 237, 27 July 1959.
151. Ibid.
152. Macmillan, *Riding the Storm*, 735.

Epilogue

1. Charles Douglas-Home, *Evelyn Baring: The Last Proconsul* (London: Collins, 1978), 311–12.
2. Michael Blundell, *So Rough a Wind* (London: Weidenfeld and Nicholson, 1964), 266.
3. Frank Heinlein notes that in late 1959 Colonial Secretary Macleod "did not think Kenya independence was likely to be granted in the near future" but a few months later conceded "it was no longer possible to ignore the black majorities." According to Heinlein, Macleod realized the "most important thing was not to lose the Africans' goodwill by delaying constitutional advance too long" if the British were to have any hope of safeguarding their commercial and strategic interests. Frank Heinlein, *British Government Policy and Decolonisation, 1945–1963—Scrutinizing the Official Mind* (London: Frank Cass, 2002), 196, 237, 243.
4. RH, Mss. Brit. Emp. s. 527/528, *End of Empire, Kenya*, vol. 2, John Wainwright, interview, 223–25.
5. Blundell, *So Rough a Wind*, 277; and RH, Mss. Brit. Emp. s. 527/528, *End of Empire, Kenya*, vol. 2, John Wainwright, interview, 225. Note that at first even Macleod believed decolonization would be another ten years, but by the time of the first Lancaster House talks he realized that such a delay did not fit, in his words, "[with] the facts of life in Africa today." Instead, he argued to the settlers and Macmillan, who believed his colonial secretary to be moving too quickly, that only rapid decolonization would ensure stability and safeguard British investments. Gradualism, in Macleod's mind, would lead to African frustration, possibly violence, and surely a loss of their much needed goodwill. Heinlein, *British Government Policy*, 255.
6. RH, Mss. Afr. s. 1574, Lord Howick (Sir Evelyn Baring) and Dame Margery Perham interview, Oxford, 19 November 1969, 20–21.
7. *Historical Survey of the Origins and Growth of Mau Mau*, Cmnd. 1030 (London: HMSO, 1960).
8. Jeremy Murray-Brown, *Kenyatta* (London: George Allen and Unwin, 1972), 300–301.
9. When Rawson Macharia submitted a sworn affidavit in October 1958 that he and others had been bribed to give false evidence at the Kapenguria trial, the British government responded by charging him with swearing a false affidavit. D. N. Pritt and Achhroo Kapila defended him; not surprisingly, they were unsuccessful. By the prosecution's reasoning, Macharia had lied for his own purposes and not with the knowledge of the Crown. Therefore, according to the British government's reasoning, the Kapenguria trial had not been rigged. For further details, see John Lonsdale, "Kenyatta's Trials: Breaking and Making an African Nationalist," in *The Moral World of the Law*, ed. Peter Cross (Cambridge: Cambridge University Press, 2000), 235–36.
10. Murray-Brown, *Kenyatta*, 304–5.
11. Hunja Njuki, interview, Ngorano, Mathira, Nyeri District, 23 January 1999.
12. Jomo Kenyatta, *Harambee! The Prime Minister of Kenya's Speeches, 1963–64* (Oxford: Oxford University Press, 1964), 2.
13. Jomo Kenyatta, *Suffering without Bitterness: The Founding of the Kenya Nation* (Nairobi: East African Publishing House, 1968), 189.
14. *East African Standard*, 13 April 1963, as quoted in Robert B. Edgerton, *Mau Mau: An African Crucible* (London: I. B. Tauris, 1990), 217.
15. PRO, CO 822/1230, Macleod to Renison, 10 November 1959.
16. PRO, CO 822/1337/10, draft memorandum by secretary of state for the colonies, "Colonial Policy Committee, Kenya: Proposed Amnesty," November 1959.
17. John Cowan, interview, London, 24 July 1998.
18. For Enoch Powell's later comments on accountability and the need for Governor

Baring and Alan Lennox-Boyd to assume blame, see RH, Mss. Brit. Emp. s. 527/528, *End of Empire, Kenya,* vol. 3, Enoch Powell, interview, 119.

19. Harold Macmillan, *Pointing the Way, 1959–1961* (London: Macmillan, 1972), 156.
20. Channel Four, "Secret History—Mau Mau," interview, John Cowan.
21. BBC Correspondent, "Kenya: White Terror," interview, Terence Gavaghan.
22. Thomas Askwith, *From Mau Mau to Harambee* (Cambridge: African Studies Centre, 1995), 118.
23. T. G. Askwith, interview, Cirencester, England, 9 June 1998.
24. Christopher Browning engages in a similar consideration with regard to the actions of German "ordinary men" during the Second World War. See Christopher Browning, *Ordinary Men: Reserve Police Battalion 101 and the Final Solution in Poland* (New York: HarperCollins, 1992).
25. Fitz de Souza, interview, Muthaiga, Kenya, 11 August 2003. For a similar recollection, see RH, Mss. Brit. Emp. s. 527/528, *End of Empire, Kenya,* vol. 1, Fitz de Souza, interview, 118.
26. The British colonial government undertook censuses of the African population in Kenya in 1948 and 1962. In 1948 the census recorded 1,554,925 Kikuyu, Embu, and Meru; in 1962 there were 2,215,805. The figures for the Kamba, Luo, and Luhya are as follows:

Ethnic group	1948	1962
Kamba	611,725	933,921
Luo	697,551	1,148,335
Luhya	653,774	1,086,409

The average growth rates of these three groups fell between 3 percent and 3.5 percent. When these growth rates are applied to the Kikuyu, Embu, and Meru 1948 population figure of 1,554,925, the projected range of growth for 1962 is found to be between 2,351,964 and 2,516,949. When this is compared to the actual 1962 population figure of 2,215,805, there is a difference ranging from 136,159 to 301,144. The colonial censuses of 1948 and 1962 are considered to be reasonably reliable, unlike earlier censuses. In fact, they have been used for backward projections of earlier African population sizes in Kenya (see Bruce Berman, *Control and Crisis in Colonial Kenya: The Dialectic of Domination* [London: James Currey, 1990], 94–95). Taking into account imperfections in the census taking/reporting and margins of error, I believe the data are suggestive when read alongside the empirical evidence of death rates and lowered fertility rates presented in this book. For 1948 population figures, see *African Population of Kenya Colony and Protectorate: Geographical and Tribal Studies* (Nairobi: East African Statistical Department, 1953), 6. For the 1962 population figures see Ministry of Economic Planning and Development, *Kenya Population Census, 1962,* vol. 3 (Nairobi: Ministry of Finance and Economic Planning, 1964), 36. I am grateful to Ulla Larsen, Heike Trappe, and John Lonsdale for their advice in assessing these figures.
27. The British government's official figure for "terrorist casualties" was 11,503 as reported in F. D. Corfield, *Historical Survey of the Origins and Growth of Mau Mau,* Cmnd. 1030 (1960), 316.
28. Mary Wambui Mbote, interview, Thigio, Kikuyu, Kiambu District, 13 August 2003.

NOTE ON METHODS

1. It was clear to me as my research progressed that the British colonial government's official figure of some 80,000 Mau Mau suspects detained during the Emergency was incorrect. When the government began publishing monthly detainee figures in 1954 it published "daily average figures," or net figures rather than gross figures. I therefore realized that if I could track the intake and release rates and apply them to the "daily average figures" provided by the colonial government I could get a more accurate sense of the numbers of detainees that passed through the Pipeline. In addition, I also had to determine how many of the Mau Mau suspects tried, convicted, and sent to prison were "Form C'ed" at the end of their sentences and sent to the detention camps in the

Pipeline. Ultimately, I determined an adjusted range for the detainee figures; that is, I found that the actual number of detainees passing through the Pipeline was between two and four times the actual figure, or between 160,000 and 320,000. The following documents were the most useful in calculating this estimation: *Documents relating to the death of eleven Mau Mau detainees at Hola Camp in Kenya*, Cmnd. 778 (London: HMSO, 1959); KNA, AH 6/8, Ministry of Defence, "Monthly Reports, 1954 to 1959"; KNA, AH 6/9, Ministry of Defence, "Monthly Reports, January 1959 to September 1959"; KNA, AH 9/19/12, minute from Eggins, "Works Camps," 4 August 1954; KNA, AH 9/32/251, memorandum from the minister of defense to the Resettlement Committee, "Movement of Detainees from Reception Centres to Works Camps," 4 May 1955; PRO, WO 276/428/103, memorandum from Heyman, chief of state, "Brief for C-in-C on Detainees," 9 September 1955; PRO, CO 822/798/53, memorandum from the Council of Ministers, Resettlement Committee, "Releases from Custody and Rate of Absorption of Landless KEM," 25 April 1956; PRO, WO 428/276/110, memorandum from Lieutenant Colonel Hope, "Mau Mau Convicts," 20 October 1955; and PRO WO 428/276/111, memorandum from Major General W. R. N. Hinde, "Mau Mau Convicts," 21 October 1955.

2. Musila Musembi, *Archives Management: The Kenyan Experience* (Nairobi: Africa Book Services, 1985), 17–22.

3. See John D. Barbour, *The Conscience of the Autobiographer* (New York: St. Martin's Press, 1992); and James Goodwin, *Autobiography: The Self-Made Text* (New York: Twayne, 1993). For a specific consideration of Mau Mau memoirs, including those written by former detainees as well as by forest fighters, see Marshall S. Clough, *Mau Mau Memoirs: History, Memory and Politics* (Boulder: Lynne Rienner, 1998).

4. Of the handful of memoirs in existence, I found the most comprehensive to be Josiah Mwangi Kariuki, *"Mau Mau" Detainee: The Account by a Kenya African of His Experiences in Detention Camps, 1953–1960* (London: Oxford University Press, 1963); Karigo Muchai and Donald Barnett, *The Hardcore: The Story of Karigo Muchai* (Richmond: Liberation Support Movement, 1973); and Gakaara wa Wanjau, *Mau Mau Author in Detention* (Nairobi: Heinemann, 1988).

5. My study of oral history and its methods first began under the tutelage of Leroy Vail, whose own research and writing engaged many of the same practical and theoretical issues that I have dealt with in the course of working on this book. For one of the most recent discussions of oral history, see Luise White, Stephan F. Miescher, and David William Cohen, eds., *African Words, African Voices: Critical Practices in Oral History* (Bloomington: Indiana University Press, 2001).

6. Daniel L. Schacter, *Searching for Memory: The Brain, the Mind, and the Past* (New York: Basic Books, 1996), 10.

7. The way in which people remember or cannot remember traumatic events has been considered extensively by a variety of social scientists and writers, including Paul Antze and Michael Lambek, eds., *Tense Past: Cultural Essays in Trauma and Meaning* (New York: Routledge, 1996); Cathy Caruth, *Trauma: Explorations in Memory* (Baltimore: Johns Hopkins University Press, 1995); Jennifer Cole, *Forget Colonialism?: Sacrifice and the Art of Memory in Madagascar* (Berkeley: University of California Press, 2001); E. Valentine Daniel, *Charred Lullabies: Chapters in an Anthropology of Violence* (Princeton: Princeton University Press, 1996); Saul Friedlander, *When Memory Comes*, translated by Helen R. Lane (New York: Farrar, Straus, Giroux, 1979); Liisa Malkki, *Purity and Exile: Violence, Memory and National Cosmology among Hutu Refugees in Tanzania* (Chicago: University of Chicago Press, 1995); and Alan Parkin, *Memory and Amnesia* (Oxford: Blackwell, 1987).

8. Schacter makes this point in *Searching for Memory* as well as in *The Seven Sins of Memory* (Boston: Houghton Mifflin, 2001), chapter 7.

9. Stephen Macharia Kinyanjui, interview, Kariokor, Nairobi, 16 December 1998.

10. Mary Nyambura, interview, Banana Hill, Kiambu District, 16 December 1998. Lawrence Langer confronted similar issues when collecting and analyzing testimonies

from "former victims," as he calls them, of the Nazi Holocaust. See Lawrence Langer, *Holocaust Testimonies: The Ruins of Memory* (New Haven: Yale University Press, 1991).

11. When one considers the usefulness of individual memories of specific events or periods of time, they must always be examined within the broader context of collective discourse. In other words, to what degree are these memories specific to an individual, and to what degree do they represent a society's collective memory of the past? All societies are susceptible to varying degrees to collective myth making, and the Kikuyu are no exception. Certainly, some individuals and events from the Pipeline have taken on mythical proportions over time. I do not believe, though, that this justifies dismissing oral testimonies as mere reflections of collective myths. Rather, I continue to be struck by the particularity in detail of these testimonies, especially given the nature of communication and the degree to which the state-imposed silencing prevented public, and to some extent private, discussions about detention camp experiences. However, even if one considers some or all of the oral evidence as collective myth, then the wide scale and brutal violence contained therein must still be explained. In considering the issues of individual and collective memories, I benefited greatly from the presentations and discussions at the conference "Violence and Memory," sponsored by Fondazione Giangiacomo Feltrinelli in Cortona, Italy, in June 2002. The conference proceedings are forthcoming in an edited volume by Alessandro Triulzi. Additional works on collective memory include: David Bakhurst, ed., *Collective Memory: Theoretical, Methodological, and Practical Issues: Proceedings of the Small-Group Meeting, European Association of Experimental Social Psychology* (Bari: Department of Psychology, University of Bari, 1997); Paul Connerton, *How Societies Remember* (Cambridge: Cambridge University Press, 1989); and David Middleton and Derek Edwards, eds., *Collective Remembering* (London: Sage, 1990).

12. Ngugi wa Thiong'o, *A Grain of Wheat* (London: Heinemann, 1967); *Writers in Politics* (London: Heinemann, 1981); *Homecoming: Essays on African Caribbean Literature, Culture and Politics* (New York: Lawrence Hill, 1973); and *Petals of Blood* (London: Heinemann, 1977). Also note that Robert Edgerton, in his book *Mau Mau: An African Crucible* (London: I. B. Tauris, 1990), suggests, like Ngugi wa Thiong'o, that the brutality perpetrated against Mau Mau was more widespread than the British government would like to admit. Edgerton stops short, however, of providing any kind of comprehensive investigation into the ruse of rehabilitation.

BIBLIOGRAPHY

PRIMARY SOURCES

Oral Sources

Some three hundred interviews were conducted with Kikuyu men and women who either had been detained in the Mau Mau detention camps, prisons, and Emergency villages or had been loyalists during the Emergency. These interviews took place between November 1998 and August 2004 in Kiambu, Murang'a (formerly Fort Hall), and Nyeri districts, as well as in various locations throughout Nairobi. The final data pool, therefore, had a wide geographical distribution in Central Province, and the gender balance was nearly equal.

My research assistant, Terry Wairimu, a Kikuyu woman whose family comes from Nyeri District, accompanied me to all of these interviews, with the exception of several in Nairobi and Kiambu that I conducted myself. I met Terry in the fall of 1998 at the Kenya National Archives, where she was working as a research assistant. She was twenty-four years old, had earned an undergraduate degree from the University of Nairobi, and was fluent in Kiswahili, Kikuyu, Maa, English, and French.

We located many of our interviewees through contacts with their descendants in Nairobi. After initial introductions were made, Terry and I would remain in the rural areas for periods that ranged from several days to several weeks. We were often hosted by our interviewees, or by one of their descendants who lived nearby. During this time, former detainees, villagers, and loyalists introduced us to kinsmen and neighbors who were also willing to speak about their experiences during Mau Mau. Nearly all of those interviewed agreed to be tape-recorded. Interviews were conducted either in English, Kiswahili, Kikuyu, or some combination thereof. In all cases, interviewees decided their language(s) of preference. Generally, English and/or Kiswahili were the preferred languages in Nairobi and its environs; as we traveled north of the city, Kiswahili and/or Kikuyu became the languages of choice. During graduate school and subsequent field trips to Kenya I acquired the Kiswahili language skills that were necessary for conducting interviews. With the help of Terry, who served as my tutor, I began learning Kikuyu in the fall of 1998. Still, I needed Terry's assistance to conduct the Kikuyu-language interviews, though I was able to follow the content of the oral narratives and engage in casual conversation.

All interviews began with the same query: "Tell us about your experiences during Mau Mau." After what were often long oral accounts, occasionally lasting several hours, follow-up questions would be asked to clarify any points or to expand further on certain details or incidents. After the formal interview was conducted, as we conversed over tea or a meal, many interviewees would recall incidences or details that they had left out; with the permission of the interviewee some of these testimonies were tape-recorded, though most were documented in my field notebook. Terry transcribed and translated the tapes in Kikuyu, whereas we shared the burden of transcribing and translating those tapes in English and/or Kiswahili. I translated and transcribed the tapes of the interviews that I conducted alone in Nairobi and its surrounding areas.

In addition to ex-detainees and villagers, several former colonial administrators, missionaries, settlers, lawyers, and politicians were interviewed between 1997 and 2004 in both the United Kingdom and Kenya. I conducted all of these interviews alone and in English. Some of those interviewed asked to remain anonymous; others spoke with the knowledge that their names would be included within this book. Most of these interviews were tape-recorded; the remainder were documented through handwritten notes or on computer. All interview tapes, transcripts, and notes remain in my possession.

Archival Sources

During the course of research, archives in Kenya, the United Kingdom, and the United States were consulted. In addition to those archives listed below, the following collections were used: Imani House, Anglican Church of Kenya, Nairobi; Presbyterian Church of East Africa, Nairobi; Macmillan Library, Nairobi; University of Nairobi Library, Nairobi; St. Paul's Theological Seminary, Limuru, Kenya; Imperial War Museum, London; British Library, London; University of Durham Library, Durham, England; School of Oriental and African Studies Library, London; Seeley Historical Library, Cambridge, England; British Museum, Colindale, England; Church Missionary Society Archive, University of Birmingham, Birmingham, England; Church of Scotland Missions Archive, Edinburgh University Library, Edinburgh, Scotland; Africa Inland Mission Archive, Billy Graham Center, Wheaton College, Wheaton, Illinois; and Harry Elkins Widener Library, Harvard University, Cambridge, Massachusetts.

KENYA NATIONAL ARCHIVES, NAIROBI, KENYA

A significant number of deposits were consulted from the Central and Rift Valley provinces, as well as from a variety of ministries, departments, and private collections. Annual reports from several departments and ministries were extremely useful in this study. These include: Native Affairs Department, later renamed African Affairs Department, 1934–63; Community Development Department and Community Development and Rehabilitation Department, 1952–60; *Report on the Treatment of Offenders*, 1950–63; and the annual reports for various provinces and districts throughout the colony during the years 1952 to 1963. In addition, the *Kenya Legislative Council Debates* were consulted at the National Archives. The deposits from the Kenya National Archives used in this book include:

Archdeacon Peter Bostock, papers
Chief Secretary's Office
Community Development Department
Department of Information
District Commissioner, Embu
District Commissioner, Fort Hall
District Commissioner, Garissa
District Commissioner, Laikipia
District Commissioner, Lokitaung
District Commissioner, Meru
District Commissioner, Naivasha
District Commissioner, Nakuru
District Commissioner, Nanyuki
District Commissioner, Nyeri
District Commissioner, Teita
District Commissioner, Thika
District Commissioner, Uasin Gishu
Labour Department
Ministry of African Affairs
Ministry of Internal Security and
    Defence
Murumbi Papers
Office of the President
Prisons Department
Probation Department
Provincial Commissioner, Central
    Province
Provincial Commissioner, Rift Valley
    Province

PUBLIC RECORD OFFICE, LONDON, ENGLAND

The *House of Commons Debates*, the *House of Lords Debates*, the *Kenya Official Gazettes*, and various newspaper microfilms were consulted at the Public Record Office (PRO). The series consulted include:

CAB 128—Cabinet minutes (CM and
    CC series)
CAB 129—Cabinet memoranda (CP
    and C series)
CO 533—Kenya, original
    correspondence
CO 822—East Africa, original
    correspondence
CO 847—Africa, correspondence
CO 859—Social Services Department
CO 912—Advisory Committee on the
    Treatment of Offenders in the
    Colonies and Related Bodies,
    minutes and papers
CO 968—Defence, original
    correspondence

CO 1022—South East Asia Department, original correspondence

CO 1030—Far East Department, registered files

WO 236—General Sir George Erskine, papers

WO 276—East Africa Command, papers

RHODES HOUSE LIBRARY, OXFORD, ENGLAND

Rhodes House (RH) contains a wealth of documentation from personal and private collections. In addition, the archive contains a variety of useful official reports and secondary materials from the period. The deposits consulted were:

Mss. Afr. s. 424—miscellaneous documents

Mss. Afr. s. 486—Sir Arthur Young, papers

Mss. Afr. s. 596—Electors' Union and the European Elected Members Organisation, papers

Mss. Afr. s. 721—Eric Frank Martin, papers

Mss. Afr. s. 746—Sir Michael Blundell, papers

Mss. Afr. s. 782—Elspeth Huxley, papers

Mss. Afr. s. 846—Mrs. J. C. Appleby, papers

Mss. Afr. s. 917—Christopher Todd, memoirs

Mss. Afr. s. 929—Kenya Emergency Liaison Committee

Mss. Afr. s. 1574—Lord Howick (Sir Evelyn Baring) and Dame Margery Perham, interview

Mss. Afr. s. 1579—S. H. Fazan, papers

Mss. Afr. s. 1580—Major General Sir Robert Hinde, KBE, CB, DSO, papers

Mss. Afr. s. 1619—Christopher L. Todd, papers

Mss. Afr. s. 1681—Africa Bureau, records

Mss. Afr. s. 1770—Thomas Askwith, *Memoirs of Kenya, 1936–61*

Mss. Afr. s. 2095—Terence Gavaghan, *Corridors of Wire*

Mss. Afr. s. 2100—Thomas Askwith, correspondence

Mss. Afr. s. 2154—Elspeth Huxley, papers

Mss. Afr. s. 2166—Thomas Askwith, papers

Mss. Afr. s. 2213—Sir Eric Griffith-Jones, papers

Mss. Brit. Emp s. 332—Arthur Creech Jones, papers

Mss. Brit. Emp s. 365—Fabian Colonial Bureau, papers

Mss. Brit. Emp. s. 525—Oliver Lyttelton (Lord Chandos), papers

Mss. Brit. Emp. s. 527/528—*End of Empire, Kenya*, transcripts

Official Publications

UNITED KINGDOM

All documents listed were published by HMSO in London.
Correspondence Relating to the Flogging of Natives by Certain Europeans in Nairobi.
    Cmnd. 3256. 1907.
Report of the Kenya Land Commission. Cmnd. 4556. 1934.
Colonial Office. *Report on Kenya.* 1945–63 (annual).
*Report to the Secretary of State for the Colonies by the Parliamentary Delegation to
    Kenya, 1954.* Cmnd. 9081. 1954.
Documents relating to the death of eleven Mau Mau detainees at Hola Camp. Cmnd.
    778. 1959.
*Record of Proceedings and Evidence in the Inquiry into the deaths of eleven Mau Mau
    detainees at Hola Camp in Kenya.* Cmnd. 795. 1959.
Report on the Nyasaland Commission of Inquiry. Cmnd. 814. 1959.
Further Documents relating to the death of eleven Mau Mau detainees at Hola Camp.
    Cmnd. 816. 1959.
Historical Survey of the Origins and Growth of Mau Mau. Cmnd. 1030. 1960.

COLONY AND PROTECTORATE OF KENYA

Unless noted, all documents listed were published by the Government Printer,
    Nairobi.
Report of the Native Labour Commission, 1912–13. 1914.
Kenya Land Commission, Evidence. 3 vols. 1934.
Report of the Committee on Juvenile Crime and Kabete Reformatory. 1934.
Report on African Education in Kenya. 1949.
African Population of Kenya Colony and Protectorate: Geographical and Tribal Studies.
    Nairobi: East African Statistical Department, 1953.
J. C. Carothers. *The Psychology of Mau Mau.* 1954.
Emergency Regulations Made under the Emergency Powers Order in Council, 1939. 1954.
Report of the Committee on African Wages. 1954.
R. J. M. Swynnerton. *A Plan to Intensify the Development of African Agriculture in
    Kenya.* 1954.
Report on the General Administration of the Prisons and Detention Camps in Kenya.
    1956.
*Administrative Enquiry into Allegations of Ill-treatment and Irregular Practices Against
    Detainees at Manyani Detention Camp and Fort Hall District Works Camps.*
    1959.
Report on the Committee on Emergency Detention Camps. 1959.

SECONDARY SOURCES

Unpublished Theses

Gachihi, Margaret Wangui. "The Role of Kikuyu Women in the Mau Mau." Master's thesis,
    University of Nairobi, 1986.
Heather, Randall. "Intelligence and Counter-insurgency in Kenya, 1952–56." Ph.D. diss.,
    Cambridge University, 1993.
Njonjo, A. L. "The Africanisation of the 'White Highlands': A Study in Agricultural Class
    Struggles in Kenya, 1950–1974." Ph.D. diss., Princeton University, 1977.
Pugliese, Christiana. "Author, Publisher and Gikuyu Nationalist: The Life and Writings of
    Gakaara wa Wanjau." Ph.D. diss., University of London, 1993.

Redley, M. G. "The Politics of Predicament: The White Community in Kenya, 1918–1932." Ph.D. diss., Cambridge University, 1976.

Books and Articles

Abbink, John, Mirjam de Bruijn, and Klaas Van Walraven, eds. *Rethinking Resistance: Revolt and Violence in African History*. Leiden: Brill, 2003.

Alexander, Jocelyn, JoAnn McGregor, and Terence Ranger. *Voice and Memory: One Hundred Years in the "Dark Forests" of Matabeleland*. Oxford: James Currey, 2000.

Allen, Michael Thad. *The Business of Genocide: The SS, Slave Labor, and the Concentration Camps*. Chapel Hill: University of North Carolina Press, 2002.

Anderson, Benedict. *Imagined Communities: Reflections on the Origin and Spread of Nationalism*. London: Verso, 1983.

Anderson, David M. "Master and Servant in Colonial Kenya, 1895–1939." *Journal of African History* 41, no. 3 (2000): 459–85.

Anderson, Perry. *Lineages of the Absolutist State*. London: New Left Books, 1974.

Andreopoulos, George J., ed. *Genocide: Conceptual and Historical Dimensions*. Philadelphia: University of Pennsylvania Press, 1994.

Antze, Paul, and Michael Lambek, eds. *Tense Past: Cultural Essays in Trauma and Meaning*. New York: Routledge, 1996.

Appiah-Kubi, Kofi, and Sergio Mendes, eds. *African Theology en Route*. New York: Orbis Books, 1983.

Applebaum, Anne. *Gulag: A History*. New York: Doubleday, 2003.

Apter, David, ed. *The Legitimization of Violence*. London: Macmillan, 1997.

Arendt, Hannah. *On Violence*. New York: Harcourt Brace, 1969.

———. *The Origins of Totalitarianism*. New York: Harcourt Brace, 1948.

Askwith, Thomas. *From Mau Mau to Harambee*. Cambridge: African Studies Centre, 1995.

———. *The Story of Kenya's Progress*. Nairobi: Eagle Press, 1957.

Asprey, Robert B. *War in the Shadows: The Guerilla in History*. New York: Doubleday, 1975.

Atieno Odhiambo, E. S. "Democracy and the Ideology of Order." In *The Political Economy of Kenya*, ed. Michael G. Schatzberg, 177–201. New York: Praeger, 1987.

———. "The Formative Years, 1945–55." In *Decolonization and Independence in Kenya, 1940–93*, ed. B. A. Ogot and W. R. Ochieng', pp. 25–47. London: James Currey, 1995.

———. "The Production of History in Kenya: The Mau Mau Debate." *Canadian Journal of African Studies* 25, 2 (1991): 300–307.

Atieno Odhiambo, E. S., and John Lonsdale, eds. *Mau Mau and Nationhood: Arms, Authority and Narration*. Oxford: James Currey, 2003.

Bakhurst, David, ed. *Collective Memory: Theoretical, Methodological, and Practical Issues: Proceedings of the Small-Group Meeting, European Association of Experimental Social Psychology*. Bari Polignana a Mare: Department of Psychology, University of Bari, May, 1997.

Baldwin, W. W. *Mau Mau Manhunt: The Adventures of the Only American Who Fought the Terrorists in Kenya*. New York: E. P. Dutton, 1957.

Barbour, John D. *The Conscience of the Autobiographer*. New York: St. Martin's Press, 1992.

Bardach, Janusz, and Kathleen Gleeson. *Man Is Wolf to Man: Surviving the Gulag*. Berkeley: University of California Press, 1998.

———. *Surviving Freedom: After the Gulag*. Berkeley: University of California Press, 2003.

Barnett, Donald L., and Karari Njama. *Mau Mau from Within*. New York: Modern Reader, 1966.

Bartov, Omer. *Mirrors of Destruction: War, Genocide, and Modern Identity*. Oxford: Oxford University Press, 2000.

Bartov, Omer, Atina Grossman, and Mary Nolan, eds. *Crimes of War: Guilt and Denial in the Twentieth Century*. New York: New Press, 2002.

Bates, Robert H. *Beyond the Miracle of the Market: The Political Economy of Agrarian Development in Kenya.* Cambridge: Cambridge University Press, 1989.

Beidelman, Thomas. *Colonial Evangelism.* Bloomington: Indiana University Press, 1982.

Bennett, George. *Kenya: A Political History, the Colonial Period.* London: Oxford University Press, 1963.

Berlin, Isaiah. *The Crooked Timber of Humanity: Chapters in the History of Ideas.* London: John Murray, 1990.

Berman, Bruce. *Control and Crisis in Colonial Kenya: The Dialectic of Domination.* London: James Currey, 1990.

———. "Nationalism, Ethnicity, and Modernity: The Paradox of Mau Mau." *Canadian Journal of African Studies* 25, no. 2 (1991): 181–206.

Berman, Bruce, and John Lonsdale. "Louis Leakey's Mau Mau: A Study in the Politics of Knowledge." *History and Anthropology* 5, no. 2 (1991): 143–204.

———. *Unhappy Valley: Conflict in Kenya and Africa.* Books 1 and 2. London: James Currey, 1992.

Bernault, Florence, ed. *A History of Prison and Confinement in Africa.* Portsmouth: Heinemann, 2003.

Betts, Raymond, ed. *The "Scramble" for Africa: Causes and Dimensions of Empire.* Boston: Heath, 1966.

Blixen, Karen. *Out of Africa.* London: Putnam, 1937.

Blundell, Michael. *A Love Affair with the Sun.* Nairobi: Kenway, 1994.

———. *So Rough a Wind.* London: Weidenfeld and Nicholson, 1964.

Boyd, Viscount [Alan Lennox-Boyd]. "Opening Address." In *The Transfer of Power: The Colonial Administrator in the Age of Decolonisation*, ed. Anthony Kirk-Greene, 2–9. Oxford: Committee for African Studies, 1979.

Brockway, Fenner. *African Journeys.* London: Victor Gollancz, 1955.

———. *Towards Tomorrow: The Autobiography of Fenner Brockway.* London: Hart-Davis, MacGibbon, 1977.

———. *Why Mau Mau? An Analysis and a Remedy.* London: Congress of Peoples Against Imperialism, 1953.

Browning, Christopher. *Ordinary Men: Reserve Police Battalion 101 and the Final Solution in Poland.* New York: HarperCollins, 1992.

Brownmiller, Susan. *Against Our Will: Men, Women and Rape.* New York: Simon and Schuster, 1975.

Buijtenhuijs, Robert. *Essays on Mau Mau: Contributions to Mau Mau Historiography.* Leiden: African Studies Center, 1982.

———. *Mau Mau Twenty Years After: The Myth and the Survivors.* The Hague: Mouton, 1973.

———. *Le mouvement "Mau Mau": Une révolte paysanne et anti-coloniale en Afrique noire.* The Hague: Mouton, 1971.

Buntman, Fran Lisa. *Robben Island and Prisoner Resistance to Apartheid.* Cambridge: Cambridge University Press, 2003

Campbell, Guy. *The Charging Buffalo: A History of the Kenya Regiment.* London: Leo Cooper, 1986.

Carnegie, V. M. *A Kenyan Farm Diary.* Edinburgh: William Blackwood and Sons, 1930.

Carothers, J. C. *The African Mind in Health and Disease: A Study in Ethnopsychiatry.* Geneva: World Health Organization, 1953.

Carruthers, Susan L. *Winning Hearts and Minds: British Governments, the Media and Colonial Counter-Insurgency, 1944–1960.* London: Leicester University Press, 1995.

Caruth, Cathy. *Trauma: Explorations in Memory.* Baltimore: Johns Hopkins University Press, 1995.

Cassese, Antonio. *Violence and Law in the Modern Age.* Princeton: Princeton University Press, 1988.

Castle, Barbara. *Fighting All the Way.* London: Macmillan, 1993.

———. "Police and Administration in Kenya." *Socialists and the Colonies Venture, Journal of the Fabian Colonial Bureau* 7, no. 9 (1956).

Chaliand, Gerard, ed. *Guerilla Strategies.* Berkeley: University of California Press, 1982.

Chalk, Frank, and Kurt Jonassohn. *The History and Sociology of Genocide: Analyses and Case Studies.* New Haven: Yale University Press, 1990.

Chang, Iris. *The Rape of Nanking: The Forgotten Holocaust of World War II.* New York: Basic Books, 1997.

Chanock, Martin. *Law, Custom, and Social Order: The Colonial Experience in Malawi and Zambia.* Cambridge: Cambridge University Press, 1985.

Chaudhuri, Nupur, and Margaret Strobel, eds. *Western Women and Imperialism: Complicity and Resistance.* Bloomington: Indiana University Press, 1992.

Chege, Michael. "Mau Mau Rebellion Fifty Years On." *African Affairs* 103 (2004): 123–36.

Chevenix-Trench, Charles. *Men Who Ruled Kenya: The Kenya Administration, 1892–1963.* London: Radcliffe Press, 1993.

Church Missionary Society. *Kenya—time for Action.* London: CMS, 1955.

Clayton, Anthony. *Counter-insurgency in Kenya: A Study of Military Operations against Mau Mau.* Nairobi: Transafrica Publishers, 1976.

Clayton, Anthony, and Donald Savage. *Government and Labour in Kenya, 1895–1963.* London: Frank Cass, 1974.

Cleary, A. S. "The Myth of Mau Mau in Its International Context." *African Affairs* 81, no. 355 (April 1990): 227–45.

Clough, Marshall S. *Fighting Two Sides: Kenyan Chiefs and Politicians, 1918–1940.* Niwot: University Press of Colorado, 1990.

———. *Mau Mau Memoirs: History, Memory and Politics.* Boulder: Lynne Rienner, 1998.

Coates, John. *Suppressing Insurgency: An Analysis of the Malayan Emergency, 1948–1954.* Boulder: Westview Press, 1992.

Cohen, David William. *The Combing of History.* Chicago: University of Chicago Press, 1994.

Cole, Jennifer. *Forget Colonialism?: Sacrifice and the Art of Memory in Madagascar.* Berkeley: University of California Press, 2001.

Comaroff, Jean. *Body of Power, Spirit of Resistance: The Culture and History of South African People.* Chicago: University of Chicago Press, 1985.

Connerton, Paul. *How Societies Remember.* Cambridge: Cambridge University Press, 1989.

Cooper, Frederick. *Decolonization and African Society: The Labor Question in French and British Africa.* Cambridge: Cambridge University Press, 1996.

———. "Mau Mau and the Discourses of Decolonization." *Journal of African History* 29 (1988): 313–20.

Cooper, Frederick, and Ann Laura Stoler, eds. *Tensions of Empire: Colonial Cultures in a Bourgeois World.* Berkeley: University of California Press, 1997.

Cranworth, Baron Bertram Francis Gurdon. *A Colony in the Making: Sport and Profit in British East Africa.* London: Macmillan, 1912.

———. *Kenya Chronicles.* London: Macmillan, 1939.

Daniel, E. Valentine. *Charred Lullabies: Chapters in an Anthropology of Violence.* Princeton: Princeton University Press, 1996.

Darwin, John. *Britain and Decolonisation: The Retreat from Empire in the Post-War Period.* New York: St. Martin's Press, 1988.

Davison, Jean. *Voices from Mutira: Lives of Rural Gikuyu Women.* Boulder: Lynne Rienner, 1989.

Deacon, Harriet, ed. *The Island: A History of Robben Island, 1488–1990.* Cape Town: David Philip and Mayibuye Books, 1996

De Silva, Cara, ed. *In Memory's Kitchen: A Legacy from the Women of Terezin.* Translated by Bianca Steiner Brown. Northvale: Jason Aronson, 1996.

Dlamini, Moses. *Hell-Hole, Robben Island, Prisoner No. 872/63: Reminiscences of a Political Prisoner.* Nottingham: Spokesman, 1994.

Dolot, Miron. *Execution by Hunger: The Hidden Holocaust.* New York: W. W. Norton, 1985.

Douglas, Mary. *Purity and Danger: An Analysis of the Concepts of Pollution and Taboo.* London: Routledge, 1966.

Douglas-Home, Charles. *Evelyn Baring: The Last Proconsul.* London: Collins, 1978.

Edgerton, Robert B. *Mau Mau: An African Crucible*. London: I. B. Tauris, 1990.

Eliot, Sir Charles. *The East Africa Protectorate*. London: Edward Arnold, 1905.

Elkins, Caroline. "Detention, Rehabilitation and the Destruction of Kikuyu Society." In *Mau Mau and Nationhood: Arms, Authority and Narration*, ed. E. S. Atieno Odhiambo and John Lonsdale, 191–226. Oxford: James Currey, 2003.

———. "The Struggle for Mau Mau Rehabilitation in Late Colonial Kenya." *International Journal of African Historical Studies* 33, no. 1 (2000): 25–57.

Elkins, Caroline, and John Lonsdale. "Memories of Mau Mau in Kenya: Public Crises and Private Shame." In *Memoria e Violenza*, ed. Alessandro Triulzi. Napoli: L'Ancora del Mediterraneo, forthcoming, 2005.

Engels, Dagmar, and Shula Marks, eds. *Contesting Colonial Hegemony: State and Society in Africa and India*. London: I. B. Tauris, 1994.

Etherington, Norman. "Natal's Black Rape Scare of the 1870s." *Journal of Southern African Studies* 15, no. 1 (1988): 36–53.

Etienne, Mona, and Eleanor Leacock. *Women and Colonization: Anthropological Perspectives*. New York: Praeger, 1980.

Evans, Peter. *Law and Disorder or Scenes of Life in Kenya*. London: Secker and Warburg, 1956.

Fabian, Johannes. *Time and the Other: How Anthropology Makes Its Object*. New York: Columbia University Press, 1983.

Fanon, Frantz. *The Wretched of the Earth*. New York: Grove Press, 1968.

Fein, Helen. *Accounting for Genocide: National Responses and Jewish Victimization during the Holocaust*. New York: Free Press, 1979.

Feldman, Allen. *Formations of Violence: The Narrative of the Body and Political Terror in Northern Ireland*. Chicago: University of Chicago Press, 1991.

Ferguson, Niall. *Empire: The Rise and Demise of the British World Order and the Lessons for Global Power*. New York: Basic Books, 2002.

Fiddes, George. *The Dominion and the Colonial Office*. London: Putnam, 1926.

Foran, W. Robert. *The Kenya Police, 1887–1960*. London: Robert Hale, 1962.

Foucault, Michel. *Discipline and Punish: The Birth of the Prison*. New York: Pantheon, 1977.

Fox, James. *White Mischief*. London: Jonathan Cape, 1982.

Freeden, Michael. *The New Liberalism—an Ideology of Social Reform*. Oxford: Clarendon Press, 1982.

Friedlander, Saul. *When Memory Comes*. Translated by Helen R. Lane. New York: Farrar, Straus, Giroux, 1979.

Frost, Richard. *Race Against Time: Human Relations and Politics in Kenya before Independence*. London: Rex Collings, 1978.

Furedi, Frank. "The African Crowd in Nairobi: Popular Movements and Elite Politics." *Journal of African History* 14 (1973): 275–90.

———. *The Mau Mau War in Perspective*. London: James Currey, 1989.

———. "The Social Composition of the Mau Mau Movement in the White Highlands." *Journal of Peasant Studies* 1 (1974): 486–505.

Gallagher, John, and Ronald Robinson. "The Imperialism of Free Trade." *Economic History Review* 6, no. 1 (1953): 1–15.

Galula, David. *Counter-Insurgency Warfare*. New York: Praeger, 1964.

Gatheru, R. Mugo. *Child of Two Worlds: A Kikuyu's Story*. New York: New American Library, 1972.

Gavaghan, Terence. *Of Lions and Dung Beetles: A "Man in the Middle" of Colonial Administration in Kenya*. Devon: Arthur H. Stockwell, 1999.

Genovese, Eugene D. *Roll, Jordan, Roll: The World the Slaves Made*. New York: Pantheon, 1974.

Gicaru, Muga. *Land of Sunshine: Scenes of Life in Kenya before Mau Mau*. London: Lawrence and Wishart, 1958.

Gikoyo, Gucu. *We Fought for Freedom/Tulipigania Uhuru*. Nairobi: East African Publishing House, 1979.

Ginzburg, Eugenia. *Within the Whirlwind.* Translated by Ian Boland. New York: Harcourt Brace Jovanovich, 1981.

Goffman, Erving. *Asylums: Essays on the Social Situation of Mental Patients and Other Inmates.* New York: Doubleday, 1961.

Goldhagen, Daniel Jonas. *Hitler's Willing Executioners: Ordinary Germans and the Holocaust.* New York: Vintage, 1997.

Goldsworthy, David. *Colonial Issues in British Politics, 1945–1961.* Oxford: Clarendon Press, 1971.

Goodwin, James. *Autobiography: The Self-Made Text.* New York: Twayne, 1993.

Gordon, David. *Decolonization and the State in Kenya.* Boulder: Westview, 1986.

Gramsci, Antonio. *Selections from the Prison Notebooks of Antonio Gramsci.* Translated and edited by Quintin Hoare and Geoffrey Nowell Smith. New York: International Publishers, 1971.

Greaves, L. B. *Carey Francis of Kenya.* London: Rex Collings, 1969.

Green, Maia. "Mau Mau Oathing Rituals and Political Ideology in Kenya: A Re-Analysis." *Africa* 60, no. 1 (1990): 69–87.

Gregory, Robert. *Sidney Webb and East Africa.* Berkeley: University of California Press, 1962.

Gupta, Partha Sarathi. *Imperialism and the British Labour Movement, 1914–1964.* New York: Holmes and Meier, 1975.

Gutierrez, Gustavo. *A Theology of Liberation: History, Politics and Salvation.* New York: Orbis Books, 1973.

Guyer, Jane. "Household and Community in African Studies." *African Studies Review* 24, nos. 2–3 (1981): 87–137.

Guyer, Jane, and Samuel Belinga. "Wealth in People as Wealth in Knowledge." *Journal of African History* 36, no. 1 (1995): 91–120.

Hannaford, Ivan. *Race: The History of an Idea in the West.* Baltimore: Johns Hopkins University Press, 1996.

Harbeson, John. *Nation-Building in Kenya: The Role of Land Reform.* Evanston: Northwestern University Press, 1973.

Harlow, Barbara. *Resistance Literature.* New York: Methuen, 1987.

Hayner, Priscilla B. *Unspeakable Truths: Confronting State Terror and Atrocity.* New York: Routledge, 2001.

Heinlein, Frank. *British Government Policy and Decolonisation, 1945–1963—Scrutinising the Official Mind.* London: Frank Cass, 2002.

Henderson, Ian. *Man Hunt in Kenya.* New York: Doubleday, 1958.

Henderson, Ian, and Philip Goodhart. *The Hunt for Kimathi.* London: Hamish Hamilton, 1958.

Herling, Gustaw. *A World Apart.* Translated by Andrzej Ciozkosz. New York: Arbor House, 1986.

Heussler, Robert. *Yesterday's Rulers: The Making of the British Colonial Service.* London: Oxford University Press, 1963.

Hewitt, Peter. *Kenya Cowboy: A Police Officer's Account of the Mau Mau Emergency.* Johannesburg: Covos Day, 2001.

Hobley, C. W. *Kenya from Chartered Company to Crown Colony.* London: Witherby, 1929.

Hobsbawm, Eric. *Primitive Rebels.* New York: W. W. Norton, 1959.

Hobsbawm, Eric, and Terence Ranger, eds. *Invention of Tradition.* Cambridge: Cambridge University Press, 1983.

Horne, Alistair. *Macmillan, 1957–1986.* London: Macmillan, 1989.

Horowitz, Irving Louis. *Taking Lives: Genocide and State Power.* New Brunswick, N.J.: Transaction, 1997.

Howarth, Anthony. *Kenyatta: A Photographic Biography.* Nairobi: East African Publishing House, 1967.

Howe, Stephen. *Anticolonialism in British Politics—the Left and the End of Empire, 1918–1964.* Oxford: Clarendon Press, 1993.

Hughes, O. E. B. "Villages in the Kikuyu Country." *Journal of African Administration* 8, no. 4 (1955): 170–74.

Huxley, Elspeth. *The Challenge of Africa*. London: Aldus, 1971.

———. *Nine Faces of Kenya*. London: Harvill Press, 1990.

———. *Race and Politics in Kenya, a Correspondence between Elspeth Huxley and Margery Perham*. London: Faber and Faber, 1944.

———. *The Red Strangers*. London: Chatto and Windus, 1944.

———. *Settlers of Kenya*. Nairobi: Highway Press, 1948.

———. *White Man's Country: Lord Delamere and the Making of Kenya*. Vols. 1–2. London: Macmillan, 1935.

Huxley, Elspeth, and Arnold Curtis, eds. *Pioneers' Scrapbook: Reminiscences of Kenya, 1890–1968*. London: Evans Brothers, 1980.

Iliffe, John. *The African Poor*. Cambridge: Cambridge University Press, 1987.

———. *The Emergence of African Capitalism*. Minneapolis: University of Minnesota Press, 1983.

Itote, Waruhiu. *"Mau Mau" General*. Nairobi: East African Publishing House, 1967.

———. *Mau Mau in Action*. Nairobi: Transafrica, 1979.

Jacobs, Dan. *The Brutality of Nations*. New York: Knopf, 1987.

James, Lawrence. *The Rise and Fall of the British Empire*. New York: St. Martin's Press, 1996.

Jonassohn, Kurt, and Karin Solveig Bjornson. *Genocide and Gross Human Rights Violations*. New Brunswick, N.J.: Transaction, 1998.

Kabiro, Ngugi. *Man in the Middle: The Story of Ngugi Kabiro*. Richmond: Liberation Support Movement, 1973.

Kaggia, Bildad. *Roots of Freedom, 1921–1963: The Autobiography of Bildad Kaggia*. Nairobi: East African Publishing House, 1975.

Kamunchula, J. T. Samuel. "The Meru Participation in Mau Mau." *Kenya Historical Review* 3, no. 2 (1975): 193–216.

Kanogo, Tabitha. "Kikuyu Women and the Politics of Protest: Mau Mau." In *Images of Women in Peace and War, Cross-Cultural and Historical Perspectives*, ed. Sharon Macdonald, Pat Holden, and Shirley Ardener, 78–96. Madison: University of Wisconsin Press, 1988.

———. *Squatters and the Roots of Mau Mau*. London: James Currey, 1987.

Kariuki, Josiah Mwangi. *"Mau Mau" Detainee: The Account by a Kenya African of His Experiences in Detention Camps, 1953–1960*. London: Oxford University Press, 1963.

Kathrada, Ahmed M. *Letters from Robben Island: A Selection of Ahmed Kathrada's Prison Correspondence, 1964–1989*, ed. Robert D. Vassen. East Lansing: Michigan State University Press, 1999.

Kelsall, R. K. *Higher Civil Servants in Great Britain*. London: Routledge, 1955.

Kennedy, Dane. "Constructing the Colonial Myth of Mau Mau." *International Journal of African Historical Studies* 25, no. 2 (1992): 241–60.

———. *Islands of White: Settler Society and Culture in Kenya and Southern Rhodesia, 1890–1939*. Durham, N.C.: Duke University Press, 1987.

Kenyatta, Jomo. *Facing Mount Kenya: The Tribal Life of the Gikuyu*. 1939; reprint, Nairobi: Heinemann, 1978.

———. *Harambee! The Prime Minister of Kenya's Speeches, 1963–64*. Oxford: Oxford University Press, 1964.

———. *Suffering without Bitterness, the founding of the Kenya Nation*. Nairobi: East African Publishing House, 1968.

Kershaw, Greet. *Mau Mau from Below*. Oxford: James Currey, 1997.

———. "Mau Mau from Below: Fieldwork and Experience, 1955–57 and 1962." *Canadian Journal of African Studies* 25, no. 2 (1991): 274–97.

Killingray, David, and David M. Anderson. "An Orderly Retreat? Policing the End of Empire." In *Policing and Decolonisation: Politics, Nationalism and the Police, 1917–65*, ed. David M. Anderson and David Killingray, 1–21. Manchester: Manchester University Press, 1992.

Kinyatti, Maina wa, ed. *Kenya's Freedom Struggle: The Dedan Kimathi Papers.* London: Zed, 1987.

———. "Mau Mau: The Peak of Political Organization in Colonial Kenya." *Kenya Historical Review* 5, no. 2 (1977): 287–311.

———, ed. *Thunder from the Mountains: Mau Mau Patriotic Songs.* London: Zed, 1980.

Kipkorir, Ben. *Biographical Essays on Imperialism and Colonialism in Colonial Kenya.* Nairobi: Kenya Literature Bureau, 1980.

———. "The Inheritors and Successors: The Traditional Background to the Modern Kenyan African Elite: Kenya circa 1890–1930." *Kenya Historical Review* 2, no. 2 (1974): 143–61.

Kirk-Greene, Anthony. "In Search of an Anatomy of African Administrators." *Public Administration and Development* 1 (1981): 271–79.

———. *On Crown Service: A History of HM Colonial and Overseas Civil Services, 1837–1997.* London: I. B. Tauris, 1999.

———, ed. *The Transfer of Power: The Colonial Administrator in the Age of Decolonisation.* Oxford: Committee for African Studies, 1979.

Kitching, Gavin. *Class and Economic Change in Kenya: The Making of an African Petite Bourgeoisie.* New Haven: Yale University Press, 1980.

Kitson, Frank. *Gangs and Counter-Gangs.* London: Barrie and Rockliffe, 1960.

Koff, David, and Anthony Howarth. *Black Man's Land: Images of Colonialism and Independence in Kenya.* Van Nuys, Calif.: Bellweather Group, 1979.

Kuper, Leo. *Genocide: Its Political Use in the Twentieth Century.* New Haven: Yale University Press, 1981.

Langer, Lawrence. *Holocaust Testimonies: The Ruins of Memory.* New Haven: Yale University Press, 1991.

Lapping, Brian. *End of Empire.* New York: St. Martin's, 1985.

Lavers, Anthony. *The Kikuyu Who Fight Mau Mau/Wakikuyu Wanopigana na Mau Mau.* Nairobi: Eagle Press, 1985.

Leakey, L. S. B. *Defeating Mau Mau.* London: Methuen, 1954.

———. *Mau Mau and the Kikuyu.* London: Methuen, 1953.

———. *The Southern Kikuyu before 1903.* Vols. 1, 2, and 3. London: Academic Press, 1977.

Leigh, Ione. *In the Shadow of the Mau Mau.* London: W. H. Allen, 1954.

Leo, Christopher. *Land and Class in Kenya.* Toronto: University of Toronto Press, 1984.

Levi, Primo. *If This Is a Man.* Translated by Stuart Woolf. New York: Vintage, 1996.

———. *The Reawakening.* Translated by Stuart Woolf. New York: Touchstone, 1995.

———. *Survival in Auschwitz.* Translated by Stuart Woolf. New York: Touchstone, 1996.

Lewis, Joanna. "'Daddy Wouldn't Buy Me a Mau Mau': The British Popular Press and the Demoralization of Empire." In *Mau Mau and Nationhood: Arms, Authority and Narration,* ed. E. S. Atieno Odhiambo and John Lonsdale, 227–50. Oxford: James Currey, 2003.

———. *Empire State-Building: War and Welfare in Kenya, 1925–52.* Oxford: James Currey, 2000.

Leys, Colin. *Underdevelopment in Kenya.* Berkeley: University of California Press, 1974.

Likimani, Muthoni. *Passbook Number F. 47927: Women and Mau Mau in Kenya.* London: Macmillan, 1985.

Lindsay, Lisa, and Stephan Miescher, eds. *Men and Masculinities in Modern Africa.* Portsmouth: Heinemann, 2003.

Lipscomb, J. F. *White Africans.* London: Faber and Faber, 1955.

Lloyd, Trevor. *Empire: The History of the British Empire.* London: Hambledon and London, 2001.

Lonsdale, John. "Agency in Tight Corners: Narrative and Initiative in African History." *Journal of African Cultural Studies* 13, no. 1 (2000): 5–16.

———. "Authority, Gender and Violence: The War Within Mau Mau's Fight for Land and Freedom." In *Mau Mau and Nationhood: Arms, Authority and Narration,* ed. E. S. Atieno Odhiambo and John Lonsdale, 46–75. Oxford: James Currey, 2003.

————. "KAU's Cultures: Imaginations of Community and Constructions of Leadership in Kenya after the Second World War." *Journal of African Cultural Studies* 13, no. 1 (2000): 107–24.

————. "Kenyatta's Trials: Breaking and Making an African Nationalist." In *The Moral World of the Law,* ed. Peter Cross, 196–239. Cambridge: Cambridge University Press, 2000.

————. "Mau Maus of the Mind: Making Mau Mau and Remaking Kenya." *Journal of African History* 31 (1990): 393–421.

————. "The Prayers of Waiyaki: Political Uses of the Kikuyu Past." In *Revealing Prophets: Prophecy in Eastern African History,* ed. David Anderson and Douglas H. Johnson, 240–91. London: James Currey, 1995.

————. "Some Origins of Nationalism in East Africa." *Journal of African History* 9, no. 1 (1968): 119–46.

Louis, William Roger, ed. *The Oxford History of the British Empire.* 5 vols. Oxford: Oxford University Press, 1998–99.

Low, D. A., and John Lonsdale. "Introduction: Towards the New Order, 1945–63." In *History of East Africa,* ed. D. A. Low and Alison Smith, 3:12–16. Oxford: Clarendon Press, 1976.

Lugard, Frederick. *The Dual Mandate in British Tropical Africa.* Edinburgh: Blackwood and Sons, 1922.

Lyttelton, Oliver [Lord Chandos]. *The Memoirs of Lord Chandos: An Unexpected View from the Summit.* New York: New American Library, 1963.

McCulloch, Jock. *Black Peril, White Virtue: Sexual Crime in Southern Rhodesia, 1902–1935.* Bloomington: Indiana University Press, 2000.

————. *Colonial Psychiatry and "the African Mind."* Cambridge: Cambridge University Press, 1995.

McEvoy, Kieran. *Paramilitary Imprisonment in Northern Ireland: Resistance, Management, and Release.* Oxford: Oxford University Press, 2001.

MacKenzie, John, ed. *Propaganda and Empire: The Manipulation of British Public Opinion, 1880–1960.* Manchester: Manchester University Press, 1984.

Macmillan, Harold. *Pointing the Way, 1959–1961.* London: Macmillan, 1972.

————. *Riding the Storm, 1956–1959.* London: Macmillan, 1971.

Maharaj, Mac, ed. *Reflections in Prison.* Cape Town: Zebra and Robben Island Museum, 2001.

Majdalany, Fred. *State of Emergency: The Full Story of Mau Mau.* Boston: Houghton Mifflin, 1963.

Malkki, Liisa. *Purity and Exile: Violence, Memory and National Cosmology among Hutu Refugees in Tanzania.* Chicago: University of Chicago Press, 1995.

Maloba, Wunyabari O. *Mau Mau and Kenya: An Analysis of a Peasant Revolt.* Bloomington: Indiana University Press, 1993.

Mamdani, Mahmood. *Citizen and Subject: Contemporary Africa and the Legacy of Late Colonialism.* Princeton: Princeton University Press, 1996.

Mandela, Nelson. *Long Walk to Freedom: The Autobiography of Nelson Mandela.* London: Little, Brown, 1994.

Mann, Kristin, and Richard Roberts, eds. *Law in Colonial Africa.* Portsmouth: Heinemann, 1991.

Mathu, Mohamed. *The Mau Mau in Kenya.* London: Hutchinson, 1954.

Maughan-Brown, David. *Land, Freedom, and Fiction: History and Ideology in Kenya.* London: Zed, 1985.

Meinertzhagen, Richard. *Kenya Diary, 1902–1906.* London: Oliver and Boyd, 1957.

Memmi, Albert. *The Colonizer and the Colonized.* Boston: Beacon Press, 1965.

————. *Racism.* Minneapolis: University of Minnesota Press, 2000.

Middleton, David, and Derek Edwards, eds. *Collective Remembering.* London: Sage, 1990.

Middleton, John, and Greet Kershaw. *The Central Tribes of the North-Eastern Bantu: The Kikuyu including Embu, Meru, Mbere, Chuka, Mwimbi, Tharaka, and the Kamba of Kenya.* London: International African Institute, 1954.

Milgram, Stanley. *Obedience to Authority: An Experimental View.* New York: Harper and Row, 1974.

Miller, Charles. *The Lunatic Express: An Entertainment in Imperialism.* New York: Macmillan, 1971.

Millet, Kate. *The Politics of Cruelty: An Essay on the Literature of Political Imprisonment.* New York: W. W. Norton, 1994.

Ministry of Economic Planning and Development. *Kenya Population Census, 1962.* 4 volumes. Nairobi: Ministry of Finance and Economic Planning, 1964–66.

Mitchell, Philip. *African Afterthoughts.* London: Hutchinson, 1954.

Moore, Barrington. *Injustice: The Social Bases of Obedience and Revolt.* White Plains, N.Y.: M. E. Sharpe, 1978.

Moss, George L. *Toward the Final Solution: A History of European Racism.* Madison: University of Wisconsin Press, 1985.

Movement for Colonial Freedom. *Truth About Kenya—an eye witness account by Eileen Fletcher.* 1956.

Muchai, Karigo, and Donald Barnett. *The Hardcore: The Story of Karigo Muchai.* Richmond: Liberation Support Movement, 1973.

Muoria, Henry. *I, the Gikuyu and the White Fury.* Nairobi: East African Educational Publishers, 1994.

Muriuki, Godfrey. *A History of the Kikuyu, 1500–1900.* Nairobi: Oxford University Press, 1974.

Murphy, Philip. *Alan Lennox-Boyd, a Biography.* London: I. B. Tauris, 1999.

———. *Party Politics and Decolonization: The Conservative Party and British Colonial Policy in Tropical Africa, 1951–1964.* Oxford: Clarendon Press, 1995.

Murray, Jocelyn. "The Church Missionary Society and the 'Female Circumcision' Issue in Kenya, 1929–1932." *Journal of Religion in Africa* 8, no. 2 (1976): 92–104.

———. *Proclaim the Good News: A Short History of the Church Missionary Society.* London: Hodder and Stoughton, 1985.

Murray-Brown, Jeremy. *Kenyatta.* London: George Allen and Unwin, 1972.

Musembi, Musila. *Archives Management: The Kenyan Experience.* Nairobi: Africa Book Services, 1985.

Neier, Aryeh. *War Crimes: Brutality, Genocide, Terror, and the Struggle for Justice.* New York: Times Books, 1998.

Ngugi wa Thiong'o. "Born Again: Mau Mau Unchained." In *Writers in Politics*, 86–93. London: Heinemann, 1981.

———. *Detained: A Writer's Prison Diary.* London: Heinemann, 1981.

———. *A Grain of Wheat.* London: Heinemann, 1967.

———. "J. M.—a Writer's Tribute." In *Writers in Politics*, 82–85. London: Heinemann, 1967.

———. "Mau Mau: Violence and Culture." In *Homecoming: Essays on African Caribbean Literature, Culture and Politics*, 26–30. New York: Lawrence Hill, 1973.

———. *Petals of Blood.* London: Heinemann, 1977.

Njama, Karari. *Mau Mau from Within: Autobiography and Analysis of Kenya's Peasant Revolt.* New York: Modern Reader, 1966.

O'Barr, Jean, "Introductory Essay." In *Passbook Number F. 47927* by Muthoni Likimani, 1–37. London: Macmillan, 1985.

Odinga, Oginga. *Not Yet Uhuru.* London: Heinemann, 1967.

Ogot, B. A. "The Decisive Years, 1952–63." In *Decolonization and Independence in Kenya, 1940–93*, ed. B. A. Ogot and W. R. Ochieng', 48–79. London: James Currey, 1995.

———. "Revolt of the Elders: An Anatomy of the Loyalist Crowd in the Mau Mau Uprising, 1952–56." In *Politics and Nationalism in Colonial Kenya*, ed. B. A. Ogot, 134–48. Nairobi: East African Publishing House, 1972.

Oliver, Roland. *The Missionary Factor in East Africa.* London: Longmans, 1954.

Ortner, Sherry B. "Resistance and the Problem of Ethnographic Refusal." *Comparative Studies in Society and History* 37, no. 1 (1995): 173–93.

Osiel, Mark. *Mass Atrocity, Collective Memory, and the Law.* New Brunswick, N.J.: Transaction, 1997.

Otieno, Wambui Waiyaki. *Mau Mau's Daughter: A Life History.* Boulder: Lynne Rienner, 1998.

Pakenham, Thomas. *The Scramble for Africa, 1876–1916.* London: Weidenfeld and Nicholson, 1991.

Parker, Mary. *How Kenya Is Governed.* Nairobi: Eagle Press, 1955.

Parkin, Alan. *Memory and Amnesia.* Oxford: Blackwell, 1987.

Parkinson, Cosmo. *The Colonial Office from Within, 1909–1945.* London: Faber, 1947.

Parsons, Timothy. *The African Rank-and-File: Social Implications of Colonial Military Service in the King's African Rifles, 1902–1964.* Portsmouth, N.H.: Heinemann, 1999.

Patterson, Orlando. *Slavery and Social Death: A Comparative Study.* Cambridge: Harvard University Press, 1982.

Perham, Margery. *The Colonial Reckoning: The End of Imperial Rule in Africa in the Light of the British Experience.* New York: Knopf, 1962.

Perkins, Anne. *Red Queen: The Authorized Biography of Barbara Castle.* London: Macmillan, 2003.

Picket, Brent L. "Foucault and the Politics of Resistance." *Polity* 28, no. 4 (1996): 445–66.

Porter, Andrew, ed. *Atlas of British Overseas Expansion.* London: Routledge, 1991.

Power, Samantha. *"A Problem from Hell": America and the Age of Genocide.* New York: Basic Books, 2002.

Presley, Cora Ann. *Kikuyu Women, the Mau Mau Rebellion and Social Change in Kenya.* Boulder: Westview Press, 1992.

———. "Labor Protest Among Kikuyu Women, 1912–1947." In *Women, Race and Class in Africa,* ed. Claire Robertson and Iris Berger, 255–73. New York: Holmes and Meier Press, 1986.

———. "Women and the Mau Mau Rebellion." In *In Resistance: Studies in African, Afro-American, and Caribbean Resistance,* ed. Gary Okihiro, 53–70. Amherst: University of Massachusetts Press, 1986.

Ranger, Terence. *Peasant Consciousness and Guerrilla War in Zimbabwe.* London: James Currey, 1985.

———. *Voices from the Rocks: Nature, Culture and History in the Matopos Hills of Zimbabwe.* Oxford: James Currey, 1999.

Rawcliffe, D. H. *The Struggle for Kenya.* London: Victor Gollancz, 1954.

Reemtsma, Jan Philipp. "On War Crimes." In *Crimes of War: Guilt and Denial in the Twentieth Century,* ed. Omer Bartov, Atina Grossman, and Mary Nolan, 8–16. New York: New York Press, 2002.

Rich, Paul. *Race and Empire in British Politics.* Cambridge: Cambridge University Press, 1986.

Roberts, Granville. *The Mau Mau in Kenya.* London: Hutchinson, 1954.

Rosberg, Carl, and John Nottingham. *The Myth of "Mau Mau": Nationalism in Kenya.* Nairobi: East African Publishing House, 1966.

Rotberg, Robert I., and Thomas G. Weiss, eds. *From Massacres to Genocide: The Media, Public Policy and Humanitarian Crises.* Washington, D.C.: Brookings Institution, 1996.

Sabar-Friedman, Galia. "The Mau Mau Myth: Kenyan Political Discourse in Search of Democracy." *Cahiers d'études africaines* 35, no. 1 (1995): 101–29.

Sandgren, David P. *Christianity and the Kikuyu: Religious Divisions and Social Conflict.* New York: P. Lang, 1989.

Santilli, Kathy. "Kikuyu Women in the Mau Mau Revolt." *Ufahamu* 8, no. 1 (1977–78): 143–59.

Santoru, Marina E. "The Colonial Idea of Women and Direct Intervention: The Mau Mau Case." *African Affairs* 95, no. 379 (1996): 253–67.

Scarry, Elaine. *The Body in Pain: The Making and Unmaking of the World.* Oxford: Oxford University Press, 1985.

Schacter, Daniel L. *Searching for Memory: The Brain, the Mind, and the Past.* New York: Basic Books, 1996.

———. *The Seven Sins of Memory.* Boston: Houghton Mifflin, 2001.

Schadenberg, Jurgen. *Voices from Robben Island.* Randburg: Ravan Press, 1994.

Scott, James. *Domination and the Arts of Resistance: Hidden Transcripts.* New Haven: Yale University Press, 1990.

———. *Weapons of the Weak: Everyday Forms of Peasant Resistance.* New Haven: Yale University Press, 1985.

Shannon, Mary. "African Education among the Kikuyu." *African World* (July 1953): 13–14.

———. "Rebuilding the Social Life of the Kikuyu." *African Affairs* 56, no. 225 (1957): 276–84.

———. "Rehabilitating the Kikuyu." *African Affairs* 54, no. 215 (1955): 129–37.

Sheleff, Leon Shaskolsky. *The Bystander: Behavior, Law, Ethics.* Lexington, Mass.: Lexington Books, 1978.

Shepherd, Robert. *Iain Macleod.* London: Random House, 1994.

Slater, Montagu. *The Trial of Jomo Kenyatta.* London: Mercury Books, 1965.

Smith, Alison, and Mary Bull, eds. *Margery Perham and British Rule in Africa.* London: Frank Cass, 1991.

Smith, David Lovatt. *My Enemy: My Friend.* Nairobi: FOCCAM, 2000.

Sofsky, Wolfgang. *The Order of Terror: The Concentration Camp.* Translated by William Templer. Princeton: Princeton University Press, 1997.

———. *Violence: Terrorism, Genocide, War.* Translated by Anthea Bell. London: Granta Books, 2003.

Solzhenitsyn, Aleksandr. *The Gulag Archipelago, 1918–1956.* Translated by Thomas P. Whitney and Harry Willetts. New York: HarperCollins, 1985.

Sorrenson, M. P. K. *Land Reform in the Kikuyu Country: A Study in Government Policy.* London: Oxford University Press, 1967.

———. *Origins of European Settlement in Kenya.* Nairobi: Oxford University Press, 1968.

Spencer, John. *The Kenya African Union.* London: KPI, 1985.

Stoler, Ann Laura. "Rethinking Colonial Categories: European Communities and the Boundaries of Rule." *Comparative Studies in Society and History* 31, no. 1 (1989): 134–61.

Stubbs, Richard. *Hearts and Minds in Guerrilla Warfare: The Malaya Emergency, 1948–1960.* New York: Oxford University Press, 1989.

Symonds, Richard. *Oxford and Empire: The Last Lost Cause?* Oxford: Clarendon Press, 1986.

Tamarkin, Mordechai. "The Loyalists in Nakuru during the Mau Mau Revolt." *Asian and African Studies* 12, no. 2 (1978): 247–61.

———. "Mau Mau in Nakuru." *Journal of African History* 17, no. 308 (1978): 297–320.

Thomas, Lynn M. *Politics of the Womb: Women, Reproduction, and the State in Kenya.* Berkeley: University of California Press, 2003.

Throup, David. "Crime, Politics and the Police in Colonial Kenya, 1939–63." In *Policing and Decolonisation: Politics, Nationalism and the Police, 1917–65,* ed. David M. Anderson and David Killingray, 127–57. Manchester: Manchester University Press, 1992.

———. *Economic and Social Origins of Mau Mau, 1945–53.* London: James Currey, 1988.

Throup, David, and Charles Hornsby. *Multi-Party Politics in Kenya.* Oxford: James Currey, 1998.

Thuku, Harry. *An Autobiography.* Nairobi: Oxford University Press, 1970.

Tignor, Robert L. *Capitalism and Nationalism at the End of Empire: State and Business in Decolonizing Egypt, Nigeria, and Kenya, 1945–1963.* Princeton: Princeton University Press, 1998.

———. *The Colonial Transformation of Kenya: The Kamba, Kikuyu and Maasai from 1900 to 1939.* Princeton: Princeton University Press, 1976.

Todorov, Tzvetan. *Facing the Extreme: Moral Life in the Concentration Camps.* Translated by Arthur Denner and Abigail Pollak. New York: Henry Holt, 1996.

Totten, Samuel, William S. Parsons, and Isreal W. Charny, eds. *A Century of Genocide: Eyewitness Accounts and Critical Views.* New York: Garland, 1997.

Trzebinski, Errol. *Kenya Pioneers.* London: Heinemann, 1985.

Turner, Victor W. *Dramas, Fields, and Metaphor: Symbolic Action in Human Society.* Ithaca: Cornell University Press, 1974.

———. *The Drums of Affliction: A Study of Religious Processes among the Ndembu of Zambia.* Oxford: Clarendon Press, 1968.

————. *The Ritual Process: Structure and Anti-Structure.* Chicago: Aldine, 1969.

Vail, Leroy. Introduction to *The Creation of Tribalism in Southern Africa,* ed. Leroy Vail. London: James Currey, 1989.

Vail, Leroy, and Landeg White. *Power and the Praise Poem: Southern African Voices in History.* London: James Currey, 1991.

Van Gennep, Arnold. *The Rites of Passage.* Chicago: University of Chicago Press, 1960.

Van Zwanenberg, R. M. A. *Colonial Capitalism and Labour in Kenya, 1919–1939.* Nairobi: East African Literature Bureau, 1975.

————. "Kenya's Primitive Colonial Capitalism: The Economic Weakness of Kenya's Settlers up to 1940." *Canadian Journal of African Historical Studies* 9, no. 2 (1975): 277–92.

Vaughan, Megan. *Curing their Ills: Colonial Power and African Illness.* Cambridge: Polity Press, 1991.

Wachanga, H. K. *The Swords of Kirinyaga: The Fight for Land and Freedom.* Nairobi: East African Literature Bureau, 1975.

Waciuma, Charity. *Daughter of Mumbi.* Nairobi: East African Publishing House, 1969.

Wamwere, Koigi wa. *Conscience on Trial. Why I was Detained: Notes of a Political Prisoner in Kenya.* Trenton N.J.: Africa World Press, 1988.

Wanjau, Gakaara wa. *Mau Mau Author in Detention.* Nairobi: Heinemann, 1988.

Wanjohi, Gerald Joseph. *The Wisdom and Philosophy of the Gikuyu Proverbs, the Kihooto World-View.* Nairobi: Paulines Publications Africa, 1997.

Wartenberg, Thomas E. *The Forms of Power: From Domination to Transformation.* Philadelphia: Temple University Press, 1990.

Weber, Max. *Politics as a Vocation.* Translated by H. H. Gerthand and C. Wright Mills. Philadelphia: Fortress Press, 1965.

Weisbord, Robert. *African Zion: The Attempt to Establish a Jewish Colony in the East Africa Protectorate, 1903–1905.* Philadelphia: Jewish Publication Society of America, 1968.

West, Cornell. "Marxist Theory and the Specificity of Afro-American Oppression." In *Marxism and the Interpretation of Cultures,* ed. Cary Nelson and Lawrence Grossberg, 17–30. Urbana: University of Illinois Press, 1988.

White, Luise. *The Comforts of Home: Prostitution in Colonial Nairobi.* Chicago: University of Chicago Press, 1990.

————. "Separating the Men from the Boys: Constructions of Gender, Sexuality, and Terrorism in Central Kenya, 1939–1959." *International Journal of African Historical Studies* 23, no. 1 (1990): 1–25.

White, Luise, Stephan F. Miescher, and David William Cohen, eds. *African Words, African Voices: Critical Practices in Oral History.* Bloomington: Indiana University Press, 2001.

Wilson, Christopher. *Before the Dawn in Kenya.* Nairobi: English Press, 1953.

Wipper, Audrey. "The Maendeleo ya Wanawake Movement: Some Paradoxes and Contradictions." *African Studies Review* 18, no. 3 (1975): 99–120.

————. "The Maendeleo ya Wanawake Movement in the Colonial Period." *Rural Africana* 29 (1975–76): 195–214.

Wolf, Eric. *Peasant Wars in the Twentieth Century.* New York: Harper and Row, 1969.

Young, Crawford. *The African Colonial State in Comparative Perspective.* New Haven: Yale University Press, 1994.

ACKNOWLEDGMENTS

IT HAS TAKEN ME NEARLY A DECADE TO COMPLETE THIS BOOK, DUR-
ing which time the list of those who have provided me with intellectual,
practical, and personal support has grown to considerable size.

While this project began in 1995, my love for African history started
long before, during my undergraduate years at Princeton. It was there that
I first met Bob Tignor, who inspired me to follow his career path, something I have never regretted. Over the years Bob has been a guiding light,
providing encouragement and gentle criticism and always leading by example. During the course of my research for this book, I had the pleasure
of spending nearly a year at the Public Record Office in London with Bob,
who was there working on his own project. Together, we spent countless
hours over lunch and during our commutes talking about African and imperial history, family and politics, and the latest sports standings back in
the United States. Since then Bob read various drafts of this book, offering
his wisdom and support. I will forever be indebted to him.

All of the research and writing for this book was done during my time
at Harvard, first as a graduate student and then as a faculty member in the
history department. To reconstruct a period of history that has been
largely purged from the official archives takes a lot of time and considerable resources. On both counts, Harvard was extraordinarily generous. I
first arrived in Cambridge in 1994 largely to work with Leroy Vail, whose
work on oral history and tradition, as well as on resistance, was pathbreak-
ing. Like Bob, he inspired by example while doing his best to temper the
renegade intellect of his graduate student. It was Leroy who was convinced
of the importance of this project, and of the need for me to be careful and
exhaustive with my research; it was he who insisted that I must perfect my
languages, live in the field, and interview survivors. It is the only way, he
would remind me, to understand history from the Africans' perspectives.
Sadly, Leroy did not live to see me finish my research. During my fieldwork
I received an early morning phone call in Nairobi with the news that he
had succumbed in his valiant struggle with lymphoma. As I was writing
this book, though, his hand guided me many times and left an imprint on
many a page.

There are many other people at Harvard to whom I am deeply indebted. Emmanuel Akyeampong has been a true friend and steadfast supporter of this project, first as an adviser and now as a colleague. Susan Pedersen offered sound advice, tough criticism, and great friendship. I am also grateful to Liz Cohen, who stepped in at several important moments in the writing of this book to provide invaluable guidance and support. And finally, the African studies crowd at Harvard is one of the most encouraging groups of people a young scholar could hope for. Everyone was extremely understanding of my absences as I finished this book and, even more remarkably, insistent that I stay away from teaching and administrative duties so that the story of detention could finally go to press. To Bob Bates, Suzanne Blier, Skip Gates, Ulla Larsen, Suzanne Grant Lewis, John Mugane, Pauline Peters, Kay Shelemay, Lucy White, and, of course, Emmanuel, thanks is but a small recompense.

I am also grateful to the numerous friends and colleagues outside of Harvard who aided in my research and writing. First among them is John Lonsdale, whose contributions to this book, not to mention my intellectual development, are far too numerous to catalog here. He is the most gifted scholar I know, and one who combines brilliance with consummate good grace. This book would not have been the same without him. My sincere thanks also goes to several other Africanists who provided advice, read drafts, and, most important, shared more than a drink or two with me over the years. They are Jocelyn Alexander, Dave Anderson, Zayde Antrim, Kelly Askew, E. S. Atieno Odhiambo, Bruce Berman, Chloe Campbell, Marshall Clough, Jean Hay, Kennell Jackson, Joanna Lewis, Julie Livingstone, Meredith McKittrick, Joe Miller, Kenda Mutongi, Jeanne Penvenne, Derek Peterson, Bill Rich, Sara Rich, Parker Shipton, Megan Vaughan, Richard Waller, and Diana Wylie. To Terence Ranger, who offered generous support during my research days at Oxford and who, like Leroy, insisted that I provide plenty of room for African voices in this book, I offer my deepest gratitude. I am also indebted to John McGhie, Giselle Portenier, and the entire production crew at the BBC, who brought my research to the screen with the production of *Kenya: White Terror* in 2002. Throughout the filming and editing, John and Giselle strove tirelessly to get this story right, and I walked away from the project with a new understanding of myself and my fieldwork. I would also like to thank Anne Perkins, who stepped in during the last stages of my writing to offer incredible insight into postwar Labour politics. My sincerest gratitude, as well, to Sharon Sundue, who is my most loyal and trusted friend, not to mention a truly fine historian.

My research assistant, Terry Wairimu, was a constant source of support, knowledge, and friendship throughout this project. We first met in the fall of 1998 and began what I would call our odyssey to find survivors upcountry. During our long car rides Terry never once complained of my hair-raising driving skills. Instead, she sat stoically in the passenger seat as I wove around potholes and passed cars on hillside curves, and discussed Kikuyu history, politics, and culture with me. Together we spent many a lengthy stretch in the field, often not knowing where we would sleep or eat, fueled instead by our shared interest in recovering the past in Kikuyuland. After our initial year of interviewing, Terry and I continued working together on this project as well as on several others, though we now spend most of our time talking about our children and our lives outside of work. Our friendship is one of the greatest by-products of the years of research that went into this book and one that will, I hope, last a lifetime.

Over the years there have been several others in Kenya who provided encouragement, support, and good humor that sustained me through my work. Every time I am in Nairobi the Campaignes—Alice, Jonathan, Sylvie, and Nico—provide me with a true home. They always welcome me with open arms, even when I work late into the evening and track red dust through their house after spending the day upcountry. Njoroge Mungai, Christina Cole, and Petal and David Allen also offered great friendship, as well as a wealth of information about Kenya, past and present. Last but not least, the Nottinghams—John, Christopher, Muthoni, Fiona, Njambi, and the late Richard—gave their friendship, wisdom, and unending logistical support, particularly during my numerous follow-up research trips during the last few years. To all of them, my deepest gratitude and respect.

During the course of my research several institutions provided funding. They include the Frank Knox Memorial Fellowship, the Krupp Foundation Fellowship in European Studies, the J. William Fulbright Fellowship, the Social Science Research Council, the International Dissertation Research Fellowship, the Foreign Language and Area Studies Fellowship, the Harvard University Cooke Fund, the Weatherhead Center for International Affairs, and Harvard's Committee on African Studies. In addition, I would like to thank my department for generously allowing me such a substantial amount of leave time to conduct my research and to finish the writing.

The staffs at several archives and libraries were instrumental at various stages of this work. Special thanks goes to Musila Musembi and his entire staff at the Kenya National Archives, Nairobi. Also extremely helpful were the librarians and archivists at the Rhodes House Library, Oxford; the Public Record Office, London; the British Museum, Colindale; the Seeley Historical Library, Cambridge; the School of Oriental and African Studies, London; the Presbyterian Church of East Africa, Nairobi; Imani House,

Nairobi; the University of Nairobi Library, Nairobi; the Macmillan Library, Nairobi; and Widener Library, Cambridge, Massachusetts.

This book would not have been completed had it not been for the year that I spent at the Radcliffe Institute for Advanced Study. There, Drew Faust, Judy Vichniac, and their staff created the closest thing to utopia that I can imagine. When I walked into my Radcliffe office in September 2003, it was the first time I had a place of my own away from my home and my department to write. But the beauties of Radcliffe extend far beyond the quiet time that it affords its fellows. It is a true community of scholars, writers, scientists, and artists who support one another in their endeavors, gently push one another to realize their best, and applaud everyone's successes. Somehow the other fellows also had the uncanny ability to know when to leave me alone in my work, and when to pester me and offer advice. Though I am grateful to all of them, I would particularly like to extend my heartfelt thanks and admiration to those who read various drafts of this book, provided important analytical insights to my work, and, most important, gave me a shoulder to lean on during some of those long, dark days of writing. They include Amy Bach, Susanna Blumenthal, Jennifer Cole, Jean Comaroff, John Comaroff, Susan Eckstein, Anne Fessler, Jane Gaines, Jacquelyn Dowd Hall, Jennifer Harbury, Darlene Clark Hine, Chris Jones-Pauly, Jennifer Knust, Soledad Loaeza, Susan Moller Okin, Katy Park, and Irene Winter. I would also like to thank my Radcliffe research partner, Jennifer Kinloch, as well as the research help and editorial advice given to me by Liz Thornberry. Special gratitude as well goes to Lindy Hess for offering me her time and wisdom on many occasions.

Several individuals were determined to see this book not just in print but in as near to perfect form as possible. Jill Kneerim, my agent, believed in me and in this project from the moment we first met. Every writer should have an advocate like Jill who pushes her project with such grace and zeal. My sincerest thanks to her and the entire staff at Kneerim and Williams. Vanessa Mobley, my editor at Henry Holt, was with me every step of the way during the writing process, providing incisive criticism and constant encouragement. Her eye for detail and desire for perfection carried over into much of this book. I would also like to thank everyone at Henry Holt who worked with us to make this project a success. They include John Sterling, Maggie Richards, Elizabeth Shreve, Denise Cronin, and Daniel Reid. At Jonathan Cape my editor, Will Sulkin, provided invaluable insights and support, for which I am very grateful. My toughest critic of all, my dear Uncle Jake, read through every draft page of this book and held no punches in telling me what needed to be improved and what needed to go. There is no doubt that this book became substantially better after it was carved up, more than once, with his red pen.

There are two remaining groups of people to whom I owe far more than gratitude. The first comprises the hundreds of men and women who survived the camps and villages and who so generously shared their lives, their homes, and countless meals with me. My deepest admiration and thanks for their bravery and willingness to return to a period in their pasts that was, as many of them said, as painful today as it was some fifty years ago.

And finally there is my family. Nothing I could possibly say or do would begin to thank them for the understanding, encouragement, and love that they have given me over the years. The final stretch of writing was particularly hard on everyone around me. I was absent for days and sometimes weeks at a time. My husband, Brent, not only took over at home but also kept cheering me on, telling me to write the best book that I possibly could. In his good hands our two young sons, Andy and Jake, thrived despite my absence, and, together, the three of them knew how to pull me away from my work when I needed it most, making me laugh and relax in the sheer joy of their company. Then during some of the toughest hours my mom, better known as Mimi, swooped in and rescued us all with home-cooked meals and countless hours of babysitting. Mary Lalli (aka Dos Mimi) was often never far behind, offering up one of her gourmet meals and lively company. I'm not certain who among them is happiest to see this book finally completed. I know, though, that of everyone it was Brent who shouldered the lion's share of our domestic life, not to mention his own career, while never once complaining. Apart from being my husband, he is simply the most wonderful person in the world.

ILLUSTRATION CREDITS

INDEX

Entries in *italics* refer to captions.

BODLEY
HEAD

THE HISTORY OF THE BODLEY HEAD

The Bodley Head was founded in 1887 by John Lane and Elkin Matthews.
Initially trading in antiquarian books in London, in 1894 Lane and Matthews
began to publish works of 'stylish decadence', including the notorious literary
periodical *The Yellow Book*. The Bodley Head became a private company in 1921
and in the 1970s formed a publishing group with Jonathan Cape and
Chatto & Windus. It was bought by Random House in 1987
and ceased trading as an adult imprint in 1990.

2008 saw the launch of an exciting and entirely new imprint within
Random House's VINTAGE division with the revival of the distinguished
Bodley Head name. In its new incarnation The Bodley Head is devoted to
excellence in non-fiction in all fields. Its two principal strands are books
of impeccable scholarship in the humanities and sciences, and books which
directly address the intellectual and cultural issues of our times.

For more information on books published by The Bodley Head please visit:
www.vintage-books.co.uk

For updates and news follow us on Twitter @TheBodleyHead